Instructor's Classroom Kit
Volume I

for

Berk

Infants, Children, and Adolescents

Sixth Edition

prepared by

Laura E. Berk
Illinois State University

Judy Ashkenaz

Sara Harris
Illinois State University

Trisha Mann
Illinois State University

Gabrielle F. Principe
Ursinus College

Mark Seidl

Diana Murphy

PEARSON

Boston   New York   San Francisco
Mexico City   Montreal   Toronto   London   Madrid   Munich   Paris
Hong Kong   Singapore   Tokyo   Cape Town   Sydney

ISBN-13: 978-0-205-54701-2
ISBN-10:   0-205-54701-X

Printed in the United States of America

10 9 8 7 6 5 4 3 2 1   11 10 09 08 07

CONTENTS

PREFACE

This *Instructor's Classroom Kit*, which accompanies *Infants, Children, and Adolescents Sixth Edition*, is designed to assist both the novice and the experienced teacher in preparing lectures and guiding students' learning. During the months that we wrote the kit, we tried to think of the kind of supports that might help instructors seasoned by years of experience bring freshness, stimulation, and inspiration to the teaching of child development. At the same time, we paid great attention to addressing the needs of beginning teachers—only a breath ahead of the syllabus in lecture preparation and scrambling to find good sources that amplify text discussion. The resources in this kit are intended to lighten the busy schedules of instructors; bring new insights and lively discussion to the classroom; and, most of all, deepen the understanding of students of child development.

The *Instructor's Classroom Kit* consists of the following instructional resources keyed to each chapter of the text:

1. Transparencies. A total of 160 overhead projector transparencies highlight key concepts and research findings. Transparency numbers and titles are page-referenced to the figures or tables in the text to which they pertain. A complete listing of transparencies can be found in the *Transparencies for Human Development* supplement that accompanies *Infants, Children, and Adolescents, Sixth Edition.*

2. Media Materials. A comprehensive, chapter-by-chapter listing of available films and videotapes is included in the manual. For each segment of *Infants, Children, and Adolescents in Action* and *A Window on Infants, Children, and Adolescents*, a synopsis is provided. Other videotapes are categorized separately with the date of production, name of the distributor, length of the presentation, and a description of content.

3. Chapter-at-a-Glance. Located at the beginning of each chapter, the Chapter-at-a-Glance tables provide easy reference to available resources in the kit as well as outside supplements. Main topics are page-referenced, and instruction ideas (Learning Objectives, Lecture Outlines, Lecture Enhancements, Learning Activities, and Ask Yourself Questions) and supplements (Test Bank Items, Transparencies, and Media Materials) relevant to each text section are listed.

4. Brief Chapter Summary. This feature is designed to provide quick familiarity with the coverage of topics in each chapter. It can serve as the basis for deciding which subjects treated by the text to review and extend in class lecture and which supplementary topics to add that reflect the instructor's unique perspective, interests, and personal experiences.

5. Learning Objectives. For each text chapter, a comprehensive set of Learning Objectives is provided. We believe that students learn best when they actively grapple with text material and integrate new information with what they already know. Students can be asked to write a paragraph or two in response to each objective, include important terms in their responses, check their answers against the text's discussion, and revise each response accordingly. This exercise yields a student-generated summary of the content of each chapter. Once completed, it provides a useful review written in the student's own words that can be referred to while preparing for examinations. Further, the objectives are tied to individual items in the accompanying Test Bank.

6. Lecture Outline. The purpose of the Lecture Outlines is to provide a detailed synopsis of each chapter. Material is organized by text headings and subheadings and page-referenced to the text. Important terms and concepts appear in boldface and in italics, as in the text narrative. The outlines permit a "quick read" of each chapter and can serve as the basis for lecture notes or PowerPoint slides.

7. Lecture Enhancements. From four to five Lecture Enhancements, page-referenced to relevant text material, accompany each chapter. Each expands on information treated in the text by addressing new theory and research, considering controversial issues that promote student discussion and debate, and extending the text's emphasis on the vital connections among theory, research, and applications. To assist instructors with the time-consuming task of lecture preparation, the Lecture Enhancements go beyond merely suggesting appropriate topics to providing the general direction of each lecture's content. Enough detail is given so that instructors who are pressed for time can integrate information from the manual directly into their lectures. Each Lecture Enhancement is accompanied by a list of current sources that can be used to develop a more extensive lecture presentation. Finally, for Lecture Enhancements calling for student participation, specific instructions have been boldfaced.

8. Learning Activities. From five to thirteen Learning Activities per chapter are included. Many of the activities provide students with opportunities to see "live" examples of research findings by observing and interviewing children and adolescents. Also included are written assignments that permit students to extend their knowledge of topics in the text.

9. Ask Yourself. The Ask Yourself feature consists of critical thinking questions, designed to support students' active engagement with the subject matter. Each can be found at the end of major sections in the text and is page-referenced in this manual. The focus of these questions is divided between theory and application. Many describe problematic situations and ask students to resolve them in light of what they have learned. In this way, the questions inspire high-level thinking and new insights.

10. Suggested Student Readings. Many instructors wish to assign or recommend supplementary readings to their students. A list of three to five additional readings complements each text chapter. The readings have been carefully selected for their interest, value, and readability; the majority are recently published. Each entry is annotated so instructors can discern the topic and general orientation of the reading prior to consulting the original source.

11. Test Bank. The Test Bank contains over 2,000 multiple choice questions, each of which is page-referenced to chapter content and classified by type (factual, applied, or conceptual). Each chapter also includes a selection of essay questions and sample answers.

12. Grade Aid Study Questions. Page-referenced and organized according to major headings in the textbook, study questions assist students in identifying main points and grasping concepts and principles. A helpful study and review aid, this feature greatly enhances students' retention of chapter material.

13. Crossword Puzzles. This unique study aid helps students master vocabulary central to the field of child development. Students can use the puzzles to test their knowledge of the important terms and concepts covered in each chapter.

14. Grade Aid Practice Tests. Practice tests are designed to reinforce key chapter concepts and to assess student understanding of chapter material. By checking their answers against the key at the back of the Grade Aid, students gain feedback that guides and improves their studying.

15. PowerPoint Presentation. The PowerPoint presentation contains illustrations and outlines of key topics for each chapter from the text, presented in a clear and visually attractive format.

Laura E. Berk
Judy Ashkenaz
Sara Harris
Diana Murphy
Trisha Mann
Gabrielle Principe
Mark Seidl

CHAPTER 1
HISTORY, THEORY, AND RESEARCH STRATEGIES

CHAPTER-AT-A-GLANCE

Chapter Outline	Instruction Ideas	Supplements
The Field of Child Development pp. 4–6 Domains of Development • Periods of Development	Learning Objectives 1.1–1.2	Test Bank Items 1–5 Please contact your Allyn and Bacon publisher's representative for a wide range of video offerings available to adopters.
Basic Issues pp. 6–10 Continuous or Discontinuous Development? • One Course of Development or Many? • Relative Influence of Nature and Nurture? • A Balanced Point of View	Learning Objective 1.3 Lecture Enhancement 1.1 Learning Activity 1.1 Ask Yourself p. 9	Transparency 1 Test Bank Items 6–15, 140
Historical Foundations pp. 11–13 Medieval Times • The Reformation • Philosophics of the Enlightenment • Scientific Beginnings	Learning Objective 1.4 Ask Yourself p. 13	Test Bank Items 16–29, 146
Mid-Twentieth-Century Theories pp. 14–21 The Psychoanalytic Perspective • Behaviorism and Social Learning Theory • Piaget's Cognitive-Developmental Theory	Learning Objective 1.5 Learning Activities 1.2–1.3 Ask Yourself p. 21	Transparencies 2–5 Test Bank Items 30–55, 145,148–149
Recent Theoretical Perspectives pp. 21 29 Information Processing • Ethology and Evolutionary Developmental Psychology • Vygotsky's Sociocultural Theory • Ecological Systems Theory • New Directions: Development as a Dynamic System	Learning Objective 1.6 Learning Activities 1.2–1.4 Ask Yourself p. 29	Transparencies 6–8 Test Bank Items 56–80, 147, 148–149
Comparing Child Development Theories pp. 29, 30	Learning Objective 1.7 Learning Activities 1.2–1.3	Test Bank Items 81–83
Studying the Child pp. 29–46 Common Methods of Gathering Information • General Research Designs • Designs for Studying Development • Ethics in Research on Children	Learning Objectives 1.8–1.11 Lecture Enhancements 1.2–1.4 Learning Activities 1.5–1.8 Ask Yourself pp. 35, 46	Transparency 9 Test Bank Items 84–139, 141–144, 150–154

BRIEF CHAPTER SUMMARY

Child development is the study of all aspects of human growth and change in the first two decades of life, from conception through adolescence. It is part of a larger, interdisciplinary field, developmental science, which looks at all changes throughout the lifespan. Researchers often divide development into three broad domains—physical, cognitive, and emotional and social—while recognizing that each domain influences and is influenced by the others. Further, researchers usually divide the first two decades of life into five age periods. In addition, some researchers identify the transition from adolescence to adulthood as a distinct period: emerging adulthood. These divisions make the vast, interdisciplinary study of human constancy more orderly and convenient.

Theories are orderly, integrated ideas, based on scientific verification, that guide and give meaning to our observations and give us a basis for practical action. This chapter provides an overview of philosophical and theoretical approaches to child study from medieval to modern times. It also reviews major research strategies used to study child behavior and development.

All major theories of child development take a stand on three basic issues: (1) Is development continuous or discontinuous? (2) Is there one universal course of development or many possible courses? (3) Are genetic or environmental factors (nature or nurture) more important in development? Modern child development theories also pay attention to the various contexts in which children grow up. Further, theories differ in the degree to which they emphasize stability versus the potential for change. Modern theories generally take a balanced point of view on these issues, recognizing the merits of both positions.

Research methods commonly used to study children include systematic observation; self-reports; the clinical, or case study, method; and ethnography. Investigators of child development may use a correlational research design, which shows a relationship but does not allow inferences about cause and effect. Or they may use an experimental design, which permits cause-and-effect inferences. To study how their participants change over time, investigators use special developmental research strategies, including longitudinal, cross-sectional, sequential, and microgenetic designs. Each method and each design has both strengths and limitations.

Conducting research with children poses special ethical dilemmas. Guidelines have been developed that can be used to determine if the benefits of research outweigh the risks and to ensure that children's rights are protected.

LEARNING OBJECTIVES

After reading this chapter, you should be able to:

1.1   Explain the importance of the terms *applied* and *interdisciplinary* as they help to define the field of child development. (p. 4)

1.2   List the age periods researchers use to study child development, and cite the three domains in which development is often divided. (pp. 4–6)

1.3   Explain the role of theories in understanding child development, and describe the three basic issues on which major theories take a stand. (pp. 6–10)

1.4   Trace historical influences on modern theories of child development, from medieval times through the early twentieth century. (pp. 11–13)

1.5   Describe the theoretical perspectives that influenced child development research in the mid-twentieth century, and cite the contributions and limitations of each. (pp. 14–21)

1.6   Describe six recent theoretical perspectives of child development, noting the contributions of major theorists. (pp. 21–29)

1.7   Identify the stand that each modern theory takes on the three basic issues of child development presented earlier in this chapter. (pp. 29, 30)

1.8   Describe the methods commonly used to study children, and cite the strengths and limitations of each. (pp. 29, 31–35)

1.9   Contrast correlational and experimental research designs, and cite the strengths and limitations of each. (pp. 35, 37–39)

1.10   Describe research designs used to study development, noting the strengths and limitations of each. (pp. 40–43)

1.11   Discuss children's research rights, and explain why research involving children raises special ethical concerns. (pp. 43, 45–46)

LECTURE OUTLINE

I. THE FIELD OF CHILD DEVELOPMENT (pp. 4–6)
    A. **Child development** is an area of study devoted to understanding all aspects of human constancy and change from conception through adolescence.
    B. It is part of a larger discipline, **developmental science,** which includes all changes experienced throughout the lifespan.
    C. Child development research is of both scientific and *applied,* or practical, importance.
    D. Child development research is *interdisciplinary*—it has grown through the combined efforts of people from many fields, including psychology, sociology, anthropology, biology, and neuroscience, as well as professionals in education, family studies, medicine, public health, and social service.
    E. Domains of Development (pp. 4–5)
        1. *Physical development:* Includes changes in body size, proportions, appearance, functioning of body systems, perceptual and motor capacities, and physical health.
        2. *Cognitive development:* Includes changes in intellectual abilities, including attention, memory, academic and everyday knowledge, problem solving, imagination, creativity, and language.
        3. *Emotional and social development:* Includes changes in emotional communication, self-understanding, knowledge about other people, interpersonal skills, friendships, intimate relationships, and moral reasoning and behavior.
        4. Each of these domains influences and is influenced by the others during a child's development.
    F. Periods of Development (pp. 5–6)
        1. *The prenatal period: from conception to birth.* In this 9-month period, the most rapid time of change, a one-celled organism is transformed into a human baby capable of adjusting to life in the surrounding world.
        2. *Infancy and toddlerhood: from birth to 2 years*: Dramatic changes in the body and brain support the emergence of a wide array of motor, perceptual, and intellectual capacities; the beginnings of language; and first intimate ties to others.
        3. *Early childhood: from 2 to 6 years.* The body becomes longer and leaner, motor skills are refined, and children become more self-controlled and self-sufficient. Make-believe play blossoms, thought and language expand, a sense of morality becomes evident, and children establish ties with peers.
        4. *Middle childhood: from 6 to 11 years.* Children master new responsibilities more similar to those they will perform as adults. Development in this period includes improved athletic abilities, participation in organized games, more logical thought processes, mastery of basic literacy skills, and advances in understanding self, morality, and friendship.
        5. *Adolescence: from 11 to 18 years.* In this period, puberty leads to an adult-sized body and sexual maturity. Thought becomes abstract and idealistic, and schooling is increasingly directed toward preparation for higher education and the world of work. Young people begin to define personal values and goals and establish autonomy from family.
        6. *Emerging adulthood: from 18 to 25 years.* For many contemporary youth in industrialized nations, this is a period of exploration of options in love, career, and personal values before making enduring commitments to adult roles.

II. BASIC ISSUES (pp. 6–10)
   A. A **theory** is an orderly, integrated set of statements that describes, explains, and predicts behavior.
       1. Theories are tools that provide organizing frameworks for our observations. They guide and give meaning to what we see, help us understand development, and give us a basis for our practical efforts to improve the welfare and treatment of children.
       2. Unlike mere opinion or belief, a theory's continued existence depends on scientific verification.
       3. Within the field of child development, the existence of many theories helps advance knowledge through researchers' efforts to support, contradict, and integrate different points of view.
       4. All theories of child development take a stand on three basic issues:
            a. Is the course of development continuous or discontinuous?
            b   Does one course of development characterize all children, or are there many possible courses?
            c. Do genetic or environmental factors have a greater influence on development?
   B. Continuous or Discontinuous Development? (pp. 7–8)
       1. If development is **continuous,** the difference in capacities and behavior between the immature and mature being is simply one of amount or complexity, not of kind; development consists of gradually adding on more of the same types of skills that were there to begin with.
       2. If development is **discontinuous,** it takes place in **stages**—qualitative changes in thinking, feeling, and behaving that characterize specific periods of development; in this view, new ways of understanding and responding to the world emerge at specific times of fairly sudden change, rather than gradually.
   C. One Course of Development or Many? (p. 8)
       1. Stage theorists assume that people everywhere follow the same sequence of development.
       2. The field of child development is becoming increasingly aware that children grow up in distinct **contexts**—unique combinations of genetic and environmental circumstances that lead to different paths of change and foster different capacities, skills, and emotions.
       3. Contemporary theorists regard the contexts that mold development as many-layered and complex, including heredity and biological makeup, the settings (immediate and more remote) within which children grow up, and broader cultural factors.
   D. Relative Influence of Nature and Nurture? (pp. 8–9)
       1. The **nature–nurture controversy** asks whether genetic or environmental factors are more important as underlying causes of development.
            a. *Nature* means inborn biological givens—the hereditary information we receive from our parents at the moment of conception, which signals the body to grow and affects all our characteristics and skills.
            b. *Nurture* means the complex forces of the physical and social world that influence our biological makeup and psychological experiences before and after birth.
       2. All theories grant at least some role to both nature and nurture, but they vary in their emphasis on each.
            a. Theorists who stress the importance of *heredity,* or nature, typically emphasize *stability*—that children who are high or low in a characteristic will remain so at later ages. If they do grant a role to environment, they generally believe that *early experiences* establish lifelong patterns of behavior that cannot be changed by later experiences.
            b. Theorists who emphasize the role of environment believe that *change* is possibly and even likely when supported by new experiences.
            c. Investigators' views on the question of *stability versus change* have great applied significance—for example, in considering the value of providing children of various ages with experiences aimed at promoting change.
   E. A Balanced Point of View (p. 9)
       1. Modern theories tend to recognize the merits of both sides, acknowledging that both continuous and discontinuous changes occur, that development has both universal features and features unique to the individual and his or her contexts, and that heredity and environment are inseparably interwoven, each affecting the potential of the other to influence the child's traits and capacities.

2. New evidence on **resilience**—the ability to adapt effectively in the face of threats to development—is receiving increasing attention as investigators look for ways to protect young people from the negative effects of life stressors; both biologically endowed characteristics and environmental factors play a role in fostering resilience.

III. HISTORICAL FOUNDATIONS (pp. 11–13)
   A. Contemporary theories of child development are the result of centuries of change in Western cultural values, philosophical thinking about children, and scientific progress. Early ideas that long preceded scientific child study still linger as important forces in current theory and research.
   B. Medieval Times (p. 11)
      1. In medieval Europe, childhood was already viewed as a separate period of life. Medieval paintings and written texts depict children as distinct from adults through clothing and occupations—for example, playing games. Child-care manuals and protective laws indicated an awareness of children as vulnerable beings.
      2. Religious writings contained contradictory beliefs about children's basic nature—sometimes depicting them as possessed by the devil, at other times as innocent and angelic—that foreshadowed later views.
   C. The Reformation (p. 11)
      1. In the sixteenth century, the Puritan belief in original sin gave rise to the view that children were born evil and stubborn and had to be civilized through harsh, restrictive child-rearing practices.
      2. The Puritans who emigrated from England to the United States brought with them the belief that child rearing was one of their most important obligations.
      3. As they trained their children in self-reliance and self-control, Puritan parents gradually adopted a view that struck a balance between severity and permissiveness.
   D. Philosophies of the Enlightenment (pp. 11–12)
      1. The seventeenth-century Enlightenment brought new philosophies that emphasized ideals of human dignity and respect, including more humane conceptions of childhood.
      2. John Locke (pp. 11–12)
         a. British philosopher John Locke viewed the child as a **tabula rasa,** or blank slate, whose character was shaped entirely by experience.
         b. Locke regarded development as continuous and championed nurture, with the possibility of many courses of development and of change at later ages due to new experiences.
         c. Locke saw parents as rational tutors, molding the child through instruction, example, and the use of praise and approval as rewards. His view led to more compassionate treatment of children, a view supported by modern research.
         d. However, Locke's view of children as passive, doing little to influence their own destiny, has been discarded.
      3. Jean-Jacques Rousseau (p. 12)
         a. Eighteenth-century French philosopher Jean-Jacques Rousseau introduced a new view of childhood in which children are not blank slates but, rather, **noble savages,** naturally endowed with a sense of right and wrong and an innate plan for orderly, healthy growth.
         b. Rousseau believed that adult training could only do harm to children's built-in moral sense and unique ways of thinking and feeling.
         c. Rousseau introduced two influential concepts: *stage* and **maturation**—the idea that there is a genetically determined, naturally unfolding course of growth.
         d. Rousseau viewed children as determining their own destinies, and he viewed development as a discontinuous, stagewise process that follows a single, unified course mapped out by nature.
   E. Scientific Beginnings (pp. 12–13)
      1. During the late nineteenth and early twentieth centuries, early observations of children were followed by improved methods and theories.
      2. Darwin: Forefather of Scientific Child Study (p. 12)
         a. The *theory of evolution* developed by British naturalist Charles Darwin was based on his observations that within a species, no two individuals are exactly alike. Darwin's theory emphasized two related principles: *natural selection* and *survival of the fittest.*

        b.   Darwin's emphasis on the adaptive value of physical characteristics and behavior eventually found its way into important developmental theories.

        c.   Darwin noticed striking similarities in the prenatal growth of many species, suggesting that all species, including human beings, were descended from a few common ancestors.

        d.   Other scientists attempted to document parallels between child development and human evolution; this effort, though unsuccessful, paved the way for scientific child study.

   3.   The Normative Period (p. 13)

        a.   American psychologist G. Stanley Hall (generally regarded as the founder of the child study movement) and his student Arnold Gesell used evolutionary ideas as the basis for their theories, which regarded development as a genetically determined process that unfolds automatically, similar to the growth of a flower.

        b.   The theories of Hall and Gesell were one-sided, but their methods launched the **normative approach** to child study, in which age-related averages based on measures of many individuals are computed to represent typical development.

        c.   Gesell was among the first to make knowledge of child development meaningful to parents, through his popular books of child-rearing advice.

   4.   The Mental Testing Movement (p. 13)

        a.   This movement emerged from the French psychologist Alfred Binet's attempts to develop an intelligence test to identify children with learning problems in the Paris school system.

        b.   Binet's test captured the complexity of children's thinking by defining intelligence in terms of components—good judgment, planning, and clinical reflection—that could be measured directly.

        c.   Binet's results sparked interest in individual differences in development and prompted research focused on comparing children's intelligence test scores to identify differences based on gender, ethnicity, birth order, family background, and other characteristics.

IV. MID-TWENTIETH CENTURY THEORIES (pp. 14–21)

   A. The Psychoanalytic Perspective (pp. 14–16)

      1.   The **psychoanalytic perspective** assumes that children move through a series of stages in which they confront conflicts between biological drives and social expectations. How they resolve these conflicts determines their psychological adjustment.

      2.   Freud's Theory (p. 14)

        a.   Sigmund Freud's **psychosexual theory** of development emphasizes that healthy personality development is determined by how parents manage their child's early sexual and aggressive drives.

        b.   In Freud's view, an individual's basic personality is determined by the relationships established between three parts of the personality—the *id,* which is the source of basic biological needs and desires; the *ego,* the conscious, rational part of personality, which develops in early infancy; and the *superego,* or conscience, which reflects the values of society.

        c.   Freud believed that over the course of childhood, sexual impulses shift their focus from the oral to the anal to the genital regions of the body. If parents strike an appropriate balance between permitting too much or too little gratification of the child's basic needs, their child will grow into a well-adjusted adult.

        d.   Freud's theory was the first to emphasize the influence of the early parent–child relationship, but because it was based on the problems of sexually repressed Victorian adults, it overemphasized the influence of sexual feelings; also, Freud did not study children directly.

      3.   Erikson's Theory (pp. 14–15)

        a.   Expanding Freud's views, Erik Erikson created his **psychosocial theory,** which emphasized the ego as a positive force in development.

        b.   Erikson, one of the first to recognize the lifespan nature of development, added three adult stages to Freud's five stages.

        c.   He recognized that normal development must be understood in relation to the individual's cultural context and that child rearing is responsive to the competencies needed and valued by the child's society.

4. Contributions and Limitations of Psychoanalytic Theory (pp. 15–16)
   a. The psychoanalytic perspective emphasizes the value of studying the individual's unique life history by using the clinical, or case study, method to develop a detailed picture of a single child's personality.
   b. Despite its contributions, this approach is no longer in the mainstream of child development research because many of its ideas are too vague to test empirically, and because it focuses too exclusively on the clinical approach.

B. Behaviorism and Social Learning Theory (pp. 16–18)
   1. Traditional Behaviorism (p. 17)
      a. John Watson, who wanted to create an objective science of psychology, initiated the North American study of **behaviorism,** which is concerned primarily with studying directly observable stimuli and responses rather than unobservable workings of the mind.
      b. Inspired by studies of animal learning carried out by Russian physiologist Ivan Pavlov, Watson investigated whether adults could use classical conditioning to mold children's behavior by controlling stimulus–response associations.
      c. B. F. Skinner's *operant conditioning theory,* another form of behaviorism, views behavior as determined by environmental reinforcers and punishments.
   2. Social Learning Theory (pp. 17–18)
      a. Albert Bandura's **social learning theory** emphasizes the role of modeling (otherwise known as *imitation* or *observational learning*) as a basis for development.
      b. Because the most recent revision of Bandura's theory stresses the importance of *cognition,* particularly how we think about ourselves and other people, he refers to it as a *social-cognitive* rather than a social learning approach.
      c. In Bandura's view, through watching others engage in self-praise and self-blame and through feedback about the worth of their own actions, children develop *personal standards* for behavior and a sense of *self-efficacy*—a belief that their own abilities and characteristics will help them succeed
   3. Contributions and Limitations of Behaviorism and Social Learning Theory (p. 18)
      a. Behaviorism and social learning theory have had a major impact on practices used with children, such as **behavior modification,** which combines conditioning and modeling to eliminate undesirable behaviors and to increase socially desirable responses.
      b. Behaviorism and social learning theory have been criticized for taking too narrow a view of environmental influences and for underestimating children's contributions to their own development.

C. Piaget's Cognitive–Developmental Theory (pp. 18–20)
   1. In Jean Piaget's **cognitive-developmental theory,** development occurs in stages as children actively manipulate and explore the environment.
   2. Piaget's Stages (pp. 18–19)
      a. Central to Piaget's theory is the biological concept of *adaptation,* whereby a child's mental structures develop to better fit with, or represent, the external world, just as body structures adapt to fit with the environment.
      b. During Piaget's *sensorimotor stage,* a baby uses the senses and movements to explore the world.
      c. In the *preoperational stage,* these action patterns evolve into symbolic but illogical thinking.
      d. School-age children, in the *concrete operational stage,* use more organized reasoning.
      e. Finally, in adolescents and adults, though becomes an abstract, systematic reasoning system in the *formal operational stage.*
   3. Piaget began by observing his own children—presenting them with problems and studying their responses.
   4. Later, Piaget conducted clinical interviews in which a child's initial response to a task was the basis for subsequent questions.
   5. Contributions and Limitations of Piaget's Theory (pp. 19–21)
      a. Piaget convinced the field that children are active learners whose minds consist of rich structures of knowledge.
      b. He explored children's reasoning about the social as well as the physical world.

        c.   Piaget's stages stimulated a wealth of research on children's conceptions of themselves, other people, and relationships, and encouraged the development of educational approaches that emphasize discovery learning and exploration of the environment.

        d.   Later research evidence indicates that Piaget underestimated the competencies of infants and preschoolers, and that children's performance on Piagetian problems can be improved with training, challenging the assumption that discovery learning is better than adult teaching in fostering development.

        e.   Piaget's stagewise account pays too little attention to the effects of social and cultural influences on children's thinking.

        f.   Today, many researchers accept a modified view in which changes in children's thinking occur more gradually than Piaget believed.

        g.   Others embrace an approach—information processing—that emphasizes continuous gains in cognition.

        h.   Still other theories highlight the role of social and cultural contexts in child development.

V.   RECENT THEORETICAL PERSPECTIVES (pp. 21–29)

    A. Information Processing (pp. 21–23)

        1.   **Information processing** is an approach to development that uses the design of digital computers as a metaphor for thought processes. In this view, the human mind is a symbol-manipulating system through which information flows.

        2.   Information is presented to the senses at input, then actively coded, transformed, and organized until it emerges as a behavioral response at output.

        3.   Concern with Rigor and Precision (pp. 21–22)

            a.   Information-processing researchers use flowcharts to map the precise steps used to solve problems and complete tasks.

            b.   Some information-processing models track children's mastery of just one or a few tasks; others, which describe the human cognitive system as a whole, are used as guides for asking questions about broad changes in children's thinking with age.

            c.   Information processing can be used to examine how individual process social information—for example, by tracking the steps children use to solve social problems and acquire gender-linked preferences.

            d.   Like Piaget's theory, information processing regards children as active, sense-making beings who modify their thinking in response to environmental demands. But, unlike Piaget's theory, it does not divide development into stages but views it as a process of continuous change.

            e.   A great strength of the information-processing approach is its commitment to rigorous research methods, which has produced precise accounts of children's thinking, leading to the development of effective teaching methods.

            f.   One limitation of information processing is that it is better at analyzing the components of thinking than at putting them together into a comprehensive theory of development. Another limitation is that it virtually ignores aspects of cognition that are not linear and logical, such as imagination and creativity.

        4.   Developmental Cognitive Neuroscience (pp. 22–23)

            a.   **Developmental cognitive neuroscience,** an area of investigation that has arisen in the past two decades, brings together researchers from psychology, biology, neuroscience, and medicine to study the relationship between brain changes and a child's cognitive processing and behavior patterns.

            b.   Improved methods for analyzing brain activity allow neuroscientists to examine how specific experiences at various ages influence brain growth and organization, and also clarify the brain bases of many learning and behavior disorders, leading to practical applications.

    B. Ethology and Evolutionary Developmental Psychology (pp. 23–24)

        1.   **Ethology** studies the adaptive, or survival, value of behavior and its evolutionary history.

        2.   Studies of *imprinting,* the early following behavior of some baby birds, reveal that this behavior must occur during an early, restricted period of development.

        3.   Observations of imprinting led to the concept of the *critical period* in child development—a limited time span during which the child is biologically prepared to acquire certain adaptive behaviors if exposed to an appropriately stimulating environment.

4. In human development, the concept of a **sensitive period**—a time that is optimal for certain capacities to emerge and in which the individual is especially responsive to environmental influences—is more accurate than the strict notion of a critical period.

5. British psychoanalyst John Bowlby applied ethological theory to understanding the human infant–caregiver relationship, suggesting that development of attachment in human babies is a lengthy process involving changes in psychological structures that lead the infant to form a deep affectionate tie with the caregiver.

6. **Evolutionary developmental psychology** seeks to understand the adaptive value of species-wide cognitive, emotional, and social competencies as those competencies change with age.

7. Evolutionary developmental psychologists want to understand the entire *organism–environment system,* not just the genetic and biological basis of development.

C. Vygotsky's Sociocultural Theory (pp. 24–25)

1. Cross-cultural and multicultural studies provide insight into the relationship of culturally specific beliefs and practices to development—whether developmental pathways apply to all children or reflect the child's particular environmental conditions.

2. Lev Vygotsky's **sociocultural theory** focuses on how culture is transmitted from one generation to the next.

3. Vygotsky believed that social interaction is essential for cognitive development, which he saw as a socially mediated process in which children depend on assistance from adults and more expert peers as they tackle new challenges.

4. A major finding of cross-cultural research is that cultures select different tasks for children's learning, helping children to master tasks that will lead to the knowledge and skills essential for success in a particular culture.

5. Vygotsky's theory reveals that children in every culture develop unique strengths, but his emphasis on culture and social experience led him to neglect biological contributions to development and children's capacity to shape their own development. Vygotsky's followers stress that children participate actively in the social interactions from which their development springs, and that they play an active role in modifying and transforming those practices.

D. Ecological Systems Theory (pp. 25–27)

1. Urie Bronfenbrenner's **ecological systems theory** views the child as developing within a complex system of relationships affected by multiple levels of the environment.

2. The Microsystem (p. 26):
   a. The innermost level of the environment, the **microsystem,** consists of activities and interaction patterns in the child's immediate environment.
   b. Within the microsystem, relationships between individuals are *bidirectional:* Adults and children affect one another's behavior.
   c. *Third parties* in the microsystem affect the quality of any two-person relationship.

3. The Mesosystem (p. 26):
   a. The **mesosystem**, the second layer in Bronfenbrenner's model, includes connections between microsystems such as home, school, and neighborhood that foster children's development.
   b. Each microsystem is more likely to support children's development when links exist between these environments.

4. The Exosystem (pp. 26–27):
   a. The **exosystem** consists of social settings that do not include children but affect their experiences in immediate settings.
   b. It includes parents' workplaces, religious institutions, and community services, as well as informal social networks.
   c. Research confirms that a breakdown in exosystem activities has a negative impact on development.

5. The Macrosystem (p. 27):
   a. The **macrosystem** is the outermost layer of Bronfenbrenner's model, consisting of a culture's laws, values, customs, and resources.
   b. The priority that the macrosystem gives to children's needs affects the support they receive at inner levels of the environment.

6. An Ever-Changing System (p. 27):
   a. In Bronfenbrenner's system, the environment is ever-changing, as important life events produce new conditions affecting development.
   b. This temporal dimension, the **chronosystem,** includes both changes in life events that are imposed on the child and changes that arise from within the child.
E. New Directions: Development as a Dynamic System (pp. 27–29)
   1. According to the **dynamic systems perspective,** the child's mind, body, and physical and social worlds form an *integrated system* that guides mastery of new skills.
   2. The system is *dynamic,* or constantly in motion.
   3. When change occurs in any part of the system, children actively reorganize their behaviors so that the various components of the system work together again, but in a more complex and effective way.
   4. Researchers who adopt this perspective study children's behavior during a transition.
   5. Dynamic systems theorists believe that within certain broad universal outlines of development, wide individual differences exist in specific skills and competencies.
   6. This view has been inspired by other scientific disciplines, especially biology and physics, and by information-processing and contextual theories.
   7. Some investigators have used the dynamic systems view to explain emotional and social development as well as development of motor and c cognitive skills—part of an effort to move closer to an all-encompassing approach to understanding change.

VI. COMPARING CHILD DEVELOPMENT THEORIES (p. 29)
   A. Theories of child development can be distinguished by the aspect of development on which they focus and by their differing points of view about the development process.
   B. All theories have strengths and limitations; no single theory provides a complete account of development. An *eclectic position,* or blend of several theories, can take into account what each of them has contributed to our knowledge of children.

VII. STUDYING THE CHILD (pp. 29–46)
   A. Research begins with a *hypothesis,* or prediction, about behavior, that is usually drawn directly from a theory, followed by research conducted according to scientifically accepted procedures.
   B. Researchers must first choose a *method of gathering information* and then decide on a *research design*— an overall plan for the research study that will permit the best possible test of the investigator's hypothesis.
   C. Learning about research strategies is important for two reasons:
      1. Knowing the strengths and limitations of various strategies is important for separating dependable information from misleading results.
      2. Individuals who work directly with children are in a unique position to make connections between research and practice by collaborating with schools and other institutions to design, implement, and evaluate interventions to enhance children's development.
   D. Common Methods of Gathering Information (pp. 31–35)
      1. Systematic Observation (pp. 31–33)
         a. **Naturalistic observation** involves going into the field, or natural environment, and observing the behavior of interest there.
            (1) An advantage is that the observed behavior is real and not contrived.
            (2) A disadvantage is that not all individuals have the same opportunity to display a particular behavior in everyday life.
         b. **Structured observations** involve setting up a laboratory situation that evokes the behavior of interest so that every participant has an equal opportunity to display the response.
            (1) An advantage is that the researcher can control the research situation in order to study behaviors that rarely occur in everyday life.
            (2) A disadvantage of all types of systematic observation is that they tell us little about the reasoning behind people's behavior.
      2. Self-Reports: Interviews and Questionnaires (pp. 33–34)
         a. Self-reports—including structured and unstructured interviews, questionnaires, and tests—ask research participants to provide information about their perceptions, thoughts, abilities, feelings, attitudes, beliefs, and past experiences.

    b.   A **clinical interview** uses a flexible, conversational style to probe for the participant's viewpoint.

        (1)   Two major strengths are that clinical interviews permit people to describe their thoughts in terms that are close to the way they think in everyday life, and that they can provide a large amount of information in a brief period.

        (2)   Limitations include the potential for participants to report their thoughts inaccurately in an attempt to please the interviewer or to have difficulty recalling past events, as well as the method's reliance on verbal ability and expressiveness.

    c.   In a **structured interview,** every participant is asked the same questions in the same way.

        (1)   This method is more efficient than the clinical interview, provides briefer answers, and can be used with groups as well as individuals.

        (2)   A limitation is that this method does not yield the same depth of information as the clinical interview, and it is also vulnerable to the problem of inaccurate reporting.

  3.   The Clinical, or Case Study, Method (p. 34)

    a.   The **clinical, or case study, method** brings together a wide range of information about a single child in an effort to obtain a comprehensive picture of that child's psychological functioning and experiences.

    b.   Strengths and limitations:

        (1)   The clinical method is well suited to studying individuals who are few in number but vary widely in characteristics, such as *prodigies.*

        (2)   Researchers' own theoretical biases may influence their interpretations of the information they gather.

        (3)   Investigators cannot generalize their findings beyond the child they are studying.

  4.   Methods for Studying Culture (pp. 34–35)

    a.   To study the impact of culture on child development, researchers adjust the methods just considered or tap procedures specially designed for cross-cultural and multicultural research.

    b.   **Ethnography,** a technique borrowed from anthropology, is a descriptive, qualitative technique directed toward understanding a culture or distinct social group through *participant observation*—the researcher's participation in the daily life of the community.

    c.   Strengths and limitations of ethnography:

        (1)   The ethnographic method assumes that through close contact with a social group, researchers can understand the beliefs and behaviors of its members more accurately.

        (2)   The researcher's presence may alter the situation being studied, or investigators' cultural values and theoretical commitments may lead them to observe selectively or misinterpret what they see.

        (3)   Ethnographic findings cannot be generalized to groups other than those studied.

E. General Research Designs (pp. 35–39)

  1.   Correlational Design (pp. 35–37)

    a.   In a **correlational design,** researchers gather information on existing groups of individuals in natural life circumstances, making no effort to alter their experiences.

    b.   Strengths and limitations of correlational studies:

        (1)   They allow researchers to study conditions that may be impossible to arrange or control, and therefore must be studied as they currently exist.

        (2)   One important limitation is that finding a correlation does not allow researchers to infer a cause-and-effect relationship.

    c.   The **correlation coefficient** is a number with a value between +1.00 and –1.00 that indicates how two variables are related.

    d.   The size of the number denotes the strength of the relationship.

        (1)   A zero correlation indicates no association.

        (2)   A value close to either +1.00 or –1.00 denotes a stronger relationship.

    e.   The number's sign indicates the direction of the relationship.

        (1)   A positive sign means that as one variable increases, the other also increases.

        (2)   A negative sign indicates that as one variable increases, the other decreases.

  2. Experimental Design (pp. 37–38)
      a. In an **experimental design,** researchers divide the events and behaviors of interest into two types.
          (1) The **independent variable** is the one the investigator manipulates to see what changes it causes in the other variable.
          (2) The **dependent variable** is the one the investigator expects to be influenced by the independent variable.
      b. Experimental design permits inferences about cause-and-effect relationships because researchers use an evenhanded procedure to assign people to two or more treatment conditions.
          (1) To control for participants' characteristics that might reduce the accuracy of their findings, researchers engage in **random assignment** of participants to treatment conditions—for example, by flipping a coin.
          (2) *Matching,* in which participants are measured before the experiment on the factor in question, is used along with random assignment to ensure that the experimental groups are equivalent on factors that might distort the results.
  3. Modified Experimental Designs: Field and Natural Experiments (pp. 38–39)
      a. Researchers use modifications of experimental design to investigate behaviors that occur more naturally outside of a laboratory setting.
      b. In *field experiments,* researchers randomly assign participants to different treatments in natural settings.
      c. In *natural, or quasi-, experiments,* investigators research preexisting treatments, choosing participant groups carefully to ensure that their characteristics are as much alike as possible.
F. Designs for Studying Development (pp. 40–43)
  1. The Longitudinal Design (p. 40)
      a. In a **longitudinal design,** participants are studied repeatedly at different ages.
      b. Researchers can identify both common patterns of development and individual differences.
      c. This design permits examination of relationships between early and later events and behaviors.
  2. Problems in Conducting Longitudinal Research (pp. 40–41)
      a. Over time, participants may move away or drop out of the research, leading to biased samples.
      b. Participants may behave unnaturally as a result of repeated exposure to a test situation (*practice effects*).
      c. Cultural–historical changes can cause **cohort effects**—particular influences on one group that may make results inapplicable to other groups.
  3. The Cross-Sectional Design (p. 41)
      a. In a **cross-sectional design,** groups of people differing in age are studied at the same point in time.
      b. Because participants are measured only once, the problems of participant dropout or practice effects are avoided.
  4. Problems in Conducting Cross-Sectional Research (pp. 41–42)
      a. It does not provide evidence about individual differences.
      b. Cohort effects may occur, reflecting unique experiences associated with the time period in which people in each age group were growing up, rather than age-related changes.
  5. Improving Developmental Designs (pp. 42–43)
      a. Sequential Designs (pp. 42–43)
          (1) In a **sequential design,** investigators conduct several similar cross-sectional or longitudinal studies (called *sequences*) at varying times.
          (2) This design detects cohort effects by comparing results for same-age participants who were born in different years.
          (3) This design permits both longitudinal and cross-sectional comparisons.
          (4) Sequential design also is efficient.

      b. Examining Microcosms of Development (p. 43)
        (1) The **microgenetic design,** an adaptation of the longitudinal approach, captures the processes that produce change by presenting children with a novel task and following their mastery over a series of closely spaced sessions.
        (2) Microgenetic studies are very difficult to carry out, and they are subject to practice effects.
      c. Combining Experimental and Developmental Designs (p. 43)
        (1) Sometimes researchers can explore the causal link between experiences and development by experimentally manipulating the experiences, producing results that may provide strong evidence for a causal relationship.
        (2) This type of combined approach is increasingly common.

   G. Ethics in Research on Children (pp. 43–46)
      1. Special ethical guidelines are needed for research with children, who are more vulnerable than adults to physical and psychological harm, to ensure that the quest for scientific knowledge does not exploit them.
      2. Children's immaturity can make it difficult for them to evaluate the meaning of their research participation.
      3. The ethical principle of *informed consent* requires special interpretation when participants are children. For children 7 years and older, their own informed consent, as well as that of their parents, should be obtained.
      4. In ethnic minority communities where deference to authority and meeting the needs of a guest (the researcher) are highly valued, special care must be taken to ensure that children and parents do not consent when they actually would rather not do so.
      5. Special precautions should be taken in the use of deception and concealment with children, which should be done only if investigators can satisfy institutional committees that such practices are necessary.
      6. *Debriefing,* providing a full account and justification of research activities, should take place with children, but does not always work as well as with adults, because their trust in adults may be undermined.

LECTURE ENHANCEMENTS

LECTURE ENHANCEMENT 1.1
Building Child Resilience Through Family Intervention (p. 10)

Time: 5–10 minutes

Objective: To highlight strategies for building resilience in families with children.

Compared to strained parent-child relationships, a warm, parent-child bond is associated with diverse benefits, including peer acceptance, higher-quality friendships, higher levels of altruism and moral development, greater problem-solving skills, and higher academic achievement. According to Sheridan, Eagle, and Dowd (2005), educators and mental health professionals can use the following strategies to build resilience in families, which greatly enhances child development:

(1) *Base intervention efforts on family-identified needs.* Professionals must be responsive to a family's most salient needs and develop both short- and long-term goals. Each family will likely have unique needs. For example, one family may need financial assistance and access to public transportation, while another family may need mental health services and high-quality child care.

(2) *Use existing family strengths and capabilities to mobilize family resources.* Although personal and/or environmental conditions (for example, mental health problems, poverty, unemployment, lack of high-quality child care, neighborhood crime) may limit a family's ability to identify or access strengths, all families have assets that can be used to build resilience. Professionals must help family members identify, access, and mobilize strengths.

(3) *Maximize social networks and supports.* Troubled families may perceive social networks and supports as inaccessible. For example, some parents view schools and unavailable and unresponsive to their family's needs. However, research shows that positive parent-school partnerships can greatly enhance child development. Professionals must help families forge positive relationships with primary systems, such as schools, child-care centers, and mental health agencies.

(4) *Concern should be with the process of family change as well as outcomes.* By helping families identify needs and goals, professionals can help promote positive outcomes. When families are actively involved in intervention efforts, they tend to be committed to following through with both short- and long-term goals.

In small groups, have students list factors that support resilience in childhood and adolescence. Next, ask students to review ecological systems theory on pages 25–27 of the text. For each factor listed, students should determine in which level of the environment it belongs. Why is it important to intervene at multiple levels of the environment?

Sheridan, S. M., Eagle, J. W., & Dowd, S. E. (2005). In S. Goldstein & R. B. Brooks (Eds.), *Handbook of resilience in children* (pp. 165–179). New York: Springer.

LECTURE ENHANCEMENT 1.2
An Illustration of the Case Study Method: A Musical Prodigy (p. 44)

Time: 5–10 minutes

Objective: To supplement text discussion of the case study method using an example of a 6-year-old musical prodigy.

As discussed in the text, the clinical, or case study, method is used to obtain as complete a picture as possible of an individual's psychological functioning and the experiences that led up to it. Often it is the only method suited to investigating the development of rare instances of human characteristics.

Although many researchers have sought to understand factors that contribute to the development of musical prodigies, no researcher has yet to explain this unusual phenomenon. In one study, Ruthsatz and Detterman (2003) observed and assessed the skills of a 6-year-old musical prodigy named Derek. Derek was an only child of an intact family in the southern United States. By age 6, Derek had released two CDs, appeared in two movies, and performed in countless recitals. Derek sang in both English and Spanish and played a variety of musical instruments, despite never having been exposed to structured music lessons. According to his parents, Derek learned music simply by listening to other performers. No one in his family had shown any accelerated music abilities. Derek's mother played the piano, but only as a recreational activity.

The researchers administered an intelligence test that assessed verbal reasoning, abstract / visual reasoning, quantitative reasoning, and short-term memory. They also administered the Intermediate Measures of Music Audiation, which measures musical aptitude, or the ability to benefit from music instruction. Results indicated that Derek's general level of intelligence was 132—in the superior range. The intelligence test also revealed that Derek had extraordinary memory skills, which is consistent with previous research reporting that exceptional memory is common in highly talented musicians. On the Intermediate Measures of Music Audiation, Derek again scored in the superior range: Derek's composite score was equal to or greater than 98 percent of his musically talented agemates. Although Ruthsatz and Detterman (2003) were unable to draw any conclusions abut the origins of Derek's prodigious talent, their results agree with other case studies: Exceptional memory skills often combine with high musical aptitude in musical prodigies.

Ruthsatz, J., & Detterman, D. K. (2003). An extraordinary memory: The case study of a musical prodigy. *Intelligence, 31,* 509–518.

LECTURE ENHANCEMENT 1.3
Illustrating Naturalistic Observation: Does Time of Day Influence Hyperactive Behavior in Children with ADHD? (pp. 31–33)

Time: 10–15 minutes

Objective: To illustrate the methodology used in a naturalistic observation.

As discussed in the text, researchers sometimes go into the field, or natural environment, to observe human behavior—a method called naturalistic observation. You can illustrate this method using the following study:

Previous research indicates that time of day is related to problem behavior in children with ADHD. However, there is little consensus on when children with ADHD experience an increase in symptoms—higher rates of hyperactivity and lower rates of attention. Some researchers report that behavior problems subside, and others that they become more pronounced, in the late afternoon. To examine the relationship between time of day and hyperactive behavior, Antrop, Roeyers, and De Baecke (2005) recruited fourteen 6- to 12-year-old boys with ADHD and fourteen controls matched on age, SES, and classroom attendance. Using one-minute intervals, two observers rated children's behavior in their classrooms for an entire day on the following dimensions:

1. The degree of out-of-seat behavior

2. The degree of nonproductive, repetitive movements

3. The degree of inattention to class activities or off-task behavior (such as playing with papers or getting up from the desk)

4. The degree of vocalization or noisiness

5. The degree of disturbing the teacher or classmates

Each rating ranged from 1 (not at all applicable) to 6 (very much applicable). In addition, two video cameras were installed in each classroom, one focused on the ADHD child and the other on the control child, to pick up any information the observers missed. Parents and teachers were asked to complete a questionnaire about each child that focused on behaviors associated with ADHD.

Results indicated that during the afternoon, the children with ADHD were more restless and noisy and got up from their seats more often than the control children. These outcomes were particularly strong following afternoon playtime. Overall, these findings suggest that time of day—particularly afternoon time—is associated with an increase in certain aspects of hyperactivity in children with ADHD.

A strength of this study is the insight it offers into the behavior of children with ADHD in natural classroom environments. Although the children were aware of the observers, the teachers indicated that the children behaved as they do on a typical day at school. Despite the benefits of naturalistic observation, however, not all children may have the same opportunity to display a particular behavior in everyday life. In this investigation, some children may have engaged in more or less hyperactivity than they might have otherwise displayed as a result of the classroom schedule of activities. Afternoon playtime, in particular, seemed to energize the activity level and disruptiveness of children with ADHD.

On the basis of these findings, ask students to consider how teachers might restructure the school day so children with ADHD are less likely to show an afternoon rise in hyperactivity. Using their knowledge of research strategies, have students design an evaluation of their restructuring plan that makes use of naturalistic observations and either the field experiment or the natural, or quasi-, experimental design.

Antrop, I., Roeyers, H., & De Baecke, L. (2005). Effects of time of day on classroom behavior in children with ADHD. *School Psychology International, 26,* 29–43.

LECTURE ENHANCEMENT 1.4
Illustrating the Longitudinal Research Design: Impact of Family Transitions on Child Adjustment (pp. 40–41)

Time: 15–20 minutes

Objective: To illustrate the features of longitudinal research.

As noted in the text, researchers often use the longitudinal research design for tracking developmental change. To demonstrate longitudinal methodology, you can present the following study in class.

To examine the impact of family transitions—such as parental separation, divorce, remarriage, or death—on children's development, Ruschena and collaborators (2005) followed 2,443 infants and their parents from 1983 to 2000. Attrition rates reduced the final sample size by nearly half—to 1,260 children and 1,310 parents. The researchers collected the following information:

(1) Demographic information, including family background, number of children, geographic location, and SES, was obtained at the beginning of the study.

(2) At several points throughout the study, parents were asked to complete behavior checklists that focused on appropriate and inappropriate behaviors for the child's age. The researchers were interested in aggression, hyperactivity, impulsivity, anxiety, depression, and fearfulness.

(3) During early childhood and adolescence, parents rated their children on various aspects of temperament, such as reactivity, persistence, and approach–withdrawal. Parents were also asked to characterize their child as easy or difficult.

(4) Parents and children provided child social-skills ratings that measured cooperation, assertiveness, responsibility, and empathy. The social-skills measure was administered when children were 11 years old and again when they were 13 years old.

(5) When children were age 15 or 16, parents completed a peer relationship scale, which assessed adolescent affiliation with substance-using and / or antisocial peers.

(6) When children were 17 or 18 years old, parents were asked about any family transitions in the child's lifetime (parental separation, death, divorce, or remarriage, the presence of stepsiblings, and the number of home and school moves). Children were then asked to describe their reactions to family transitions, such as ambivalence, regret, relief, or anger. During this time, parents were also asked to complete a school problems checklist, a parent-adolescent conflict scale, and a marital conflict scale, and children completed an attachment-to-parents questionnaire.

Findings revealed that children who experienced a major transition in the first 18 years of life did not exhibit more academic, peer, or behavioral difficulties than children who did not experience a major transition. The one exception pertained to children who experienced multiple and frequent transitions early in life: Several closely spaced transitions predicted later academic difficulties, parent–child conflict, and behavioral problems. These effects were particularly strong for children who had experienced parental divorce.

Parental ratings of child temperament indicated that children seen as difficult in early childhood had higher rates of behavior problems than children viewed as easy, and these problems persisted into adolescence. A difficult temperament was also associated with strained parent–child relations and peer difficulties. Parental reports of marital conflict did not necessarily predict negative child outcomes. Instead, children with an easy temperament and a positive relationship who had at least one parent showed more favorable academic, social, and behavioral development than children with a difficult temperament and strained relations with parents. Overall, these findings suggest that a major life transition does not necessarily put children at risk for negative developmental outcomes. Instead, it seems that multiple transitions and a difficult temperament predict a variety of adjustment difficulties, particularly when parent–child relations are strained.

Implementing a longitudinal design to answer the researchers' questions was beneficial for several reasons. Perhaps most importantly, the longitudinal design permitted an examination of the impact of major life transitions on later development. The investigators were also able to identify individual and group differences in development. For example, children with an easy temperament developed more favorably than children with a difficult temperament. In addition, children who experienced only one major transition fared much better than children who experienced several closely spaced transitions. Despite these benefits, the study had one important limitation: Between 1983 and 2000, the researchers lost nearly half of their original sample. High attrition rates, common in longitudinal studies, can lead to biased samples that no longer represent the intended population. As a result, generalization of findings becomes more difficult.

Ruschena, E., Prior, M., Sanson, A., & Smart, D. (2005). A longitudinal study of adolescent adjustment following family transitions. *Journal of Child Psychology and Psychiatry, 46,* 353–363.

LEARNING ACTIVITIES

LEARNING ACTIVITY 1.1
What Is Your Stance on the Three Basic Issues of Human Development? (pp. 6–9)

To help students better understand the three basic issues of human development, present this activity as an in-class assignment. The exercise will help students express their own viewpoints on some of the controversies in the field of human development.

Directions: Listed below are four pairs of statements related to basic issues about human development. Read each statement carefully. Then circle the statement in each pair that more closely reflects your own view.

1. A. Development is a continuous, gradual progression, with new abilities, skills, and knowledge gradually added at a relatively uniform pace.
   B. Development occurs at different rates, alternating between periods of little change and periods of abrupt, rapid change.

2. A. All humans follow the same general sequence of development.
   B. Each individual has a unique course of development.

3. A. Children respond to the world in much the same way as adults. The main difference is that children's thinking is less sophisticated and complex than adults'.
   B. Children have unique ways of thinking about and responding to the world that are very different from those of adults.

4. A. An individual's personality is mostly determined by heredity.
   B. An individual's personality can be modified through caregiving experiences.

Next, have students break into small groups and discuss their answers. What is their stance on the three basic issues of human development? Which theories take a stance similar to their own? If students had to choose a theory that best represents their own view of development, would they choose a single theory or would they select certain components of several theories? What aspects of their chosen theory (or theories) make it more attractive than the others?

LEARNING ACTIVITY 1.2
Keeping a Theory / Research Notebook (pp. 14–29)

Given the many developmental theories that exist, students are likely to find some more appealing and plausible than others. Encourage students to construct a systematic list of their theoretical likes and dislikes by keeping a theory / research notebook. For each theory, students should list the concepts and principles they find important and those they believe to be inadequate or incorrect. As they learn more throughout the course, they can revise their opinions, noting research that supports their changing views. At the end of the course, students should have developed a personal perspective on human development, which may emphasize one theory or blend aspects of several or many theories.

LEARNING ACTIVITY 1.3
Mid-Twentieth-Century Theories and Recent Theoretical Perspectives (pp. 14–29)

Present the following exercise to students as a quiz or in-class activity.

Directions: Read each of the following statements and indicate whether it is *True* (T) or *False* (F).

Statements:

_____ 1. According to Freud, in each stage of psychosexual development, parents walk a fine line between permitting too much or too little gratification of their child's basic needs.

_____ 2. Both Freud and Erikson pointed out that normal development must be understood in relation to each culture's life situation.

_____ 3. Behaviorism and social learning theory have been praised for acknowledging people's contributions to their own development.

_____ 4. In Piaget's theory, as the brain develops and children's experiences expand, they move through four broad stages, each characterized by qualitatively distinct ways of thinking.

_____ 5. Research indicates that Piaget underestimated the competencies of infants and preschoolers.

_____ 6. Information-processing researchers view the mind as a symbol-manipulating system through which information flows.

_____ 7. Evolutionary psychologists are solely concerned with the biological bases of development.

_____ 8. According to Vygotsky, social interaction is necessary for children to acquire the ways of thinking and behaving that make up a community's culture.

_____ 9. The mesosystem is made up of social settings that do not contain the developing person but nevertheless affect experiences in immediate settings.

_____ 10. According to Bronfenbrenner, the environment is dynamic and ever-changing.

Answers:

1. T
2. F
3. F
4. T
5. T
6. T
7. F
8. T
9. F
10. T

LEARNING ACTIVITY 1.4
Applying Ecological Systems Theory to a "Hot Topic" in Child Development (pp. 25–27)

Have students form small groups and select a "hot topic" in child development, such as the effects of divorce, child abuse and neglect, child-care quality, the obesity epidemic, public policies for children, or sex education programs in the schools. Once students have selected their topic, ask them to consider how each level of the environment may affect development, including bidirectional influences and the role of third parties.

LEARNING ACTIVITY 1.5
Thinking About Research Methods and Designs (pp. 29, 31–43)

Pose the following questions to students for an in-class discussion:

1. An investigator is interested is determining whether infant child care leads to an insecure attachment bond between children and their mothers during the first year of life as well as into the preschool years. What research method and design would you use for this study, and why? Would there be any special ethical considerations with this type of study? If so, what are they?

2. An investigator is interested in determining whether sociability in children is related to school achievement and whether this relationship varies for children in preschool, grade school, and middle school. What research method and design would you use for this study, and why? Would there be any special ethical considerations with this type of study? If so, what are they?

LEARNING ACTIVITY 1.6
Critiquing Journal Articles (pp. 29, 31–43)

Have students select and read two articles about child development published during the past four years. Each article should present an empirical study on a topic related to child development. Some journals to consider for this activity are *American Psychologist*, *Child Development*, *Developmental Psychology*, *Early Childhood Research Quarterly*, *Journal of Adolescence*, *Journal of Applied Developmental Psychology*, and *Developmental Science*.

Next, have students (1) prepare a brief summary of the problem, method, results, discussion, and conclusions of the two articles; (2) indicate the type of research method(s) and design(s) used; and (3) identify any potential problems for achieving accurate results posed by the research design(s). Students can then discuss their findings in small groups or as a class.

LEARNING ACTIVITY 1.7
Cross-Sectional, Longitudinal, and Sequential Research Designs (pp. 40–43)

Present the following exercise as a quiz or in-class activity.

Directions: Listed below are descriptions, challenges, and examples of cross-sectional, longitudinal, and sequential research designs. For each statement, determine which research design is being described.

Statements:

1. The researcher studies groups of participants who differ in age at the same point in time.
2. The researcher is interested in whether or not frequent exposure to violent television in early childhood predicts aggressive and antisocial behavior in adulthood.
3. May have the same problems as longitudinal and cross-sectional strategies, but the design itself helps identify difficulties.
4. Age-related changes may be distorted because of biased sampling, participant dropout, practice effects, or cohort effects. Theoretical and methodological changes in the field can make findings obsolete.
5. The researcher follows a sequence of samples (two or more age groups), collecting data on them at the same points in time.
6. Does not permit the study of individual developmental trends. Age differences may be distorted because of cohort effects.
7. The researcher is interested in age-related changes in children's problem-solving skills. The researcher selects three samples—preschool-age children, school-age children, and adolescents—and tracks them for five years.
8. The researcher is interested in how children of different ages process traumatic events, such as terrorism or natural disasters. The researcher recruits children in grades 3, 6, 9, and 12 for the study and interviews them about the London terrorist attacks, the Asian tsunami, and Hurricane Katrina.
9. The researcher studies the same group of participants repeatedly at different ages.

Answers:

1. Cross-sectional
2. Longitudinal
3. Sequential
4. Longitudinal
5. Sequential
6. Cross-sectional
7. Sequential
8. Cross-sectional
9. Longitudinal

LEARNING ACTIVITY 1.8
Exploring Ethical Guidelines for Research with Children (pp. 43, 45–46)

To supplement the text coverage of ethics in child research, have students visit the following website: *http://www. srcd.org/ethicalstandards.html.* As students review the website, have them compare ethical guidelines for children with those presented in the text. What are some special ethical considerations for research with children? Do the ethical guidelines presented in the website adequately protect child research participants from undue risk? Explain.

ASK YOURSELF . . .

REVIEW: Why are there many theories of child development? Cite three basic issues on which almost all theories take a stand. (pp. 6–9)

The field of child development contains many theories with very different ideas about what children are like and how they change. The study of child development provides no ultimate truth because investigators do not always agree on the meaning of what they see. In addition, children are complex beings, who change physically, cognitively, emotionally, and socially. As yet, no single theory has explained all these aspects. However, the existence of many theories helps advance knowledge because researchers are continually trying to support, contradict, and integrate these different points of view.

Almost all theories take a stand on three basic issues: (1) Is the course of development continuous or discontinuous? (2) Does one course of development characterize all children, or are there many possible courses? (3) Are genetic or environmental factors more important in influencing development?

APPLY: Anna, a high school counselor, has devised a program that integrates classroom learning with vocational training to help adolescents at risk for school dropout stay in school and transition smoothly to work life. What is Anna's position on *stability versus change* in development? Explain. (p. 9)

Anna's program reflects a belief in the possibility of *change* in development. First, she takes the position that environmental influences, not just heredity, are important. Second, by establishing a program for adolescents, she rejects the view that early experiences establish lifelong behavioral patterns that cannot be fully overcome by later, more positive experiences. Taking a more optimistic view of development, Anna believes that change is possible and even likely if it is supported by new experiences. She believes that high school students who are at risk for dropout will be able to benefit from the program she has developed, because it will provide positive experiences that will enable them to overcome the powerful negative events of their first few years.

CONNECT: Provide an example of how one domain of development (physical, cognitive, or emotional/social) can affect development in another domain. (pp. 4–5)

Development is often divided into three broad domains: physical, cognitive, and emotional and social, each of which influences and is influenced by the others. For example, new motor capacities, such as reaching, sitting, crawling, and walking (physical), contribute greatly to infants' understanding of their surroundings (cognitive). When babies think and act more competently, adults stimulate them more with games, language, and expressions of delight at their new achievements (emotional and social). These enriched experiences, in turn, promote all aspects of development.

REFLECT: Cite an aspect of your development that differs from a parent's or grandparent's when he or she was your age. How might contexts explain this difference? (p. 9)

This is an open-ended question with no right or wrong answer.

REVIEW: Suppose we could arrange a debate between John Locke and Jean-Jacques Rousseau on the nature–nurture controversy. Summarize the argument that each historical figure is likely to present. (pp. 11–12)

JOHN LOCKE: Locke believed that each child begins as a blank slate (*tabula rasa*), who is neither good nor evil and whose character will be shaped entirely by experience. He championed nurture—the power of the environment to shape the child—and believed that parents can mold their child as they wish through careful instruction, effective example, and rewards (such as praise) for good behavior.

JEAN-JACQUES ROUSSEAU: Rousseau, in contrast, believed that the role of nature is paramount: He viewed children as noble savages, born with a sense of right and wrong and an innate plan for orderly, healthy growth. In this view, adult training has no value; it can only harm or delay a child's genetically determined, naturally unfolding course of growth.

CONNECT: What do the ideas of Rousseau, Darwin, and Hall have in common? (pp. 12–13)

Rousseau, Darwin, and Hall all emphasized the importance of nature over nurture in development. Rousseau saw development as a discontinuous, stagewise process; he believed that children determine their own destiny and that they develop according to a naturally unfolding course of growth.

Darwin's theory also emphasized the innate characteristics of a species. He believed in survival of the fittest—the idea that those individuals who best meet the survival requirements of their environment will live long enough to reproduce, passing on their more beneficial characteristics to future generations.

Hall, inspired by Darwin's ideas about evolution, also saw development as a genetically determined process, which he imagined unfolding automatically, much like a flower.

REFLECT: Find out whether your parents read Gesell, Spock, or other parenting advice books when you were growing up. What questions most concerned them? Do you think today's parents have concerns that differ from those of your parents? Explain. (pp. 4, 13)

This is an open-ended question with no right or wrong answer.

REVIEW: What aspect of behaviorism made it attractive to critics of psychoanalytic theory? How did Piaget's theory respond to a major limitation of behaviorism? (pp. 16–18)

The early behaviorists rejected the psychoanalytic concern with the unseen workings of the mind. They sought, instead, to create an objective science of psychology in which directly observable events—stimuli and responses—are the appropriate focus of study. As psychologists became interested in whether behaviorism might offer a more direct and effective explanation of children's social behavior than the less precise concepts of psychoanalytic theory, several kinds of social learning theory emerged, with an emphasis on modeling, or observational learning, as a powerful source of development.

However, modeling and reinforcement—two important themes of behaviorism—were criticized in turn for providing an incomplete account of development. Many theorists believed that behaviorism offered too narrow a view of important environmental influences, while also underestimating children's contributions to their own development.

Piaget responded to these concerns by maintaining that knowledge could not be imposed on a child through reinforcement or rewards. Rather, children actively construct knowledge as they manipulate and explore their world. Besides investigating children's understanding of their physical environment, Piaget explored their reasoning about the social world. His cognitive-developmental perspective convinced the field that children are active learners whose minds consist of rich structures of knowledge.

APPLY: A 4-year-old becomes frightened of the dark and refuses to go to sleep at night. How would a psychoanalyst and a behaviorist differ in their views of how this problem developed? (pp. 14–18)

According to the psychoanalytic approach, children move through a series of stages in which they confront conflicts between biological drives and social expectations. In this view, fear of the dark reflects an unconscious motive or deep-seated anxiety within the child. A psychoanalyst might conclude, for example, that the child's fear really represents anxiety about nighttime separation from the parent. Once the anxiety is resolved, the fear will subside.

In contrast, behaviorists look at environmental contingencies and behavioral responses, not at the inner workings of the mind. From this perspective, a child would be scared of the dark if previous experiences in the dark were negative. Perhaps the child heard a sharp, loud noise at night or was frightened by the concrete visual images of a nightmare. Based on these previous experiences, the child would be conditioned to respond fearfully to being in the dark.

CONNECT: Although social learning theory focuses on social development and Piaget's theory on cognitive development, each has enhanced our understanding of other domains. Mention an additional domain addressed by each theory. (pp. 17–20)

Social learning theory emphasizes modeling, or observational learning, as a source of development. In addition to its original emphasis on the emotional/social domain, however, the theory has evolved to stress the importance of cognition, or thinking. As a result, it is often known as a social-cognitive, rather than a social learning, approach. In addition to explaining children's social development, social-cognitive theory provides insight into how individuals control their own development in the cognitive domain through the attitudes, values, and convictions they acquire about themselves.

Piaget's cognitive-developmental theory focuses on cognitive development but also explores how children reason about the social world. It has sparked a great deal of research on children's conceptions of themselves, other people, and human relationships—all aspects of the social/emotional domain.

REVIEW: What features of Vygotsky's sociocultural theory distinguish it from Piaget's theory and from information processing? (pp. 18–20, 21–22, 24–25)

Vygotsky's sociocultural theory focuses on how culture—the values, beliefs, customs, and skills of a social group—is transmitted to the next generation. In his view, social interaction—in particular, cooperative dialogues with more knowledgeable members of society—is necessary for children to acquire the ways of thinking and feeling that make up their community's culture. Like both Piaget and the information-processing theorists, Vygotsky saw children as active, constructive beings. But whereas Piaget's theory and the information-processing view emphasize children's *independent* efforts to make sense of their world, Vygotsky regarded cognitive development as a *socially mediated process*, dependent on the support of adults and more-expert peers as children tackle new tasks. In contrast to both of these views, Vygotsky's theory considers the various environmental contexts that contribute to children's development.

REVIEW: Explain how each recent theoretical perspective regards children as active contributors to their own development. (pp. 21–28)

INFORMATION PROCESSING: Like Piaget's cognitive-developmental theory, information processing regards children as active, sense-making beings. In this view, from presentation to the senses at input to behavioral responses at output, the information is actively coded, transformed, and organized, similar to the functioning of a computer program. When presented with a task, children perform a set of mental operations and experiment with various strategies in their attempts to solve the problem.

ETHOLOGY AND EVOLUTIONARY DEVELOPMENTAL PSYCHOLOGY: Both ethologists and evolutionary developmental psychologists are interested in how individuals respond to their environment by learning adaptive behavior patterns—that is, behaviors that promote survival. For instance, newborns come into the world equipped with certain behaviors, such as smiling, babbling, grasping, and crying, that serve as built-in social signals, encouraging the caregiver to approach, care for, and interact with the baby. By actively working to keep the parent near, these behaviors help ensure that the baby will be fed, protected from danger, and provided with stimulation and affection necessary for growth.

VYGOTSKY'S SOCIOCULTURAL THEORY: Vygotsky's theory focuses on how *culture*—the values, beliefs, customs, and skills of a social group—is transmitted to the next generation. According to Vygotsky, social interaction—in particular, cooperative dialogues with more knowledgeable members of society—is necessary for children to acquire the ways of thinking and behaving that make up a community's culture. Like Piaget, Vygotsky saw children as active, constructive beings. But whereas Piaget emphasized children's independent efforts to make sense of their world, Vygotsky viewed cognitive development as a socially mediated process, dependent on assistance provided by adults and more expert peers as children tackle new challenges.

ECOLOGICAL SYSTEMS THEORY: Ecological systems theory views the child as developing within a complex system of relationships affected by multiple levels of the surrounding environment. Specifically, the child's biologically influenced dispositions join with environmental forces to mold development. Changes in life events can be imposed on the child or they can arise from within the child, since as children get older they select, modify, and create many of their own settings and experiences. How they do so depends on their physical, intellectual, and personality characteristics and their environmental opportunities. In ecological systems theory, children are both products and producers of their environments.

DYNAMIC SYSTEMS PERSPECTIVE: According to the dynamic systems perspective, the child's mind, body, and physical and social worlds form an *integrated system* that guides mastery of new skills. The system is *dynamic,* or constantly in motion. A change in any part of it disrupts the current organism–environment relationship. When this happens, the child actively reorganizes his or her behavior so the various components of the system work together again but in a more complex, effective way.

CONNECT: Return to the Biology and Environment box on page 10. How does the story of John and Gary illustrate bidirectional influences within the microsystem, as described in ecological systems theory? (pp. 10, 25–27)

The microsystem consists of activities and interaction patterns in the child's immediate surroundings. Bronfenbrenner emphasizes that to understand child development at this level, we must keep in mind that all relationships are *bidirectional:* Adults affect children's behavior, but children's biologically and socially influenced characteristics—their physical attributes, personalities, and capacities—also affect adults' behavior. In the example on page 10, both John and Gary experienced similar environmental stressors during their childhood and adolescence. But whereas Gary was able to overcome the odds and forge a happy, healthy, well-adapted life, John fell victim to the effects of the adversity he had experienced in his earlier years. Gary's personal qualities, such as his ability to make new friends and adapt to new surroundings each time his family moved, likely contributed to his resilience. John, in contrast, responded to similar changes by becoming anxious and angry. Gary's close relationship with his grandfather may have helped him overcome the effects of a stressful home life while also providing him with a positive role model with whom he could relate. And unlike John, Gary had opportunities to participate in community life—for example, by volunteering for Habitat for Humanity—which likely strengthened his resilience.

REFLECT: To illustrate the chronosystem in ecological systems theory, select an important event from your childhood, such as a move to a new neighborhood, a class with an inspiring teacher, or parental divorce. How did the event affect you? How might its impact have differed had you been five years younger? How about five years older? (p. 27)

This is an open-ended question with no right or wrong answer.

REVIEW: Why might a researcher choose structured observation over naturalistic observation? How about the reverse? What might lead the researcher to opt for clinical interviewing over systematic observation? (pp. 31–33)

Naturalistic observations allow investigators to see directly the everyday behaviors they hope to explain. However, not all individuals have the same opportunity to display a particular behavior in everyday life. To deal with this limitation, researchers sometimes choose *structured observation,* in which the investigator sets up a laboratory situation that evokes the behavior of interest so that every participant has an equal opportunity to display the response. Although structured observation permits more control over the research situation, there is no way to ensure that participants will behave in the laboratory as they do in everyday life.

Some researchers are less concerned with directly observable behavior. Instead, they are interested in exploring the perceptions, thoughts, abilities, feelings, attitudes, beliefs, or past experiences of their participants. In these instances, researchers often select a clinical interview—a flexible, conversational style used to probe for the participant's point of view. The clinical interview not only permits people to display their thoughts in terms as close as possible to the way they think in everyday life but also provides a great deal of information in a fairly brief period of time.

APPLY: A researcher wants to study the thoughts and feelings of children who have a parent on active duty in the military. Which method is best suited for investigating this question? Why? (pp. 33–34)

The clinical interview is best suited to investigating this research question, because the researcher wants to learn about children's thoughts and feelings. The clinical interview permits children to display their thoughts in terms that are as close as possible to they way they think in everyday life. It can also provide a large amount of information in a fairly brief period.

Another possible method is the structured interview, in which each participant is asked the same questions in the same way. The structured interview reduces the risk of distorting the results that can occur when questions are phrased differently for each participant. It is also more efficient—answers are briefer and take less time to gather. However, the procedure does not yield the same depth of information as the clinical interview.

CONNECT: What strengths and limitations do the clinical, or case study, method and ethnography have in common? (pp. 34–35)

Like the clinical method, ethnography is a descriptive, qualitative research technique. But instead of aiming to understand a single individual, it is directed toward understanding a culture or distinct social group through participant observation. However, as with clinical research, investigators' cultural values and theoretical commitments sometimes lead them to observe selectively or misinterpret what they see.

REVIEW: Explain how cohort effects can distort the findings of both longitudinal and cross-sectional studies. How does the sequential design reveal cohort effects? (pp. 40–43)

Both longitudinal and cross-sectional studies can be influenced by cohort effects—the particular set of historical and cultural conditions that influence individuals born in the same time period. Therefore, results based on one cohort may not apply to children developing at other times. For example, a longitudinal study of social development carried out around the time of World War II would probably result in quite different findings than if it were carried out in the first decade of the twenty-first century, during the decade of the 1960s, or during the Great Depression of the 1930s. Similarly, a cross-sectional design that compares 5-year-old cohorts and 15-year-old cohorts—groups born and reared in different years—may not really identify age-related changes. Rather, the results may reflect unique experiences associated with the different historical time period in which each age group grew up.

In sequential designs, researchers overcome some of these limitations by conducting several similar longitudinal or cross-sectional studies, or sequences, at varying times. Sequential designs permit researchers to find out whether cohort effects are operating by comparing people of the same age who were born in different years. If the samples do not differ on the measured variables, the researcher can rule out cohort effects.

APPLY: A researcher compares children who went to summer leadership camps with children who attended athletic camps. She finds that those who attended leadership camps are friendlier. Should the investigator tell parents that sending children to leadership camps will cause them to be more sociable? Why or why not? (pp. 35, 37)

No. This particular study is a correlational design, in which the researcher looks at relationships between participants' characteristics and their behavior or development. Although this type of design allows researchers to gather information on individuals in their natural life circumstances, it has one major limitation: We cannot infer cause and effect. Therefore, the researcher cannot conclude that attending summer leadership camps is superior to attending athletic camps. Perhaps more sociable children choose to attend leadership camps over athletic camps. It is also possible that a third variable that the researcher did not even consider contributed to the research findings.

CONNECT: Review the experiment on music lessons and intelligence reported in the Social Issues: Education box on page 44. Why was it ethically important for the researchers to offer music lessons to the no-lessons control group during the year after completion of the study? (*Hint:* Refer to Table 1.7.) (pp. 43–46)

One of the research rights established by the American Psychological Association states that when researchers are investigating experimental treatments believed to be beneficial, children in control groups have the right to alternative beneficial treatments if they are available. In this case, music lessons were found to have beneficial effects on children's intelligence. Therefore, it was important that the no-lessons control group have an opportunity that was similar to the advantage provided the experimental group, once the favorable impact of music lessons was known.

REFLECT: Suppose a researcher asks you to enroll your baby in a 10-year longitudinal study. What factors would lead you to agree and stay involved? Do your answers shed light on why longitudinal studies often have biased samples? Explain. (pp. 40–41)

This is an open-ended question with no right or wrong answer.

SUGGESTED STUDENT READINGS

Boyden, J., de Berry, J. (Eds.). (2004). *Children and youth on the front lines: Ethnography, armed conflict, and displacement.* New York: Berghahn Books. Presents fascinating, ethnographic accounts of children's experiences with violence, war, and trauma.

Bronfenbrenner, U. (Ed.). (2005). *Making human beings human.* Thousand Oaks, CA: Sage. An excellent resource for anyone interested in psychology, sociology, education, family studies, or related fields, this book examines the complexity of human development, including one's ability to influence and be influenced by many layers of the environment.

Greene, S., & Hogan, D. (Eds.). (2005). *Researching children's experiences: Approaches and methods.* Thousand Oaks: Sage. Examines the various methods and designs for conducting research with children, including strengths, limitations, and ethical concerns.

Schoon, I. (2006). *Risk and resilience: Adaptations in changing times.* New York: Cambridge University Press. Using findings from Britain's National Child Development and British Cohort Studies, this book examines factors that promote and undermine resilience in childhood and during the transition to adulthood.

TRANSPARENCIES

T-1 **Is Development Continuous or Discontinuous?** Figure 1.2 (p. 7)

T-2 **Freud's Psychosexual Stages** Table 1.1 (p. 15)

T-3 **Erikson's Psychosexual Stages (Part One)** Table 1.2 (p. 16)

T-4 **Erikson's Psychosexual Stages (Part Two)** Figure 1.2 (p. 16)

T-5 **Piaget's Stages of Cognitive Development** Table 1.3 (p. 20)

T-6 **Information-Processing Flowchart Showing the Steps That a 5-Year-Old Used to Solve a Bridge-Building Problem** Figure 1.3 (p. 22)

T-7 **Structure of the Environment in Ecological Systems Theory** Figure 1.4 (p. 26)

T-8 **The Dynamic Systems View of Development** Figure 1.5 (p. 28)

T-9 **Does the Way Adults End Their Angry Encounters Affect Children's Emotional Reactions?** Figure 1.7 (p. 38)

MEDIA MATERIALS

DVDs AND VIDEOTAPES

Bandura's Social Cognitive Theory: An Introduction (2003, Davidson Films, 38 min.). Albert Bandura narrates this film, which uses archival materials and new footage to introduce students to the vocabulary and innovative methods of his work. Using examples from his own life, Bandura illustrates the role of chance is shaping the life course. His warm humor and intellectual authority are evident as he introduces his early work with Bobo dolls and his later research on self-efficacy. The four processes of observational learning are reviewed. A Learning Guide is available.

B. F. Skinner: A Fresh Appraisal (1999, Davidson Films, 30 min.). Other than Freud, no psychologist has been so discussed, critiqued, and, at times, maligned as B. F. Skinner. Using both archival and new footage, this program takes a fresh look at who Skinner was and what he said in his 20 books. The vocabulary Skinner invented to describe his ideas and feelings is introduced in context so the student understands how the terms were intended to be used and the research that produced them. The program also lays to rest some myths about Skinner and credits him with contributions not often attributed to him.

Cognitive Development (1995, Cambridge Educational, 58 min.). This program examines and critically evaluates Piaget's theory in light of subsequent research. It clearly describes Piaget's central themes, reviews the cognitive stages of development from birth to age 12, and illustrating children's behavior at each level. Research relevant to each stage is examined, leading to the conclusion that children are more cognitively capable than Piaget believed.

Contexts of Development (1992, RMI Media Productions, 30 min.). This program illustrates how biological factors and social, economic, and cultural influences work together to influence development.

The Developing Child (2001, WGBH Boston with the American Psychological Association, 30 min.). This program, Part 5 of the 12-part series Discovering Psychology, reviews the nature–nurture debate and shows how developmental psychologists study the contributions of both heredity and environment to child development.

Discovering Childhood (1993, RMI Media Productions, 60 min.). Part 1 of the series Developmental Psychology. This program summarizes the history, themes, theories, methodology, and perspectives of the field of developmental psychology. It looks at historical changes in attitudes toward children and provides an overview of major developmental theorists, including Erikson, Hull, Piaget, Skinner, Havighurst, and Lewin.

Do Parents Matter? Judith Harris on the Power of Peers (1999, Films Media Group, 12 min.). In this news segment, *ABC News* correspondent Sylvia Chase interviews Judith Rich Harris, author of *The Nurture Assumption* (1998), about her controversial theory of development, in which Harris argues for the powerful effect of the child's adaptation to peer groups and maintains that parents have relatively little impact on their children's development. The film notes that Steven Pinker, director of the Center for Cognitive Neuroscience at MIT, supports the author's hypothesis, while Harvard child psychologist Jerome Kagan strongly disagrees, citing flaws in Harris's evidence and noting her lack of scientific credentials.

Endless Questions: Critical Thinking and Research (2006, Aquarius Health Care Media, 30 min.). This program, part of the Inside Out series, shows how researchers investigate the question, "Does happiness lead to good health?" using multiple methods: case study, survey, naturalistic observation, correlational studies, and controlled experiments.

Erik H. Erikson: A Life's Work (1992, Davidson Films, 30 min.). This program uses archival material and newly shot footage to give viewers a complete introduction to Erikson's work. The program, which includes commentary by Erikson's colleague Margaret Brenman-Gibson, illustrates how genetics, cultural influences, and unique experiences interact in an individual's life.

How We Study Children (1996, Insight Media, 24 min.). This program illustrates several research methods for investigating children's behavior. It discusses advantages and drawbacks of observational and experimental techniques, as well as ways to address methodological problems.

Infant and Child Development (2001, RMI Media Productions, 30 min.). This program provides an overview of Piaget's four stages of cognitive development.

John Locke (2004, Films Media Group, 21 min.). This program chronicles the life and work of the seventeenth-century English philosopher and political theorist John Locke, whose belief that human character is shaped entirely by experience served as the forerunner of the behaviorist perspective on human development.

Learning: Observational and Cognitive Approaches (2001, RMI Media Productions, 30 min.). This program discusses observational learning and uses the research of B. F. Skinner to illustrate the cognitive process of learning.

The Lily Videos: A Longitudinal View of Life with Down Syndrome (1997, Davidson Films, 3 vols., 33 min. total). This documentary examines the life of Lily, a child born with Down syndrome, from age 10 to 30. It illustrates particular aspects of development throughout childhood, adolescence, and young adulthood, focusing on the challenges Lily faced because of her disability.

Nature and Nurture of Development, Parts I and II (1993, GPN, 30 min. each). Programs 23 and 24 of the Worlds of Childhood series. This program shows how aspects of biology, history, economics, family, peers, school, community, and culture combine to have an impact on individual development.

The Nature of Human Nature (1995, Films Media Group, 58 min.). Evolutionary psychologists believe that the brain, like the body, is a product of natural selection, reflecting successful solutions to the challenges our ancestors faced in the course of millions of years of evolution. This program explores our new understanding of the evolutionary history of the human brain—what series host Roger Bingham describes as a "second Darwinian Revolution."

Research Methods (2001, RMI Media, 30 min.). This program provides an overview of observational and descriptive research by illustrating how the scientific method is used to study the relationship between violent video games and aggression.

Research Methods for the Social Sciences (1995, Insight Media, 33 min.). This program provides an introduction to various research methods, including suggestions for the appropriate use of each method. It discusses key experimental concepts such as control groups; independent and dependent variables; and clinical, correlational, and field methodology. It also examines ethical issues in social science research.

Resiliency: Beating the Odds (1998, Films Media Group, 19 min.). This program investigates resilience—the elusive quality that gives an individual the capacity to rise above extremely difficult life events. It explores the question of why some people thrive despite challenges such as poverty, abuse, and disabilities. The program identifies some personality traits of resilient people and considers ways that individuals can learn to nurture those qualities within themselves.

Study of the Child: History and Trends (1997, Magna Systems, 28 min.). This module lays out the history of child development, starting with early philosophies and exploring changes in beliefs about human nature, with a look at the nature–nurture question. It examines the move away from myths and toward scientific investigation, presents two methods of study, and concludes with six overarching principles derived from child development research.

Study of the Child: Observation (1993, Magna Systems, 37 min.). This program outlines the reasons for observing children as well as techniques, basic components of naturalistic observations, difficulties in observing and recording, and the various types of naturalistic and subjective observations.

Study of the Child: Theories of Development (1997, Magna Systems, 27 min.). This module, which includes brief clips of parents talking about their parenting beliefs and of children in child-care centers, provides an overview of the major theories of child development—cognitive, psychosexual, psychosocial, behaviorist, social learning, and sociocultural—in action. Linking theory to application, it explores the way in which the perspectives of various theorists, including Piaget, Freud, Erikson, Gesell, Skinner, and Vygotsky, may encourage caregivers to focus on isolated aspects of the child rather than on the development of the whole child.

Theories of Development (1997, Insight Media, 29 min.). This film surveys the cognitive, psychosexual, psychosocial, behavioral, social-learning, and sociocultural theories of child development, including the ideas of Piaget, Freud, Erikson, Gesell, Skinner, and Vygotsky. It also discusses how most theories focus on only one aspect of development.

Vygotsky's Developmental Theory: An Introduction (1994, Davidson Films, 28 min.). This program introduces the life and concepts of Lev Vygotsky and illustrates ideas integral to his work: that children construct knowledge in collaboration with more expert partners; that learning leads to development; that development cannot be separated from its social context; and that language plays a central role in cognitive development. The film also provides classroom examples, which are ideally suited for education majors, along with a Learning Guide.

Why Study Human Behavior? (2001, RMI Media, 30 min.). This program introduces psychology as a science of behavior and mental processes. It explains how our lives are enhanced when we understand why we think and act as we do.

Young Minds: Is Zero-to-Three Destiny? (1999, Films Media Group, 11 min.). The idea that Mozart's music could have a lasting impact on the growth of a baby's brain captured the imagination of parents and policymakers alike. In this brief segment, NewsHour correspondent Betty Ann Bowser talks with advocates on both sides of the zero-to-three debate, including Yale child psychiatrist Kyle Pruett, who argues that the child's first three years are crucial, and skeptics John Bruer, author of *The Myth of the First Three Years,* and Harvard child psychologist Jerome Kagan.

TEST BANK

MULTIPLE CHOICE

1) The field of child development is
    A) motivated more by scientific curiosity than practical concerns.
    B) part of a larger field known as developmental science.
    C) not considered an interdisciplinary field because researchers in psychology rarely collaborate with researchers in other fields.
    D) driven largely by theoretical questions about children's behavior.
    Answer: B
    Page Ref: 4
    Skill: Factual
    Objective: 1.1

2) Of the following, which is true regarding the domains of development?
    A) The field of child development is divided into two broad domains: cognitive and social.
    B) The domains of development do not influence one another.
    C) Each period of development is made up of a new set of domains.
    D) The domains of development combine in an integrated, holistic fashion.
    Answer: D
    Page Ref: 4
    Skill: Conceptual
    Objective: 1.1

3) Which period of human development is the most rapid time of change?
    A) the prenatal period
    B) infancy and toddlerhood
    C) middle childhood
    D) adolescence
    Answer: A
    Page Ref: 5
    Skill: Factual
    Objective: 1.2

4) During early childhood,
    A) children form their first intimate ties to others.
    B) a sense of morality becomes evident.
    C) children master basic literacy skills.
    D) thought becomes abstract and idealistic.
    Answer: B
    Page Ref: 6
    Skill: Conceptual
    Objective: 1.2

5) The period of emerging adulthood has been posited by some researchers to
    A) reflect the increasingly prolonged transition to adult roles among youth in many nations.
    B) capture the maturity of youth growing up in many developing nations.
    C) describe those children who take on adult roles early in their adolescent years.
    D) label those adults who act in many ways as if they were still adolescents.
    Answer: A
    Page Ref: 6
    Skill: Conceptual
    Objective: 1.2

6) Theories that are verified by research are vital to the field of child development because they
    A) ensure the proper use of rigorous research procedures.
    B) provide the ultimate truth regarding the development of children.
    C) often serve as a basis for practical action.
    D) are resistant to the influence of cultural values and belief systems.
Answer: C
Page Ref: 6
Skill: Conceptual
Objective: 1.3

7) In the field of child development, a theory's continued existence depends on whether
    A) the general public accepts its predictions as common sense.
    B) it has been tested using a fair set of procedures agreed on by the scientific community and its findings are replicated.
    C) respected authors agree with its predictions.
    D) the popular press buys into its predictions.
Answer: B
Page Ref: 7
Skill: Conceptual
Objective: 1.3

8) The existence of many theories in the field of child development
    A) interferes with practical applications to help children and their families.
    B) helps advance knowledge.
    C) is due to variations in research procedures among investigators.
    D) hinders attempts to organize data from diverse scientific studies.
Answer: B
Page Ref: 7
Skill: Conceptual
Objective: 1.3

9) Jude believes that his 1-year-old daughter's memory works very much the same as his, but that she simply cannot remember as much as he does. Jude views the development of memory as
    A) discontinuous.
    B) determined by nature.
    C) continuous.
    D) determined by nurture.
Answer: C
Page Ref: 8
Skill: Applied
Objective: 1.3

10) When 3-year-old Liam puts on his mother's dress and shoes, he explains to her that he has changed into a girl. Rather than correcting Liam, his mother recognizes that he does not yet understand that gender is not changed by physical appearances. Liam's mother most likely views development as
    A) driven by nature.
    B) a continuous process.
    C) taking place in stages.
    D) stable.
Answer: C
Page Ref: 8
Skill: Applied
Objective: 1.3

11) The concept of _____ is characteristic of _____ theories.
 A) nurture; continuous
 B) stability; stage
 C) change; heredity
 D) stage; discontinuous
Answer: D
Page Ref: 8
Skill: Conceptual
Objective: 1.3

12) In his research, Dr. Peer explores how gregarious children elicit different responses from others compared to reserved children. Dr. Peer most likely emphasizes _____ in his research.
 A) the role of distinct contexts
 B) the nature-nurture controversy
 C) the concept of stage
 D) continuous development
Answer: A
Page Ref: 8
Skill: Applied
Objective: 1.3

13) Theorists who emphasize _____ as the driving force of development typically emphasize _____.
 A) nurture; stages
 B) heredity; stability
 C) nature; early experiences
 D) continuity; heredity
Answer: B
Page Ref: 9
Skill: Conceptual
Objective: 1.3

14) American black children score, on average, 15 points below American white children on measures of general intelligence. Dr. Jensen argues that this difference is due to genetics and that no amount of intervention could boost the IQ scores of black children. Dr. Jenson believes that intelligence is largely due to
 A) nurture.
 B) nature.
 C) stages.
 D) early experiences.
Answer: B
Page Ref: 8
Skill: Applied
Objective: 1.3

15) Marcus was physically abused by his parents during his early years. Now in elementary school and living with a foster family, his school counselor believes that the negative events of his first few years can be overcome by his current positive life circumstances. The counselor emphasizes the role of _____ in development.
 A) nurture
 B) stages
 C) nature
 D) stability
Answer: A
Page Ref: 9
Skill: Applied
Objective: 1.3

16) During medieval times,
    A) children dressed and acted like adults.
    B) the courts gave severe punishments to lawbreaking youths.
    C) laws recognized that children needed protection from people who might mistreat them.
    D) childhood was not regarded as a distinct developmental period.
Answer: C
Page Ref: 11
Skill: Factual
Objective: 1.4

17) During the Reformation, the Puritans
    A) characterized children as innocent and close to angels.
    B) regarded children as fully mature by the time they were 7 or 8 years old.
    C) suggested that parents reward children with praise and approval rather than with money or sweets.
    D) believed that children were born evil and had to be civilized.
Answer: D
Page Ref: 11
Skill: Factual
Objective: 1.4

18) As the Puritans emigrated from England to America, they brought the belief that
    A) children's characters are shaped entirely by experience.
    B) child rearing was one of adults' most important obligations.
    C) children are naturally endowed with a sense of right and wrong.
    D) children never should be punished harshly for their wrongdoings.
Answer: B
Page Ref: 11
Skill: Conceptual
Objective: 1.4

19) John Locke viewed the child as
    A) born with original sin.
    B) a noble savage.
    C) a tabula rasa.
    D) close to angels.
Answer: C
Page Ref: 11–12
Skill: Factual
Objective: 1.4

20) John Locke's philosophy emphasized the use of
    A) praise and approval as rewards for good behavior.
    B) harsh and repressive punishment for misbehavior.
    C) material rewards, such as sweets or money, for good behavior.
    D) time out as a compassionate form of punishment for misbehavior.
Answer: A
Page Ref: 12
Skill: Conceptual
Objective: 1.4

21) _____'s ideas served as the forerunner of _____.
   A) Arnold Gesell; the psychoanalytic perspective
   B) Jean-Jacques Rousseau; ecological system theory
   C) John Locke; behaviorism
   D) G. Stanley Hall; Piaget's theory
Answer: C
Page Ref: 11
Skill: Conceptual
Objective: 1.4

22) All contemporary child development theories have discarded
   A) Charles Darwin's emphasis on the adaptive value of behavior.
   B) Jean-Jacques Rousseau's view of development as discontinuous.
   C) Konrad Lorenz's notion of sensitive periods in development.
   D) John Locke's view of the child as a tabula rasa.
Answer: D
Page Ref: 12
Skill: Conceptual
Objective: 1.4

23) According to Jean-Jacques Rousseau's concept of noble savage,
   A) the human child follows the same general plan as the evolution of the species.
   B) children are naturally endowed with a sense of right and wrong.
   C) children are born as blank slates to be filled by adult instruction.
   D) children must learn to redirect their naturally evil tendencies into socially acceptable behaviors.
Answer: B
Page Ref: 12
Skill: Conceptual
Objective: 1.4

24) Jean-Jacques Rousseau's philosophy characterized development as a
   A) discontinuous process that is mapped out by nature.
   B) continuous process that follows many possible courses of development.
   C) stagewise process that is determined by nurture.
   D) continuous process that follows a single, unified course of development.
Answer: A
Page Ref: 12
Skill: Conceptual
Objective: 1.4

25) During his explorations to distant parts of the world, Charles Darwin discovered that
   A) certain species of baby birds will imprint on their mothers during a critical period.
   B) the development of attachment in human infants is driven primarily by the baby's innate desire for closeness to the mother.
   C) the early prenatal growth of many species is similar.
   D) major human developments take place during a sensitive period when the child is especially responsive to environmental influences.
Answer: C
Page Ref: 12
Skill: Factual
Objective: 1.4

26) Charles Darwin is considered the forefather of scientific child study because
   A) he established the first research laboratory to carry out rigorous, controlled experiments on children.
   B) his discovery that early prenatal growth is strikingly similar in many species prompted other researchers to directly observe children's behavior.
   C) he constructed the first comprehensive theory of child growth and development.
   D) he was the first scientist to compute statistics to represent typical development at different ages.
   Answer: B
   Page Ref: 12
   Skill: Factual
   Objective: 1.4

27) Inspired by Charles Darwin's work, G. Stanley Hall and his student, Arnold Gesell,
   A) were the first theorists to focus on the role of nurture in human development.
   B) computed age-related averages on large numbers of children to represent typical development.
   C) developed the concept of a sensitive period in human development.
   D) constructed the first intelligence test.
   Answer: B
   Page Ref: 13
   Skill: Factual
   Objective: 1.4

28) Both _____ and _____ believed that children were naturally endowed with knowledge of their own needs.
   A) Darwin; Bronfenbrenner
   B) Watson; Binet
   C) Rousseau; Gesell
   D) Locke; Piaget
   Answer: C
   Page Ref: 12, 13
   Skill: Conceptual
   Objective: 1.4

29) Binet and Simon's intelligence test originally was constructed to
   A) predict which children were most likely to become adult geniuses.
   B) measure individual differences in IQ as a function of variables like race, gender, and family background.
   C) document developmental improvements in children's intellectual functioning.
   D) identify children with learning problems who needed to be placed in special classes.
   Answer: D
   Page Ref: 13
   Skill: Factual
   Objective: 1.4

30) According to the psychoanalytic perspective, personality development is greatly influenced by
   A) children's ability to listen, remember, and abstract general rules from observed behaviors.
   B) children's efforts to achieve equilibrium between internal structures and information they encounter in their everyday worlds.
   C) how children resolve conflicts between biological drives and social expectations.
   D) cultural values, laws, customs, and resources.
   Answer: C
   Page Ref: 14
   Skill: Conceptual
   Objective: 1.5

31) Sigmund Freud constructed his psychosexual theory
    A) on the basis of his adult patients' memories of painful childhood events.
    B) by carrying out studies of animal behavior.
    C) on the basis of interviews with institutionalized children and adolescents.
    D) by carefully observing his own children.
Answer: A
Page Ref: 14
Skill: Factual
Objective: 1.5

32) According to Freud, the _____ work(s) to reconcile the demands of the _____ and the _____.
    A) id; ego; superego
    B) ego; id; superego
    C) superego; id; ego
    D) sexual impulses, ego; id
Answer: B
Page Ref: 14
Skill: Conceptual
Objective: 1.5

33) Freud's theory was the first theory to stress the influence of _____ in development.
    A) observational learning
    B) the early parent-child relationship
    C) humans' evolutionary history
    D) genetic processes
Answer: B
Page Ref: 14
Skill: Conceptual
Objective: 1.5

34) In contrast to Freud, Erikson
    A) viewed children as taking an active role in their own development.
    B) emphasized the lifespan nature of development.
    C) minimized the role of culture in individual development.
    D) focused on the impact of early experiences on later behavior.
Answer: B
Page Ref: 15
Skill: Conceptual
Objective: 1.5

35) One reason that the psychoanalytic perspective is no longer in the mainstream of child development is because
    A) the theory ignores the role of early experience in later social and emotional functioning.
    B) most psychoanalysts believe that development is complete by the end of adolescence.
    C) modern researchers have demonstrated that personality development does not take places in stages.
    D) of the failure to consider research methods other than the clinical approach.
Answer: D
Page Ref: 16
Skill: Conceptual
Objective: 1.5

36) According to behaviorism, _____ are the appropriate focus of psychological research.
   A) directly observable events
   B) unconscious impulses and drives
   C) adaptive evolutionary behavior patterns
   D) stagewise transformations

Answer: A
Page Ref: 16–17
Skill: Factual
Objective: 1.5

37) In classical conditioning,
   A) a neutral stimulus is paired with another stimulus that produces a reflexive response.
   B) an innate reflex is extinguished.
   C) no new associations between stimuli are learned.
   D) a reflexive response is paired with a nonreflexive response to produce a new stimulus.

Answer: A
Page Ref: 17
Skill: Conceptual
Objective: 1.5

38) Ivan Pavlov taught dogs to salivate at the sound of a bell by using
   A) operant conditioning.
   B) modeling.
   C) classical conditioning.
   D) behavior modification.

Answer: C
Page Ref: 17
Skill: Factual
Objective: 1.5

39) In a historic experiment with Little Albert, John Watson demonstrated that
   A) both human and animal behavior can be affected by the principles of classical conditioning.
   B) infants as young as a few days old will repeat a behavior to obtain a desirable reward.
   C) children can be conditioned to fear a formerly neutral stimulus
   D) humans have an innate, inborn fear of white furry objects.

Answer: C
Page Ref: 17
Skill: Conceptual
Objective: 1.5

40) On a few occasions, Razi's mother gave him a lollipop to keep him quiet when she took him to the grocery store. Now every time Razi goes to the grocery store, he asks his mother for a lollipop. This is an example of
   A) classical conditioning.
   B) operant conditioning.
   C) behavior modification.
   D) modeling.

Answer: A
Page Ref: 17
Skill: Applied
Objective: 1.5

41) According to operant conditioning theory,
    A) neutral stimuli can bring about a response if paired with a stimuli that produces a reflex.
    B) the frequency of a behavior can be decreased if it is preceded by a punishment.
    C) a reflexive response can bring about a neutral response if paired with a new stimuli.
    D) the frequency of a behavior can be increased if it is followed by a reinforcer.
Answer: D
Page Ref: 17
Skill: Conceptual
Objective: 1.5

42) Each time 20-month-old Gage picks up a block and returns it to his toy box, his mother claps and exclaims, "Good boy, Gage!" In response to his mother's praise, Gage excitedly picks up the remaining blocks. Gage's behavior is an example of
    A) classical conditioning.
    B) modeling.
    C) behavior modification.
    D) operant conditioning.
Answer: D
Page Ref: 17
Skill: Applied
Objective: 1.5

43) Albert Bandura's social learning theory stresses the importance of
    A) stimulus-response associations.
    B) sensitive periods.
    C) cognition.
    D) reinforcers and punishments.
Answer: C
Page Ref: 17
Skill: Factual
Objective: 1.5

44) At his preschool, Haru sees his classmates using paper towel rolls as pretend swords. At home, his mother wonders how Haru learned this behavior that she did not teach him. According to social learning theory, Haru is displaying
    A) observational learning.
    B) operant conditioning.
    C) behavior modification.
    D) classical conditioning.
Answer: A
Page Ref: 17
Skill: Applied
Objective: 1.5

45) According to social learning theory, as children grow older,
    A) they become more selective in what they imitate.
    B) they depend more on their friends rather than adults for encouragement and praise.
    C) operant conditioning becomes more effective than classical conditioning in influencing behavior.
    D) they play an increasingly passive role in their own development.
Answer: A
Page Ref: 18
Skill: Conceptual
Objective: 1.5

46) Which of the following is an example of behavior modification?
    A) Letting children with acute burn injuries play a virtual reality game while nurses engage in the painful process of changing their bandages.
    B) Putting children into time out for increasing durations following repeated occurrences of pushing their classmates.
    C) Talking with children about their early attachment experiences with their parents in an attempt to uncover the underlying cause of thumb sucking.
    D) Taking away a treasured toy for an increased amount of time each time a child bites his or her nails.
Answer: A
Page Ref: 18
Skill: Applied
Objective: 1.5

47) One important criticism of behaviorism and social learning theory is that they
    A) offer too narrow a view of important environmental influences.
    B) are relevant only to children's behavior in the laboratory, not in everyday, natural settings.
    C) put too much emphasis on children's innate genetic inheritance.
    D) can be used as the basis for training animals, but rarely influence human behavior.
Answer: A
Page Ref: 18
Skill: Conceptual
Objective: 1.5

48) According to Piaget's cognitive-developmental theory,
    A) development must be understood in relation to each child's culture.
    B) children's sense of self-efficacy guides their responses in particular situations.
    C) children actively construct knowledge as they interact with their world.
    D) rapid development occurs during sensitive periods.
Answer: C
Page Ref: 18
Skill: Conceptual
Objective: 1.5

49) Piaget believed that
    A) cognitive processes are similar at all ages but present to a greater or lesser extent.
    B) with age, children's minds become better adapted to the external world.
    C) social interaction with adults and more expert peers is the best way to promote cognitive development.
    D) wide variation exists in thinking among children of the same age.
Answer: B
Page Ref: 18
Skill: Conceptual
Objective: 1.5

50) According to Piaget, _____ lead(s) to more advanced ways of thinking.
    A) cooperative dialogues between children and more knowledgeable members of society
    B) brain growth
    C) changes in the organism-environment relationship
    D) children's efforts to achieve equilibrium
Answer: D
Page Ref: 19
Skill: Conceptual
Objective: 1.5

51) In Piaget's theory, _____ during the sensorimotor period.
   A) children are able to use symbols to represent their experiences
   B) children's reasoning becomes logical
   C) children's thinking becomes abstract
   D) children "think" by acting on the world with their eyes, ears, hands, and mouth
Answer: D
Page Ref: 19, 20
Skill: Factual
Objective: 1.5

52) According to Piaget's theory, in the concrete operational stage,
   A) children can think of all possible outcomes in a scientific problem.
   B) children's reasoning becomes logical.
   C) children develop the capacity for abstract thought.
   D) children can evaluate the logic of verbal statements without referring to real-world circumstances.
Answer: B
Page Ref: 20
Skill: Conceptual
Objective: 1.5

53) Early in his career, Piaget derived his ideas about cognitive change during the first two years by
   A) conducting clinical interviews with children and their parents.
   B) carrying out laboratory experiments on large numbers of children.
   C) performing mental tests on children in his clinical practice.
   D) making observations of his own children.
Answer: D
Page Ref: 19
Skill: Factual
Objective: 1.5

54) A classroom environment based on Piaget's theory of cognitive development would be likely to emphasize
   A) joint problem solving with older children or adults.
   B) reinforcing children for giving the right answers.
   C) formal mathematics and language drills.
   D) discovery learning and direct contact with the environment.
Answer: D
Page Ref: 20
Skill: Applied
Objective: 1.5

55) Modern research on Piaget's theory shows that
   A) he overestimated the competencies of infants and young children.
   B) he overemphasized the role of social and cultural influences on development.
   C) he ignored children's active role in their own development.
   D) children's performances on Piagetian tasks can be improved with training.
Answer: D
Page Ref: 20
Skill: Conceptual
Objective: 1.5

56) The design of digital computers was associated with the development of
    A) the information-processing framework.
    B) ecological systems theory.
    C) behaviorism.
    D) ethology.
Answer: A
Page Ref: 21
Skill: Conceptual
Objective: 1.6

57) In one study, researchers asked children to solve novel math problems. Careful tracking of the children's efforts revealed that experimentation with several strategies usually led to successful answers. This study is illustrative of research in the _____ tradition.
    A) behaviorist
    B) information-processing
    C) social learning
    D) ecological systems
Answer: B
Page Ref: 21
Skill: Conceptual
Objective: 1.6

58) _____ researchers often use flowcharts to track children's problem-solving efforts.
    A) Ecological systems
    B) Evolutionary developmental
    C) Information-processing
    D) Sociocultural
Answer: C
Page Ref: 21
Skill: Factual
Objective: 1.6

59) Piaget's theory and the information-processing perspective emphasize
    A) children as playing an active role in their own development.
    B) cognitive development as a continuous process.
    C) the role of stimulus-response associations in intellectual development.
    D) the importance of equilibration in producing higher levels of thinking.
Answer: A
Page Ref: 22
Skill: Conceptual
Objective: 1.6

60) A major strength of the information-processing approach to development is its commitment to
    A) field work.
    B) clinical interviews.
    C) rigorous research methods.
    D) structured observations.
Answer: C
Page Ref: 22
Skill: Conceptual
Objective: 1.6

61) A major weakness of the information-processing perspective is that
    A) it overemphasizes nonlinear aspects of cognition, such as creativity and imagination.
    B) it has had difficulty developing a comprehensive theory of cognitive development.
    C) investigators have failed to study cognition under rigorous experimental conditions.
    D) it views the child as playing a passive role in his or her own development.

Answer: B
Page Ref: 22
Skill: Conceptual
Objective: 1.6

62) Dr. Mnemonic uses brain-imaging techniques to study the relationship between brain development and the emergence of language in young children. Dr. Mnemonic would most likely consider himself to be a(n)
    A) behaviorist.
    B) information-processing researcher.
    C) evolutionary developmental psychologist.
    D) developmental cognitive neuroscientist.

Answer: D
Page Ref: 22–23
Skill: Applied
Objective: 1.6

63) Sociocultural theory, ethology, ecological systems theory, and dynamic system theory all focus on
    A) the adaptive value of behavior.
    B) contexts for development.
    C) children's biological makeup.
    D) historical and cultural influences on development.

Answer: B
Page Ref: 23–28
Skill: Conceptual
Objective: 1.6

64) Observations of _____ led to the concept of _____ in child development.
    A) learned behaviors in dogs; equilibration
    B) imprinting; the critical period
    C) nonhuman primates; adaptation
    D) modeling; microsystem

Answer: B
Page Ref: 23
Skill: Factual
Objective: 1.6

65) During early childhood, children develop language rapidly and are especially responsive to conversational interactions. Based on these observations, one could argue that
    A) language acquisition is due to the unfolding of a genetic blueprint.
    B) language learning develops in stages.
    C) early childhood is a sensitive period for language development.
    D) children play a passive role in language acquisition.

Answer: C
Page Ref: 23
Skill: Conceptual
Objective: 1.6

66) John Bowlby advocated which of the following explanations of mother-infant attachment?
   A) Behaviors like smiling, babbling, and crying are innate social signals that encourage parents to interact with their infants.
   B) Infants become attached to their mothers because mothers are associated with the reduction of primary drives, such as hunger and thirst.
   C) Mothers and infants are both instinctively attached to each other at birth.
   D) Mothers' behaviors like smiling, hugging, and vocalizing reinforce their infants' social engagement.
   Answer: A
   Page Ref: 24
   Skill: Conceptual
   Objective: 1.6

67) Dr. Genus studies the adaptive value of newborn's preference for facelike stimuli. Dr. Genus most likely considers his research to be within the realm of
   A) ecological systems theory.
   B) sociocultural theory.
   C) evolutionary developmental psychology.
   D) dynamic systems theory.
   Answer: C
   Page Ref: 24
   Skill: Conceptual
   Objective: 1.6

68) Vygotsky's theory focuses on
   A) the impact of nested environmental structures.
   B) children's capacity to shape their own development.
   C) the adaptive value of behavior.
   D) how culture is transmitted to the next generation.
   Answer: D
   Page Ref: 24
   Skill: Factual
   Objective: 1.6

69) Vygotsky believed that _____ produce development.
   A) cooperative dialogues between children and more knowledgeable members of society
   B) bidirectional influences within the chronosystem
   C) environmental influences that occur during a sensitive period
   D) children's active, independent efforts
   Answer: A
   Page Ref: 24
   Skill: Conceptual
   Objective: 1.6

70) Unlike Piaget, Vygotsky
   A) emphasized children's capacity to shape their own development.
   B) focused on the social transmission of knowledge.
   C) emphasized that all child-environment relationships are bidirectional.
   D) focused on discontinuous change.
   Answer: B
   Page Ref: 25
   Skill: Conceptual
   Objective: 1.5

71) Which of the following behaviors is consistent with Vygotsky's theory?
   A) When his mother takes him to the grocery store, Tom is well behaved because he knows that his mother will reward him for his good behavior with a lollipop.
   B) When playing in her sandbox, Amy builds the same sort of castle that she had seen her best friend build yesterday.
   C) When building a tower with blocks, Ted produces the same kind of guiding comments that an adult has used previously to help him build block towers.
   D) When working on her math homework, Michelle tries several solutions before she arrives at the correct answer.
Answer: C
Page Ref: 25
Skill: Conceptual
Objective: 1.6

72) Cross-cultural research stimulated by Vygotsky's theory has shown that
   A) the developmental sequences observed in Western cultures are universal.
   B) children in Western cultures are intellectually superior to those in other cultures.
   C) adults begin to encourage culturally valued skills as soon as children begin school.
   D) children in every culture develop unique strengths.
Answer: D
Page Ref: 25
Skill: Conceptual
Objective: 1.6

73) In Bronfenbrenner's ecological systems theory,
   A) all interactions between children and adults are bidirectional.
   B) immediate reinforcement, punishment, and modeled behaviors are the most important environmental influences.
   C) the same environmental influences affect children in uniform ways.
   D) children acquire culturally valued practices from interactions with adults.
Answer: A
Page Ref: 26
Skill: Conceptual
Objective: 1.6

74) In Bronfenbrenner's ecological systems theory, connections between parents and school are in the
   A) microsystem.
   B) mesosystem.
   C) exosystem.
   D) macrosystem.
Answer: B
Page Ref: 26
Skill: Applied
Objective: 1.6

75) In Bronfenbrenner's ecological systems theory,
   A) all relationships in the microsystem are unidirectional.
   B) the macrosystem encompasses connections between microsystems.
   C) development is controlled by environmental forces.
   D) social settings in the exosystem do not contain children.
Answer: D
Page Ref: 26–27
Skill: Conceptual
Objective: 1.6

76) According to ecological systems theory, a nation's child protection system is in the
    A) microsystem.
    B) mesosystem.
    C) exosystem.
    D) macrosystem.
    Answer: D
    Page Ref: 27
    Skill: Applied
    Objective: 1.6

77) Angela's grades in school have been affected negatively by her parents' recent divorce. In ecological systems theory, the divorce represents a change in Angela's
    A) exosystem.
    B) chronosystem.
    C) mesosystem.
    D) macrosystem.
    Answer: B
    Page Ref: 27
    Skill: Applied
    Objective: 1.6

78) According to the dynamic systems perspective,
    A) a change in any part of the system promotes the reorganization of skills.
    B) children model the behaviors of others.
    C) children engage in cooperative dialogues with adults or more knowledgeable peers.
    D) children are in the sensitive period for a particular behavior.
    Answer: A
    Page Ref: 27
    Skill: Conceptual
    Objective: 1.6

79) Dynamic systems theorists emphasize that
    A) children are driven mainly by instincts and unconscious motives.
    B) different children master the same skills in unique ways.
    C) sensitive periods are key to understanding development.
    D) development can be best understood in terms of its adaptive value.
    Answer: B
    Page Ref: 28
    Skill: Conceptual
    Objective: 1.6

80) Which of the following theoretical perspectives can best explain why some toddlers never crawl on their hands and knees before they learn how to walk?
    A) ecological systems theory
    B) sociocultural theory
    C) evolutionary developmental psychology
    D) dynamic systems perspective
    Answer: D
    Page Ref: 28
    Skill: Conceptual
    Objective: 1.6

81) Which major theory of development takes the strongest position on one side of the nature versus nurture issue?
    A) psychoanalytic theory
    B) ethology
    C) behaviorism
    D) ecological systems theory
Answer: C
Page Ref: 30
Skill: Conceptual
Objective: 1.7

82) Both _____ and _____ emphasize discontinuous development.
    A) behaviorism; social learning theory
    B) Piaget's theory; information-processing theory
    C) Piaget's theory; psychoanalytic theory
    D) Vygotsky's theory; ecological systems theory
Answer: C
Page Ref: 30
Skill: Conceptual
Objective: 1.7

83) Which of the following theories emphasizes many possible courses of development?
    A) information-processing perspective
    B) evolutionary developmental theory
    C) Piaget's cognitive-developmental theory
    D) Vygotsky's sociocultural theory
Answer: D
Page Ref: 30
Skill: Conceptual
Objective: 1.7

84) Dr. Seuss observes children's naturally occurring reactions to stressful medical procedures in an attempt to develop ways to help children cope with these types of experiences. This is an example of
    A) the clinical method.
    B) a structured observation.
    C) a naturalistic observation.
    D) an ethnography.
Answer: C
Page Ref: 31
Skill: Applied
Objective: 1.8

85) The greatest advantage of naturalist observation is that it
    A) can reveal how children actually behave in everyday life.
    B) can be used with infants and toddlers.
    C) provides insight into the thinking that underlies observed behaviors.
    D) permits inferences about cause and effect in everyday settings.
Answer: A
Page Ref: 31, 32
Skill: Conceptual
Objective: 1.8

86) A major limitation of naturalistic observation is that
    A) the findings cannot be generalized beyond the participants and settings in which the research was originally conducted.
    B) researchers cannot expect that participants will behave in the laboratory as they do in their natural environments.
    C) not all participants have the same opportunity to display a particular behavior in everyday life.
    D) people may not accurately report their thoughts, feelings, and experiences.
Answer: C
Page Ref: 31, 32
Skill: Conceptual
Objective: 1.8

87) A major advantage of structured observations is that they
    A) are useful for studying behaviors that investigators rarely have an opportunity to see in everyday life.
    B) permit participants to display their thoughts in terms that are as close as possible to the way they think in everyday life.
    C) yield richly detailed narratives that offer valuable insight into the many factors that affect development.
    D) allow researchers to see the behavior of interest as it occurs in natural settings.
Answer: A
Page Ref: 32, 33
Skill: Conceptual
Objective: 1.8

88) Professor Springfield is interested in examining personality factors associated with children's willingness to talk to strangers. Which of the following methods is best suited to explore this question?
    A) naturalistic observation
    B) a case study
    C) structured observation
    D) an ethnography
Answer: C
Page Ref: 32, 33
Skill: Applied
Objective: 1.8

89) A researcher is likely to choose a structured observation over a naturalistic observation when he
    A) wants to eliminate the possibility that observers may see and record behaviors that are expected rather than what participants actually do.
    B) is interested in studying a behavior that he rarely would have an opportunity to see in everyday life.
    C) is interested in obtaining as complete a picture as possible of a child's psychological functioning and the experiences that led up to it.
    D) is concerned that his research participants will behave differently than they do in their natural environments.
Answer: B
Page Ref: 32
Skill: Factual
Objective: 1.8

90) A researcher interested in children's beliefs about Santa Claus and the Easter Bunny begins each child's interview with the same question, but subsequent questions are determined by each child's answers. This is an example of a(n)
   A) ethnography.
   B) case study.
   C) structured interview.
   D) clinical interview.
Answer: D
Page Ref: 33
Skill: Applied
Objective: 1.8

91) A strength of the clinical interview is that
   A) it permits children to display their thoughts in terms that are close to the way they think in everyday life.
   B) it provides highly objective and generalizable data.
   C) it accurately assesses even those participants who have low verbal ability and expressiveness.
   D) each participant is asked the same questions in the same way.
Answer: A
Page Ref: 33
Skill: Factual
Objective: 1.8

92) One major limitation of the clinical interview is
   A) it does not provide much insight into participants' reasoning or ideas.
   B) different responses may reflect the manner of interviewing rather than real differences in the way children think about a topic.
   C) the questions are phrased the same for each participant, regardless of verbal ability.
   D) the lack of flexibility in the interview protocol.
Answer: B
Page Ref: 33
Skill: Conceptual
Objective: 1.8

93) Structured interviews
   A) eliminate the possibility that an interviewer might prompt some participants more than others.
   B) yield a greater depth of information than clinical interviews.
   C) are more time consuming to carry out compared to clinical interviews.
   D) have been criticized because of their flexibility.
Answer: A
Page Ref: 33
Skill: Conceptual
Objective: 1.8

94) A researcher is likely to choose a structured interview over a clinical interview when he
   A) wants to use a flexible, conversational tone to probe for the participants' point of view.
   B) wants to collect information on children with limited verbal skills.
   C) plans to collect data from an entire class of children at the same time.
   D) is interested in obtaining very in depth information about a child's thoughts, feelings, and experiences.
Answer: C
Page Ref: 33
Skill: Conceptual
Objective: 1.8

95) Which of the following methods is best suited to studying the development of prodigies?
    A) a naturalistic observation
    B) a cross-sectional study
    C) a field experiment
    D) the clinical method
Answer: D
Page Ref: 34
Skill: Factual
Objective: 1.8

96) Of the following, which is a limitation of the clinical method?
    A) Information collected using the clinical method often lacks in descriptive detail.
    B) The clinical method does not provide evidence about development at the level of the individual.
    C) The clinical method requires intensive study of participants' moment-by-moment behaviors.
    D) Because information often is collected unsystematically and subjectively, researchers' theoretical preferences may bias their interpretations.
Answer: D
Page Ref: 34
Skill: Conceptual
Objective: 1.8

97) Dr. Plaque studies cultural differences in myths and rituals that are practiced when children lose their primary teeth. Dr. Plaque most likely relies on
    A) ethnography.
    B) natural experiments.
    C) the clinical method.
    D) the case study method.
Answer: A
Page Ref: 34
Skill: Applied
Objective: 1.8

98) Researchers who use the _____ method rely on _____ to achieve their goals.
    A) ethnographic; participant observation
    B) microgenetic; clinical interviews
    C) ethnographic; clinical interviews
    D) microgenetic; participant observation
Answer: A
Page Ref: 34
Skill: Conceptual
Objective: 1.8

99) Ethnographers strive to minimize their influence on the culture that they are observing by
    A) employing rigorous experimental procedures.
    B) minimizing the time spent with the cultural community they are studying.
    C) relying on unobtrusive techniques, such as surveillance cameras and one-way mirrors.
    D) becoming part of the cultural community they are studying.
Answer: D
Page Ref: 34
Skill: Conceptual
Objective: 1.8

100) To study the effects of divorce on children's school performance, Professor Nuptial examined differences in grades among children of divorce versus children of intact families. This is an example of a
    A) case study.
    B) correlational design.
    C) cross-sectional design.
    D) field experiment.
Answer: B
Page Ref: 35, 37
Skill: Applied
Objective: 1.9

101) The major limitation of correlational designs is that
    A) the findings do not provide information about how people behave outside of the laboratory.
    B) investigators' theoretical beliefs frequently lead them to misinterpret their observations.
    C) they do not permit inferences about cause and effect.
    D) the results cannot be generalized to other people and settings.
Answer: C
Page Ref: 37
Skill: Conceptual
Objective: 1.9

102) Professor Pedagogy's research shows that participation in extracurricular activities is POSITIVELY correlated with grades in school. Based on the findings from this one study, of the following statements, which can Professor Pedagogy conclude?
    A) Participation in extracurricular activities causes grades to increase.
    B) Higher grades cause students to participate in extracurricular activities.
    C) Students who participate in more extracurricular activities have higher grades.
    D) A third variable, such as intelligence, is causing both participation in extracurricular activities and grades to increase.
Answer: C
Page Ref: 37
Skill: Applied
Objective: 1.9

103) Dr. Sim's research shows that videogame play is NEGATIVELY related to physical activity during childhood. Based on the findings from this one study, of the following statements, which can Dr. Sim's conclude?
    A) Playing videogames causes children to engage in less physical activity.
    B) Children who engage in more physical activity play more videogames.
    C) Engaging in less physical activity causes children to play videogames.
    D) Children who engage in less physical activity play more videogames.
Answer: D
Page Ref: 37
Skill: Applied
Objective: 1.9

104) A correlation of -.79 between self-esteem and delinquency in adolescence indicates that
    A) the higher an adolescent's self-esteem, the more likely he or she is to be delinquent.
    B) self-esteem and delinquency are only weakly correlated during adolescence.
    C) the lower an adolescent's self-esteem, the more likely he or she is to be delinquent.
    D) self-esteem and delinquency are not related during adolescence.
Answer: C
Page Ref: 37
Skill: Applied
Objective: 1.9

105) A(n) _____ permits inferences about cause and effect.
    A) naturalistic observation
    B) natural experiment
    C) correlational design
    D) experimental design
Answer: D
Page Ref: 37
Skill: Factual
Objective: 1.9

106) In an experiment of the effects of realistic (e.g., trucks, dolls) versus nonspecific (pipe cleaners, paper bags) play materials on peer interaction, the independent variable would be
    A) type of play material.
    B) a measure of peer interaction.
    C) the number of toys used in the study.
    D) the number of children in the study.
Answer: A
Page Ref: 37
Skill: Applied
Objective: 1.9

107) In an experiment to determine whether children would be more likely to break a promise to work when they thought no one was present to observe their transgression, the dependent variable would be
    A) the number of children who thought that no one was present during the experiment.
    B) the intervention.
    C) whether an experimenter was present once the children promised to work.
    D) the number of children who broke the promise to work.
Answer: D
Page Ref: 37
Skill: Applied
Objective: 1.9

108) In an experiment examining whether a certain type of intervention improves the psychological adjustment of shy children, the dependent variable would be
    A) the type of intervention.
    B) the number of children in the subject pool who are shy.
    C) the number of shy children who benefit from the intervention.
    D) a measure of psychological adjustment.
Answer: D
Page Ref: 37
Skill: Applied
Objective: 1.9

109) Cause-and-effect inferences can be made in experiments because
    A) participants in all treatment conditions are treated exactly alike except for the independent variable.
    B) an experimenter holds the dependent variable constant throughout an experiment.
    C) participants are systematically assigned to experimental conditions.
    D) the independent variable varies randomly throughout the experiment.
Answer: A
Page Ref: 37
Skill: Conceptual
Objective: 1.9

110) Random assignment in an experimental design increases the likelihood that the
    A) independent variable will have a measurable effect.
    B) participants' all will have similar characteristics.
    C) experimental groups will differ systematically on the variable(s) of interest.
    D) participants' characteristics will be equally distributed across treatment groups.

Answer: D
Page Ref: 38
Skill: Conceptual
Objective: 1.9

111) One way to randomly assign participants to experimental conditions would be to
    A) flip a coin.
    B) assign participants to experimental groups in the order that they show up for an experiment.
    C) let parents choose in which experimental group they would like their children to participate.
    D) let children choose in which experimental group they would like to participate.

Answer: A
Page Ref: 38
Skill: Applied
Objective: 1.9

112) Professor Atari is studying whether playing videogames that require mental rotation of visual images fosters success of spatial reasoning tests. The BEST method for Professor Atari to use to be able to infer cause and effect would be to
    A) compare the number of hours of videogame play among children who score high on spatial reasoning tests with those who score low on spatial reasoning tests.
    B) calculate a correlation between children's scores of spatial reasoning and the number of hours of videogame play.
    C) select a group of children who already play a lot of videogames and a second group who never play video games and compare their scores of spatial reasoning.
    D) randomly choose half of the participants to play videogames and the remaining half to play no videogames and later compare measures of spatial reasoning for each group.

Answer: D
Page Ref: 38
Skill: Applied
Objective: 1.9

113) To examine the effects of single-sex versus mixed-sex classrooms on intelligence test performance, Dr. Tutor compared the IQ scores of children in a suburban single-sex school with those of children in an urban mixed-sex school. He found that the children in the single-sex school outperformed those in the mixed-sex school, and concluded that single-sex schooling heightens IQ. This is an erroneous conclusion because
    A) the children were not randomly assigned to levels of the dependent variable.
    B) the researcher should have examined only those from urban schools or only those from suburban schools.
    C) the dependent variable was measured incorrectly.
    D) the children were not randomly assigned to levels of the independent variable.

Answer: D
Page Ref: 38
Skill: Applied
Objective: 1.9

114) An investigator set out to test the hypothesis that moderate levels of stress have a facilitative effect on IQ test performance, and that high levels of stress have a detrimental effect on IQ test performance. Using a technique called "matching" to assign participants to treatment conditions, it would be BEST to match participants on
   A) level of stress experienced during the IQ test.
   B) occupation.
   C) gender.
   D) a measure of intelligence.
   Answer: A
   Page Ref: 38
   Skill: Applied
   Objective: 1.9

115) In one study, researchers randomly assigned non-English-speaking students to either a bilingual education classroom or an English-only immersion classroom. This is an example of a
   A) naturalistic observation.
   B) structured observation.
   C) natural experiment.
   D) field experiment.
   Answer: D
   Page Ref: 38
   Skill: Applied
   Objective: 1.9

116) Researchers may do _____ as a complement to _____ to ensure that their findings are applicable to everyday life.
   A) field experiments; laboratory experiments
   B) naturalistic observations; natural experiments
   C) naturalistic observations; structured observations
   D) natural experiments; field experiments
   Answer: A
   Page Ref: 38
   Skill: Conceptual
   Objective: 1.9

117) Researchers at Acme University compared family dynamics in "typical" versus "troubled" families by observing families during dinner. Income, education, number of siblings, and children's ages were matched. This is an example of a
   A) natural experiment.
   B) structured observation.
   C) field experiment.
   D) microgenetic design.
   Answer: A
   Page Ref: 39
   Skill: Applied
   Objective: 1.9

118) Natural experiments differ from correlational research in that
   A) participants are randomly assigned to treatment conditions in natural settings.
   B) researchers present participants with a novel task and follow their mastery over a series of closely spaced sessions.
   C) investigators assign participants with similar characteristics in equal numbers to each treatment condition.
   D) groups of people are carefully chosen to ensure that their characteristics are as much alike as possible.
   Answer: D
   Page Ref: 39
   Skill: Conceptual
   Objective: 1.9

119) Two major strengths of the longitudinal design are that researchers can _____ and _____.
   A) collect a large amount of data in a short time span; identify both common patterns and individual differences
   B) explore similarities among children of different cohorts; examine relationships between early and later behaviors
   C) examine relationships between early and later behaviors; explore similarities among children of different cohorts
   D) identify both common patterns and individual differences; examine relationships between early and later behaviors
   Answer: D
   Page Ref: 40
   Skill: Conceptual
   Objective: 1.10

120) To examine whether children's popularity is stable or changes across the years, Dr. Clique followed a group of children from ages 5 to 18 years. This is an example of a _____ design.
   A) sequential
   B) microgenetic
   C) longitudinal
   D) cross-sectional
   Answer: C
   Page Ref: 40
   Skill: Applied
   Objective: 1.10

121) Which of the following would result in a cohort effect in a longitudinal study?
   A) selective loss of participants during the duration of the study
   B) changes in participants' natural responses as a result of repeated testing
   C) failure to select participants who are representative of the population of interest
   D) cultural-historical change
   Answer: D
   Page Ref: 40–41
   Skill: Conceptual
   Objective: 1.10

122) Dr. Farina is studying whether her company's new formula increases intelligence in infants. She tests a group of infants before and after using the formula. She finds that the infants' scores increase from the first to the second testing session. She should think twice about declaring the formula a success because _____ is/are the MOST likely threat to the accuracy of her findings.
   A) practice effects
   B) cohort effects
   C) participant dropout
   D) the correlational nature of her study
Answer: A
Page Ref: 40–41
Skill: Applied
Objective: 1.10

123) A study in the 1950s demonstrated that the vast majority of adolescent girls had positive body images, even if they were overweight. One should be cautious about generalizing these findings to today's adolescent girls because of
   A) the lack of random assignment.
   B) practice effects.
   C) cohort effects.
   D) participant dropout.
Answer: C
Page Ref: 41
Skill: Applied
Objective: 1.10

124) To explore how friendship changes with age, Professor Buddy asked sixth through twelfth graders at several different schools to name their best friend and up to ten other friends at the school. The results showed that the older children named fewer friends, but those they named were more likely to name them as friends as well. This is an example of a _____ study.
   A) cross-sectional
   B) longitudinal
   C) longitudinal-sequential
   D) sequential
Answer: A
Page Ref: 41
Skill: Applied
Objective: 1.10

125) An advantage of cross-sectional designs is that
   A) researchers do not have to be concerned about practice effects.
   B) their validity cannot be threatened by cohort effects.
   C) the effects of early experience on later development can be examined.
   D) it is an efficient strategy for examining individual development.
Answer: A
Page Ref: 41
Skill: Conceptual
Objective: 1.10

126) A major disadvantage of cross-sectional research is that
    A) age-related changes cannot be examined.
    B) participant dropout often limits the generalizability of the findings.
    C) factors affecting individual development cannot be explored.
    D) practice effects often compromise the accuracy of a researcher's findings.
Answer: C
Page Ref: 41
Skill: Conceptual
Objective: 10.10

127) The findings of cross-sectional studies that cover a wide age span are MOST likely to be affected by which of the following threats to validity?
    A) selective attrition
    B) biased sampling
    C) cohort effects
    D) practice effects
Answer: C
Page Ref: 41–42
Skill: Conceptual
Objective: 1.10

128) A sequential design
    A) does not allow inferences about individual differences.
    B) permits researchers to check if cohort effects are operating.
    C) is less efficient than a longitudinal design.
    D) assures researchers that the findings are generalizable beyond the cohorts studied.
Answer: B
Page Ref: 42
Skill: Conceptual
Objective: 1.10

129) To examine age-related changes in memory strategy use, Professor Cerebellum presented 5-, 6-, and 7-year-olds with various memory tasks several times over a period of three years. This is an example of a _____ study.
    A) cross-sectional
    B) microgenetic
    C) sequential
    D) longitudinal
Answer: C
Page Ref: 42
Skill: Applied
Objective: 1.10

130) A microgenetic design
    A) is the most practical approach to use over a long developmental period.
    B) offers insights into how developmental change occurs.
    C) is a variation of the cross-sectional design.
    D) offers insights into the cause of cohort effects.
Answer: B
Page Ref: 43
Skill: Conceptual
Objective: 1.10

131) Dr. Sum is interested in documenting individual differences in the factors leading up to the emergence of children's understanding of the principle of cardinality—that the last number in a counting sequence indicates the quantity of items in the set. The BEST design for Dr. Sum to use would be a
   A) correlational study.
   B) microgenetic study.
   C) cross-sectional design.
   D) case study.
Answer: B
Page Ref: 43
Skill: Applied
Objective: 1.10

132) A major limitation of microgenetic research is that
   A) participant dropout often distorts developmental trends.
   B) it is often difficult to anticipate the time required for development to take place.
   C) microgenetic studies often create ethical issues.
   D) cohort effects often limit the generalizability of the findings.
Answer: B
Page Ref: 43
Skill: Conceptual
Objective: 1.10

133) The ultimate responsibility for the ethical integrity of research with children lies with the
   A) children's parents.
   B) institution's review committee.
   C) study participants.
   D) investigator.
Answer: D
Page Ref: 45
Skill: Factual
Objective: 1.11

134) Researchers can honor school-age children's research rights with respect to knowledge of results by
   A) giving the parents of study participants a copy of the results of the study.
   B) using simple language to explain the results of the research to the study participants.
   C) giving information to the parents of potential study participants so they can decide what and how to tell their children about the research.
   D) trying to explain in highly scientific language the results of the research to the children who participated in the study.
Answer: B
Page Ref: 45
Skill: Applied
Objective: 1.11

135) A researcher had planned to examine children's memories for traumatic events by showing his participants a videotape of a violent crime, but his project was rejected by his university's ethics committee. The committee MOST likely rejected this study because it violated which of the following research rights?
   A) privacy
   B) beneficial treatments
   C) informed consent
   D) protection from harm
Answer: D
Page Ref: 45
Skill: Applied
Objective: 1.11

136) An investigator interested in romantic relationships during adolescence calls up teenagers from a local high school and asks them a variety of questions without first asking their parents' permission. This investigator has violated which of the following children's research rights?
   A) informed consent
   B) protection from harm
   C) privacy
   D) beneficial treatments
Answer: A
Page Ref: 45
Skill: Applied
Objective: 1.11

137) A researcher wishes to inform children of the intelligence test scores that they received in his experiment by posting a list of names and scores outside their classroom. This violates which of the following children's research rights?
   A) privacy
   B) beneficial treatments
   C) informed consent
   D) knowledge of results
Answer: A
Page Ref: 45
Skill: Applied
Objective: 1.11

138) In a study examining the effectiveness of an intervention teaching social problem-solving skills to antisocial children, the participants who received this intervention showed improved peer relations. At the conclusion of the experiment, the researchers did NOT offer the intervention to those who did not receive it in the study. This violates the children's _____ research right.
   A) informed consent
   B) privacy
   C) beneficial treatments
   D) knowledge of results
Answer: C
Page Ref: 45
Skill: Applied
Objective: 1.11

139) Some researchers have suggested that debriefing does not work well with children because it
   A) often leads to cohort effects.
   B) is unethical to debrief children.
   C) can bias the effects of an experimental manipulation.
   D) may undermine children's belief in the honesty of adults.
Answer: D
Page Ref: 46
Skill: Factual
Objective: 1.11

140) According to research on resilience, which of the following factors is associated with protection against the damaging effects of stressful life conditions?
    A) high self-esteem
    B) multiple siblings
    C) social support outside the immediate family
    D) an emotionally reactive personality
Answer: C
Page Ref: 10
Skill: Conceptual
Objective: (B&E Box) Resilient Children

141) In the United States and Canada, children who are first generation and second generation
    A) are more likely than children who are native-born to have missed school because of illness.
    B) report more emotional distress compared to native-born children.
    C) achieve in school as well as or better than children with native-born parents.
    D) are more likely than children who are native-born to commit delinquent acts.
Answer: C
Page Ref: 36
Skill: Conceptual
Objective: (CI Box) Immigrant Youths: Amazing Adaptation

142) Adolescents from immigrant families _____ compared to adolescents with native-born parents.
    A) view school success as less important
    B) more strongly stress individual over community goals
    C) feel less a sense of obligation to their parents
    D) endorse their parents' values of education more strongly
Answer: D
Page Ref: 36
Skill: Conceptual
Objective: (CI Box) Immigrant Youths: Amazing Adaptation

143) Of the following, which is supported by research on the Mozart effect?
    A) Exposing infants to classical music can produce lifelong intellectual benefits.
    B) The Mozart effect lasts only 15 minutes.
    C) Listening to classical music immediately before taking a test can boost the test performance of school-age children.
    D) Listening to classical music while studying for a test can boost the test performance of school-age children.
Answer: B
Page Ref: 44
Skill: Conceptual
Objective: (SI Box) Can Musical Experiences Enhance Intelligence?

144) Studies show that
    A) music lessons can lead to increases in children's intelligence that do not arise from drama lessons.
    B) drama lessons can boost children's intelligence test performance above and beyond the effects of music lessons.
    C) piano, but not voice, lessons can lead to gains in children's intelligence test performance.
    D) music lessons can boost children's performance on spatial but not verbal abilities.
Answer: A
Page Ref: 44
Skill: Conceptual
Objective: (SI Box) Can Musical Experiences Enhance Intelligence?

ESSAY

145) Describe three larger questions about the nature of the person and the course of human development that emerge from comparisons of major theories. Indicate the stance of psychoanalytic theory, behaviorism, and cognitive-developmental theory on each of these issues.

Answer: Almost all of the major twentieth-century theories take a stand on the following three basic issues of child development: (1) Is development a continuous or discontinuous process? (2) Is there one course of development or are there many courses? (3) Is nature or nurture a more important determinant of development?

Psychoanalytic theory holds that (1) development is discontinuous, proceeding through a series of psychosexual and psychosocial stages; (2) there is one course of development because the stages are universal; and (3) both nature and nurture determine development as innate impulses are channeled and controlled through child-rearing experiences. According to this theory, individual development is stable because early experiences set the course of later development.

Behaviorism assumes that (1) the course of development is continuous because it is the result of increases in learned behaviors; (2) there are many possible courses of development because behaviors reinforced and modeled may vary from child to child; and (3) development is determined primarily by nurture. Behaviorism holds that individual development is open to change because both early and later experiences are important.

According to cognitive-developmental theory, (1) development is discontinuous because children proceed through stages of cognitive development; (2) it is possible to have one course of development because the stages are universal; and (3) development is determined by both nature and nurture because development occurs as the brain matures and children exercise their innate drive to discover reality in a generally stimulating environment. Development is as open to change because both early and later experiences influence development.

Page Ref: 14–21

146) Describe John Locke's and Jean-Jacques Rousseau's early philosophies of childhood, and name the twentieth-century theories foreshadowed by each.

Answer: John Locke viewed the child as a tabula rasa, or blank slate. In his view, children are nothing at all to begin with, and their characters are shaped entirely by experience. Locke described parents as rational tutors who could mold the child in any way they wished through careful instruction, effective example, and rewards for good behavior. Regarding child-rearing practices, Locke suggested that parents reward children not with physical rewards, such as money or candy, but with praise and approval. Locke also opposed physical punishment, and his philosophy led to a change from harshness toward children to kindness and compassion. Locke's ideas laid the groundwork for twentieth-century behaviorism.

Jean-Jacques Rousseau viewed children as noble savages—noble because they are endowed with an innate sense of right and wrong, and savages because they have unique, natural ways of thinking and feeling that are harmed by adult training and restriction. Rousseau's child-centered philosophy held that adults should be receptive to the child's needs at each of four stages of development. Rousseau's ideas include two important concepts found in modern theories. The first is the concept of stage or qualitative changes that characterize different time periods of development. The second is the concept of maturation, which refers to a genetically determined, naturally unfolding course of growth. Rousseau's philosophy emphasized that children are unique and different from adults and that their development is determined by their own inner nature. Rousseau's ideas are found in Piaget's cognitive-developmental theory.

Page Ref: 11–12

147) Compare and contrast the terms "critical period" and "sensitive period," and discuss how observations of imprinting led to the development of these concepts.

Answer: Watching animals in their natural habitats, Konrad Lorenz and Niko Tinbergen developed the concept of imprinting to describe the early following behavior of certain baby birds that ensures that the young will stay close to the mother and be fed and protected from danger. Imprinting takes place during an early, restricted time period of development. If the mother is not present during this time, but an objected resembling her in important features is, young birds may imprint on it instead.

The term critical period refers to a limited time span during which the child is biologically prepared to acquire certain adaptive behaviors but needs the support of an appropriately stimulating environment. A sensitive period refers to a time that is optimal for certain capacities to emerge because the individual is especially responsive to environment. The idea of a sensitive period offers a better account of human development than does the strict notion of a critical period. Development may occur later, but it is harder to induce.

Page Ref: 23–24

148) Both traditional behaviorism and Urie Bronfenbrenner's ecological systems theory view the environment as playing a vital role in development. However, each theory describes the influence of the environment quite differently. Explain.

Answer: Behaviorists view the environment fairly narrowly—as limited to events and conditions immediately surrounding the child. In other words, they focus on immediate reinforcements and modeled behaviors. In contrast, Bronfenbrenner expands this view by envisioning the environment as a series of nested structures that includes but also extends beyond home, school, and neighborhood settings in which children spend their lives. Ecological systems theory views the child as developing within a complex system of relationships affected by multiple levels of the surrounding environment, with each level having a powerful impact on development. In addition, ecological systems theory emphasizes that the interaction between the child and the environment is a two-way street involving bidirectional and reciprocal relationships.

Page Ref: 16–17, 25–27

149) Describe the similarities and differences between Piaget's cognitive-developmental theory and Vygotsky's sociocultural theory.

Answer: Piaget did not regard direct teaching by adults as important for cognitive development. Instead, he emphasized children's active, independent efforts to make sense of their world. Vygotsky agreed with Piaget that children are active, constructive beings. But unlike Piaget, he viewed cognitive development as a socially mediated process—as dependent on the support that adults and more mature peers provide as children try new tasks. Additionally, Vygotsky did not regard all children as moving through a universal sequence of stages of cognitive development, as Piaget did. Vygotsky believed that as soon as children acquire language, their enhanced ability to communicate with others leads to continuous changes in thought and behavior that can vary greatly from culture to culture. Unlike Piaget, Vygotsky also emphasized that children in every culture develop unique strengths that are not present in other cultures. Vygotsky argued that this is the case because different cultures select and value different tasks for children's learning.

Page Ref: 18–21, 24–25

150) Two types of systematic observation used in child development research are naturalistic and structured observation. Explain the benefits and limitations of each.

Answer: The great strength of naturalistic observation is that investigators can see directly the everyday behaviors they hope to explain. One limitation of this research method is that not all children have the same opportunity to display a particular behavior in everyday life. Researchers commonly deal with this difficulty by making structured observations in a laboratory. In this approach, the investigator sets up a situation that evokes the behavior of interest so that every participant has equal opportunity to display the response. The major benefit of this method is that it permits greater control over the research situation than does naturalistic observation. In addition, structured observation is especially useful for studying behaviors that investigators rarely have an opportunity to see in everyday life. The great disadvantage of structured observations is that children may not behave in the laboratory as they do in their natural environment.

Page Ref: 31–33

151) Describe the ethnographic method and its major benefits and limitations.

Answer: Ethnography is a descriptive, qualitative technique directed toward understanding a culture or distinct cultural group through participant observation. Typically, the researcher lives with the cultural community for a period of months or years, participating in all aspects of daily life. By making extensive field notes, the investigator tries to capture the culture's unique values and social processes.

The major strength of the ethnographic method is that it provides a more complex and accurate description than can be derived from a single observational visit, interview, or questionnaire. Two limitations of this approach are that the findings may be biased by the researcher's cultural values, and that the results cannot be applied to individuals and settings other than the ones studied.

Page Ref: 32, 34–35

152) Explain why inferences about cause and effect can be made in experiments but not in correlational studies.

Answer: Correlational studies do not permit inferences about cause-and-effect relationships; they simply permit study of the strength and direction of an association between variables. For example, a positive correlation indicates that as one variable increases, the other also increases. A negative correlation indicates that as one variable increases, the other decreases. In an experiment, inferences about cause-and-effect relationships are possible because the researcher directly controls or manipulates changes in the independent variable. This is done by exposing participants to two or more treatment conditions and comparing their performance on measures of the dependent variable. Random assignment of participants to treatment conditions increases the chances that the characteristics of participants will be equally distributed across treatment groups. Random assignment also increases the likelihood that any differences in the dependent variable will be due to the manipulation of the independent variable rather than systematic differences in composition of the treatment groups.

Page Ref: 35, 37

153) Explain why reliability and validity are keys to scientifically sound research.

Answer: Reliability refers to the consistency, or repeatability, of measures of behavior. Validity refers to the extent to which research methods accurately measure characteristics that the investigator set out to measure. Reliability is essential for valid research because methods that are implemented carelessly, unevenly, and inconsistently cannot possibly represent what an investigator originally intended to study. Validity is essential because if, during any phase of carrying out a study—selecting participants, choosing research settings and tasks, and implementing procedures—the researcher permits factors unrelated to the hypothesis to influence behavior, then the validity of the results is in doubt, and they cannot be considered a fair test of the investigator's theory.

Page Ref: 35, 37–39

154) Describe and contrast longitudinal, cross-sectional, and sequential designs. Cite the strengths and weaknesses of each.

Answer: In a longitudinal design, the investigator studies the same group of participants repeatedly at different ages. The strengths of this approach are that it permits study of common patterns and individual differences in development and relationships between early and later events and behaviors. The limitations of this design are that age-related changes may be distorted because of participant dropout, practice effects, and cohort effects. In a cross-sectional design, the investigator studies groups of participants differing in age at one point in time. This approach is more efficient than the longitudinal design and is not plagued by such problems as participant dropout and practice effects. The weaknesses of this method are that it does not permit study of individual developmental trends, and age differences may be distorted because of cohort effects.

In a sequential design, the investigator repeatedly studies two or more groups of participants born in different years. The strengths of this approach are that it permits both longitudinal and cross-sectional comparisons and reveals the existence of cohort effects. This design may have the same problems as longitudinal and cross-sectional strategies, but the design itself helps identify difficulties.

Page Ref: 40–43

STUDY QUESTIONS

The Field of Child Development

1. True or False: Research on child development has been stimulated by both scientific curiosity and social pressures to better children's lives. (p. 4)

2. Child development is an *interdisciplinary* field. Explain what this means. (p. 4)

    _____

    _____

    _____

Domains of Development

1. List the three broad domains in which development is often divided. (p. 4)

    A. _____

    B. _____

    C. _____

Periods of Development

1. List the six age periods used to segment the first two-and-a-half decades of life. (pp. 5–6)

    A. _____   Age span: _____

    B. _____   Age span: _____

    C. _____   Age span: _____

    D. _____   Age span: _____

    E. _____   Age span: _____

    F. _____   Age span: _____

Basic Issues

1. What are the three elements of a good theory? (p. 6)

    A. _____

    B. _____

    C. _____

2. Cite two reasons that theories are important to the study of child development. (pp. 6–7)

    A. _____

    B. _____

3. Explain how theories differ from opinions. (p. 7)

    _____

    _____

    _____

Continuous or Discontinuous Development?

1.   Describe the two views theories use to explain the course of development. (pp. 7–8)

A.   _____

   _____

B.   _____

   _____

2.   The (continuous / discontinuous) perspective maintains the belief that development occurs in stages. Explain what this means. (p. 8)

   _____

   _____

One Course of Development or Many?

1.   Explain how distinct *contexts* can influence child development. (p. 8)

   _____

   _____

   _____

2.   Describe both personal and environmental factors that shape the context of a child's development. (p. 8)

Personal: _____

Environmental: _____

   _____

   _____

Relative Influence of Nature or Nurture?

1.   Briefly discuss the two views theories use to explain the underlying causes of development. (p. 8)

A.   _____

   _____

B.   _____

   _____

2.   Describe how a theory's position on nature and nurture affects whether there is an emphasis on stability or change. (p. 9)

A.   _____

   _____

B.   _____

   _____

A Balanced Point of View

1.   True or False: Theorists today regard heredity and environment as interwoven, each affecting the potential of the other to modify the child's traits and capacities. (p. 9)

Biology and Environment: Resilient Children

1. Define *resilience,* and explain why researchers are increasingly interested in this concept. (p. 10)

   A. _____

   _____

   B. _____

   _____

2. List and briefly describe the four broad factors that appear to offer protection from the damaging effects of stressful life events. (p. 10)

   A. _____

   _____

   B. _____

   _____

   C. _____

   _____

   D. _____

   _____

Historical Foundations

Medieval Times

1. In medieval times, childhood (was / was not) regarded as a distinct developmental period. Cite evidence to support your response. (p. 11)

   _____

   _____

The Reformation

1. True or False: Puritan doctrine stressed the innate goodness of all children. Briefly explain your response. (p. 11)

   _____

   _____

2. True or False: The Puritans placed a high value on the development of reasoning in children. (p. 11)

Philosophies of the Enlightenment

1. During the Enlightenment, the British philosopher John Locke regarded the child as a tabula rasa, which means _____. Explain his view. (pp. 11–12)

   _____

   _____

   _____

2. Summarize Locke's stance on each of the three basic issues of human development. (p. 12)

   Continuous or discontinuous development?

   _____

   _____

   _____

   One course of development or many?

   _____

   _____

   _____

   Relative influence of nature or nurture?

   _____

   _____

   _____

3. Jean-Jacques Rousseau, a French philosopher during the Enlightenment, introduced the notion of children as *noble savages*. Explain what he meant by this term. (p. 12)

   _____

   _____

   _____

4. Describe some of the key differences in the theories put forth by John Locke and Jean-Jacques Rousseau. (p. 11)

   _____

   _____

   _____

5. Cite two concepts included in Rousseau's theory that remain important to modern theories of child development. (p. 12)

   A. _____

   B. _____

Scientific Beginnings

1. Briefly describe the two principles emphasized in Darwin's theory of evolution. (p. 12)

   A. _____

   _____

   _____

   _____

   B. _____

   _____

   _____

   _____

2. Who is generally regarded as the founder of the child study movement? (p. 13)

_____

3. The _____ *approach* to child development uses age-related averages to represent typical development. (p. 13)

4. Who constructed the first successful intelligence test? (p. 13)

_____

5. Why did this test succeed, while previous efforts to create a useful intelligence test had failed? (p. 13)

_____

_____

6. A translated version of this test was developed for use with English-speaking children. What is the name of this instrument? (p. 13)

_____

Mid-Twentieth-Century Theories

The Psychoanalytic Perspective

1. Summarize the basic concepts of the *psychoanalytic perspective.* (p. 14)

_____

_____

_____

2. Freud's _____ *theory* emphasized that how parents manage their child's sexual and aggressive drives in the first few years of life is crucial for healthy personality development. (p. 14)

3. Name and briefly describe the three components of personality outlined in Freud's theory. (p. 14)

A. _____

_____

B. _____

_____

C. _____

_____

4. Match each of the following stages of psychosexual development with the appropriate description. (p. 15)

_____ Stage in which sexual instincts die down	1. Oral
_____ Stage in which the infant desires sucking activities	2. Anal
_____ Stage in which the Oedipal and Electra conflicts take place	3. Phallic
_____ Stage marked by mature sexuality	4. Latency
_____ Stage in which toilet training becomes a major issue between parent and child	5. Genital

5. Cite one contribution and three limitations of Freud's theory. (p. 14)

Contribution: _____

_____

_____

Limitation: _____

_____

_____

Limitation: _____

_____

_____

Limitation: _____

_____

_____

6. In what ways did Erikson build upon and improve Freud's theory? (pp. 14–15)

_____

_____

_____

_____

7. Match each of Erikson's stages with the appropriate description. (p. 16)

_____ Successful resolution of this stage depends on the adult's
success at caring for other people or productive work.

_____ The primary task of this stage is the development of a sense
of self and a sense of one's place in society.

_____ Successful resolution of this stage depends on a warm, loving
relationship with the caregiver.

_____ In this stage, children experiment with adult roles through
make-believe play.

_____ Successful resolution of this stage depends on parents
granting the child reasonable opportunities for free choice.

_____ Successful resolution of this stage involves reflecting on
life's accomplishments.

_____ The development of close relationships with others helps
ensure successful resolution of this stage.

_____ Children who develop the capacity for cooperation and productive
work will successfully resolve this stage.

1. Basic trust vs. mistrust
2. Autonomy vs. shame and doubt
3. Initiative vs. guilt
4. Industry vs. inferiority
5. Identity vs. role confusion
6. Intimacy vs. isolation
7. Generativity vs. stagnation
8. Integrity vs. despair

8. Cite two contributions of psychoanalytic theory. (p. 15)

A. _____

B. _____

9. Discuss two reasons why psychoanalytic theory is no longer in the mainstream of child development research. (p. 16)

    A. _____

    _____

    B. _____

    _____

Behaviorism and Social Learning Theory

1. True or False: Behaviorism focuses on the inner workings of the mind. (p. 16)

2. True or False: Watson's study of little Albert, an 11-month-old baby who was taught to fear a white rat by associating it with a loud noise, supported Pavlov's concept of *classical conditioning*. (p. 17)

3. Summarize B. F. Skinner's *operant conditioning theory*. (p. 17)

    _____

    _____

    _____

4. Describe the concept of modeling, also known as *imitation* or *observational learning*, as emphasized in Bandura's *social learning theory*. (p. 17)

    _____

    _____

    _____

5. Summarize Bandura's revisions to his social learning theory, which stress the importance of *cognition* in the learning process. (pp. 17–18)

    _____

    _____

    _____

6. Behaviorism and social learning theory have had a major applied impact on the field of child development through the introduction of *behavior modification*. Explain this procedure. (p. 18)

    _____

    _____

    _____

7. Discuss two limitations of behaviorism and social learning theory. (p. 18)

    A. _____

    _____

    B. _____

    _____

Piaget's Cognitive-Developmental Theory

1. True or False: Piaget's *cognitive-developmental theory* is consistent with the principles of behaviorism; that is, Piaget believed that knowledge is imparted to children through the use of reinforcement. Briefly explain your response. (p. 18)

    _____

    _____

2. Define Piaget's concept of *adaptation*. (pp. 18–19)

    _____

    _____

3. Match each of Piaget's stages with the appropriate description. (p. 20)

    _____ During this stage, thought becomes more complex, and children develop   1. Sensorimotor
    the capacity for abstract reasoning.   2. Preoperational
    _____ This stage is characterized by the use of eyes, ears, hands, and mouth to   3. Concrete operational
    explore the environment.   4. Formal operational
    _____ During this stage, children use symbols and engage in make-believe play.
    _____ This stage is marked by the development of logical, organized reasoning
    skills.

4. What did Piaget use as his chief method for studying child and adolescent thought? (p. 19)

    _____

5. Discuss contributions of Piaget's theory. (pp. 19–20)

    _____

    _____

6. Cite three recent challenges to Piaget's theory. (p. 20)

    A. _____

    _____

    B. _____

    _____

    C. _____

    _____

Recent Theoretical Perspectives

Information Processing

1. Briefly describe the *information-processing* view of child development. (p. 21)

    _____

    _____

    _____

2. How are flowcharts used by information-processing researchers? (p. 21)

    _____

    _____

3. In what basic way are information processing and Piaget's theory alike? In what basic way are they different? (p. 22)

Alike: _____

Different: _____

4. Cite one strength and two limitations of the information-processing approach. (p. 22)

Strength: _____

Limitation: _____

Limitation: _____

5. Briefly describe a new area of investigation, called *developmental cognitive neuroscience.* (pp. 22–23)

_____

_____

_____

6. List three areas in which developmental cognitive neuroscientists are making rapid progress in the field of child development. (p. 23)

A. _____

B. _____

C. _____

Ethology and Evolutionary Developmental Psychology

1. *Ethology* is the study of (p. 23)

_____

_____

2. Name the two European zoologists who laid the modern foundations of ethology. (p. 23)

A. _____

B. _____

3. Contrast the notion of a *critical period* with that of a *sensitive period.* (p. 23)

Critical period: _____

_____

_____

_____

Sensitive period: _____

_____

_____

_____

4. Explain how John Bowlby used the principles of ethology to understand the infant-caregiver relationship. (pp. 23–24)

_____

_____

_____

5. Briefly explain the primary focus of *evolutionary developmental psychology,* and list a question that may be asked by an evolutionary developmental psychologist. (p. 24)

    A. _____

    _____

    B. _____

    _____

Vygotsky's Sociocultural Theory

1. Explain the importance of social interaction in Vygotsky's *sociocultural theory.* (p. 24)

    _____

    _____

    _____

2. Compare and contrast the theories of Piaget and Vygotsky. (pp. 24–25)

    _____

    _____

    _____

    _____

3. True or False: Because cultures select tasks for children's learning, children in every culture develop unique strengths not present in others. (p. 25)

4. Vygotsky's emphasis on culture and social experience led him to neglect _____ contributions to development. (p. 25)

Ecological Systems Theory

1. Summarize the core tenet of Bronfenbrenner's *ecological systems theory.* (p. 25)

    _____

    _____

2. To explain the contribution of both biological and environmental influences on development, Bronfenbrenner recently characterized his perspective as a _____ model. (p. 25)

3. Match each level of ecological systems theory with the appropriate description or example. (pp. 26–27)

    _____ Relationship between the child's home and school   1. Microsystem
    _____ The influence of cultural values   2. Mesosystem
    _____ The parent's workplace   3. Exosystem
    _____ The child's interaction with parents   4. Macrosystem

4. Provide examples of factors in each system that can enhance development. (pp. 26–27)

    Microsystem: _____

    Mesosystem: _____

    Exosystem: _____

    Macrosystem: _____

5. Bronfenbrenner's _____ system refers to temporal changes that affect development, such as the timing of the birth of a sibling. (p. 27)

6. In ecological systems theory, development is controlled by (environmental circumstances / inner dispositions / the interaction of environmental circumstances and inner dispositions). (p. 27)

New Directions: Development as a Dynamic System

1. Describe the *dynamic systems perspective.* (p. 27)

_____

_____

_____

2. Based on the dynamic systems perspective, explain how individuals develop both universal traits and individual abilities. (p. 28)

Universal traits: _____

_____

Individual abilities: _____

_____

Comparing Child Development Theories

1. Identify the stances that the following modern theories take on the three basic issues of childhood and child development: (p. 30)

Theory	Continuous or Discontinuous Development?	One Course of Development or Many?	Nature or Nurture as More Important?
Psychoanalytic perspective	_____	_____	_____
Behaviorism and social learning theory	_____	_____	_____
Piaget's cognitive-developmental theory	_____	_____	_____
Information processing	_____	_____	_____
Ethology and evolutionary developmental psychology	_____	_____	_____
Vygotsky's sociocultural theory	_____	_____	_____
Ecological systems theory	_____	_____	_____
Dynamic systems perspective	_____	_____	_____

Studying the Child

1. Research usually begins with a _____, or a prediction about behavior drawn from a theory. (p. 29)

Common Methods of Gathering Information

1. Compare and contrast *naturalistic* and *structured* observation techniques, noting one strength and one limitation of each approach. (pp. 31–33)

    Naturalistic: _____

    _____

    Strength: _____

    _____

    Limitation: _____

    _____

    Structured: _____

    _____

    Strength: _____

    _____

    Limitation: _____

    _____

2. Explain how *clinical interviews* differ from structured interviews, and note the benefits and limitations of each technique. (pp. 33–34)

    Clinical: _____

    _____

    Benefits: _____

    _____

    Limitations: _____

    _____

    Structured: _____

    _____

    Benefits: _____

    _____

    Limitations: _____

    _____

3. Cite the primary aim of the *clinical, or case study, method,* and note the procedures often used to achieve this goal. (p. 34)

    Aim: _____

    _____

    Procedures: _____

    _____

4. What are the drawbacks of using the clinical method? (p. 34)

    _____

    _____

5. _____is a research method aimed at understanding a culture or distinct social group. This goal is achieved through _____, a technique in which the researcher lives with the cultural community and participates in all aspects of daily life. (p. 34)

6. Cite two limitations of the ethnographic method. (p. 35)

   A. _____

   B. _____

Cultural Influences: Immigrant Youths: Amazing Adaptation

1. True or False: Students who are first-generation (foreign-born) and second-generation (American- or Canadian-born, with immigrant parents) achieve in school as well as or better than students of native-born parents. (p. 36)

2. On average, adolescents from immigrant families are (more / less) likely to commit delinquent and violent acts, to use drugs and alcohol, or to have early sex. (p. 36)

3. Discuss two ways in which family and ethnic community influence the academic achievement of adolescents from immigrant families. (p. 36)

   A. _____

   _____

   B. _____

   _____

General Research Designs

1. Explain the basic features of the *correlational design*. (pp. 35, 37)

   _____

   _____

2. True or False: The correlational design is preferred by researchers because it allows them to infer cause and effect. Explain your response. (p. 37)

   _____

   _____

   _____

3. Investigators examine the relationships among variables using a(n) _____ , a number that describes how two measures, or variables, are associated with one another. (p. 37)

4. A *correlation coefficient* can range from _____ to _____. The magnitude of the number shows the (strength / direction) of the relationship between the two variables, whereas the sign indicates the (strength / direction) of the relationship. (p. 37)

5. For a correlation coefficient, a positive sign means that as one variable increases, the other (increases / decreases); a negative sign indicates that as one variable increases, the other (increases / decreases). (p. 37)

6. A researcher determines that the correlation between warm, consistent parenting and child delinquency is –.80. Explain what this indicates about the relationship between these two variables. (p. 37)

   _____

   _____

   _____

7. If the same researcher had found a correlation of +.45, what would this have indicated about the relationship between warm, consistent parenting and child delinquency? (p. 37)

_____

_____

_____

8. What is the primary distinction between a *correlational design* and an *experimental design*? (p. 37)

_____

9. Describe the difference between an *independent* and a *dependent* variable. (p. 37)

Independent: _____

_____

Dependent: _____

_____

10. What is the feature of an experimental design that enables researchers to infer a cause-and-effect relationship between the variables? (p. 37)

_____

_____

11. Researchers engage in _____ *assignment* of participants to treatment conditions. Why is this important in experimental studies? (p. 38)

_____

_____

12. In _____ *experiments,* researchers randomly assign people to treatment conditions in natural settings. (p. 38)

13. True or False: Natural experiments differ from correlational research in that groups of participants are carefully chosen to ensure that their characteristics are as much alike as possible. (p. 39)

Designs for Studying Development

1. In a _____ *design,* participants are studied repeatedly at different ages, and changes are noted as the participants get older. (p. 40)

2. List two advantages of the longitudinal design. (p. 40)

A. _____

_____

B. _____

_____

3. Describe three problems in conducting longitudinal research. (p. 40)

A. _____

_____

B. _____

_____

C. _____

_____

4. In what way do *cohort effects* threaten the accuracy of longitudinal research findings? (pp. 40–41)

_____

_____

_____

5. Describe the *cross-sectional design.* (p. 41)

_____

_____

_____

6. In cross-sectional designs, researchers (do / do not) need to worry about participant dropout and practice effects. (p. 41)

7. Summarize two drawbacks of the cross-sectional design. (pp. 41–42)

A. _____

_____

B. _____

_____

8. In _____ *designs*, researchers conduct several similar cross-sectional or longitudinal studies at varying times. List three advantages of this design. (p. 42)

A. _____

_____

B. _____

_____

C. _____

_____

9. In a _____ design, researchers present children with a novel task and follow their mastery over a series of closely spaced sessions. (p. 43)

10. Microgenetic research is especially useful for studying (physical / cognitive / emotional and social) development. (p. 43)

11. List three reasons why microgenetic studies are difficult to carry out. (p. 43)

A. _____

_____

B. _____

_____

C. _____

_____

Social Issues: Education: Can Musical Experiences Enhance Intelligence?

1. True or False: The "Mozart effect" has a long-lasting influence on intelligence. (p. 44)

2. To produce lasting gains in mental test scores, interventions must have the following two features: (p. 44)

    A. _____

    _____

    B. _____

    _____

3. Explain how enrichment activities, such as music or chess lessons, can aid a child's developing intelligence. (p. 44)

_____

_____

_____

Ethics in Research on Children

1. Why are ethical concerns especially complex when children take part in research? (p. 43)

_____

_____

_____

2. Briefly describe the following children's research rights. (p. 45)

    A. Protection from harm:

    _____

    B. Informed consent:

    _____

    C. Privacy:

    _____

    D. Knowledge of results:

    _____

    E. Beneficial treatments:

    _____

3. For children _____ years and older, their own informed consent should be obtained in addition to parental consent prior to participation in research. (pp. 45–46)

4. What is *debriefing*, and why does it rarely work well with children? (p. 46)

    A. _____

    _____

    B. _____

    _____

PUZZLE 1.1 TERM REVIEW

Across

2. Genetically determined, naturally unfolding course of growth

3. Information-_____ approach: views the human mind as a symbol-manipulating machine

7. Freud's theory focusing on early sexual and aggressive drives

9. Erikson's stage theory of development entailing resolution of psychological conflicts

10. Social _____ theory: emphasizes the role of observational learning in the development of behavior

11. In ecological systems theory, temporal changes in a child's environment

14. Theory that focuses on how social interaction contributes to development

16. Theory concerned with the adaptive value of behavior

20. _____ developmental psychology seeks to understand the adaptive value of species-wide cognitive, emotional, and social competencies as those competencies change with age

21. _____ savages: view of children as possessing an innate plan for healthy growth

23. Development as a process in which new ways of understanding and responding to the world emerge at specific times

25. Nature-_____ controversy

26. In ecological systems theory, social settings that do not contain the child but that affect their experiences in immediate settings

Down

1. Unique combinations of personal and environmental circumstances that can result in different paths of change

4. _____ development: field of study devoted to understanding constancy and change from conception through adolescence and emerging adulthood

5. Theory that emphasizes the unique developmental history of each child

6. View of the child as a blank slate: tabula _____

8. In ecological systems theory, activities and interaction patterns in the child's immediate surroundings

12. In ecological systems theory, cultural values, laws, customs, and resources that influence experiences and interactions at inner levels of the environment

13. _____ systems theory: view of the child as developing within a complex system of relationships

15. Emphasizes the study of directly observable events

17. In ecological systems theory, connections between the child's immediate settings

18. Ability to adapt effectively in the face of threats to development

19. Piaget's _____-developmental theory suggests that children actively construct knowledge as they manipulate and explore their world

22. Development as gradually adding on more of the same types of skills that were there to begin with

23. _____ systems perspective: the child's mind, body, and physical and social worlds form an integrated system

24. Qualitative change characterizing a particular time period of development

PUZZLE 1.2 TERM REVIEW

Across

6. _____ period: a time that is optimal for certain capacities to emerge

7. Developmental cognitive _____ is the study of relationships between changes in the brain and the developing child's cognitive processes and behavior

9. Design in which the same participants are studied repeatedly, at different ages

11. _____ observation: observing a behavior of interest in the natural environment

12. Design that permits inferences about cause and effect

13. Behavior _____: procedures that combine conditioning and modeling to eliminate undesirable behaviors and increase desirable responses

15. Design in which researchers present children with a novel task and follow their mastery over a series of closely spaced sessions

20. Design in which researchers gather information without altering the participants' experience

22. Developmental _____: an interdisciplinary field that includes all changes throughout the lifespan

23. Describes, explains, and predicts behavior

Down

1. Variable manipulated by the researcher

2. _____ designs allow researchers to conduct several similar cross-sectional or longitudinal studies at varying times

3. Participant observation of a culture

4. Variable expected to be influenced by the experimental manipulations

5. _____ effects refer to the impact of cultural historical change on the accuracy of findings

8. Design in which groups of people differing in age are studied at the same point in time

10. The clinical method or _____ study approach

14. Structured _____: the researcher sets up a situation that evokes a behavior of interest and observes that behavior in a laboratory setting

16. Approach that uses age-related averages to represent typical development

17. _____ interview: each participant is asked the same questions in the same way

18. A number describing how two variables are related is called a correlation _____

19. In a _____ interview, the researcher uses a flexible, conversational style to probe for a participant's point of view

21. _____ assignment helps researchers control characteristics of participants that could reduce the accuracy of their findings

CROSSWORD PUZZLE SOLUTIONS

PUZZLE 1.1

PUZZLE 1.2

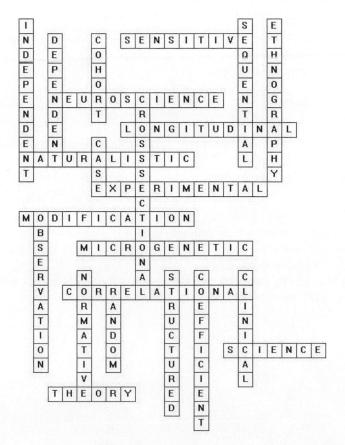

PRACTICE TEST #1

1. Our knowledge of child development is interdisciplinary. What does this mean? (p. 4)
   a. Our knowledge of child development is based exclusively on research conducted by people in the field of child development.
   b. Child development is not recognized as a distinct field of study.
   c. **It has grown through the combined efforts of people from many fields.**
   d. Child development is part of a larger discipline known as developmental psychology.

2. The domains in which children develop (p. 4)
   a. involve only cognitive skills.
   b. occur sequentially.
   c. pertain to infants and toddlers alone.
   d. **combine in an integrated, holistic fashion.**

3. The period of infancy and toddlerhood lasts from (p. 6)
   a. conception to birth.
   b. **birth to 2 years.**
   c. 2 to 6 years.
   d. 6 to 11 years.

4. Researchers have posited a developmental period called emerging adulthood because (p. 6)
   a. most societies encourage prolonged immaturity.
   b. **younger adults have moved beyond adolescence but not yet assumed adult roles.**
   c. they no longer consider adolescence a useful category.
   d. young people now tend to defer exploration of love, career, and personal values.

5. A good theory is a useful tool of research because it (p.7)
   a. stands outside cultural values and belief systems.
   b. is not subject to further testing.
   c. **describes, explains, and predicts behavior.**
   d. distills complex observations into a single statement.

6. Researchers who view development as continuous would maintain that the difference between immaturity and maturity is essentially (p. 7)
   a. longer developmental periods.
   b. stages.
   c. a sense of morality.
   d. **amount or complexity.**

7. A researcher who emphasizes the role of nature in development would examine the effects of (p. 8)
   a. **inborn biological givens.**
   b. a single theory of development.
   c. the physical and social world.
   d. stages.

8. Research shows that resilient children tend to (p. 10)
   a. come from broken families.
   b. bond with grandparents.
   c. **have biologically endowed characteristics that help them cope with stressful events.**
   d. change their environments often to reduce their exposure to risk.

9. During medieval times, (p. 11)
   a. **religious writings presented contradictory depictions of children's natures.**
   b. the concept of childhood was shaped by the notion of original sin.
   c. children were regarded as small adults.
   d. children were viewed as essentially angelic innocents.

10. John Locke encouraged parents to (p. 12)
    a. use physical punishment to foster obedience.
    b. allow children to follow their own inclinations.
    c. **use praise and approval as rewards.**
    d. keep their children's minds a tabula rasa for as long as possible.

11. G. Stanley Hall and Arnold Gesell are best known for (p. 13)
    a. reintroducing the idea of original sin into the study of child development.
    b. **launching the normative approach, in which measures of behavior are taken on large numbers of individuals and computed to represent typical development.**
    c. developing a more sophisticated theory of the mind as a tabula rasa.
    d. challenging Darwin's theory.

12. Psychoanalytic theorists accept the clinical, or case study, method because (p. 15)
    a. without it, psychoanalytic theories are too vague to be tested empirically.
    b. it is the best way to chart how experience imprints the blank mind.
    c. it allows them to avoid the constraints of mental testing.
    d. **it accords with their view that the individual's unique life history must be studied.**

13. According to Piaget, children move from the preoperational stage to concrete operational stage when (p. 19)
    a. they begin to use their senses and movement to explore the world.
    b. their action patterns become symbolic though illogical.
    c. **their cognition transforms into more organized reasoning.**
    d. they develop powers of abstract, systematic reasoning.

14. Like Piaget's theory, the information-processing approach regards children as (p. 22)
    a. struggling to accommodate their sexual and aggressive drives to the needs of society.
    b. **active, sense-making beings who modify their thought in response to environmental demands.**
    c. involved in a process of increasingly selective imitation.
    d. largely influenced by culture.

15. Developmental cognitive neuroscience has made rapid progress in (p. 23)
    a. **identifying the types of experiences that support or undermine brain development.**
    b. clearing away the lingering influence of psychoanalysis.
    c. analyzing thought into components and reassembling those into a comprehensive theory.
    d. demonstrating with greater nuance the effects of operant conditioning.

16. Ethological theory proposes that during the critical period, the child needs appropriate stimulation in order to (p. 23)
    a. undergo the brain changes that enable various behavior patterns.
    b. begin the process of psychosocial development.
    c. **acquire certain adaptive behaviors.**
    d. conform to social norms.

17. Vygotsky viewed cognitive development as a (p. 25)
    a. process that occurs within a large organism-environment system.
    b. **socially mediated process in which children depend on assistance from adults.**
    c. process free of social or cultural contexts.
    d. process that occurs rapidly during the critical period.

18. According to Bronfenbrenner, relationships at the level of the microsystem (p. 26)
    a.   are more important than those at the mesosystem level.
    b.   involve only parents.
    c.   shield children from forces that originate in the exosystem.
    d.   are bidirectional.

19. The dynamic systems view proposes that children (p. 27)
    a.   undergo the most profound changes when the microsystem clashes with the macrosystem.
    b.   reorganize their behavior in response to changes in the organism-environment relationship.
    c.   learn primarily through social interaction.
    d.   actively code, transform, and organize information.

20. The greatest limitation of naturalistic observation is that (p. 31)
    a.   not all individuals will be able to display a particular behavior in everyday life.
    b.   it does not distinguish between human and animal behavior.
    c.   it relies too heavily on self-reports.
    d.   too often parents intervene to make children perform a particular behavior.

21. Researchers employing the ethnographic method try to minimize their influence on the culture they are studying by (p. 34)
    a.   confining themselves to systematic observation.
    b.   observing only one or two aspects of children's experience in that culture.
    c.   describing, rather than interpreting, cultural meanings.
    d.   becoming part of the culture.

22. According to ethnographies, one of the reasons that children of immigrant parents often succeed in school is that the (p. 36)
    a.   children inherited high intelligence from their parents.
    b.   parents often studied with them.
    c.   parents believe that education is the surest way to improve life chances.
    d.   children have thoroughly assimilated the values of their new homeland.

23. The correlational design enables researchers to (p. 35)
    a.   eliminate the influence of the correlation coefficient.
    b.   examine relationships between participants' characteristics and their behavior or development.
    c.   infer cause and effect.
    d.   understand the interactions among independent and dependent variables.

24. The major problem with the cross-sectional design is that it (p. 41)
    a.   can be influenced by cohort effects.
    b.   relies too heavily on quasi-experiments.
    c.   does not provide evidence of change at the individual level.
    d.   too often yields results that cannot be assembled into general theories.

25. Microgenetic studies are difficult to conduct because (p. 43)
    a.   the time required for children to change their behavior is hard to anticipate.
    b.   combining longitudinal and cross-sectional designs is very difficult.
    c.   such studies require a large number of random assignments.
    d.   researchers must control so many independent variables.

PRACTICE TEST #2

1. In the period of middle childhood, (p. 6)
   a. language begins to develop.
   b. make-believe play blossoms.
   c. the child masters basic literacy skills.
   d. the young person establishes autonomy from the family.

2. The existence of many theories of child development (p. 7)
   a. helps advance knowledge by engaging the efforts of many researchers.
   b. prevents researchers from developing coherent explanations.
   c. suggests that development is always discontinuous.
   d. inhibits researchers' efforts to improve the welfare and treatment of children.

3. Theories of discontinuous development propose that development (p. 8)
   a. concludes in middle childhood.
   b. is a process of gradually augmenting skills present since birth.
   c. proceeds through five domains.
   d. occurs through sudden and rapid periods of transformation.

4. A theorist who argues that personality is shaped by intellectual stimulation from teachers holds which of the following views of development? (pp. 8–9)
   a. nature
   b. nurture
   c. continuous
   d. discontinuous

5. In America, the efforts to teach children self-reliance and self-control led Puritan parents to (p. 11)
   a. adopt a moderate balance between severity and permissiveness.
   b. use extremely harsh, repressive measures.
   c. reject the idea of original sin.
   d. put children to work as soon as they could walk.

6. According to Rousseau, (p. 12)
   a. child development is very similar to the evolution of other species.
   b. children can be ranked on an intelligence scale.
   c. parents should be receptive to children's needs at each of four stages of development.
   d. children have little influence on their own development.

7. Darwin's theory influenced theories of child development as researchers (p. 12)
   a. borrowed his conception of children as angelic.
   b. applied his emphasis on the adaptive value of physical and behavioral characteristics to child development.
   c. adapted his techniques of mental testing to children.
   d. came to view play as an example of survival of the fittest.

8. Freud proposed that children develop through stages in which they (p. 14)
   a. confront conflicts between biological drives and social expectations.
   b. become active, contributing members of society.
   c. conform to a greater or lesser extent to statistical norms.
   d. respond to reinforcers.

9. Erikson's psychosocial theory departed from Freud's theory by emphasizing (p. 15)
    a. the limited role of the superego.
    b. the case study method.
    c. the lifespan nature of development.
    d. empirically verifiable concepts.

10. According to Albert Bandura, (p. 18)
    a. development must be understood in relation to each culture's life situation.
    b. behavior can be shaped with operant conditioning.
    c. children develop a superego as they strive to meet parental and social expectations.
    d. children gradually become more selective in which behaviors they imitate.

11. A major limitation of Piaget's theory is that it (p. 20)
    a. discounts the role of the child's social world in its development.
    b. rests on limited use of clinical interviews.
    c. underestimates the competencies of infants and preschoolers.
    d. overemphasizes the effects of reinforcers on behavior.

12. The information-processing approach views development as a process of continuous change because it (p. 22)
    a. regards thought processes as similar at all ages but present to a greater or lesser extent.
    b. views environment as the supreme force in development.
    c. emphasizes stages through which children acquire new skills.
    d. assumes that personality emerges through maturation.

13. One criticism of the information-processing approach is that it (p. 22)
    a. fails to account sufficiently for the influence of unconscious drives.
    b. relies too heavily on intelligence tests.
    c. pays too much attention to nonlinear and illogical aspects of children's cognition.
    d. is better at analyzing thinking into its components than at reassembling them into a comprehensive theory.

14. Which of the following approaches draws upon diverse disciplines to study the relationship between changes in the brain and the child's cognitive processing and behavior patterns? (pp. 22–23)
    a. the normative approach
    b. behaviorism
    c. developmental cognitive neuroscience
    d. the information-processing approach

15. John Bowlby originated the ethological theory of attachment, pointing out that (pp. 23–24)
    a. infant smiling and babbling are built-in social signals that encourage caregivers to interact with them.
    b. facelike stimuli play a crucial role in infants' survival.
    c. children are most ready to develop important capacities during sensitive periods.
    d. imprinting is less important than previously thought.

16. An evolutionary developmental psychologist would seek to answer which of the following questions? (p. 24)
    a. What happens to the brain to enable imaginative play?
    b. What does play tell about children's sexual and aggressive drives?
    c. How can play be shaped by the application of reinforcers?
    d. What do children learn from play that might lead to adult gender-typed behaviors?

17. Unlike Vygotsky's sociocultural theory, Bronfenbrenner's ecological systems theory considers (p. 25)
    a. the effects of imprinting during the critical period.
    b. the child's biologically influenced dispositions.
    c. children's cooperative dialogues with more experienced elders.
    d. the adaptive value of species-wide competencies.

18. The dynamic systems perspective (p. 28)
    a. draws upon every field of science except physics.
    b. rejects the ecological systems emphasis on the effects of the chronosystem.
    c. draws upon information-processing and contextual theories.
    d. had been applied mainly to the study of language acquisition.

19. Structured observation deals with the limitation of naturalistic observation by (p. 31)
    a. establishing a laboratory situation that evokes the behavior of interest.
    b. employing clinical interviews.
    c. studying parents as well as children.
    d. rewarding children who display the behavior of interest.

20. The major advantage of the clinical, or case study, method is that it (p. 34)
    a. allows people to express their thoughts in terms as close as possible to the way they think in everyday life.
    b. isolates the subject of study from the effects of culture.
    c. fits with nearly all research designs.
    d. yields detailed narratives that offer insights into the array of factors affecting development.

21. Immigrant adolescents who had arrived in Canada often described their first year as very difficult because (p. 36)
    a. they did not speak English or French.
    b. their parents did not immediately establish close ties to an ethnic community.
    c. they could not get into good schools.
    d. their parents had to work too many hours to supervise them.

22. Experimental design enables researchers to (p. 37)
    a. gauge the effects of subtle changes in dependent variables.
    b. minimize their cultural influence.
    c. perceive cause-and-effect relationships by controlling the independent variable.
    d. free themselves from the constraints of laboratory experiments.

23. Researchers can minimize the influence of cohort effects by employing _____ designs. (p. 42)
    a. longitudinal
    b. sequential
    c. cross-sectional
    d. ethnographic

24. Research into the effect of music on children's intelligence suggests that (p. 44)
    a. sustained musical experiences can lead to small increases in intelligence.
    b. both music and drama lessons produced the same intelligence gains.
    c. listening to classical music will increase intelligence.
    d. music lessons can lead to gains in social maturity.

25. One of the most important ethical issues in research on children is (p. 43)
    a. parental involvement in the research design.
    b. the role of the federal government in the research process.
    c. the lack of guidelines from research-oriented associations.
    d. children often cannot evaluate for themselves what participation in research will mean.

POWERPOINT SLIDES

Domains of Development

Domain	Changes in
Physical	▪Body size & proportions, appearance ▪Functioning of body systems, health ▪Perceptual & motor capacities
Cognitive	▪ Intellectual abilities
Emotional and Social	▪Emotional communication ▪Self-understanding, knowledge about others ▪Interpersonal skills & relationships ▪Moral reasoning & behavior

Copyright © Allyn & Bacon 2008

Periods of Development

Prenatal	Conception to birth
Infancy and Toddlerhood	Birth to 2 years
Early Childhood	2 to 6 years
Middle Childhood	6 to 11 years
Adolescence	11 to 18 years
Emerging Adulthood	18 to 25 years

Copyright © Allyn & Bacon 2008

Theory

An orderly, integrated set of statements that
- Describes
- Explains
- Predicts behavior

Basic Issues in Development

1. **Continuous or discontinuous?**
2. **One course of development or many possible courses?**
3. **Relative influence of nature and nurture?**

Continuous or Discontinuous Development

(a) Continuous Development

(b) Discontinuous Development

Infancy   Adulthood   Infancy   Adulthood

Nature and Nurture

Nature
- Inborn, biologic givens
- Based on genetic inheritance

Nurture
- Physical and social world
- Influence biological and psychological development

Resilient Children

- Personal Characteristics
- A Warm Parental Relationship
- Social Support Outside the Immediate Family
- Community Resources and Opportunities

Historical Views of Childhood

Medieval Era	Childhood (to age 7 or 8) regarded as separate phase with special needs
16th Century	Puritan "child depravity" views
17th Century	John Locke "tabula rasa" or "blank slate" view
18th Century	Jean-Jacques Rousseau "noble savages" view

Early Scientific Study of Development

Evolutionary Theory	Darwin's ideas of natural selection and survival of the fittest are still influential.
Normative Approach	Hall & Gesell: Age-related averages based on measurements of large numbers of children.
Mental Testing Movement	Binet & Simon: Early developers of intelligence tests

Copyright © Allyn & Bacon 2008

Freud's Three Parts of the Personality

Id	▪Largest portion of the mind ▪Unconscious, present at birth ▪Source of biological needs & desires
Ego	▪Conscious, rational part of mind ▪Emerges in early infancy ▪Redirects id impulses acceptably
Superego	▪The conscience ▪Develops from ages 3 to 6, from interactions with caregivers

Copyright © Allyn & Bacon 2008

Freud's Psychosexual Stages

- Oral
- Anal
- Phallic
- Latency
- Genital

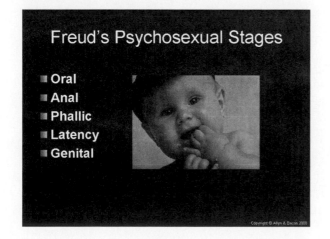

Copyright © Allyn & Bacon 2008

Erikson's Psychosocial Stages

Basic trust v. mistrust	Birth–1 year	Identity v. role confusion	Adolescence
Autonomy v. shame and doubt	1–3 years	Intimacy v. isolation	Emerging Adulthood
Initiative v. guilt	3–6 years	Generativity v. stagnation	Adulthood
Industry v. inferiority	6–11 years	Integrity v. despair	Old Age

Copyright © Allyn & Bacon 2008

Behaviorism & Social Learning

Classical Conditioning	Stimulus – Response
Operant Conditioning	Reinforcers and Punishments
Social-Cognitive Approach	Modeling Self-efficacy

Copyright © Allyn & Bacon 2008

Social Learning Theory

Modeling or Observational Learning	A baby claps her hands after her mother does so, a teenager dresses like her friends.
Cognition	Stressed today *Social-cognitive approach.*
Personal Standards	Children begin to believe their own abilities will help them succeed.

Copyright © Allyn & Bacon 2008

Behavior Modification

- Behavior modification: combines conditioning and modeling to eliminate undesirable behaviors and increase desirable responses.
- Examples: 4- and 5- year-olds' unruliness in preschool was reduced using tokens that could be traded for candy in exchange for good behavior.
- Children being treated for acute burn injuries played a virtual reality game that distracted them from the procedure and caused their levels of pain and anxiety to drop dramatically.

Copyright © Allyn & Bacon 2008

Limitations of Behaviorism and Social Learning Theory

- Too narrow a view of important environmental influences
- Bandura's work is unique in that it grants children an active role in their own learning.

Copyright © Allyn & Bacon 2008

Piaget's Stages of Cognitive Development

STAGE	PERIOD OF DEVELOPMENT	DESCRIPTION
Sensorimotor	Birth–2 years	Infants "think" by acting on the world with their eyes, ears, hands, and mouth. As a result, they invent ways of solving sensorimotor problems, such as pulling a lever to hear the sound of a music box, finding hidden toys, and putting objects in and taking them out of containers.
Preoperational	2–7 years	Preschool children use symbols to represent their earlier sensorimotor discoveries. Development of language and make-believe play takes place. However, thinking lacks the logic of the two remaining stages.
Concrete operational	7–11 years	Children's reasoning becomes logical. School-age children understand that a certain amount of lemonade or play dough remains the same even after its appearance changes. They also organize objects into hierarchies of classes and subclasses. However, thinking falls short of adult intelligence. It is not yet abstract.
Formal operational	11 years on	The capacity for abstract, systematic thinking enables adolescents, when faced with a problem, to start with a hypothesis, deduce testable inferences, and isolate and combine variables to see which inferences are confirmed. Adolescents can also evaluate the logic of verbal statements without referring to real-world circumstances.

Jean Piaget

Copyright © Allyn & Bacon 2008

Information-Processing Flowchart

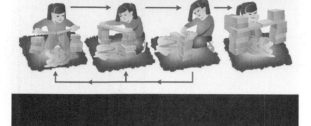

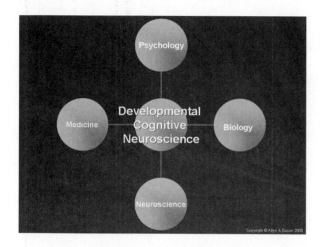

Neuroscientists

- Making rapid progress in identifying the types of experiences that support or undermine brain development at various ages.
- Clarifying the brain bases of many learning and behavioral disorders.
- Contributing to treatments for children with disabilities.

Ethology

- Concerned with the adaptive, or survival value of behavior and its evolutionary history.
- Roots traced to Darwin:
  - Imprinting
  - Critical Period

Evolutionary Developmental Psychology

- Seeks to understand adaptive value of human competencies
- Studies cognitive, emotional and social competencies as they change with age
- Expands upon ethology

Sensitive Period

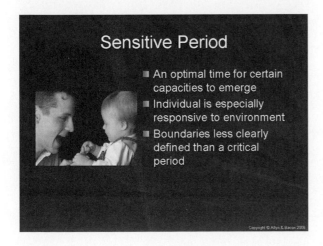

- An optimal time for certain capacities to emerge
- Individual is especially responsive to environment
- Boundaries less clearly defined than a critical period

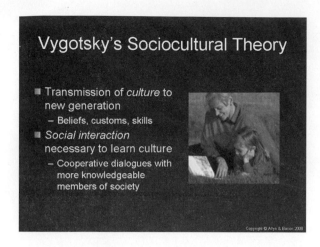

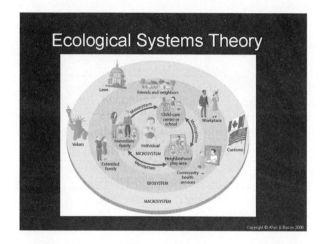

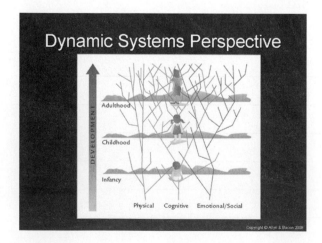

Comparing Child Development Theories

THEORY	CONTINUOUS OR DISCONTINUOUS DEVELOPMENT?	ONE COURSE OF DEVELOPMENT OR MANY?	NATURE OR NURTURE AS MORE IMPORTANT?
Psychoanalytic perspective	*Discontinuous:* Psychosexual and psychosocial development takes place in stages.	*One course:* Stages are assumed to be universal.	*Both nature and nurture:* Innate impulses are channeled and controlled through child-rearing experiences. *Early experiences set the course of later development.*
Behaviorism and social learning theory	*Continuous:* Development involves an increase in learned behaviors.	*Many possible courses:* Behaviors reinforced and modeled may vary from child to child.	*Emphasis on nurture:* Development results from conditioning and modeling. *Both early and later experiences are important.*
Piaget's cognitive-developmental theory	*Discontinuous:* Cognitive development takes place in stages.	*One course:* Stages are assumed to be universal.	*Both nature and nurture:* Development occurs as the brain matures and children exercise their innate drive to discover reality in a generally stimulating environment. *Both early and later experiences are important.*
Information processing	*Continuous:* Children gradually improve in perception, attention, memory, and problem-solving skills.	*One course:* Changes studied characterize most or all children.	*Both nature and nurture:* Children are active, sense-making beings who modify their thinking as the brain matures and they confront new environmental demands. *Both early and later experiences are important.*

Comparing Child Development Theories (continued)

Ethology and evolutionary developmental psychology	*Both continuous and discontinuous:* Children gradually develop a wider range of adaptive behaviors. Sensitive periods occur, in which qualitatively distinct capacities emerge fairly suddenly.	*One course:* Adaptive behaviors and sensitive periods apply to all members of a species.	*Both nature and nurture:* Evolution and heredity influence behavior, and learning lends greater flexibility and adaptiveness to it. In sensitive periods, early experiences set the course of later development.
Vygotsky's sociocultural theory	*Both continuous and discontinuous:* Language acquisition and schooling lead to stagewise changes. Dialogues with more expert members of society also lead to continuous changes that vary from culture to culture.	*Many possible courses:* Socially mediated changes in thought and behavior vary from culture to culture.	*Both nature and nurture:* Heredity, brain growth, and dialogues with more expert members of society jointly contribute to development. Both early and later experiences are important.
Ecological systems theory	*Not specified.*	*Many possible courses:* Children's characteristics join with environmental forces at multiple levels to mold development in unique ways.	*Both nature and nurture:* Children's characteristics and the reactions of others affect each other in a bidirectional fashion. Layers of the environment influence child-rearing experiences. Both early and later experiences are important.
Dynamic systems perspective	*Both continuous and discontinuous:* Change in the system is always ongoing. Stagelike transformations occur as children reorganize their behavior so components of the system work as a functioning whole.	*Many possible courses:* Biological makeup, everyday tasks, and social experiences vary, yielding wide individual differences in specific skills.	*Both nature and nurture:* The child's mind, body, and physical and social surroundings form an integrated system that guides mastery of new skills. Both early and later experiences are important.

Systematic Observation

Naturalistic Observation

- In the "field" or natural environment where behavior happens

Structured Observations

- Laboratory situation set up to evoke behavior of interest
- All participants have equal chance to display behavior

Interviews

Clinical Interview

- Flexible, conversational style
- Probes for participant's point of view

Structured Interview

- Each participant is asked same questions in same way
- May use questionnaires, get answers from groups

Copyright © Allyn & Bacon 2008

Cultural Influences: Immigrant Youths Adaptation

- Academic achievement and adjustment: many children of immigrant parents from diverse countries adapt amazingly well.
- The experience of these children is not problem-free, but family and community cohesion, supervision, and high expectations combine to promote favorable outcomes.

Copyright © Allyn & Bacon 2008

Correlational Design

- Researchers gather information and make no effort to alter their experiences.
- Limited because cause and effect can not be inferred.

Copyright © Allyn & Bacon 2008

Correlation Coefficients

- The magnitude of the number indicates the **strength** of the relationship.
- The sign of the number (+ or -) indicates the **direction** of the relationship.

+ 1.00	Strong positive relationship between two variables
0	No relationship
−1.00	Strong negative relationship between two variables

Copyright © Allyn & Bacon 2008

Correlation Coefficients

Magnitude
- Size of the number between 0 and 1.
- Closer to one (positive or negative) is a stronger relationship

Direction
- Indicated by + or - sign.
- Positive (+) means, as one variable increases, so does the other
- Negative (-) means, as one variable increase, the other decreases.

Copyright © Allyn & Bacon 2008

Independent and Dependent Variables

Independent
- Experimenter changes, or manipulates
- Expected to cause changes in another variable.

Dependent
- Experimenter measures, but does not manipulate
- Expected to be influenced by the independent variable

Copyright © Allyn & Bacon 2008

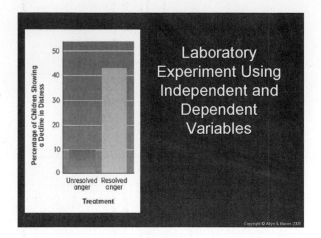

Laboratory Experiment Using Independent and Dependent Variables

Modified Experiments

Field Experiments
- Use rare opportunities for random assignment in natural settings

Natural Experiments
- Compare differences in treatment that already exist
- Groups chosen to match characteristics as much as possible

Designs for Studying Development

Longitudinal	Same participants studied repeatedly at different ages.
Cross-sectional	Participants of differing ages all studied at the same time.
Sequential	Several similar cross-sectional or longitudinal studies are conducted at varying times.
Microgenetic	Participants are presented with a novel task and their mastery is followed over a series of sessions.

Strengths and Limitations of Research Designs

DESIGN	DESCRIPTION	STRENGTHS	LIMITATIONS
General			
Correlational	This investigator obtains information on participants without altering their experiences.	Permits study of relationships between variables.	Does not permit inferences about cause-and-effect relationships.
Experimental	The investigator manipulates an independent variable and looks at its effect on a dependent variable; can be conducted in the laboratory or in the natural environment.	Permits inferences about cause-and-effect relationships.	When conducted in the laboratory, findings may not apply to the real world. When conducted in the field, control is usually weaker, and results may be due to variables other than the treatment.
Developmental			
Longitudinal	The investigator studies the same group of participants repeatedly at different ages.	Permits study of common patterns and individual differences in development and relationships between early and later events and behaviors.	Age-related changes may be distorted because of dropout and test-wiseness of participants and because of cohort effects.
Cross-sectional	The investigator studies groups of participants differing in age at the same point in time.	More efficient than the longitudinal design.	Does not permit study of individual developmental trends. Age differences may be distorted because of cohort effects.
Sequential design	The investigator follows a sequence of samples (two or more age groups), collecting data on them at the same points in time.	Permits both longitudinal and cross-sectional comparisons. Reveals cohort effects. Permits tracking of age-related changes more efficiently than the longitudinal design.	May have the same problems as longitudinal and cross-sectional strategies, but the design itself helps identify difficulties.
Microgenetic design	The investigator presents children with a novel task and follows their mastery over a series of closely spaced sessions.	Offers insights into the process of development.	Requires intensive study of participants' moment-by-moment behaviors. The time required for participants to change is difficult to anticipate. Practice effects may distort developmental trends.

Copyright © Allyn & Bacon 2008

Sequential Designs

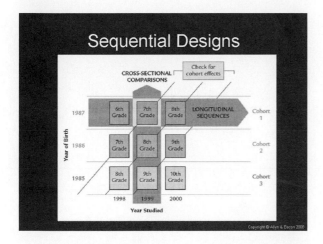

Copyright © Allyn & Bacon 2008

Can Musical Experience Enhance Intelligence?

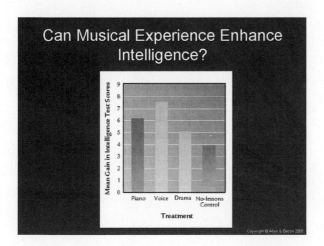

Copyright © Allyn & Bacon 2008

99

Children's Research Rights

- Protection from harm
- Informed consent
- Privacy
- Knowledge of results
- Beneficial treatments

Copyright © Allyn & Bacon 2008

CHAPTER 2
BIOLOGICAL AND ENVIRONMENTAL FOUNDATIONS

CHAPTER-AT-A-GLANCE

Chapter Outline	Instruction Ideas	Supplements
Genetic Foundations pp. 52–62 The Genetic Code • The Sex Cells • Boy or Girl? • Multiple Births • Patterns of Genetic Inheritance • Chromosomal Abnormalities	Learning Objectives 2.1–2.8 Learning Activities 2.1–2.3 Ask Yourself p. 62	Transparencies 12–16 Test Bank Items 1–39, 99–100 Please contact your Allyn and Bacon publisher's representative for a wide range of video offerings available to adopters.
Reproductive Choices pp. 63–69 Genetic Counseling • Prenatal Diagnosis and Fetal Medicine • The Alternative of Adoption	Learning Objective 2.9 Lecture Enhancement 2.1 Learning Activities 2.4–2.5 Ask Yourself p. 69	Transparency 17 Test Bank Items 40–43, 89–93
Environmental Contexts for Development pp. 69–82 The Family • Socioeconomic Status and Family Functioning • Affluence • Poverty • Beyond the Family: Neighborhoods and Schools • The Cultural Context	Learning Objectives 2.10–2.13 Lecture Enhancements 2.2–2.4 Learning Activities 2.6–2.7 Ask Yourself p. 82	Test Bank Items 44–65, 94–98, 102
Understanding the Relationship Between Heredity and Environment pp. 82–89 The Question, "How Much?" • The Question, "How?"	Learning Objective 2.14 Learning Activity 2.8 Ask Yourself p. 89	Transparencies 19–21, 23 Test Bank Items 66–88, 103–105

BRIEF CHAPTER SUMMARY

This chapter examines the foundations of development: heredity and environment. The principles of genetic transmission determine the characteristics that make us human and contribute to individual differences in appearance and behavior. Inheritance of harmful recessive genes and abnormalities of the chromosomes are major causes of serious developmental problems. Genetic counseling and prenatal diagnosis help people at risk for transmitting hereditary disorders assess their chances of giving birth to a healthy baby.

Environmental influences on development are no less complex than hereditary factors. The family has an especially powerful impact. It operates as a complex, dynamic social system in which members exert direct, indirect, and third-party effects on one another. Socioeconomic status influences child-rearing practices: Poverty and homelessness undermine effective family functioning and children's well-being, while affluence may lead to overscheduling and lack of emotional closeness, which also have negative effects. The quality of community life, from neighborhoods and schools to small towns and cities, is another influence on children's development. Cultural values—for example, the degree to which a society emphasizes collectivism versus individualism—combine with public policies, laws, and government programs to shape experiences in all of these contexts.

Some child development specialists believe that it is useful and possible to determine "how much" heredity and environment contribute to individual differences. Others think that the effects of heredity and environment cannot be clearly separated. Instead, they want to discover "how" these two major determinants of development work together in a complex, dynamic interplay.

LEARNING OBJECTIVES

After reading this chapter, you should be able to:

2.1   Distinguish between genotypes and phenotypes. (p. 51)

2.2   Describe the structure and function of chromosomes and DNA molecules. (p. 52)

2.3   Explain the process of mitosis. (pp. 52–53)

2.4   Describe the process of meiosis, and explain how it leads to genetic variability. (pp. 53–54)

2.5   Describe the genetic events that determine the sex of the new organism. (pp. 54–55)

2.6   Identify two types of twins, and explain how each is created. (pp. 55–56)

2.7   Explain how alleles influence the inheritance of traits, such as through dominant–recessive inheritance, incomplete dominance, X-linked inheritance, polygenic inheritance, mutation, and genetic imprinting. (pp. 56–60)

2.8   Describe the origins and consequences of Down syndrome and abnormalities of the sex chromosomes. (pp. 60–62)

2.9   Discuss reproductive choices available to prospective parents, noting the pros and cons of reproductive technologies. (pp. 63–68)

2.10   Describe family functioning from the ecological systems perspective, citing direct and indirect family influences and explaining the view of the family as a dynamic, changing system. (pp. 69–71)

2.11   Discuss the impact of socioeconomic status, including affluence and poverty, on family functioning. (pp. 71–75)

2.12   Summarize the role of neighborhoods and schools in the lives of children. (pp. 75–77)

2.13   Discuss how cultural values and public policies influence the well-being of children. (pp. 77–82)

2.14   Explain the various ways heredity and environment may combine to influence complex human traits. (pp. 82–89)

LECTURE OUTLINE

I. GENETIC FOUNDATIONS (pp. 52–62)
   A. The foundations of development are heredity and environment.
      1. Heredity supplies our **genotype** (genetic makeup).
      2. Our **phenotype** (directly observable characteristics) reflects the combined effects of heredity and environment.
      3. Each human being is made up of trillions of *cells*. **Chromosomes**—rodlike structures in the *nucleus* of each cell—store and transmit genetic information.
   B. The Genetic Code (pp. 52–53)
      1. Chromosomes are made up of molecules of **deoxyribonucleic acid (DNA)**, which resembles a twisted ladder, with each "rung" containing a pair of chemical substances called *bases*.
      2. A **gene** is a segment of DNA along the length of the chromosome, which contains instructions for making proteins.
      3. DNA duplicates itself through the process of **mitosis**, during which chromosomes copy themselves, so that each new cell receives an exact copy of the original chromosomes.
      4. Genes send instructions for making a rich assortment of proteins to the *cytoplasm* surrounding the cell nucleus. The number and variety of proteins made by human genes account for the complexity of our species.
   C. The Sex Cells (pp. 53–54)
      1. New individuals are created when the sex cells, or **gametes** (the sperm cells in males and the ova in females), combine.
      2. Each gamete—formed through a cell division process called **meiosis**—contains only 23 chromosomes.
      3. When the gametes combine at conception, the resulting cell, called a **zygote,** again has 46 chromosomes.
      4. In meiosis, the chromosomes pair up and exchange segments in a process called **crossing over**, so that genes from one are replaced by genes from another, creating new hereditary combinations. Then chance determines which member of each pair will gather with others and end up in the same gamete.
      5. Meiosis is responsible for the variability among nontwin offspring of the same two parents.
      6. The cells from which sperm arise are produced throughout life, allowing a healthy man to father a child at any age after sexual maturity.
      7. Because the female is born with all her ova (1 to 2 million) already present in her ovaries, she can bear children for only a three to four decades, during which 350 to 450 ova will mature.
   D. Boy or Girl? (pp. 54–55)
      1. The 22 matching pairs of chromosomes within a human cell are called the **autosomes**.
      2. The twenty-third pair consists of **sex chromosomes**, called XX in females and XY in males.
      3. The sex of the new organism is determined by whether an X-bearing or a Y-bearing sperm fertilizes the ovum.
   E. Multiple Births (pp. 55–56)
      1. **Fraternal**, or **dizygotic**, **twins,** the most common type of multiple birth, result when two separate ova are released and fertilized by two separate sperm.
      2. **Identical**, or **monozygotic**, **twins,** who have the same genetic makeup, result when a single zygote that has started to duplicate separates into two clusters of cells that develop into two individuals.
      3. During their early years, children of single births are often healthier and develop more rapidly than twins, who tend to be born early.
   F. Patterns of Genetic Inheritance (pp. 56–60)
      1. Two forms of each gene, each called an **allele,** occur at the same place on the chromosomes—one inherited from the mother and one from the father.
      2. If the alleles from both parents are alike, the child is **homozygous** and will display the inherited trait.
      3. If the alleles are different, the child is **heterozygous**, and the phenotype, or visible trait, depends on the relationships between the alleles.

4. Dominant–Recessive Inheritance (pp. 56–57)

   a. Many heterozygous pairings show a pattern of **dominant–recessive inheritance,** in which only one allele, called *dominant,* affects the child's characteristics, while the other allele, called *recessive,* has no effect.

   b. An individual who inherits a heterozygous pair of alleles for a trait will be a **carrier** for the recessive trait; carriers do not exhibit the trait but can pass it to their children.

   c. One of the most frequently occurring recessive disorders is *phenylketonuria,* or *PKU,* which appears in children whose parents both carry the recessive allele for the trait. The severity of this and other recessive disorders may depend on the action of **modifier genes,** which act on other alleles, slightly altering their effects.

   d. Serious diseases are rarely due to dominant alleles, because the affected individual rarely lives long enough to pass the gene to the next generation. An exception is *Huntington disease,* in which the symptoms do not appear until age 35 or later, when the person has already passed the dominant allele to his or her children.

5. Incomplete Dominance (p. 57)

   a. **Incomplete dominance** is a pattern of inheritance in which both alleles are expressed in the phenotype, resulting in a combined trait or one that is intermediate between the two.

   b. An example is the *sickle cell trait,* a heterozygous condition present in many black Africans. *Sickle cell anemia* occurs in full form when a child inherits two recessive alleles. In heterozygous individuals, the disease may occur when they experience oxygen deprivation—for example, at high altitudes.

   c. The sickle cell allele is common among black Africans because carriers of this allele are more resistant to malaria than individuals who are homozygous for normal red blood cells. In Africa, where malaria is common, sickle cell carriers are more likely to survive to maturity.

6. X–linked Inheritance (pp. 57, 59)

   a. **X-linked inheritance** applies when a recessive allele is carried on the X chromosome. Males are more likely to be affected because the Y chromosome, which is shorter than the X, may not have a corresponding dominant allele to override the recessive allele.

   b. A well-known example is *hemophilia,* a disorder in which the blood fails to clot normally.

   c. Besides X-linked disorders, the male is at a disadvantage in other ways, including higher rates of miscarriage, infant and childhood deaths, birth defects, learning disabilities, behavior disorders, and mental retardation.

   d. Although the male disadvantage is generally offset by higher rates of male than female births, recent declines in the proportion of male births in industrialized countries may reflect a rise in stressful living conditions, which heighten spontaneous abortions, especially of male fetuses.

7. Genetic Imprinting (pp. 59–60)

   a. In a pattern of inheritance called **genetic imprinting**, some alleles are *imprinted,* or chemically *marked,* in such a way that one pair member (either the mother's or the father's) is activated, regardless of its makeup.

   b. Imprinting helps us understand certain puzzling genetic patterns—for example, why children are more likely to develop diabetes if their father, rather than their mother, suffers from it, whereas the reverse is true for other diseases, such as asthma and hay fever.

   c. Imprinting is involved in several childhood cancers and in *Prader-Willi syndrome,* a disorder with symptoms of mental retardation and severe obesity. It may also influence the onset and progression of Huntington disease.

   d. Genetic imprinting can also operate on the sex chromosomes, as seen in *fragile X syndrome*, a disorder linked to some cases of autism, which occurs only when the defective gene is passed from mother to child.

8. Mutation (p. 60)

   a. **Mutation** is a sudden but permanent change in a DNA segment through which harmful genes are created. It may occur spontaneously or may be caused by hazardous environmental agents, such as ionizing (high-energy) radiation.

   b. In *germline mutation,* which occurs in the cells that give rise to gametes, the defective DNA is passed on to the next generation when the affected individual mates.

      c.   In *somatic mutation,* which can occur at any time of life, normal body cells mutate, and the DNA defect spreads to every cell derived form the affected body cell, eventually leading to disease or disability.

    9. Polygenic Inheritance (p. 60)

      a.   Complex traits result from **polygenic inheritance**, in which many genes are involved in determining the characteristic.

      b.   Characteristics that vary continuously among people, such as height, weight, and intelligence, are due to polygenic inheritance.

G. Chromosomal Abnormalities (pp. 60–62)

    1. Most chromosomal defects results from mistakes during meiosis, when the ovum and sperm are formed. Because these abnormalities involve more DNA than single-gene disorders, they usually produce many mental and physical symptoms.

    2. Down Syndrome (pp. 60–61)

      a.   *Down syndrome,* the most common chromosomal disorder, usually results from a failure of the twenty-first pair of chromosomes to separate during meiosis, so that the new individual inherits three, rather than two, of these chromosomes.

        (1) For this reason, this disorder is sometimes called *trisomy 21.*

        (2) Less commonly, an extra twenty-first chromosome is attached to part of another chromosome (*translocation* pattern), or an error in the early stages of mitosis causes the defective chromosomal makeup to occur in some, but not all, body cells (*mosaic* pattern).

      b.   Symptoms of Down syndrome include mental retardation, memory and speech problems, limited vocabulary, slow motor development, and distinct physical features.

      c.   Affected individuals who live past age 40 are likely to show symptoms of *Alzheimer's disease,* the most common form of dementia, which is also linked to genes on chromosome 21.

      d.   The risk of bearing a Down syndrome baby rises dramatically with maternal age, probably because the woman's ova weaken over time. In some cases, the extra genetic material originates with the father, and some studies indicate a role for advanced paternal age, though this is still unclear.

    3. Abnormalities of the Sex Chromosomes (pp. 61–62)

      a.   Most disorders of the autosomes, other than Down syndrome, disrupt development so severely that miscarriage occurs. Disorders of the sex chromosomes usually lead to fewer problems and often are not recognized until adolescence, when some cause delayed puberty.

      b.   Contrary to common myths about individuals with sex chromosome disorders, males with *XYY syndrome* are not always more aggressive and antisocial than XY males, and most children with sex chromosome disorders do not suffer from mental retardation. Rather, they have specific intellectual problems—verbal difficulties in *triple X syndrome* and *Klinefelter syndrome,* problems with spatial relationships in *Turner syndrome.*

II. REPRODUCTIVE CHOICES (pp. 63–69)

A. Genetic Counseling (p. 63)

    1. **Genetic counseling** is a communication process designed to help a couple assess the likelihood of giving birth to a baby with a hereditary disorder and to choose the best course of action in view of risks and family goals.

    2. The genetic counselor interviews the couple and prepares a *pedigree,* a picture of the family tree in which affected relatives are identified. The pedigree is used to estimate the likelihood that parents will have an abnormal child.

B. Prenatal Diagnosis and Fetal Medicine (pp. 63–65, 66)

    1. **Prenatal diagnostic methods** are medical procedures that permit detection of developmental problems before birth. They include *amniocentesis, chorionic villus sampling,* and *maternal blood analysis.*

    2. Prenatal diagnosis has led to advances in fetal medicine, permitting some problems to be treated before birth.

    3. However, these techniques frequently result in complications, most commonly premature labor and miscarriage. To avoid these risks, prenatal diagnosis—except for maternal blood analysis—should not be used routinely.

4. Advances in *genetic engineering* offer new hope of correcting hereditary defects.
   a. Researchers involved in the Human Genome Project are "annotating" the genome in an effort to understand the estimated 4,000 human disorders due to either single genes or an interplay of genetic and environmental factors. They have identified the genes involved in cystic fibrosis, Duchenne muscular dystrophy, Huntington disease, Marfan syndrome, and hundreds of other diseases.
   b. New treatments being explored include *gene therapy* to correct genetic abnormalities and *proteomics,* modification of gene-specified proteins involved in disease.
5. Increasing numbers of individuals are turning to reproductive technologies—alternative methods of conception and childbearing that include *donor insemination, in vitro fertilization,* and *surrogate motherhood.* Laws are needed to regulate these practices, raise complex ethical issues.

C. The Alternative of Adoption (pp. 65, 67–69)
   1. Because the availability of healthy babies needing adoptive families has declined in North America and Western Europe, more people are adopting from other countries or accepting children who are past infancy or who have known developmental problems.
   2. Adopted children and adolescents tend to have more learning and emotional difficulties than other children, a difference that increases with the child's age at adoption.
   3. Despite these risks, most adopted children fare well, and international adoptees, overall, fare better than birth siblings or institutionalized agemates who stay behind.
   4. Most adopted children have happy childhoods and grow up to be well-adjusted adults. In early adulthood, marriage and childbirth may trigger adoptees' desire to search for their birth parents.

III. ENVIRONMENTAL CONTEXTS FOR DEVELOPMENT (pp. 69–82)
   A. The child's environment consists of many influences that combine to affect the course of development, as described in ecological systems theory—from the *microsystem* (immediate settings) to the *macrosystem,* or broad climate of society.
   B. The Family (pp. 69–71)
      1. In power and breadth of influence, no other context for development equals the family.
      2. The family is a network of interdependent relationships within which the behaviors of each member affect those of others through *bidirectional influences.*
      3. Direct Influences (p. 70)
         a. Research on the family system shows how parents and children directly affect each other.
         b. When parents are firm but also warm and affectionate, children tend to cooperate; when children willingly comply with parental requests, parents are likely to be warm and gentle in the future. Harsh discipline tends to increase children's misbehavior, which in turn may lead to greater use of harsh punishment. Both examples show how parent–child interaction can promote or undermine children's well-being.
      4. Indirect Influences (p. 70–71)
         a. The effect of *third parties* can either support or undermine other family relationships.
         b. These relationships, including the parents' marital relationship and the influence of grandparents, can serve as supports for or barriers to development.
      5. Adapting to Change (p. 71)
         a. The family is a dynamic, ever-changing system in which each member adapts to the development of other members.
         b. The developmental status of each family member and the historical time period also contribute to a dynamic family system.
         c. In industrialized nations, socioeconomic status is an important factor in general patterns of family functioning, even as families have become increasingly diverse.
   C. Socioeconomic Status and Family Functioning (pp. 71–73)
      1. **Socioeconomic status (SES)** is an index of individuals' and families' social position and economic well-being that combines years of education, the prestige of one's job and the skill it requires, and income.

2. SES is linked to timing of parenthood and to family size, as well as to child-rearing values and expectations—differences that reflect their varying life conditions and differing educational levels.
   a. Higher-SES parents are more likely to emphasize psychological traits, such as curiosity and happiness, and to take an interest in verbal stimulation and nurturing inner traits.
   b. Lower-SES parents, who lack power and influence in their relationships beyond the home, tend to value external characteristics, such as obedience and neatness, and are more likely to use coercive discipline.
   c. In diverse cultures, education of women fosters patterns of thinking that improve quality of life for both parents and children.
3. Higher SES is associated with enhanced cognitive and language development, academic success, and reduced incidence of emotional and behavior problems. These characteristics make higher educational attainment more likely—outcomes that appear to reflect differences in family functioning.

D. Affluence (p. 73)
1. Children of affluent parents with professionally and socially demanding lives may experience adjustment problems if these parents fail to engage in family interaction and parenting that promote development.
2. Poorly adjusted affluent young people report less emotional closeness and supervision from their parents than better-adjusted counterparts, especially when parents value their accomplishments more than their character.
3. Among affluent teenagers, substance use is correlated with anxiety and depression, suggesting that these youths use drugs to self-medicate.
4. The simple routine of eating dinner with parents is associated with a reduction in adjustment difficulties for both affluent and low-SES youths.
5. Interventions are needed to make affluent parents aware of the high costs of a competitive lifestyle that deemphasizes family time.

E. Poverty (pp. 74–75)
1. Today about 12 percent of people in Canada and 13 percent in the United States are poor.
2. Those most affected by poverty are parents under age 25 with young children, elderly people who live alone, ethnic minorities, and women, especially single mothers with preschool children, for whom the poverty rate in both countries is nearly 50 percent.
3. The poverty rate is higher among children than any other age group, a circumstance that is particularly worrisome because the earlier poverty begins, the deeper it is, and the longer it lasts, the more devastating are its effects on physical and mental health.
4. The constant stresses accompanying poverty weaken the family system.
   a. Daily hassles and crises reduce parents' ability to deal effectively with their children.
   b. Poor housing and dangerous neighborhoods increase stress levels and reduce social support networks.
   c. Homelessness, which has become more common in the past 25 years, has particularly devastating effects on children, who suffer from developmental delays, emotional stress, health problems, school absenteeism, and poor academic performance.

F. Beyond the Family: Neighborhoods and Schools (pp. 75–77)
1. Child abuse and neglect are greatest in areas where community life is disrupted.
2. Strong family ties to the community, through friends, relatives, and religious affiliations, reduce family stress and adjustment problems.
3. Neighborhoods (pp. 75–76)
   a. Children are better adjusted socially and emotionally when their neighborhood experiences are more varied.
   b. Neighborhood resources have a greater impact on young people growing up in economically disadvantaged than well-to-do neighborhoods, because low-SES young people are more dependent on their immediate surroundings.
   c. In low-income neighborhoods, in-school and after-school programs can compensate for a lack of other resources by providing art, music, sports, and other enrichment activities.

        d.   In low-income areas, social ties linking families to one another and to other institutions are weak or absent. Consequently, informal social controls over young people weaken, giving rise to antisocial activities. Community-based programs (such as the Better Beginnings, Better Futures Project in Ontario, Canada) can help prevent these effects of poverty.

    4.   Schools (pp. 76–77)

        a.   School is a formal institution designed to transmit knowledge and skills that children in the developed world need to become productive members of their society.

        b.   Schools are complex social systems that vary in the quality of their physical environments, educational philosophies, and social life.

        c.   Regular parent–school contact supports children's development. In low-SES communities, teachers and administrators must take extra steps to promote these family–school ties.

G. The Cultural Context (pp. 77–82)

    1.   Cultural Values and Practices (pp. 77–79)

        a.   Cultures shape all aspects of daily life—family interaction, school experiences, and community settings beyond the home.

        b.   The North American cultural context reflects the central values of independence, self-reliance, and the privacy of family life.

        c.   In large industrialized countries such as the United States, **subcultures** exist in which groups of people share beliefs and customs different from those of the larger culture.

        d.   The African-American cultural tradition of **extended-family households**, in which parent and child live with one or more adult relatives, has helped members of this subculture to overcome the effects of prejudice and economic deprivation.

        e.   In **collectivist societies**, which value an *interdependent self,* people define themselves as part of a group and stress group over individual goals.

        f.   In **individualistic societies**, which value an *independent self,* people think of themselves as separate entities and are largely concerned with their own personal needs. The United States is more individualistic than most other industrialized nations, while Canada is somewhat less individualistic, but more so than most Western European countries.

        g.   Collectivist versus individualistic values have a powerful impact on a nation's approach to protecting the well-being of children and families.

    2.   Public Policies and Child Development (pp. 79–80, 81)

        a.   **Public policies** are laws and government programs designed to improve conditions by responding to current social problems.

        b.   The United States and Canada lag behind other developed nations in policies that benefit children and families. This is the result of a complex set of political and economic forces, including cultural values of self-reliance and privacy and the high cost of good social programs.

        c.   Compared with the United States, Canada devotes considerably more of its resources to education and health. But like the United States, Canada has been slow to move toward national standards and funding for child care.

    3.   Looking Toward the Future (pp. 80, 82)

        a.   Public policies aimed at fostering children's development can be justified on the grounds that children represent a society's future, as well as on humanitarian grounds—children's basic rights as human beings, as outlined in the 1989 United Nations *Convention on the Rights of the Child.* However, the United States is one of only two countries whose legislature has not yet ratified the Convention, reflecting American individualism and fears that the provisions of the Convention would shift the burden of child rearing from the family to the state.

        b.   In the United States, one of the most influential interest groups devoted to the well-being of children is the Children's Defense Fund, which publishes *The State of America's Children,* an annual document providing a comprehensive analysis of children's condition and suggestions for improving programs for children.

        c.   Canada's public education movement, *Campaign 2000,* works to build nationwide awareness of child poverty and to lobby government representatives for improved public policies benefiting children, including raising basic living standards, ensuring affordable, appropriate housing for all children, and strengthening child care and other community resources.

IV. UNDERSTANDING THE RELATIONSHIP BETWEEN HEREDITY AND ENVIRONMENT (pp. 82–89)
   A. **Behavioral genetics** is a field devoted to uncovering the contributions of nature and nurture to the great diversity that exists in human traits and abilities.
   B. Some investigators focus on the question of *how much each factor contributes* to differences between individuals, but a growing consensus regards this question as unanswerable and focuses instead on *how nature and nurture work together.*
   C. The Question, "How Much?" (pp. 83–85)
      1. Heritability (p. 83)
         a. **Heritability estimates** measure the extent to which individual differences in complex traits, such as intelligence and personality, within a population are due to genetic factors.
         b. Heritability estimates are obtained from **kinship studies**, which compare the characteristics of family members, most commonly identical and fraternal twins.
         c. Most kinship studies support a moderate role for heredity, but findings are controversial.
      2. Concordance (p. 84)
         a. The **concordance rate** is the percentage of instances in which both twins show a trait when it is present in one twin. For a trait to be attributed solely to heredity, the concordance rate for identical twins would have to be 100 percent.
         b. Concordance and adoption research, taken together, suggest that genetic factors play a role in the tendency for schizophrenia, depression, and criminality to run in families, although the environment is also involved.
      3. Limitations of Heritability and Concordance (pp. 84–85)
         a. Serious questions have been raised about the accuracy of heritability estimates and concordance rates, which can overestimate the impact of heredity while underestimating the importance of environment.
         b. It is difficult to generalize the twin pair study results to the general population.
         c. Although they provide useful information, they do not address the process of development. Results can easily be misapplied to suggest that ethnic differences in intelligence have a genetic basis.
         d. Heritability estimates and concordance rates also have limited usefulness, because they do not provide precise information on how intelligence and personality develop or how children might respond to interventions designed to enhance their experiences.
   D. The Question, "How?" (pp. 85–88)
      1. Today, most researchers believe that that development is the result of a dynamic interplay between heredity and environment. They focus on the question of *how* nature and nurture work together.
      2. Reaction Range (pp. 85–86)
         a. **Range of reaction** refers to each person's unique, genetically determined response to the environment, accounting for children's varying responses to the same environment.
         b. Reaction range reveals that unique blends of heredity and environment lead to both similarities and differences in behavior.
      3. Canalization (p. 86)
         a. **Canalization** is the tendency of heredity to restrict development to one or a few potential outcomes. It is highly adaptive, ensuring that children will develop certain species-typical skills (such as walking) under a wide range of rearing conditions.
         b. Strongly canalized behaviors develop similarly in a wide range of environments, requiring extreme environmental conditions to modify them or cause them not to appear.
         c. Intelligence and personality are less strongly canalized, varying widely with environmental changes.
      4. Genetic–Environmental Correlation (pp. 86–87)
         a. According to the concept of **genetic–environmental correlation,** our genes influence the environments to which we are exposed.

       b.   Passive and Evocative Correlation (p. 86)

          (1) *Passive* correlation is common in young children, who do not have control over the environment available to them. Parents create an environment compatible with their own heredity.

          (2) In *evocative* correlation, children behave in ways consistent with their own heredity, evoking responses from others that, in turn, strengthen the child's original response.

       c.   Active Correlation (pp. 86–87)

          (1) *Active* correlation is more common at older ages, when children extend their experiences beyond the immediate family and can choose environments that complement their genetic tendencies.

          (2) This tendency to actively choose environments that complement our heredity is called **niche-picking**. It explains why pairs of identical twins who are reared apart nevertheless develop similar food preferences, hobbies, and vocations.

          (3) With age, genetic factors may become more important in determining the environments we experience and choose for ourselves.

    5.   Environmental Influences on Gene Expression (pp. 87–88)

       a.   Growing evidence reveals that the relationship between heredity and environment is not a one-way street, from genes to environment to behavior, but is *bidirectional:* Genes affect children's behavior and experiences, but experiences and behavior also affect gene expression.

       b.   Stimulation—both *internal* to the child and *external* (home, neighborhood, school, and society) triggers gene activity.

       c.   This view of the relationship between heredity and environment is called the *epigenetic framework.* **Epigenesis** means development resulting from ongoing, bidirectional exchanges between heredity and all levels of environment.

       d.   The success of any attempt to improve development depends on the characteristics we want to change, the genetic makeup of the child, and the type and timing of our intervention.

LECTURE ENHANCEMENTS

LECTURE ENHANCEMENT 2.1
Should Psychiatric Risk Assessment Be Included in Genetic Counseling? (p. 63)

Time: 10–15 minutes

Objective: To examine the use of psychiatric risk assessment in genetic counseling.

As noted in the text, genetic factors contribute to a wide variety of traits, including personality, intelligence, and mental health. According to Pestka (2006), certain psychiatric illnesses like schizophrenia probably involve multiple genes that, when combined with environmental factors, often manifest into serious mental health problems.

    Because mental health problems tend to run in families, more couples are seeking genetic counseling to assess their risk of having offspring with a serious psychiatric condition. Like traditional genetic counseling, risk assessment includes the development of a family pedigree. However, since multiple genes are likely involved and researchers have yet to identify specific genes that contribute to psychiatric disorders, risk assessment must be used with caution. Pestka (2006) adds that genetic counselors should not ignore the potential contribution of environmental factors. For example, a child with a family history of chronic depression is more likely to develop mental health problems when his or her home environment is disorganized and replete with stressors (i.e., poverty, poor caregiver mental health, few social supports). If the same child is raised in a stable and supportive environment, he or she may never develop depressive symptoms. Moreover, most clients lack an adequate understanding of risk. For example, in one study, clients with bipolar disorder estimated their offspring's risk of inheriting the disorder to be 45 percent, while the actual risk was only 17.5 percent.

    According to Pestka (2006), researchers have much to learn about the link between genes and mental health. While genetic factors certainly play an important role, we have yet to identify specific genes that contribute to most psychiatric disorders. Therefore, physicians and other professionals who include mental health risk assessment in genetic counseling are ethically obligated to educate clients on the many factors that contribute to psychiatric conditions, as well as dispel any myths that clients may have.

Ask students to reflect on these findings. Do they think genetic counseling should include a risk assessment for mental health disorders? If so, should genetic counseling only focus on severe psychiatric illnesses like bipolar disorder and schizophrenia or should all mental health disorders be considered? Explain.

Pestka, E. L. (2006). Genetic counseling for mental health disorders. *Journal of the American Psychiatric Nurses Association, 11,* 338–343.

LECTURE ENHANCEMENT 2.2
More on Environmental Contexts for Development: Peer Influences and Adolescent Risk Behavior (pp. 69–71)

Time: 15–20 minutes

Objective: To examine the influence of peers on adolescent sexual activity and binge drinking.

As noted in the text, in power and breadth of influence, no context equals the family. However, when children enter school, peers become increasingly influential. But are peers more influential than family when basic values are at stake? To find out, Jaccard, Blanton, and Dodge (2005) recruited 1,700 friendship dyads in grades 7 through 11. The study lasted one year and focused on the extent to which close friends encourage sexual activity and binge drinking in each other. The researchers collected the following information:

(1) *Nominations and peer linking.* Each participant was asked to list five same-sex friends. To determine how close the participant was to each friend, the researchers asked a series of such questions, such as "Did you go to [name]'s house during the past week?" "Did you talk to [name] on the phone during the past week?" Questions were scored a 0 for a no and 1 for yes. The higher scores represented the participant's closest friends. The friend with the highest score became the participant's target friend.

(2) *Adolescent satisfaction with maternal relationship.* Participants were asked to respond on a 5-point agree/disagree scale to the following question: "Overall, I am satisfied with my relationship with my mother."

(3) *Adolescent perceptions of parental control.* To determine how controlling participants perceived their parents to be, the researchers asked, "Do your parents let you make your own decisions about (1) the time you come home on weekend nights, (2) the people you hang out with, (3) what you wear, (4) how much TV you watch, (5) which TV programs you watch, (6) what time you go to bed on weeknights, and (7) what you eat?" Questions were scored 1 for a no and 0 for a yes, with higher scores indicating greater parental control.

(4) *Physical development.* Participants reported on their physical maturity by responding to several statements about pubertal development—for example, extent of body hair (boys) and degree of breast development (girls).

(5) *Adolescent perceptions of mothers' attitudes about sex.* Participants were asked to rate their perceptions of their mother's attitudes toward sex and contraception, using the following questions: "How would your mother feel about your having sex at this time in your life?" "How would your mother feel about your using birth control at this time in your life?" Answers were scored on a scale of 1 to 5 from strongly approve to strongly disapprove.

(6) *Academic achievement.* To measure academic achievement, the researchers obtained self-reported grades during the previous grading period.

(7) *Involvement in romantic relationships.* Participants were asked to provide the first and last initials of individuals with whom they had a romantic relationship during the past 18 months.

(8) *Behavioral outcomes.* Participants were asked if they had yet engaged in sexual intercourse and, if so, how recently. To determine if participants had engaged in binge drinking, they were asked, "Over the past 12 months, on how many days did you drink five or more drinks in a row?"

(9) *Peer similarity on the surrounding dimension.* If both the participant and the target friend reported engaging in sexual activity or binge drinking, they were classified as similar on that dimension.

Results indicated that although friend behavior did have some impact on participants' sexual activity and binge drinking, the effects were small. According to Jaccard and colleagues (2005), unlike clothing preferences and extracurricular activities, sexual activity and binge drinking often represent fundamental value systems. Previous research indicates that adolescents are less vulnerable to peer pressure when personal values are at stake. At the same time, the small number of participants who engaged in binge drinking were very similar to their target friend in behavioral outcomes (how often they engaged in binge drinking) and in reports of low maternal warmth. This is consistent with other research in which peer influences are greater when parental bonds are strained.

Using information in this study and their own experiences, ask students to discuss factors that contribute to adolescent risk taking. Some students may even be willing to discuss their own experiences with peer pressure.

Jaccard, J., Blanton, H., & Dodge, T. (2005). Peer influences on risk behavior: An analysis of the effects of a close friend. *Developmental Psychology, 41,* 135–147.

LECTURE ENHANCEMENT 2.3
Why Do Affluent Youths Have Problems? (p. 73)

Time: 10–15 minutes

Objective: To highlight factors that contribute to problems in affluent youths.

As discussed in the text, despite the advantages that children of affluent parents enjoy (education, material wealth), they may be at risk for adjustment problems, such as substance abuse, anxiety, and depression. The text also notes that excessive achievement pressures and isolation from adults often contribute to these difficulties.

According to Luthar and Latendresse (2005), the following factors may also explain why many affluent youths display serious problems:

- *Problems may be hidden.* Unless the problems are conspicuous, affluent parents may be unwilling to delve into their own or their children's problems. It is also possible that these parents are less likely to seek help for internalizing problems, such as depression, than externalizing problems, such as aggression or disobedience.

- *Social concerns may discourage getting help.* Some affluent parents may be hesitant to seek help for less visible problems because of embarrassment or privacy concerns. Moreover, some parents may feel that, since they are financially well off, they should be able to handle their own problems.

- *Affluent families may be overscheduled.* Affluent youths often have hectic and stressful schedules and their parents are frequently involved in demanding, high-stress careers. As a result, affluent parents may have less time to devote to their children and may miss warning signs that something is wrong.

- *Mental-health providers may not raise concerns.* School psychologists and counselors may be hesitant to express concerns to affluent parents, perhaps fearing resistance or even threats of lawsuits. Moreover, clinicians may minimize problems and dismiss affluent children as "not needing help."

Luthar, S. S., & Latendresse, S. J. (2005). Children of the affluent: Challenges to well-being. *Current Directions in Psychological Science, 14,* 49–53.

LECTURE EHANCEMENT 2.4
Is Kindergarten an Overlooked Social Policy? (pp. 79–80, 82)

Time: 10–15 minutes

Objective: To highlight social policy issues surrounding kindergarten programs in the United States and Canada.

Because children's access to kindergarten depends on U.S. state or Canadian province and school district rules and resources, kindergarten is an important policy issue (Vecchiotti, 2003). The variability in kindergarten programs contributes to inequalities in children's early educational experiences. In the United States and Canada, kindergarten classes are either full-day, part-day, or alternate-day, and not all states and provinces mandate kindergarten attendance.

According to Vecchiotti (2003), to reduce inequalities in children's earliest educational experiences, the following policy issues surrounding kindergarten must be addressed:

(1) *Should the kindergarten year be required for all children?* By mandating kindergarten attendance, educators and policymakers can establish a uniform set of standards for what children need to know by the time they enter first grade.

(2) *Should there be a uniform entrance age?* Cut-off ages for kindergarten entry differ across states and provinces. In some classrooms, children range in age from 4 to 6 years, which makes it highly challenging for teachers to implement a developmentally appropriate curriculum, especially when teachers have large classes. A uniform entrance age would reduce inequalities in early education.

(3) *Curriculum instructional methods: What is appropriate?* Because there are no federal standards for appropriate kindergarten and instructional materials, children's academic experiences often vary considerably from one program to the next. General consensus about what children should learn in kindergarten can help better prepare children for school entry and reduce inequalities in early education.

(4) *Screening and assessment: What are appropriate practices?* Early screening and assessment can be difficult tasks. Young children learn and acquire skills at different rates, and educators too often rely on assessment results without considering developmental history, background, and early experiences. State and school district policies should adopt assessment practices that utilize multiple sources of information, including observations of teachers and parental reports.

(5) *Is there a persistent shortage of qualified kindergarten teachers?* Nearly all kindergarten teachers have completed college and a supervised teaching experience, but many have not specialized in teaching kindergarten. To reduce class size in the early elementary grades, U.S. schools often hire teachers with emergency or temporary certification or certification in areas other than early education. Previous research has documented a relationship between teacher quality and academic achievement. Specifically, achievement test scores tend to be higher in schools with highly qualified teachers. To reduce the number of insufficiently qualified teachers in kindergarten programs, state and federal governments should develop more stringent standards for teacher qualifications.

In small groups, have students discuss whether kindergarten attendance and kindergarten program quality should be elevated to a federal policy issue. Should kindergarten entry age and kindergarten curricular standards be nationally specified? Should kindergarten attendance be mandatory? Why or why not?

Vecchiotti, S. (2003). Kindergarten: An overlooked educational policy priority. *Social Policy Report: Society for Research in Child Development, 17,* 3–19.

LEARNING ACTIVITIES

LEARNING ACTIVITY 2.1
Observing Similarities and Differences in Phenotypes Among Family Members (pp. 51–54)

Have students jot down the most obvious similarities in physical characteristics and behavior for several children and parents whom they know well (for example, height, weight, eye and hair color, personality, interests, hobbies). Did they find that one child shows combined features of both parents, another resembles just one parent, on another is unlike either parent?

Next, ask students to trace a visible genetic trait (phenotype), such as hair or eye color, through as many of their family members as possible. When the genetic family tree is complete, try to determine genotypes. Note that you must begin with the most recent generation and work back. Also note that inferences must be made because homozygosity and heterozygosity cannot be determined for some dominant traits. For example, it may not be known whether someone is homozygous for dark hair or heterozygous—that is, a genetic makeup consisting of a dominant dark-hair and a recessive light-hair gene. Have students explain how differences among family members in the first activity may have occurred. Integrate the terms *phenotype, genotype, meiosis,* and *crossing over* into the discussion.

LEARNING ACTIVITY 2.2
Demonstrating Environmental Influence by Comparing Identical Twins (p. 55)

As discussed in the text, identical, or monozygotic, twins have the same genetic makeup—that is, they are genetically identical clones. Phenotypic variation of identical twins is perhaps the best evidence of the extent to which environmental influences can modify genetic expression. To demonstrate, invite a pair of identical twins (who are friends or relatives of a class member) to join your class for observation and interviews. Before the visit, have students generate a list of questions that they would like to ask each twin. These questions should be based on attributes or abilities that are thought to have a strong genetic component. For example, students may want to ask each twin questions about IQ, personality, interests, and talents. Students should also note any physical differences between the twins (for example, height, weight, handedness). After the visit, engage students in a discussion about similarities and differences among the twins, including how the environment may have contributed to differences.

LEARNING ACTIVITY 2.3
Matching: Patterns of Genetic Inheritance (pp. 56–60)

To help students better understand patterns of genetic inheritance, present the following activity as a quiz or in-class assignment.

Directions: Match each of the following terms with its definition.

Terms:

1. Allele
2. Homozygous
3. Heterozygous
4. Dominant-recessive inheritance
5. Carriers
6. Incomplete dominance
7. X-linked inheritance
8. Genetic imprinting
9. Mutation
10. Polygenic inheritance

Definitions:

A. Traits in which many genes influence the characteristics in question.
B. Alleles are imprinted, or chemically marked, in such a way that one member of the pair is activated, regardless of its makeup.
C. Refers to each form of a gene.
D. When heterozygous individuals with just one recessive allele can pass that trait to their children.
E. A pattern of inheritance in which both alleles are expressed, resulting in a combined trait, or one that is intermediate between the two.
F. If the alleles from both parents are alike, the child will display the inherited trait.
G. In many heterozygous pairings, only one allele affects the child's characteristics. It is called dominant; the second allele, which has no effect, is called recessive.
H. A sudden change in a segment of DNA.
I. If the alleles differ, the relationships between the alleles determine the trait that will appear.
J. When a harmful allele is carried on the X chromosome.

Answers:
1. C
2. F
3. I
4. G
5. D
6. E
7. J
8. B
9. H
10. A

LEARNING ACTIVITY 2.4
More on The Human Genome Project (pp. 64–66)

The Human Genome Project has identified thousands of genes, including those involved in hundreds of diseases. To extend the text discussion of the Human Genome Project, have students visit the website *http://www.ornl.gov/sci/ techresources/Human_Genome/home.shtml*, which provides current research, progress in DNA sequence mapping, and ethical, legal, and social concerns. Have students read one or two current research studies and summarize the findings. What are the benefits of the Human Genome Project? What are some ethical and legal concerns? How do students feel about genetic research?

LEARNING ACTIVITY 2.5
True or False: The Pros and Cons of Reproductive Technology (p. 65)

As an in-class assignment or quiz, present the following activity to students:

Directions: Read each of the following statements and determine if it is *True* (T) or *False* (F).

_____ 1. One-fourth of all couples who try to conceive discover that they are sterile.
_____ 2. Donor insemination is 30 to 40 percent successful.
_____ 3. About one percent of all children in developed countries are conceived through in vitro fertilization.
_____ 4. In vitro fertilization can only be used to overcome female fertility problems.
_____ 5. A "sex sorter" method of in vitro fertilization helps ensure that couples who carry X-linked diseases have a daughter.
_____ 6. In the United States and Canada, donors are always screened for genetic and sexually transmitted diseases.
_____ 7. Because surrogacy favors the wealthy as contractors for infants and the less economically advantaged as surrogates, it may promote the exploitation of financially needy women.
_____ 8. Most recipients of in vitro fertilization are in their fifties and sixties.
_____ 9. In the past decade, scientists have successfully cloned human infants.
_____ 10. At present, nothing is known about the psychological consequences of being a product of reproductive technologies.

Answers:

1. F
2. F
3. T
4. F
5. T
6. F
7. T
8. F
9. F
10. T

LEARNING ACTIVITY 2.6
Conducting a Survey of Attitudes Toward Government Intervention into Family Life (pp. 69–71)

Have students interview two or three family members, friends, or acquaintances and ask the following questions:

(1) Who should be responsible for raising young children?
(2) Should the government provide money and resources to low-income families with young children? If so, should the money come from tax dollars?

When students return to class with their responses, instruct them to classify each answer on the basis of whether parents are viewed as solely responsible for children's upbringing or whether society should play an important role. Compile the findings and discuss them in relation to evidence that government support for children and families has been more difficult to realize in the United States and Canada than in other industrialized nations. How do students feel about their findings? Do they agree with the findings? Why or why not?

LEARNING ACTIVITY 2.7
Researching Social Indicators of Children's Well-Being in the United States and Canada (pp. 77–82)

Although the United States and Canada are two of the wealthiest nations in the world, they do not rank among the top countries on any measure of children's health and well-being. Direct students to a website sponsored by the Children's Defense Fund: *http://www.childrensdefense.org/*. By clicking on *State Data*, students can find out their state's raking on several leading social indicators of children's well-being. If students are not from the United States, they can choose a state to research. Next, direct students to a website sponsored by Canada's National Child Benefit: *http://www.nationalchildbenefit.ca*. By clicking on *National Child Benefit Progress Report*, students can find out how their province or territory ranks on various social indicators. If students are not from Canada, they can choose a territory or province to research.

Using information from the websites, have students answer the following questions: How do public policies for children in the United States compare to those in Canada? How are cultural values, special interests, and economic conditions reflected in these policies? Do students think that these policies reflect current research in the field of child development? How large is the gap between what we know and its application to public policy?

LEARNING ACTIVITY 2.8
Exploring Epigenesis (pp. 87–88)

Have students review the definition and example of epigenesis on page 88 of the text. Next, ask them to form small groups and create two scenarios—one that would likely enhance gene expression and one that would likely dampen gene expression. For example, providing an economically at-risk preschooler with intensive early intervention promotes cognitive and social / emotional growth, which translates into better academic performance and peer relations on entering school, thereby transforming gene expression. In contrast, not providing the same preschooler with early intervention and denying him or her appropriate environmental stimulation can dampen gene expression so severely that later intervention has little impact. As this example illustrates, environment–gene exchanges can contribute to vastly different outcomes in the same child.

ASK YOURSELF . . .

REVIEW: Explain the genetic origins of PKU and Down syndrome. Cite evidence indicating that both heredity and environment contribute to the development of children with these disorders. (pp. 56–57, 60–61)

PKU: Phenylketonuria, or PKU, is one of the most frequently occurring recessive disorders. Infants born with two recessive alleles lack an enzyme that converts one of the basic amino acids that make up proteins (phenylalanine) into a byproduct essential for body functioning (tyrosine). Without this enzyme, phenylalanine quickly builds to toxic levels that damage the central nervous system. By 1 year, infants with PKU are permanently mentally retarded. But despite its potentially damaging effects, PKU provides an illustration of the fact that inheriting unfavorable genes does not always lead to an untreatable condition. Newborns diagnosed with PKU and placed on a diet low in phenylalanine usually attain an average level of intelligence and have a normal lifespan, although they still show mild cognitive deficits.

DOWN SYNDROME: Down syndrome usually results from a failure of the twenty-first pair of chromosomes to separate during meiosis. As a result, the new individual inherits three of these chromosomes rather than the normal two. In other, less frequent forms, an extra broken piece of twenty-first chromosome is attached to part of another chromosome (called *translocation* pattern). Or an error occurs during the early stages of mitosis, causing some but not all body cells to have the defective chromosomal makeup (called a *mosaic* pattern). Because less genetic material is involved in the mosaic type, symptoms of the disorder are less extreme.

Although Down syndrome leads to mental retardation and other cognitive, motor, and physical problems, environment plays a role in the development of affected children. Children with Down syndrome do best when their parents take extra steps to encourage them to become interested in their surroundings. They also benefit from infant and preschool intervention programs, although emotional, social, and motor skills improve more than intellectual performance.

In sum, though both PKU and Down syndrome are due to heredity, environmental factors affect how well these children fare.

REVIEW: Using your knowledge of X-linked inheritance, explain why males are more vulnerable to miscarriage, infant death, genetic disorders, and other problems. (pp. 57, 59)

When a harmful allele is carried on the X chromosome, X-linked inheritance applies. Males are more likely to be affected because their sex chromosomes do not match. In females, any recessive allele on one X chromosome has a good chance of being suppressed by a dominant allele on the other X. But the Y chromosome is only about one-third as long and therefore lacks many corresponding alleles to override those on the X.

Besides X-linked disorders, many sex differences reveal the male to be at a disadvantage. Rates of miscarriage, infant and childhood deaths, birth defects, learning disabilities, behavior disorders, and mental retardation are greater for boys. It is possible that these sex differences can be traced to the genetic code. The female, with two X chromosomes, benefits from a greater variety of genes.

APPLY: Gilbert's genetic makeup is homozygous for dark hair. Jan's is homozygous for blond hair. What color is Gilbert's hair? How about Jan's? What proportion of their children are likely to be dark-haired? Explain. (p. 56)

Because homozygous individuals inherit similar genes from both parents, they will always display the inherited trait. As a result, Gilbert will have dark hair, while Jan will have blond hair. Because Gilbert can pass on only the dominant dark-hair gene, all of Gilbert and Jan's children will have dark hair. Their children, however, have a 50 percent chance of being heterozygous—carriers of the gene for blond hair, which they can pass on to their own children.

CONNECT: Referring to ecological systems theory (see Chapter 1, pages 25–27), explain why parents of children with genetic disorders often experience increased stress. What factors, within and beyond the family, can help these parents support their children's development? (pp. 60–61)

Ecological systems theory views the child as developing within a complex system of relationships affected by multiple levels of the surrounding environment. Caring for a disabled child can be expensive, exhausting, and stressful for parents. For example, infants with Down syndrome are more difficult to care for than normal infants. Their facial deformities often lead to breathing and feeding difficulties. Also, these infants smile less readily, show poorer eye-to-eye contact, and explore objects less persistently than other children. When parents take extra steps to encourage them to engage with their surroundings, Down syndrome children develop more favorably. From the viewpoint of ecological systems theory, factors in the mesosystem—for example, the availability of specialized infant and preschool intervention programs—can help these parents support their children's development, both by providing experiences that promote the child's physical and cognitive development and by relieving the parent of the sole burden of caring for the child.

REVIEW: Why is genetic counseling called a *communication process*? Who should seek it? (p. 63)

Genetic counseling is called a communication process because it is designed to help couples assess their chances of giving birth to a baby with a hereditary disorder and then choose the best course of action in view of risks and family goals. If a family history of mental retardation, physical defects, or inherited diseases exists, the genetic counselor interviews the couple and prepares a *pedigree*—a picture of the family tree identifying affected relatives. Blood tests or genetic analyses may also be used to reveal whether the parent is a carrier of the harmful gene. Once all the relevant information has been gathered, the genetic counselor explains the results and helps prospective parents consider appropriate options and explore the possible consequences of each.

Individuals likely to seek counseling are those who have had difficulties bearing children, such as repeated miscarriages, or who know that genetic problems exist in their families. Women who delay childbearing past age 35 are also candidates for genetic counseling.

APPLY: Imagine that you must counsel a couple considering in vitro fertilization using the wife's ova and sperm from an anonymous man to overcome the husband's infertility. What medical and ethical risks would you raise? (p. 64)

The couple should be told that in vitro fertilization poses greater risks than natural conception to infant survival and healthy development. More than 50 percent of in vitro procedures result in multiple births, usually twins but also triplets and higher-order multiples, making the rate of low birth weight 2.6 times as high for in vitro babies as in the general population. The risk of major birth defects is also double. Further, the couple should be told that the success rate of in vitro fertilization declines steadily with age, from about 40 percent in women younger than age 35 to only 7 percent in those age 43 and older. They should be informed that because few legal guidelines govern the procedure, donors are not always screened for genetic or sexually transmitted diseases. Finally, they should be made aware of the serious ethical concerns surrounding the in vitro "sex sorter" method, which may encourage parental sex selection.

CONNECT: How does research on adoption reveal resilience? Which of the factors related to resilience (see Chapter 1, page 10) is central in positive outcomes for adoptees? (pp. 66–68)

Research shows that adopted children and adolescents have more learning and emotional difficulties than other children, a difference that increases with the child's age at time of adoption. But despite the risks, most adopted children are resilient, and those with problems usually make rapid progress. For example, in a study of internationally adopted children in the Netherlands, sensitive maternal care and secure attachment in infancy predicted cognitive and social competence at age 7. Further, international adoptees fare better in development than birth siblings or institutionalized agemates who are not adopted. Although later-adopted children are more likely than agemates to have persistent cognitive, emotional, and social problems, when these children feel loved and supported in their new families, they develop feelings of trust and affection for their adoptive parents.

REFLECT: Imagine that you are a woman who is a carrier of fragile X syndrome but who wants to have children. Would you become pregnant, adopt, use a surrogate mother, or give up your desire for parenthood? If you became pregnant, would you opt for prenatal diagnosis? Explain your decisions. (pp. 63–68)

This is an open-ended question with no right or wrong answer.

REVIEW: Links between family and community are essential for children's well-being. Provide examples and research findings from our discussion that support this idea. (pp. 73, 75–76)

Connections between family and community are vital for children's well-being. For example, research shows that in poverty-stricken urban areas, community life is usually disrupted: Families move often, parks and playgrounds are in disarray, and community centers providing organized leisure time activities do not exist. In such neighborhoods, family violence, child abuse and neglect, children's problem behavior, and youth antisocial activity are especially high. Informal social controls, such as adults who keep an eye on children's activities, are likely to disintegrate. In contrast, when family ties to the community are strong—as indicated by regular church, synagogue, or mosque attendance, frequent contact with friends and relatives, and organized youth activities—family stress and youth adjustment are reduced.

APPLY: Check your local newspaper or one or two national news magazines or news websites to see how often articles on the condition of children and families appear. Why is it important for researchers to communicate with the general public about children's needs? (pp. 79–82)

When widespread social problems arise, such as poverty, homelessness, hunger, and disease, nations attempt to solve them by developing public policies—laws and government programs designed to improve current conditions. Besides depending on strong advocacy, public policies that enhance child development flow from policy-relevant research that documents needs and evaluates programs to spark improvements. By collaborating with community and government agencies, researchers help create a sense of immediacy about the conditions of children and families that is necessary to spur a society into action. Public understanding of the conditions of children and families can mobilize voters to demand action from their lawmakers.

CONNECT: How does poverty affect the functioning of the family system, placing all aspects of development at risk? (pp. 73, 75)

Poverty is accompanied by constant stresses that gradually weaken the family system. Poor families have many daily hassles—bills to pay, the car breaking down, loss of welfare and unemployment payments, something stolen from the house, to name just a few. When daily crises arise, parents become depressed, irritable, and distracted, hostile interactions increase, and children's development suffers. Negative outcomes are especially severe in single-parent families and those that must live in poor housing and dangerous neighborhoods—conditions that make everyday existence even more difficult while reducing social supports that assist in coping with economic hardship.

Another factor placing children and families at risk is homelessness, which has become more common in the past 25 years. Most homeless families consist of women with children under age 5. Besides health problems (which affect most homeless people), homeless children suffer from developmental delays and serious emotional stress. An estimated 25 to 30 percent of those who are old enough do not go to school, and those who do enroll achieve less well than other poverty-stricken children because of poor attendance and severe health and emotional difficulties.

REFLECT: Do you agree with the widespread North American sentiment that government should not become involved in family life? Explain. (p. 80)

This is an open-ended question with no right or wrong answer.

REVIEW: What is epigenesis, and how does it differ from range of reaction and genetic–environmental correlation? Provide an example of epigenesis. (pp. 85, 86, 88)

Epigenesis means development resulting from ongoing, bidirectional exchanges between heredity and all levels of the environment. For instance, providing a baby with a healthy diet promotes brain growth, leading to new connections between nerve cells, which transform gene expression. This opens the door to new gene–environment exchanges—for example, advanced exploration of objects and interaction with caregivers, which further enhance brain growth and gene expression. These ongoing bidirectional influences foster cognitive and social development.

Although range of reaction and genetic-environmental correlation also emphasize the relationship between heredity and environment, both grant priority to heredity. In range of reaction, heredity limits each person's response to varying environments. In genetic–environmental correlation, our genes influence the environments to which we are exposed. Some theorists regard genetic–environmental correlation as entirely driven by genetics. They believe that children's genetic makeup causes them to receive, evoke, or seek experiences that actualize their inborn tendencies. In contrast, the concept of epigenesis does not give priority to either heredity or environment. Rather, it reminds us that development is best understood as a series of complex exchanges between nature and nurture.

APPLY: Bianca's parents are accomplished musicians. At age 4, Bianca began taking piano lessons. By age 10, she was accompanying the school choir. At age 14, she asked if she could attend a special music high school. Explain how genetic–environmental correlation promoted Bianca's talent. (pp. 86–87)

According to the concept of genetic–environmental correlation, our genes influence the environments to which we are exposed. Early in her development, Bianca probably experienced *passive* genetic–environmental correlation. Her parents, as dedicated musicians, exposed her to musical activities, such as attending concerts and listening to classical music. They also provided her first piano lessons and opportunities for other music-related experiences. Because Bianca was receptive to this abundance of musical stimulation, she undoubtedly evoked positive responses from her parents, who continued to promote her musical development—an example of *evocative* genetic–environmental correlation. As Bianca grew older, she became more active in choosing her own environments. She decided to accompany the school choir and later to attend a special music high school. Bianca's inherited musical talent led her to engage in *niche-picking,* in which she selected activities that complemented her heredity. In these ways, heredity and environment worked together to advance Bianca's musical endeavors.

CONNECT: Explain how each of the following concepts supports the conclusion that genetic influences on human characteristics are not constant but change over time: somatic mutation (page 60), niche-picking (page 86), and epigenesis (page 88).

Somatic mutation occurs when normal body cells mutate, as happens in many cancers and other diseases. Unlike germline mutation, which occurs only in the cells that give rise to gametes, somatic mutation can take place at any time of life, perhaps reflecting a genetic susceptibility in some individuals that causes body cells to mutate easily in the presence of triggering events. Somatic mutation increases with age, providing evidence that individuals do not have a single, permanent genotype but that each cell's genetic makeup can change over time.

Niche-picking is the tendency to actively choose environments that complement our heredity. It is not seen in infants and young children, who cannot choose their own environments. But older children and adolescents, who are increasingly in charge of their environments, can express their preferences through niche-picking, explaining why pairs of identical twins reared apart in childhood and later reunited often share preferences in food, hobbies, and vocations.

Epigenesis refers to development resulting from ongoing bidirectional exchanges between heredity and all levels of the environment. For example, giving a baby a healthy diet promotes brain growth, leading to new connections between brain cells, which transform gene expression, opening the door to new gene–environment exchanges, which in turn further enhance brain growth and gene expression.

REFLECT: What aspects of your own development—for example, interests, hobbies, college major, or vocational choice—are probably due to niche-picking? Explain. (pp. 86–87)

This is an open-ended question with no right or wrong answer.

SUGGESTED STUDENT READINGS

Lindsey, D. (2007). *Future of children: Wealth, poverty, and opportunity in America.* New York: Oxford University Press. Presents an overview of child and family poverty in the United States, including the role of public policy in child development.

Mundy, L. (2007). *Everything conceivable: How assisted reproduction is changing men, women, and the world.* New York: Knopf. A compelling look at reproductive technologies, this book examines current research, as well as controversies, surrounding assisted reproduction. The author also includes personal narratives, myths, and the social consequences of assisted reproduction.

Peters, R. D., Leadbeater, B., & McMahon, R. J. (Eds.). (2005). *Resilience in children, families, and communities: Linking context to practice and policy.* New York: Kluwer Academic. An ecological approach to the study of resilience, this book examines empirical research, intervention efforts, and the role of public policy in fostering resilience in children and families.

Segal, N. L. (2005). *Indivisible by two: Lives of extraordinary twins.* Cambridge, MA: Harvard University Press. A fascinating look into the lives of multiples, this book follows 12 sets of twins, triplets, and quadruplets. The author not only describes the unique experiences of multiples, but she also highlights the many challenges faced by the parents, friends, and spouses of these extraordinary individuals.

TRANSPARENCIES

T-12   **A Karyotype, or Photograph, of Human Chromosomes** Figure 2.1 (p. 52)

T-13   **DNA's Ladderlike Structure** Figure 2.2 (p. 53)

T-14   **The Cell Division Process of Meiosis Leading to Gamete Formation** Figure 2.3 (p. 54)

T-15   **Dominant-Recessive Mode of Inheritance, as Illustrated by PKU** Figure 2.4 (p. 59)

T-16   **X-Linked Inheritance** Figure 2.5 (p. 59)

T-17   **Amniocentesis and Chorionic Villus Sampling** Figure 2.6 (p. 65)

T-19   **Concordance Rates for Schizophrenia, Severe Depression, and Antisocial Behavior and Criminality** Figure 2.8 (p. 84)

T-20   **Intellectual Ranges of Reaction (RR) for Three Children in Environments That Vary from Extremely Unstimulating to Highly Enriched** Figure 2.9 (p. 85)

T-21   **Similarity in Mothers' Interactions for Pairs of Siblings Differing in Genetic Relatedness** Figure 2.10 (p. 87)

T-23   **The Epigenetic Framework** Figure 2.11 (p. 88)

MEDIA MATERIALS

INFANTS, CHILDREN, AND ADOLESCENTS IN ACTION

Biological and Environmental Foundations, Prenatal Development, and Birth

This section of the Observation Program contains three parent interviews: (1) Steve and Tonya faced a tragedy rare among couples in their twenties. Their first child, Kristin, was born with Down syndrome. Tonya and Steve describe their reaction to Kristin's birth and how they adjusted to caring for a baby with serious disabilities and health problems. (2) Gina and Lindrey experience the birth of their second child. After having her first baby by cesarean section, Gina is determined to have a vaginal delivery with her second. Her husband, Lindrey, describes the experience as Gina progresses through labor and delivery. (3) Adena and Cooper discuss the transition to parenthood. Their son, Charlie, is 4 months old. The section concludes with newborn reflexes, which help ensure that the baby will survive and receive care and attention from adults.

DVDs AND VIDEOTAPES

Body Doubles: The Twin Experience (1997, Films Media Group, 51 min.). This HBO documentary, which explores the extent to which personality is influenced by heredity, includes interviews with numerous twins. It also reviews the history of twin research, with a focus on the research conducted at the University of Minnesota Twin Research Center. The film received positive reviews from *Booklist* and *MC Journal: The Journal of Academic Media Librarianship.*

Hand-Me-Down Genes: Family Patterns (1997, Films Media Group, 28 min.). This is Part 1 of the two-part series Hand-Me-Down Genes: An Introduction to Genetics, which is designed to give students a basic understanding of genetics. This first part examines how our genetic makeup is determined by the formation of sex cells, from the first gamete to chromosome pairs, and explores the role of genes in family resemblances, both within and across generations. Finally, it looks at some genetic deviations, such as cystic fibrosis, Huntington's disease, achondroplasia, Klinefelter syndrome, and Turner syndrome.

Hand-Me-Down Genes: How Genes Work (1997, Films Media Group, 25 min.). Part 2 of Hand-Me-Down Genes: An Introduction to Genetics begins by considering the nucleus of a single cell and goes on to explain all the other components the cell needs to function: chromosomes, genes, DNA, and ribosomes. The program uses animated graphics to explore the basic genetic building blocks and how they work.

Heredity and Environment (2005, Magna Systems, 29 min.). This program provides a biological explanation of conception and offers information on a variety of related topics, including the job of genes, dominant and recessive traits chromosomal abnormalities such as Down syndrome, genetic disorders such as dwarfism, who is a candidate for genetic counseling, how nature and nurture interact, and how the environment shapes the brain.

Infertility and IVF (1995, Films Media Group, 20 min.). This program explores the topic of infertility, with a focus on in vitro fertilization. It tells the story of one young couple who successfully underwent IVF and had a child. An infertility specialist explains the process and describes what infertile couples can do to increase the odds of pregnancy. Other topics include the importance of counseling and criteria for choosing an infertility clinic.

Making Better Babies: Genetics & Reproduction (2003, Films for the Humanities and Sciences, 58 min.). This program is part of the three-part PBS series Our Genes/Our Choices. Moderated by *Dateline NBC* correspondent John Hockenberry, it explores the ethical dilemmas posed by prenatal testing and the implications of other genetic options, such as cloning, that may be available in the near future. Panelists include Francis Collins, director of the National Human Genome Research Institute; ABC correspondent Meredith Vieira; Princeton University professor Lee Silver; Paul Miller, Commissioner of the U.S. Equal Employment Opportunity Commission; Wellesley College professor Adrienne Asch; Faye Wattleton, president of the Center for Gender Equality; and Zev Rosenwaks, director of the Center for Reproductive Medicine and Infertility at the New York Weill Cornell Medical Center.

TEST BANK

MULTIPLE CHOICE

1) Eye color is an example of a(n)
    A) gamete.
    B) phenotype.
    C) autosome.
    D) genotype.
Answer: B
Page Ref: 51
Skill: Applied
Objective: 2.1

2) Chromosomes
    A) are located inside the cell nucleus.
    B) are inherited from the mother only.
    C) come in 46 matching pairs.
    D) always come in XY pairs.
Answer: A
Page Ref: 52
Skill: Factual
Objective: 2.2

3) Chromosomes are made up of a chemical substance called
    A) genes.
    B) DNA.
    C) genotype.
    D) gametes.
Answer: B
Page Ref: 52
Skill: Factual
Objective: 2.2

4) Although the bases in the DNA ladder must always pair up in the same way across the ladder rungs,
    A) they can occur in any order along its sides.
    B) the pairs change during mitosis.
    C) A does occasionally pair with C, causing Down syndrome.
    D) C never pairs with G.
Answer: A
Page Ref: 52
Skill: Factual
Objective: 2.2

5) Genes are made up of
    A) thousands of chromosomes.
    B) parts of many different cells.
    C) segments of DNA of varying lengths.
    D) either X cells or Y cells.
Answer: C
Page Ref: 52
Skill: Factual
Objective: 2.2

6) The DNA of humans and chimpanzees is between _____ percent identical.
   A) 20 and 25
   B) 50 and 55
   C) 75 and 80
   D) 98 and 99
Answer: D
Page Ref: 52
Skill: Factual
Objective: 2.2

7) People around the world are about _____ percent genetically identical.
   A) 35
   B) 50
   C) 75
   D) 99
Answer: D
Page Ref: 52
Skill: Factual
Objective: 2.2

8) During mitosis,
   A) each new body cell is 50% genetically identical to the original cell.
   B) the number of chromosomes in each body cell is halved.
   C) each new body cell contains 23 chromosomes.
   D) each new body cell contains the same number of chromosomes as the original cell.
Answer: D
Page Ref: 52
Skill: Factual
Objective: 2.3

9) Research demonstrates that
   A) environmental factors can modify genetic expression.
   B) approximately 50% of chimpanzee and human DNA is identical.
   C) simpler and more complex species roughly produce the same number of proteins.
   D) one's phenotype is entirely determined by one's phenotype.
Answer: A
Page Ref: 53
Skill: Factual
Objective: 2.3

10) _____ contain _____ chromosomes.
   A) Gametes; 23 pairs of
   B) Gametes; 23
   C) Body cells; 23
   D) Body cells; 46 pairs of
Answer: B
Page Ref: 53
Skill: Factual
Objective: 2.4

11) Crossing over results in
    A) higher rates of fraternal twins for women with X-linked disorders.
    B) incredible variability among offspring.
    C) reduced adaptive abilities in some species.
    D) the production of more female zygotes than male zygotes.
Answer: B
Page Ref: 53
Skill: Factual
Objective: 2.4

12) The genetic variability produced by _____ increase(s) the chances that at least some members of a species will cope with ever changing environments and survive.
    A) meiosis
    B) genetic imprinting
    C) modifier genes
    D) dominant-recessive inheritance
Answer: A
Page Ref: 53
Skill: Factual
Objective: 2.3

13) _____ sperm and _____ ova/ovum are produced each time meiosis is completed.
    A) One; four
    B) Four; one
    C) Millions of; two
    D) Millions of; several hundred
Answer: B
Page Ref: 53
Skill: Factual
Objective: 2.4

14) A person whose 23rd pair of chromosomes is XY
    A) has Down syndrome.
    B) is male.
    C) cannot be a fraternal twin.
    D) has PKU.
Answer: B
Page Ref: 54
Skill: Factual
Objective: 2.5

15) The sex of a baby is determined by
    A) genes on the X chromosome.
    B) whether the ovum is carrying an X chromosome or a Y chromosome.
    C) whether an X-bearing or a Y-bearing sperm fertilizes the ovum.
    D) whether the sperm fertilizes an X-bearing or Y-bearing egg.
Answer: C
Page Ref: 55
Skill: Factual
Objective: 2.5

16) A zygote that separates into two clusters of cells instead of just one produces
    A) Klinefelter syndrome.
    B) identical twins.
    C) fraternal twins.
    D) triple X syndrome.
Answer: B
Page Ref: 55
Skill: Factual
Objective: 2.6

17) The most common type of multiple birth occurs when
    A) two different ova are fertilized by two different sperm.
    B) a zygote separates into two clusters of cells.
    C) one ovum is fertilized by two different sperm cells.
    D) two ova are released from the ovaries and fertilized.
Answer: D
Page Ref: 55
Skill: Factual
Objective: 2.6

18) _____ is one of the major causes of the dramatic rise in fraternal twins and other multiple births in industrialized nations over the past few decades.
    A) Poor maternal diet
    B) Use of fertility drugs
    C) Younger maternal age
    D) Radiation exposure
Answer: B
Page Ref: 55
Skill: Factual
Objective: 2.6

19) In dominant-recessive inheritance relationships,
    A) both alleles influence the person's characteristics.
    B) individuals with two dominant alleles are carriers of the trait.
    C) the influence of only one allele is apparent under heterozygous conditions.
    D) harmful alleles are carried on the X chromosome.
Answer: C
Page Ref: 56
Skill: Applied
Objective: 2.7

20) Carriers are
    A) homozygous individuals with one dominant allele.
    B) heterozygous individuals with two dominant alleles.
    C) heterozygous individuals with one recessive allele.
    D) homozygous individuals with one recessive allele.
Answer: C
Page Ref: 56
Skill: Factual
Objective: 2.7

21) Children born with two recessive PKU alleles
    A) appear normal until age 35 or later, when the nervous system begins to degenerate.
    B) show symptoms of the disorder only if their mother, but not their father, has PKU.
    C) usually attain an average level of intelligence and a normal lifespan if placed on a diet low in phenylalanine beginning in infancy.
    D) are protected from the disease except when they experience oxygen deprivation.
Answer: C
Page Ref: 56
Skill: Conceptual
Objective: 2.7

22) The case of PKU demonstrates that
    A) serious inherited disorders are more often due to dominant than to recessive genes.
    B) most inherited disabilities and disorders are untreatable.
    C) even if we know the genetic makeup of the parents, it is difficult to predict the likelihood that children in a family will display a disorder.
    D) changes in the environment can alter the severity of an inherited disorder.
Answer: D
Page Ref: 56
Skill: Conceptual
Objective: 2.7

23) Children with PKU vary in the extent to which they respond to treatment. This is due to
    A) a codominance pattern of inheritance.
    B) genetic imprinting.
    C) a mutation.
    D) the action of modifier genes.
Answer: D
Page Ref: 56
Skill: Conceptual
Objective: 2.7

24) Serious diseases are only rarely due to dominant alleles. This is because
    A) individuals who inherit these disorders seldom live long enough to reproduce.
    B) prenatal testing has virtually eliminated these disorders.
    C) the harmful allele is eliminated from the family's heredity after several generations.
    D) children who inherit the dominant allele do not always develop the disorder.
Answer: A
Page Ref: 57
Skill: Conceptual
Objective: 2.7

25) _____ has endured in some families because its symptoms usually do not appear until after the person already has passed the dominant gene to his or her children.
    A) Huntington disease
    B) Tay-Sachs disease
    C) Cystic fibrosis
    D) Hemophilia
Answer: A
Page Ref: 57
Skill: Factual
Objective: 2.7

26) In incomplete dominance,
    A) most children show a full form of the disease.
    B) only the dominant allele affects the individual's characteristics.
    C) children have a 50% chance of inheriting the disorder if one parent has the trait.
    D) both the dominant and the recessive alleles are expressed in the phenotype.
Answer: D
Page Ref: 57
Skill: Factual
Objective: 2.7

27) _____ is a case of incomplete dominance.
    A) Sickle cell trait
    B) PKU
    C) Down syndrome
    D) Color blindness
Answer: A
Page Ref: 57
Skill: Factual
Objective: 2.7

28) The sickle cell allele
    A) is more common among European Americans than African Americans.
    B) is decreasing in regions of the world where the risk of malaria is high.
    C) puts individuals at increased risk of malaria.
    D) is more common among black Africans than African Americans.
Answer: D
Page Ref: 57
Skill: Conceptual
Objective: 2.7

29) Males are more likely than females to be negatively affected by X-linked disorders because
    A) the Y chromosome lacks many corresponding alleles to override those carried on the X chromosome.
    B) the Y chromosome is much longer than the X chromosome.
    C) their sex chromosomes match.
    D) males are more likely to inherit recessive alleles.
Answer: A
Page Ref: 57, 59
Skill: Conceptual
Objective: 2.7

30) Studies of sex differences show that
    A) worldwide, more girls than boys are born.
    B) the proportion of male births has declined in many industrialized countries in recent decades.
    C) approximately equal numbers of males and females are conceived.
    D) rates of miscarriage, infant death, and birth defects are higher among females than males.
Answer: B
Page Ref: 59
Skill: Conceptual
Objective: 2.7

31) People with asthma or hay fever tend to have mothers, not fathers, with the illness. The pattern of inheritance is best explained by
   A) X-linked inheritance.
   B) genetic mutation.
   C) polygenic inheritance.
   D) genetic imprinting.

Answer: D
Page Ref: 59
Skill: Conceptual
Objective: 2.7

32) Fragile X syndrome
   A) affects females more severely than males.
   B) is linked to over half of the cases of autism.
   C) is expressed only when it is passed from father to child.
   D) is the most common inherited cause of mental retardation.

Answer: D
Page Ref: 60
Skill: Factual
Objective: 2.7

33) Repeated exposure to high doses of radiation can cause
   A) incomplete dominance.
   B) mutation.
   C) crossing over.
   D) genetic imprinting.

Answer: B
Page Ref: 60
Skill: Conceptual
Objective: 2.7

34) Mutations
   A) can be triggered by smoking or exposure to environmental pollutants.
   B) cannot be passed onto an individual's offspring.
   C) happen only during the prenatal period.
   D) cannot be caused by psychological stress.

Answer: A
Page Ref: 60
Skill: Conceptual
Objective: 2.7

35) Down syndrome is most commonly caused by
   A) increased age of the father.
   B) failure of the 21st pair of chromosomes to separate during meiosis.
   C) mutation of the genetic material on the 23rd chromosomal pair.
   D) trauma at birth.

Answer: B
Page Ref: 60
Skill: Factual
Objective: 2.8

36) Research on Down syndrome demonstrates that
   A) carriers are protected from the disease unless they experienced oxygen deprivation.
   B) its symptoms usually do not appear in affected individuals until age 35 or later.
   C) a diet low in phenylalanine can prevent nervous system damage in affected individuals.
   D) more than half of affected individuals who live past age 40 show symptoms of Alzheimer's disease.
Answer: D
Page Ref: 61
Skill: Conceptual
Objective: 2.8

37) _____ is associated with a dramatic increase in the risk of having a child with Down syndrome.
   A) Prenatal tobacco exposure
   B) Maternal infectious disease
   C) Maternal age over 35
   D) Prenatal malnutrition
Answer: C
Page Ref: 61
Skill: Conceptual
Objective: 2.8

38) Research on sex chromosome disorders shows that
   A) verbal difficulties are common among females who are missing an X chromosome.
   B) most children with these disorders suffer from mental retardation.
   C) males, but not females, with an extra X chromosome are sterile.
   D) males with XYY syndrome are more aggressive and antisocial than are XY males.
Answer: C
Page Ref: 62
Skill: Conceptual
Objective: 2.8

39) _____ syndrome in females and _____ syndrome in males are due to an extra X chromosome.
   A) Triple X; Klinefelter
   B) Klinefelter; triple X
   C) Turner; triple X
   D) Triple X; Turner
Answer: A
Page Ref: 62
Skill: Conceptual
Objective: 2.8

40) Mr. and Mrs. Kohn would like to have a baby but are concerned about the prevalence of Tay-Sachs in their family. Which of the following would you recommend to help them determine their chances of having a baby with this disorder?
   A) amniocentesis
   B) genetic engineering
   C) chorionic villus sampling
   D) genetic counseling
Answer: D
Page Ref: 63
Skill: Applied
Objective: 2.9

41) Amniocentesis
    A) is the most widely used prenatal diagnostic technique.
    B) can be performed as early as 9 weeks after conception.
    C) entails a slightly greater risk of miscarriage than does chorionic villus sampling.
    D) can be used to detect an elevated level of alpha-fetoprotein.
    Answer: A
    Page Ref: 64
    Skill: Factual
    Objective: 2.9

42) To date, gene therapy has had some success in relieving symptoms in patients with
    A) Alzheimer's disease.
    B) Down syndrome.
    C) hemophilia.
    D) Klinefelter syndrome.
    Answer: C
    Page Ref: 64
    Skill: Conceptual
    Objective: 2.9

43) Most adopted children
    A) search for their birth parents during early adolescence.
    B) appear well-adjusted as adults.
    C) do better if they are adopted after infancy.
    D) have trouble developing feelings of trust and affection toward their adoptive parents.
    Answer: B
    Page Ref: 68
    Skill: Conceptual
    Objective: 2.9

44) Many studies show that when parents' requests are firm but made with warmth and affection, children tend to cooperate. And when children willingly comply, their parents tend to be warm and gentle in the future. This is an example of a(n) _____ influence between parents and their children.
    A) macrosystem
    B) indirect
    C) microsystem
    D) direct
    Answer: D
    Page Ref: 70
    Skill: Conceptual
    Objective: 2.10

45) When marital relationships are warm and loving, mothers and fathers tend to praise and stimulate their children more. This is an example of a(n) _____ influence between parents and their children.
    A) direct
    B) microsystem
    C) indirect
    D) macrosystem
    Answer: C
    Page Ref: 70
    Skill: Applied
    Objective: 2.10

46) Parents relate to their children differently as their children age. These changes in ways of interacting take place in Bronfenbrenner's
    A) mesosystem.
    B) exosystem.
    C) macrosystem.
    D) chronosystem.
Answer: D
Page Ref: 71
Skill: Conceptual
Objective: 2.10

47) When asked about the personal qualities they desire for their children, lower-SES parents emphasize _____ and higher-SES parents emphasize _____.
    A) psychological traits; external characteristics
    B) psychological traits; intellectual abilities
    C) intellectual abilities; psychological traits
    D) external characteristics; psychological traits
Answer: D
Page Ref: 71
Skill: Conceptual
Objective: 2.11

48) Research on SES demonstrates that
    A) higher-SES parents are more likely than lower-SES parents to use coercive discipline.
    B) children of affluent parents are more likely than low-SES youths to engage in alcohol and drug use.
    C) lower-SES parents tend to feel a lack of authority at home, just as they do at their jobs.
    D) lower-SES parents talk to their infants more than higher-SES parents do.
Answer: B
Page Ref: 73
Skill: Conceptual
Objective: 2.11

49) For _____ children, eating dinner with parents is associated with a reduction in adjustment difficulties.
    A) both affluent and low-SES
    B) only low-SES
    C) only high-SES
    D) only middle-SES
Answer: A
Page Ref: 73
Skill: Conceptual
Objective: 2.11

50) In both the United States and Canada, the poverty rate for single mothers with preschool children is nearly _____ percent.
    A) 50
    B) 35
    C) 25
    D) 10
Answer: A
Page Ref: 74
Skill: Factual
Objective: 2.11

51) Of all Western nations, _____ has the highest percentage of extremely poor children.
    A) the United States
    B) Brazil
    C) Canada
    D) Germany
Answer: A
Page Ref: 74
Skill: Factual
Objective: 2.11

52) One of the central causes of the recent rise in homeless families with children is the
    A) lack of blue-collar jobs.
    B) increase in alcoholism and illicit drug abuse.
    C) release of large numbers of mentally ill people from hospitals.
    D) rising cost of health care.
Answer: C
Page Ref: 75
Skill: Conceptual
Objective: 2.11

53) Community resources have _____ impact on the development of young people in economically
    disadvantaged neighborhoods compared to those in well-to-do neighborhoods.
    A) a greater
    B) a lesser
    C) no measurable
    D) a similar
Answer: A
Page Ref: 75
Skill: Conceptual
Objective: 2.12

54) Research on low-income neighborhoods indicates that
    A) the stressors that come from living in a poverty-stricken neighborhood usually do not undermine parental
       warmth and involvement.
    B) involvement in religious youth groups and special-interest clubs does not boost school achievement.
    C) informal social controls usually remain strong despite high population turnover.
    D) involvement in after-school programs is associated with improved school performance.
Answer: D
Page Ref: 76
Skill: Conceptual
Objective: 2.12

55) Parents who are involved in school activities and who attend parent-teacher conferences tend to
    A) display an authoritarian parenting style.
    B) have children who show superior academic achievement.
    C) hold an educational philosophy that regards children as passive learners.
    D) have children who are highly competitive.
Answer: B
Page Ref: 76–77
Skill: Conceptual
Objective: 2.12

56) One reason that Americans have been slow to accept the idea of publicly supported child care is because
   A) most grandparents regularly participate in child rearing.
   B) few mothers of young children work outside the home.
   C) it is widely believed that daily separation from the mother is harmful to young children.
   D) of the widely held belief that the care of young children and the paying for that care are the duty of parents, and only parents.

Answer: D
Page Ref: 77
Skill: Conceptual
Objective: 2.13

57) The African-American tradition of extended-family households
   A) rarely occurs in the modern era.
   B) has enabled its members to survive, despite a long history of prejudice and economic deprivation.
   C) is limited to only this subculture in North America.
   D) rarely includes grandparents.

Answer: B
Page Ref: 77
Skill: Conceptual
Objective: 2.13

58) Among African Americans, living with an extended family tends to produce
   A) children with insecure attachments.
   B) more families on welfare and fewer people with jobs.
   C) higher levels of divorce and teenage pregnancy.
   D) improved childrearing.

Answer: D
Page Ref: 77
Skill: Conceptual
Objective: 2.13

59) Cross-cultural research demonstrates that
   A) collectivism tends to increase as cultures become increasingly complex.
   B) people stress group over individual goals in collectivist cultures.
   C) the United States, Canada, and most of Western Europe stress collectivist values.
   D) collectivist cultures emphasize personal exploration and discovery.

Answer: B
Page Ref: 77
Skill: Conceptual
Objective: 2.13

60) Public policy research indicates that
   A) the United States and Canada rank above most Western countries on nearly all measures of children's well-being.
   B) poverty is not a major problem affecting children's well-being in the United States and Canada.
   C) American and Canadian public policies that protect children have lagged behind policies in other developed nations.
   D) both the United States and Canada have excellent systems in place for guaranteeing high-quality child care to all citizens.

Answer: C
Page Ref: 79
Skill: Conceptual
Objective: 2.13

61) _____ is the only industrialized nation in the world that does not have a universal, publicly funded health care system.
   A) Sweden
   B) China
   C) Canada
   D) The United States
   Answer: D
   Page Ref: 79
   Skill: Factual
   Objective: 2.13

62) Public policies safeguarding children and youth have been _____ in the United States than in other Western industrialized nations.
   A) enacted earlier
   B) more protective
   C) more successful
   D) slower to emerge
   Answer: D
   Page Ref: 79
   Skill: Factual
   Objective: 2.13

63) Of the following, which country has the highest infant death rate?
   A) Spain
   B) Singapore
   C) Hong Kong
   D) the United States
   Answer: D
   Page Ref: 79
   Skill: Factual
   Objective: 2.13

64) In both the United States and Canada,
   A) much child care is substandard in quality.
   B) national standards for child care have been slow to develop.
   C) child care is funded by the federal government.
   D) less than 5 percent of adolescents leave high school without a diploma.
   Answer: A
   Page Ref: 79
   Skill: Conceptual
   Objective: 2.13

65) Which of the following is TRUE regarding the Convention on the Rights of the Child?
   A) The United States did not participate in drawing up the Convention.
   B) Canada's Parliament has not yet ratified the Convention.
   C) The United States is one of only two countries in the world whose legislature has not yet ratified the Convention.
   D) Opponents argue that the Convention's provisions would shift the burden of childrearing to the family.
   Answer: C
   Page Ref: 80
   Skill: Conceptual
   Objective: 2.13

66) Behavioral geneticists
    A) have identified the DNA sequences for most psychological disorders.
    B) argue that the effects of the environment account for only a small amount of variation in human behavior.
    C) generally are still limited to investigating the impact of genes on complex characteristics indirectly.
    D) have identified the genes that underlie most polygenetic traits, such as intelligence and personality.
Answer: C
Page Ref: 83
Skill: Factual
Objective: 2.14

67) In kinship studies, the average correlation in IQ is
    A) higher for identical twins than for fraternal twins.
    B) positive for identical twins but negative for fraternal twins.
    C) about the same for both identical and fraternal twins.
    D) higher for fraternal twins than for identical twins.
Answer: A
Page Ref: 83
Skill: Conceptual
Objective: 2.14

68) A heritability estimate of .6 for intelligence in twin samples suggests that
    A) there is a 60 percent chance that the intelligence level of twins will be the same.
    B) differences in environmental influences explain 60 percent of the variation in intelligence.
    C) there is a 60 percent chance that the intelligence level of twins will be significantly different.
    D) differences in genetic makeup explain 60 percent of the variation in intelligence.
Answer: D
Page Ref: 83
Skill: Applied
Objective: 2.14

69) Suppose the heritability estimate for shoe size is .4. This would indicate that differences in _____ could explain _____ percent of the variation in shoe size.
    A) the environment; 40
    B) heredity; 60
    C) heredity; 40
    D) the environment; 4
Answer: C
Page Ref: 83
Skill: Applied
Objective: 2.14

70) A _____ refers to the percentage of instances in which both twins have a trait when it is present in one twin.
    A) kinship rate
    B) heritability estimate
    C) factor analysis
    D) concordance rate
Answer: D
Page Ref: 84
Skill: Factual
Objective: 2.14

71) A concordance rate of 100 percent for schizophrenia would mean that
    A) neither twin has schizophrenia.
    B) if one twin has schizophrenia, the other one always has it.
    C) heredity does not play a major role in schizophrenia.
    D) if one twin has schizophrenia, the other twin never has it.
Answer: B
Page Ref: 84
Skill: Applied
Objective: 2.14

72) Critics of heritability estimates and concordance rates argue that
    A) the rearing environments of most twin pairs are too diverse to determine the role of heredity.
    B) these measures overestimate the role of the environment.
    C) the effects of heredity and environment are inseparable.
    D) heredity plays only a small role in the development of complex traits.
Answer: C
Page Ref: 84–85
Skill: Conceptual
Objective: 2.14

73) Heritability estimates
    A) cannot be computed on twins reared apart, only on twins reared together.
    B) are likely to exaggerate the role of heredity.
    C) decrease as parental education and income increase.
    D) tend to overestimate the importance of the environment.
Answer: B
Page Ref: 84
Skill: Applied
Objective: 2.14

74) It is inappropriate to use heritability estimates to explain ethnic differences in intelligence because
    A) heritabilities computed on mostly white twin samples do not provide information relevant to test score differences between ethnic groups.
    B) ethnic group differences in intelligence are largely due to heredity.
    C) twinning occurs with a higher frequency among some racial and ethnic groups.
    D) the environments of twin pairs are more diverse than those of the general population.
Answer: A
Page Ref: 85
Skill: Conceptual
Objective: 2.14

75) The most serious criticism of heritability estimates is that they
    A) cannot be computed for complex traits, such as personality and intelligence.
    B) underestimate the impact of heredity on development.
    C) are difficult to compute for racial and ethnic minorities.
    D) provide no precise information on how complex traits develop.
Answer: D
Page Ref: 85
Skill: Conceptual
Objective: 2.14

76) The concept of range of reaction explains that children who are exposed to the same environmental conditions
   A) may respond to them differently because of their genetic makeup.
   B) will tend to show the same pattern of responses over time.
   C) tend to overcome their inheritance, so their genes have no effect.
   D) will become genetically more similar than other children are.
   Answer: A
   Page Ref: 85
   Skill: Conceptual
   Objective: 2.14

77) Consider the following hypothetical situations: In an extremely understimulating environment, both Sally and Sam would have low intelligence. However, in a highly simulating environment, Sally's performance would greatly exceed that of Sam's. This example illustrates the concept of
   A) niche-picking.
   B) range of reaction.
   C) concordance.
   D) kinship.
   Answer: B
   Page Ref: 85
   Skill: Applied
   Objective: 2.14

78) _____ seem(s) to be highly canalized.
   A) Intelligence
   B) Cognition
   C) Infant perceptual and motor development
   D) Personality
   Answer: C
   Page Ref: 86
   Skill: Applied
   Objective: 2.14

79) According to the concept of genetic-environmental correlation,
   A) the environment to which we are exposed determines which genes are expressed in our phenotypes.
   B) our genes influence the environments to which we are exposed.
   C) we tend to seek out environments that contain others with a similar genetic makeup.
   D) our genes affect how we respond to the environment.
   Answer: B
   Page Ref: 86
   Skill: Conceptual
   Objective: 2.14

80) Elena and Aidan are both professional dancers. Their daughter Katrin is enrolled in ballet, tap, and jazz dance classes. This is an example of
   A) a passive correlation.
   B) an evocative correlation.
   C) an active correlation.
   D) niche-picking.
   Answer: A
   Page Ref: 86
   Skill: Applied
   Objective: 2.14

81) A friendly, cheerful child will probably receive more social stimulation than a shy, reserved child. This is an example of a(n) _____ genetic-environmental correlation.
   A) evocative
   B) passive
   C) dynamic
   D) active
   Answer: A
   Page Ref: 86
   Skill: Applied
   Objective: 2.14

82) Ada, who is well-coordinated and muscular, joins both the swim and gymnastics teams in college. This is an example of a(n) _____ genetic-environmental correlation.
   A) evocative
   B) passive
   C) dynamic
   D) active
   Answer: D
   Page Ref: 86
   Skill: Applied
   Objective: 2.14

83) *Niche-picking* is an example of a(n) _____ genetic-environmental correlation.
   A) evocative
   B) passive
   C) dynamic
   D) active
   Answer: D
   Page Ref: 86
   Skill: Conceptual
   Objective: 2.14

84) Of the following age groups, which does the most niche-picking?
   A) infants
   B) toddlers
   C) preschoolers
   D) adolescents
   Answer: D
   Page Ref: 86
   Skill: Conceptual
   Objective: 2.14

85) The concept of niche-picking explains why
   A) identical twins reared apart during childhood are likely to have similar hobbies, food preferences, and vocations.
   B) identical twins become somewhat less alike with age.
   C) fraternal twins reared together are more alike than identical twins reared apart.
   D) identical twins reared apart tend to differ more than those who are reared together.
   Answer: A
   Page Ref: 87
   Skill: Conceptual
   Objective: 2.14

86) In one study, boys with a gene known to predispose humans to aggression were no more aggressive than boys without this gene, *unless* they had a history of severe child abuse. This finding supports the concept of
   A) niche-picking.
   B) epigenesis.
   C) canalization.
   D) range of reaction.
   Answer: B
   Page Ref: 88
   Skill: Conceptual
   Objective: 2.14

87) According to the concept of epigenesis,
   A) development results from bidirectional interactions between heredity and the environment.
   B) children's genetic makeup causes them to receive, evoke, and seek experiences that actualize their inborn tendencies.
   C) heredity restricts the development of some behaviors to just one or a few outcomes.
   D) children's genetic inheritance constrains responsiveness to varying environments.
   Answer: A
   Page Ref: 88
   Skill: Factual
   Objective: 2.14

88) Halina provides her baby with plenty of age-appropriate stimulation, which increases brain growth and transforms gene expression. This series of interactions leads to new gene-environment exchanges, which further enhance brain growth and gene expression. This is an example of
   A) niche-picking.
   B) canalization.
   C) epigenesis.
   D) range of reaction.
   Answer: C
   Page Ref: 88
   Skill: Applied
   Objective: 2.14

89) Of the following, which is true concerning donor insemination and in vitro fertilization?
   A) Children conceived through these methods will be genetically related to at least one parent.
   B) The overall rate of successful pregnancies using these methods is near 100 percent.
   C) Sperm donors are always screened for genetic disorders and sexually transmitted infections.
   D) More than 50 percent of in vitro procedures result in multiple births.
   Answer: D
   Page Ref: 66–67
   Skill: Conceptual
   Objective: (SI Box) The Pros and Cons of Reproductive Technologies

90) An ethical concern with in vitro fertilization is that
   A) in vitro children and adolescents are less well-adjusted than their counterparts who were naturally conceived.
   B) babies conceived using this procedure are particularly susceptible to the effects of teratogens.
   C) in vitro infants are less securely attached to their parents than children who were naturally conceived.
   D) the in vitro "sex sorter" method will lead to parental sex selection.
   Answer: D
   Page Ref: 66–67
   Skill: Conceptual
   Objective: (SI Box) The Pros and Cons of Reproductive Technologies

91) Of the following, which is supported by research on in vitro fertilization?
   A) Most in vitro babies are singletons.
   B) The risk of major birth defects is doubled in in vitro babies.
   C) Caregiving is warmer for naturally conceived children than for in vitro babies.
   D) The rate of low birth weight is higher in the general population than among in vitro babies.

Answer: B
Page Ref: 66–67
Skill: Conceptual
Objective: (SI Box) The Pros and Cons of Reproductive Technologies

92) _____ is banned in Australia, Canada, and many European nations.
   A) In vitro fertilization
   B) Donor insemination
   C) Abortion
   D) Surrogate motherhood

Answer: D
Page Ref: 66–67
Skill: Factual
Objective: (SI Box) The Pros and Cons of Reproductive Technologies

93) Of the following, which is true?
   A) Scientists have not yet successfully cloned mammals, only invertebrate organisms.
   B) At donor banks, customers cannot select ova or sperm on the basis of physical characteristics.
   C) Doctors have used donor ova in combination with in vitro fertilization to help postmenopausal women become pregnant.
   D) All nations allow some degree of genetic alteration of human gametes.

Answer: C
Page Ref: 66–67
Skill: Conceptual
Objective: (SI Box) The Pros and Cons of Reproductive Technologies

94) In developing nations,
   A) girls are more likely than boys to go to school.
   B) language and literacy skills do little to open up new life opportunities.
   C) the percentage of children who go to school has been decreasing in recent decades.
   D) years of schooling strongly predicts women's preventive health behavior.

Answer: D
Page Ref: 72
Skill: Conceptual
Objective: (CI Box) Worldwide Education of Girls: Transforming Current and Future Generations

95) According to a recent United Nations report, _____ is the most effective means of combating the most profound, global threats to human development.
   A) the education of boys
   B) family planning services
   C) the education of girls
   D) medical care

Answer: C
Page Ref: 72
Skill: Conceptual
Objective: (CI Box) Worldwide Education of Girls: Transforming Current and Future Generations

96) African-American adolescent mothers living in extended families are _____ than mothers living on their own.
   A) more likely to be on welfare
   B) less likely to get a job
   C) more likely to complete high school
   D) less likely to be effective parents
   Answer: C
   Page Ref: 78
   Skill: Conceptual
   Objective: (CI Box) The African-American Extended Family

97) Research on the welfare-to-work program demonstrates that
   A) the lives of children are improved when their parents move off of welfare, even if their incomes remained below the poverty threshold.
   B) low-SES families fare best when they receive welfare assistance for at least 5 years, regardless of their employment status.
   C) the incomes of the poorest single-mother families have been increasing in recent years.
   D) a combination of welfare and work is often more beneficial to children than a total reliance on work.
   Answer: D
   Page Ref: 81
   Skill: Conceptual
   Objective: (SI Box) Welfare Reform, Poverty, and Child Development

98) In Canada, but not in the United States,
   A) welfare benefits increase if family size increases.
   B) teenage single mothers can be denied welfare benefits.
   C) most of its citizens are guaranteed a modest minimum income.
   D) single parents receive extra income during the child's first three years.
   Answer: A
   Page Ref: 81
   Skill: Conceptual
   Objective: (SI Box) Welfare Reform, Poverty, and Child Development

ESSAY

99) How does phenylketonuria (PKU) provide an excellent illustration of the fact that inheriting unfavorable genes does not always lead to an untreatable condition?
   Answer: Infants born with PKU lack an enzyme that converts one of the basic amino acids that make up proteins (phenylalanine) into a byproduct essential for body functioning. Without this enzyme, phenylalanine quickly builds to toxic levels that damage the central nervous system. U.S. states and Canadian provinces require that each newborn be given a blood test for PKU. If the disease is found, the baby is placed on a diet low in phenylalanine. Although children who receive this treatment show mild cognitive deficits, they usually attain an average level of intelligence and have a normal lifespan as long as dietary treatment begins early and continues.
   Page Ref: 56–59

100) Is there a sex difference in the likelihood of inheriting recessive disorders carried on the autosomes or on the sex chromosomes? Explain.
   Answer: Males and females have an equal chance of inheriting recessive disorders, such as PKU or sickle cell anemia, carried on the autosomes. But when a harmful gene is carried on the X chromosome, X-linked inheritance applies. Males are more likely than females to be affected because their sex chromosomes do not match. In females, any recessive gene on one X has a good chance of being suppressed by a dominant gene on the other X. But the Y chromosome is only about one-third as long and therefore lacks many corresponding genes to override those on the X.
   Page Ref: 54–55, 56–59

101) What are direct and indirect influences in terms of family functioning? Provide an example of each.

Answer: Direct influences occur when the behavior of one family member helps sustain a form of interaction in the other that either promotes or undermines psychological well-being. For example, when warmth and affection accompany parents' requests, children tend to cooperate. When children willingly comply, their parents are likely to be warm and gentle in the future. In contrast, parents who discipline with hostility usually have children who refuse and rebel. Because children's misbehavior is stressful for parents, they may increase their use of punishment, leading to more unruliness by the children. In these examples, each of the children's reactions, in turn, prompts a new link in the interactive chain. Indirect influences occur when interactions between any two family members are affected by others who are present in the setting, known as third parties. For example, when the parents' marital relationship is warm and considerate, mothers and fathers praise and stimulate their children more, and nag and scold them less. In contrast, when a marriage is tense and hostile, parents are likely to express anger, criticize, and punish.

Page Ref: 69–71

102) How do the United States and Canada compare to other nations on indicators of child health and well-being?

Answer: The United States does not rank well on any key measures of children's health and well-being, such as the childhood poverty rate, the infant death rate, and the teenage pregnancy rate. The United States is the only industrialized country in the world that does not have a universal, publicly funded health care system. About 11 percent of U.S. children have no health insurance.

Canada, which devotes considerably more of its resources to education and health, fares somewhat better. For example, all Canadian citizens have access to government-funded health care.

Both the United States and Canada have been slow to move toward national standards and funding for child care. In both countries, much child care is substandard in quality. In families affected by divorce, weak enforcement of child support payments heightens poverty in mother-headed households. And about 11 percent of U.S. and Canadian adolescents leave high school without a diploma. Those who do not finish their education are at risk for lifelong poverty.

Page Ref: 77–82

103) Discuss the limitations of heritability estimates and concordance rates.

Answer: One criticism of heritability estimates and concordance rates is that they refer only to the particular population studied and its unique range of genetic and environmental influences. If the range of either heredity or environment changes, then heritability and concordance values will change as well. Second, the accuracy of these statistics depends on the extent to which the twin pairs on which they are computed reflect genetic and environmental variation in the population. Because the environments of most twin pairs do not represent the broad range of environments found in the general population, it is often difficult to generalize these heritability and concordance findings to the population as a whole. Third, heritability estimates can easily be misapplied. For example, high heritabilities have been used to suggest that ethnic differences in intelligence have a genetic basis. However, this line of reasoning is incorrect because heritabilities computed on mostly white twin samples do not tell us what is responsible for test score differences between ethnic groups. A final criticism is that these statistics give us no information about how these traits develop or how individuals might respond to environments designed to help them develop as far as possible.

Page Ref: 83–85

104) Describe the concepts of range of reaction and canalization. Explain how each of these concepts provides a way of understanding how heredity and the environment interact.

Answer: A range of reaction refers to each person's unique, genetically determined response to a range of environmental conditions. Reaction range highlights two important points about the relationship between heredity and the environment. First, it shows that because each of us has a unique genetic makeup, we respond differently to the same environment. Second, sometimes different genetic-environmental combinations can make two people look about the same. Canalization refers to the tendency of heredity to restrict the development of some characteristics to just one or, at most, a few outcomes. A behavior that is strongly canalized follows a genetically set growth plan, and only powerful environmental forces can change it. Over time, even very flexible behaviors can become fixed and canalized, depending on the environments to which the individuals were exposed. Recently, scientists have expanded the notion of canalization to include environmental influences.

Page Ref: 85–86

105) Describe the epigenetic framework, and provide an example of epigenesis.

Answer: According to the epigenetic framework, individual development is the result of ongoing, bidirectional exchanges between heredity and the environment. That is, genes affect the individual's behavior and experiences, and the individual's experiences also affect gene expression. Stimulation at all levels of the environment—both internal to the individual and external to the individual—trigger gene activity. For example, providing an infant with a healthy diet increases brain growth, which translates into new connections and faster message transfer between nerve cells and, in turn, transformed gene expression. This series of interactions opens the door to new gene-environment interactions. For example, advanced exploration of objects and interaction with caregivers further enhance brain growth and gene expression.

Page Ref: 88

STUDY QUESTIONS

1. _____ are directly observable characteristics that depend in part on the _____, the complex blend of genetic information that determines our species and also influences all of our unique characteristics. (p. 51)

Genetic Foundations

1. Rodlike structures in the nuclei of cells that store and transmit genetic information are called _____. (p. 52)

2. Humans have (23 / 46) pairs of chromosomes in each cell. (p. 52)

The Genetic Code

1. Chromosomes are made up of a chemical substance called _____. It looks like a twisted ladder and is composed of segments called _____. (p. 52)

2. The process through which DNA duplicates itself so that each new body cell contains the same number of chromosomes is called _____. (p. 52)

The Sex Cells

1. Sex cells, or _____, are formed through the process of (mitosis / meiosis). (p. 53)

2. True or False: Sex cells contain only half the number of chromosomes normally present in body cells. (p. 53)

3. When the sperm and ova unite at conception, the cell that results is called a _____. (p. 53)

4. During meiosis, the process of _____, in which chromosomes next to each other break at one or more points and exchange segments, creates new hereditary combinations unique to the individual. (p. 53)

5. Explain why the genetic variability produced by meiosis is important in an evolutionary sense. (p. 53)

_____

_____

Boy or Girl?

1. The twenty-two matching pairs of chromosomes are called _____. (p. 54)

2. The twenty-third pair of chromosomes, also called the sex chromosomes, determine the sex of the child. In females, this pair is called _____, whereas in males it is called _____. (p. 54)

Multiple Births

1. Match each of the following terms with the appropriate description. (p. 55)

   _____ This type of twinning may result from environmental influences like temperature changes, variations in oxygen levels, or late fertilization of the ovum.

   _____ This is the most common type of multiple birth.

   _____ Older maternal age and use of fertility drugs and in vitro fertilization are major causes of this type of twinning.

   _____ These twins are genetically no more alike than ordinary siblings.

   _____ These twins share the same genetic makeup.

   1. Fraternal, or dizygotic, twins
   2. Identical, or monozygotic, twins

2. True or False: During the early years of life, children of single births are often healthier and develop more rapidly than twins. (p. 55)

Patterns of Genetic Inheritance

1. Each of two forms of a gene located at the same place on the autosome is called a(n) _____. (p. 56)

2. If the alleles from both parents are alike, the child is _____ and will display the inherited trait. If the alleles inherited from the mother and father are different, then the child is _____, and the relationship between the alleles will determine the trait, or phenotype. (p. 56)

3. Describe *dominant–recessive inheritance*, and provide one example of this type of inheritance. (pp. 56–57)

    A. _____

    _____

    B. _____

    _____

4. One of the most common recessive disorders is _____, which affects the way the body breaks down proteins contained in many foods. (p. 56)

5. _____ *genes* enhance or dilute the effects of other genes. (p. 56)

6. True or False: Serious diseases typically result from dominant alleles. Briefly explain your response. (p. 57)

    _____

    _____

7. Describe *incomplete dominance*, and name one condition that results from this pattern of inheritance. (p. 57)

    A. _____

    _____

    B. _____

    _____

8. (Males / Females) are more likely to be affected by *X-linked inheritance.* Why is this the case? (p. 57)

    _____

    _____

9. Name one X-linked disorder. (pp. 57, 58)

    _____

10. True or False: In recent decades, the proportion of male births has declined in many industrialized countries. Explain your answer. (p. 59)

    _____

    _____

    _____

11. _____ occurs when alleles are chemically marked in such a way that one pair member is activated, regardless of its makeup. (p. 59)

12. List three conditions or diseases that are caused by *genetic imprinting.* (pp. 59–60)

    A. _____   B. _____

    C. _____

13. Explain how harmful genes are created. (p. 60)

_____

_____

14. Describe *polygenic inheritance*, and give an example of a trait that is determined by this pattern of inheritance. (p. 60)

A. _____

_____

B. _____

_____

Chromosomal Abnormalities

1. Most chromosomal defects are the result of mistakes during _____, when the ovum and sperm are formed. (p. 60)

2. _____, the most common chromosomal abnormality, often results from a failure of the twenty-first pair of chromosomes to separate during meiosis. For this reason, the disorder is sometimes called Trisomy 21. (p. 60)

3. List the physical and behavioral characteristics of Down syndrome. (p. 61)

Physical: _____

_____

Behavioral: _____

_____

4. True or False: The risk of Down syndrome rises with maternal age. (p. 61)

5. Disorders of the sex chromosomes result in (more / less) serious consequences than do disorders of the autosomes. (p. 61)

6. Identify whether the following myths about individuals with sex chromosome disorders are true or false. (pp. 61–62)

A. Males with XYY syndrome are more aggressive and antisocial than XY males.   True or False

B. Most children with sex chromosome disorders suffer from mental retardation.   True or False

C. Girls with Turner syndrome have trouble with spatial relationships, such as drawing pictures and noticing changes in facial expressions.   True or False

D. Children with sex chromosome disorders have intellectual problems that are usually very specific.   True or False

Reproductive Choices

Genetic Counseling

1. What is the purpose of genetic counseling, and who is most likely to seek this service? (p. 63)

_____

_____

_____

Biology and Environment: The Pros and Cons of Reproductive Technologies

1. Briefly describe the following reproductive technologies: (p. 66)

    Donor insemination: _____

    _____

    _____

    _____

    In vitro fertilization: _____

    _____

    _____

    _____

    Surrogate motherhood: _____

    _____

    _____

    _____

2. True or False: Children conceived through in vitro fertilization typically exhibit a variety of behavioral and adjustment problems and have insecure attachments to their parents. (p. 66)

3. Discuss some of the concerns surrounding the use of donor insemination and in vitro fertilization. (p. 66)

    _____

    _____

    _____

4. Describe some of the risks involved with surrogate motherhood. (p. 66)

    _____

    _____

    _____

5. Briefly describe several new reproductive technologies, and note ethical dilemmas associated with each. (pp. 66–67)

    A. _____

    _____

    B. _____

    _____

Prenatal Diagnosis and Fetal Medicine

1. _____ are medical procedures that permit detection of developmental problems before birth. (p. 63)

2. Cite six types of prenatal diagnostic methods. (p. 64)

   A. _____

   B. _____

   C. _____

   D. _____

   E. _____

   F. _____

3. True or False: The techniques used in fetal medicine rarely result in complications like premature labor or miscarriage. (p. 64)

4. Summarize the goals of the Human Genome Project, and explain why this program offers hope for correcting hereditary defects. (pp. 64–65)

   _____

   _____

   _____

5. Describe three steps that prospective parents can take before conception to increase their chances of having a healthy baby. (p. 68)

   A. _____

   B. _____

   C. _____

The Alternative of Adoption

1. Why has the availability of healthy babies declined in North America and Western Europe? (p. 65)

   _____

   _____

2. Adopted children and adolescents have (fewer / more) learning and emotional difficulties than other children. Cite two possible reasons for this trend. (pp. 65, 67)

   A. _____

   B. _____

3. Discuss research findings on international adoptees' development in comparison to birth siblings or agemates who stay behind. (pp. 67–68)

   _____

   _____

   _____

4. True or False: Most adoptees have serious, long-term adjustment problems that are evident well into adulthood. (p. 68)

Environmental Contexts for Development

The Family

1. Distinguish between direct and indirect familial influences. (pp. 69–70)

    Direct: _____

    _____

    Indirect: _____

    _____

2. Discuss some ways in which the family system must adapt over time. (pp. 70–71)

    _____

    _____

    _____

Socioeconomic Status and Family Functioning

1. List the three variables that determine a family's *socioeconomic status (SES)*. (p. 71)

    A. _____   B. _____

    C. _____

2. Compare child characteristics emphasized in lower-SES families with those emphasized in higher-SES families. (pp. 71–73)

    Lower-SES: _____

    _____

    Higher-SES: _____

    _____

3. Describe the influence of SES on parenting practices and parent-child interaction. (pp. 71–73)

    _____

    _____

    _____

4. Summarize the factors that explain SES differences in family interaction. (pp. 71–73)

    _____

    _____

    _____

5. True or False: Higher-SES children show more advances in cognitive development and tend to perform better in school than their lower-SES peers. (p. 73)

Social Issues: Education: Worldwide Education of Girls: Transforming Current and Future Generations

1. Cite two ways that educating girls benefits the welfare of families, societies, and future generations. (p. 72)

   A. _____

   _____

   B. _____

   _____

2. How does education influence family health? (p. 72)

   _____

   _____

   _____

3. True or False: The empowerment that education provides women is associated with more equitable husband-wife relationships and a reduction in harsh disciplining of children. (p. 72)

Affluence

1. Discuss two factors that contribute to poor adjustment in affluent youths. (p. 73)

   A. _____

   _____

   B. _____

   _____

2. What simple routine does research associate with a reduction in adjustment difficulties for both affluent and low-SES youths? (p. 73)

   _____

Poverty

1. What subgroups of the population are hardest hit by poverty? (p. 74)

   A. _____ B. _____

   C. _____ D. _____

2. The poverty rate is (higher / lower) among children than any other age group. (p. 74)

3. Describe how the constant stresses that accompany poverty gradually weaken the family system. (pp. 74–75)

   _____

   _____

   _____

4. Summarize the developmental risks that homeless children face. (p. 75)

   _____

   _____

   _____

Beyond the Family: Neighborhoods and Schools

1. Neighborhood resources have a greater impact on children growing up in (disadvantaged / well-to-do) areas. Why is this the case? (pp. 75–76)

    _____

    _____

2. Summarize features of the Better Beginnings, Better Futures Project of Ontario, Canada, and note major outcomes of the program. (p. 76)

    Features: _____

    _____

    _____

    Outcomes: _____

    _____

    _____

3. List four broad features of the school environment that impact students' developmental outcomes. (pp. 76–77)

    A. _____

    B. _____

    C. _____

    D. _____

4. Why are higher-SES parents more likely to have regular contact with teachers than lower-SES parents? (p. 77)

    _____

    _____

The Cultural Context

1. What are *subcultures*? (p. 77)

    _____

    _____

2. The African-American _____ *household*, in which one or more adult relatives live with the parent-child nuclear family unit, is a vital feature of black family life. (p. 77)

3. Distinguish the characteristics of collectivist versus individualistic societies. (pp. 77–78)

    Collectivist: _____

    _____

    Individualistic: _____

    _____

4. What are *public policies*? (p. 79)

    _____

5. True or False: Among developed nations, the United States and Canada have served as forerunners in the development of public policies to safeguard children. (p. 79)

6. List some of the areas in which American and Canadian public policies regarding children are deficient. (pp. 79–80)

_____

_____

_____

7. Cite three reasons why attempts to help children and youth in the United States and Canada have been difficult to realize. (p. 80)

A. _____

B. _____

C. _____

8. The _____ is a legal agreement that commits each cooperating country to work toward guaranteeing environments that foster children's development, protect them from harm, and enhance their community participation and self-determination. The United States (is / is not) one of the two countries in the world that has not yet ratified this agreement. (p. 80)

9. How are researchers helping to improve public policies that enhance child development? (p. 82)

_____

_____

Cultural Influences: The African-American Extended Family

1. Cite characteristics of the African-American extended family that help reduce the stress of poverty and single parenthood. (p. 78)

_____

_____

_____

2. How does the African-American extended family help transmit cultural values? (p. 78)

_____

_____

_____

Social Issues: Health: Welfare Reform, Poverty, and Child Development

1. Briefly summarize features of welfare-to-work programs. (p. 81)

_____

_____

_____

2. True or False: To date, the welfare-to-work programs have been successful in making all welfare recipients financially independent. (p. 81)

3. True or False: A welfare-work combination, in which individuals retain some welfare support while working, seems to have the greatest benefit for children and families. Explain your answer. (p. 81)

_____

_____

_____

4. Explain how welfare policies in other Western nations, such as France and Canada, attempt to protect children from the damaging effects of poverty. (p. 81)

France: _____

_____

_____

Canada: _____

_____

_____

Understanding the Relationship Between Heredity and Environment

1. _____ is a field devoted to uncovering the contributions of nature and nurture as they relate to individual differences in human traits and abilities. (p. 83)

The Question, "How Much?"

1. Name the two methods used by behavioral geneticists to infer the role of heredity in complex human characteristics. (p. 83)

   A. _____   B. _____

2. What are *heritability estimates*? (p. 83)

_____

_____

_____

3. Heritability estimates are obtained from _____ *studies*, which compare characteristics of family members. (p. 83)

4. True or False: Heritability estimates for intelligence and personality are approximately .50, indicating that genetic makeup can explain half of the variance in these traits. (p. 83)

5. What is a *concordance rate*? (p. 84)

_____

_____

6. What do concordance rates of 0 and of 100 mean? (p. 84)

   0: _____

   100: _____

7. When a concordance rate is much higher for (identical / fraternal) twins, then heredity is believed to play a major role. (p. 84)

8. Discuss three limitations of heritability estimates and concordance rates. (pp. 84–85)

   A. _____

   _____

   B. _____

   _____

   C. _____

   _____

The Question, "How?"

1. In *range of reaction,* heredity (limits / increases) responsiveness to varying environments. In *canalization,* heredity (restricts / expands) the development of certain behaviors. (pp. 85–86)

2. Range of reaction highlights two important points. List them. (pp. 85–86)

   A. _____

   _____

   B. _____

   _____

3. Describe the concept of *canalization.* (p. 86)

   _____

   _____

   _____

4. Which is more strongly canalized: infant perceptual and motor development or intelligence and personality? (p. 86)

5. According to the concept of _____, our genes influence the environments to which we are exposed. (p. 86)

6. Match the following types of genetic-environmental correlations with the appropriate descriptors. (p. 86)

   _____ Children increasingly seek out environments that fit their genetic tendencies (niche-picking).
   _____ A child's style of responding influences other's responses, which then strengthens the child's original style.
   _____ Parents provide an environment consistent with their own heredity.

   1. Passive correlation
   2. Evocative correlation
   3. Active correlation

7. The tendency to choose environments that complement our heredity is called _____. (p. 86)

8. _____ means development resulting from ongoing, bidirectional exchanges between heredity and all levels of the environment. Researchers call this view of the relationship between heredity and the environment the _____ framework. (p. 88)

9. Provide an example of *epigenesis.* (p. 88)

   _____

   _____

PUZZLE 2.1 TERM REVIEW

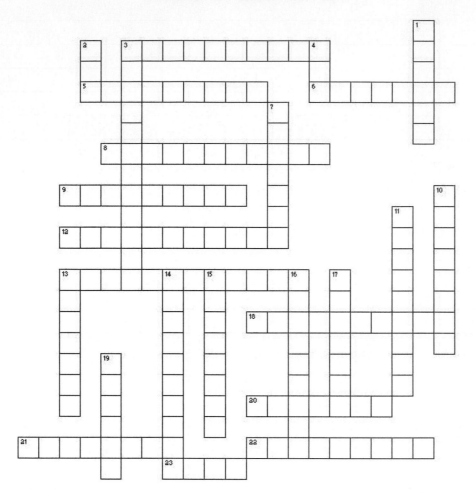

Across

3. Having two identical alleles at the same place on a pair of chromosomes
5. The 22 matching chromosomes pairs in each human cell
6. _____ inheritance: the recessive gene is carried on the X chromosome
8. _____ twins have the same genetic makeup
9. Fraternal, or _____, twins
12. Rodlike structures in the cell nucleus that store and transmit genetic information
13. An exchange of genes between chromosomes next to each other during meiosis (2 words)
18. _____ dominance: a pattern of inheritance in which both alleles are expressed in the phenotype
20. The process of cell division
21. A sudden but permanent change in a segment of DNA
22. Directly observable characteristics
23. A segment of a DNA molecule that contains hereditary instructions

Down

1. Each of two forms of a gene located at the same place in the autosomes
2. Long, double-stranded molecules that make up chromosomes (abbr.)
3. Having two different alleles at the same place on a pair of chromosomes
4. _____ chromosomes: The 23rd pair of chromosomes; XX in females, XY in males
7. The process of cell duplication
10. Genes that enhance or dilute the effects of other genes
11. _____ inheritance: Many genes determine a characteristic
13. A heterozygous individual who can pass a recessive trait to his or her children
14. Genetic _____: alleles are chemically marked in such a way that one pair member is activated, regardless of its makeup
15. The genetic makeup of an individual
16. Dominant-_____ inheritance: in heterozygous pairings, only one allele affects the child's traits
17. Human sperm and ova
19. Cell formed by the union of the sperm and the ovum at conception

PUZZLE 2.2 TERM REVIEW

Across

2. _____-environmental correlation: the notion that heredity influences the environments to which an individual is exposed
6. Genetic _____ is designed to help couples assess their chances of giving birth to a baby with a hereditary disorder.
7. Group of people with beliefs and customs that differ from those of the larger culture
11. A measure of a family's social position and economic well-being (abbr.)
14. In _____ societies, people think of themselves as separate entities and are largely concerned with their own personal needs
15. _____ policies: laws and government programs designed to improve the condition of children and families
16. _____ studies compare the characteristics of family members to obtain heritability estimates.
17. _____ diagnostic methods are medical procedures that permit detection of problems before birth.

Down

1. Development resulting from ongoing, bidirectional exchanges between heredity and environment
3. Range of _____: a person's genetically determined response to a range of environmental conditions
4. In _____-family households, parent and child live with one or more adult relatives
5. Tendency for individuals to actively choose environments that complement their heredity (2 words; hyph.)
8. In _____ societies, people define themselves as part of a group and stress group over individual goals
9. _____ rate: percentage of instances in which both members of a twin pair show a trait when it is present in one pair member
10. _____ genetics: field devoted to uncovering the contributions of nature and nurture to individual differences in human traits and abilities
12. _____ estimate: measure of the extent to which individual differences in complex traits in a specific population are due to genetic factors
13. Tendency of heredity to restrict the development of some characteristics to just one or a few outcomes

CROSSWORD PUZZLE SOLUTIONS

PUZZLE 2.1

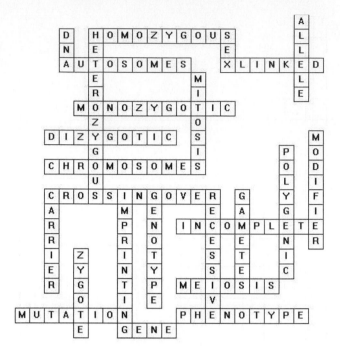

PUZZLE 2.2

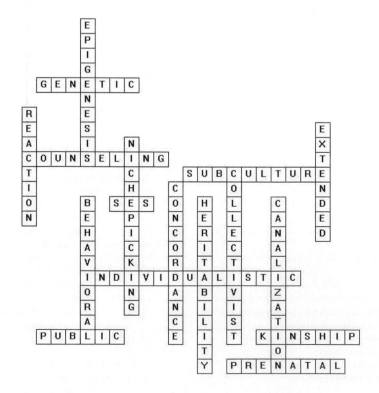

PRACTICE TEST #1

1. The paired bases of the DNA molecule (p. 52)
   a. take shapes that are determined by phenotypes.
   b. can occur in any order along its sides.
   c. join in various ways across the ladder rungs.
   d. determine how nurture will affect the individual.

2. Of the following factors, which is responsible for the complexity of human beings? (p. 53)
   a. the number of human genes
   b. the richness of human cytoplasm
   c. the length of human chromosomes
   d. the variety of proteins made by human genes

3. In the male, meiosis produces (p. 53)
   a. one ovum.
   b. several gametes.
   c. four sperm.
   d. two zygotes.

4. In industrialized nations, older maternal age, fertility drugs, and in vitro fertilization are major causes of (p. 55)
   a. the rise in fraternal twinning.
   b. slowed cell mitosis after conception.
   c. a decline in the production of autosomes.
   d. late fertilization of the ovum.

5. In heterozygous children, (p. 56)
   a. traits inherited from both parents dominate.
   b. gametes often combine to produce zygotes that twin.
   c. Y chromosomes are more common than X chromosomes.
   d. relationships between the alleles determine the phenotype.

6. Serious diseases rarely result from dominant alleles because (p. 57)
   a. modifier genes are more likely to cancel out the gene carrying the disease.
   b. children who develop the disease often die before they reproduce, thus eliminating the harmful allele from the family's heredity.
   c. heterozygous individuals often carry the dark hair gene that also makes them more resistant to certain diseases.
   d. using in vitro fertilization helps parents avoid producing harmful combinations of alleles.

7. Males are more likely to suffer from X-linked disorders because (p. 57)
   a. they are less likely to die in infancy than females.
   b. the proportion of male births is rising in many industrialized countries.
   c. they are more prone to patterns of incomplete dominance.
   d. their sex chromosomes do not match.

8. After germline mutation occurs, (p. 60)
   a. a DNA defect appears in every cell derived from the affected body cell.
   b. an individual is more likely to develop a serious illness as a result of smoking.
   c. the defective DNA is passed on to the next generation when the individual mates.
   d. the range of possible polygenetic inheritance decreases.

9. Individuals with Down syndrome who live past age 40 often show symptoms of (p. 61)
   a. **Alzheimer's disease.**
   b. trisomy 21.
   c. fragile X syndrome.
   d. hemophilia.

10. The pedigree that results from genetic counseling (p. 63)
    a. traces the descent of X-linked inheritance.
    b. predicts the outcome of polygenetic inheritance.
    c. determines traits, such as hair and eye color, that a child will get from his or her parents.
    d. **uses fundamental genetic principles to estimate the likelihood that parents will have an abnormal child.**

11. New reproductive technologies have caused many to worry that (p. 67)
    a. surrogate motherhood will no longer be available to financially needy women.
    b. too much genetic information will be widely available.
    c. **those methods could lead to selective breeding of babies with particular traits.**
    d. governments' restrictions on their use will become too stringent.

12. Amniocentesis can help identify genetic defects by (p. 64)
    a. removing a small plug of tissue from the end of one or more chorionic villi.
    b. **obtaining a sample of fluid from the uterus.**
    c. beaming high-frequency sound waves at the uterus.
    d. obtaining a sample of fetal blood.

13. By middle childhood, international adoptees placed in homes in infancy (p. 68)
    a. **have mental test scores similar to those of their nonbiological siblings.**
    b. fare about as well in development as their birth siblings who stayed behind.
    c. are more prone to emotional difficulties.
    d. tend to have problems trusting their adoptive parents.

14. According to Bronfenbrenner's theory, forces that comprise the chronosystem confront a family with (p. 71)
    a. powerful social values.
    b. different and sometimes conflicting parenting styles.
    c. **constant change to which each member must adapt.**
    d. isolation, alienation, and the behavioral problems that can result from those.

15. For both affluent and low-SES youths, adjustment difficulties can be reduced by (p. 73)
    a. longer school days.
    b. **a simple routine like eating dinner with parents.**
    c. more social activities with friends outside the home.
    d. stronger discipline.

16. According to a United Nations report, the education of girls (p. 72)
    a. has declined slightly in the developed world.
    b. is most effective in one-room rural schools.
    c. has made little headway in Latin America.
    d. **is the most effective means of combating maternal and child mortality.**

17. Of the following Western nations, which has the highest percentage of extremely poor children? (p. 74)
    a. **the United States**
    b. Canada
    c. France
    d. Switzerland

18. The Better Beginnings, Better Futures Project of Ontario, Canada, has (p. 76)
    a. done little to alleviate the effects of poverty on children.
    b. focused particularly on neighborhood recreation facilities, such as playgrounds.
    c. **yielded gains in family functioning, effective parenting, and children's reading skills.**
    d. yet to reduce the overall frequency of emotional and behavior problems.

19. Of the following indicators, both Canada and the United States rank higher than Ireland and Singapore in (p. 79)
    a. childhood poverty.
    b. **infant deaths in the first year of life.**
    c. teenage pregnancy rates.
    d. expenditures on health care as a percentage of gross domestic product.

20. Compared with nuclear-family households, extended-family arrangements (p. 78)
    a. add to the stress of childrearing.
    b. weaken children's relationships with people outside the family.
    c. prepare girls more effectively than boys for the work of managing a separate household.
    d. **place more emphasis on cooperation and moral and religious values.**

21. Most heritability estimates come from kinship studies that compare (p. 83)
    a. parents and children.
    b. **identical and fraternal twins.**
    c. brothers and sisters.
    d. children and their cousins.

22. Researchers generally use concordance rates to (p. 84)
    a. **study the contribution of heredity to emotional and behavioral disorders.**
    b. compare heritability estimates.
    c. quantify the effects of parental stress on children's learning.
    d. demonstrate the extremely powerful influence of heredity on criminality.

23. The most serious criticism of heritability estimates and concordance rates is that (p. 85)
    a. twin studies cannot necessarily be applied to the general population.
    b. they tell us too much about nature and not enough about nurture.
    c. **the statistics they produce give no precise information about how intelligence and personality develop.**
    d. they tend to overestimate the influence of environmental factors on intelligence and behavior.

24. Intelligence and personality are less strongly canalized because (p. 86)
    a. they are shaped by passive correlation.
    b. **they vary significantly with changes in the environment.**
    c. they display a narrow reaction range.
    d. the process of niche-picking changes them very little.

25. The concept of epigenesis can help researchers (p. 88)
    a. make sense of how internal stimulation triggers gene activity.
    b. to extend an individual's range of reaction.
    c. trace the effects of evocative correlation.
    d. **understand development as a series of complex changes between nature and nurture.**

PRACTICE TEST #2

1. Humans share most of their DNA with (p. 52)
    a.   bacteria.
    b.   reptiles.
    c.   pigs.
    d.   primates.

2. The essential function of meiosis is to (p. 53)
    a.   ensure that each generation receives a constant quantity of genetic material.
    b.   stimulate the production of zygotes.
    c.   prevent damaged genes from crossing over to the next generation.
    d.   regulate the process of mitosis.

3. Gametes that form in females carry (p. 55)
    a.   either an X or a Y chromosome.
    b.   only short chromosomes.
    c.   an X chromosome.
    d.   all the genetic material the human organism needs.

4. The frequency of identical twins is (p. 55)
    a.   much higher in industrialized nations.
    b.   slightly lower in Asia than elsewhere.
    c.   the same around the world.
    d.   steadily rising in North America.

5. The example of PKU illustrates the fact that (p. 56)
    a.   conditions once thought to be due to dominant-recessive inheritance actually result from multiple genes.
    b.   heterozygous individuals are not always carriers of recessive traits.
    c.   hair color and facial features are reasonably accurate predictors of inherited disabilities.
    d.   inherited recessive disorders do not always lead to untreatable conditions.

6. The sickle cell carrier rate is believed to be higher in Canada than in the United States because (p. 57)
    a.   the risk of malaria is slightly higher in Canada.
    b.   more African Canadians are recent immigrants than African Americans.
    c.   incomplete dominance patterns are more common throughout the entire Canadian population.
    d.   more African Canadians live at higher altitudes than African Americans.

7. The concept of genetic imprinting helps to explain why (p. 59)
    a.   children inherit certain parent-specific diseases.
    b.   the rate of sickle cell anemia is rising among North Americans of European descent.
    c.   females are more likely to suffer the effects of X-linked inheritance.
    d.   fragile X syndrome results in 2 to 3 percent of autism cases.

8. Most chromosomal defects result from (p. 60)
    a.   radiation.
    b.   mistakes during meiosis.
    c.   somatic mutation.
    d.   Prader-Willi syndrome.

9. Adding or subtracting from the usual number of X chromosomes results in (p. 62)
    a.   Down syndrome.
    b.   facial abnormalities.
    c.   incomplete dominance.
    d.   particular intellectual deficits.

10. Candidates for genetic counseling typically are (p. 63)
    a. women who have had three or more pregnancies.
    b. men with XYY syndrome.
    c. women of advanced maternal age.
    d. individuals with Down syndrome.

11. The overall success rate of in vitro fertilization is 30 percent, but (p. 66)
    a. it often requires more ova than most women produce.
    b. success declines steadily with age.
    c. that rate is far lower when the man has fertility problems.
    d. it can increase the risk of X-linked disease.

12. More people in North America and Western Europe are adopting from other countries because (p. 65)
    a. the availability of healthy babies in those regions has declined.
    b. adoptable children in their own countries are often past infancy.
    c. adopted children tend to have fewer learning and emotional difficulties.
    d. they can select children like themselves in personality and background.

13. The family is the most powerful context of development because it (p. 69)
    a. constitutes a macrosystem.
    b. protects children from environmental stressors.
    c. introduces children to the physical world, creates unique bonds, and teaches fundamental skills and values.
    d. guards children from most indirect influences.

14. Compared to low-SES parents, high-SES parents tend to (p. 71)
    a. expect their children to be polite and obedient before all else.
    b. talk to and stimulate their infants and preschoolers more.
    c. encourage their female children more than their male children.
    d. pass on higher levels of stress to their children.

15. In North America, poverty is highest among (p. 74)
    a. Native-American children.
    b. Hispanic children.
    c. African-American children.
    d. Canadian-Aboriginal children.

16. Most homeless families consist of (p. 75)
    a. women with children under age 5.
    b. ethnic minorities.
    c. one or more members with mental illness.
    d. people turned away from government-supported housing.

17. Studies have shown that children whose families moved into low-poverty neighborhoods (p. 75)
    a. had trouble adjusting to their new surroundings.
    b. showed little change in their behavior.
    c. showed substantially better health and school achievement.
    d. improved more in social interaction than in academic performance.

18. Higher-SES parents tend to interact frequently with their children's teachers because (p. 77)
    a. they generally live in small towns.
    b. their backgrounds and values are often similar to those of the teachers.
    c. their children and the teachers' children often go to the same schools.
    d. they can more easily take time off work than lower-SES parents.

19. U.S. opponents of the United Nations Convention on the Rights of the Child maintain that it (p. 80)
    a. **would shift the burden of child rearing from the family to the state.**
    b. is insufficiently collectivist.
    c. does not go as far toward protecting children as U.S. policies already in place.
    d. forces the United States to adopt principles that few other nations observe.

20. The results of welfare reform in Canada and the United States suggest that (p. 81)
    a. the faster parents leave welfare for work, the faster their children's lives will improve.
    b. work requirements should be more stringent.
    c. **welfare reform promotes children's development only when it results in a more adequate standard of living.**
    d. both countries' commitment to providing affordable child care helped to decrease their welfare roles.

21. Currently, most kinship studies find that heredity (p. 83)
    a. plays hardly any role in intelligence.
    b. has a strong influence on intelligence.
    c. cannot be conclusively linked to many traits.
    d. **plays a moderate role in intelligence.**

22. Heritability estimates are controversial because they (p. 84)
    a. are too dependent on the extent to which twin pairs reflect genetic and environmental variation.
    b. **can easily be misapplied to suggest dubious genetic bases for certain traits.**
    c. employ simplistic statistical procedures.
    d. tell us nothing about personality traits.

23. Reaction range highlights that (p. 86)
    a. strongly canalized behavior develops similarly in diverse environments.
    b. concordance rates are likely to exaggerate the role of heredity.
    c. **different genetic-environmental combinations can make two people look the same.**
    d. despite our highly varied genetic makeups, we tend to respond in similar ways to different environments.

24. In older children, active genetic-environmental correlation becomes common because (p. 86)
    a. **as they gain more freedom, they seek environments that fit their genetic tendencies.**
    b. their heredity evokes stronger responses that, in turn, prompt them to display certain behaviors even more.
    c. their hereditary traits become less strongly canalized.
    d. they cease to engage in niche-picking.

25. Theorists who emphasize the effects of canalization and range of reaction would most likely believe that (p. 87)
    a. unfavorable genetic-environmental correlations can be uncoupled.
    b. active correlation has little bearing on genetic tendencies.
    c. heritability estimates are the most accurate predictors of intelligence.
    d. **genetic-environmental correlation is driven largely by genetics.**

POWERPOINT SLIDES

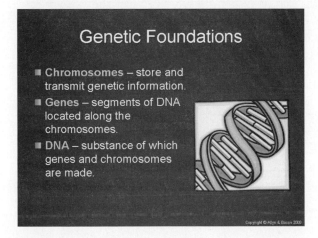

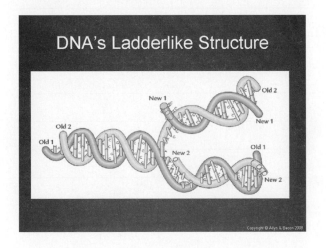

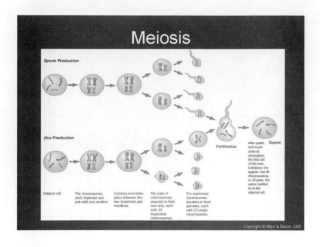

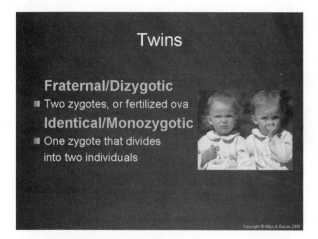

Maternal Factors Related to Fraternal Twinning

FACTOR	DESCRIPTION
Ethnicity	Occurs in 4 per 1,000 births among Asians, 8 per 1,000 births among whites, 12 to 16 per 1,000 births among blacks[a]
Family history of twinning	Occurs more often among women whose mothers and sisters gave birth to fraternal twins
Age	Rises with maternal age, peaking between 35 and 39 years, and then rapidly falls
Nutrition	Occurs less often among women with poor diets; occurs more often among women who are tall and overweight or of normal weight as opposed to slight body build
Number of births	Is more likely with each additional birth
Season and geographic region	Increases with exposure to sunlight: Occurs more often in conceptions during summer months and in regions near the equator
Fertility drugs and in vitro fertilization	Is more likely with fertility hormones and in vitro fertilization (see page 66), which also increase the chances of triplets to quintuplets

[a]Worldwide rates, not including multiple births resulting from use of fertility drugs.

Sources: Bortolus et al., 1999; Hall, 2003.

166

Examples of Dominant and Recessive Characteristics

DOMINANT	RECESSIVE
Dark hair	Blond hair
Normal hair	Pattern baldness
Curly hair	Straight hair
Nonred hair	Red hair
Facial dimples	No dimples
Normal hearing	Some forms of deafness
Normal vision	Nearsightedness
Farsightedness	Normal vision
Normal vision	Congenital eye cataracts
Normally pigmented skin	Albinism
Double-jointedness	Normal joints
Type A blood	Type O blood
Type B blood	Type O blood
Rh-positive blood	Rh-negative blood

Note: Many normal characteristics that were previously thought to be due to dominant–recessive inheritance, such as eye color, are now regarded as due to multiple genes. For the characteristics listed here, there still seems to be general agreement that the simple dominant–recessive relationship holds.

Source: McKusick, 2002.

Copyright © Allyn & Bacon 2008

Dominant and Recessive Diseases

DISEASE	DESCRIPTION	MODE OF INHERITANCE	INCIDENCE	TREATMENT
Autosomal Diseases				
Cooley's anemia	Pale appearance, retarded physical growth, and lethargic behavior begin in infancy.	Recessive	1 in 500 births to parents of Mediterranean descent	Frequent blood transfusion; death from complications usually occurs by adolescence.
Cystic fibrosis	Lungs, liver, and pancreas secrete large amounts of thick mucus, leading to breathing and digestive difficulties.	Recessive	1 in 2,000 to 2,500 Caucasian births; 1 in 16,000 births to North Americans of African descent	Bronchial drainage, prompt treatment of respiratory infection, dietary management. Advances in medical care allow survival with good life quality into adulthood.
Phenylketonuria (PKU)	Inability to metabolize the amino acid phenylalanine, contained in many proteins, causes severe central nervous system damage in the first year of life.	Recessive	1 in 8,000 births	Placing the child on a special diet results in average intelligence and normal lifespan. Subtle difficulties with planning and problem solving are often present.
Sickle cell anemia	Abnormal sickling of red blood cells causes oxygen deprivation, pain, swelling, and tissue damage. Anemia and susceptibility to infections, especially pneumonia, occur.	Recessive	1 in 600 births to North Americans of African descent	Blood transfusions, pain-killers, prompt treatment of infection. No known cure; 50 percent die by age 20.
Tay-Sachs disease	Central nervous system degeneration, with onset at about 6 months, leads to poor muscle tone, blindness, deafness, and convulsions.	Recessive	1 in 3,600 births to Jews of European descent and to French Canadians	None; death by 3 to 4 years of age.
Huntington disease	Central nervous system degeneration leads to muscular coordination difficulties, mental deterioration, and personality changes. Symptoms usually do not appear until age 35 or later.	Dominant	1 in 18,000 to 25,000 births	None; death 10 to 20 years after symptom onset.
Marfan syndrome	Tall, slender build; thin, elongated arms and legs; and heart defects and eye abnormalities, especially of the lens. Excessive lengthening of the body results in a variety of skeletal defects.	Dominant	1 in 20,000 births	Correction of heart and eye defects sometimes possible. Death from heart failure in early adulthood is common.

Copyright © Allyn & Bacon 2008

Incomplete Dominance and Dominant and Recessive Diseases (continued)

X-Linked Diseases				
Duchenne muscular dystrophy	This degenerative muscle disease causes abnormal gait, with loss of ability to walk between 7 and 13 years of age.	Recessive	1 in 3,000 to 5,000 male births	None; death from respiratory infection or weakening of the heart muscle usually occurs in adolescence.
Hemophilia	Blood fails to clot normally; can lead to severe internal bleeding and tissue damage.	Recessive	1 in 4,000 to 7,000 male births	Blood transfusions; safety precautions to prevent injury.
Diabetes insipidus	Insufficient production of the hormone vasopressin results in excessive thirst and urination. Dehydration can cause central nervous system damage.	Recessive	1 in 2,500 male births	Hormone replacement.

Note: For recessive disorders, carrier status can be detected in prospective parents through a blood test or genetic analyses. For all disorders listed, prenatal diagnosis is available (see page 00).

Sources: Behrman, Kliegman, & Arvin, 1996; Chodirker et al., 2001; Gott, 1998; Grody, 1999; Knoers et al., 1993; McKusick, 2002; Schulman & Black, 1997.

Copyright © Allyn & Bacon 2008

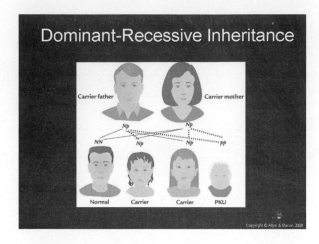

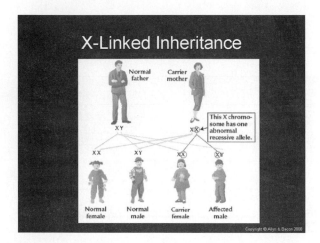

X-Linked Disorders

- About 105 boys are born for every 100 girls, worldwide.
- In recent decades, the proportion of male births has declined in many industrialized countries. Many researchers attribute the decline to a rise in stressful living conditions.

Genetic Imprinting and Mutation

Imprinting

- **Chemical marker that activates either father's or mother's gene**
- **Often temporary**

Mutation

- **Sudden, permanent change in a DNA segment**

Copyright © Allyn & Bacon 2008

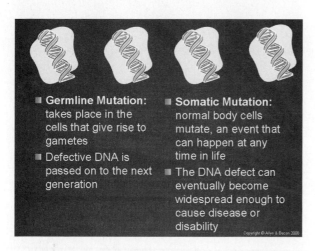

- **Germline Mutation:** takes place in the cells that give rise to gametes
- Defective DNA is passed on to the next generation

- **Somatic Mutation:** normal body cells mutate, an event that can happen at any time in life
- The DNA defect can eventually become widespread enough to cause disease or disability

Copyright © Allyn & Bacon 2008

Chromosomal Abnormalities

- Down Syndrome—results from problems with the 21st chromosome
- Sex Chromosome Abnormalities—problems with the X or Y chromosomes

Copyright © Allyn & Bacon 2008

MATERNAL AGE	RISK
20	1 in 1,900 births
25	1 in 1,200
30	1 in 900
33	1 in 600
36	1 in 280
39	1 in 130
42	1 in 65
45	1 in 30
48	1 in 15

Risk of Giving Birth to a Down Syndrome Child by Maternal Age

Note: The risk of giving birth to a Down syndrome baby after age 35 has increased slightly over the past 20 years as a result of improved medical interventions during pregnancy and consequent greater likelihood that a Down syndrome fetus will survive to be liveborn.

Sources: Adapted from Halliday et al., 1995; Meyers et al., 1997.

Copyright © Allyn & Bacon 2008

Sex Chromosomal Disorders

DISORDER	DESCRIPTION	INCIDENCE	TREATMENT
XYY syndrome	Extra Y chromosome. Above-average height, large teeth, and sometimes severe acne. Intelligence, male sexual development, and fertility are normal.	1 in 1,000 male births	No special treatment necessary.
Triple X syndrome (XXX)	Extra X chromosome. Tallness and impaired verbal intelligence. Female sexual development and fertility are normal.	1 in 500 to 1,250 female births	Special education to treat verbal ability problems.
Klinefelter syndrome (XXY)	Extra X chromosome. Tallness, body fat distribution resembling females, incomplete development of sex characteristics at puberty, sterility, and impaired verbal intelligence.	1 in 900 male births	Hormone therapy at puberty to stimulate development of sex characteristics; special education to treat verbal ability problems.
Turner syndrome (XO)	Missing X chromosome. Short stature, webbed neck, incomplete development of sex characteristics at puberty, sterility, and impaired spatial intelligence.	1 in 2,500 to 8,000 female births	Hormone therapy in childhood to stimulate physical growth and at puberty to promote development of sex characteristics; special education to treat spatial ability problems.

Sources: Geerts, Steyaert, & Feyns, 2003; Rovet et al., 1996; Saitta & Zackai, 2005; Simpson et al., 2003.

Copyright © Allyn & Bacon 2008

Prenatal Diagnostic Methods

- Amniocentesis
- Chorionic Villus Sampling
- Fetoscopy
- Ultrasound
- Maternal Blood Analysis
- Preimplantation Genetic Diagnosis

Copyright © Allyn & Bacon 2008

Fetal Medicine

- Drugs delivered into uterus
- Surgery
- Bone marrow transplants
- Genetic engineering and gene therapy

Genetic Engineering

The Human Genome Project

Gene Therapy

Reproductive Technologies

- Donor Insemination and In Vitro Fertilization
- Surrogate Motherhood
- New Frontiers in Reproductive Technology
  – ethical concerns

The Alternative of Adoption

- Adopted children tend to have more learning and emotional difficulties than other children.
- The child's age at adoption correlates to learning and emotional difficulties experienced.
- Most adopted children eventually fare well.

Copyright © Allyn & Bacon 2008

Environmental Contexts for Development

- Family
- Socioeconomic Status
- Neighborhoods
- Towns and Cities
- Cultural Context

Copyright © Allyn & Bacon 2008

Family Influences on Development

- Direct
  - Two-person relationships
- Indirect
  - Third parties
- Adapting to Change
  - Changes from within and outside the family

Copyright © Allyn & Bacon 2008

Socioeconomic Status and Family Functioning

- Timing of Family Life Cycle
- Values and Expectations
- Father's Involvement
- Communication and Discipline Styles
- Children's Cognitive Development

Copyright © Allyn & Bacon 2008

Worldwide Education of Girls

- 135 million children in the world, mostly poverty-stricken girls, receive no education at all.
- Providing education benefits girls by providing them with enhanced verbal skills and the empowerment to improve their life.
- Also improves:
  - Family Health
  - Family Relationships and Parenting
- According to the United Nations, educating girls will have a profound impact on combating poverty, maternal and child mortality, and disease.

Copyright © Allyn & Bacon 2008

Affluence

- Many affluent parents are not physically and emotionally available for their children.
- These parents often make excessive demands for achievement.
- Adolescents whose parents value achievement over character often have academic and emotional problems.

Copyright © Allyn & Bacon 2008

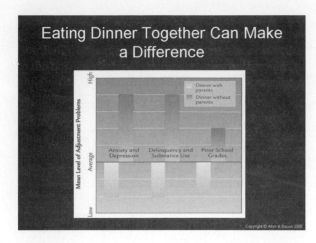

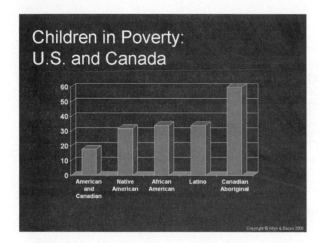

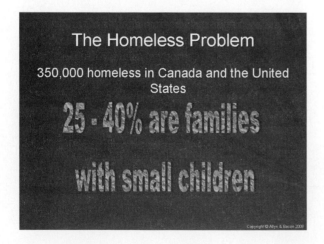

Neighborhoods

- Neighborhoods offer resources and social ties that play an important part in children's development.
- Higher-SES families are less dependent on their immediate surroundings than are low-SES families.
- Social ties linking families together break down in areas with unemployment, crime, and population turnover.

Copyright © Allyn & Bacon 2008

Schools

- Children spend an average of 14,000 hours in school by the time they reach high school graduation.
- Parent-school contact supports development at all ages.

Copyright © Allyn & Bacon 2008

The Cultural Context

- Culture shapes every aspect of daily life.
- Different cultures have different values. For example, the North American culture values the independence, self-reliance, and privacy of the family.
- Subcultures
- Extended family households

Copyright © Allyn & Bacon 2008

The African-American Extended Family

- Today, more black than white adults have relatives other than their own children living in the same household.
- Extended family system provides emotional support and the sharing of resources, and helps reduce the stress of poverty and single parenthood.
- These arrangements also place a high value on cooperation and moral and religious values.

Copyright © Allyn & Bacon 2008

Individualist and Collectivist Societies

Individualist

- People think of themselves as separate from other people.
- Concerned with personal goals.

Collectivist

- People define themselves as part of a group.
- Concerned with group goals over individual goals.

Copyright © Allyn & Bacon 2008

Public Policy Shortcomings

- Children without health insurance
- Substandard child care
- Poor vocational preparation
- High-school dropouts

Copyright © Allyn & Bacon 2008

Comparing the United States and Canada to Other Countries

INDICATOR	U.S. RANK*	CANADIAN RANK*	SOME COUNTRIES THE UNITED STATES AND CANADA TRAIL
Childhood poverty[b] (among 23 industrialized nations considered)	23rd	16th	Australia, Czech Republic, Germany, Norway, Sweden, Taiwan
Infant deaths in the first year of life (worldwide)	26th	16th	Hong Kong, Ireland, Singapore, Spain
Teenage pregnancy rate (among 45 industrialized nations considered)	28th	21st	Albania, Australia, Czech Republic, Denmark, Poland, Netherlands
Expenditures on education as a percentage of gross domestic product[c] (among 22 industrialized nations considered)	10th	6th	For Canada: Israel, Sweden / For the United States: Australia, France, New Zealand, Sweden
Expenditures on health as a percentage of gross domestic product[c] (among 22 industrialized nations considered)	16th	4th	For Canada: Iceland, Switzerland / For the United States: Austria, Australia, Hungary, New Zealand

*1 = highest, or best, rank.
[b]North American childhood poverty rates—18 percent in both the United States and Canada—greatly exceed those of any of these nations. For example, the rate is 12 percent in Australia, 6 percent in the Czech Republic, 4 percent in Norway, and 2.5 percent in Sweden.
[c]Gross domestic product is the value of all goods and services produced by a nation during a specified time period. It provides an overall measure of a nation's wealth.
Sources: Luxembourg Income Study, 2005; Perie et al., 2000; UNICEF, 2001; U.S. Census Bureau, 2007; U.S. Department of Education, 2006.

Copyright © Allyn & Bacon 2008

Welfare Reform, Poverty, and Child Development

- Welfare-to-work programs

- Welfare reform promotes children's development only when it results in better standards of living for the family.

Copyright © Allyn & Bacon 2008

Children's Rights

- 1989 Convention on the Rights of the Child
- 1991 Canada initiated Campaign 2000 to build awareness of the plight of child poverty and to lobby for improved policies

Copyright © Allyn & Bacon 2008

How Much Does Heredity Contribute to Behavior?

Heritability Estimates

- Portion of individual differences attributable to genetics
- Ranges from 0 to 1.00

Concordance

- What percent of the time do twins both show a trait?
- Ranges from 0 to 100%

Copyright © Allyn & Bacon 2008

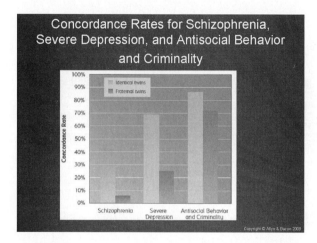

Concordance Rates for Schizophrenia, Severe Depression, and Antisocial Behavior and Criminality

Copyright © Allyn & Bacon 2008

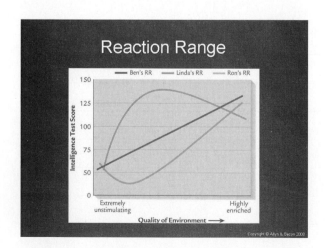

Reaction Range

Copyright © Allyn & Bacon 2008

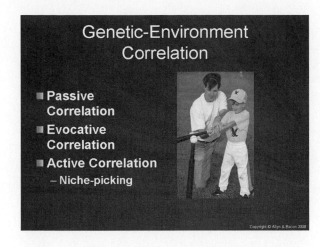

Genetic-Environment Correlation

- **Passive Correlation**
- **Evocative Correlation**
- **Active Correlation**
  - Niche-picking

Copyright © Allyn & Bacon 2008

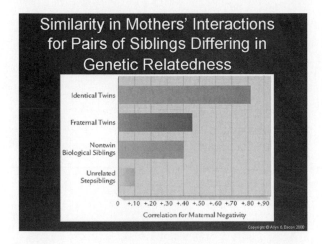

Similarity in Mothers' Interactions for Pairs of Siblings Differing in Genetic Relatedness

Correlation for Maternal Negativity

Copyright © Allyn & Bacon 2008

Environmental Influences on Gene Expression

- Parents and other caring adults can uncouple unfavorable genetic-environmental correlations.
- For example, twins who displayed aggressive behavior could be positively affected by mothers who practiced good, positive parenting.

Copyright © Allyn & Bacon 2008

CHAPTER 3
PRENATAL DEVELOPMENT

CHAPTER-AT-A-GLANCE

Chapter Outline	Instruction Ideas	Supplements
Motivations for Parenthood pp. 93–97 Why Have Children? • How Large a Family? • Is There a Best Time During Adulthood to Have a Child?	Learning Objectives 3.1–3.2 Learning Activity 3.5 Ask Yourself p. 97	Transparencies 24–25, 27 Test Bank Items 1–10, 93 Please contact your Allyn and Bacon publisher's representative for a wide range of video offerings available to adopters.
Prenatal Development pp. 97–104 Conception • The Period of the Zygote • The Period of the Embryo • The Period of the Fetus	Learning Objective 3.3 Learning Activities 3.1–3.2, 3.5 Ask Yourself p. 104	Transparencies 28–29 Test Bank Items 11–42, 94–96
Prenatal Environmental Influences pp. 104–122 Teratogens • Other Maternal Factors • The Importance of Prenatal Health Care	Learning Objectives 3.4–3.7 Lecture Enhancements 3.1–3.3 Learning Activities 3.3, 3.5 Ask Yourself p. 122	Transparencies 31–33 Test Bank Items 43–81, 85–92, 97–100
Preparing for Parenthood pp. 122–124 Seeking Information • The Baby Becomes a Reality • Models of Effective Parenthood • The Parental Relationship	Learning Objective 3.8 Lecture Enhancement 3.4 Learning Activity 3.6 Ask Yourself p. 124	Test Bank Items 82–84

BRIEF CHAPTER SUMMARY

This chapter begins with a discussion of motivations for parenthood and current changes in birth patterns. Today, men and women are more likely to weigh the pros and cons of having children than they were in previous generations. The American family has declined in size over time, a trend that has benefits for child rearing. Births to women over age 30 have increased, a change associated with both advantages and disadvantages for children.

At no other time is change as rapid as it is before birth. Prenatal development takes place in three phases: (1) the period of the zygote, during which the newly fertilized ovum travels down the fallopian tube and attaches itself to the uterine wall; (2) the period of the embryo, during which the groundwork for all body structures is laid down; and (3) the period of the fetus, the "growth and finishing" phase.

The prenatal period is a vulnerable time. The developing organism can be endangered by teratogens, including drugs, cigarettes, alcohol, radiation, and environmental pollution, as well as infectious disease, inadequate exercise and nutrition, maternal stress, Rh blood incompatibility, and maternal age. Prenatal health care is vitally important to ensure the health of mother and baby.

For most expectant parents, however, the prenatal period is not a time of medical hazard. Rather, it is a time of major life change in which mothers and fathers prepare for parenthood.

LEARNING OBJECTIVES

After reading this chapter, you should be able to:

3.1   Cite advantages and disadvantages of parenthood mentioned by modern North American couples. (pp. 93–95)

3.2   Review current trends in family size and childbearing age, and discuss their impact on child development. (pp. 95–97)

3.3   List the three phases of prenatal development, and describe the major milestones of each. (pp. 97–104)

3.4   Define the term *teratogen*, and summarize the factors that affect the impact of teratogens. (pp. 104–107)

3.5   List agents known to be or suspected of being teratogens, and discuss evidence supporting the harmful effects of each. (pp. 107–115)

3.6   Discuss maternal factors other than exposure to teratogens that can affect the developing embryo or fetus. (pp. 115–119)

3.7   Discuss the importance of prenatal health care, and cite some of the barriers to seeking such care. (pp. 119–122)

3.8   Explain the factors that contribute to personal adjustment as expectant mothers and fathers prepare for parenthood. (pp. 122–124)

LECTURE OUTLINE

I.   MOTIVATIONS FOR PARENTHOOD (pp. 93–97)
  A. Why Have Children? (pp. 94–95)
    1.   In the past, many adults had children because it was biologically and culturally expected.
    2.   Today, in Western industrialized nations, childbearing decisions are a matter of personal choice because of the availability of effective birth control techniques. Also, changes in cultural values allow people to remain childless with much less fear of social criticism.
    3.   North Americans mention the following as advantages of having children:
      a.   Giving and receiving warmth and affection
      b.   Experiencing the stimulation and fun that children add to life
      c.   Being accepted as a responsible, mature community member

      d.   Experiencing new growth and learning opportunities that add meaning to life

      e.   Having someone to provide care in old age

      f.   Gaining a sense of accomplishment and creativity from helping children grow

      g.   Learning to become less selfish and to sacrifice

      h.   Having someone carry on after one's own death

    4.   They cite the following as disadvantages of having children:

      a.   Loss of freedom; being tied down

      b.   Financial strain of rearing a child from birth to age 18, with additional expense for higher education and financial dependency during emerging adulthood

      c.   Family–work conflict—not enough time to meet both child-rearing and job responsibilities

      d.   Interference with mother's career progress

      e.   Concerns about children's health, safety, and well-being

      f.   Risks of bringing up children in a dangerous world

      g.   Reduced time to spend with one's spouse

      h.   Loss of privacy

      i.   Fear that children will turn out badly

    5.   Careful weighing of the pros and cons of having children means that many more couples are making informed and personally meaningful decisions.

  B. How Large a Family? (pp. 95–96)

    1.   In 1960, the average number of children per North American couple was 3.1; currently, it is 1.8 in the United States and 1.6 in Canada. The average is even lower in Japan (1.4), Germany (1.4), and Italy (1.3).

    2.   Smaller family size is more compatible with a woman's decision to divide her energies between family and work. Marital instability has also contributed to smaller families.

    3.   Research shows that large families do not create less intelligent children, as many people believe. Rather, the link between larger family size and lower mental test scores is explained by the trend for mothers who are low in intelligence to have more children.

    4.   Research also challenges the popular belief that only children will become spoiled or selfish.

  C. Is There a Best Time During Adulthood to Have a Child? (pp. 96–97)

    1.   First births to women in their thirties have increased greatly over the past quarter century, as more people delay childbearing until their education is complete and their careers established.

    2.   Older parents may be financially better off and more mature emotionally than younger parents. But because fertility problems increase with age, those who postpone childbirth until their late thirties or early forties run the risk of not having children at all.

II. PRENATAL DEVELOPMENT (pp. 97–104)

  A. Conception (p. 98)

    1.   About every 28 days, in the middle of a woman's menstrual cycle, an ovum bursts from one of her ovaries and is drawn into one of two *fallopian tubes.* The *corpus luteum* (the spot on the ovary from which the ovum was released) then secretes hormones that prepare the lining of the uterus to receive a fertilized ovum.

    2.   Sperm are produced in a male's *testes,* two glands located in the *scrotum,* sacs lying just behind the penis.

    3.   Following intercourse, sperm travel through the *cervix* and into the fallopian tube, where fertilization usually occurs.

    4.   Sperm can remain viable for up to 6 days, but conception most often results from intercourse during the three-day period before and during ovulation.

  B. The Period of the Zygote (pp. 99–100)

    1.   The period of the zygote lasts about two weeks, from fertilization until the cell mass drifts out of the fallopian tubes and attaches itself to the uterine wall.

    2.   By the fourth day, 60 to 70 cells exist, forming a hollow, fluid-filled ball called a **blastocyst.**

    3.   The **embryonic disk** (the cells on the inside of the blastocyst) will become the new organism; the outer ring of cells, called the **trophoblast,** will become the structures that provide protective covering.

4. Implantation (p. 99)
   a. **Implantation** occurs between the seventh and ninth days, when the blastocyst burrows deep into the uterine lining.
   b. The trophoblast forms a membrane, called the **amnion,** that encloses the developing organism in **amniotic fluid,** which cushions the developing organism and regulates the temperature of the prenatal world.
   c. A *yolk sac* emerges that produces blood cells until the liver, spleen, and bone marrow are mature enough to take over this function.
   d. As many as 30 percent of zygotes do not survive this period. In this way, nature eliminates most prenatal abnormalities.
5. The Placenta and Umbilical Cord (pp. 99–100)
   a. By the end of the second week, the **chorion,** a protective membrane surrounding the amnion, develops, and tiny blood vessels called *villi* emerge from it and burrow into the uterine wall.
   b. The **placenta** now develops; this special organ permits food and oxygen to reach the developing organism and waste products to be carried away.
   c. The placenta is connected to the developing organism by the **umbilical cord,** which to a length of 1 to 3 feet during pregnancy.

C. The Period of the Embryo (p. 101)
1. The period of the **embryo,** which lasts from implantation through the eighth week of pregnancy, is the time of the most rapid prenatal changes, when the groundwork is laid for all body structures and internal organs.
2. Last Half of the First Month (p. 101)
   a. In the third week of pregnancy (the first week of the period of the embryo), the embryonic disk forms three layers of cells:
      (1) The *ectoderm* will become the nervous system and skin.
      (2) The *mesoderm* will become the muscles, skeleton, circulatory system, and other internal organs.
      (3) The *endoderm* will become the digestive system, lungs, urinary tract, and glands.
   b. At first, the nervous system develops fastest. The ectoderm folds over, forming the **neural tube,** or spinal cord.
3. The Second Month (p. 101)
   a. Rapid development continues in the second month, when the eyes, ears, nose, jaw, and neck form.
   b. Tiny buds become arms, legs, fingers, and toes, and the internal organs become more distinct.
   c. Changing body proportions cause the embryo's posture to become more upright.
   d. The embryo can now move, and it responds to touch, especially in the mouth area and on the soles of the feet.

D. The Period of the Fetus (pp. 102–104)
1. The longest prenatal period is the period of the **fetus,** the "growth and finishing" phase, which lasts from the ninth week to the end of pregnancy.
2. The Third Month (p. 102)
   a. The organs, muscles, and nervous system start to become organized and connected.
   b. By the twelfth week, the external genitals are well-formed, and the sex of the fetus can be determined using ultrasound.
   c. The end of the third month marks the completion of the first of the three **trimesters**—the three equal time periods into which prenatal development is divided.
3. The Second Trimester (p. 102)
   a. By the middle of the second trimester (between 17 and 20 weeks), the fetus is large enough that the mother can feel its movements.
   b. A white, cheeselike substance called **vernix** covers the skin of the fetus, protecting it from chapping in the amniotic fluid.
   c. White, downy hair called **lanugo** also covers the fetus, helping the vernix stick to the skin.

d. At the end of the second trimester, many organs are well-developed and most of the brain's neurons are in place. After this time, few neurons will be produced, but *glial cells,* which support and feed the neurons, continue to increase at a rapid rate throughout the remainder of the prenatal period and even after birth.

e. Because brain growth leads to new behavioral capacities, the fetus can now be both stimulated and irritated by sounds and light, but a fetus born at this time cannot yet survive.

4. The Third Trimester (pp. 102–104)

a. The **age of viability,** between 22 and 26 weeks, is the point at which the baby can first survive if born early.

b. A baby born between the seventh and eighth month usually needs oxygen assistance to breathe.

c. The brain continues to make great strides during the last three months. The *cerebral cortex* enlarges and the fetus spends more time awake. By 28 weeks, fetuses are awake about 11 percent of the time, a figure that rises to 16 percent just before birth.

d. Between 30 and 34 weeks, fetuses show rhythmic alternations between sleep and wakefulness.

e. Higher fetal activity in the last weeks of pregnancy predicts a more active infant in the first month of life—a relationship that persist into early childhood in boys. Fetal activity has also been linked to higher tolerance for frustration in 1-year-olds and less fearfulness in 2-year-olds.

f. Between 23 and 30 weeks, connections form between the cerebral cortex and brain regions involved in pain sensitivity, so that the fetus can feel pain.

g. By 28 weeks, fetuses blink their eyes in response to nearby sounds, and within the next 6 weeks, they can distinguish different voices and sounds by tone and rhythm, showing systematic heart rate changes in response to different speakers.

h. As the growing fetus fills the uterus, it moves less often. Brain development contributes to a decline in physical activity by enabling the fetus to inhibit behavior.

i. In the eighth month, a layer of fat develops under the skin to assist with temperature regulation, and the fetus receives antibodies from the mother's blood to protect against illnesses.

j. In the last weeks, most fetuses assume an upside-down position. Growth slows, and birth is about to take place.

III. PRENATAL ENVIRONMENTAL INFLUENCES (pp. 104–122)

A. Teratogens (pp. 105–115)

1. A **teratogen** is any environmental agent that causes damage during the prenatal period. The harm done by teratogens depends on several factors:

a. Larger doses over longer time periods usually have more negative effects.

b. The genetic makeup of the mother and the developing organism affect the individual's ability to withstand harmful environments.

c. The presence of several negative factors at once, such as poor nutrition, lack of medical care, and additional teratogens, can worsen the impact of a single harmful agent.

d. The effects of teratogens vary with the age of the organism at the time of exposure, in line with the concept of a *sensitive period*—a limited time span in which a part of the body or a behavior is biologically prepared to develop rapidly and, therefore, is especially sensitive to its surroundings.

(1) Serious defects are most likely to occur during the embryonic period, when the foundations for all body parts are being laid down.

(2) Some parts of the body, such as the brain and the eye, have long sensitive periods that extend throughout prenatal development, while other sensitive periods are much shorter.

e. The effects of teratogens may be subtle and delayed and may include indirect psychological consequences, which can be harder to identify than physical damage.

(1) Experiments reveal that low birth weight is associated with cardiovascular disease and diabetes in middle adulthood, probably as a result of complex factors.

(2) High birth weight is associated with later development of breast cancer.

2. Prescription and Nonprescription Drugs (pp. 107–108)
    a. **Thalidomide,** a sedative used widely in the 1960s and still prescribed to treat certain diseases, caused severe limb deformations in embryos when taken by mothers 4 to 6 weeks after conception.
    b. When taken during pregnancy, Accutane, a vitamin A derivative prescribed to treat severe acne, causes extensive damage to the fetus, including abnormalities of the eye, ear, skull, brain, heart, central nervous system, and immune system. The U.S. federal government now requires that doctors enter every patient who takes Accutane into an Internet database, in an effort to limit use during pregnancy.
    c. The synthetic hormone *diethylstilbestrol (DES)* was widely prescribed between 1945 and 1970 to prevent miscarriages. Daughters of mothers who had taken DES showed unusually high rates of cancer of the vagina, malformations of the uterus, infertility, and pregnancies resulting in prematurity, low birth weight, and miscarriage.
    d. Several studies have linked regular aspirin use to low birth weight, infant death around the time of birth, poorer motor development, and lower intelligence test scores in early childhood, although other research fails to confirm these findings.
    e. Heavy caffeine intake is associated with low birth weight, miscarriage, and newborn withdrawal symptoms, such as irritability and vomiting.
    f. The safest course of action is to cut down on or avoid these drugs entirely.
3. Illegal Drugs (pp. 108, 110)
    a. As many as 3 to 7 percent of American and Canadian babies born in large cities, and 1 to 2 percent of all North American newborns, have been exposed to cocaine prenatally.
    b. Babies born to users of cocaine, heroin, or methadone are at risk for prematurity, low birth weight, physical defects, breathing difficulties, and death around the time of birth. In addition, these infants are often born drug-addicted.
    c. Throughout the first year, heroin- and methadone-exposed infants are less attentive to the environment than nonexposed babies, and their motor development is slow. In some children, problems persist.
    d. Evidence on cocaine suggests that prenatal exposure causes lasting difficulties in some babies, including eye, bone, genital, urinary tract, kidney, and heart deformities; brain hemorrhages and seizures; and severe growth retardation.
        (1) Several studies report perceptual, motor, attention, memory, and language problems in infancy that persist into the preschool years.
        (2) Other studies report no major negative effects of prenatal cocaine exposure. It is difficult to isolate the precise impact of cocaine, because users often take several drugs and engage in other high-risk behaviors.
    e. Several researchers have linked prenatal marijuana exposure to smaller head size; sleep, attention, memory, and academic achievement difficulties; childhood depression; and poorer problem-solving performance in adolescence, but lasting consequences are not well-established.
4. Tobacco (pp. 110–111)
    a. Although smoking rates have declined in Western nations, an estimated 12 percent of American women and 17 percent of Canadian women smoke during their pregnancies.
    b. Effects of smoking during pregnancy include low birth weight and increased risk of miscarriage, prematurity, impaired heart rate and breathing during sleep, infant death, and asthma and cancer later in childhood.
    c. The more cigarettes a mother smokes, the greater the chances that her baby will be affected. If a pregnant woman stops smoking at any time, she immediately reduces the likelihood that her infant will be born underweight and suffer from future problems.
    d. Newborns of smoking mothers are less attentive to sounds, display more muscle tension, are more excitable when stimulated, and more often have colic—findings suggesting subtle effects on brain development.
    e. Some studies report that prenatally exposed children and adolescents have shorter attention spans, poorer memories, lower mental test scores, and more behavior problems.

    f.   The nicotine in tobacco constricts blood vessels, lessens blood flow to the uterus, and causes the placenta to grow abnormally, reducing the transfer of nutrients, so the fetus gains weight poorly.

    g.   Nicotine also raises the concentration of carbon monoxide in the bloodstreams of both mother and fetus. Carbon monoxide displaces oxygen from red blood cells, which has been shown to damage the central nervous system and slow body growth in the fetuses of laboratory animals.

    h.   Pregnant women should also avoid "passive smoking" by husbands, relatives, or co-workers, since it is also related to low birth weight, infant death, childhood respiratory illnesses, and possible long-term impairments in attention and learning.

5.   Alcohol (pp. 111–112)

    a.   **Fetal alcohol spectrum disorder (FASD)** encompasses a range of physical, mental, and behavioral outcomes caused by prenatal alcohol exposure.

        (1)   **Fetal alcohol syndrome (FAS),** the most severe diagnosis, typically occurs when the mother drinks heavily throughout pregnancy. It is distinguished by slow physical growth, facial abnormalities, and brain injury causing impairment in at least three areas of functioning.

        (2)   **Partial fetal alcohol syndrome (p-FAS)** is seen in children whose mothers drank alcohol in smaller quantities, and in some cases of paternal alcohol use. It is characterized by two of the three facial abnormalities seen in FAS, as well as brain injury.

        (3)   **Alcohol-related neurodevelopmental disorder (ARND)** results when prenatal alcohol exposure is less pervasive than in FAS. It is characterized by impairment in at least three areas of mental functioning, despite typical physical growth and absence of facial abnormalities.

    b.   The more alcohol a woman consumes during pregnancy, the poorer the child's motor coordination, speed of information processing, reasoning, and intelligence and achievement test scores during the preschool and school years.

    c.   In adolescence and early adulthood, FASD is associated with persisting deficits in motor coordination, poor school performance, trouble with the law, inappropriate sexual behavior, alcohol and drug abuse, and lasting mental health problems.

    d.   Alcohol produces its harmful effects in two ways:

        (1)   It interferes with cell duplication and migration in the primitive neural tube.

        (2)   It requires large quantities of oxygen to metabolize, which draws away oxygen that the developing organism needs for cell growth.

    e.   About 25 percent of American and Canadian mothers report drinking some alcohol during pregnancy.

        (1)   Higher rates of alcohol abuse seen in poverty-stricken women.

        (2)   The incidence of FAS is as high as 10 percent on some Native American and Canadian First Nations reservations.

        (3)   The poor judgment associated with FASD means that affected girls who later become pregnant may not understand why they should avoid alcohol, so that the cycle is repeated.

    f.   Because even mild drinking during pregnancy affects the child's head size and body growth, expectant mothers should avoid alcohol entirely.

6.   Radiation (pp. 112–113)

    a.   When mothers are exposed to radiation during pregnancy, the embryo or fetus can suffer harm, as was seen in children born to pregnant Japanese women who survived the bombing of Hiroshima and Nagasaki and to women who experienced the nuclear power plant accident in Chernobyl.

    b.   Exposure to radiation leads to a higher incidence of miscarriage and babies born with underdeveloped brains, physical deformities, and slow physical growth.

    c.   Even when a radiation-exposed baby appears normal, problems may appear later, including increased risk of childhood cancer, lower intelligence test scores, and high rates of language and emotional disorders.

    d.   Women should avoid medical X-rays as much as possible during pregnancy, and should insist on the use of an abdominal X-ray shield if X-rays are absolutely necessary during pregnancy.

7. Environmental Pollution (p. 113)
   a. In industrialized nations, an astounding number of potentially dangerous chemicals are released into the environment, with many new pollutants introduced each year.
   b. Established teratogens causing brain damage and other defects include *mercury, polychlorinated biphenyls (PCBs),* and *lead.*
8. Infectious Disease (pp. 114–115)
   a. Certain diseases, when contracted by the expectant mother during pregnancy, are major causes of miscarriage and birth defects.
   b. Viruses (p. 114)
      (1) **Rubella** (three-day or German measles) can cause a wide variety of abnormalities, especially when it occurs during the embryonic period.
      (2) The *human immunodeficiency virus (HIV),* can lead to **acquired immune deficiency syndrome (AIDS),** a disease that destroys the immune system and that has infected increasing numbers of women. When HIV-infected women become pregnant, they pass the virus to the developing organism 20 to 30 percent of the time.
      (3) The developing organism is especially sensitive to the family of herpes viruses, particularly *cytomegalovirus* and *herpes simplex 2.*
   c. Bacterial and Parasitic Diseases (p. 115)
      (1) **Toxoplasmosis** is a parasitic disease caused by eating undercooked or raw meat or from contact with the feces of infected cats.
      (2) During the first trimester, toxoplasmosis can lead to eye and brain damage as well as later learning and visual disabilities.
B. Other Maternal Factors (pp. 115–119)
   1. Exercise (pp. 115–116)
      a. In healthy, physically fit women, regular moderate exercise is related to increased birth weight, but very vigorous, extended exercise, especially late in pregnancy, results in lower birth weight than in healthy controls.
      b. Because the growing fetus places some strain on the back, abdominal, pelvic, and thigh muscles, exercises that strengthen these areas are particularly helpful.
      c. In most cases, expectant mothers who remain fit experience fewer physical discomforts late in pregnancy.
   2. Nutrition (pp. 116–117)
      a. A healthy prenatal diet, consisting of a gradual increase in calories, helps ensure the health of mother and baby.
      b. Consequences of Prenatal Malnutrition (p. 116)
         (1) Studies show a sensitive period for nutrition in the first trimester, when maternal malnutrition is more likely to result in miscarriage or physical defects.
         (2) Prenatal malnutrition can damage the central nervous system and the structure of the liver, kidneys, pancreas, and other organs, and can suppress development of the immune system, leaving babies susceptible to disease.
         (3) Prenatally malnourished babies are often irritable and unresponsive to stimulation, and may have long-lasting learning problems.
      c. Prevention and Treatment (pp. 116–117)
         (1) Many studies show that providing pregnant women with adequate food has a substantial impact on the health of their newborn babies.
         (2) Optimizing maternal nutrition through vitamin–mineral enrichment as early as possible is also crucial.
            (a) Folic acid can prevent abnormalities of the neural tube, and adequate folate during the last 10 weeks of pregnancy cuts in half the risk of premature delivery and low birth weight.
            (b) U.S. and Canadian guidelines recommend that all women of childbearing age consume 0.4 milligrams of folic acid daily, and 4 milligrams of folate beginning one month before conception.

(3) When poor nutrition continues throughout pregnancy, successful intervention after birth must not only provide nutrients but also break the cycle of strained and apathetic mother–infant interactions.

3. Emotional Stress (pp. 117–118)

   a. Intense stress during pregnancy is associated with higher rates of miscarriage, prematurity, low birth weight, newborn irritability, respiratory illness, digestive disturbances, and certain physical defects.

   b. When an expectant mother experiences fear and anxiety, blood supply to the brain, heart, and limbs increases, resulting in decreased blood supply to the uterus. Consequently, the fetus is deprived of oxygen and nutrients. Stress hormones also cross the placenta, causing a rise in fetal heart rate and activity.

   c. Stress-related prenatal complications are greatly reduced when mothers receive support from significant others to whom they can turn for emotional support.

4. Blood Incompatibility (p. 118)

   a. The most common blood incompatibility problem is **Rh factor incompatibility,** in which the Rh protein is present in the blood of the fetus but not in the mother's blood. In this case, the mother forms antibodies to the foreign Rh protein, which can return to the fetus's system, where they destroy red blood cells.

   b. The danger of Rh incompatibility increases with each additional pregnancy because it takes time for the mother to produce Rh antibodies.

   c. In most cases, the harmful effects of Rh incompatibility can be prevented through routine vaccination of Rh-negative mothers.

5. Maternal Age and Previous Births (pp. 118–119)

   a. Women who delay having children until their thirties or forties face a greater risk of infertility, miscarriage, and babies born with chromosomal defects.

   b. Women in their late thirties and early forties who have no serious health difficulties are no more likely to experience prenatal and birth problems than mothers in their twenties.

   c. Once a girl can conceive, her body is physically ready to carry and give birth to a baby, but teenagers have a higher rate of problems related to lack of access to medical care or fear of seeking care.

C. The Importance of Prenatal Health Care (pp. 119–122)

   1. Regular prenatal checkups help ensure the health of the mother and fetus by monitoring the mother's general health and weight gain, and growth of the fetus.

   2. Women with diabetes need careful monitoring because extra sugar in the mother's bloodstream can lead to pregnancy and birth problems.

   3. **Toxemia,** also called *preeclampsia,* is a complication that occurs in 5 to 10 percent of pregnant women, in which blood pressure increases sharply in the second half of pregnancy. If untreated, it can cause convulsions in the mother and death of the fetus.

   4. Inadequate prenatal care may result from lack of health insurance, from situational barriers such as lack of transportation, and personal barriers such as psychological stress, demands of taking care of other young children, family crises, ambivalence about the pregnancy, and lack of belief in the benefits of care.

   5. In countries with universally available affordable health care, maternal and infant health problems are greatly reduced.

   6. Culturally sensitive prenatal care, including *group prenatal care,* can be beneficial, especially for minority women, by providing a relaxed, informal atmosphere in which women can ask questions and learn about important health issues.

IV. PREPARING FOR PARENTHOOD (pp. 122–124)

A. Psychological preparation for childbirth has important long-term consequences for the parent–child relationship.

B. Seeking Information (p. 122)

   1. Reading books and talking to doctors about pregnancy and childbirth promote parental adjustment.

   2. Information can make a pregnant woman feel more confident about her ability to be a good mother.

189

C. The Baby Becomes a Reality (p. 123)
1. As the mother's body gradually changes, the baby becomes a current reality.
2. Fathers and siblings can share the reality of the baby by seeing the fetus through ultrasound images and by feeling the fetal movements when touching the mother's abdomen.
3. In these ways, parents get to know the fetus as an individual and may form an emotional attachment to the new being.
D. Models of Effective Parenthood (pp. 123–124)
1. Expectant parents who have had good relationships with their own parents already have positive parental models to emulate.
2. Prospective parents who had negative experiences in childhood can often rely on other examples in developing an optimistic view of themselves as parents, and may also benefit from special intervention programs to help them come to terms with these experiences.
E. The Parental Relationship (p. 124)
1. Evidence indicates that if a marriage is in danger of falling apart, pregnancy adds to rather than lessening family conflict.
2. Pregnancy changes established roles and expectations for both expectant mothers and fathers.
3. When a marriage is based on love and respect, parents are well-equipped for the challenges of pregnancy and those that will occur after the baby is born.

LECTURE ENHANCEMENTS

LECTURE ENHANCEMENT 3.1
More on the Long-Term Effects of Prenatal Alcohol Exposure (pp. 111–112)

Time: 5–10 minutes

Objective: To examine the long-term effects of prenatal alcohol exposure on cognitive ability, academic achievement, and behavior.

As noted in the text, even mild alcohol consumption during pregnancy can cause harm to the developing organism. To extend existing research on the long-term effects of prenatal alcohol exposure, Howell and colleagues (2006) recruited 265 adolescents (ages 13–17 years) from low-SES backgrounds. One hundred and twenty-eight participants were prenatally exposed to alcohol and had some physical features of fetal alcohol spectrum disorder (FASD), such as growth retardation and facial abnormalities. Fifty-three participants were prenatally exposed to alcohol but demonstrated no physical features of the disorder. To control for the effects of disability on behavior and academic achievement, an additional 84 participants were recruited from special education programs in three urban school districts.

To measure cognitive ability, participants completed a standardized IQ test. A standardized achievement test was administered to assess achievement in five subject areas—basic reading, spelling, mathematics, math reasoning, and numerical operations. Because children with FASD often demonstrate impairments in adaptive behavior, caregivers completed the Vineland Adaptive Behavior Scales, which assesses communication, daily living skills, and socialization. Finally, the researchers reviewed school records (attendance, conduct problems, report cards, special education assignment) and medical history.

Results indicated that participants who were prenatally exposed to alcohol and showed physical features of FASD had significantly lower IQ scores than the other two groups. These participants also showed significant deficits in math achievement. Interestingly, there were no significant differences in conduct problems and absenteeism between the three groups of participants. That is, all three groups had similar rates of conduct problems and school absences. In addition, all three groups scored similarly on the Vineland Adaptive Behavior Scales. Overall, these findings suggest that alcohol-affected youth (i.e., those who have physical features of FASD) have more severe impairments in overall cognitive ability and math achievement than youth who were prenatally exposed to alcohol but show no physical features of FASD and special education youth who were not prenatally exposed to alcohol.

Howell, K. K., Lynch, M. E., Platzman, K. A., Smith, G. H., & Coles, C. D. (2006). Prenatal alcohol exposure and ability, academic achievement, and school functioning in adolescence: A longitudinal follow-up. *Journal of Pediatric Psychology*, 31, 116–126.

LECTURE ENHANCEMENT 3.2
Does Exposure to Certain Teratogens During Pregnancy Increase the Risk of ADHD? (pp. 110–111)

Time: 10–15 minutes

Objective: To explore the link between prenatal exposure to teratogens and ADHD in childhood.

As discussed in the text, smoking during pregnancy is associated with low birth weight, preterm delivery, infant death, childhood asthma, and learning difficulties. But does prenatal exposure to nicotine put children at risk for attention-deficit hyperactivity disorder (ADHD)? In one study, Thapar and colleagues (2003) recruited 1,452 twins between the ages of 5 and 16 years and collected the following information: family history of ADHD, parent and teacher ratings of children's ADHD symptoms, maternal smoking during pregnancy, conduct disorder symptoms, and aspects of family adversity like poverty and single-parent households. Although family history mostly accounted for ADHD in children, smoking during pregnancy remained a significant predictor, even after controlling for conduct disorder and family factors.

In a related study, Linnet and colleagues (2003) examined the literature on the relationship between prenatal exposure to nicotine, alcohol, caffeine, and psychosocial stress and a child's developing ADHD symptoms. The review included 24 studies on nicotine, 9 on alcohol, 5 on psychosocial stress, and 1 on caffeine. Although the studies employed inconsistent methods for collecting data, research on smoking during pregnancy revealed a moderate risk for ADHD symptoms in childhood. Alcohol and caffeine were not predictive of ADHD. Results from studies on psychosocial stress were inconsistent but indicated a possible link between high levels of maternal stress during pregnancy and ADHD in children.

Taken together, these findings suggest that prenatal exposure to nicotine and to maternal stress may contribute to the development of ADHD symptoms in childhood. However, further research is needed in order to rule out other maternal lifestyle factors that might explain these associations.

Ask students to reflect on the findings of these two studies. Do they find the evidence on prenatal exposure to nicotine and stress and the development of ADHD in children to be compelling? If researchers continue to find a strong link between prenatal nicotine exposure and ADHD, should tobacco companies be forced to report these findings on warning labels? Why or why not?

Linnet, K. M., Dalsgaard, S., Obel, C., Wisborg, K., Henriksen, T. B., Rodriguez, A., Kotimaa, A., Moilanen, I., Thomsen, P. H., Olsen, J., & Javelin, M. R. (2003). Maternal lifestyle factors in pregnancy risk of attention deficit hyperactivity disorder and associated behaviors: Review of the current evidence. *American Journal of Psychiatry, 160,* 1028–1040.

Thapar, A., Fowler, T., Rice, F., Scourfield, J., van den Bree, M., Thomas, H., Harold, G., & Hay, D. (2003). Maternal smoking during pregnancy and attention deficit hyperactivity disorder symptoms in offspring. *American Journal of Psychiatry, 160,* 1985–1989.

LECTURE ENHANCEMENT 3.3
Does Posttraumatic Stress Disorder During Pregnancy Result in Low Infant Cortisol Levels? (pp. 117–118)

Time: 5–10 minutes

Objective: To examine the effects of intense anxiety during pregnancy on infant cortisol levels.

As discussed in the text, intense anxiety during pregnancy is associated with a higher rate of miscarriage, prematurity, low birth weight, infant respiratory illness, digestive disturbances, and several commonly occurring physical defects, such as cleft lip and palate. To further examine the effects of prenatal stress and anxiety on infants, Yehuda and colleagues (2005) recruited 38 pregnant women who were directly exposed to the September 11, 2001, World Trade Center collapse.

To determine probable posttraumatic stress disorder (PTSD) and severity of PTSD, participants completed a PTSD checklist. Participants also completed a depression inventory and provided demographic and medical information. When the infants were 9 months old, researchers collected salivary cortisol levels from both mothers and their infants. The primary goal of the study was to determine if maternal PTSD symptoms and cortisol levels were related to infant cortisol levels.

Results indicated that infants whose mothers experienced severe PTSD after the disaster had abnormally low cortisol levels. Moreover, cortisol levels were especially low in babies whose mothers were in their third trimester of pregnancy on September 11, 2001. This is an important finding for several reasons. First, it seems that severe stress in the third trimester of pregnancy is more damaging to infants than severe stress in the first two trimesters. Second, low cortisol levels are linked to a reduced physiological capacity to manage stress. As noted in the text, maternal emotional stress during pregnancy predicts anxiety, anger and aggression, and overactivity in school-age children.

Yehuda, R., Engel, S. M., Brand, S. R., Seckl, J., Marcus, S. M., & Berkowitz, G. S. (2005). Transgenerational effects of posttraumatic stress disorder in babies of mothers exposed to the World Trade Center Attacks during pregnancy. *The Journal of Clinical Endocrinology & Metabolism, 90,* 4115–4118.

LECTURE ENHANCEMENT 3.4
Depressive Symptoms and Stress During Pregnancy and Across the Transition to Parenthood (pp. 122–124)

Time: 10–15 minutes

Objective: To examine the course of depressive symptoms and feelings of stress for first-time parents.

The text points out that the transition to parenthood can be both an exciting and stressful time for couples. For some, this transition triggers depression and other mental health problems. To further examine the course of depressive symptoms and feelings of stress for first-time parents, Perren and colleagues (2005) recruited 74 couples and administered a standardized depression scale and stress questionnaire at five different intervals—during the second trimester of pregnancy and again when infants were 1 month, 3 months, 12 months, and 18 months of age. Because adults with a history of mental health problems are more likely to experience severe stress and depression with the transition to parenthood than adults without such a history, participants completed a self-report on the number and severity of psychiatric symptoms during pregnancy. Finally, because depressed tend to perceive their infants as more difficult and fussy than nondepressed parents, participants completed the Infant Characteristics Questionnaire (ICQ) at 3, 12, and 18 months postpartum. The ICQ measures perceptions of fussiness, difficulty, crying, and ability to be soothed.

Results indicated that both mothers and fathers experienced some symptoms of depression during pregnancy and in the first few months after birth, although women reported higher levels of depression than men. Not surprisingly, men and women who experienced a greater number and severity of psychiatric symptoms during pregnancy reported more depressive symptoms throughout the study than other participants. For women who experienced few psychiatric symptoms during pregnancy, depression scores decreased from pregnancy to 18 months postpartum. Overall, child difficulty seemed to affect fathers more than mothers, as men reported higher levels of stress when they identified their babies as difficult. This finding remained even after controlling for psychiatric symptoms and depression. Finally, mothers with psychiatric symptoms during pregnancy and fathers (with and without psychiatric symptoms) reported the highest levels of stress one year after birth.

Taken together, these findings indicate that the transition to parenthood is a stressful time for both men and women. Women tend to experience more depressive symptoms than men, while men report higher levels of stress. For men and women without a history of psychiatric symptoms, feelings of depression declined from birth to 18 months postpartum, with men continuing to report high levels of stress into the first year.

Ask students to reflect on information in this study and research presented in Lecture Enhancement 3.3. Why is social support important during pregnancy? How might social support offset some of the stress and depressive symptoms that accompany the transition to parenthood?

Perren, S., von Wyl, A., Burgin, D., Simoni, H., & von Klitzing, K. (2005). Depressive symptoms and psychosocial stress across the transition to parenthood: Associations with parental psychopathology and child difficulty. *Journal of Psychosomatic Obstetrics & Gynecology, 26,* 173–183.

LEARNING ACTIVITIES

LEARNING ACTIVITY 3.1
True or False: Prenatal Development (pp. 97–104)

As an in-class assignment or quiz, present the following activity to students:

Directions: Read each of the following statements and determine if it is *True* (T) or *False* (F).
Statements:

_____ 1. Fertilization usually takes place in the fallopian tube.
_____ 2. As many as 50 percent of zygotes do not survive the first two weeks.
_____ 3. During the period of the fetus, the most rapid prenatal changes take place.
_____ 4. At first, the nervous system develops the fastest.
_____ 5. In the second month of pregnancy, the eyes, ears, nose, jaw, and neck form.
_____ 6. The period of the fetus is the longest prenatal period.
_____ 7. Brain weight doubles from the 20th week until birth.
_____ 8. The age of viability occurs sometime between 22 and 26 weeks.
_____ 9. By 28 weeks, fetuses are awake about 30 percent of the time.
_____ 10. Higher fetal activity in the last weeks of pregnancy predict a more passive infant in the first month of life.

Answers:

1. T
2. F
3. F
4. T
5. T
6. T
7. F
8. T
9. F
10. F

LEARNING ACTIVITY 3.2
Viewing Ultrasound Pictures and Videotapes (pp. 97–104)

Ultrasound examinations have become a routine screening device during pregnancy. Students may have access to their own or others' ultrasound pictures or videotapes. Ask students to share these pictures or videotapes in class, noting the observable physical features of fetuses of different prenatal ages. Videotapes of the ultrasounds of twins and triplets are especially interesting. Ask students to describe the types of information that can be learned through ultrasound examinations. If students bring videotapes to class, have them preview the tapes so that they know when to "fast forward" to a new prenatal age or physical feature.

LEARNING ACTIVITY 3.3
Examining Genetic and Environmental Vulnerability to Teratogens (pp. 105–115)

The term *teratogen* refers to any environmental agent that causes damage during the prenatal period. However, genes influence the extent to which the developing organism is affected by teratogens. In small groups, have student generate a list of genetic and environmental factors that might contribute to a developing baby's susceptibility to the effects of teratogens. Once students have completed the activity, ask them to share some examples with the class.

LEARNING ACTIVITY 3.4
Speaking to Pregnant Women About Prenatal Environmental Influences (pp. 105–115)

Present the following scenario to students:

You have been asked by a local health department to speak to a group of newly pregnant women about prenatal environmental influences. What information would you include in your discussion? For example, what should the women know about teratogens? How about maternal disease, exercise, and nutrition? What recommendations would you give to promote a healthy pregnancy? Use research in your text to support your answers.

LEARNING ACTIVITY 3.5
Creating a Pamphlet for Expectant Fathers

Using research throughout the chapter, ask students to create a pamphlet for expectant fathers on what to expect during pregnancy and childbirth. For example, what changes can the father expect in his partner? What changes does the baby undergo during each trimester? Why are health and nutrition so important during pregnancy? What will the newborn look like? How can he support the mother during pregnancy and childbirth, and why is social support important for both mother and baby?

LEARNING ACTIVITY 3.6
Applying Ecological Systems Theory to the Transition to Parenthood (pp. 122–124)

As noted in the text, the arrival of a new baby is often exciting but stressful. A number of factors, such as social support, influence the transition to parenthood. Have students review ecological systems theory on pages 25–27 of Chapter 1. Next, ask them to describe factors at each level of the environment that may influence the transition to parenthood. Encourage students to consider bidirectional influences and third parties. Once student have completed the activity, ask them to share some examples with the class.

ASK YOURSELF . . .

REVIEW: Using research findings, explain why the common assumption that larger families make less intelligent children is incorrect. What accounts for the link between family size and mental test scores? (pp. 95–96)

The U.S. National Longitudinal Survey of Youth studied a large, representative sample of 14- to 22-year-olds and, later, their offspring in a two-generation longitudinal study that examined the relationship of sibling birth order to mental test scores. Researchers found that mental test performance did not decline with later birth order, contradicting the belief that having more children depresses children's intellectual ability. However, the study did show that the larger the family, the lower the scores of all siblings. The link can be explained by the strong trend for mothers who are low in intelligence to bear more children: Young people with lower mental test scores are more likely to drop out of school, live in poverty, and fail to engage in family planning—and, as a result of all of these factors, to have larger families.

APPLY: Rhonda and Mark are career-oriented, 35-year-old parents of an only child. They are thinking about having a second baby. What factors should they keep in mind as they decide whether to add to their family at this time in their lives? (pp. 96–97)

Older parents may be somewhat less energetic than they were at earlier ages, but they are financially better off and more mature emotionally. For these reasons, they may be better able to invest in parenting.

Nevertheless, reproductive capacity does decline with age. Fertility problems among women increase from ages 15 to 50, with a sharp rise in the mid-thirties. About 26 percent of 35- to 44-year-olds are affected. Age also affects male reproductive capacity. Amount of semen and concentration of sperm in each ejaculation gradually decline after age 30.

CONNECT: Why is it incorrect for couples who postpone childbearing until age 40 to conclude that medical advances can overcome fertility problems? (See Chapter 2, page 64.) (p. 97)

A growing number of couples choose to delay parenthood to complete educational or career goals. However, just as fertility declines with age, so does the effectiveness of reproductive technologies. For example, in vitro fertilization has a 40 percent success rate in women under age 35, but the rate drops to 7 percent in women 43 and older. Male fertility also begins to decline after age 30. Men hoping to become fathers in their forties may have lower sperm counts and, as a result, require the use of reproductive technologies like in vitro fertilization. This method increases the chance of multiple births, posing greater risks to infant survival and health than natural conception.

REFLECT: Ask one of your parents or grandparents to list their motivations for having children. How do those motivations compare with your own? What factors—for example, education or cultural changes—might account for any differences? (pp. 94–95)

This is an open-ended question with no right or wrong answer.

REVIEW: Why is the period of the embryo regarded as the most dramatic prenatal phase? Why is the period of the fetus called the "growth and finishing" phase? (p. 101)

The period of the embryo lasts from implantation through the eighth week of pregnancy. During these brief 6 weeks, the most rapid prenatal changes take place, as the groundwork is laid for all body structures and internal organs. The period of the fetus is the longest prenatal period, extending from the ninth week to the end of the pregnancy. During this period, the developing organism increases rapidly in size, and the organs, muscles, and nervous system become organized and connected.

APPLY: Amy, who is two months pregnant, wonders how the developing organism is being fed and what parts of the body have formed. "I don't look pregnant yet, so does that mean not much development has taken place?" she asks. How would you respond to Amy? (pp. 99–101)

The first trimester is the time of the most rapid prenatal changes. By the end of the second week, tiny blood vessels called villi emerge from a protective membrane called the chorion. As these villi burrow into the uterine wall, the placenta starts to develop. The placenta permits food and oxygen to reach the developing organism and waste products to be carried away. The placenta is connected to the developing organism by the umbilical cord. During the period of the embryo, from the second through the eighth week of pregnancy, the foundation is laid for all body structures and internal organs. In the second month, the eyes, ears, nose, jaw, neck, arms, legs, fingers, and toes form. Internal organs become more distinct; for example, the heart develops separate chambers. Also, the embryo responds to touch and it can move. In these first two months—often, before the mother even knows that she is pregnant—the developing organism has become a complex being.

CONNECT: How is brain development related to fetal capacities and behavior? What implications do individual differences in fetal behavior have for the baby's temperament after birth? (pp. 102–104)

Brain growth allows new behavioral capacities to emerge. The 20-week-old fetus, for example, can be stimulated as well as irritated by sound. If a doctor looks inside the uterus using fetoscopy, fetuses try to shield their eyes from the light with their hands, indicating that the sense of sight has begun to emerge.

The brain continues to make great strides during the last three months. The *cerebral cortex,* the seat of human intelligence, enlarges. As neurological organization improves, the fetus spends more time awake. At 20 weeks, the heart rate reveals no periods of alertness; by 28 weeks, fetuses are awake about 11 percent of the time, a figure that rises to 16 percent just before birth. Between 30 and 34 weeks, fetuses show rhythmic alternations between sleep and wakefulness.

By the end of pregnancy, the fetus shows the beginnings of a personality. Higher fetal activity in the last weeks of pregnancy predicts a more active infant in the first month of life. Fetal activity is also linked to infant temperament. In one study, more active fetuses in the third trimester became 1-year-olds who could better handle frustration and 2-year-olds who were less fearful.

REVIEW: Why is it difficult to determine the effects of some environmental agents, such as drugs and pollution, on the embryo and fetus? (pp. 105–106)

It is difficult to determine the effects of some environmental agents on the unborn because the harm done by teratogens is not simple and straightforward. The harm done by teratogens depends on several factors, including dose, heredity, other negative influences, and age. For example, larger doses over longer time periods usually have more negative effects. The genetic makeup of both the mother and the developing organism plays a vital role, as some individuals are more resistant to harmful environments. Also, the presence of other negative influences, such as poor nutrition, lack of prenatal care, and additional teratogens, can worsen the negative effects of a single harmful agent, and often, the compounding effects of several teratogens cannot be separated from one another. Moreover, the effects of harmful agents vary by the age of the organism at the time of exposure, so determining effects of specific agents is complicated and must take sensitive periods into account. Finally, the effects of teratogens go beyond immediate physical damage. Long-term effects, including psychological consequences, that are not readily apparent, may show up later in development or as indirect effects of physical damage.

APPLY: Nora, pregnant for the first time, has heard about the teratogenic impact of alcohol and tobacco. But she still believes that a few cigarettes and a glass of wine a day won't be harmful. Provide Nora with research-based reasons for not smoking or drinking. (pp. 110–112)

Nora should be told that the harm done by teratogens is not always simple and straightforward. It depends on dose, heredity, other negative influences, such as poor nutrition and lack of prenatal care, and age of the organism at the time of exposure.

Both smoking and drinking alcohol can be harmful to the developing baby. Low birth weight, miscarriage, prematurity, impaired heart rate and breathing during sleep, infant death, and asthma and cancer later in childhood are all associated with prenatal exposure to smoking. Even when the baby of a smoking mother appears to be in good physical condition, slight behavioral abnormalities may threaten the child's development. Newborns of smoking mothers are less attentive to sounds and display more muscle tension. Some studies also report that prenatally exposed children have shorter attention spans, poorer memories, lower mental test scores, and more behavior problems in childhood and adolescence, even after many other factors have been controlled. "Passive smoking," too, can be harmful to the fetus. As with maternal smoking, exposure to smoke-filled environments is associated with low birth weight, infant death, and possible long-term impairments in attention and learning.

Prenatal maternal drinking is linked to fetal alcohol spectrum disorder (FASD), including fetal alcohol syndrome (FAS), partial fetal alcohol syndrome (p-FAS), and a less severe form, alcohol-related neurodevelopmental disorder (ARND). While varying in severity, all forms of FASD involve some physical, mental, and behavioral impairment. Because even less than one drink per day is associated with reduced head size and body growth, Nora should avoid tobacco and alcohol altogether.

CONNECT: How do teratogens illustrate the notion of epigenesis, presented in Chapter 2, that environments can affect gene expression (see pages 105–106 to review)? (p. 111)

Epigenesis refers to development resulting from ongoing, bidirectional exchanges between heredity and all levels of the environment. When positive, these exchanges promote cognitive and social development. For example, providing a baby with a healthy diet increases brain growth, which leads to new connections between nerve cells, which in turn transform gene expression. This permits new gene–environment exchanges, which further enhance brain growth and gene expression. In contrast, harmful environments, as in the case of prenatal exposure to teratogens, can dampen gene expression. Sometimes this effect is so profound that later experiences can no longer change characteristics that originally were flexible, such as intelligence and personality. As an example, a child born with fetal alcohol spectrum disorder will not catch up in physical size or in mental ability, even when provided with an enriched diet, because the harmful environment created by prenatal alcohol exposure has affected the individual's gene expression.

REFLECT: If you had to choose five environmental influences in a campaign aimed at promoting healthy prenatal development, which ones would you choose, and why? (pp. 104–121)

This is an open-ended question with no right or wrong answer.

APPLY: Muriel, who is expecting her first child, recalls her own mother as cold and distant. Muriel is worried about whether she will be effective at caring for her new baby. What factors during pregnancy are related to maternal behavior? (pp. 122–124)

How effectively individuals construct a parental identity during pregnancy has important consequences for the parent–infant relationship. Seeking information (for example, by reading books, accessing relevant websites, asking friends, or attending a prenatal class) can help an expectant mother feel more confident that she will be a good parent. And seeing an ultrasound image of the fetus can make the pregnancy more of a reality for both parents.

If their own parental relationships are mixed or negative, expectant mothers and fathers may have trouble building a healthy picture of themselves as parents. Some adults handle this problem constructively, by seeking other examples of effective parenthood. Many people come to terms with negative experiences in their own childhoods, recognize that other options are available to them as parents, and build healthier and happier relationships with their children.

REFLECT: Ask your parents and/or your grandparents to describe attitudes and experiences that fostered or interfered with their capacity to build a positive parental identity when they were expecting their first child. Do you think building a healthy picture of oneself as a parent is more challenging today than it was in your parents' or grandparents' generation? (pp. 122–124)

This is an open-ended question with no right or wrong answer.

SUGGESTED STUDENT READINGS

Curtis, G. B., & Schuler, J. (2005). *Your pregnancy for the father-to-be.* New York: Perseus Publishing. Written for a general audience, this book provides information to expectant fathers about physical changes during pregnancy, medical tests and procedures, and the importance of providing the mother with social support during pregnancy and after the baby arrives. Other topics include: costs of having a baby, child-care expenses, planning for the future, and the impact of pregnancy on a couple's relationship.

Hopkins, B., & Johnson, S. P. (Eds.). (2005). *Prenatal development of postnatal functions.* Westport, CT: Praeger. Examines the link between prenatal and postnatal development, including brain development, the effects of maternal stress, the importance of nutrition, and learning experiences before and after birth.

Miller, M. W. (2006). *Brain development: Normal processes and the effects of alcohol and nicotine.* New York: Oxford University Press. Examines the effects of alcohol and nicotine on the developing nervous system. The author explores the immediate and long-term consequences of prenatal exposure to alcohol and nicotine, including research on brain plasticity and resilience.

TRANSPARENCIES

T-24   **Advantages and Disadvantages of Parenthood Mentioned by American Couples** Table 3.1 (p. 94)

T-25   **Advantages and Disadvantages of a One-Child Family** Table 3.2 (p. 96)

T-27   **First Births to American Women of Different Ages in 1970 and 2001** Figure 3.2 (p. 97)

T-28   **Female Reproductive Organs, Showing Fertilization, Early Cell Duplication, and Implantation** Figure 3.3 (p. 98)

T-29   **Cross-Section of the Uterus, Showing Detail of the Placenta** Figure 3.4 (p. 101)

T-31   **Sensitive Periods in Prenatal Development** Figure 3.5 (p. 105)

T-32   **Relationship of Birth Weight to Breast Cancer Risk in Adulthood** Figure 3.6 (p. 106)

T-33   **Expectant Mothers in the United States with Late (after the First Trimester) or No Prenatal Care** Figure 3.8 (p. 120)

MEDIA MATERIALS

INFANTS, CHILDREN, AND ADOLESCENTS IN ACTION

Biological and Environmental Foundations, Prenatal Development, and Birth

This section of the Observation Program contains three parent interviews: (1) Steve and Tonya faced a tragedy rare among couples in their twenties. Their first child, Kristin, was born with Down syndrome. Tonya and Steve describe their reaction to Kristin's birth and how they adjusted to caring for a baby with serious disabilities and health problems. (2) Gina and Lindrey experience the birth of their second child. After having her first baby by cesarean section, Gina is determined to have a vaginal delivery with her second. Her husband, Lindrey, describes the experience as Gina progresses through labor and delivery. (3) Adena and Cooper discuss the transition to parenthood. Their son, Charlie, is 4 months old. The section concludes with newborn reflexes, which help ensure that the baby will survive and receive care and attention from adults.

DVDs AND VIDEOTAPES

Baby Love (1996, Films Media Group, 57 min.). In this intimate program, a diverse group of teen mothers—some as young as 13—speak out on a wide range of topics, including love, virginity, sex, pregnancy, birth, parenting, their families, and their babies' fathers. Their experiences, attitudes, and insights provide a glimpse of the personal side of the complex social problem of teen pregnancy. This documentary, which contains explicit language, is an indispensable resource for use in teen pregnancy prevention, intervention, and parenting programs.

Babywatching (Films Media Group, 50 min.). This program, featuring zoologist Desmond Morris and based on his best-selling book of the same name, tries to capture the neonatal experience not just by observing babies but actually through the eyes of a newborn. Focusing on infants from several different cultural and economic backgrounds, the program examines the physical condition of the newborns, infant psychology, anthropological issues, and the bonding and interaction between a newborn baby and its family.

Birth (1999, Cambridge Educational, 54 min.; not available in French-speaking Canada). This program brings together footage of many women's experiences of childbirth, along with commentary from obstetricians, midwives, psychologists, counselors, and recent mothers and fathers. Topics include sonograms, prenatal examinations, changing attitudes toward the role of pain during childbirth, postpartum depression, and various birth scenarios—in-hospital, at-home, and cesarean births. The program contains some nudity associated with childbirth.

Birth: Eight Women's Stories (1993, Films Media Group, 70 min.). This program follows eight women, ranging in age from 27 to 45, who are giving birth in a variety of circumstances, including natural births at home and in the hospital, a cesarean delivery of twins under epidural anesthesia, induced labor with vaginal delivery, and water birth in the hospital. Each of the eight stories is presented as a triumph, with no attempt to promote one method of childbirth over another. The program includes both explicit footage of childbirth and commentaries by mothers, fathers, midwives, and obstetricians.

Child Development: From Prenatal to Birth (1998, Films Media Group; CD-ROM, available for Windows only). This program, part of the Child Development Interactive CD-ROM Series, provides an overview of prenatal development from fertilization to birth. The program also explores prenatal diagnostic methods and the effect of the mother's health on the developing fetus.

Conception to Birth (Discovery Channel, 50 min.). This program, focusing on one young couple and their child-to-be, follows the journey of human life from the moment of conception to the moment of birth. With its dramatic visual examples of what is happening in the womb, starting with the division of cells in the first few hours of pregnancy, this DVD has been described by viewers as "amazing" and "incredible."

Conception to Neonate: Birth and the Newborn (1992, Concept Media, 27 min.). This program contrasts today's typical birth experiences with those of a generation ago. It describes family-sensitive birth practices and looks at the initial interaction between parents and newborns. The program includes a discussion of the physical care of the newborn immediately after birth and a review of the newborn's innate reflexes and some other common characteristics of neonates.

Conception to Neonate: Pregnancy (1991, Concept Media, 26 min.). This program follows a couple from conception to birth, describing their emotional and psychological reactions as well as the physical changes in both the mother and the fetus.

Conception to Neonate: Reducing Risk Factors (1991, Concept Media, 34 min.). This program focuses on environmental factors that can contribute to low birth weight and birth defects. It presents several approaches to prevention—making lifestyle changes, seeking early prenatal care, avoiding harmful substances, and seeking information about personal risks.

David with Fetal Alcohol Syndrome (1996, Films Media Group, 45 min.). This program is an in-depth profile of David Vandenbrink, a 21-year-old man who suffers from fetal alcohol syndrome (FAS), a condition that went undiagnosed for the first 18 years of his life. Through the words and experiences of David and his adoptive family, viewers are given an intimate look at what it is like to grow up with the effects of FAS.

Fetal Abuse: The Effects of Drugs and Alcohol (1997, Films Media Group, 18 min.). This program illustrates the severe physical, mental, and behavioral problems that may occur in children born to substance-abusing mothers. Mothers who drink alcohol during pregnancy may give birth to children with fetal alcohol syndrome, while those who use drugs during pregnancy may have babies who are addicted at birth. Longer-term issues of prenatal substance abuse include learning disabilities and delayed motor, speech, and language development. The program presents a clear message—that women should avoid using drugs and alcohol both before and during pregnancy.

Fetal Alcohol Exposure: Changing the Future (2006, Films for the Humanities & Sciences, 31 min.). This program looks at the prenatal effects of maternal drinking and the primary and secondary disabilities—including neurological, cognitive, and behavioral characteristics—associated with fetal alcohol spectrum disorders (FASD). It draws on the firsthand experiences of several experts: Ann Streissguth, director of the University of Washington's Fetal Alcohol and Drug Unit; Kathy Mitchell, vice president of NOFAS; Erica Lara, who works at a residential drug and alcohol treatment facility for women with young children; and Erica Gitis-Miles, a college student with FASD.

Fetal Alcohol Syndrome and Other Drug Use During Pregnancy (1992, Films Media Group, 19 min.). This program focuses on Native American populations, profiling an 8-year-old Apache boy who was born with FAS. It shows how alcohol consumed by the mother crosses the placenta into the fetal bloodstream and describes common birth defects associated with the disorder. The program also looks at babies born to cocaine-addicted mothers.

In the Womb (2005, National Geographic, 100 min.). Making use of revolutionary 3D and 4D ultrasound imagery, this program opens a window into the delicate, dark world of the fetus, exploring each trimester of pregnancy in astonishing detail—including a view of a fetoscope operation performed in utero to correct life-threatening complications before birth.

The Newborn: Development and Discovery (2005, 1996, Magna Systems, 29 min.). This program presents the most current thinking about newborn infants and their developmental needs. The updated version of this module covers new research on brain development, including reaction time and pain sensitivity, and new methods of assessing the newborn, including the revised Brazelton Neonatal Assessment Scale. There is also information on reflexes, bonding, and development of cognitive and emotional skills, as well as updated information on treatment of premature and other low-birth-weight newborns.

NOVA: Life's Greatest Miracle (2001, PBS Home Video, 52 min.). This completely updated version of Lennart Nilsson's world-famous *Miracle of Life* video uses the latest technological advances in microscopy and medical imaging to chronicle the inside-the-womb story of the growth of a baby from embryo to newborn.

Pediatric AIDS (1997, Films Media Group, 21 min.). In this program, which focuses on the estimated 800,000 children worldwide who are infected with HIV, Dr. Philip Pizzo of Children's Hospital, Boston, describes how children contract HIV from their mothers and what can be done to block prenatal infection. The program looks at various preventive measures, including administration of the anti-retroviral drug AZT during pregnancy and the use of intravenous medications during delivery. A nurse at a children's AIDS hospice is seen demonstrating treatments to alleviate the symptoms of the disease.

Pregnancy and Substance Abuse (1990, Films Media Group, 28 min.). This program looks at pregnancy in relation to the sensitive-period concept. It includes footage of several couples as they go through pregnancy and receive prenatal care. Former U.S. Surgeon General C. Everett Koop talks about the risks of smoking during pregnancy. Michael Dorris, author of *The Broken Cord,* talks about his experiences raising an adopted son with fetal alcohol syndrome.

Prenatal Development (2001, Films Media Group, 21 min.). This video looks at the nine months of prenatal development, from conception to the birth of a healthy baby. It provides information on the major physical milestones that occur during pregnancy, with an emphasis on the importance of the expectant mother's health, nutrition, and care, and on the proper development of the baby.

The Right Way to Be Pregnant (1995, Films Media Group, 19 min.). This program focuses on a young pregnant woman to illustrate how women can improve their chances of a healthy pregnancy and a healthy baby. An obstetrician and a nurse provide up-to-date information for women who are contemplating pregnancy, with an emphasis on the need for a pre-conception physical, the dangers of smoking or drinking during pregnancy, and the importance of good medical care, a healthy diet, and regular exercise. Addressing the issues associated with high-risk and problem pregnancies, the program emphasizes the importance of getting prenatal care and of following the individual guidelines set by medical personnel.

Unborn Addicts (1994, Films Media Group, 47 min.). This program presents case studies of two pregnant women, both lifelong addicts, who have entered methadone programs. The women are followed throughout pregnancy and delivery. One newborn is drug-free, but the other is given opium to relieve the intense symptoms of drug withdrawal after birth. Scenes of infant drug withdrawal may be disturbing to some viewers. *Unborn Addicts* is recommended by *MC Journal: The Journal of Academic Media Librarianship.*

TEST BANK

MULTIPLE CHOICE

1) Today, _____ percent of North American married couples bear children.
   A) 60
   B) 70
   C) 80
   D) 90
   Answer: B
   Page Ref: 94
   Skill: Factual
   Objective: 3.1

2) According to a conservative estimate, today's new parents will spend about _____ in the United States and _____ in Canada rear a child from birth through age 18.
   A) $75,000; $100,000
   B) $200,000; $100,000
   C) $190,000; $170,000
   D) $500,000; $400,000
   Answer: C
   Page Ref: 95
   Skill: Factual
   Objective: 3.1

3) In 1960, the average number of children per North American couple was _____. Today it is between _____ in the United States and Canada.
   A) 5.5; 2.5 and 2.7
   B) 3.1; 1.6 and 1.8
   C) 5.5; 1.8 and 2
   D) 3.1; 2.5 and 3
   Answer: B
   Page Ref: 95
   Skill: Factual
   Objective: 3.2

4) A major reason for the declining family size in the United States is
   A) increases in infertility.
   B) the increasing divorce rate.
   C) increases in the financial burden of children.
   D) the increasing number of women in the work force.
   Answer: D
   Page Ref: 95
   Skill: Conceptual
   Objective: 3.2

5) Children who grow up in smaller families _____ than children who grow up in larger families.
   A) do worse in school
   B) have higher mental test scores
   C) attain lower levels of education
   D) are less socially competent
   Answer: B
   Page Ref: 96
   Skill: Conceptual
   Objective: 3.2

6) Which of the following is supported by research on family size?
    A) Children in larger families tend to do better in school than children in smaller families.
    B) Small families are usually less well off economically than larger families.
    C) Parents with lower intelligence test scores tend to have larger families than parents with higher scores.
    D) Parents who have many children tend to be more patient and less punitive than those who have few children.

Answer: C
Page Ref: 96
Skill: Conceptual
Objective: 3.2

7) The unfavorable outcomes associated with large family size are eliminated when
    A) siblings are spaced widely apart.
    B) children are placed in early, high-quality child care.
    C) a third party, such as a grandparent, lives with the family.
    D) children are raised by bright, economically advantaged parents.

Answer: D
Page Ref: 96
Skill: Conceptual
Objective: 3.2

8) Research on only children demonstrates that they _____ children with siblings.
    A) are more spoiled and selfish than
    B) perform more poorly on mental tests than
    C) are more economically disadvantaged than
    D) are as well-adjusted as

Answer: D
Page Ref: 96
Skill: Conceptual
Objective: 3.2

9) Research on childbearing reveals that
    A) first births to women in their thirties have increased greatly over the past quarter century.
    B) fertility problems among women do not show any increase until age 40.
    C) reproductive technologies are equally successful among younger and older parents.
    D) a 45-year-old man is as fertile as a 25-year-old man.

Answer: A
Page Ref: 96–97
Skill: Conceptual
Objective: 3.2

10) In men, the amount of semen and concentration of sperm in each ejaculation begins to decline after age
    _____.
    A) 18
    B) 25
    C) 30
    D) 35

Answer: C
Page Ref: 97
Skill: Factual
Objective: 3.3

11) The corpus luteum
    A) is where fertilization usually takes place.
    B) secretes hormones that prepare the lining of the uterus to receive a fertilized egg.
    C) is a thin, long structure that leads to the uterus.
    D) is where implantation occurs.
    Answer: B
    Page Ref: 98
    Skill: Factual
    Objective: 3.3

12) Fertilization usually takes place in the
    A) fallopian tube.
    B) uterus.
    C) cervix.
    D) vaginal canal.
    Answer: A
    Page Ref: 98
    Skill: Factual
    Objective: 3.3

13) The male produces an average of _____ sperm a day, yet only _____ reach the ovum.
    A) 1 million; 5 or fewer
    B) 300 million; 300 to 500
    C) 300 to 500; 3
    D) 1 billion; 1 million
    Answer: B
    Page Ref: 98
    Skill: Factual
    Objective: 3.3

14) The period of the zygote lasts about _____, beginning with _____.
    A) 3 months; fertilization
    B) 2 weeks; implantation
    C) 3 months; implantation
    D) 2 weeks; fertilization
    Answer: D
    Page Ref: 99
    Skill: Conceptual
    Objective: 3.3

15) Inside the blastocyst, the _____ will become the new organism and the _____ will become the structures that provide nourishment and protective covering.
    A) amnion; chorion
    B) chorion; amnion
    C) embryonic disk; trophoblast
    D) trophoblast; embryonic disk
    Answer: C
    Page Ref: 99
    Skill: Factual
    Objective: 3.3

16) _____ occurs seven to nine days after _____.
    A) The period of the fetus; implantation
    B) Fertilization; implantation
    C) Implantation; fertilization
    D) The period of the embryo; fertilization
Answer: C
Page Ref: 99
Skill: Conceptual
Objective: 3.3

17) Amniotic fluid
    A) helps keep the temperature of the prenatal world constant.
    B) produces blood cells until the developing liver, spleen, and bone marrow are mature enough to take over this function.
    C) provides nourishment to the prenatal organism.
    D) separates the mother's bloodstream from the embryo or fetal bloodstream.
Answer: A
Page Ref: 99
Skill: Conceptual
Objective: 3.3

18) During the period of the zygote, villi emerge from the _____ that burrow into the uterine wall.
    A) trophoblast
    B) chorion
    C) placenta
    D) amnion
Answer: B
Page Ref: 99
Skill: Factual
Objective: 3.3

19) The placenta
    A) permits food and oxygen to reach the developing organism and waste products to be carried away.
    B) provides a cushion against any jolts caused by the mother's movements.
    C) produces blood cells until the developing liver, spleen, and bone marrow are mature enough to take over this function.
    D) encloses the blastocyst in amniotic fluid.
Answer: A
Page Ref: 99
Skill: Factual
Objective: 3.3

20) The umbilical cord
    A) permits the blood of the mother and the embryo to mix directly.
    B) seldom tangles because it is firm like a garden hose.
    C) contains one large artery that delivers nutrients to the embryo.
    D) grows to a length of 6 inches to 1 foot during the course of pregnancy.
Answer: B
Page Ref: 100
Skill: Factual
Objective: 3.3

21) The period of the embryo lasts from
    A) fertilization to implantation.
    B) implantation through the eighth week of pregnancy.
    C) weeks two through twelve of pregnancy.
    D) the eight week of pregnancy through birth.
Answer: B
Page Ref: 101
Skill: Factual
Objective: 3.3

22) During the period of the embryo, the ectoderm will become the
    A) digestive system, lungs, and urinary tract.
    B) brain and central nervous system.
    C) muscles and the skeleton.
    D) nervous system and the skin.
Answer: D
Page Ref: 101
Skill: Conceptual
Objective: 3.3

23) At _____, the top of the _____ swells to form a brain.
    A) 3 1/2 weeks; neural tube
    B) 2 1/2 months; embryonic disk
    C) 3 1/2 weeks; embryonic disk
    D) 2 1/2 months; neural tube
Answer: A
Page Ref: 101
Skill: Factual
Objective: 3.3

24) At the beginning of the period of the embryo, the _____ system develops fastest.
    A) nervous
    B) circulatory
    C) endocrine
    D) skeletal
Answer: A
Page Ref: 101
Skill: Conceptual
Objective: 3.3

25) The heart begins to pump blood during the _____ month of pregnancy.
    A) first
    B) second
    C) third
    D) fourth
Answer: A
Page Ref: 101
Skill: Factual
Objective: 3.3

26) During the second month of pregnancy, the embryo
   A) reacts to light.
   B) kicks and bends its arms.
   C) is stimulated by sounds.
   D) responds to touch.
Answer: D
Page Ref: 101
Skill: Conceptual
Objective: 3.3

27) The most rapid prenatal changes take place during the period of the _____, whereas the developing organism increases rapidly in size during the period of the _____.
   A) zygote; fetus
   B) fetus; embryo
   C) embryo; fetus
   D) zygote; embryo
Answer: C
Page Ref: 101, 102
Skill: Conceptual
Objective: 3.3

28) During the third month of pregnancy,
   A) the fetus can suck its thumb.
   B) the heart begins to pump blood.
   C) neuron production begins.
   D) the eyes, ears, and nose form.
Answer: A
Page Ref: 102
Skill: Conceptual
Objective: 3.3

29) Iris wonders when she will first be able to hear her baby's heartbeat with a stethoscope. You tell her that she should be able to hear it as early as the _____ month of pregnancy.
   A) third
   B) fourth
   C) fifth
   D) sixth
Answer: A
Page Ref: 102
Skill: Applied
Objective: 3.3

30) Radsheda wonders when she will first be able to feel her baby's movements. You tell her that this should happen by the
   A) end of the first trimester.
   B) middle of the second trimester.
   C) end of the second trimester.
   D) beginning of the third trimester.
Answer: B
Page Ref: 102
Skill: Applied
Objective: 3.3

31) By the middle of the second trimester,
    A) a fetus born early has a chance for survival.
    B) vernix and lanugo cover the fetus's skin.
    C) most of the brain's neurons are in place.
    D) glial cell production is nearly complete.
Answer: B
Page Ref: 102
Skill: Conceptual
Objective: 3.3

32) At the end of the second trimester, nearly all of the brain's _____ are in place. However, the brain's _____ continue to increase at a rapid rate throughout pregnancy and after birth.
    A) glial cells; neurons
    B) neural tubes; neurons
    C) neurons; glial cells
    D) neurons; neural tubes
Answer: C
Page Ref: 102
Skill: Conceptual
Objective: 3.3

33) Melissa is 20 weeks pregnant and her obstetrician is about to perform a fetoscopy. How will the fetus MOST likely react?
    A) The fetus will try to open its mouth.
    B) The fetus will feel pain if it is not given painkillers.
    C) The fetus will react with body movements to the sound.
    D) The fetus will try to shield its eyes with the hands.
Answer: D
Page Ref: 102
Skill: Applied
Objective: 3.3

34) The age of viability occurs sometime between
    A) 19 and 23 weeks.
    B) 22 and 26 weeks.
    C) 25 and 29 weeks.
    D) 28 and 32 weeks.
Answer: B
Page Ref: 102
Skill: Factual
Objective: 3.3

35) During the last three months of pregnancy,
    A) the neural tube swells to form the brain.
    B) glial cell production is nearly complete.
    C) neurons begin to form and travel to their permanent locations in the brain.
    D) convolutions and groves in the surface of the cerebral cortex appear.
Answer: D
Page Ref: 103
Skill: Conceptual
Objective: 3.3

36) At 28, but not 20, weeks, fetuses
    A) are awake about 11 percent of the time.
    B) respond to light.
    C) can form a fist and curl their toes.
    D) react to sound.
Answer: A
Page Ref: 103
Skill: Conceptual
Objective: 3.3

37) Between 30 and 34 weeks, fetuses
    A) develop a layer of fat that assists with temperature regulation.
    B) show rhythmic alternations between sleep and wakefulness.
    C) show no periods of alertness.
    D) have no chance of survival if born early.
Answer: B
Page Ref: 103
Skill: Conceptual
Objective: 3.3

38) In one study, more active fetuses during the third trimester became 1-year-olds who
    A) were more fearful.
    B) were more fussy and difficult.
    C) had irregular eating schedules.
    D) could better handle frustration.
Answer: D
Page Ref: 103
Skill: Conceptual
Objective: 3.3

39) During the third trimester,
    A) taste and odor preferences are acquired from bathing in and swallowing amniotic fluid.
    B) painkillers need not be used during surgical procedures because the fetus cannot yet feel pain.
    C) fetuses can hear bodily noises but not noises that occur outside of the womb.
    D) higher fetal activity is linked with abnormal neurological development.
Answer: A
Page Ref: 103
Skill: Conceptual
Objective: 3.3

40) During the last 6 weeks of pregnancy,
    A) reading aloud and playing classical music has long-term positive effects on cognitive development.
    B) the sound quality is not good enough for the fetus to distinguish different voices.
    C) fetuses show no evidence that they can hear noises that occur outside of the womb.
    D) fetuses show systematic heart rate changes in response to their mother's voice versus a stranger's voice.
Answer: D
Page Ref: 103
Skill: Conceptual
Objective: 3.3

41) In the final month of pregnancy,
   A) most fetuses show an increase in physical activity.
   B) the fetus's immune system is fully functioning.
   C) most fetuses assume an upright position.
   D) a layer of fat is added to the fetus to assist with temperature regulation.
Answer: D
Page Ref: 104
Skill: Conceptual
Objective: 3.3

42) A baby born early in the eight month of pregnancy would be especially susceptible to infection because the
   A) brain's respiratory center is not yet mature.
   B) fetus begins to receive disease-fighting antibodies from the mother's blood in the eight month.
   C) brain is not sufficiently developed until the end of the ninth month to assist with digestion of food.
   D) air sacs of the lungs are not sufficiently mature to exchange carbon dioxide for oxygen until the end of the ninth month.
Answer: B
Page Ref: 104
Skill: Conceptual
Objective: 3.3

43) Of the following, which has the longest sensitive period to teratogens during pregnancy?
   A) the heart
   B) the central nervous system
   C) the eyes
   D) the ears
Answer: B
Page Ref: 105–106
Skill: Conceptual
Objective: 3.4

44) During the first two weeks of pregnancy, teratogens
   A) cause the most serious damage to the developing organism.
   B) usually affect the growth of sensory organs, such as the eyes and ears.
   C) rarely have any impact on the developing organism.
   D) typically result in malformations of internal organs, such as the brain and heart.
Answer: C
Page Ref: 106
Skill: Factual
Objective: 3.4

45) The period of the _____ is the time when serious defects from teratogens are most likely to occur because _____ this time.
   A) fetus; birth takes place soon after
   B) zygote; implantation occurs during
   C) fetus; the prenatal organism is developing most rapidly during
   D) embryo; the foundations for all body parts are laid down during
Answer: D
Page Ref: 106
Skill: Conceptual
Objective: 3.4

46) During the fetal period,
    A) teratogenic damage is usually minor.
    B) structures such as the ears, eyes, and teeth are protected from the damaging effects of teratogens.
    C) serious defects due to teratogens are most likely to occur.
    D) teratogenic damage usually causes miscarriage.
Answer: A
Page Ref: 106
Skill: Conceptual
Objective: 3.4

47) Thalidomide, a sedative prescribed to pregnant mothers in the 1960s, often produced
    A) serious behavioral disorders.
    B) cancer of the reproductive organs.
    C) gross limb defects.
    D) growth retardation.
Answer: C
Page Ref: 107
Skill: Conceptual
Objective: 3.5

48) Men and women whose mothers _____ during pregnancy have an increased risk of cancer of the genitals.
    A) were prescribed DES
    B) regularly smoked cigarettes
    C) drank alcohol heavily
    D) took aspirin
Answer: A
Page Ref: 108
Skill: Conceptual
Objective: 3.5

49) Heavy _____ intake is associated with newborn withdrawal symptoms, such as irritability and vomiting.
    A) aspirin
    B) tobacco
    C) alcohol
    D) caffeine
Answer: D
Page Ref: 108
Skill: Conceptual
Objective: 3.5

50) Most babies born to mothers who used cocaine regularly during pregnancy
    A) are born drug addicted.
    B) survive only a few days.
    C) are extremely placid and calm.
    D) have abnormally low pitched and dull cries.
Answer: A
Page Ref: 108
Skill: Conceptual
Objective: 3.5

51) Following a high dose of cocaine during pregnancy,
    A) the embryonic or fetal heart rate slows down to a dangerously low level.
    B) the concentration of carbon dioxide is raised to unsafe levels in the bloodstream of the developing organism.
    C) oxygen delivered to the developing organism falls for 15 minutes.
    D) the placenta slows down production of nutrients needed to sustain the developing organism.
    Answer: C
    Page Ref: 108, 110
    Skill: Conceptual
    Objective: 3.5

52) Of the following, which is supported by research on prenatal cocaine exposure?
    A) Some studies reveal no major negative effects of prenatal cocaine exposure.
    B) Infants born to mothers who used cocaine during their pregnancies are often very calm and sleepy.
    C) Most studies reveal that the negative effects of prenatal cocaine exposure disappear by the preschool years.
    D) The effects of prenatal cocaine exposure are usually so extreme that they are not affected by quality of caregiving.
    Answer: A
    Page Ref: 110
    Skill: Conceptual
    Objective: 3.5

53) A recent estimate indicates that about _____ percent of American women and _____ percent of Canadian women smoke during their pregnancies.
    A) 2; 6
    B) 20; 5
    C) 12; 17
    D) 35; 15
    Answer: C
    Page Ref: 110
    Skill: Factual
    Objective: 3.5

54) Complications due to cigarette smoking by pregnant women include
    A) infants born addicted to nicotine.
    B) deformed facial features.
    C) low birth weight, infant death, and childhood cancer.
    D) delayed language development and poor fine motor skills.
    Answer: C
    Page Ref: 110
    Skill: Factual
    Objective: 3.5

55) The likelihood of negative effects due to smoking during pregnancy are
    A) reduced immediately if the mother decides to stop smoking.
    B) reduced only if the mother stops before the period of the embryo.
    C) not reduced unless the mother stops before the placenta begins carrying food and oxygen to the prenatal organism.
    D) not reduced if the mother stops smoking, because the damage has likely already been done.
    Answer: A
    Page Ref: 110
    Skill: Factual
    Objective: 3.5

56) Research on the effects of smoking demonstrates that
   A) a woman whose husband smoked during her pregnancy is no more likely to have a low-birth-weight baby than a woman whose husband did not smoke.
   B) if a pregnant mother waits until the third trimester to stop smoking, she does not reduce the likelihood of negative effects of nicotine.
   C) an infant whose mother smoked a pack of cigarettes a day during pregnancy is no more likely to show negative effects from smoking than is an infant whose mother smoked a pack a week.
   D) passive smoking is related to low birth weight, infant death, and childhood respiratory illnesses.
   Answer: D
   Page Ref: 111
   Skill: Conceptual
   Objective: 3.5

57) _____ is/are typical of children born with fetal alcohol syndrome (FAS).
   A) Paternal alcohol use
   B) Large eyelid openings and a thick upper lip
   C) Typical physical growth
   D) Brain injury
   Answer: D
   Page Ref: 111
   Skill: Conceptual
   Objective: 3.5

58) Of the following, which is supported by research on alcohol use during pregnancy?
   A) When provided with enriched diets, FAS babies catch up in physical size during infancy and childhood.
   B) The defects of children born with FASD vary as a function of the length and timing of their mother's drinking during pregnancy.
   C) Mental impairment in children whose mothers drank heavily during pregnancy is usually not permanent.
   D) Mild drinking is not associated with lasting negative effects.
   Answer: B
   Page Ref: 111
   Skill: Conceptual
   Objective: 3.5

59) Alcohol use during pregnancy adversely affects the prenatal organism by
   A) causing the placenta to grow abnormally and interfering with brain development.
   B) interfering with brain development and drawing away oxygen that the developing organism needs to metabolize the alcohol.
   C) causing the placenta to grow abnormally and raising the concentration of carbon monoxide in the bloodstream.
   D) raising the concentration of carbon monoxide in the bloodstream and drawing away oxygen that the developing organism needs to metabolize the alcohol.
   Answer: B
   Page Ref: 112
   Skill: Conceptual
   Objective: 3.5

60) On some Native American and Canadian First Nation reservations, the incidence of FAS is as high as _____ percent.
   A) 10
   B) 5
   C) 3
   D) 1
Answer: A
Page Ref: 112
Skill: Factual
Objective: 3.5

61) Studies on radiation exposure during pregnancy reveal that
   A) an abdominal X-ray shield does not provide protection against the damaging effects of dental X-rays.
   B) the prenatally exposed Chernobyl children had normal brain wave activity by childhood.
   C) exposure to low-level radiation, such as medical X-rays, does not produce negative effects.
   D) stressful rearing conditions can worsen the damaging effects of prenatal radiation.
Answer: D
Page Ref: 113
Skill: Conceptual
Objective: 3.5

62) Pregnant women are advised to avoid _____ to reduce the likelihood of mercury exposure.
   A) changing cat litter boxes
   B) exposure to paint flaking off the walls of old buildings
   C) inhaling car exhaust
   D) long-lived predatory fish, such as swordfish, albacore tuna, and shark.
Answer: D
Page Ref: 113
Skill: Conceptual
Objective: 3.5

63) Wanda, who is pregnant, lives in an old apartment building where multiple layers of paint are flaking off the walls. To protect her baby, Wanda should have the paint tested for
   A) polychlorinated biphenyls (PCBs).
   B) mercury.
   C) phosphorus.
   D) lead.
Answer: D
Page Ref: 113
Skill: Applied
Objective: 3.5

64) The greatest damage to the developing organism occurs when rubella strikes the mother
   A) during the period of the zygote.
   B) before implantation.
   C) during the embryonic period.
   D) during the second trimester.
Answer: C
Page Ref: 114
Skill: Factual
Objective: 3.5

65) Research on HIV/AIDS reveals that
  A) about half of all new HIV infections occur in developing countries.
  B) the incidence of AIDS is increasing in industrialized nations.
  C) in South Africa, one-fourth of all pregnant women are HIV-positive.
  D) women account for about half of all AIDS cases in North America and Western Europe.
Answer: C
Page Ref: 114
Skill: Conceptual
Objective: 3.5

66) Of the following, which is supported by research on prenatal HIV/AIDS transmission?
  A) HIV-positive pregnant women invariably pass the virus to their baby.
  B) HIV-positive babies usually do not show symptoms of AIDS until 5 to 8 months.
  C) Zidovudine (ZDV) reduces prenatal AIDS transmission by as much as 95 percent.
  D) Most prenatal HIV babies survive for many years after AIDS symptoms appear.
Answer: C
Page Ref: 114
Skill: Conceptual
Objective: 3.5

67) _____ is the most frequent prenatal infection.
  A) Rubella
  B) Toxoplasmosis
  C) Cytomegalovirus
  D) Herpes simplex 2
Answer: C
Page Ref: 114
Skill: Factual
Objective: 3.5

68) To avoid _____, Rini's obstetrician advises her to make sure that the meat she eats is well-cooked and to have other family members change the cat's litter box.
  A) rubella
  B) cytomegalovirus
  C) polychlorinated biphenyls
  D) toxoplasmosis
Answer: D
Page Ref: 115
Skill: Applied
Objective: 3.5

69) Research on exercise during pregnancy shows that
  A) most women engage in sufficient moderate exercise during pregnancy to promote their own and their baby's health.
  B) an expectant mother who remains fit experiences fewer physical discomforts in the final weeks.
  C) frequent, vigorous exercise is associated with positive birth outcomes.
  D) pregnant women should not exercise late in pregnancy.
Answer: B
Page Ref: 116
Skill: Conceptual
Objective: 3.6

70) Jija is pregnant with her first child and wonders how much weight she should gain to ensure a healthy outcome. You should recommend that _____ pounds is a sensible and safe amount of weight to gain.
   A) 15 to 20
   B) 25 to 30
   C) 35 to 40
   D) 45 to 50
Answer: B
Page Ref: 116
Skill: Applied
Objective: 3.6

71) Research on prenatal malnutrition indicates that
   A) poor nutrition suppresses the development of the immune system.
   B) malnutrition during the first trimester is associated with central nervous system damage.
   C) the sensitive-period concept does not operate with nutrition.
   D) malnutrition during the third trimester is associated with physical defects.
Answer: A
Page Ref: 116
Skill: Conceptual
Objective: 3.6

72) _____ supplementation can prevent abnormalities of the neural tube, such as anencephaly and spina bifida.
   A) Vitamin B6
   B) Iron
   C) Potassium
   D) Folic acid
Answer: D
Page Ref: 116–117
Skill: Factual
Objective: 3.6

73) Taking vitamin C and iron beginning early in pregnancy
   A) promotes growth of the placenta and adequate birth weight.
   B) helps prevent neural tube defects.
   C) reduces the risk of cretinism, a common cause of mental retardation.
   D) helps prevent maternal high blood pressure.
Answer: A
Page Ref: 117
Skill: Factual
Objective: 3.6

74) Intense prenatal anxiety is related to
   A) Down syndrome.
   B) sickle cell disease.
   C) cleft lip and palate.
   D) neural tube defects.
Answer: C
Page Ref: 117
Skill: Conceptual
Objective: 3.6

75) Babies whose mothers were directly exposed to the September 11, 2001, World Trade Center collapse during their pregnancies had abnormally
   A) low cortisol levels if their mothers had reacted to the disaster with severe anxiety.
   B) high cortisol levels if their mothers had reacted to the disaster with severe anxiety.
   C) low cortisol levels regardless of their mother's reaction to the disaster.
   D) high cortisol levels regardless of their mother's reaction to the disaster.
   Answer: A
   Page Ref: 118
   Skill: Conceptual
   Objective: 3.6

76) Of the following, which is true when the mother is Rh-negative and her fetus is Rh-positive?
   A) The damage caused by Rh incompatibility can be avoided if the mother is given several blood transfusions containing the Rh protein during the last trimester of pregnancy.
   B) First-born children are rarely affected by Rh incompatibility.
   C) Rh-positive babies are routinely given a vaccine at birth to prevent the buildup of harmful Rh antibodies.
   D) The harmful effects of Rh incompatibility can be prevented if the newborn is immediately placed on a diet low in phenylalanine.
   Answer: B
   Page Ref: 118
   Skill: Conceptual
   Objective: 3.6

77) Danica is a healthy 35-year-old woman who is pregnant with her first child. Based on the text, you can tell her that
   A) her baby is more likely than a younger woman's baby to be low birth weight.
   B) she is likely to have a longer and more difficult labor than a younger woman.
   C) she is more likely to have prenatal complications than a woman in her twenties.
   D) she is more likely than a younger woman to have a baby born with a chromosomal defect.
   Answer: D
   Page Ref: 118
   Skill: Applied
   Objective: 3.6

78) Teenage mothers are at greater risk than older mothers for prenatal complications because
   A) their reproductive organs are not yet mature enough to support a pregnancy.
   B) their uterus is not developed enough to maintain a pregnancy for the full 38 to 40 weeks.
   C) many pregnant teenagers do not receive adequate prenatal care.
   D) their egg cells, or ovum, are not yet mature enough to successfully conceive.
   Answer: C
   Page Ref: 119
   Skill: Conceptual
   Objective: 3.6

79) Toxemia during pregnancy is caused by
   A) the mother's contact with the feces of infected cats.
   B) extra sugar in the mother's bloodstream.
   C) Rh incompatibility between the blood type of the mother and fetus.
   D) a sharp increase in the mother's blood pressure.
   Answer: D
   Page Ref: 119
   Skill: Factual
   Objective: 3.7

80) Infants who receive inadequate prenatal care are five times more likely to _____ than babies whose mothers receive early medical attention.
   A) be born overweight
   B) die
   C) be born at home
   D) have chromosomal abnormalities
   Answer: B
   Page Ref: 119
   Skill: Conceptual
   Objective: 3.7

81) Of the following, which is supported by research on prenatal care?
   A) Over 90 percent of pregnant women in the United States receive prenatal care during their first trimester.
   B) Lack of health insurance is one common reason why low-income pregnant women do not seek early prenatal care.
   C) Most pregnant women do not need to arrange prenatal care until the second trimester.
   D) Most women who engage in high-risk behaviors, such as smoking and drug abuse, seek out early prenatal care.
   Answer: B
   Page Ref: 119
   Skill: Conceptual
   Objective: 3.7

82) A study of more than 100 first-time expectant married couples revealed that
   A) about one-third reported a negative reaction to learning that they were expecting.
   B) no participants felt negatively by the third trimester.
   C) as the pregnancy moved along, negative reactions increased.
   D) over 90 percent of the couples reported a positive reaction to learning that they were expecting.
   Answer: B
   Page Ref: 122
   Skill: Conceptual
   Objective: 3.8

83) Studies on parenting show that
   A) when men and women have had good relationships with their own parents, they are more likely to be effective parents during infancy and early childhood.
   B) mothers' and fathers' attachment to their fetus was not associated with their later relationship with their baby.
   C) mothers and fathers who have had negative relationships with their own parents usually are unsuccessful at building happier and healthier relationships with their own children.
   D) mothers' and fathers' relationships with their own parents had no effect on their parenting.
   Answer: A
   Page Ref: 123
   Skill: Conceptual
   Objective: 3.8

84) Expectant couples who are unhappy in their marriages during pregnancy
   A) often are brought closer together by the birth of their child.
   B) tend to have more children than those who are satisfied with their marriages.
   C) are as effective parents as those who are happy in their marriages.
   D) continue to be distant and dissatisfied after their baby is born.
   Answer: D
   Page Ref: 124
   Skill: Conceptual
   Objective: 3.8

85) _____ is associated with _____ in adulthood.
   A) Low birth weight; cancer
   B) High birth weight; diabetes
   C) High birth weight; Alzheimer's disease
   D) Low birth weight; cardiovascular disease
Answer: D
Page Ref: 106–107
Skill: Conceptual
Objective: (SI Box) The Prenatal Environment and Health in Later Life

86) Sabrina weighed nine pounds when she was born. Research shows that she is at an increased risk of _____ in adulthood.
   A) breast cancer
   B) stroke
   C) heart disease
   D) diabetes
Answer: A
Page Ref: 106–107
Skill: Applied
Objective: (SI Box) The Prenatal Environment and Health in Later Life

87) High birth weight is associated with an increased risk of _____, whereas low birth weight is predictive of
   _____.
   A) prostate cancer; cardiovascular disease
   B) diabetes; breast cancer
   C) cardiovascular disease; diabetes
   D) breast cancer; cardiovascular disease
Answer: D
Page Ref: 106–107
Skill: Conceptual
Objective: (SI Box) The Prenatal Environment and Health in Later Life

88) _____ is the most widely used teratogenic drug in current years.
   A) Thalidomide
   B) Diethylstilbestrol
   C) Accutane
   D) Toxoplasmosis
Answer: C
Page Ref: 109
Skill: Factual
Objective: (SI Box) The Teratogenic Effects of Accutane

89) Research on Accutane use indicates that
   A) it can cause extensive damage if taken during pregnancy, including skull, brain, heart, and immune system abnormalities.
   B) women who take the drug cannot get pregnant.
   C) its teratogenic effects were unknown until after the drug was marketed.
   D) it causes damage only if used during the third trimester of pregnancy.
Answer: A
Page Ref: 109
Skill: Conceptual
Objective: (SI Box) The Teratogenic Effects of Accutane

90) Research on Accutane use during pregnancy shows that
   A) over two-thirds of women who take Accutane always use a form of contraception during sexual intercourse.
   B) Accutane's packaging does not warn users to avoid during pregnancy.
   C) the drug company who makes Accutane will pay for birth control counseling and contraceptives.
   D) bottles of Accutane do not have a teratogen symbol like the drug thalidomide does.
   Answer: C
   Page Ref: 109
   Skill: Conceptual
   Objective: (SI Box) The Teratogenic Effects of Accutane

91) When asked to describe their prenatal-care visits, many low-SES ethnic minority expectant and new mothers reported that
   A) group prenatal care discouraged them from sustaining regular prenatal visits.
   B) most of the care that they received was sensitive and personal.
   C) they experienced belittling interactions with medical staff and impersonal, hurried checkups.
   D) women receiving traditional 15-minute appointments engaged in fewer health-damaging behaviors than those in group prenatal care.
   Answer: C
   Page Ref: 121
   Skill: Conceptual
   Objective: (CI Box) Culturally Sensitive Prenatal Care Promotes Healthy Pregnancies

92) In ethnic minority women, group prenatal care is
   A) associated with a reduced incidence of prematurity and low birth weight.
   B) less effective than the traditional 15-minute individual appointments in providing adequate prenatal care.
   C) often hurried and impersonal.
   D) associated with a lower rate of health-promoting behavior than traditional prenatal care.
   Answer: A
   Page Ref: 121
   Skill: Conceptual
   Objective: (CI Box) Culturally Sensitive Prenatal Care Promotes Healthy Pregnancies

ESSAY

93) Describe the relationship between intelligence and family size. Does this research suggest good reasons for limiting family size?
   Answer: Generally, the larger the family, the lower the mental test scores of all siblings. The link between family size and children's scores can be explained by the strong trend for mothers who are low in intelligence to give birth to more children. Among children of bright, economically advantaged mothers, the family size-intelligence correlation disappears. Although many good reasons exist for limited family size, the concern that additional births will reduce children's intelligence and life chances is not warranted. Rather, young people with lower scores—many of whom dropped out of school, live in poverty, or lack hope for their future, are most likely to have large families.
   Page Ref: 95–96

94) Describe the major milestones of the period of the zygote.

Answer: The period of the zygote lasts about 2 weeks, from conception until the blastocyst attaches itself to the uterine wall. During this time, structures that support prenatal growth emerge. The embryonic disk is surrounded by the amnion, which fills with amniotic fluid to regulate temperature and cushion against the mother's movements. From the chorion, villi emerge that burrow into the uterine wall, and the placenta begins to develop. The developing organism is connected to the placenta by the umbilical cord.

Page Ref: 99–101

95) Describe brain growth during the final three prenatal months and its consequences for the sleep-wake cycle.

Answer: During the last three months of pregnancy, the cerebral cortex enlarges. Convolutions and grooves in its surface appear, permitting a dramatic increase in surface area. As neurological organization improves, the fetus spends more time awake. At 20 weeks, the fetal heart rate reveals no periods of alertness. But by 28 weeks, fetuses are awake about 11 percent of the time, a figure that rises to 16 percent just before birth. Between 30 and 34 weeks, fetuses show rhythmic alterations between sleep and wakefulness that gradually increase in organization.

Page Ref: 102–104

96) During the last few months of pregnancy, describe the fetus's responsiveness to external stimulation. Given their sensitivity to specific forms of stimulation, should expectant mothers provide fetuses with extra stimulation?

Answer: In the third trimester, fetuses acquire taste and odor preferences from bathing in and swallowing amniotic fluid. By 28 weeks, fetuses blink their eyes in reaction to nearby sounds. Within the next six weeks, fetuses distinguish the tone and rhythm of different voices and sounds. They show systematic heart rate changes in response to a male versus a female speaker, to the mother's voice versus a stranger's, and to a simple familiar melody versus an unfamiliar melody. However, specific forms of fetal stimulation, such as reading aloud and playing classical music, are unlikely to have a long-lasting impact on cognitive development because of the developing child's constantly changing capacities and experiences, which can override the impact of fetal stimulation. Further, animal studies indicate that although ordinary stimulation contributes to the functioning of sensory systems, excessive input can be dangerous.

Page Ref: 102–104

97) Describe the physical, cognitive, and social characteristics of fetal alcohol syndrome (FAS).

Answer: Babies born to mothers who drank heavily during pregnancy often have FAS. Characteristics of FAS are slow mental growth, a pattern of three facial abnormalities (short eyelid openings, a thin upper lip, a smooth or flattened philtrum, or indentation running from the bottom of the nose to the upper lip), and brain injury, evident in a small head and impairment in at least three areas of functioning, such as memory, language, and communication, attention span and activity level, planning and reasoning, motor coordination, or social skills. Other defects—of the eyes, ears, nose, throat, heart, genitals, urinary tract, or immune system—may also be present. In adolescence and early adulthood, FAS is linked with persisting motor coordination deficits, poor school performance, trouble with the law, inappropriate sexual behavior, drug and alcohol abuse, and lasting mental health problems.

Page Ref: 111

98) Describe outcomes and treatments for infants born to HIV-infected mothers.

Answer: HIV-positive pregnant women pass on the virus to their baby 20 to 30 percent of the time. In older children and adults, AIDS symptoms take years to emerge, but in infants, the disease progresses rapidly. By 6 months, weight loss, diarrhea, and repeated respiratory illnesses are common. The virus also causes brain damage, as indicated by seizures, a gradual loss in brain weight, and delayed mental and motor development. Most prenatal AIDS babies survive for only 5 to 8 months after the appearance of these symptoms. The antiviral drug zidovudine (ZDV) reduces prenatal AIDS transmission by as much as 95 percent, even in women with advanced disease.

Page Ref: 114

99) Describe the effects of prenatal malnutrition and interventions that are most effective.

Answer: Prenatal malnutrition can cause damage to the central nervous system and can distort the structure of other organs, including the liver, kidney, and pancreas, thereby increasing the risk of heart disease, stroke, and diabetes in adulthood. Prenatally malnourished babies frequently catch respiratory illnesses, because poor nutrition suppresses development of the immune system. Also, these infants are irritable and unresponsive to stimulation and emit a high-pitched cry that is particularly distressing to caregivers. With age, low intelligence test scores and serious learning problems become apparent.

Studies have shown that providing pregnant women with adequate food has a positive impact on the health of their newborn babies. In addition, maternal nutrition can be optimized through use of vitamin-mineral enrichment, such as folic acid. Programs that teach parents how to interact effectively help break the cycle of apathetic mother-baby interaction.

Page Ref: 116–117

100) Describe the impact of emotional stress during pregnancy, and explain how stress affects the prenatal organism.

Answer: Emotional stress during pregnancy is associated with an increased rate of miscarriage, prematurity, low birth weight, newborn irritability, respiratory illness, and digestive disturbances. It is also related to physical defects, such as cleft lip and palate, heart deformities, and pyloric stenosis. During a stressful experience, large amounts of blood are sent to parts of the body involved in the defensive response, including the brain, the heart, and muscles in the arms, legs, and trunk. Blood flow to other organs, including the uterus, is reduced. As a result, the fetus is deprived of a full supply of oxygen and nutrients. Also, stress hormones released under stress cross the placenta, leading the fetus's heart rate and activity to rise dramatically. Additionally, stress weakens the immune system, making pregnant women more susceptible to infectious disease. Finally, women who experience long-term anxiety are more likely to smoke, drink, eat poorly, and engage in other behaviors that harm the developing organism.

Page Ref: 117–118

STUDY QUESTIONS

Motivations for Parenthood

Why Have Children?

1. List five advantages and five disadvantages of parenthood mentioned by North American couples. (p. 95)

    Advantages:

    A. _____

    B. _____

    C. _____

    D. _____

    E. _____

    Disadvantages:

    A. _____

    B. _____

    C. _____

    D. _____

    E. _____

How Large a Family?

1. List two major reasons that family size has declined in industrialized nations. (p. 95)

    A. _____

    B. _____

2. Describe the benefits of growing up in a small family. (p. 95)

    _____

    _____

    _____

3. True or False: Children's mental test performance tends to decline with later birth order. (pp. 95–96)

4. Describe factors that contribute to lower intelligence scores for children in large families. (p. 96)

    _____

    _____

    _____

5. Discuss some of the pros and cons of living in a one-child family, including perspectives of both parents and children. (p. 96)

    Pros (children): _____

    _____

    Cons (children): _____

    _____

Pros (parents): _____

_____

Cons (parents): _____

_____

Is There a Best Time During Adulthood to Have a Child?

1. Cite reasons why many modern couples are delaying childbearing into their thirties and beyond. (pp. 96–97)

_____

_____

2. True or False: Both males and females experience a decline in reproductive capacity with age. (p. 97)

Prenatal Development

Conception

1. Approximately once every 28 days, an ovum is released from one of a woman's two _____, and it travels through one of the two _____, which are long, thin structures that lead to the uterus. (p. 98)

2. The male produces vast numbers of sperm in the _____, two glands located in the scrotum. (p. 98)

3. True or False: Sperm live for up to 10 days and can lie in wait for the ovum, which survives for 3 days after being released in the fallopian tube. (p. 98)

The Period of the Zygote

1. The period of the zygote lasts about _____ weeks, from fertilization until the tiny mass of cells drifts down and out of the fallopian tube and attaches itself to the wall of the uterus. (p. 99)

2. Match each term with the appropriate definition. (p. 99)

   _____ Will become the structures that provide protective covering and nourishment to the new organism   1. Blastocyst

   _____ Hollow, fluid-filled ball that is formed by a tiny mass of cells four days after fertilization   2. Embryonic disk

   _____ Will become the new organism   3. Trophoblast

3. List two functions of the *amniotic fluid.* (p. 99)

   A. _____

   B. _____

4. True or False: As many as 30 percent of zygotes do not make it through the first two weeks. (p. 99)

5. The _____ permits food and oxygen to reach the developing organism and waste products to be carried away. (p. 99)

6. The *placenta* is connected to the developing organism by the _____. (p. 100)

The Period of the Embryo

1. The period of the *embryo* lasts from implantation through the _____ week of pregnancy. (p. 101)

2. True or False: The most rapid prenatal changes take place during the period of the embryo. (p. 101)

3. Why is the embryo especially vulnerable to interference with healthy development? (p. 101)

_____

_____

4. List the organs and structures that will be formed from each of the three layers of the embryonic disk. (p. 100)

Ectoderm: _____

Mesoderm: _____

Endoderm: _____

5. Briefly summarize the events that take place during the second month of pregnancy. (p. 101)

_____

_____

_____

The Period of the Fetus

1. True or False: The period of the *fetus* is the longest prenatal period. (p. 102)

2. Prenatal development is divided into _____, or three equal time periods. (p. 102)

3. The white, cheeselike substance that protects the skin from chapping in the amniotic fluid is called _____. (p. 102)

4. _____ is a white, downy hair that covers the entire body of the fetus. (p. 102)

5. The age at which the baby can first survive if born early is called the *age of* _____. When does this typically occur? (p. 102)

_____

6. Summarize research findings on the relationship between fetal activity patterns and temperament in early childhood. (p. 103)

_____

_____

_____

7. True or False: During the third trimester, fetuses are able to distinguish the tone and rhythm of different voices and sounds. Briefly explain your response. (p. 103)

_____

_____

_____

8. Describe major changes in the fetus during the final three months of pregnancy. (pp. 103–104)

_____

_____

_____

Prenatal Environmental Influences

Teratogens

1. Define the term *teratogen,* and describe four factors that affect the impact of teratogens on prenatal development. (p. 105)

   Teratogen: _____

   _____

   A. _____

   B. _____

   C. _____

   D. _____

2. A _____ *period* is a limited time span in which a part of the body or a behavior is biologically prepared to develop rapidly and is especially sensitive to its surroundings. (p. 105)

3. True or False: The period of the zygote is the time when teratogens are most likely to cause serious defects. (p.106)

4. When taken by mothers four to six weeks after conception, _____, a sedative widely available in some countries during the early 1960s, produced deformities of the embryo's developing arms and legs, and less frequently, caused damage to the ears, heart, kidneys, and genitals. (p. 107)

5. True or False: Heavy caffeine intake during pregnancy is associated with low birth weight, miscarriage, and newborn withdrawal symptoms. (p. 108)

6. Describe the difficulties faced by babies who are prenatally exposed to cocaine, heroine, or methadone. (pp. 108, 110)

   _____

   _____

   _____

   _____

7. Explain why it is difficult to isolate the precise damage caused by prenatal drug exposure. (p. 110)

   _____

   _____

   _____

8. Summarize physical and behavioral effects of maternal smoking during the prenatal period. (p. 110)

   _____

   _____

   _____

   _____

9. True or False: If the mother stops smoking at any time during her pregnancy, even during the last trimester, she reduces the chances that her baby will be negatively impacted. (p. 110)

10. Explain the mechanisms through which smoking harms the fetus. (p. 111)

    _____

    _____

    _____

11. Why should expectant mothers, even those who do not smoke, avoid smoke-filled environments? (p. 111)

_____

_____

12. Infants who have a range of physical and behavioral abnormalities and whose mothers drank heavily throughout most or all of pregnancy are said to have _____ . (p. 111)

13. Match the following characteristics with the proper diagnosis. (p. 111)

_____ At least three areas of mental functioning are impaired, despite typical physical growth and absence of facial abnormalities

_____ Characterized by two of the three facial abnormalities and brain injury

_____ Distinguished by slow physical growth, a pattern of three facial abnormalities, and brain injury

A. Fetal alcohol syndrome (FAS)
B. Partial fetal alcohol syndrome (p-FAS)
C. Alcohol-related neurodevelopmental disorder (ARND)

14. Describe physical and mental impairments associated with fetal alcohol spectrum disorders that persist from the preschool years through early adulthood. (pp. 111–112)

Preschool and school years: _____

_____

Adolescence and early adulthood: _____

_____

15. Describe two ways in which alcohol produces its devastating effects. (p. 112)

A. _____

_____

B. _____

_____

16. True or False: Mild drinking, less than one alcoholic drink, is associated with poor outcomes for the child. Therefore, no amount of alcohol is safe to drink during pregnancy. (p. 112)

17. True or False: Low doses of radiation exposure, such as through medical x-rays, are believed to be safe for the developing fetus and have not been linked to any negative outcomes. (p. 112)

18. Match each of the following environmental pollutants with its effect on development. (p. 113)

_____ This teratogen, commonly found in paint chippings from old buildings and other industrial materials, is related to low birth weight, prematurity, brain damage, and physical defects.

_____ In the 1950s, children prenatally exposed to this teratogen in a Japanese community displayed mental retardation, abnormal speech, and uncoordinated movements.

_____ Women who ate fish contaminated with this substance gave birth to babies with slightly reduced birth weights, smaller heads, more intense physiological reactions to stress, less interest in their surroundings, and later memory and intellectual deficits.

1. Mercury
2. PCBs
3. Lead

19. Describe the outcomes associated with embryonic and fetal exposure to *rubella*. (p. 114)

Embryonic: _____

_____

_____

Fetal: _____

_____

_____

20. When women carrying the AIDS virus become pregnant, they pass on the disease to their baby approximately
_____ to _____ percent of the time. (p. 114)

21. True or False: Most infants prenatally exposed to the AIDS virus survive eight to ten years after the appearance
of symptoms. (p. 114)

22. Pregnant women can become infected with _____, a parasitic disease found in many
animals, from eating raw or undercooked meat or from contact with the feces of infected cats. (p. 115)

Biology and Environment: The Prenatal Environment and Health in Later Life

1. True or False: Numerous studies have identified a link between low birth weight and serious health problems
later in life, including heart disease, stroke, and diabetes. (p. 107)

2. List the consequences of high birth weight on adult health. (p. 107)

_____

_____

3. What can individuals do to prevent prenatal risks from becoming a reality? (p. 107)

_____

_____

Social Issues: Health: Can a Thalidomide-Like Tragedy Occur Again?
The Teratogenic Effects of Accutane

1. What is Accutane? (p. 109)

_____

_____

2. Summarize pregnancy complications and birth defects associated with Accutane use. (p. 109)

Pregnancy complications: _____

_____

Birth defects: _____

_____

3. Describe barriers to preventing prenatal exposure to Accutane. (p. 109)

_____

_____

_____

4. Cite three strategies for preventing prenatal Accutane exposure. (p. 109)

A. _____

B. _____

C. _____

Other Maternal Factors

1. Regular, moderate exercise during pregnancy is associated with (increased / decreased) birth weight. (p. 115)

2. Summarize the behavioral and health problems of prenatally malnourished babies. (p. 116)

_____

_____

3. List the vitamin and mineral supplements that have been found to reduce prenatal complications and birth defects. (pp. 116–117)

A. _____   B. _____

C. _____   D. _____

E. _____   F. _____

4. True or False: Prenatal malnutrition is currently limited to developing countries, and it has been entirely eradicated in the United States through government programs for low-income pregnant women. (p. 117)

5. Describe the mechanisms through which maternal stress affects the developing organism, and note outcomes associated with severe emotional stress during pregnancy. (pp. 117–118)

Mechanisms: _____

_____

_____

Outcomes: _____

_____

_____

6. Under what conditions can *Rh factor incompatibility* cause problems for the developing fetus? (p. 118)

_____

_____

_____

7. Problems resulting from the Rh factor are more likely to affect (first-born / later-born) children. (p. 118)

8. True or False: Healthy women in their thirties experience far more prenatal difficulties than women in their twenties. (p. 118)

9. The physical immaturity of teenage mothers (does / does not) lead to pregnancy complications. (p. 119)

The Importance of Prenatal Health Care

1. Describe two potential complications that can arise during pregnancy. (p. 119)

A. _____

_____

B. _____

_____

2. Name two groups of women who often do not receive adequate prenatal care, and note the consequences for their babies. (p. 119)

A. _____   B. _____

Consequences: _____

_____

3. Discuss some of the barriers to obtaining prenatal health care mentioned by expectant mothers who delay or never seek such care. (p. 119)

_____

_____

_____

Cultural Influences:
Culturally Sensitive Prenatal Care Promotes Healthy Pregnancies

1. Why is the lack of patient-sensitive prenatal care particularly disturbing to many ethnic minority women? (p. 121)

_____

_____

2. Describe the benefits of group prenatal care for minority expectant mothers. (p. 121)

_____

_____

_____

Preparing for Parenthood

1. Over _____ percent of pregnancies in industrialized nations result in healthy newborn babies. (p. 122)

Seeking Information

1. Pregnant mothers regard _____ as an extremely valuable source of information, second in importance only to their doctors. (p. 122)

The Baby Becomes a Reality

1. What changes and experiences help expectant parents come to view the baby as a reality? (p. 123)

_____

_____

_____

Models of Effective Parenthood

1. True or False: Men and women who have had good relationships with their own parents are more likely to develop positive images of themselves as parents during pregnancy. (p. 123)

2. Cite three benefits of participating in special intervention programs for expectant mothers and fathers. (p. 124)

   A. _____

   B. _____

   C. _____

The Parental Relationship

1. True or False: Having a baby typically improves a troubled marital relationship. (p. 124)

2. Describe some of the ways in which pregnancy changes a marital relationship. (p. 124)

_____

_____

_____

PUZZLE 3.1 TERM REVIEW

Across

2. The _____ cord connects the prenatal organism to the placenta
5. Zygote four days after fertilization, when it forms a hollow, fluid-filled ball
6. _____ fluid: keeps the temperature in the womb constant and provides a cushion against jolts
7. Age of _____: age at which the fetus can first survive if born early
11. The prenatal organism from two to eight weeks after conception
12. Ring of cells which will become the structures that provide protective covering and nourishment to the new organism
13. White, cheeselike substance that covers the fetus and prevents chapping
14. Membrane that encloses the developing organism in amniotic fluid
15. White, downy hair that covers the fetus

Down

1. _____ tube: primitive spinal chord
3. The blastocyst burrows deep into the uterine lining during _____
4. Embryonic _____: cluster of cells inside the blastocyst which will become the new organism
8. The prenatal organism from the ninth week to the end of pregnancy
9. Outer membrane that forms a protective covering and sends out villi from which the placenta emerges
10. Separates the mother's bloodstream from that of the fetus while permitting the exchange of nutrients and waste products

PUZZLE 3.2 TERM REVIEW

Across

2. Environmental agent that causes damage during the prenatal period
3. Fetal Alcohol _____: Mental retardation, slow growth, and facial abnormalities resulting from maternal alcohol consumption during pregnancy
4. German measles; causes a variety of prenatal abnormalities
5. Fetal alcohol _____ disorder: A range of physical, mental, and behavioral outcomes caused by prenatal alcohol exposure
6. Illness marked by increased maternal blood pressure and swelling of the face, hands, and feet
7. Sedative available in the early 1960s that caused deformities of the arms and legs when taken between the fourth and sixth week after conception
9. Three equal periods of time in prenatal development
10. Parasitic disease caused by eating raw or undercooked meat or through contact with the feces of infected cats

Down

1. Alcohol-related _____ disorder: The least severe form of fetal alcohol spectrum disorders that involves brain injury, but with typical physical growth and absence of facial abnormalities
4. When present in the fetus's blood but not in the mother's, the _____ factor may cause the mother to build up antibodies that destroy the fetus's red blood cells
8. _____ fetal alcohol syndrome: A form of fetal alcohol spectrum disorder characterized by facial abnormalities and brain injury, but less severe than fetal alcohol syndrome; usually seen in children whose mothers drank alcohol in smaller quantities during pregnancy
11. Viral infection that destroys the immune system (abbr.)

CROSSWORD PUZZLE SOLUTIONS

PUZZLE 3.1

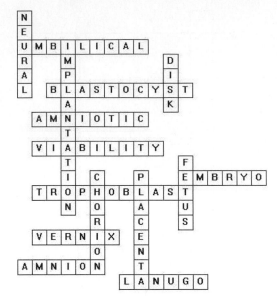

PUZZLE 3.2

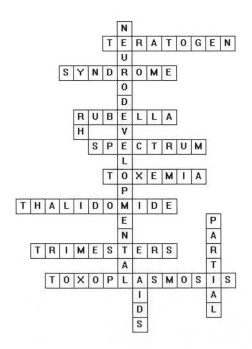

PRACTICE TEST #1

1. Today, in Western industrialized nations, the issue of whether to have children is a(n) (p. 94)
   a. unavoidable cultural demand.
   b. individual choice.
   c. biological given.
   d. religious imperative.

2. Today, to rear a child from birth to age 18, new parents in the United States will have to spend about (p. 95)
   a. $150,000.
   b. $170,000.
   c. $190,000.
   d. $210,000.

3. Between 1960 and the present, the average number of children per North American couple declined because of (p. 95)
   a. fewer marriages.
   b. cultural prohibitions on larger families.
   c. people marrying at later ages.
   d. more effective birth control, a woman's decision to work, and marital instability.

4. In the past quarter century, births have greatly increased to women in their (p. 96)
   a. teens.
   b. twenties.
   c. thirties.
   d. forties.

5. About once every 28 days, in the middle of the menstrual cycle, an ovum bursts from one of the woman's (p. 98)
   a. ovaries.
   b. fallopian tubes.
   c. corpus luteum.
   d. uterine linings.

6. The male produces sperm in the (p. 98)
   a. cervix.
   b. penis.
   c. embryonic disk.
   d. testes.

7. How long can sperm live in the fallopian tubes waiting for an ovum? (p. 98)
   a. no more than 6 hours
   b. 3 days
   c. up to 6 days
   d. as much as 2 weeks

8. The placenta starts to develop (p. 99)
   a. when the yolk sac emerges to produce blood cells.
   b. when villi emerge from the chorion and burrow into the uterine wall.
   c. when the blastocyst develops into the trophoblast.
   d. within 24 hours after implantation occurs.

9. Early in the period of the embryo, the embryonic disk develops the ectoderm, which will become the (p. 101)
   a. nervous system.
   b. muscles.
   c. urinary tract.
   d. circulatory system.

10. By the end of the second trimester, (p. 102)
    a.   the placenta has been replaced by the vernix.
    b.   the organs, muscles, and nervous system have begun to connect.
    c.   most of the brain's billions of neurons are in place.
    d.   the growth of glial cells slows and gradually stops.

11. By 28 weeks, fetuses (p. 103)
    a.   are awake about 20 percent of the time.
    b.   are no longer irritated by sudden loud noises.
    c.   make tiny flutters that are still too light to be felt by the mother.
    d.   blink their eyes in reaction to nearby sounds.

12. Defects resulting from teratogens can affect emotional and social development because they (p. 106)
    a.   often cause malformations of the arms and legs.
    b.   can damage critical parent-child interactions, peer relations, and opportunities to explore.
    c.   strike during sensitive periods.
    d.   tend to cluster during the embryonic period.

13. Researchers suspect that high birth weight may promote which of the following conditions in adult women? (pp. 106–107)
    a.   breast cancer
    b.   diabetes
    c.   heart disease
    d.   stroke

14. Several studies suggest that regular aspirin use during pregnancy is linked to (p. 108)
    a.   erythema nodosum in children.
    b.   high rates of vaginal cancer in daughters of mothers who used it.
    c.   low birth weight and infant death around the time of birth.
    d.   newborn withdrawal symptoms.

15. To help prevent Accutane-related fetal malformations, doctors often counsel women to (p. 109)
    a.   refrain from taking other vitamin A-derived drugs.
    b.   abstain from sex or use two forms of birth control.
    c.   monitor their vitamin A levels closely.
    d.   reduce their doses of Accutane.

16. The principal difference between fetal alcohol syndrome (FAS) and alcohol-related neurodevelopmental disorder (ARND) is that (p. 111)
    a.   FAS involves two, rather than three, facial abnormalities.
    b.   ARND involves only short eyelid openings.
    c.   FAS involves no brain injuries.
    d.   ARND involves at least three areas of mental functioning despite typical physical growth and absence of facial abnormalities.

17. Of the following environmental teratogens, which is responsible for prematurity and brain damage? (p. 113)
    a.   mercury
    b.   PCBs
    c.   lead
    d.   carbon dioxide

18. If a pregnant woman catches rubella, her child (p. 114)
    a. **risks developing eye cataracts, organ defects, and mental retardation.**
    b. may be especially sensitive to herpes simplex 2.
    c. has a better chance of being born with the rubella antibody.
    d. will be more vulnerable to toxoplasmosis.

19. Most prenatal AIDS babies survive only (p. 114)
    a. a few hours after birth.
    b. 3 to 5 days.
    c. 4 to 6 weeks.
    d. **5 to 8 months.**

20. Maternal stress can cause a variety of problems, including miscarriage, because (p. 118)
    a. it can suppress the mother's production of folic acid.
    b. **stress hormones crossing the placenta can dramatically increase the fetal heart rate.**
    c. it can cause the mother to exercise too vigorously.
    d. stress has been linked to increased risk of viral infection.

21. Inadequate prenatal care is most common among (p. 119)
    a. women age 50 to 55.
    b. white, middle-class women.
    c. women who suffer from preeclampsia.
    d. **adolescent, low-income, and ethnic minority women.**

22. Evaluations of group prenatal care have revealed that the participants (p. 121)
    a. prefer the group leaders to be men from the participants' culture.
    b. **engage in fewer health-damaging behaviors.**
    c. tend to be young mothers.
    d. are less likely to ask questions for fear of embarrassment.

23. Men and women are more likely to develop positive images of themselves as parents when they (p. 123)
    a. have had more than one child.
    b. have experience caring for children prior to having one of their own.
    c. **have had good relationships with their own parents.**
    d. wait to have children until they feel secure in their careers.

24. Research suggests that in a troubled marriage, pregnancy (p. 124)
    a. **adds to rather than lessens family conflict.**
    b. can help the parents improve their relationship.
    c. often prompts the mother and father to seek out models of effective parenting.
    d. causes the parents to turn from their troubles and focus on preparing for the changes that will occur as soon as the baby is born.

25. During pregnancy, women typically look to their partners for (p. 124)
    a. expressions of masculine strength and protectiveness.
    b. deeper commitment to providing a steady income.
    c. emotional calm and reserve.
    d. **demonstrations of affection and interest in the pregnancy.**

PRACTICE TEST #2

1. Between 1958 and the present, the percentage of North American couples that bear children declined from 78 percent to (p. 94)
   a.   62 percent.
   b.   65 percent.
   c.   70 percent.
   d.   74 percent.

2. Of the following factors, which is a cause of declining family size in industrialized nations? (p. 95)
   a.   earlier marriage
   b.   marital instability
   c.   sexual abstinence
   d.   government policy

3. According to the U.S. National Longitudinal Survey of Youth, in general, the larger the family, the lower the mental test scores of the all the siblings, because (p. 96)
   a.   mothers who are low in intelligence tend to give birth to more children.
   b.   the parents of such families are more likely to divorce.
   c.   mothers tend to be too busy to foster their children's education.
   d.   the homes of large families tend to be full of noise and other distractions.

4. Male reproductive capacity gradually declines after age (p. 97)
   a.   15.
   b.   20.
   c.   25.
   d.   30.

5. The largest cell in the human body is the (p. 98)
   a.   fallopian tube.
   b.   ovum.
   c.   zygote.
   d.   sperm.

6. Most conceptions result from intercourse (p. 98)
   a.   within 6 hours before or after ovulation.
   b.   during the week of ovulation.
   c.   on the day of or during the 2 days preceding ovulation.
   d.   during the 2 hours before or after ovulation.

7. During the period of the zygote, implantation occurs when the (p. 99)
   a.   blastocyst burrows into the uterine lining.
   b.   sperm penetrates and fertilizes the ovum.
   c.   trophoblast forms the chorion.
   d.   amnion encloses the developing organism.

8. In the second month of the period of the embryo, the (p. 101)
   a.   organism develops the endoderm.
   b.   neural tube and neurons develop.
   c.   heart begins to pump blood.
   d.   liver and spleen assume production of blood cells.

9. During the last three months of pregnancy, (p. 103)
   a. the genitals form so that the sex of the fetus becomes evident.
   b. grooves and convolutions form in the surface of the cerebral cortex.
   c. the fetus tends to rest quietly because of decreasing space in the womb.
   d. the lanugo grows over the fetus's body.

10. During the eighth month of pregnancy, a layer of fat develops to assist with (p. 104)
    a. temperature regulation.
    b. antibody production.
    c. blood circulation.
    d. waste filtration.

11. The effects of teratogens (p. 106)
    a. usually kill the fetus in the womb.
    b. mostly cause malformations of the limbs.
    c. can be subtle and delayed for years.
    d. tend to concentrate during the first two weeks after conception.

12. Research indicates that high birth weight is associated with (p. 107)
    a. excessive weight gain in adulthood.
    b. lower maternal estrogen during pregnancy.
    c. greatly increased risk of cardiovascular disease in adulthood.
    d. increases in digestive and lymphatic cancer in both men and women.

13. Throughout the first year, infants who were exposed to heroine and methadone are (p. 108)
    a. less attentive to the environment than nonexposed babies.
    b. more likely to develop respiratory distress than nonexposed babies.
    c. likely to develop genital abnormalities during adolescence.
    d. more prone to irritability and vomiting than nonexposed babies.

14. Of the following, which factor accounts for continued prenatal exposure to the teratogenic drug Accutane? (p. 109)
    a. Manufacturers have failed to provide adequate warnings.
    b. The drug's teratogenic effects have only recently been established.
    c. The pregnancies were unplanned, and women who become pregnant without planning are often less responsive to teratogen counseling.
    d. The pregnant women smoked while taking the drug.

15. Newborns of smoking mothers (p. 110)
    a. tend to have smaller head sizes than newborns of mothers who do not smoke.
    b. are less attentive to sounds.
    c. often have facial abnormalities.
    d. have abnormally high birth weights.

16. Low levels of radiation, such as those resulting from medical X-rays, can increase the risk of (p. 112)
    a. adult diabetes.
    b. a smooth or flattened philtrum.
    c. smaller head size.
    d. childhood cancer.

17. In industrialized nations, how many commonly used chemicals are potentially dangerous to the developing organism?
    (p. 113)
    a. less than 20,000
    b. about 50,000
    c. more than 75,000
    d. nearly 1,000,000

18. Pregnant women may become infected with toxoplasmosis (p. 115)
    a.   from contact with the urine of infected dogs.
    b.   by eating raw or undercooked meat.
    c.   through unprotected sex with an infected person.
    d.   through drug abuse.

19. In addition to adequate quantities of food, which of the following nutritional factors is crucial to the health of newborns? (p. 116)
    a.   vitamin-mineral enrichment
    b.   reduced consumption of dairy products
    c.   food that has been thoroughly irradiated
    d.   foods that are low in folic acid

20. Women age 50 to 55 experience high rates of pregnancy complications because (p. 118)
    a.   they and the fetus tend to develop Rh factor incompatibility.
    b.   their systems often produce high levels of cortisol.
    c.   their bodies have had more time to absorb environmental teratogens.
    d.   menopause and aging reproductive organs often prevent them from conceiving naturally.

21. If untreated, toxemia in pregnant women can cause (p. 119)
    a.   extreme facial malformations in babies.
    b.   high birth weight.
    c.   convulsions in the mother and fetal death.
    d.   higher levels of stress hormones crossing the placenta.

22. Lack of patient-sensitive prenatal care is particularly disturbing to women from cultures that (p. 121)
    a.   value large families.
    b.   emphasize warm, personalized styles of interaction and a relaxed sense of time.
    c.   encourage them to begin bearing children early.
    d.   stress indirect discussion of intimate matters like pregnancy.

23. Of the following factors, which is especially likely to spark negative or ambivalent feelings about parenthood? (p. 122)
    a.   an unplanned pregnancy
    b.   if the mother is over age 35
    c.   the parents' levels of education
    d.   a pregnancy in the third trimester

24. Expectant mothers tend to rank which of the following sources of information as second only to their doctors? (p. 122)
    a.   friends who have already had children
    b.   nurses
    c.   mothers and grandmothers
    d.   books

25. During their partner's pregnancy, men typically look for (p. 124)
    a.   interest in the pregnancy.
    b.   help with household chores.
    c.   expressions of warmth from their partner.
    d.   willingness to put aside career and other personal goals for motherhood.

POWERPOINT SLIDES

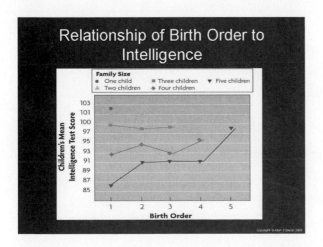

Advantages and Disadvantages of a One-Child Family

ADVANTAGES		DISADVANTAGES	
Mentioned by Parents	**Mentioned by Children**	**Mentioned by Parents**	**Mentioned by Children**
Having time to pursue one's own interests and career	Having no sibling rivalry Having more privacy	Walking a "tightrope" between healthy attention and overindulgence	Not getting to experience the closeness of a sibling relationship
Less financial pressure	Enjoying greater affluence	Having only one chance to "make good" as a parent	Feeling too much pressure from parents to succeed
Not having to worry about "playing favorites" among children	Having a closer parent–child relationship	Being left childless in case of the child's death	Having no one to help care for parents when they get old

Source: Hawke & Knox, 1978.

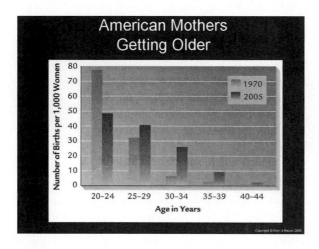

American Mothers Getting Older

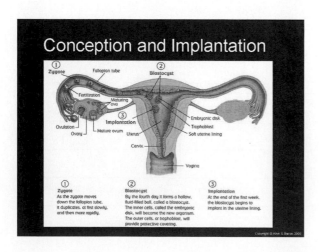

Conception and Implantation

Periods of Prenatal Development

Period	Length	Key Events
Zygote	2 weeks	■Fertilization ■Implantation ■Start of Placenta
Embryo	6 weeks	■Arms, legs, face, organs, muscles all develop ■Heart begins beating
Fetus	30 weeks	■"Growth and finishing"

Copyright © Allyn & Bacon 2003

TRIMESTER	PERIOD	WEEKS	LENGTH AND WEIGHT	MAJOR EVENTS
First	Zygote	1		The one-celled zygote multiplies and forms a blastocyst.
		2		The blastocyst burrows into the uterine lining. Structures that feed and protect the developing organism begin to form—amnion, chorion, yolk sac, placenta, and umbilical cord.
	Embryo	3–4	¼ inch (6 mm)	A primitive brain and spinal cord appear. Heart, muscles, ribs, backbone, and digestive tract begin to develop.
		5–8	1 inch (2.5 cm); ⅐ ounce (4 g)	Many external body structures (face, arms, legs, toes, fingers) and internal organs form. The sense of touch begins to develop, and the embryo can move.
	Fetus	9–12	3 inches (7.6 cm); less than 1 ounce (28 g)	Rapid increase in size begins. Nervous system, organs, and muscles become organized and connected, and new behavioral capacities (kicking, thumb sucking, mouth opening, and rehearsal of breathing) appear. External genitals are well-formed, and the fetus's sex is evident.
Second		13–24	12 inches (30 cm); 1.8 pounds (820 g)	The fetus continues to enlarge rapidly. In the middle of this period, fetal movements can be felt by the mother. Vernix and lanugo keep the fetus's skin from chapping in the amniotic fluid. Most of the brain's neurons are present by 24 weeks. Eyes are sensitive to light, and the fetus reacts to sound.
Third		25–38	20 inches (50 cm); 7.5 pounds (3,400 g)	The fetus has a good chance of survival if born during this time. Size increases. Lungs mature. Rapid brain development causes sensory and behavioral capacities to expand. In the middle of this period, a layer of fat is added under the skin. Antibodies are transmitted from mother to fetus to protect against disease. Most fetuses rotate into an upside-down position in preparation for birth.

Source: Moore & Persaud, 2003.
Photos (from top to bottom) © Claude Cortier/Photo Researchers, Inc.; © G. Moscoso/Photo Researchers, Inc.; © John Watney/Photo Researchers, Inc.; © James Stevenson/Photo Researchers, Inc.; © Lennart Nilsson, A Child Is Born/ Bonniers.

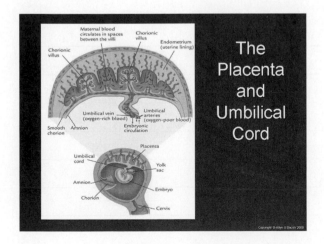

The Placenta and Umbilical Cord

Copyright © Allyn & Bacon 2003

Discussion

- Would you recommend that expectant mothers provide their fetuses with certain kinds of stimulation to enhance later mental development? Why or why not?

Sensitive Periods in Prenatal Development

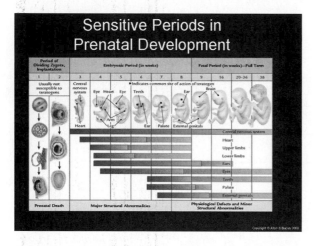

Prenatal Environmental Influences: Teratogens

Teratogen—any environmental agent that causes damage during the prenatal period.

- Dose
- Heredity
- Other negative influences
- Age

Prenatal Development and Later Health

- Low Birth Weight
  Greater chance of
  - Heart Disease
  - Stroke
  - Diabetes
- High Birth Weight
  - Greater chance of breast cancer

Relationship of Birth Weight to Breast Cancer Risk in Adulthood

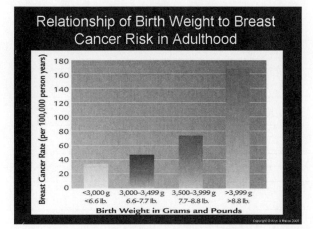

Teratogens

- Drugs
  - Prescription
  - Nonprescription
  - Illegal
- Tobacco
- Alcohol
- Radiation
- Pollution
- Infectious Disease

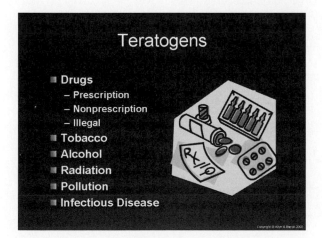

Can a Thalidomide-Like Tragedy Occur Again?

- Accutane—toxic to developing organisms
- Efforts to control its damaging prenatal risks include:
  - Restriction of this and other drugs for the treatment of severe conditions.
  - Improved public and patient education.
  - Interventions that promote widespread, effective contraceptive use.

Fetal Alcohol Spectrum Disorder: Criteria for Diagnosis

Criteria	FAS	p-FAS	ARND
Slow physical growth	Yes	No	No
Facial abnormalities: • Short eyelid openings • Thin upper lip • Smooth or flattened philtrum	All three are present	Two of the three are present	None are present
Brain injury	Impairment in a minimum of three areas of functioning	Impairment in a minimum of three areas of functioning	Impairment in a minimum of three areas of functioning

Source: Loock et al., 2005.

The Effects of Environmental Pollution

- More than 75,000 chemicals are in common use in the United States, and many new pollutants are introduced each year.
- Many babies are "born polluted" by chemicals that can impair development and increase the chances of life-threatening diseases and health problems later on.

Effects of Some Infectious Diseases During Pregnancy

DISEASE	PHYSICAL MISCARRIAGE	MENTAL MALFORMATIONS	RETARDATION	LOW BIRTHWEIGHT AND PREMATURITY
Viral				
Acquired immune deficiency syndrome (AIDS)	0	?	+	?
Chicken pox	0	+	+	+
Cytomegalovirus	+	+	+	+
Herpes simplex 2 (genital herpes)	+	+	+	+
Mumps	+	?	0	0
Rubella (German measles)	+	+	+	+
Bacterial				
Chlamydia	+	?	0	+
Syphilis	+	+	+	?
Tuberculosis	+	?	+	+
Parasitic				
Malaria	+	0	0	+
Toxoplasmosis	+	+	+	+

+ = established finding, 0 = no present evidence, ? = possible effect that is not clearly established.

Sources: Behrman, Kliegman, & Jenson, 2000; Jones, Lopez, & Wilson, 2003; Mardh, 2002; O'Rahilly & Müller, 2001.

Copyright © Allyn & Bacon 2006

Maternal Factors in Healthy Prenatal Development

- Exercise
- Nutrition
- Prevention and Treatment
- Emotional Stress
- Rh Blood Factor
- Age
- Previous Births

Copyright © Allyn & Bacon 2006

The Effects of Emotional Stress on the Developing Fetus

- Stress hormones cross the placenta, causing a dramatic rise in fetal heart rate and activity.
- Fetal neurological functioning can be permanently altered.
- Maternal emotional stress predicts anxiety, short attention span, anger, aggression, and overactivity among preschoolers and young children above and beyond the impact of other risk factors.
- Stress-related prenatal complications can be greatly reduced when mothers receive the support of family members and friends.

Copyright © Allyn & Bacon 2006

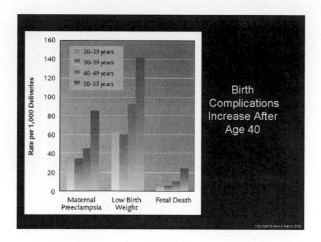

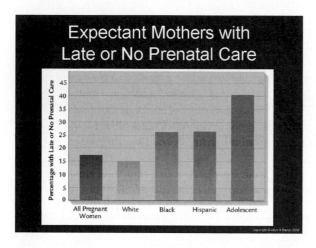

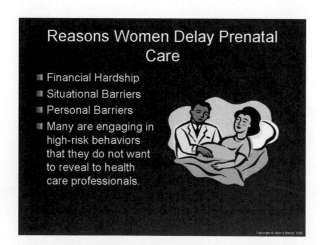

Culturally Sensitive Prenatal Care Promotes Healthy Pregnancies

- Low-SES ethnic minority expectant and new mothers were not receiving warm prenatal care and expressed difficulty getting questions answered.
- Group prenatal care offers a sensitive alternative.

Copyright © Allyn & Bacon 2008

Preparing for Parenthood

Expectant Parents:
- Seek information.
- Get to know the baby as a reality.
- Look for models of effective parenthood.
- Adjust couples' relationships.

Copyright © Allyn & Bacon 2008

CHAPTER 4
BIRTH AND THE NEWBORN BABY

CHAPTER-AT-A-GLANCE

Chapter Outline	Instruction Ideas	Supplements
The Stages of Childbirth pp. 130–133 Stage 1: Dilation and Effacement of the Cervix • Stage 2: Delivery of the Baby • Stage 3: Birth of the Placenta • The Baby's Adaptation to Labor and Delivery • The Newborn Baby's Appearance • Assessing the Newborn's Physical Condition: The Apgar Scale	Learning Objectives 4.1–4.3 Ask Yourself p. 133	Transparency 35 Test Bank Items 1–15, 104 Please contact your Allyn and Bacon publisher's representative for a wide range of video offerings available to adopters.
Approaches to Childbirth pp. 133–135 Natural, or Prepared, Childbirth • Home Delivery	Learning Objectives 4.4–4.5 Learning Activity 4.1	Transparency 36 Test Bank Items 16–22
Medical Interventions pp. 136–138 Fetal Monitoring • Labor and Delivery Medication • Instrument Delivery • Induced Labor • Cesarean Delivery	Learning Objective 4.6 Learning Activity 4.1 Ask Yourself p. 138	Transparency 37 Test Bank Items 23–35, 105
Birth Complications pp. 138–146 Oxygen Deprivation • Preterm and Low-Birth-Weight Infants • Birth Complications, Parenting, and Resilience	Learning Objectives 4.6–4.9 Learning Activity 4.2 Ask Yourself p. 146	Transparencies 38, 40 Test Bank Items 36–49, 90–95, 106
Precious Moments After Birth pp. 146–147	Learning Objective 4.10	Test Bank Items 50–53
The Newborn Baby's Capacities pp. 147–157 Reflexes • States • Sensory Capacities • Neonatal Behavioral Assessment	Learning Objectives 4.11–4.14 Lecture Enhancement 4.1 Learning Activities 4.3–4.7 Ask Yourself p. 157	Test Bank Items 54–83, 96–99, 107–110
The Transition to Parenthood pp. 157–161 Changes in the Family System • Single-Mother Families • Parent Interventions	Learning Objective 4.15 Lecture Enhancements 4.2–4.4 Ask Yourself p. 161	Test Bank Items 84–89, 100–103

BRIEF CHAPTER SUMMARY

Childbirth takes place in three stages: (1) dilation and effacement of the cervix, (2) delivery of the baby, and (3) birth of the placenta. Production of stress hormones helps the infant withstand the trauma of childbirth. The Apgar Scale permits assessment of the baby's physical condition immediately after birth.

Natural, or prepared, childbirth and delivery in a birth center are increasingly popular alternatives to traditional hospital delivery in Western industrial societies; some women choose home birth as a noninstitutional option. Social support during labor and delivery can promote a successful childbirth experience. However, various medical interventions are commonly a part of childbirth in the United States. These procedures help save the lives of many babies but can introduce new problems when used routinely.

Although most births proceed normally, serious complications sometimes occur. The most common complications result from oxygen deprivation and prematurity. Fortunately, many babies who experience severe birth trauma recover with the help of favorable child-rearing environments, which can be supported by high-quality intervention. Infant mortality rates are higher in the United States than in many other industrialized nations. Affordable, available prenatal care is a key factor in reducing infant mortality.

Infants begin life with a remarkable set of skills for relating to the surrounding world. Newborns display a wide variety of reflexes—automatic responses to specific forms of stimulation. In the early weeks, babies move in and out of different states of arousal (degrees of sleep and wakefulness) frequently but spend the most time in either rapid-eye-movement REM sleep, during which the brain stimulates itself, and non-REM (NREM) sleep.

Crying is the first way that babies communicate their needs. With experience, parents become better at interpreting the meaning of the infant's cries. Newborns' senses of touch, taste, smell, and sound are well developed. Vision is the least mature sensory capacity. Tests such as the Neonatal Behavioral Assessment Scale (NBAS) have been developed to assess the newborn's reflexes, state changes, responsiveness to stimuli, and other reactions.

The baby's arrival brings profound changes for the family system, which do not significantly strain a happy marriage but may cause distress in a troubled marriage. Special interventions exist to ease the transition to parenthood. Couples who support each other in their new roles typically adjust well.

LEARNING OBJECTIVES

After reading this chapter, you should be able to:

4.1   Describe the events leading up to childbirth and the three stages of labor. (pp. 130–131)

4.2   Discuss the baby's adaptation to labor and delivery, and describe the newborn baby's appearance. (pp. 131–132)

4.3   Explain the purpose and main features of the Apgar Scale. (pp. 132–133)

4.4   Discuss the concept of natural childbirth, noting the typical features of a natural childbirth program, the benefits of the natural childbirth experience, and the importance of social support. (pp. 133–135)

4.5   Discuss the benefits and concerns associated with home delivery. (p. 135)

4.6   List common medical interventions used during childbirth, circumstances that justify their use, and any dangers associated with each. (pp. 136–138)

4.7   Discuss the risks associated with oxygen deprivation, preterm, small-for-date, and low-birth-weight births, and review the developmental outlook for infants born under such circumstances. (pp. 138–141)

4.8   Describe several interventions for preterm infants, including infant stimulation and parent training. (pp. 141–143, 144)

4.9 Summarize the findings of the Kauai Study relating to the long-term consequences of birth complications. (pp. 143, 145)

4.10 Discuss parents' feelings of involvement with their newborn babies, noting research on bonding and rooming in. (pp. 146–147)

4.11 Name and describe major newborn reflexes, noting the functions served by each, and discuss the importance of assessing newborn reflexes. (pp. 147–149)

4.12 Summarize the five infant states of arousal, with particular attention to sleep and crying. (pp. 149–150)

4.13 Describe the newborn baby's responsiveness to touch, taste, smell, sound, and visual stimulation. (pp. 150–156)

4.14 Describe Brazelton's Neonatal Behavioral Assessment Scale (NBAS), and explain its usefulness. (pp. 156–157)

4.15 Discuss typical changes in the family system after the birth of a new baby, along with interventions that foster the transition to parenthood. (pp. 157–161)

LECTURE OUTLINE

I. THE STAGES OF CHILDBIRTH (pp. 130–133)
   A. Several signs indicate that labor is near.
      1. Brief, unpredictable contractions called *false labor* or *prelabor* begin several weeks before the actual birth.
      2. About two weeks before birth, an event called *lightening* occurs, when the baby's head drops low into the uterus as the cervix begins to soften in preparation for delivery.
      3. A signal that labor will occur soon is the *bloody show,* a reddish discharge released when the mucus plug that sealed the cervix during pregnancy is released.
   B. Stage 1: Dilation and Effacement of the Cervix (p. 131)
      1. Stage 1 is the longest stage of labor, lasting an average of 12 to 14 hours with a first birth and 4 to 6 hours with later births.
      2. As uterine contractions become more frequent and powerful, they lead to **dilation and effacement of the cervix**—the opening (dilation) and thinning (effacement) of the cervix, forming a clear channel from the uterus into the vagina.
      3. The uterine contractions are now forceful and regular. They start out 10 to 20 minutes apart and lasting about 15 to 20 seconds. Gradually, they get closer together, occurring every 2 to 3 minutes, and become more powerful, lasting as long as 60 seconds.
      4. **Transition,** the climax of Stage 1 and the most uncomfortable part of childbirth, is reached when the frequency and strength of contractions are at their peak and the cervix opens completely.
   C. Stage 2: Delivery of the Baby (p. 131)
      1. In Stage 2, which lasts approximately 50 minutes for a first baby and 20 minutes in later births, the infant is born.
      2. Strong uterine contractions continue, but the mother also feels a natural urge to squeeze and push with her abdominal muscles, forcing the baby down and out.
      3. The baby's head *crowns* when the vaginal opening stretches around the entire head.
   D. Stage 3: Birth of the Placenta (p. 131)
      1. This final stage of labor lasts about 5 to 10 minutes.
      2. A few final contractions and pushes cause the placenta to separate from the uterine wall and be delivered.
   E. The Baby's Adaptation to Labor and Delivery (pp. 131–132)
      1. The force of the uterine contractions exposes the infant's head to a great deal of pressure and repeatedly squeezes the placenta and umbilical cord, temporarily reducing the infant's oxygen supply with each contraction.

      2.   In response to the force of the contractions, the infant produces high levels of stress hormones, which help the baby withstand oxygen deprivation by sending a rich supply of blood to the brain and heart.

      3.   In addition, this prepares the baby to breathe effectively by causing the lungs to absorb any remaining fluid and by expanding the bronchial tubes.

      4.   Stress hormones also arouse the baby into alertness.

  F. The Newborn Baby's Appearance (p. 132)

      1.   The average newborn is 20 inches long and weighs 7½ pounds; boys tend to be slightly longer and heavier than girls.

      2.   The head is large in comparison to the trunk and legs, which are short and bowed.

      3.   Newborns' round faces, chubby cheeks, large foreheads, and big eyes make adults feel like picking them up and cuddling them—which is essential since, unlike most other mammals, they will not be able to get around on their own until much later.

  G. Assessing the Newborn's Physical Condition: The Apgar Scale (pp. 132–133)

      1.   Infants who have difficulty making the transition to life outside the uterus must be given help at once.

      2.   The **Apgar Scale** is used to assess the infant's physical condition on five criteria, each of which is rated from 0 to 2; a combined score of 7 or better indicates that the baby is in good physical condition.

      3.   Two Apgar ratings are given, at 1 minute and again at 5 minutes after birth, because some babies have trouble adjusting at first but do quite well after a few minutes.

II. APPROACHES TO CHILDBIRTH (pp. 133–135)

  A. Childbirth practices vary according to the society to which mother and baby belong.

      1.   In some village and tribal cultures, expectant mothers are well-acquainted with the childbirth process.

      2.   In most nonindustrialized cultures, women are assisted by others—not necessarily medical personnel—during labor and delivery.

      3.   In Western nations, childbirth has changed dramatically over the centuries.

         a. Until the late 1800s, birth usually took place in the home and was a family-centered event.

         b. The industrial revolution led to greater crowding and new health problems in cities, so childbirth moved from home to hospital, and doctors assumed responsibility for childbirth.

         c. By the 1950s and 1960s, many women were questioning the routine use of medical procedures during labor and, and a natural childbirth movement arose in Europe and spread to North America.

           (1) Today, most hospitals offer birth centers that are family-centered and homelike.

           (2) *Freestanding birth centers* operate independently of hospitals and offer less backup medical care.

         d. A small number of North American women reject institutional birth entirely and choose to have their babies at home.

  B. Natural, or Prepared, Childbirth (pp. 134–135)

      1.   **Natural,** or **prepared, childbirth** is an approach designed to reduce pain and medical intervention while making childbirth a rewarding experience for parents.

      2.   In typical natural childbirth programs, the expectant mother and a companion participate in three activities:

         a. *Classes* educate parents about the anatomy and physiology of labor and delivery.

         b. The expectant mother learns *relaxation and breathing techniques* that help her counteract the pain of the contractions.

         c. A *labor coach* is trained to offer physical and emotional support to the mother during the birth.

      3.   Social Support and Natural Childbirth (p. 134)

         a. Social support, such as the presence of a trained companion, is important to the success of natural childbirth techniques.

         b. In one study, mothers with support had fewer birth complications and significantly shorter labors than those without supportive companionship.

         c. Continuous rather than intermittent support of a trained companion during labor and delivery strengthens these outcomes.

4. Positions for Delivery (pp. 134–135)
    a. During natural childbirth in a birth center or at home, mothers often give birth in an upright, sitting position rather than lying flat on their backs with their feet in stirrups. Research favors the sitting position, for several reasons:
        (1) This position shortens labor by making pushing easier and more effective.
        (2) The baby benefits from a richer supply of oxygen because blood flow to the placenta is increased.
    b. In water birth, the mother sits in a warm tub of water, an approach that is associated with shorter labor, lower rate of episiotomy, and greater likelihood of giving birth without medication.

C. Home Delivery (p. 135)
    1. Home birth has always been popular in England, the Netherlands, Sweden, and other industrialized nations, but is chosen by only about 1 percent of women in North America.
    2. Many home births are handled by certified nurse-midwives who have degrees in nursing and training in childbirth management.
    3. For healthy women aided by a well-trained doctor or midwife, complications rarely occur during home birth. But when mothers are at risk for any kind of complication, the appropriate place for labor and delivery is the hospital, where life-saving treatment is available.

III. MEDICAL INTERVENTIONS (pp. 136–138)
    A. Childbirth in North America, more than anywhere else in the world, is a medically monitored and controlled event.
    B. Fetal Monitoring (p. 136)
        1. **Fetal monitors** are electronic instruments that track the baby's heart rate during labor.
        2. Fetal monitoring is a safe medical procedure that has saved the lives of many babies in high-risk situations, but the routine use of fetal monitors is controversial.
            a. In healthy pregnancies, continuous monitoring does not reduce rates of infant brain damage and death.
            b. Critics worry that fetal monitors falsely identify babies as being in danger.
            c. Monitoring is linked to an increase in the number of instrument and cesarean (surgical) deliveries.
            d. Some women complain that the monitors are uncomfortable and restrictive.
        3. Routine use of monitoring is likely to continue, as evidence that doctors and hospitals have done everything possible to protect the baby.
    C. Labor and Delivery Medication (pp. 136–137)
        1. Some form of medication is used in more than 80 percent of North American births.
            a. **Analgesics** are pain-relieving drugs used to help a mother relax during labor.
            b. **Anesthetics** are stronger painkillers that block sensation.
                (1) Currently, the most common anesthetic used during labor is *epidural analgesia*, which reduces pain in the pelvic region, while preserving the mother's ability to feel the pressure of contractions and to push during the second stage of labor.
                (2) Nevertheless, epidural analgesia weakens uterine contractions, thereby prolonging labor, and drugs cross the placenta, affecting newborns' Apgar scores and responsiveness.
        2. Some researchers claim that the use of childbirth medication has a lasting impact on physical and mental development, but their findings have been challenged.
        3. Because of these drugs' negative effects on newborn adjustment, the current trend is to limit their use.
    D. Instrument Delivery (p. 137)
        1. **Forceps** are metal clamps placed around the baby's head to pull the infant from the birth canal, a method that has been used since the sixteenth century to hasten delivery.
        2. A **vacuum extractor** consists of a suction tube attached to a plastic cup that is placed on the baby's head.
        3. Instrument delivery is used when the mother's pushing during the second stage of labor does not cause the baby to move through the birth canal in a reasonable amount of time.

4. Forceps or vacuum extractors are used in about 7 percent of births in the United States and 17 percent of births in Canada, compared with less than 5 percent of births in Western Europe.

5. Because the use of forceps or vacuum extractors can result in head injury or brain damage, these methods should not be used when mothers can be encouraged to deliver normally and there is no special reason to hurry.

E. Induced Labor (p. 137)

1. An **induced labor** is started artificially by breaking the amnion and giving the mother a hormone that stimulates contractions. About 20 percent of North American labors are induced.

2. Induced labor is justified when continuing the pregnancy threatens the well-being of mother or baby. Too often, however, labor is induced for the doctor's or patient's convenience.

3. The contractions of an induced labor are longer, harder, and closer together than in a naturally occurring labor.

4. As a result, labor and delivery medication is more likely to be used in larger amounts, and there is a greater chance of instrument delivery.

5. When induction is performed before the mother is physically ready, a cesarean delivery is necessary.

6. Levels of the placental hormone *corticotropin-releasing hormone (CRH)* help predict the success of induction procedures.

F. Cesarean Delivery (p. 138)

1. A **cesarean delivery** is a surgical birth in which the doctor makes an incision in the mother's abdomen and lifts the baby out of the uterus.

2. Forty years ago, cesarean delivery was rare. Today, cesarean births account for 30 percent of U.S. births and 19 percent of births in Canada.

3. Cesareans have always been warranted by medical emergencies, such as Rh incompatibility, but in other instances, surgical birth is not always.

4. When the baby is in a breech position (turned so that the buttocks or feet would be delivered first), a cesarean is usually justified.

5. Although the operation is safe, mothers need more time for recovery after a caesarean, and cesarean newborns are more likely to be sleepy and unresponsive and to have breathing difficulties.

6. Also, doctors are now beginning to caution women about attempting a vaginal birth after a cesarean because of slightly increased rates of uterine rupture and infant death. Therefore, women who have had one caesarean delivery are likely to do so again in subsequent births.

IV. BIRTH COMPLICATIONS (pp. 138–146)

A. Oxygen Deprivation (pp. 139–140)

1. **Cerebral palsy** is a general term for a variety of problems, all involving muscle coordination, that result from brain damage before, during, or just after birth.

2. A common cause of cerebral palsy is **anoxia,** inadequate oxygen supply during labor and delivery. It may be caused by squeezing of the umbilical cord, *placenta abruptio* (premature separation of the placenta), or *placenta previa,* in which the placenta covers the cervical opening, causing part of the placenta to detach as the cervix dilates and effaces.

3. Researchers are experimenting with ways to prevent secondary brain damage from occurring after initial brain injury from anoxia—for example, cooling the brain with a special head-cooling cap, or having anoxic newborns lie on a precooled water blanket.

4. The greater the oxygen deprivation, the poorer children's cognitive and language skills in early and middle childhood, although many improve over time.

5. In **respiratory distress syndrome,** a disorder of infants born more than 6 weeks early, the baby's lungs are so immature that the air sacs collapse, causing serious breathing difficulties.

B. Preterm and Low-Birth-Weight Infants (pp. 140–143)

1. Premature babies—those who are born 3 weeks or more before the end of a full 38-week pregnancy or who weigh less than 5½ pounds at birth—are at risk for many physical, cognitive, emotional, and behavioral problems.

2. About 1 in 13 American infants and 1 in 18 Canadian infants are born underweight, with the highest rates among poverty-stricken women, who are more likely to be undernourished and exposed to harmful environmental influences.

3. Preterm versus Small-for-Date Infants (pp. 140–141)
   a. **Preterm infants** are those born several weeks or more before their due date. Their weight may be appropriate based on time spent in the uterus.
   b. **Small-for-date infants** are below their expected weight when length of the pregnancy is taken into account. They usually have more serious problems than preterm infants.
4. Consequences for Caregiving (p. 141)
   a. The appearance and behavior of preterm babies can lead parents to be less sensitive and responsive in caring for them.
   b. Mothers may resort to interfering pokes and verbal commands in an effort to obtain a higher level of response from a baby who is passive, unresponsive, or irritable.
   c. This may explain why preterm babies as a group are at risk for child abuse, especially when they are born to isolated, poverty-stricken mothers who cannot provide good nutrition, health care, or parenting.
   d. How well preterm babies develop has a great deal to do with the parent–child relationship, and the most effective interventions support both parents and infants.
5. Interventions for Preterm Infants (pp. 141–143)
   a. Preterm babies are cared for in special Plexiglas-enclosed beds called *isolettes* that protect the baby from infection and carefully control temperature.
   b. Physical needs that ordinarily would lead to close human contact are met mechanically.
   c. Special Infant Stimulation (p. 142)
      (1) Gentle motion, touch, or audio stimulation can promote growth, more predictable sleep patterns, and alertness in preterm infants.
      (2) Skin-to-skin "kangaroo care," in which the infant is placed in a vertical position against the parent's chest, is widely used in developing countries and, in Western nations, is increasingly used as a valuable supplement to hospital intensive care.
      (3) Kangaroo care fosters improved oxygenation of the baby's body, temperature regulation, sleep, feeding, alertness, and infant survival.
   d. Training Parents in Infant Caregiving Skills (pp. 142–143)
      (1) Interventions that support parents of preterm infants generally teach them about the infant's characteristics and promote caregiving skills.
      (2) Warm parenting that helps preterm infants sustain attention promotes early cognitive and language development.
      (3) When preterm infants live in stressed, low-income households, long term, intensive intervention is necessary.
6. Very Low Birth Weight, Environmental Advantages, and Long-Term Outcomes (pp. 143, 144–145)
   a. Home, school, and societal advantages are responsible for excellent outcomes seen in a study of Canadian young adults who, as newborns, weighed between 1 and 2.2 pounds.
   b. However, despite advanced medical technology and new ways of helping parents, most very-low-birth-weight infants either die or end up with serious disabilities.
   c. The United States has made less progress than other industrialized nations in reducing **infant mortality**—number of deaths in the first year of life per 1,000 live births. It is currently twenty-sixth in international rankings, with members of poor ethnic minorities at greatest risk.
   d. Canada, with a much lower infant mortality rate, ranks sixteenth, although First Nations and Inuit babies have much higher infant mortality rates than Canadian babies in general.
   e. **Neonatal mortality,** the rate of death within the first month of life, accounts for 67 percent of infant deaths in the United States and 80 percent in Canada.
   f. Universal, high-quality health care, generous parental leave, and other social services have a powerful positive impact on infant well-being.
C. Birth Complications, Parenting, and Resilience (pp. 143, 145)
   1. Research on infants who experienced birth complications indicates that, as long as birth injuries are not overwhelming, a supportive home environment can restore children's growth. However, negative home environments can have lasting effects on even the sturdiest newborn.

2.   Some children with serious birth complications and troubled family environments are resilient and, as a result, fare well as adults. These children often rely on factors outside their immediate families and within themselves to overcome stress, sometimes forming relationships with relatives, neighbors, and peers.

V.   PRECIOUS MOMENTS AFTER BIRTH (pp. 146–147)
   A.   Regardless of SES or participation in childbirth classes, fathers touch, look at, talk to, and kiss their newborn infants just as much as mothers do.
   B.   Parental hormonal changes in the presence of the newborn help foster parents' involvement and sensitivity. Studies have shown hormonal changes in father that were compatible with those of mothers, including slight increases in *prolactin* and *estrogens,* and a drop in *androgens.*
   C.   **Bonding**—parents' feelings of affection and concern for their newborn baby—does not depend on a specific period of togetherness immediately following the birth, although contact with the baby after birth may be one of several factors that helps build a good parent–infant relationship.
   D.   Today, hospitals offer an arrangement called **rooming in,** in which the newborn stays in the mother's hospital room all or most of the time.

VI.   THE NEWBORN BABY'S CAPACITIES (pp. 147–157)
   A.   Reflexes (pp. 147–149)
      1.   A **reflex** is an inborn, automatic response to a particular form of stimulation. Reflexes are the newborn baby's most obvious organized patterns of behavior.
      2.   Adaptive Value of Reflexes (p. 147)
         a.   Some reflexes have survival value. For example, the rooting reflex helps a breast-fed baby find the mother's nipple.
         b.   Some reflexes (e.g., the Moro, or "embracing," reflex) may have helped babies survive earlier in our evolutionary past but no longer serve a special purpose.
         c.   Several reflexes help parents and infants establish gratifying interaction.
      3.   Reflexes and the Development of Motor Skills (pp. 147–149)
         a.   A few reflexes form the basis for motor skills that will develop later. For example, the tonic neck reflex may prepare the baby for voluntary reaching.
         b.   Other reflexes drop out early, but the motor functions involved are renewed later. For example, when stepping is exercised regularly, babies tend to walk several weeks earlier than if it is not practiced.
      4.   The Importance of Assessing Newborn Reflexes (p. 149)
         a.   Researchers believe that most newborn reflexes disappear during the first six months of life because of the infant's gradual increase in voluntary control over behavior.
         b.   Assessing reflexes along with other characteristics can reveal the health of the baby's nervous system.
   B.   States (pp. 149–152)
      1.   Newborn infants move in and out of the five **states of arousal,** or degrees of sleep and wakefulness, throughout the day and night.
      2.   Striking individual differences in daily rhythms exist that affect parents' attitudes toward and interactions with the baby.
      3.   Sleep (pp. 149–151)
         a.   During irregular, or **rapid-eye-movement (REM),** sleep, which accounts for 50 percent of the newborn's sleep time, the brain and parts of the body are active, much as in the waking state.
         b.   During regular, or **non-rapid-eye-movement (NREM),** sleep, the body is almost motionless, and heart rate, breathing, and brain-wave activity are slow and even.
         c.   Researchers believe that the stimulation of REM sleep is vital for growth of the central nervous system in young infants, because they spend little time in an alert state, where they can get input from the environment. Also, the rapid eye movements of REM sleep protect the health of the eye.
         d.   Because normal sleep behavior in newborns is patterned, observations of sleep states can help identify central nervous system abnormalities.

    e. **Sudden infant death syndrome (SIDS)** is the unexpected death, usually during the night, of an infant younger than 1 year of age that remains unexplained after thorough investigation. Possible causes include preexisting physical problems, problems in brain functioning, exposure to cigarette smoke, prenatal drug abuse, and sleep position. Preventive practices include putting babies down on their backs and using a pacifier.

   4. Crying (pp. 151–153)

    a. Crying is the first way that babies communicate their needs, especially physical needs. It typically increases during the early weeks, peaks at about 6 weeks, and then declines.

    b. Crying stimulates strong feelings of arousal and discomfort in men and women, parents and nonparents.

     (1) Soothing Crying Infants (p. 152)

      (a) The most effective technique usually used by Western parents is lifting the baby to the shoulder and rocking or walking.

      (b) Another common soothing method is swaddling—wrapping the baby snugly in a blanket.

      (c) In many non-Western societies, infants spend most of the time in close physical contact with caregivers, and show shorter bouts of crying.

     (2) Abnormal Crying (pp. 152–153)

      (a) The cries of brain-damaged babies and those who have experienced prenatal and birth complications are often shrill and piercing.

      (b) *Colic,* or persistent crying, occurs in newborns who react especially strongly to unpleasant stimuli, and usually subsides between 3 and 6 months of age.

 C. Sensory Capacities (pp. 153–156)

  1. Touch (pp. 153–154)

    a. Touch helps stimulate early physical and emotional development.

    b. Sensitivity to touch, pain, and temperature change is present at birth.

    c. Allowing infants to endure severe pain overwhelms the nervous system with stress hormones, which can disrupt the child's developing capacity to handle common, everyday stressors.

  2. Taste and Smell (pp. 154–155)

    a. Babies are born with the ability to communicate their taste preferences.

    b. Infant facial expressions indicate they can distinguish among several tastes.

    c. Newborns can readily learn to like a taste that at first evoked either a neutral or a negative response—for example, when a previously disliked taste is paired with relief of hunger.

    d. Infants' responsiveness to the smell of certain foods is similar to that of adults, suggesting that some odor preferences are innate.

    e. Newborn infants are attracted to the odor of their own mother's lactating breast, which helps the baby find a food source and to distinguish the mother from other people.

  3. Hearing (p. 155)

    a. Newborns can hear a wide variety of sound, and they prefer complex sounds such as voices and noises, to pure tones.

    b. Newborns can detect the sounds of any human language and make fine-grained distinctions among many speech sounds.

    c. Responsiveness to sound supports the newborn's exploration of the environment. Infants as young as 3 days turn their eyes and head in the general direction of a sound.

    d. Newborns prefer speech that is high-pitched and expressive and respond more strongly to their mother's voice than to that of an unfamiliar woman.

  4. Vision (pp. 155–156)

    a. Vision is the least developed of the newborn's senses.

    b. Newborns cannot focus their eyes very well and have limited **visual acuity,** or fineness of discrimination.

    c. Although their eye movements are slow and inaccurate, newborns actively explore their environment by scanning it for interesting sights and tracking moving objects.

    d. Newborns prefer colored to gray stimuli, but they are not yet good at discriminating colors.

D.   Neonatal Behavioral Assessment (pp. 156–157)

1.   The **Neonatal Behavioral Assessment Scale (NBAS)** is a test developed by T. Berry Brazelton to assess the baby's reflexes, muscle tone, state changes, responsiveness to physical and social stimuli, and other reactions.

2.   The *Neonatal Intensive Care Unit Network Neurobehavioral Scale (NNNS)* is a similar instrument used with newborns at risk for developmental problems.

3.   The NBAS has been used in many cultures worldwide, providing information about both individual and cultural differences in newborn behavior.

4.   Because newborn behavior and parenting styles combine to shape development, changes in NBAS scores over the first week or two of life provide the best estimate of a baby's ability to recover from the stress of birth.

5.   The NBAS and NNNS have also been used to help parents get to know their infants, promoting more effective interaction with their newborn.

VII.   THE TRANSITION TO PARENTHOOD (pp. 157–161)

A.   In the first weeks after childbirth, the mother needs to recover physically and adjust to massive hormonal shifts in her body.

B.   The father needs to become a part of this new threesome while supporting the mother in her recovery.

C.   Changes in the Family System (pp. 158, 160)

1.   The demands of new parenthood do not significantly strain a happy marriage, but troubled marriages usually become more distressed after the baby is born.

2.   Parenthood generally leads husbands and wives to assume more traditional gender roles.

3.   Many women experience a period of letdown after the initial excitement of the baby's arrival, and about 10 percent experience **postpartum depression,** mild to severe feelings of sadness and withdrawal that last for weeks or months. Paternal depression can also occur. Early treatment of parental depression is vital to prevent the disorder from interfering with the parent–child relationship.

4.   Postponing parenthood until the late twenties or thirties eases the transition to parenthood. And fathers' participation in infant care enhances the marital relationship, adjustment to parenthood, and sensitivity to the baby.

5.   A second birth typically requires that fathers take an even more active role in parenting, and fathers' willingness to take on this role is linked to mothers' adjustment after the arrival of a second baby.

D.   Single-Mother Families (pp. 158–159)

1.   About 37 percent of babies in the United States and Canada are born to single mothers.

2.   Teenage mothers and their newborns are at high risk for developmental problems, and in general, single mothers living in poverty are likely to experience a stressful transition to parenthood.

3.   In contrast, older single women who give birth or adopt generally encounter few parenting difficulties because of economic well-being and psychological maturity.

E.   Parent Interventions (pp. 159, 161)

1.   Special interventions exist to ease the transition to parenthood, such as counselor-led parenting groups for low-risk parents and more intensive programs to enhance social support and the parent–child relationship for high-risk parents.

2.   When couples have a positive marital relationship, available social support, and sufficient income, the stress caused by the birth of a baby remains manageable.

LECTURE ENHANCEMENTS

LECTURE ENHANCEMENT 4.1
Do Daytime Activity Level and Exposure to Light Predict Nighttime Sleep in Infants? (pp. 149–150)

Time: 5–10 minutes

Objective: To examine the impact of daytime activity level and light exposure on nighttime sleep in infants.

In adults, exposure to natural and artificial light affects melatonin secretion and sleep-wake cycles. However, it is unclear whether or not light exposure has the same effect on young infants. To find out, Harrison (2004) recruited parents of 56 full-term infants who were healthy and free from medication. The infants were observed in their homes for 3 consecutive days at 6 weeks, 9 weeks, and 12 weeks of age. During each 3-day block:

1. Parents kept a daily diary to record infant sleep, wakefulness, crying, and feeding.

2. Infants were fitted with an ankle-worn actiwatch that recorded 24-hour activity rates.

3. The Actiwatch-L, which is sensitive to a wide range of light waves, was attached to a small toy and was kept near the infant at all times.

Results from the cry diaries indicated that 6-week-old infants cried substantially more than 9- to 12-week-old infants. Infants who had high levels of evening crying also slept less at night. Although total sleep declined between 6 and 12 weeks, a greater proportion of sleep was at night. The amount of light exposure did not predict crying, but infants who were exposed to considerable early afternoon light slept longer and more soundly at night. In addition, babies with high activity levels during the day slept better at night than babies with low activity levels.

Overall, this study supports previous research in that young infants cry significantly more than older infants and nighttime sleep increases during the first 3 months of life. In addition, the results suggest that daytime light exposure and high daytime activity levels contribute to longer and sounder sleep in healthy infants.

Harrison, Y. (2004). The relationship between daytime exposure to light and night-time sleep in 6-to-12-week-old infants. *Journal of Sleep Research, 13,* 345–352.

LECTURE ENHANCEMENT 4.2
Maternal Depression and its Effects on Newborn Behavior (p. 160)

Time: 10–15 minutes

Objective: To examine the effects of maternal depression on depressive behavior in newborns.

Research on the newborns of depressed mothers shows that depressive symptoms (irritability, low activity levels, poor feeding and sleeping) are sometimes present at birth. To further examine the relationship between maternal depression and depressive symptoms in newborns, Field and colleagues (2004) recruited 140 pregnant women (70 depressed and 70 nondepressed) in their second trimester of pregnancy. At two separate intervals—in the second trimester and again shortly after birth—the researchers administered standardized depression, anxiety, and anger scales. Because certain neurotransmitters and hormones like norepinephrine, epinephrine, cortisol, dopamine, and seratonin are related to general mood and depression, urine samples were collected during a routine ultrasound visit and 24 hours after birth. Infant urine samples were also collected 24 hours after birth. To assess infant behavior, the researchers recorded sleep and wake cycles, administered the Brazelton Neonatal Behavior Assessment Scale, recorded EEG activity (since depressed individuals tend to show increased right frontal EEG activation), and measured heart rate. Finally, the researchers recorded maternal EEG activity and heart rate following birth.

Findings indicated that depressed mothers and their newborns had higher cortisol levels and lower dopamine and seratonin levels than the nondepressed mother-infant pairs. Depressed mothers and their babies also had higher heart rates and greater right frontal EEG activity than nondepressed mothers and infants. Not surprisingly, Brazelton scores, which include infant habituation, orientation, and motor behavior, were lower in infants of depressed mothers.

And consistent with previous research, depressed mothers were more likely to deliver prematurely and have low-birth-weight babies. Taken together, these findings show that depressed mothers are more likely than nondepressed mothers to experience birth complications, and their infants are at-risk for depressive symptoms immediately following birth.

Ask students to reflect on these findings. How might maternal and newborn depression affect the transition to parenthood? What are some long-term consequences of maternal and paternal depression on child development?

Field, T., Diego, M., Dieter, J., Hernandez-Reif, M., Schanberg, S., Kuhn, C., Yando, R., & Bendell, D. (2004). Prenatal depression effects on the fetus and the newborn. *Infant Behavior & Development, 27,* 216–229.

LECTURE ENHANCEMENT 4.3
The Transition to Siblinghood: A Developmental Ecological Systems Approach (p. 158)

Time: 15–20 minutes

Objective: To highlight environmental factors that contribute to the transition to siblinghood.

As noted in the next, the early weeks after a new baby enters the family are full of profound changes. While the arrival of a newborn sibling is a normative life event for many children, the transition to siblinghood can result in a mixture of positive and negative emotions. Some children welcome the new arrival, while others experience a developmental setback in a specific area like toilet training.

To extend existing research on the transition to siblinghood, Volling (2005) provides a developmental ecological systems approach to examine changes in both child and family functioning that occur with the birth of a new baby.

- Significant changes occur within the immediate family (microsystem). Because the mother may spend most of the early weeks after the birth caring for the newborn, the quality of the father-child relationship may be particularly important for sibling adjustment.

- Changes in the family system may also affect connections between home and school or home and child-care setting (mesosystem). For example, a supportive child-care arrangement that recognizes child and family needs helps promote favorable sibling adjustment. Talking to the child about the new baby, the new roles that mom and dad have, and validating the child's feelings are important.

- Social settings, such as the parents' workplace (exosystem), can have an indirect effect on sibling adjustment. A supportive work environment that provides paid maternity and paternity leave helps relieve the parents' stress, which translates into more effective parenting. Supportive neighbors and relatives can also offer stress relief to parents and siblings as they adjust to the changing family structure.

- Cultural values and customs (macrosystem) can have a profound effect on the transition to siblinghood—both directly and indirectly. For example, some families involve siblings in nearly all aspects of the pregnancy and birth. Children who are actively involved in the pregnancy and know what to expect following birth tend to adjust more favorably to the new baby than children who are excluded from the process. In addition, when fathers take an active role in household duties and child care, mothers tend to experience less stress and engage in more effective parenting.

- Children and families are involved in dynamic and ever-changing environmental contexts (chronosystem). An additional birth, moving to a new home, a parent changing jobs, and the child's age will affect the entire family system. For instance, toddlers react to the birth of a sibling very differently than school-age children or adolescents. There will also be adjustments to the marital and parental relationship following the birth.

Ask students to reflect on their own experiences with siblinghood. How did they deal with the arrival of a new baby? What role did environmental supports play in the transition? Did they have a smooth transition to siblinghood or was it a stressful time? Explain.

Volling, B. L. (2005). The transition to siblinghood: A developmental ecological systems perspective and directions for future research. *Journal of Family Psychology, 19,* 542–549.

LECTURE ENHANCEMENT 4.4
More on the Transition to Parenthood: Do Beliefs About Birth Order and Birth Rank Affect Parenting and Child Development? (pp. 157–161)

Time: 10–15 minutes

Objective: To explore beliefs and stereotypes associated with birth order, as well as the accuracy of these stereotypes.

In an interesting series of studies, Herrera and colleagues (2003) examined beliefs and stereotypes about birth order and birth rank. In one investigation, participants were asked about the personality traits of firstborns, only children, middle-borns, and last-borns. In two other studies, participants were asked what occupations are likely to be held by people of different birth ranks. In a final study, the researchers examined actual occupations held by individuals differing in birth rank.

Results of the first study indicated that "(1) firstborns are believed to be the most intelligent, obedient, stable, and responsible and the least emotional; (2) only children are believed to be the most disagreeable; (3) middle-borns are believed to be the most envious and the least bold and talkative; and (4) last-borns are believed to be the most creative, emotional, extraverted, disobedient, irresponsible, and talkative" (p. 149). However, it is important to note that despite these perceptions, research on birth order does not support such stereotypes.

Results of the next two studies indicated that participants' beliefs about occupations were consistent with their perceptions of personality differences. Even more interesting, results of the last study showed that participants' ideas about birth order were, at least to some degree, reflected in reality. Individuals with an earlier birth rank tend to attain more years of education and to have more prestigious occupations. The researchers noted that these results indicate that people's beliefs about birth order are predictable, strong, and consistent. Moreover, if parents (and others) react differently to firstborn and later-born children, their behaviors might shape the child's development to fit the stereotypes.

Ask students to think of additional stereotypes about birth order and to consider the extent to which their parents, and other family members, held such stereotypes. In their view, did such stereotyping affect their own development?

Herrera, N. C., Zajonc, R. B., Wieczorkowska, G., & Cichomski, B. (2003). Beliefs about birth rank and their reflection in reality. *Journal of Personality & Social Psychology, 85,* 142–150.

LEARNING ACTIVITIES

LEARNING ACTIVITY 4.1
Discussing Birth Experiences (pp. 133–138)

Invite students or former students who have recently given birth to come to class to discuss their experiences. If no one is available, students often have friends or relatives who are willing to come to class. If possible, invite at least two women or couples who have recently given birth. Students in the class should prepare questions in advance to ask of the panel of guests. For example, how active was the fetus during the pregnancy? Did the mother experience morning sickness? Did the mother experience any complications during her pregnancy or delivery? Did she have the baby at home, in a birthing center, or in a hospital? Who was present at the birth? What did she think about the newborn's appearance? If you can recruit more than one mother or couple, students can examine differences in birth experiences by asking questions such as: How long were you in labor? How many children have you had? What were the differences in length of each labor? Did you use medication during labor and delivery? Did you take natural childbirth classes, and if so, were the classes helpful? What was the father's (or other coach's) role during labor and delivery?

LEARNING ACTIVITY 4.2
Identifying the Multiple Origins of Low Birth Weight (p. 140–143)

One cause of low birth weight is unpreventable physical defects. However, many other causes are preventable, such as maternal drug use, cigarette smoking, and emotional stress. In addition, mothers from poverty-stricken ethnic minority homes have increased chances of having underweight babies due to malnutrition and exposure to harmful environmental influences.

In small groups, have students list factors that increase the chances that a baby will be born underweight. Which of the factors cited could be prevented by better health care for mothers and babies? What interventions are available to babies born underweight?

LEARNING ACTIVITY 4.3
Observing Newborn Reflexes (pp. 147–149)

Arrange for parents to bring an infant to class for a demonstration of newborn reflexes. As you demonstrate each reflex, engage students in a discussion of its adaptive value. Also, point out that pediatricians often use infant reflexes as a way of assessing the health of the baby's nervous system.

LEARNING ACTIVITY 4.4
Matching Newborn Reflexes with Their Function (p. 148)

As an in-class assignment or quiz, present the following activity to students:

Directions: Match the each newborn reflex with its function.

Reflex:

1. Eye blink
2. Rooting
3. Sucking
4. Moro
5. Palmar grasp
6. Tonic neck
7. Stepping
8. Babinski

Function:

A. May prepare infant for voluntary reaching
B. Unknown
C. Helps infant find the nipple
D. Permits feeding
E. Prepares infant for voluntary walking
F. Protects infant from strong stimulation
G. Prepares infant for voluntary grasping
H. In human evolutionary past, may have helped infant cling to mother

Answers:

1. G
2. D
3. E
4. I
5. H
6. B
7. F
8. C

LEARNING ACTIVITY 4.5
True or False: Newborn States and Sensory Capacities (pp. 149–156)

Present the following exercise to students as a quiz or an in-class activity:

Directions: Read each of the following statements and indicate whether each is *True* (T) or *False* (F).

Statements:

_____ 1. Newborns sleep about 22 hours a day.
_____ 2. Researchers believe that the stimulation of REM sleep is vital for growth of the central nervous system.
_____ 3. In many tribal and village societies and non-Western developed nations, infants spend most of the day and night in close physical contact with caregivers.
_____ 4. The cries of healthy infants tend to be shrill and piercing.
_____ 5. At birth, infants are insensitive to pain.
_____ 6. Like adults, newborns relax their facial muscles in response to sweetness, purse their lips when the taste is sour, and show a distinct archlike mouth opening when it is bitter.
_____ 7. Newborns' dual attraction to the odors of their mother and of the lactating breast helps them locate an appropriate food source and, in the process, begin to distinguish their caregiver from other people.
_____ 8. Young infants listen longer to nonspeech sounds than to human speech.
_____ 9. Vision is the least developed of the newborn baby's senses.
_____ 10. Newborns' eye movements are surprisingly quick and accurate.

Answers:

1. F
2. T
3. T
4. F
5. F
6. T
7. T
8. F
9. T
10. F

LEARNING ACTIVITY 4.6
Speaking to Parents About Newborn Sleep and Crying (pp. 149–153)

Ask students to pretend they have been asked by a local social service agency to speak to new parents about newborn sleep and crying. For example, how much sleep does a typical newborn need? Why do newborns sleep so much? Why do babies cry, and what can parents do to comfort them? When is crying cause for alarm? Students should prepare an easy-to-understand presentation that is supported by research in the text.

LEARNING ACTIVITY 4.7
Demonstrating the Neonatal Behavioral Assessment Scale (NBAS) (pp. 156–157)

If you have access to a Neonatal Behavioral Assessment Scale (NBAS) and are familiar with its administration, arrange for parents to bring an infant to class. Demonstrate a sampling of items, including reflexes, state changes, and sensory and motor capacities. If you have not had prior experience administering the NBAS, you may want to visit the Brazelton Institute website at *http://www.brazelton-institute.com*. Explain how this instrument is being used by some hospitals to teach parents about their newborn baby's capacities and unique characteristics. Additionally, discuss why a single NBAS score is not a good predictor of later development and why "recovery curves" are better predictors.

ASK YOURSELF . . .

REVIEW: Name and briefly describe the three stages of labor. (p. 131)

Stage 1: Dilation and Effacement of the Cervix. Stage 1 is the longest, lasting an average of 12 to 14 hours with a first birth and 4 to 6 hours with later births. During Stage 1, uterine contractions gradually become more frequent and powerful. As a result, the cervix opens (dilates) and thins (effaces), forming a clear channel from the uterus into the birth canal, or vagina. The climax of Stage 1 is a brief phase called transition, in which the frequency and strength of contractions are at their peak and the cervix opens completely.

Stage 2: Delivery of the Baby. In Stage 2, which lasts about 50 minutes for a first baby and 20 minutes in later births, the infant is born. Strong contractions of the uterus continue, but the mother also feels a natural urge to squeeze and push with her abdominal muscles. As she does so with each contraction, she forces the baby down and out.

Stage 3: Birth of the Placenta. Stage 3 brings labor to an end with a few final contractions and pushes, which cause the placenta to separate from the wall of the uterus and be delivered in about 5 to 10 minutes.

APPLY: On seeing her newborn baby for the first time, Caroline exclaimed, "Why is she so out of proportion?" What observations prompted Caroline to ask this question? Explain why her baby's appearance is adaptive. (p. 132)

The newborn's body proportions are often surprising to first-time parents. The infant's head is large in comparison to the trunk and legs, which are short and bowed. This combination of a large head (with its well-developed brain) and a small body is adaptive, equipping human infants to learn quickly in the first few months of life. And other aspects of newborns' appearance—round faces, chubby cheeks, large foreheads, and big eyes—make adults feel like picking them up and cuddling them, which is also adaptive since unlike most other mammals, human babies cannot get around on their own until much later.

CONNECT: Contrast the positive impact of the baby's production of stress hormones during childbirth with the negative impact of maternal stress on the fetus, discussed on page 117 in Chapter 3. (pp. 131–132)

During pregnancy, maternal stress hormones cross the placenta, causing a dramatic rise in fetal heart rate and activity and possibly altering fetal neurological functioning in ways that heighten stress reactivity in later life. During childbirth, the force of the contractions causes the infant to produce high levels of cortisol and other stress hormones. This cortisol production is adaptive because, by sending a rich supply of blood to the brain and heart, it helps the baby withstand the oxygen deprivation that is caused by each contraction.

REVIEW: Describe the features and benefits of natural childbirth. What aspect contributes greatly to favorable outcomes, and why? (p. 134)

In a typical natural, or prepared, childbirth program, the expectant mother and a companion (a partner, relative, or friend) participate in three activities:

Classes. Expectant mothers and their companions attend classes in which they learn about the anatomy and physiology of labor and delivery. Knowledge about the birth process reduces a mother's fear.

Relaxation and breathing techniques. During each class, mothers are taught relaxation and breathing exercises aimed at counteracting the pain of uterine contractions.

Labor coach. The mother's companion learns to serve as a labor coach, assisting the expectant mother during childbirth by reminding her to relax and breathe, massaging her back, supporting her body, and offering encouragement and affection.

Studies reveal many benefits for mothers who experience natural childbirth compared with those who do not. Because mothers feel more in control of labor and delivery, their attitudes toward the childbirth experience are more positive. They also feel less pain and , as a result, require little or no pain-relieving medication.

Social support is an important to the success of natural childbirth techniques. Research shows that having a trained companion who stays with the mother throughout labor and delivery results in fewer birth complications and shorter labor compared with mothers who have no social support. Other studies indicate that mothers supported during labor less often have cesarean (surgical) deliveries, and their babies' Apgar scores are higher.

APPLY: Sharon, a heavy smoker, has just arrived at the hospital in labor. Which one of the medical interventions discussed in the preceding sections is her doctor justified in using? (For help in answering this question, review the prenatal effects of tobacco on page 110 in Chapter 3.) (p. 136)

Research has established that maternal smoking results in low birth weight, prematurity, miscarriage, and infant death. Consequently, a doctor would be justified in using a fetal monitor, an electronic instrument that tracks the baby's heart rate during labor. An abnormal heartbeat pattern may indicate that the baby is in distress due to a lack of oxygen and needs to be delivered immediately.

CONNECT: Use of any one medical intervention during labor increases the chances that others will also be used. Provide as many examples as you can to illustrate this idea. (pp. 136–138)

Most infants have some heartbeat irregularities during labor, and critics worry that fetal monitors identify babies as being in danger who actually are not. As a result, monitoring is linked to an increase in the number of instrument and cesarean (surgical) deliveries.

Although induced labor is justified when continuing the pregnancy threatens the well-being of a mother or baby, often labor is induced unnecessarily, for the doctor's or the patient's convenience. An induced labor often proceeds differently from a naturally occurring one. Contractions are longer, harder, and closer together, increasing the possibility of inadequate oxygen supply to the baby. In addition, mothers often find it more difficult to stay in control of an induced labor, even when they have been coached in natural childbirth techniques. As a result, labor and delivery medication is likely to be used in larger amounts, and the chances of instrument delivery are slightly greater.

Until recently, many women with a previous cesarean delivery were offered the option of a vaginal birth in subsequent pregnancies. Though once considered safe, this practice has recently been questioned because of new evidence indicating that compared with repeated cesareans, a natural labor after a cesarean is associated with slightly higher rates of rupture of the uterus and infant death. If labor is induced, these risks multiply. As a result, there has been a shift back to the old rule, "Once a cesarean, always a cesarean." But when a mother does have a cesarean delivery, she and her baby need extra support. The operation itself is safe, but more time is needed for recovery. And because anesthetic may have crossed the placenta, cesarean newborns are more likely to be sleepy and unresponsive and are at increased risk for breathing difficulties.

REFLECT: If you were an expectant parent, would you choose home birth? Why or why not? (p. 135)

This is an open-ended question with no right or wrong answer.

REVIEW: Sensitive care can help preterm infants recover, but unfortunately they are less likely than full-term newborns to receive such care. Explain why. (pp. 140–141)

Preterm infants have a special need for sensitive attention and for certain kinds of stimulation that can help them develop. However, the appearance and behavior of these babies can lead parents to be less sensitive and responsive in caring for them. Compared to full-term infants, preterm babies—especially those who are very ill at birth—are less often held close, touched, and talked to gently. Their unresponsiveness may prompt mothers to resort to interfering pokes and verbal commands in an effort to obtain a response, putting preterm babies as a group at greater risk for child abuse.

APPLY: Cecilia and Adena each gave birth to a three-pound baby seven weeks preterm. Cecilia is single and on welfare. Adena and her husband are happily married and earn a good income. Plan an intervention appropriate for helping each baby develop. (pp. 141–143)

Skin-to-skin "kangaroo care," in which the preterm infant is placed in a vertical position close to the chest, under the parent's clothing, would be an appropriate intervention for both Cecilia and Adena. This technique is widely used in developing nations and is also widely offered in Western nations as a supplement to hospital intensive care. It fosters improved oxygenation of the baby's body, temperature regulation, breathing, feeding, alertness, and infant survival. In addition, mothers and fathers practicing kangaroo care feel more confident about meeting their infants' needs and interact more sensitively and affectionately with them. Their babies, in turn, develop more favorably during the first year than preterm infants not receiving such care.

Because of Cecilia's difficult financial situation, she and her baby would also benefit from long-term, intensive intervention, including medical follow-ups, weekly parent training sessions, and cognitively stimulating child care from 1 to 3 years of age.

Because Adena and her husband have sufficient income, their baby should remain in the hospital until he or she is in stable condition, receiving special stimulation, which has been linked to faster weight gain, more predictable sleep patterns, and greater alertness in preterm infants. In the hospital, a Plexiglas-enclosed isolette will be used to control body temperature and protect the baby from infection. Once they leave the hospital, Adena and her husband should also receive several sessions of coaching in recognizing and responding to their baby's needs.

CONNECT: List factors discussed in this chapter and in Chapter 3 that increase the chances that an infant will be born underweight. How many of these factors could be prevented by better health care for mothers and babies? (pp. 140–143)

Low-birth-weight babies can be divided into two groups: preterm and small-for-date. Preterm infants are born several weeks or more before their due date. Although they are small, their weight may still be appropriate, based on time spent in the uterus. Small-for-date babies are below their expected weight when length of the pregnancy is taken into account. Of the two types of babies, small-for-date infants usually have more serious problems. These infants probably experienced inadequate nutrition before birth. Perhaps their mothers did not eat properly, the placenta did not function normally, or the babies themselves had defects that prevented them from growing as they should. They are especially likely to suffer from prenatal neurological impairments that permanently weaken their capacity to manage stress.

Factors discussed in Chapter 3 that increase the chances that an infant will be born underweight can be divided into two general categories: teratogens and other maternal factors. A teratogen is any environmental agent that causes damage during the prenatal period, including prescription and nonprescription medications, caffeine, illegal drugs, tobacco, alcohol, radiation, environmental pollution, and infectious diseases. Other maternal factors include poor health, lack of exercise, malnutrition, and emotional stress.

To create a safe environment for prenatal development, it is important for a woman to make healthy lifestyle choices even before she becomes pregnant. These include regular exercise, good nutrition, and elimination of or avoidance of exposure to teratogens. Furthermore, although some premature births are unavoidable, many others can be prevented by improving prenatal nutrition and prenatal health care, and by avoiding teratogens before and during the pregnancy.

REFLECT: Many people object to the use of extraordinary medical measures to save extremely low-birth-weight babies because of their high risk for serious and persistent developmental problems. Do you agree or disagree? Explain. (pp. 140–143)

This is an open-ended question with no right or wrong answer.

REVIEW: What functions does REM sleep serve in young infants? Can sleep tell us anything about the health of the newborn's central nervous system? Explain. (p. 150)

Because babies probably do not dream, at least not in the way that older children and adults do, sleep researchers believe that the stimulation of REM sleep is vital for growth of the central nervous system. Young infants seem to have a special need for this stimulation because they spend so little time in an alert state, when they can get input from the environment. Whereas the brain-wave activity of REM sleep safeguards the central nervous system, the rapid eye movements protect the health of the eye by ensuring that all parts of the eye are fully oxygenated.

Because the normal sleep behavior of the newborn baby is organized and patterned, observations of sleep states can help identify central nervous system abnormalities. In infants who are brain damaged or who have experienced serious birth trauma, disturbed REM-NREM sleep cycles are often present. Babies with poor sleep organization are likely to be behaviorally disorganized and, therefore, to have difficulty learning and eliciting caregiver interactions that enhance their development. And the brain-functioning problems that underlie newborn sleep irregularities may culminate in sudden infant death syndrome, a major cause of infant mortality.

APPLY: After a difficult delivery, Jackie observes her 2-day-old daughter, Kelly, being given the NBAS. Kelly scores poorly on many items. Seeing this, Jackie wonders if Kelly will develop normally. How would you respond to Jackie's concern? (pp. 156–157)

A single NBAS score is not a good predictor of later development. Because Kelly experienced a difficult birth, she probably needs time to recover. In addition, Kelly's behavior will combine with Jackie's parenting style to shape development. Therefore, changes in NBAS scores over the first week or two of life (rather than a single score) will provide the best estimate of Kelly's ability to recover from the stress of birth. Unlike a single score, NBAS "recovery curves" predict intelligence and absence of emotional and behavior problems with moderate success well into the preschool years.

CONNECT: How do the diverse capacities of newborn babies contribute to their first social relationships? Provide as many examples as you can. (pp. 147–155)

Reflexes. Reflexes are the newborn baby's most obvious organized patterns of behavior. Several reflexes help parents and infants establish gratifying interaction. A baby who searches for and successfully finds the nipple, sucks easily during feedings, and grasps when her hand is touched encourages parents to respond lovingly and feel competent as caregivers. Reflexes can also make it easier for parents to comfort the baby by permitting infants to control distress and amount of stimulation.

States of Arousal. A baby's cry can have a powerful effect on the formation of social relationships. The sound stimulates strong feelings of arousal and discomfort in just about anyone—men and women, parents and nonparents. This powerful response is probably innately programmed in all human beings to make sure that babies receive the care and protection they need to survive.

Sensory Capacities. A newborn's responsiveness to touch, preference for high-pitched human speech, and the ability to track moving objects (such as the parent) evoke interaction with caregivers, laying the foundation for their first social relationships.

REFLECT: Are newborns more competent than you thought they were before you read this chapter? Which of their capacities most surprised you? (pp. 147–155)

This is an open-ended question with no right or wrong answer.

REVIEW: Explain how persisting postpartum depression seriously impairs children's development. (p. 160)

Postpartum depression in mothers is characterized by mild to severe feelings of sadness and withdrawal that continue for weeks or months. Depression in either the mother or the father can interfere with effective parenting and seriously impair children's development. In the weeks after birth, infants of depressed mothers sleep poorly, are less attentive to their surroundings, and have elevated stress-hormone levels. When maternal depression persists, the parent–child relationship declines.

Depressed parents view their infants more negatively than do independent observers. And they use inconsistent discipline—sometimes lax, at other times too forceful. Children who experience these maladaptive parenting practices often have serious adjustment difficulties. To avoid their parent's insensitivity, they may withdraw into a depressive mood themselves or may become impulsive and antisocial.

Over time, children of depressed parents may develop a pessimistic world view, in which they lack self-confidence and perceive their parents and other people as threatening. Children who constantly feel in danger are more likely to become overly aroused in stressful situations, easily losing control in the face of cognitive and social challenges. Although children of depressed parents may inherit a tendency to develop emotional and behavioral problems, quality of parenting is a major factor in their adjustment.

APPLY: Derek, father of a 3-year-old and a newborn, reported that he had a harder time adjusting to the birth of his second child than to that of his first child. Explain why this might be so. (p. 158)

Whereas parents often take on more traditional roles after the first child is born, well-functioning families with a newborn second child typically show a pulling back from this traditional division of responsibilities. Specifically, a second birth typically requires fathers, such as Derek, to take an active role in parenting—for example, by caring for the older child while the mother is recuperating and by sharing in the high demands of tending to both a baby and a young child. Support and encouragement from family, friends, and his spouse will be crucial for reducing Derek's stress and helping him adapt to a second child.

CONNECT: Louise has just given birth to her first child. Because her husband works long hours and is seldom available to help, she feels overwhelmed by the pressures of caring for a new baby. Why does Louise's 4-week maternity leave pose a risk to her mental health? (Hint: Consult the Social Issues: Health box on page 151.) (pp. 157–161)

The early weeks after a new baby enters the family are full of profound changes. The mother needs time to recover from childbirth and adjust to the massive hormone shifts in her body. The father needs to become part of the new threesome while supporting the mother in her recovery. Because of the infant's needs, the family schedule becomes irregular and uncertain. The demands of new parenthood—disrupted sleep schedules, less time for husband and wife to devote to each other, and new financial responsibilities—usually does not cause significant marital strain for couples who have a gratifying, mutually supportive marriage. But troubled marriages usually become more distressed after a baby is born. Because Louise receives little social support from her husband while she is adjusting to the baby's arrival, she feels overwhelmed with the demands of caring for an infant. When a family is stressed by a baby's arrival, a short employment leave of 6 weeks or less is linked to maternal anxiety and depression and to negative interactions with the baby. A longer leave (12 weeks or more) predicts more favorable maternal mental health and sensitive, responsive caregiving.

REFLECT: If you are a parent, what was the transition to parenthood like for you? What factors helped you adjust to this major life change? What factors made it more difficult? If you are not a parent, pose these questions to someone you know who recently became a parent. (pp. 157–161)

This is an open-ended question with no right or wrong answer.

SUGGESTED STUDENT READINGS

Mifflin, P. C. (2004). *Saving very premature babies: Ethical issues.* London, UK: Butterworth-Heinemann. Examines the ethical and legal issues surrounding medical interventions for extremely premature babies. The author also addresses the challenges faced by parents of these babies, including the emotional and financial toll of long-term care.

Reed, R. K. (2005). *Birthing fathers: The transformation of men in American rites of birth.* New Brunswick, NJ: Rutgers University Press. Presents a historical overview of men's involvement in pregnancy and childbirth, including personal experiences and the transition to fatherhood.

Simonds, W., Rothman, B. K., Norman, B. M. (2006). *Laboring on: Birth in transition.* New York: Taylor & Francis. Examines a variety of issues concerning pregnancy and labor, including approaches to childbirth, medical interventions, debates over midwifery, and women's healthcare reform.

TRANSPARENCIES

T-35 **The Three Stages of Labor** Figure 4.1 (p. 130)

T-36 **Sitting Position often Used for Delivery in a Birth Center or at Home** Figure 4.2 (p. 135)

T-37 **Instrument Delivery** Figure 4.3 (p. 137)

T-38 **Incidence of Major and Minor Disabilities by Birth Weight, Obtained from Studies of Low-Birth-Weight Children at School Age** Figure 4.4 (p. 141)

T-40 **Infant Mortality in 29 Nations** Figure 4.6 (p. 144)

MEDIA MATERIALS

INFANTS, CHILDREN, AND ADOLESCENTS IN ACTION

Biological and Environmental Foundations, Prenatal Development, and Birth

This section of the Observation Program contains three parent interviews: (1) Steve and Tonya faced a tragedy rare among couples in their twenties. Their first child, Kristin, was born with Down syndrome. Tonya and Steve describe their reaction to Kristin's birth and how they adjusted to caring for a baby with serious disabilities and health problems. (2) Gina and Lindrey experience the birth of their second child. After having her first baby by cesarean section, Gina is determined to have a vaginal delivery with her second. Her husband, Lindrey, describes the experience as Gina progresses through labor and delivery. (3) Adena and Cooper discuss the transition to parenthood. Their son, Charlie, is 4 months old. The section concludes with newborn reflexes, which help ensure that the baby will survive and receive care and attention from adults.

A WINDOW ON INFANTS, CHILDREN, AND ADOLESCENTS

Segment 1: The Newborn Baby's Capacities: Anna, 2 weeks

In this segment, 2-week-old Anna exhibits a variety of newborn reflexes and capacities. Anna's mother carefully attends to the newborn, responding to Anna's signals by speaking softly and asking if she is hungry when she begins to suck on her fingers. Next, Professor Berk holds Anna while her mother shakes a rattle, illustrating the newborn's responsiveness to sound and visual stimulation. The segment concludes with Anna demonstrating the crawling motion, Moro reflex, and stepping reflex.

DVDs AND VIDEOTAPES

Baby Love (1996, Films Media Group, 57 min.). In this intimate program, a diverse group of teen mothers—some as young as 13—speak out on a wide range of topics, including love, virginity, sex, pregnancy, birth, parenting, their families, and their babies' fathers. Their experiences, attitudes, and insights provide a glimpse of the personal side of the complex social problem of teen pregnancy. This documentary, which contains explicit language, is an indispensable resource for use in teen pregnancy prevention, intervention, and parenting programs.

Babywatching (Films Media Group, 50 min.). This program, featuring zoologist Desmond Morris and based on his best-selling book of the same name, tries to capture the neonatal experience not just by observing babies but actually through the eyes of a newborn. Focusing on infants from several different cultural and economic backgrounds, the program examines the physical condition of the newborns, infant psychology, anthropological issues, and the bonding and interaction between a newborn baby and its family.

Birth (1999, Cambridge Educational, 54 min.; not available in French-speaking Canada). This program brings together footage of many women's experiences of childbirth, along with commentary from obstetricians, midwives, psychologists, counselors, and recent mothers and fathers. Topics include sonograms, prenatal examinations, changing attitudes toward the role of pain during childbirth, postpartum depression, and various birth scenarios—in-hospital, at-home, and cesarean births. The program contains some nudity associated with childbirth.

Birth: Eight Women's Stories (1993, Films Media Group, 70 min.). This program follows eight women, ranging in age from 27 to 45, who are giving birth in a variety of circumstances, including natural births at home and in the hospital, a cesarean delivery of twins under epidural anesthesia, induced labor with vaginal delivery, and water birth in the hospital. Each of the eight stories is presented as a triumph, with no attempt to promote one method of childbirth over another. The program includes both explicit footage of childbirth and commentaries by mothers, fathers, midwives, and obstetricians.

Child Development: From Prenatal to Birth (1998, Cambridge Educational; CD-ROM, available for Windows only). This program, part of the Child Development Interactive CD-ROM Series, provides an overview of prenatal development from fertilization to birth. The program also explores prenatal diagnostic methods and the effect of the mother's health on the developing fetus.

Conception to Neonate: Birth and the Newborn (1991, Concept Media, 27 min.). This program contrasts today's birth experiences with those of 30 years ago. It describes family-sensitive birth practices and looks at the initial interaction between parents and newborns. The program includes a discussion of the physical care of the newborn immediately after birth and a review of the newborn's innate reflexes and some other common characteristics of neonates.

First Adaptations (1992, RMI Media Productions, 30 min.). This program explores the tools the newborn brings to the challenge of survival. Experts discuss the growth of the infant brain and the cognitive capabilities that emerge as the nervous system develops and grows. We see research evidence that newborns just a few hours old are already able to learn critical facts about the world around them.

Great Expectations (1992, RMI Media Productions, 30 min.). This program focuses on the birth experience and how parents prepare for it. Experts discuss birth techniques, environmental contexts, and prematurity. Live footage shows viewers both vaginal and cesarean births, as well as a Lamaze class in progress.

Nature's Child: Biological Growth (1991, RMI Media Productions, 60 min.). Part 2 in the series Developmental Psychology focuses on the biological processes that occur before birth. Examines genetics and genetic abnormalities and how they affect behavior and prenatal development. The three stages of labor and the birth process are shown, along with such complications as prematurity and anoxia.

The Newborn (Films for the Humanities & Sciences, 23 min.). This program examines the reactions of the newborn 10 days after birth. It illustrates how the most important functions—sitting, standing, walking, grasping, and social contact—can already be identified in incipient form in the neonate, as a result of innate reflexes. The program demonstrates how initial medical examinations may provide evidence of developmental disorders.

The Newborn: Development and Discovery (2005, 1996, Magna Systems, 29 min.). This program presents the most current thinking about newborn infants and their developmental needs. The updated version of this module covers new research on brain development, including reaction time and pain sensitivity, and new methods of assessing the newborn, including the revised Brazelton Neonatal Assessment Scale. There is also information on reflexes, bonding, and development of cognitive and emotional skills, as well as updated information on treatment of premature and other low-birth-weight newborns.

Physical Examination of the Neonate (1995, Concept Media, 28 min.). This program demonstrates the immediate assessment of the newborn, including use of the Apgar scoring system. It also shows a detailed newborn assessment that includes measurement of weight, length, and head circumference; vital signs; heart and breath sounds; and posture, proportions, and color. Throughout, the program differentiates normal variations from those that are not.

Preemies (2000, Films Media Group, 22 min.). This program explores the concerns that arise when babies are born more than three months prematurely, giving them low chances of survival and, when they do survive, the potential for lifelong medical issues. Looking at the struggle for life of babies in a high-tech neonatal care unit, the program offers ideas for how parents of these fragile infants can find support.

Pregnancy and Birth (2005, Magna Systems, 29 min.). This program provides a contemporary look at pregnancy and the birth process, and how advances in technology and knowledge affect both. Topics include childbirth choices in hospitals and at home, the role of childbirth classes, the importance of a childbirth coach, the three stages of labor, the difference between analgesia and anesthesia, and the reasons for cesarean section.

Prenatal Development and the Birth Process (1993, GPN Educational Media, 30 min.). This program, Module 3 of GPN's Worlds of Childhood series, examines research on the developmental significance of the prenatal period in light of the principles of human genetics, the availability of prenatal care, and other risk factors. Families in various cultures—Brazil, Russia, and the United States—are seen preparing for birth and going through delivery.

The Process of Birth (1993, Films for the Humanities & Sciences, 30 min.). This program, part of the series The Psychological Development of the Child, shows how different cultures hold varying beliefs about what is best for mother and infant during and shortly after birth. The program includes a look at birth positions, places, and personnel and addresses the issue of when bonding begins.

Shaping Youngest Minds (1999, Learning Seed, 24 min.). This program reviews the physical development of the brain from its earliest stages. It contends that the shaping of behavior begins in the womb and stresses the importance of stimulating learning and growth from infancy. It outlines an approach to child development using specific examples that capitalize on current brain research.

Sudden Infant Death Syndrome (1995, Films for the Humanities & Sciences, 49 min.). This program presents the views of parents who have lost infants to SIDS, and of doctors and researchers working to understand and defeat this silent killer. Specialists provide up-to-date information on which infants are at highest risk and what precautions parents can take to protect them.

Sudden Infant Death Syndrome: An Update (1998, Films for the Humanities & Sciences, 17 min.). This program explores what is currently known about sudden infant death syndrome (SIDS) and suggests steps that parents and other caregivers can take to reduce the risk factors for this deadly and still-mysterious illness. Physicians and other health experts discuss appropriate prenatal care as well as the importance of child sleeping positions, parental smoking, and other factors. The is an excellent program for future parents, child-care providers, and anyone else who is responsible for the care of infants.

Wonder Years: First Steps in Autonomy (1995, Films Media Group, 25 min.). This classic program identifies the three key factors in shaping a child's development and providing stepping stones to adult independence: extreme biological changes, psychological advances, and physical surroundings. The program looks at both prenatal and postnatal differences, as well as the dangers of premature birth. A video experiment shows infants' remarkable sensitivity to communication and to their environment. The impact of postnatal depression on mother and child is discussed.

TEST BANK

MULTIPLE CHOICE

1) The onset of uterine contractions
   A) occurs during the first stage of labor.
   B) often occurs several weeks before delivery of the baby.
   C) occurs in the lower part of the mother's uterus.
   D) begins with regular and strong contractions of the uterus.
   Answer: B
   Page Ref: 130
   Skill: Conceptual
   Objective: 4.1

2) Bloody show occurs when the
   A) amniotic sac is ruptured.
   B) mucus plug is released from the cervix.
   C) fetus's head drops low into the uterus.
   D) first uterine contractions take place.
   Answer: B
   Page Ref: 130
   Skill: Factual
   Objective: 4.1

3) For first time mothers, stage 1 lasts an average of
   A) 1 to 2 hours.
   B) 4 to 6 hours.
   C) 12 to 14 hours.
   D) 24 to 48 hours.
   Answer: C
   Page Ref: 131
   Skill: Factual
   Objective: 4.1

4) During the first stage of labor, the
   A) mother feels a natural urge to push.
   B) baby's head crowns.
   C) placenta is delivered.
   D) cervix dilates and effaces.
   Answer: D
   Page Ref: 131
   Skill: Factual
   Objective: 4.1

5) During transition, the
   A) baby is forced down and out of the birth canal.
   B) placenta is delivered.
   C) frequency and strength of contractions are at their peak.
   D) cervix begins to dilate and efface.
   Answer: C
   Page Ref: 131
   Skill: Conceptual
   Objective: 4.1

6) During the second stage of labor, the
    A) uterus begins to contract regularly.
    B) baby is born.
    C) cervix starts to dilate.
    D) placenta is delivered.
Answer: B
Page Ref: 131
Skill: Factual
Objective: 4.1

7) _____ occurs when the vaginal opening is stretched around the baby's entire head.
    A) Lightening
    B) Bloody show
    C) Crowning
    D) False labor
Answer: C
Page Ref: 131
Skill: Factual
Objective: 4.1

8) During the third stage of labor,
    A) contractions occur 10 to 20 minutes apart.
    B) the mucus plug is released from the cervix.
    C) the expulsion of the placenta takes place.
    D) lightening occurs.
Answer: C
Page Ref: 131
Skill: Factual
Objective: 4.1

9) The third stage of labor typically lasts
    A) 5 to 10 minutes.
    B) 30 minutes to an hour.
    C) 1 to 2 hours.
    D) 12 to 14 hours.
Answer: A
Page Ref: 131
Skill: Factual
Objective: 4.1

10) High levels of stress hormones produced by infants during childbirth
    A) can lead to anoxia, or inadequate oxygen supply, during delivery.
    B) lead to irritability and digestive disturbances in newborns.
    C) cause infants' heart rate and activity level to increase to dangerously high levels during childbirth.
    D) help infants withstand oxygen deprivation by sending a rich supply of blood to the brain and the heart.
Answer: D
Page Ref: 131
Skill: Conceptual
Objective: 4.1

11) The average newborn baby weighs _____ and is _____ inches long.
    A) 4 1/2 pounds; 15
    B) 7 1/2 pounds; 20
    C) 9 pounds; 22
    D) 12 to 13 pounds; 24
Answer: B
Page Ref: 132
Skill: Factual
Objective: 4.2

12) A newborn's round face, chubby cheeks, and large forehead
    A) are attractive to adults and ensure that babies will be picked up and cuddled.
    B) make it difficult for babies to pass through the birth canal during delivery.
    C) can lead to anoxia, or inadequate oxygen supply, during delivery.
    D) is the result of a well-developed brain that leads to greater independence than most other mammals.
Answer: A
Page Ref: 132
Skill: Conceptual
Objective: 4.2

13) The Apgar Scale rates characteristics of a newborn, including the baby's
    A) heart rate, color, and muscle tone.
    B) length and weight.
    C) vision, hearing, and sense of touch.
    D) reflexes, state changes, and responsiveness to physical and social stimuli.
Answer: A
Page Ref: 133
Skill: Conceptual
Objective: 4.3

14) Baby Amir's Apgar score is 7. The medical professionals should
    A) immediately provide medical attention because he is in serious danger.
    B) tell Amir's parents that he is in good physical condition.
    C) ask his parents if they will allow extensive life-saving efforts performed on their son.
    D) immediately put him on a ventilator because Apgar scores below 8 indicate lack of oxygen.
Answer: B
Page Ref: 132
Skill: Conceptual
Objective: 4.3

15) Two Apgar ratings are given in the minutes following birth
    A) to ensure inter-rater reliability.
    B) because some babies have trouble adjusting immediately but do well after a few minutes.
    C) because the two scores are combined to arrive at an average assessment of the newborn's well-being.
    D) because many babies who test well immediately will rapidly decline in physical condition and require emergency medical attention.
Answer: B
Page Ref: 132
Skill: Conceptual
Objective: 4.3

16) How did childbirth customs change after the industrial revolution?
   A) Women's knowledge of childbirth declined as doctors assumed responsibility.
   B) More children were born at home than in hospitals.
   C) The focus of childbirth expanded to include family and friends.
   D) The return to natural childbirth increased and fewer women requested medication during delivery.
   Answer: A
   Page Ref: 133
   Skill: Conceptual
   Objective: 4.4

17) Freestanding birth centers
   A) permit a choice of delivery positions.
   B) do not allow family members and friends to participate in the birth.
   C) offer the same level of backup medical care as hospitals.
   D) encourage childbirth medication and delivery instruments.
   Answer: A
   Page Ref: 133
   Skill: Conceptual
   Objective: 4.4

18) One of the fundamental beliefs about prepared approaches is that birth is more likely to be problem free and rewarding when mothers
   A) are knowledgeable about the types of labor medications that can be used to reduce the pain of childbirth.
   B) are comfortable with medical devices that are often used to deliver infants, such as forceps and vacuum extractors.
   C) learn about newborn care and breastfeeding.
   D) understand the process of labor and delivery.
   Answer: D
   Page Ref: 134
   Skill: Conceptual
   Objective: 4.4

19) Mothers who _____ have fewer birth complications and shorter labors.
   A) are administered epidural analgesia during childbirth
   B) give birth at home
   C) are accompanied by a trained companion during childbirth
   D) give birth lying flat on their backs with their feet in stirrups
   Answer: C
   Page Ref: 134
   Skill: Conceptual
   Objective: 4.4

20) An upright, sitting position for delivery
   A) shortens labor.
   B) puts a great deal of pressure on the mother's spinal cord.
   C) weakens uterine contractions.
   D) increases the likelihood of an episiotomy.
   Answer: A
   Page Ref: 135
   Skill: Conceptual
   Objective: 4.4

21) Home delivery is
    A) usually attended by a doctor.
    B) typically used only in developing countries.
    C) not appropriate if the mother is at risk for any kind of complication.
    D) safe only if the baby is in a breech position.
Answer: C
Page Ref: 135
Skill: Conceptual
Objective: 4.5

22) Of the following, which mother should give birth in a hospital rather than at home?
    A) Elizabeth, a healthy 25-year-old whose baby is in a breech position
    B) Michelle, a 40-year-old, assisted by a well-trained midwife
    C) Debra, a 19-year-old, with a family history of sickle cell anemia
    D) Alexandra, a 30-year-old who had a previous miscarriage
Answer: A
Page Ref: 135
Skill: Applied
Objective: 4.5

23) Fetal monitors
    A) measure the baby's blood oxygen levels during labor.
    B) have saved the lives of many high-risk babies.
    C) are linked to a decreased rate of cesarean deliveries.
    D) reduce the rate of infant brain damage and death in all pregnancies.
Answer: B
Page Ref: 136
Skill: Factual
Objective: 4.6

24) In healthy pregnancies, fetal monitoring
    A) reduces the rate of infant death.
    B) is necessary to detect hidden problems with the baby.
    C) reduces the rate of infant brain damage and death.
    D) reduces the likelihood of cesarean delivery.
Answer: C
Page Ref: 136
Skill: Conceptual
Objective: 4.6

25) What is the difference between analgesic and anesthetic use during childbirth?
    A) Analgesics are given in mild doses to relieve pain, while anesthetics block sensation entirely.
    B) Analgesics are used by doctors in hospital deliveries, while anesthetics are mainly used by midwifes in home deliveries.
    C) Analgesics are typically used when birth complications occur, while anesthetics are used in normal deliveries.
    D) Anesthetics are usually administered after the mother's request, while analgesics are administered as part of the standard birthing room procedures.
Answer: A
Page Ref: 136
Skill: Conceptual
Objective: 4.6

26) Epidural analgesia
   A) numbs the entire lower half of the body.
   B) weakens uterine contractions.
   C) renders the mother incapable of pushing during the second stage of labor.
   D) shortens labor.
   Answer: B
   Page Ref: 136
   Skill: Factual
   Objective: 4.6

27) Newborns exposed to epidural analgesia tend to
   A) have trouble falling asleep.
   B) be hyperactive and animated.
   C) have lower Apgar scores.
   D) suck more aggressively when feeding.
   Answer: C
   Page Ref: 137
   Skill: Conceptual
   Objective: 4.6

28) Instrument delivery
   A) has declined considerably over the past decade.
   B) is used in about 30 percent of North American births.
   C) is a reasonable method to speed up delivery if the mother is fatigued.
   D) is much safer for the baby than surgical delivery.
   Answer: A
   Page Ref: 137
   Skill: Conceptual
   Objective: 4.6

29) Using forceps during delivery to help pull the infant through most or all of the birth canal
   A) greatly increases the risk of brain damage.
   B) is a highly effective way to deliver a breech baby.
   C) is a reasonable method to speed up delivery if the mother is fatigued.
   D) seldom results in even minor complications.
   Answer: A
   Page Ref: 137
   Skill: Conceptual
   Objective: 4.6

30) Typically, labor is induced by giving the mother synthetic oxytocin and
   A) dislodging the mucus plug.
   B) breaking the amnion.
   C) massaging the uterus to stimulate contractions.
   D) using a balloon catheter to open the cervix.
   Answer: B
   Page Ref: 137
   Skill: Factual
   Objective: 4.6

31) In the past decade, the percentage of North American labors that _____ has more than doubled.
   A) use vacuum extraction
   B) are induced
   C) are done with spinal blocks
   D) use forceps
   Answer: B
   Page Ref: 137
   Skill: Conceptual
   Objective: 4.6

32) In induced labors,
   A) contractions are shorter and more widely spaced apart than in spontaneous labors.
   B) the rate of cesarean delivery is only half of that in spontaneous labors.
   C) the possibility of inadequate oxygen supply is greater than in spontaneous labors.
   D) the chances of an instrument delivery are less than in spontaneous labors.
   Answer: C
   Page Ref: 137
   Skill: Conceptual
   Objective: 4.6

33) Labor and delivery medication is likely to be used in larger amounts
   A) when the mother is accompanied by a trained companion during labor and delivery.
   B) in prepared childbirth.
   C) when the mother is in an upright, sitting position during delivery.
   D) in an induced labor.
   Answer: D
   Page Ref: 137
   Skill: Conceptual
   Objective: 4.6

34) Of the following, which is supported by research on cesarean delivery?
   A) Cesarean delivery is much less likely to be used in the United States than in other industrialized countries.
   B) Breech babies should always be delivered by a cesarean.
   C) Vaginal birth after a previous cesarean is associated with an increased rate of uterine rupture and infant death.
   D) Cesarean delivery has become less common with the invention and regular use of fetal monitoring.
   Answer: C
   Page Ref: 138
   Skill: Conceptual
   Objective: 4.6

35) If the fetus is in the breech position,
   A) the baby will have to be delivered by a cesarean section.
   B) fetal monitoring techniques will not be successful.
   C) labor and delivery medication will be necessary.
   D) the baby can sometimes be turned head down by the doctor during the early part of labor.
   Answer: D
   Page Ref: 138
   Skill: Factual
   Objective: 4.6

36) _____ can be caused by anoxia during labor and delivery.
   A) Cerebral palsy
   B) Toxoplasmosis
   C) Rubella
   D) Cytomegalovirus
Answer: A
Page Ref: 139
Skill: Factual
Objective: 4.7

37) _____ during pregnancy is associated with placenta abruption.
   A) Tobacco and cocaine use
   B) Exposure to PCBs
   C) High maternal stress
   D) HIV infection
Answer: A
Page Ref: 139
Skill: Conceptual
Objective: 4.7

38) Which of the following is supported by research on labor and delivery?
   A) Healthy newborns can survive periods of little or no oxygen longer than adults can.
   B) In most children, the initial damage from anoxia at birth disappears during the first year of life.
   C) Because of newborn's rapid metabolic rate, brain damage will occur if the baby does not begin breathing immediately at birth.
   D) Brain damage is likely to occur if regular breathing is delayed more than 5 minutes.
Answer: A
Page Ref: 139
Skill: Conceptual
Objective: 4.7

39) After initial brain injury from anoxia, placing newborns in a(n) _____ shortly after birth for 72 hours can substantially reduce brain injury.
   A) head-cooling device
   B) suspended hammock
   C) isolette
   D) warm waterbed
Answer: A
Page Ref: 139
Skill: Conceptual
Objective: 4.7

40) Respiratory distress syndrome
   A) is linked with folic acid use during pregnancy.
   B) can lead to permanent brain damage.
   C) rarely causes serious breathing difficulties.
   D) is a common risk for babies who are breastfed.
Answer: B
Page Ref: 140
Skill: Factual
Objective: 4.7

41) _____ is the best available predictor of infant survival and healthy development.
   A) Apgar score
   B) Birth weight
   C) Adequacy of prenatal care
   D) Socioeconomic status
Answer: B
Page Ref: 140
Skill: Factual
Objective: 4.7

42) Of the following, which best explains the difference between preterm and small-for-date infants?
   A) Some small-for-date infants are full-term.
   B) Preterm babies tend to have more serious problems than small-for-date infants.
   C) Small-for-date infants are born several weeks before their due date.
   D) Preterm infants are below their expected weight when the length of the pregnancy is taken into account.
Answer: A
Page Ref: 140
Skill: Conceptual
Objective: 4.7

43) Preterm infants
   A) are more likely than small-for-date infants to have experienced inadequate nutrition before birth.
   B) are more often held close, touched, and talked to gently than full-term infants.
   C) born at 34 weeks do not show an increased rate of illness compared to infants born at 35 weeks.
   D) usually have less serious problems than small-for-date infants.
Answer: D
Page Ref: 140
Skill: Conceptual
Objective: 4.7

44) Rocking in suspended hammocks or lying in waterbeds
   A) is a common intervention for preterm infants used in nonindustrialized countries that do not have ready access to pharmaceutics or surgical techniques.
   B) is a dangerous intervention for fragile, preterm infants.
   C) promotes faster weight gain and greater alertness in preterm infants.
   D) interferes with the development of predictable sleep patterns in preterm infants.
Answer: C
Page Ref: 142
Skill: Conceptual
Objective: 4.8

45) Stimulating which of the following senses leads to the release of certain brain chemicals that promote physical growth?
   A) sight
   B) hearing
   C) taste
   D) touch
Answer: D
Page Ref: 142
Skill: Conceptual
Objective: 4.8

46) Kangaroo skin-to-skin care
    A) is not commonly used in industrialized nations who have ready access to drugs and surgical techniques.
    B) fosters improved oxygenation of the baby's body, temperature regulation, sleep, feeding, alertness, and infant survival.
    C) does not lead to any benefits that can be seen past the first few months of life.
    D) can be dangerous for preterm newborns who are fragile and sickly.
    Answer: B
    Page Ref: 142
    Skill: Conceptual
    Objective: 4.8

47) Research on interventions for parents of preterm newborns shows that
    A) interventions are not needed for economically advantaged parents to promote healthy development.
    B) the benefits of any intervention wash out by the time the children enter elementary school.
    C) interventions that combine stimulating child care and weekly parent training sessions can boost the intellectual functioning of children born into poverty.
    D) only a few, early training sessions for low-income new parents can lead to strong lifelong benefits for their children.
    Answer: C
    Page Ref: 142–143
    Skill: Conceptual
    Objective: 4.8

48) Of the following, which summarizes the long-term consequences of birth complications found in the Kauai study?
    A) Children who experienced birth trauma never fully acquired the same levels of cognitive development as the children in the control group.
    B) Children raised in supportive home environments overcame the effects of mild or moderate birth trauma.
    C) Even children who experienced severe trauma eventually tested commensurately with their agemates on measures of intellectual development.
    D) None of the children with serious birth complications and troubled family environments achieved at the same rate as controls.
    Answer: B
    Page Ref: 143
    Skill: Conceptual
    Objective: 4.9

49) In the Kauai study, a few children with both serious birth complications and troubled families grew into competent adults. These children
    A) were adopted by high-SES families during infancy.
    B) participated in a high number of extracurricular school-based activities during the school years.
    C) were enrolled in high-quality child care during the first year of life.
    D) relied on factors outside the family and within themselves to overcome stress.
    Answer: D
    Page Ref: 145
    Skill: Conceptual
    Objective: 4.9

50) Research shows that around the time of birth,
  A) first-time fathers show increases in androgens.
  B) first-time mothers stop producing oxytocin.
  C) hormonal changes among first-time fathers are associated with negative emotional reactions to infants.
  D) first-time fathers show increases in prolactin and estrogens.
  Answer: D
  Page Ref: 146
  Skill: Conceptual
  Objective: 4.10

51) Studies on bonding show that
  A) the human mother-infant relationship depends largely on what happens during a sensitive period immediately after birth.
  B) for some parents, deep feelings of affection emerge gradually and for others these emotions are felt when first holding their babies.
  C) skin-to-skin contact between mother and baby is vital for the mother to feel affection and concern for her infant.
  D) adoptive parents have difficulty developing warm, affective relationships when the child enters the family months after birth.
  Answer: B
  Page Ref: 146
  Skill: Conceptual
  Objective: 4.10

52) Research on bonding suggests that skin-to-skin contact between a mother and her baby in the minutes after birth
  A) guarantees immediate emotional closeness between the new mother and the newborn.
  B) is especially important for mothers who have had difficult or surgical births.
  C) provides a short window of opportunity during which a newborn will spontaneously latch on to the mother's breast and begin sucking.
  D) is not essential for the development of a lasting mother-child bond.
  Answer: D
  Page Ref: 147
  Skill: Conceptual
  Objective: 4.10

53) Many parents choose rooming in
  A) when their babies have experienced severe birth trauma.
  B) because early contact supports their feeling of caring and affection for their baby.
  C) to promote weight gain in extremely premature babies.
  D) to prevent the need for labor and delivery medication.
  Answer: B
  Page Ref: 147
  Skill: Conceptual
  Objective: 4.10

54) The rooting reflex
  A) may prepare the baby for voluntary reaching.
  B) helps babies adjust their sucking pressure to how easily milk flows from the nipple.
  C) may have helped the infant cling to the mother in our evolutionary past.
  D) helps a breastfed baby find the mother's nipple.
  Answer: D
  Page Ref: 147, 148
  Skill: Conceptual
  Objective: 4.11

55) Babies display the rooting reflex
    A) when there is a sudden loud sound on a surface that supports the infant.
    B) only when hungry and touched by another.
    C) when the baby's head is to one side and the infant is lying awake on his or her back.
    D) when the sole of the foot is stroked from toe towards heel.
Answer: B
Page Ref: 147
Skill: Applied
Objective: 4.11

56) During the first week of life,
    A) the stepping reflex is strong enough to support the infant's entire weight on his or her feet.
    B) babies display the Moro reflex only when hungry and touched by another person.
    C) the palmar grasp reflex is strong enough to support the baby's entire weight.
    D) the sucking reflex is replaced by voluntary sucking.
Answer: C
Page Ref: 147, 148
Skill: Conceptual
Objective: 4.11

57) The _____ reflex may prepare the infant for voluntary reaching.
    A) rooting
    B) Moro
    C) Babinski
    D) tonic neck
Answer: D
Page Ref: 147, 148
Skill: Factual
Objective: 4.11

58) Research findings on newborn reflexes suggest that
    A) the stepping reflex appears even with the newborn's body in an upside-down position.
    B) early practice of the swimming reflex can produce a strong swimmer by the age of 2.
    C) parents should deliberately exercise newborn stepping reflexes to encourage early walking.
    D) unlike other reflexes, the tonic neck reflex appears in a wide range of situations.
Answer: A
Page Ref: 148
Skill: Conceptual
Objective: 4.11

59) Pediatricians usually test newborn reflexes carefully because weak, absent, or exaggerated reflexes in an infant may indicate
    A) ineffective parenting.
    B) poor gross motor skills.
    C) poor muscle tone.
    D) damage to the cerebral cortex.
Answer: D
Page Ref: 149
Skill: Conceptual
Objective: 4.11

60) The average newborn sleeps _____ hours a day.
    A) 8 to 10
    B) 12 to 15
    C) 16 to 18
    D) 20 to 22
Answer: C
Page Ref: 149
Skill: Factual
Objective: 4.12

61) Baby Noah moves his arms and legs gently and grimaces while he sleeps. His breathing is irregular with occasional eye movements. He is MOST likely in which of the following states?
    A) regular sleep
    B) drowsiness
    C) quiet alertness
    D) irregular sleep
Answer: D
Page Ref: 150
Skill: Applied
Objective: 4.12

62) Of the following, which is supported by research on REM sleep?
    A) REM sleep accounts for 5 to 10 percent of the newborn's sleep time.
    B) Newborns spend 2 to 3 hours a day in REM sleep.
    C) Infants spend far more time in REM sleep than they ever will again.
    D) During REM sleep, babies dream much in the same way adults do.
Answer: C
Page Ref: 150
Skill: Conceptual
Objective: 4.12

63) Why do infants spend so much time in REM sleep?
    A) REM sleep is necessary to refine fine muscle development of the eye.
    B) REM sleep allows the body to conserve needed energy for growth.
    C) REM is a form of self-stimulation that is vital for growth of the central nervous system.
    D) REM sleep assists with temperature regulation and digestion.
Answer: C
Page Ref: 150
Skill: Conceptual
Objective: 4.12

64) Who is likely to spend the greatest amount of time in REM sleep?
    A) a fetus
    B) a full-term newborn baby
    C) a preschool-age child
    D) an adolescent
Answer: A
Page Ref: 150
Skill: Conceptual
Objective: 4.12

65) Newborn infants who are brain damaged often
    A) display disturbed REM-NREM sleep cycles.
    B) cry one to two hours a day.
    C) spend about 10% of their total sleep time in REM sleep.
    D) rarely cry.
Answer: A
Page Ref: 150
Skill: Conceptual
Objective: 4.12

66) Of the following, which is supported by research on crying?
    A) Gas is the most common cause of crying among newborns.
    B) As early as the first few weeks of life, an infant can be identified by the unique vocal "signature" of his or her cry.
    C) Swaddling is an ineffective technique for soothing a crying newborn.
    D) Crying is typically at its peak in the days after birth and declines over the first few weeks.
Answer: B
Page Ref: 152
Skill: Conceptual
Objective: 4.12

67) Newborn Sonjita cries at the sound of another crying baby. Some researchers believe that she is
    A) demonstrating an early ability to model the behavior of others.
    B) acting on an inborn capacity to react to the suffering of others.
    C) trying to get an adult's attention to alleviate the bothersome loud crying of the other baby.
    D) confusing her identity with that of the crying infant.
Answer: B
Page Ref: 152
Skill: Applied
Objective: 4.12

68) Swaddling
    A) is an effective method of soothing a crying baby.
    B) interferes with sleep in infants.
    C) hinders the development of early motor abilities.
    D) promotes an insecure attachment relationship between mother and baby.
Answer: A
Page Ref: 152
Skill: Conceptual
Objective: 4.12

69) Infants in cultures where they spend much time in close bodily contact with their mothers _____ than their North American counterparts.
    A) show shorter bouts of crying
    B) show delayed development of motor skills
    C) display higher rates of colic
    D) evidence more sleep difficulties
Answer: A
Page Ref: 152
Skill: Conceptual
Objective: 4.12

70) Which of the following is true of colic?
    A) Colic is usually a sign of central nervous system damage.
    B) Colic usually persists throughout the first year of life.
    C) Colic is more common in babies who react especially strongly to unpleasant stimuli.
    D) Babies with colic tend to have dull-sounding, low-pitched cries.
Answer: C
Page Ref: 152
Skill: Conceptual
Objective: 4.12

71) A newborn is particularly sensitive to touch on the
    A) stomach, back, and legs.
    B) arms and hands.
    C) mouth, palms, and soles of feet.
    D) face, arms, and legs.
Answer: C
Page Ref: 153
Skill: Conceptual
Objective: 4.13

72) Research on pain during infancy shows that
    A) newborn males do not perceive pain during circumcision.
    B) offering a nipple that delivers a sugar solution reduces discomfort during circumcision.
    C) local anesthetics cannot be used during newborn circumcisions because these drugs elevate the heart rate to dangerous levels.
    D) newborns not given a local anesthetic during circumcision react less intensely to later routine vaccinations.
Answer: B
Page Ref: 153–154
Skill: Conceptual
Objective: 4.13

73) Newborns
    A) prefer salty water to regular water.
    B) purse their lips when they taste something sour.
    C) have difficulty learning to like a taste that first evoked a negative response.
    D) tend to reject or react indifferently to sweet tastes.
Answer: B
Page Ref: 154
Skill: Conceptual
Objective: 4.13

74) Research on early taste and odor preferences shows that
    A) the tastes and smells of amniotic fluid do not vary with the mother's diet.
    B) newborns do not exhibit taste or smell preferences until a few weeks after birth.
    C) unlike adults, the odor of rotten eggs is not unpleasant to most infants.
    D) variations in the tastes and smells of the amniotic fluid influence newborn preferences.
Answer: D
Page Ref: 154
Skill: Conceptual
Objective: 4.13

75) Which of the following is supported by research on newborn odor preferences?
   A) Most newborns cannot distinguish between the smell of their mother's breast and that of an unfamiliar lactating woman.
   B) Babies who are exposed to the smell of their mother's amniotic fluid cry less than babies who are not.
   C) Newborns cannot distinguish the smell of their mother's amniotic fluid from that of another mother.
   D) Only breastfed babies prefer the smell of a lactating mother's breast to formula.
   Answer: B
   Page Ref: 154
   Skill: Conceptual
   Objective: 4.13

76) Studies on newborn odor preferences demonstrate that
   A) both breastfed and bottle-fed babies prefer the smell of unfamiliar human milk over the smell of formula milk.
   B) bottle-fed babies prefer the smell of formula over the smell of their own mother's milk.
   C) only breastfed babies prefer the odor of unfamiliar human milk over the odor of formula milk.
   D) bottle-fed babies prefer the odor of formula over the odor of an unfamiliar mother's milk.
   Answer: A
   Page Ref: 155
   Skill: Conceptual
   Objective: 4.13

77) Research on newborn hearing shows that
   A) newborns can perceive only those sounds that are found in their own native language.
   B) newborns prefer pure tones to complex sounds.
   C) babies only a few days old can tell the difference between utterances with two versus three syllables.
   D) newborns prefer to listen to music than to human speech sounds.
   Answer: C
   Page Ref: 155
   Skill: Conceptual
   Objective: 4.13

78) Of the following, which is supported by research on newborn hearing?
   A) Newborns' ability to perceive sounds not found in their own language is more precise than adults.
   B) Babies are unable to locate the general direction of a sound until at least 3 months of age.
   C) Newborns prefer to hear a foreign language as opposed to their native language.
   D) Young babies are more attentive to speech when it is spoken in a low-pitched, monotone manner.
   Answer: A
   Page Ref: 155
   Skill: Conceptual
   Objective: 4.13

79) _____ is the least developed of the senses at birth.
   A) Hearing
   B) Taste
   C) Vision
   D) Touch
   Answer: C
   Page Ref: 155
   Skill: Factual
   Objective: 4.13

80) At birth, infants perceive objects at a distance of 20 feet about as clearly as adults do at _____ feet.
  A) 100
  B) 200
  C) 300
  D) 600
Answer: D
Page Ref: 155
Skill: Factual
Objective: 4.13

81) Research on vision in newborns demonstrates that
  A) newborns are attracted to muted colors, such as gray rather than colored stimuli.
  B) color vision becomes adultlike at about 4 months of age.
  C) newborns can discriminate between the fine-grained features of their mother's face and those of a stranger.
  D) newborns see more clearly close up than at far distances.
Answer: B
Page Ref: 156
Skill: Conceptual
Objective: 4.13

82) _____ provide(s) the best estimate of a baby's ability to recover from the stress of birth.
  A) Two NBAS scores, one taken at birth and then again at six months,
  B) A single NBAS score taken in the moments immediately after birth
  C) Changes in NBAS scores over the first week or two of life
  D) A single NBAS score taken at about one week of age
Answer: C
Page Ref: 157
Skill: Conceptual
Objective: 4.14

83) In some hospitals, health professionals use the NBAS to
  A) screen infants for possible intellectual giftedness.
  B) measure the newborn's physical condition at 1 and 5 minutes after birth.
  C) demonstrate to parents the capacities of their newborn infant.
  D) teach new mothers how to breastfeed their infants.
Answer: C
Page Ref: 157
Skill: Conceptual
Objective: 4.14

84) Of the following, which is supported by research on new parenthood?
  A) After the birth of a baby, the gender roles of husband and wife generally become less traditional.
  B) For most new parents, the arrival of a baby causes significant marital strain.
  C) Sharing caregiving predicts greater parental happiness and sensitivity to the baby.
  D) New parents in troubled marriages usually show an increase in marital satisfaction after a baby is born.
Answer: C
Page Ref: 158
Skill: Conceptual
Objective: 4.15

85) Men who postpone childbearing until the late twenties or thirties _____ than those who have children earlier in life.
   A) are more willing to participate in child-care responsibilities
   B) tend to experience greater marital conflict
   C) are usually less enthusiastic about becoming fathers
   D) show a greater decline in mental health after childbirth
   Answer: A
   Page Ref: 158
   Skill: Conceptual
   Objective: 4.15

86) Following the birth of a second child,
   A) well-functioning families usually show a pulling back from the traditional gender roles of husband and wife.
   B) most fathers take a less active role in parenting.
   C) most preschool-age children are still too unsophisticated to react with jealously or anger to the new arrival.
   D) men are less enthusiastic about being fathers.
   Answer: A
   Page Ref: 158
   Skill: Conceptual
   Objective: 4.15

87) The stress of adapting to parenthood
   A) is generally more difficult for men than it is for women.
   B) lasts for three or four years after birth.
   C) usually can be managed when parents support each other.
   D) is not as great as most people believe it to be.
   Answer: C
   Page Ref: 158
   Skill: Conceptual
   Objective: 4.15

88) Research on single-mother families shows that
   A) less than a quarter of babies in the United States and Canada are born to single mothers.
   B) planned births and adoptions by single 30- to 45-year-old women are decreasing.
   C) most young, single mothers whose pregnancies were unplanned have incomes below the poverty level.
   D) single 30- to 45-year-old women experience a more stressful transition to parenthood than single women in their twenties.
   Answer: C
   Page Ref: 159
   Skill: Conceptual
   Objective: 4.15

89) Studies on new parent interventions demonstrate that
   A) many low-income parents require tangible support, such as food, transportation, and affordable child care, to allow them to engage in effective parenting.
   B) counselor-led parent groups are highly effective for parents who are at high risk for problems.
   C) home visits do little to boost the effectiveness of programs for high-risk parents struggling with a child with disabilities.
   D) counselor-led parent groups can ease the stress of parenting among fathers but usually not among mothers.
   Answer: A
   Page Ref: 161
   Skill: Conceptual
   Objective: 4.15

90) In international rankings, the infant death rate in the United States has slipped from seventh in the 1950s to twenty-sixth in 2006. Every country that outranks the United States provides which of the following?
   A) government-sponsored health care benefits
   B) stronger crime prevention and family planning programs
   C) more funding for prenatal surgery and postpartum depression research
   D) higher numbers of well-trained pediatric nurses and midwives
Answer: A
Page Ref: 144
Skill: Conceptual
Objective: (SI Box) A Cross-National Perspective on Health Care and Other Policies for Parents and Newborn Babies

91) Of the following, which is supported by research on infant mortality?
   A) In Canada, First Nations babies die at twice the rate of Canadian babies in general.
   B) The infant mortality rates in the United States and Canada are very high relative to other countries.
   C) In the United States and Canada, the leading cause of infant mortality is sudden infant death syndrome.
   D) In the United States, the infant mortality rate is about the same in all ethnic and racial groups.
Answer: A
Page Ref: 144
Skill: Conceptual
Objective: (SI Box) A Cross-National Perspective on Health Care and Other Policies for Parents and Newborn Babies

92) In the United States and Canada, the second leading cause of neonatal mortality is
   A) birth defects.
   B) largely preventable.
   C) sudden infant death syndrome.
   D) unintentional injuries.
Answer: B
Page Ref: 144
Skill: Factual
Objective: (SI Box) A Cross-National Perspective on Health Care and Other Policies for Parents and Newborn Babies

93) Of the following, which is true?
   A) The United States and Canada guarantee women a certain number of prenatal visits at very low or no cost.
   B) The United States mandates 12-week paid maternity leave for all new mothers.
   C) In all Western European nations, a health professional routinely visits the home to provide counseling about infant care and to arrange continuing medical services.
   D) In less developed nations like China, parental leave is unpaid.
Answer: C
Page Ref: 144
Skill: Conceptual
Objective: (SI Box) A Cross-National Perspective on Health Care and Other Policies for Parents and Newborn Babies

94) Gwen is employed by a New York advertising agency with 30 employees. She is pregnant and is wondering about her rights regarding employment leave once her baby is born. You would tell her that the federal government
   A) does not guarantee any paid or unpaid leave for employees in businesses with less than 50 workers.
   B) mandates 12 weeks of paid leave for all workers.
   C) grants 3 months at full pay and an additional 9 months at no pay.
   D) guarantees 12 weeks of paid leave only in businesses with 50 or more employees.
Answer: A
Page Ref: 145
Skill: Applied
Objective: (SI Box) A Cross-National Perspective on Health Care and Other Policies for Parents and Newborn Babies

95) Of the following, which is true?
  A) In 2002, California became the first U.S. state to guarantee a mother or father paid parental leave.
  B) Longer parental leaves are not associated with more favorable mental health or effective caregiving.
  C) The United States mandates 12 weeks of paid maternity leave for all new mothers.
  D) Studies demonstrate that for most new mothers, 6 weeks of maternity leave is enough.

Answer: A
Page Ref: 145
Skill: Conceptual
Objective: (SI Box) A Cross-National Perspective on Health Care and Other Policies for Parents and Newborn Babies

96) In industrialized nations, _____ is/are the leading cause of infant mortality between 1 week and 12 months.
  A) sudden infant death syndrome
  B) automobile accidents
  C) congenital defects
  D) falls

Answer: A
Page Ref: 151
Skill: Factual
Objective: (SI Box) Sudden Infant Death Syndrome

97) One hypothesis is that SIDS is most likely to occur between 2 and 4 months of age because this is when
  A) infants begin rolling over in their sleep.
  B) reflexes decline and are replaced by voluntary responses.
  C) babies begin to spend an increasing amount of time in REM sleep.
  D) infants are most susceptible to respiratory infections.

Answer: B
Page Ref: 151
Skill: Conceptual
Objective: (SI Box) The Mysterious Tragedy of Sudden Infant Death Syndrome

98) An estimated 30 percent of SIDS cases would be prevented if women would
  A) refrain from smoking while pregnant.
  B) prevent their infants from using pacifiers during sleep.
  C) place their infants to sleep on their stomachs.
  D) dress babies more warmly during sleep.

Answer: A
Page Ref: 151
Skill: Factual
Objective: (SI Box) The Mysterious Tragedy of Sudden Infant Death Syndrome

99) Parents can reduce the likelihood of SIDS by
  A) dressing their infants warmer during sleep.
  B) sleeping in the same bed as their infants.
  C) preventing their infants from sucking on a pacifier during sleep.
  D) placing infants to sleep on their backs.

Answer: D
Page Ref: 151
Skill: Applied
Objective: (SI Box) The Mysterious Tragedy of Sudden Infant Death Syndrome

100) Postpartum blues
    A) occur only in first-time mothers.
    B) appear in 50 to 80 percent of first-time mothers.
    C) affect only mothers who lack a strong social support system.
    D) impact only breastfeeding mothers because of hormonal changes due to milk production.
Answer: B
Page Ref: 160
Skill: Factual
Objective: (B&E Box) Parental Depression and Child Development

101) Babies of mothers suffering from postpartum depression often
    A) have decreased stress hormone levels.
    B) are more attentive to their surroundings.
    C) spend an increased amount of time sleeping.
    D) show delays in mental development.
Answer: D
Page Ref: 160
Skill: Conceptual
Objective: (B&E Box) Parental Depression and Child Development

102) Children of depressed parents tend to
    A) perceive their parents and other people as threatening.
    B) seek out positive relationships with peers and other adults.
    C) fair quite well if they are healthy children.
    D) develop a positive world view in spite of their parent's negativity.
Answer: A
Page Ref: 160
Skill: Conceptual
Objective: (B&E Box) Parental Depression and Child Development

103) Which of the following is true regarding treatment for maternal depression?
    A) Antidepressant medication is rarely prescribed.
    B) Children of depressed mothers are typically involved in therapy sessions with the mother.
    C) Long-term treatment is usually necessary.
    D) When mothers do not respond to treatment, a warm relationship with another caregiver can safeguard
        their children's development.
Answer: D
Page Ref: 160
Skill: Conceptual
Objective: (B&E Box) Parental Depression and Child Development

ESSAY

104) Describe the signs that indicate that labor is near and then define the three stages of childbirth.

Answer: False labor contractions often occur briefly and at unpredictable intervals for several weeks before true labor. About 2 weeks before birth, lightening, or the dropping of the fetus's head low into the uterus, occurs. Bloody show, or the dislodging of the mucus plug that seals the cervix during pregnancy, takes place before true labor. The first stage of labor lasts an average of 12 to 14 hours for first babies and 4 to 6 hours with later births. During this stage, uterine contractions work to dilate and efface the cervix so a clear channel from the uterus into the birth canal is formed. Contractions start out at 10 to 20 minutes apart, each lasting 15 to 20 seconds. They become more powerful over time, continuing for as long as 60 seconds and occurring every 2 to 3 minutes. The climax of the first stage occurs during transition when the frequency and strength of contractions are at the peak, and the cervix opens and thins completely. Stage 2 lasts for about 50 minutes for a first baby and 20 minutes in later births. Strong uterine contractions continue during this stage as the mother pushes the baby out of her uterus. During Stage 3, a few final contractions and pushes cause the placenta to separate from the wall of the uterus and to be delivered in about 5 to 10 minutes.

Page Ref: 130–131

105) Describe circumstances that justify the use of fetal monitoring, labor and delivery medication, and cesarean delivery, and explain any risks associated with each.

Answer: Fetal monitoring is a safe medical procedure that has saved the lives of many high-risk babies. However, when used routinely, monitoring may identify infants as in danger who in fact, are not. Monitoring is linked to an increased rate of cesarean deliveries, and some women complain that the devices are uncomfortable, prevent them from moving easily, and interfere with the normal course of labor. Although labor and delivery medication to relieve pain is necessary in complicated or surgical deliveries, they can cause problems when given routinely. Anesthesia weakens uterine contractions during the first stage of labor and interferes with the mother's ability to feel contractions and push during the second stage. When given in large doses, it produces a depressed state in the newborn, which affects the early mother-infant relationship. Cesarean deliveries are justified in cases of medical emergency and serious maternal illness, and sometimes when fetuses are in the breech position. Many unnecessary cesareans are performed in the United States. In cesarean deliveries, mothers need extra time for recovery, and since medication may have crossed the placenta, babies may be sleepy, unresponsive, and have breathing difficulties.

Page Ref: 136–138

106) Describe the two types of low-birth-weight infants and the risks associated with each type. Then, describe interventions for low-birth-weight infants that have been successful in fostering development.

Answer: There are two types of low-birth-weight babies—preterm and small-for-date. Preterm infants are infants born several weeks or more before their due date. Small-for-date infants are below their expected weight when the length of the pregnancy is taken into account. Compared with preterm babies, whose weight is appropriate for the amount of time spent in the uterus, small-for-date infants are more likely to develop poorly. During the first year, they are more likely to die, catch infections, and show evidence of brain damage. By middle childhood, they have lower intelligence test scores, are less attentive, and do not achieve as well in school. One type of intervention provides for special stimulation in the intensive care nursery. Some examples of this type of intervention are suspended hammocks and waterbeds designed to imitate the gentle motion babies would have received while still in the mother's uterus. Other types include attractive mobiles; recordings of a heartbeat, soft music, or the mother's voice; and infant massage. Skin-to-skin "kangaroo care," which involves placing the infant in a vertical position against the parent's chest, is widely used in developing countries where hospitalization is not always possible. Kangaroo care provides gentle stimulation of all sensory modalities (hearing, smell, touch, and visual). It also promotes improved oxygenation of the baby's body, temperature regulation, sleep, feeding, alertness, and infant survival. Additional interventions teach parents about the preterm infant's characteristics and promote caregiving skills.

Page Ref: 140–143

107) Describe how some newborn reflexes promote the development of motor skills.

Answer: The tonic neck reflex likely prepares the infant for voluntary reaching. When babies lie on their backs in this "fencing position," they naturally gaze at the hand in front of their eyes. The reflex may encourage them to combine vision with arm movements and, eventually, reach for objects.

Reflexes like the palmar grasp, swimming, and stepping drop out early. But, the motor functions involved in each seem to be renewed later. For example, the stepping reflex looks like a primitive walking response. When the stepping reflex is exercised regularly, babies display more spontaneous stepping movements and gain muscle strength. Consequently, they tend to walk several weeks earlier than if the stepping reflex is not practiced.

Page Ref: 147–149

108) Why do pediatricians test newborn reflexes carefully?

Answer: Most newborn reflexes disappear in the first 6 months of life due to a gradual increase in voluntary control over behavior as the cerebral cortex develops. Weak or absent reflexes, overly rigid or exaggerated reflexes, and reflexes that persist beyond the point in development when they should normally disappear can signal brain damage. However, individual differences in reflexive responses exist that are no cause for concern. Newborn reflexes must be observed along with other characteristics to accurately distinguish normal from abnormal central nervous system functioning.

Page Ref: 150

109) How does REM sleep differ between infants and older children and adults? Why do infants spend so much time in REM sleep?

Answer: In older children and adults, the REM state is associated with dreaming. Babies probably do not dream, at least not in the same way older children and adults do. Young infants are believed to have a special need for the stimulation of REM sleep because they spend little time in an alert state, when they can get input from the environment. REM sleep seems to be a way in which the brain stimulates itself. This stimulation is thought to be vital for growth of the central nervous system. In support of this idea, the percentage of REM sleep is especially great in fetuses and in preterm babies, who are even less able to take advantage of external stimulation than are full-term newborns.

Page Ref: 150

110) What is the Neonatal Behavioral Assessment Scale and why is it useful?

Answer: Brazelton's Neonatal Behavioral Assessment Scale (NBAS) evaluates the baby's reflexes, state changes, responsiveness to physical stimuli, and other reactions. The NBAS has been used to help researchers learn about individual and cultural differences in newborn behavior and how child-rearing practices can maintain or change a baby's reactions. Physicians use changes in NBAS scores over the first week or two of life (rather than a single score) to estimate the baby's ability to recover from the stress of birth. The NBAS has also been used to help new parents get to know their infants. In some hospitals, the test is given in the presence of parents to teach them about their newborn's capacities.

Page Ref: 156–157

STUDY QUESTIONS

The Stages of Childbirth

1. Describe three signs that indicate that labor is near. (p. 130)

   A. _____

   B. _____

   C. _____

Stage 1: Dilation and Effacement of the Cervix

1. Describe the events that take place during Stage 1 of childbirth. (p. 131)

   _____

   _____

   _____

2. The climax of Stage 1 is called _____, in which the frequency and strength of contractions are at their peak and the cervix opens completely. (p. 131)

Stage 2: Delivery of the Baby

1. True or False: Stage 2 lasts about 50 minutes for the first child and 20 minutes in later births. (p. 131)

2. Describe the events that take place during Stage 2 of childbirth. (p. 131)

   _____

   _____

   _____

Stage 3: Birth of the Placenta

1. What happens during Stage 3 of childbirth? (p. 131)

   _____

   _____

   _____

The Baby's Adaptation to Labor and Delivery

1. True or False: The infant's production of stress hormones is especially harmful during childbirth. Explain your answer. (pp. 131–132)

   _____

   _____

The Newborn Baby's Appearance

1. The average newborn baby is _____ inches long and weighs _____ pounds. (p. 132)

2. Explain why the newborn's head is large in comparison to the trunk and legs. (p. 132)

   _____

   _____

Assessing the Newborn's Physical Condition: The Apgar Scale

1. List the five characteristics assessed by the Apgar Scale. (pp. 132–133)

    A. _____

    B. _____

    C. _____

    D. _____

    E. _____

2. On the Apgar Scale, a score of _____ or better indicates that the infant is in good physical condition; a score between _____ and _____ indicates that the baby requires special assistance; a score of _____ or below indicates a dire emergency. (p. 132)

Approaches to Childbirth

1. True or False: In many village and tribal cultures, expectant mothers know very little about the childbirth process. (p. 133)

2. Explain how childbirth practices have changed over time in Western societies. (p. 133)

    _____

    _____

Natural, or Prepared, Childbirth

1. What is the goal of *natural childbirth*? (p. 134)

    _____

2. List and describe three features of a typical natural childbirth program. (p. 134)

    A. _____

    _____

    B. _____

    _____

    C. _____

    _____

3. Mothers who go through natural childbirth have (more / less) favorable attitudes toward the childbirth experience than those who do not. (p. 134)

4. Summarize the benefits of social support during childbirth. (p. 134)

    _____

    _____

    _____

5. Name the childbirth position favored by research findings, and cite the benefits of using this position. (pp. 134–135)

    Position: _____

    Benefits: _____

    _____

6. Describe some benefits of water birth. (p. 135)

_____

_____

Home Delivery

1. Home births are typically handled by certified _____, who have degrees in nursing and additional training in childbirth management. (p. 135)

2. True or False: For healthy women assisted by a trained professional, it is just as safe to give birth at home as in a hospital. (p. 135)

Medical Interventions

Fetal Monitoring

1. Explain the purpose of *fetal monitoring*. (p. 136)

_____

_____

2. Cite four reasons why fetal monitoring is a controversial procedure. (p. 136)

   A. _____

   B. _____

   C. _____

   D. _____

Labor and Delivery Medication

1. True or False: Some form of medication is used in more than 80 percent of North American births. (p. 136)

2. The most common approach to controlling pain during labor is _____ analgesia, in which a regional pain-relieving drug is delivered continuously through a catheter into a small space in the lower spine. (p. 136)

3. Discuss three problems with the routine use of labor and delivery medication. (pp. 136–137)

   A. _____

   _____

   B. _____

   _____

   C. _____

   _____

Instrument Delivery

1. In what circumstance is delivery with *forceps* or a *vacuum extractor* appropriate? (p. 137)

_____

_____

2.   Summarize the risks associated with instrument delivery using forceps and vacuum extraction. (p. 137)

Forceps: _____

_____

Vacuum extractor: _____

_____

Induced Labor

1.   Briefly describe an induced labor. (p. 137)

_____

_____

2.   Describe two ways that an induced labor differs from a naturally occurring labor. (p. 137)

A. _____

_____

B. _____

_____

Cesarean Delivery

1.   What is a *cesarean delivery*? (p. 138)

_____

_____

2.   In what circumstances is a cesarean delivery warranted? (p. 138)

_____

_____

3.   A natural labor after a cesarean is associated with slightly (decreased / increased) rates of rupture of the uterus and infant death. (p. 138)

Birth Complications

Oxygen Deprivation

1.   Describe the physical difficulties associated with *cerebral palsy*. (p. 139)

_____

_____

2.   _____ refers to inadequate oxygen supply during the birth process. (p. 139)

3.   Placenta _____ refers to a premature separation of the placenta, whereas placenta _____ refers to a detachment of the placenta resulting from implantation of the blastocyst low in the uterus so that the placenta covers the cervical opening. (p. 139)

4.   Discuss techniques used to prevent secondary damage after the initial brain injury from anoxia. (p. 139)

_____

_____

_____

5. True or False: The vast majority of children who experience anoxia display life-long impairments in cognitive and linguistic skills. (p. 139)

6. Infants born more than six weeks early are at risk for _____, a condition in which the baby's lungs are so poorly developed that the air sacs collapse, causing serious breathing difficulties. (p. 140)

Preterm and Low-Birth-Weight Infants

1. Babies are considered premature if they are born _____ weeks or more before the end of a full 38-week pregnancy or if they weigh less than _____ pounds. (p. 140)

2. True or False: Birth weight is the best available predictor of infant survival and healthy development. (p. 140)

3. List the problems associated with low birth weight that persist through childhood and adolescence and into adulthood. (p. 140)

_____

_____

_____

_____

4. Distinguish between *preterm* and *small-for-date* babies. (p. 140)

Preterm: _____

_____

Small-for-date: _____

_____

5. Of the two types of babies, (preterm / small-for-date) infants usually have more serious problems. (p. 140)

6. Describe the characteristics of preterm infants, and explain how those characteristics may influence the behavior of parents. (p. 141)

A. _____

_____

B. _____

_____

7. Discuss several interventions for preterm infants. (p. 142)

_____

_____

_____

_____

8. Briefly describe the concept of kangaroo care, and discuss the benefits associated with this type of infant stimulation. (p. 142)

    A. _____

    _____

    B. _____

    _____

9. True or False: Research suggests that all preterm children, regardless of family characteristics, require continuous, high-quality interventions well into the school years in order to maintain developmental gains. (p. 143)

Social Issues: Health: A Cross-National Perspective on Health Care and Other Policies for Parents and Newborn Babies

1. _____ *mortality* refers to the number of deaths in the first year of life per 1,000 live births. (p. 144)

2. True or False: African-American and Native-American infants are more than twice as likely as white infants to die in the first year of life. (p. 144)

3. _____ *mortality*, the rate of death in the first month of life, accounts for 67 percent of the infant death rate in the United States and 80 percent in Canada. (p. 144)

4. List the two leading causes of neonatal mortality. (p. 144)

    A. _____

    B. _____

5. Discuss the factors largely responsible for the relatively high rates of infant mortality in the United States. (p. 144)

    _____

    _____

    _____

6. Discuss factors linked to lower infant mortality rates. (pp. 144–145)

    _____

    _____

    _____

Birth Complications, Parenting, and Resilience

1. In the Kauai longitudinal study, what factors predicted long-term difficulties following birth trauma? What factors predicted favorable outcomes? (pp. 143, 145)

    A. _____

    _____

    _____

    B. _____

    _____

    _____

2. True or False: In the Kauai study, children with serious birth complications and troubled family environments developed severe mental health problems, despite social support. (p. 145)

Precious Moments After Birth

1. True or False: Fathers provide their infants with as much stimulation and affection as mothers do. (p. 146)

2. True or False: The parent–infant relationship is highly dependent on close physical contact in the hours after birth in order for bonding to develop. (p. 146)

3. _____ is an arrangement in which the infant stays in the mother's hospital room all or most of the time. (p. 147)

The Newborn Baby's Capacities

Reflexes

1. What is a *reflex*? (p. 147)

   _____

2. Match each reflex with the appropriate response or function. (p. 148)

_____ Spontaneous grasp of adult's finger	1.	Eye blink
_____ When the sole of the foot is stroked, the toes fan out and curl	2.	Rooting
_____ Helps infant find the nipple	3	Sucking
_____ Prepares infant for voluntary walking	4	Swimming
_____ Permits feeding	5.	Moro
_____ Infant lies in a "fencing position"	6.	Palmar grasp
_____ Protects infant from strong stimulation	7.	Tonic neck
_____ In our evolutionary past, may have helped infant cling to mother	8.	Stepping
_____ Helps infants survive if dropped in water	9.	Babinski

3. Briefly explain the adaptive value of three newborn reflexes. (p. 147)

   A. _____

   B. _____

   C. _____

4. Explain how some reflexes form the basis for complex motor skills that will develop later. (p. 147)

   _____

   _____

   _____

   _____

5. When do most newborn reflexes disappear? (p. 148)

   _____

6. Explain the importance of assessing newborn reflexes. (p. 149)

   _____

   _____

   _____

States

1. Name and describe the five infant *states of arousal.* (p. 150)

   A. _____

   B. _____

   C. _____

   D. _____

   E. _____

2. Describe the characteristics of *REM* and *NREM sleep.* (p. 150)

   REM: _____

   _____

   NREM: _____

   _____

3. Why do infants spend so much time in REM sleep? (p. 150)

   _____

   _____

4. What is the most effective way to soothe a crying baby when feeding and diaper changing do not work? (p. 152)

   _____

5. True or False: Rapid parental responsiveness reduces infant crying. Explain your answer. (pp. 152–153)

   _____

   _____

6. How do the cries of brain-damaged babies and those who have experienced prenatal and birth complications differ from those of healthy infants, and how might this difference affect parental responding? (pp. 152–153)

   _____

   _____

   _____

7. Persistent crying, or _____, is a fairly common problem in newborns characterized by intense crying and difficulty calming down, which generally subsides between ___ to ___ months of age. Describe an intervention aimed at reducing colic. (p. 152)

   _____

   _____

   _____

Social Issues: Health: The Mysterious Tragedy of Sudden Infant Death Syndrome

1. What is *Sudden Infant Death Syndrome (SIDS)*? (p. 151)

   _____

   _____

2. True or False: In industrialized countries, SIDS is the leading cause of infant mortality between one week and twelve months of age. (p. 151)

3. True or False: Researchers have recently determined the precise cause of SIDS. (p. 151)

4. Describe some early physical problems that are common among SIDS victims. (p. 151)

   _____

   _____

   _____

5. Explain how impaired brain functioning might cause SIDS. (p. 151)

   _____

   _____

   _____

6. Describe four environmental factors associated with SIDS. (p. 151)

   A. _____

   _____

   B. _____

   _____

   C. _____

   _____

   D. _____

   _____

7. List three ways to reduce the incidence of SIDS. (p. 151)

   A. _____

   B. _____

   C. _____

Sensory Capacities

1. True or False: Infants are born with a poorly developed sense of touch, and consequently, they are not sensitive to pain. (p. 153)

2. True or False: Infants not only have taste preferences, but they are also capable of communicating these preferences to adults through facial expressions. (p. 154)

3. True or False: Certain odor preferences are innate. (p. 154)

4. Explain the survival value of a newborn's sense of smell. (pp. 154–155)

   _____

   _____

5. At birth, infants prefer (pure tones / complex sounds). (p. 155)

6. True or False: Infants can discriminate almost all of the speech sounds of any human language. (p. 155)

7. Cite the characteristics of human speech preferred by infants. (p. 155)

_____

_____

8. Vision is the (most / least) mature of the newborn baby's senses. (p. 155)

9. Describe the newborn baby's *visual acuity*. (pp. 155–156)

_____

_____

10. True or False: Infants have well-developed color vision at birth, and they are immediately capable of discriminating colors. (p. 156)

Neonatal Behavioral Assessment

1. Which areas of behavior does the Neonatal Behavioral Assessment Scale (NBAS) evaluate? (p. 156)

_____

_____

2. What is the Neonatal Intensive Care Unit Network Neurobehavioral Scale (NNNS) specifically designed to evaluate? (p. 156)

_____

_____

3. Since the NBAS is given to infants all around the world, researchers have been able to learn a great deal about individual and cultural differences in newborn behavior and the ways in which various child-rearing practices affect infant behavior. Briefly discuss these findings. (pp. 156–157)

_____

_____

_____

4. Why is a single NBAS score not a good predictor of later development, and what should be used in place of a single score? (p. 157)

A. _____

B. _____

5. How are NBAS interventions beneficial for the early parent–infant relationship? (p. 157)

_____

The Transition to Parenthood

1. Discuss several changes in the family system following the birth of a new baby. (p. 157)

_____

_____

_____

_____

Changes in the Family System

1. True or False: For most new parents, the arrival of a baby causes significant marital strain. (p. 158)

2. Describe changes in the division of labor in the home following childbirth. (p. 158)

   _____

   _____

   _____

3. In what ways does postponing childbearing until the late twenties or thirties ease the transition to parenthood? (p. 158)

   _____

   _____

   _____

4. Explain how a second birth affects the family system. (p. 158)

   _____

   _____

Biology and Environment: Parental Depression and Child Development

1. Differentiate between postpartum blues and postpartum depression, noting the prevalence rate of each. (p. 160)

   Postpartum blues: _____

   _____

   Postpartum depression: _____

   _____

2. Describe how the mother's depressed mood affects her newborn infant in the first months of life. (p. 160)

   _____

   _____

3. Describe parenting practices associated with persistent maternal depression, and note how these parenting behaviors impact the development of the child. (p. 160)

   Parenting practices: _____

   _____

   _____

   Impact on child: _____

   _____

   _____

4. True or False: Persistent paternal depression is a strong predictor of child behavior problems. (p. 160)

5. Briefly summarize interventions for postpartum depression. (p. 160)

   _____

   _____

Single-Mother Families

1.   True or False: Planned births and adoptions by single 30- to 45-year-old women are increasing. (p. 158)

2.   The majority of nonmarital births are (planned / unplanned) and to women in their _____. (p. 159)

3.   Describe common stressors associated with being a single mother. (p. 159)

_____

_____

_____

Parent Interventions

1.   Describe five strategies that couples can use to ease the transition to parenthood. (p. 159)

A.   _____

_____

B.   _____

_____

C.   _____

_____

D.   _____

_____

E.   _____

_____

2.   Discuss how interventions for low-risk parents differ from interventions for high-risk parents. (pp. 159, 161)

Low-risk: _____

_____

_____

High-risk: _____

_____

_____

PUZZLE 4.1 TERM REVIEW

Across

4. A strong pain-killing drug that blocks sensation
6. Inadequate oxygen supply
7. Climax of the first stage of labor; the frequency and strength of contractions peak and the cervix opens completely
14. _____ labor: a labor started artificially by breaking the amnion and giving the mother a hormone that stimulates contractions
15. General term for a variety of problems that result from brain damage before, during, or just after birth (2 words)

Down

1. A mild pain-relieving drug
2. Positioning of the baby in the uterus such that the buttocks or feet would be delivered first
3. _____ and effacement of the cervix: widening and thinning of the cervix during the first stage of labor
5. Infants whose birth weight is below normal when length of pregnancy is taken into account (3 words)

6. The _____ Scale is used to assess the newborn immediately after birth
8. _____ distress syndrome: disorder of preterm infants in which the lungs are so immature that the air sacs collapse, causing breathing difficulties
9. _____ extractor: a plastic cup attached to a suction tube; used to assist in delivering the baby
10. Natural, or _____, childbirth: approach designed to overcome the idea that birth is a painful ordeal requiring extensive medical intervention
11. _____ delivery: a surgical delivery in which the doctor makes an incision in the mother's abdomen and lifts the baby out of the uterus
12. Metal clamps placed around the baby's head; used to pull the baby from the birth canal
13. _____ monitors: electronic instruments that track the baby's heart rate during labor

PUZZLE 4.2 TERM REVIEW

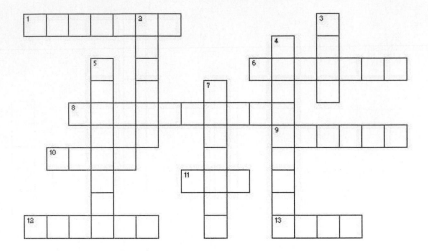

Across

1. States of _____: different degrees of sleep and wakefulness
6. Parents' feelings of affection and concern for the newborn baby
8. _____ depression: feelings of sadness and withdrawal that appear shortly after childbirth and continue for weeks or months
9. _____ mortality: the number of deaths in the first year of life per 1,000 live births
10. Test developed to assess the behavior of the infant during the newborn period (abbr.)
11. An "irregular" sleep state in which brain wave activity is similar to that of the waking state (abbr.)
12. An inborn, automatic response to a particular form of stimulation
13. A "regular" sleep state in which the heart rate, breathing, and brain wave activity are slow and regular (abbr.)

Down

2. Visual _____: fineness of visual discrimination
3. The unexpected death of an infant younger than one year of age that remains unexplained after thorough investigation (abbr.)
4. Arrangement in which the baby stays in the mother's hospital room all or most of the time (2 words)
5. _____ mortality: the number of deaths in the first month of life per 1,000 live births
7. Infants born several weeks or months before their due date

CROSSWORD PUZZLE SOLUTIONS

PUZZLE 4.1

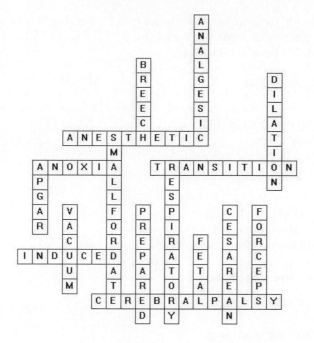

PUZZLE 4.2

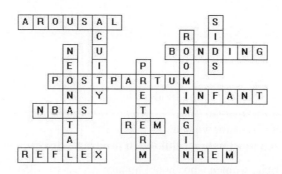

PRACTICE TEST #1

1. Early contractions of the upper part of the uterus are often called prelabor because they (p. 130)
   a. draw the baby's head into the uterus in preparation for labor.
   b. remain brief and unpredictable for several weeks.
   c. force out the bloody show.
   d. soften the cervix just before labor begins.

2. During the transition phase, before the cervix has completely dilated and effaced, the mother must relax and refrain from bearing down because she might (p. 131)
   a. bruise the cervix and slow her labor.
   b. prevent lightening from occurring.
   c. induce false labor.
   d. reharden the cervix.

3. Healthy babies adapt to the stress of childbirth by (p. 131)
   a. dropping their heads low in the uterus to hasten their passage out.
   b. curling into the so-called fetal position that protects their delicate organs.
   c. reducing the amount of blood passing to the brain and heart.
   d. producing cortisol and other stress hormones.

4. An Apgar score of between 4 and 6 means that the baby (p. 132)
   a. is in good physical condition.
   b. requires assistance in establishing vital signs.
   c. needs emergency medical attention.
   d. is close to death.

5. In Western nations, before the late 1800s, birth usually took place (p. 133)
   a. at home.
   b. in primitive hospitals.
   c. with the help of a "head helper."
   d. under a doctor's supervision.

6. Grantly Dick-Read and Fernand Lamaze (p. 134)
   a. established the first freestanding birth centers in the 1950s.
   b. introduced natural childbirth to North America.
   c. argued that natural childbirth is dangerous for women.
   d. developed the methods from which most natural childbirth programs draw.

7. Since 1970, the number of North American women who choose home birth has (p. 135)
   a. risen dramatically and now exceeds the number of women in Europe.
   b. remained constant at about 5 percent.
   c. risen but remains small, at about 1 percent.
   d. declined as doctors and hospitals have worked to discourage the practice.

8. In Canada, continuous fetal monitoring is (p. 136)
   a. used in all home births.
   b. usually reserved for babies at risk for birth complications.
   c. required in most hospitals.
   d. usually not recommended by certified nurse-midwives.

9. The most common labor-pain medication, the epidural analgesia, (p. 136)
   a. allows the mother to feel contraction pressure and move her trunk and legs.
   b. numbs the entire lower half of the mother's body.
   c. strengthens uterine contractions.
   d. has no effect on the infant's Apgar score.

10. A major reason for the rise in induced labors in North America is (p. 137)
    a. the increasing rate of birth complication in older mothers.
    b. that instrument deliveries have declined in popularity.
    c. that many doctors and patients find them convenient.
    d. improvements in delivery drugs.

11. A cause of anoxia, placenta abruptio, occurs when the (p. 139)
    a. umbilical cord wraps around the baby's neck.
    b. blastocyst implants so low that the placenta covers the cervical opening.
    c. baby, just after birth, fails to start breathing.
    d. placenta separates prematurely.

12. Compared with preterm infants, small-for-date infants are more likely to (pp. 140–141)
    a. have been born at 34 to 35 weeks.
    b. be well below average in physical growth during early childhood.
    c. have lower intelligence scores by middle childhood.
    d. experience moderately delayed cognitive development.

13. Kangaroo care can promote preterm babies' survival and recovery by (p. 142)
    a. keeping the babies upright.
    b. enabling parents to serve as human incubators through skin-to-skin touch.
    c. regulating the babies' oxygen intake.
    d. allowing parents to feed their babies through isolettes.

14. Which of the following factors is largely responsible for the high neonatal mortality rate in the United States? (p. 144)
    a. widespread poverty and weak health-care programs for mothers and young children
    b. the steady rise in maternal age
    c. the high mortality rate of Inuit babies
    d. increasing levels of harmful pollution

15. Several studies report that around the time of birth, first-time fathers (p. 146)
    a. begin producing oxytocin.
    b. produce less estrogen.
    c. experience a drop in androgens.
    d. produce less prolactin than mothers.

16. Babies display the rooting reflex when they (p. 147)
    a. place a finger in their mouths.
    b. are held under the arms.
    c. face a bright light.
    d. are hungry and are touched by another person.

17. Babies' sleep-wake cycles are affected largely by (p. 149)
    a. fullness-hunger.
    b. their parents' emotional state.
    c. the time of day.
    d. their sensitivity to external stimuli.

18. The incidence of SIDS peaks between ages (p. 151)
    a. 7 days to three weeks.
    b. 1 to 3 months.
    c. 2 to 4 months.
    d. 6 to 8 months.

19. In Western nations, the most common and effective method of soothing a crying baby is (p. 152)
    a. swaddling.
    b. taking the baby for a short car ride.
    c. massaging the baby's body.
    d. lifting the baby to the shoulder and rocking or walking.

20. Newborns show through _____ that they can distinguish several basic tastes. (p. 154)
    a. facial expressions
    b. sounds that indicate preferences
    c. hand and foot movements
    d. sucking and pushing out with the tongue

21. Allowing newborns to endure severe pain may result in (p. 154)
    a. the release of endorphins.
    b. sleep disturbances and feeding problems.
    c. decreased responsiveness to touch.
    d. reflexive fear.

22. The NBAS test has enabled researchers to (p. 156)
    a. predict intelligence into the preschool years with a high rate of success.
    b. measure how newborns discriminate colors.
    c. learn how different cultures' child-rearing practices can change or maintain a baby's reactions.
    d. draw conclusions about how babies link certain smells to particular bodies or objects.

23. Researchers believe that most newborn reflexes disappear during the first six months as (p. 149)
    a. the baby's weight exceeds its muscle strength.
    b. voluntary control over behavior increases with the development of the cerebral cortex.
    c. parental interaction stimulates more advanced motor skills.
    d. the child learns to block out certain kinds of stimuli.

24. Postponing parenthood until the late twenties or thirties can ease the transition to parenthood because waiting (p. 158)
    a. reduces the chance of emotionally devastating birth complications.
    b. helps to ensure that the new parents will not suffer violated expectations.
    c. women have time to withdraw from their careers gradually.
    d. permits couples to pursue occupational goals and gain life experience.

25. About what percent of babies in the United States and Canada are born to single mothers? (p. 158)
    a. 22
    b. 37
    c. 39
    d. 42

PRACTICE TEST #2

1. During Stage 1 of childbirth, the uterine contractions begin (p. 131)
   a. 2 to 3 minutes apart.
   b. 7 to 8 minutes apart.
   c. 10 to 20 minutes apart.
   d. 30 to 40 minutes apart.

2. During Stage 2 of childbirth, the mother
   a. feels a natural urge to squeeze and push with her abdominal muscles. (p. 131)
   b. pushes out the placenta.
   c. has contractions 8 to 10 minutes apart.
   d. transitions as her cervix opens completely.

3. The combination of small body and large head means that the infant (p. 132)
   a. received too little oxygen during the birthing process.
   b. has a well-developed brain that enables quick learning in the first few months.
   c. bruised the mother's cervix.
   d. produced the proper amount of cortisol.

4. The Apgar scale measures which of the following signs? (p. 133)
   a. mental alertness and hand-eye coordination
   b. the speed with which the infant begins nursing
   c. breathing, blinking, and kicking
   d. heart rate, respiratory effort, reflex irritability, muscle tone, and color

5. The purpose of the natural childbirth movement that arose during the 1950s and 1960s was to (p. 133)
   a. make hospital birth as comfortable and rewarding as possible.
   b. introduce European-style freestanding birth centers to North America.
   c. remove doctors entirely from the birthing experience.
   d. persuade women to have their babies at home.

6. Research indicates that mothers who are supported during labor (p. 134)
   a. are more likely to have an episiotomy.
   b. prefer lying flat on their backs with their feet in stirrups.
   c. are less likely to have cesarean births.
   d. tend to be more nervous and, therefore, experience more birth complications. (p. 135)

7. Most home births are handled by (p. 136)
   a. doctors.
   b. certified nurse-midwives.
   c. experienced family members.
   d. childbirth managers.

8. Fetal monitoring is controversial because it (p. 136)
   a. can cause the baby to produce too many stress hormones.
   b. is extremely painful for the mother.
   c. may identify babies as being in danger, when, in fact, they are not.
   d. disrupts the home birth experience.

9. Low-forceps delivery is associated with risk of (p. 137)
    a. bleeding beneath the baby's skin and external to the skull.
    b. low Apgar scores in infants.
    c. neck and torso deformities.
    d. injury to the baby's head and the mother's tissues.

10. The rise in cesarean births in Western industrialized nations is largely due to (p. 138)
    a. an increase in Rh incompatibility between mothers and their babies.
    b. medical control over childbirth.
    c. complications during natural childbirth.
    d. an increase in the number of babies in breech position.

11. Research suggests that oxygen deprivation just before, during, or just after birth can result in (p. 139)
    a. poor cognitive and language skills in early and middle childhood.
    b. respiratory distress syndrome.
    c. placenta previa.
    d. Apgar scores low in heart rate but high in color.

12. Research indicates that preterm babies stimulated with attractive mobiles, special waterbeds, and other means achieved (p. 142)
    a. few significant developmental gains.
    b. greater mental advancement by the end of their first year.
    c. faster weight gain, more predictable sleep patterns, and greater alertness.
    d. slower weight gain than preterm babies cared for in an isolette.

13. Research findings suggest that both preterm and economically disadvantaged babies need (pp. 142–143)
    a. kangaroo care.
    b. intensive intervention to achieve necessary developmental gains.
    c. help developing the rooting and sucking reflexes.
    d. more time in an isolette than economically advantaged babies.

14. Research indicates that six weeks or less of childbirth leave (p. 145)
    a. is linked to maternal depression, anxiety, and sense of role overload.
    b. can help new parents establish essential bonds with their child.
    c. is the norm in the United States and Canada.
    d. is especially detrimental to middle-SES parents.

15. The Kauai study, begun in 1955, reveals that children's personal characteristics and social experiences (pp. 143, 145)
    a. vary in their impact according to ethnic background.
    b. have a measurable impact on the neonatal mortality rate.
    c. reveal the significant effects of universal, high-quality health care and generous parental leave.
    d. increasingly contribute to the successful functioning of children who suffer serious birth problems.

16. Reflexes can help parents comfort their baby because they (p. 147)
    a. put infants to sleep.
    b. function as a shared language between parent and child.
    c. help infants control distress and amount of stimulation.
    d. enable parents to manage their own anxieties.

17. Newborns spend most of their sleep time in (p. 150)
    a. quiet alertness.
    b. the REM state.
    c. drowsiness.
    d. regular sleep.

18. A strong predictor of SIDS is (p. 151)
    a. extremely deep NREM sleep.
    b. abnormally high birth weight.
    c. abnormalities in the brain center than controls heart rate.
    d. smoking by mothers and other caregivers.

19. According to many researchers, crying peaks around 6 weeks, and then declines because (p. 152)
    a. normal readjustments of the central nervous system occur during that period.
    b. babies begin to learn more mature ways of expressing their desires.
    c. after 6 weeks, babies sleep more.
    d. around that time, parents generally feel more confident in their soothing techniques.

20. Newborns most susceptible to colic are those who (p. 152)
    a. have brain damage.
    b. cannot achieve normal REM sleep.
    c. react strongly to unpleasant stimuli.
    d. experienced anoxia at birth.

21. The least developed of the senses at birth is (p. 155)
    a. taste.
    b. vision.
    c. hearing.
    d. smell.

22. Marriages most likely to be distressed after a baby is born are those (p. 158)
    a. in which gender roles become more traditional than they were before.
    b. confronted with a baby who has severe birth defects.
    c. of older parents.
    d. troubled before the birth of the child.

23. Babies of depressed mothers often (p. 160)
    a. show delays in mental development.
    b. develop a heightened sensitivity to pain.
    c. get low NNNS scores.
    d. become unusually attached to their parents.

24. The majority of nonmarital births are (p. 159)
    a. to older women with secure careers.
    b. to couples who are ethnic minorities.
    c. unplanned and to women in their twenties.
    d. to teenage mothers.

25. Programs in which a trained intervener visits the home of high-risk parents have (p. 161)
    a. had greater success in Canada than in the United States.
    b. resulted in improved parent-infant interaction.
    c. been generally less effective than counselor-led parenting groups.
    d. done little to improve children's cognitive and social development.

POWERPOINT SLIDES

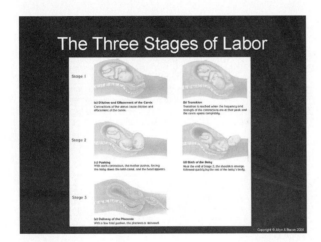

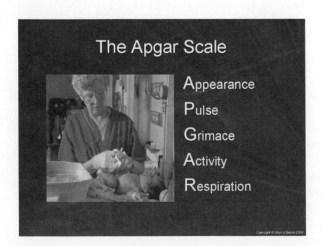

The Apgar Scale

SIGN*	SCORE		
	0	1	2
Heart rate	No heartbeat	Under 100 beats per minute	100 to 140 beats per minute
Respiratory effort	No breathing for 60 seconds	Irregular, shallow breathing	Strong breathing and crying
Reflex irritability (sneezing, coughing, and grimacing)	No response	Weak reflexive response	Strong reflexive response
Muscle tone	Completely limp	Weak movements of arms and legs	Strong movements of arms and legs
Color*	Blue body, arms, and legs	Body pink with blue arms and legs	Body, arms, and legs completely pink

*To remember these signs, you may find it helpful to use a technique in which the original labels are reordered and renamed as follows: color = Appearance, heart rate = Pulse, reflex irritability = Grimace, muscle tone = Activity, and respiratory effort = Respiration. Together, the first letters of the new labels spell Apgar.

*The skin tone of nonwhite babies makes it difficult to apply the "pink" color criterion. However, newborns of all races can be rated for pinkish glow resulting from the flow of oxygen through body tissues.

Source: Apgar, 1953.

Copyright © Allyn & Bacon 2008

Elements of Natural, or Prepared, Childbirth

- Classes
- Relaxation & Breathing Techniques
- Labor Coach
  - Social Support

Copyright © Allyn & Bacon 2008

Other Natural Childbirth Practices

- Positions for delivery might include sitting upright or using a birthing stool.
- Water births are associated with shorter labors and a greater likelihood of a medication-free delivery than other approaches.
- North American women choosing home delivery remains a small percentage.

Copyright © Allyn & Bacon 2008

Medical Interventions in Childbirth

- **Fetal Monitoring**
- **Medication**
  - Analgesics
  - Anesthetics
- **Instrument Delivery**
- **Induced Labor**

Copyright © Allyn & Bacon 2003

Instrument Delivery

Forceps

Vacuum Extraction

Copyright © Allyn & Bacon 2003

Cesarean Delivery

- Cesarean deliveries were rare 40 years ago, now they account for 30% of births in North America.
- Cesareans are warranted in medical emergencies such as:
  - Rh incompatibility
  - Premature separation of the placenta from the uterus
  - Infection
  - Baby in breech position

Copyright © Allyn & Bacon 2003

Anoxia

- Oxygen deprivation at birth
- Can lead to brain damage or later cognitive, language problems
  - Cerebral palsy
- Causes include:
  - Squeezing by umbilical cord
  - Placenta abruptio, placenta previa
  - Failing to breathe after birth
    - Respiratory distress syndrome in preterm infants

Preventing Brain Cell Death From Anoxia

- Researchers are experimenting with ways to prevent this secondary damage.
- Anoxic newborns placed in a head-cooling device shortly after birth for 72 hours substantially reduced brain injury and increased their assessment scores.
- Precooled water blankets are also being used to reduce the rates of death and severe disabilities.

Preterm and Small-for-Date Babies

Preterm

- Born weeks before their due date.

- May be appropriate weight for length of pregnancy.

Small-for-Date

- May be born at due date or preterm.
- Below expected weight for length of pregnancy. Some small-for-date babies have weakened abilities to manage stress.

Low Birth Weight and Disabilities

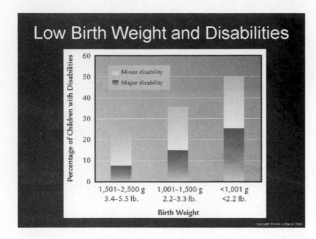

Preterm Infants

- 7 days in the womb—from 34 to 35 weeks can contribute greatly to infant health.
- Babies born at 35 weeks show substantially reduced rates of illness and lengthy hospital stays compared to those born at 34 weeks.

Interventions for Preterm Infants

- Isolette
- Respirator
- Feeding tube
- Intravenous medication
- Special infant stimulation
- Kangaroo skin-to-skin contact
- Parent training in caregiving

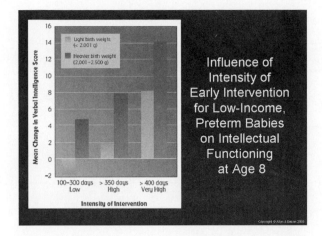

Influence of Intensity of Early Intervention for Low-Income, Preterm Babies on Intellectual Functioning at Age 8

Health Care for Parents and Newborn Babies

- Infant Mortality: in spite of the most up-to-date technology in the world, the United States has made little progress in reducing infant death-rates.

- Neonatal Mortality: low-birth rate is the second highest contributor to infant mortality, and it is largely preventable.

Infant Mortality Around the World

Health Care Programs and Policies for Mothers and Newborns

- Weak health care programs in the U.S. contribute to health problems.
- Paid, job-protected employment leave is another area where the U.S. lags far behind other countries.
- In Sweden, parents have the right to paid birth leave of 2 weeks for fathers and 18 months of paid leave to share between the parents. Even China provides a mother 3 months leave at regular pay, and Germany allows parents to supplement the standard 3-month paid leave with 2 more years at a flat rate and a third year at no pay.

Copyright © Allyn & Bacon 2008

Precious Moments After Birth

- Oxytocin causes the breasts to "let down" milk and heightens the mother's response to the baby.
- First-time fathers also show hormonal changes, including an increase in prolactin and decrease in androgens that are associated with positive emotional reactions to infants.

Copyright © Allyn & Bacon 2008

Newborn Reflexes

- Eye Blink
- Withdrawal
- Rooting
- Sucking
- Swimming
- Moro
- Palmar Grasp
- Tonic Neck
- Stepping
- Babinski

Copyright © Allyn & Bacon 2008

Infant States of Arousal

- Regular Sleep
- Irregular Sleep
- Drowsiness
- Quiet Alertness
- Waking Activity and Crying

Copyright © Allyn & Bacon 2008

The Mysterious Tragedy of Sudden Infant Death Syndrome

- SIDS is the leading cause of infant mortality between 1 week and 12 months in industrialized nations.

- Its occurrence tends to peak between 2 and 4 months of age.

Copyright © Allyn & Bacon 2008

How Can SIDS be Lessened?

- Quitting smoking, putting babies to sleep on their backs, and removing bedclothes can reduce SIDS incidents.
- Pacifiers are another protective measure.

Copyright © Allyn & Bacon 2008

Ways to Soothe a Crying Baby

- Hold on shoulder and rock or walk
- Swaddle
- Pacifier
- Ride in carriage, car, swing
- Combine methods
- Let cry for short time

Newborn Sense of Touch

- Reflexive response to touch on mouth, palms, soles, genitals
- Sensitive to pain
  - Pain can affect later behavior
  - Relieve pain with anesthetics, sugar, gentle holding

Newborn Senses of Taste and Smell

- Prefer sweet tastes at birth
- Quickly learn to like new tastes
- Have odor preferences from birth
- Can locate odors and identify mother by smell from birth

Newborn Sense of Hearing

- Can hear a wide variety of sounds at birth
- Prefer complex sounds to pure tones
- Learn sound patterns within days
- Sensitive to voices and biologically prepared to learn language

Newborn Sense of Vision

- Least developed of senses at birth
- Unable to see long distances, focus clearly
- Scan environment and try to track interesting objects
- Color vision improves in first two months

Adjustments to Parenthood

- Gender roles
- Sharing caregiving predicts greater happiness and sensitivity to the baby.
- Postponing parenthood until the late twenties or thirties eases the transition.

Adjusting to Second Births

- Fathers must take an even more active role in parenting.
- Both parents must help their first-born child adjust.

Copyright © Allyn & Bacon 2006

Parental Depression and Child Development

- 50 to 80% of first-time mothers experience postpartum depression after the birth of their baby.
- 4% of fathers also report depression after the birth of a child.
- Parental depression can have a negative effect on a child's world view.
- Early treatment is vital.

Copyright © Allyn & Bacon 2006

Changes in the Family System

- About 37% of babies in the United States and Canada are born to single-mother families.
- Planned births and adoptions by single 30-to 45-year-old women are increasing.

Copyright © Allyn & Bacon 2006

Transitioning to Parenthood

- Pre-birth counseling can ease the transition to parenthood. High-risk parents struggling with poverty or a baby with disabilities will benefit from intensive home interventions.

Copyright © Allyn & Bacon 2008

CHAPTER 5
PHYSICAL DEVELOPMENT
IN INFANCY AND TODDLERHOOD

CHAPTER-AT-A-GLANCE

Chapter Outline	Instruction Ideas	Supplements
Body Growth pp. 166–168 Changes in Body Size and Muscle–Fat Makeup • Changes in Body Proportions • Skeletal Growth	Learning Objectives 5.1–5.2	Test Bank Items 1–10 Transparencies 44, 45 ICAIA: Infancy and Toddlerhood
Brain Development pp. 168–178 Development of Neurons • Neurophysiological Methods • Development of the Cerebral Cortex • Sensitive Periods in Brain Development • Changing States of Arousal	Learning Objectives 5.3–5.7 Lecture Enhancements 5.1–5.2 Learning Activity 5.1 Ask Yourself p.178	Test Bank Items 11–44, 124–129, 133 Transparencies 46, 47
Influences on Early Physical Growth pp. 178–182 Heredity • Nutrition • Malnutrition • Emotional Well-Being	Learning Objectives 5.8–5.11 Learning Activity 5.2 Ask Yourself p. 182	Test Bank Items 45–59, 134
Learning Capacities pp. 183–187 Classical Conditioning • Operant Conditioning • Habituation • Imitation	Learning Objective 5.12 Lecture Enhancement 5.3 Learning Activities 5.3–5.4 Ask Yourself p.187	Test Bank Items 60–78 Transparencies 55, 55, 56
Motor Development pp. 187–193 The Sequence of Motor Development • Motor Skills as Dynamic Systems • Dynamic Motor Systems in Action • Cultural Variations in Motor Development • Fine Motor Development: Reaching and Grasping • Bowel and Bladder Control	Learning Objectives 5.13–5.15 Lecture Enhancement 5.4 Learning Activities 5.5–5.7 Ask Yourself p. 193	Test Bank Items 79–97, 135–136 Transparencies 48–51, 53
Perceptual Development pp. 193–203 Hearing • Vision • Object Perception • Intermodal Perception • Understanding Perceptual Development	Learning Objectives 5.16–5.20 Learning Activities 5.8–5.9 Ask Yourself p.203	Test Bank Items 98–123, 130–132, 137–138 Transparencies 57, 58, 60, 61, 63, 64

BRIEF CHAPTER SUMMARY

During the first two years, body size increases dramatically, following organized patterns of growth. The skull also grows rapidly, accommodating large increases in brain size. Neurons in the brain form an elaborate communication system, sending messages to one another by releasing neurotransmitters across the synapses. Myelination—the coating of neural fibers with myelin—improves the efficiency of message transfer. Neurophysiological methods that detect brain-wave activity allow researchers to identify relationships between the brain and psychological development.

The cerebral cortex surrounding the rest of the brain is the largest and most complex brain structure. Each hemisphere specializes in different functions, but brain plasticity allows some recovery of abilities lost to damage in one hemisphere. During sensitive periods in brain development, the rapidly growing brain must receive appropriate stimulation in order to reach its full potential. Rapid brain growth also causes substantial changes in organization of sleep and wakefulness during the first two years.

Various factors affect early physical growth. Heredity contributes to height, weight, and rate of physical maturation. Nutrition is crucial: Rapidly growing babies need extra calories to keep their developing organs functioning properly. Breast milk, which is ideally suited to meet infants' needs, is especially important in promoting infant survival and health in poverty-stricken regions. Rapid weight gain in infancy appears to be related to later overweight and obesity; malnutrition in the early years can lead to permanent stunting of physical growth and of brain development. Affection and stimulation are also essential for healthy physical growth.

Babies are born with built-in learning capacities that allow them to benefit from experience immediately after birth. Classical conditioning, operant conditioning, habituation and recovery, and imitation are important early learning capacities that infants use to explore their physical and social worlds.

Motor development, like physical growth, follows an organized sequence, with large individual differences in rate of motor progress. According to dynamic systems theory, mastery of motor skills involves acquiring increasingly complex systems of action in which each new skill is a joint product of central nervous system development, the body's movement possibilities, the goals the child has in mind, and environmental supports for the skill. Cultural variations in infant rearing practices also influence motor development. Of all motor skills, reaching may play the greatest role in infant cognitive development because it opens up a new way of exploring the environment. Reaching improves as depth perception advances and infants gain control of body movements. Early experience also plays a role.

Hearing and vision undergo major advances in the first year. Babies begin to organize sounds into complex patterns, detecting regularities that facilitate later language learning. Newborns prefer human speech to nonspeech sounds, and infants have a remarkable ability to extract regularities from complex, continuous speech, which prepares them to utter their first words around age 12 months. Visual development is supported by maturation of the eye and visual centers in the cerebral cortex. Depth perception develops gradually, helping infants avoid falling. Pattern perception begins at birth; newborns prefer to look at patterned rather than plain stimuli. Babies' tendency to look for structure in a pattern stimulus also applies to face perception; they quickly learn to prefer their mother's face to that of an unfamiliar woman. Size constancy and object constancy also begin in the first week of life. Through intermodal perception, babies perceive input from different sensory systems in a unified way. Perception is guided by the discovery of affordances—the action possibilities that a situation affords.

LEARNING OBJECTIVES

After reading this chapter, you should be able to:

5.1 Describe changes in body size, body proportions, and muscle–fat makeup during the first two years of life. (pp. 166–167)

5.2 Discuss skeletal growth during the first two years of life, including the growth of the skull and the appearance of teeth. (pp. 167–168)

5.3 Describe brain development during infancy and toddlerhood at the level of individual brain cells and at the level of the cerebral cortex. (pp. 168–172)

5.4 Summarize research on brain lateralization and brain plasticity. (pp. 172–173)

330

5.5   Describe research findings related to the existence of sensitive periods in brain development, and note the evidence of brain growth spurts and need for appropriate stimulation. (pp. 173–176)

5.6   Describe current methods of measuring brain functioning, and identify which measure is most appropriate during infancy and toddlerhood. (pp. 170–171)

5.7   Explain how the organization of sleep and wakefulness changes over the first two years. (pp. 176–178)

5.8   Discuss the impact of heredity on early physical growth. (p. 178)

5.9   Discuss the nutritional needs of infants and toddlers, the advantages of breastfeeding, and the extent to which chubby babies are at risk for later overweight and obesity. (pp. 178–180)

5.10   Discuss the impact of severe malnutrition on the development of infants and toddlers, and cite two dietary diseases associated with this condition. (pp. 180–182)

5.11   Describe the growth disorder known as nonorganic failure to thrive, noting common symptoms and family circumstances surrounding the disorder. (p. 182)

5.12   Explain how infants learn through classical conditioning, operant conditioning, habituation and recovery, and imitation. (pp. 183–187)

5.13   Describe the general course of motor development during the first two years, along with factors that influence it. (pp. 187–188)

5.14   Explain the dynamic systems theory of motor development, highlighting cultural variations in motor development. (pp. 189–190)

5.15   Describe the development of reaching and grasping, and explain how early experiences affect these skills. (pp. 190–193)

5.16   Summarize the development of hearing in infancy, giving special attention to speech perception. (pp. 193–194)

5.17   Summarize the development of vision in infancy, with particular attention to depth perception and pattern perception. (pp. 195–200)

5.18   Discuss the development of object perception during the first year of life. (pp. 200–201)

5.19   Explain the concept of intermodal perception. (p. 202)

5.20   Explain the Gibsons' differentiation theory of perceptual development. (pp. 202–203)

LECTURE OUTLINE

I. BODY GROWTH (pp. 166–168)
    A. Changes in Body Size and Muscle-Fat Makeup (pp. 166–167)
        1. During the first two years, the body grows more rapidly than at any time after birth.
        2. By the end of the first year, the typical infant's length is 50 percent greater than it was at birth, and by age 2 years, it is 75 percent greater.
        3. Birth weight doubles by 5 months of age, triples by 1 year, and quadruples by 2 years.
        4. Body fat, which helps the infant maintain a constant body temperature, increases after birth, peaking around 9 months of age. During the second year, toddlers slim down, a trend that continues into middle childhood.
        5. In contrast, muscle tissue increases slowly during infancy and does not peak until adolescence.
        6. In infancy, girls are slightly shorter and lighter than boys, with a higher ratio of fat to muscle. Ethnic differences in body size are apparent as well.
    B. Changes in Body Proportions (p. 167)
        1. The **cephalocaudal trend** is a pattern of physical growth and motor control that proceeds from head to tail; growth of the head and chest occurs before that of the trunk and legs.

       2.   The **proximodistal trend** is a pattern of physical growth and motor control that proceeds from the center of the body outward; the arms and legs grow before the hands and feet.

  C. Skeletal Growth (pp. 167–168)

       1.   Children of the same age differ in *rate* of physical growth, but current body size is not an accurate indication of physical maturity.

       2.   General Skeletal Growth (pp. 167–168)

          a.   The best way to estimate a child's physical maturity is to use **skeletal age,** a measure of the body's bone development.

          b.   Growth centers in the bone, called **epiphyses,** appear just before birth; new cartilage cells are produced at the growth plates of the epiphyses throughout childhood.

          c.   Eventually, the epiphyses thin and disappear; after that, no more growth of the bone is possible.

          d.   Skeletal age can be estimated by X-raying the bones and seeing the number of epiphyses and the extent to which they are fused.

          e.   African-American children tend to be slightly ahead of Caucasian-American children in skeletal age, and girls are considerably ahead of boys in both skeletal age and development of other organs.

       3.   Growth of the Skull (p. 168)

          a.   Because of the large increases in brain size, skull growth is especially rapid during the first two years.

          b.   At birth, the bones of the skull are separated by six gaps called **fontanels,** which gradually shrink and close.

       4.   Appearance of Teeth (p. 168)

          a.   An infant's first tooth usually appears between 4 to 6 months of age; by age 2, the average child has 20 teeth.

          b.   A child who gets teeth early is likely to be advanced in physical maturity.

II. BRAIN DEVELOPMENT (pp. 168–178)

  A. At birth, the brain is nearer to its adult size than any other physical structure, and it continues to develop at an astounding pace during infancy and toddlerhood.

  B. Development of Neurons (pp. 168–170)

       1.   The human brain has 100 to 200 billion **neurons**—nerve cells that store and transmit information.

       2.   Between the neurons are tiny gaps or **synapses,** where fibers from different neurons come close together but do not touch.

       3.   Neurons send messages to one another by releasing chemicals called **neurotransmitters,** which cross the synapse.

       4.   Neurons that are *stimulated* by input from the surrounding environment continue to establish new synapses, while those that are seldom stimulated soon lose their synapses, in a process called **synaptic pruning.**

       5.   About half of the brain's volume is made up of **glial cells,** which do not carry messages but are responsible for **myelination,** the coating of neural fibers with an insulating fatty sheath (*myelin*) that improves the efficiency of message transfer.

       6.   Brain development can be compared to molding a "living sculpture" as cell death and synaptic pruning sculpt away excess building material to form the mature brain.

  C. Neurophysiological Methods (pp. 170–171)

       1.   There are five major methods of measuring brain functioning:

          a.   *Electroencephalogram (EEG)* and *event-related potentials (ERPs)* detect changes in electrical activity in the cerebral cortex.

          b.   *Neuroimaging techniques*, including PET, fMRI, and NIROT, yield detailed, three-dimensional computerized pictures of the brain and its active areas, providing information about which brain regions are specialized for certain capacities.

  D. Development of the Cerebral Cortex (pp. 171–173)

       1.   The **cerebral cortex,** which surrounds the rest of the brain, is the largest, most complex brain structure, accounting for 85 percent of the brain's weight.

       2.   The cerebral cortex contains the greatest number of neurons and synapses and is responsible for the unique intelligence of our species.

3. Because it is the last brain structure to stop growing, the cerebral cortex is sensitive to environmental influences for much longer than other parts of the brain.
4. Regions of the Cortex (p. 172)
   a. The order in which cortical regions develop corresponds to the order in which various capacities emerge in infancy and childhood.
   b. The cortical regions with the most extended period of development are the *frontal lobes,* which are responsible for thought and consciousness.
5. Lateralization and Plasticity of the Cerebral Cortex (pp. 172–173, 174)
   a. **Lateralization** refers to the specialization of functions of the left and right sides, or *hemispheres,* of the cortex.
      (1) A lateralized brain is adaptive, enabling humans to cope successfully with changing environmental demands.
      (2) The two hemispheres work together in complex ways; the concept of a "right-brained" or "left-brained" person is an oversimplification.
   b. **Brain plasticity** refers to the ability of other areas of the brain to reorganize and take over functions of a damaged part.
   c. Research on brain-damaged children and on deaf adults provides dramatic evidence of early brain plasticity.
   d. During the first few years, the brain is more plastic than at any later time of life, perhaps because many of its synapses are not yet established.
E. Sensitive Periods in Brain Development (pp. 173, 175–176)
   1. Animal studies verify the existence of sensitive periods in the development of the cerebral cortex.
   2. Children Born with Cataracts and Orphanage Children (pp. 173, 175)
      a. Children who lived in deprived early environments that were later rectified confirm the importance of a generally stimulating physical and social environment for all domains of development.
      b. Evidence also shows that the chronic stress of early deprivation disrupts the brain's capacity to manage stress, with long-term negative consequences.
   3. Appropriate Stimulation (pp. 175–176)
      a. In addition to impoverished environments, ones that overwhelm children with expectations beyond their current capacities fail to capitalize on the brain's potential. Trying to prime infants with such excessive stimulation can cause them to withdraw, creating conditions much like stimulus deprivation.
      b. **Experience-expectant brain growth** the young brain's rapidly developing organization—depends on ordinary experiences—opportunities to see and touch objects, hear language, and explore the environment.
      c. **Experience-dependent brain growth** is a lifelong process consisting of additional growth and refinement of established brain structures as a result of specific learning experiences.
      d. Experience-expectant brain growth provides the foundation for later-occurring, experience-dependent development.
F. Changing States of Arousal (pp. 176–178)
   1. During the first two years, the organization of sleep and wakefulness changes, and fussiness and crying decline, as a result of rapid brain growth.
   2. Over time, infants remain awake for longer daytime periods and need fewer naps until finally, around age 4 or 5, napping subsides.
   3. Although brain maturation is largely responsible for changes in sleep and wakefulness, the social environment also contributes: When babies sleep with their parents, as they do in most parts of the world, they do not develop adultlike sleep–wake patterns until the end of the first year.
   4. Even infants who sleep through the night continue to wake occasionally, but these behaviors subside when parents offer comfort.

III. INFLUENCES ON EARLY PHYSICAL GROWTH (pp. 178–182)
   A. Heredity (p. 178)
      1. When diet and health are adequate, height and rate of physical growth are largely determined by heredity.

2. *Catch-up growth* refers to physical growth that returns to its genetically determined path after being delayed by temporary environmental factors.

3. Weight is also affected by genetic makeup, but the environment—especially nutrition—plays an important role.

B. Nutrition (pp. 178–180)

1. A baby's energy needs, pound for pound, are twice as great as an adult's.

2. Twenty-five percent of an infant's caloric intake is devoted to growth.

3. Breastfeeding versus Bottle-Feeding (pp. 178–180)

   a. Breast milk is ideally suited to infants' needs; breastfeeding offers many nutritional and health advantages over bottle-feeding.

   b. Breastfed babies in impoverished regions of the world are less likely to be malnourished and more likely to survive the first year of life. However, many mothers in the developing world do not know about these benefits.

   c. Today, 71 percent of American and 75 percent of Canadian mothers breastfeed, but less than half of them do so for the first six months, as is recommended by U.S. and Canadian national health agencies.

   d. Because breast milk is easily digestible, breastfed babies become hungry more often than bottle-fed infants, making breastfeeding inconvenient for many employed mothers.

   e. Infants benefit from the antibodies and easy digestibility of breast milk, and breast milk provides nutrients ideally suited for early brain development.

   f. However, breast- and bottle-fed children in industrialized nations do not differ in emotional adjustment.

4. Are Chubby Babies at Risk for Later Overweight and Obesity? (p. 180)

   a. Most chubby infants thin out during toddlerhood and the preschool years when they become more active.

   b. Infants and toddlers can eat nutritious foods freely, without risk of becoming too fat.

   c. However, recent evidence shows a strengthening relationship between rapid weight gain in infancy and obesity at older ages, possibly due to the rise in overweight and obesity among adults, who promote unhealthful eating habits in their young children.

   d. Breastfeeding for the first six months, limiting unhealthy foods, and promoting physical exercise are ways that parents can prevent their infants from becoming overweight children.

C. Malnutrition (pp. 180–182)

1. About one-third of the world's children suffer from malnutrition before age 5, with 9 percent severely affected, suffering from one of two dietary diseases, marasmus and kwashiorkor.

   a. **Marasmus** is a wasted condition of the body usually appearing in the first year of life that is caused by a diet low in all essential nutrients.

   b. **Kwashiorkor** is a disease usually appearing between 1 and 3 years of age, caused by a diet very low in protein. Symptoms include an enlarged belly, swollen feet, hair loss, skin rash, and irritable, listless behavior.

2. Children who survive these extreme forms of malnutrition grow to be smaller in all body dimensions and, when their diets do improve, are at risk for excessive weight gain.

3. Malnutrition during infancy and toddlerhood also seriously affects learning and behavior by interfering with growth of neural fibers and myelination.

4. *Iron-deficiency anemia,* a condition common among poverty-stricken infants and children, interferes with many central nervous system processes.

5. Early nutritional intervention is important and should focus on improving the family situation before the effects of early malnutrition are allowed to run their course.

6. Inadequate nutrition is not confined to developing countries. An estimated 16 percent of U.S. children and 13 percent of Canadian children suffer from *food insecurity*—uncertain access to enough food for a healthy, active life.

D. Emotional Well-Being (p. 182)

1. **Nonorganic failure to thrive** is a growth disorder, usually present by 18 months of age, that is caused by lack of parental love.

2. Infants suffering this disorder show the signs of marasmus, but no organic (or biological) cause can be found.

3. Family circumstances surrounding failure to thrive help explain the typical reactions in afflicted individuals.

4. If the disorder is not corrected in infancy, some children remain small and have lasting cognitive and emotional problems.

IV. LEARNING CAPACITIES (pp. 183–187)

A. *Learning* refers to changes in behavior as the result of experience. Babies are born with built-in learning capacities that allow them to benefit from experience immediately.

B. Classical Conditioning (pp. 183–184)

1. Newborn reflexes make **classical conditioning** possible in young infants. In this form of learning, a neutral stimulus is paired with a stimulus that triggers a reflexive response, ultimately allowing the new stimulus to produce the behavior.

2. The steps for learning by classical conditioning are as follows:

    a. An **unconditioned stimulus** (**UCS**) consistently produces a reflexive, or **unconditioned response** (**UCR**).

    b. A *neutral stimulus,* which does not lead to the reflexive response, is presented at the same time as or just before the UCS.

    c. The neutral stimulus, now called a **conditioned stimulus** (**CS**), produces the reflexive response, now called a **conditioned response** (**CR**).

3. *Extinction* refers to a decline in the CR as a result of presenting the CS repeatedly without the UCS.

4. For a baby to learn easily, the association between a UCS and a CS must have survival value—for example, in a feeding situation.

C. Operant Conditioning (p. 184)

1. **Operant conditioning** is a form of learning in which the infant acts, or *operates,* on the environment, and their spontaneous behavior is followed by a stimulus that changes the probability that they will repeat the behavior.

2. A **reinforcer** is a stimulus that increases the occurrence of a response.

3. **Punishment** refers to removing a desirable stimulus or presenting an unpleasant one to decrease the occurrence of a response.

4. Operant conditioning is a powerful tool for finding out what stimuli babies can perceive and which ones they prefer.

5. Operant conditioning also plays a vital role in the formation of social relationships, as infant and adult gaze into each other's eyes and smile—an interaction that contributes to the development of infant–caregiver attachment.

D. Habituation (pp. 185–186)

1. **Habituation** refers to a gradual reduction in the strength of a response due to repetitive stimulation.

2. **Recovery** is an increase in responsiveness after a new stimulus appears.

3. Habituation and recovery enable us to focus on those aspects of the environment we know least about, making learning more efficient.

4. Studying infants' habituation and recovery allows researchers to explore their understanding of the world.

E. Imitation (pp. 186–187)

1. **Imitation** is learning by copying the behavior of another person.

2. Research indicates that newborns can imitate adult facial expressions as well as certain gestures, such as head movements.

3. Some investigators regard the capacity for imitation as little more than an automatic response that declines with age; however, newborns imitate diverse facial expressions and head movements with effort and determination, and, unlike reflexes, imitation does not decline.

4. However limited at birth, imitation is a powerful means of learning and helps get the infant's relationship with parents off to a good start.

V. MOTOR DEVELOPMENT (pp. 187–193)

A. The Sequence of Motor Development (pp. 187–188)

1. *Gross motor development* refers to control over actions that help an infant move around in the environment, such as crawling, standing, and walking.

2. *Fine motor development* involves smaller movements, such as reaching and grasping.
3. Although the *sequence* of motor development is fairly uniform across children, large individual differences exist in *rate* of motor progress.
4. Motor control of the head precedes control of the arms and trunk, which precedes control of the legs (*cephalocaudal trend*).
5. Head, trunk, and arm control appear before coordination of the hands and fingers (*proximodistal trend*).
6. However, deviations from both of these trends exist.

B. Motor Skills as Dynamic Systems (p. 189)
1. According to **dynamic systems theory of motor development**, mastery of motor skills involves acquiring increasingly complex *systems of action*.
2. Each new skill is a joint product of central nervous system development, movement capacities of the body, the goal the child has in mind, and environmental supports for the skill.
3. After a skill is first acquired, the infant must refine it so until the skill becomes smooth and accurate.
4. Dynamic systems theory illustrates why motor development cannot be genetically determined.
   a. Heredity maps it out only at a general level.
   b. Behaviors are not *hardwired* into the nervous system but, rather, are *softly assembled*, motivated by exploration and the desire to master new tasks.

C. Dynamic Motor Systems in Action (pp. 189–190)
1. To find out how infants acquire motor capabilities, researchers conduct microgenetic studies, following babies from their first attempts at a skill until it becomes smooth and effortless.
2. By holding sounding toys alternately in front of infants' hands and feet, James Galloway and Esther Thelen found that infants reach with their feet as early as 8 weeks of age—at least a month before reaching with their hands.
3. These findings illustrate that rather than following a strict cephalocaudal pattern, the order of motor skills development depends on the anatomy of the body part, the surrounding environment, and the baby's efforts.

D. Cultural Variations in Motor Development (p. 190)
1. Cross-cultural research shows that early movement opportunities and a stimulating environment contribute to motor development.
2. Cultural beliefs vary concerning the necessity and advisability of deliberately teaching motor skills to babies.
3. The current Western practice of putting babies to sleep on their backs (to prevent SIDS) delays gross motor milestones by decreasing exposure to "tummy time."

E. Fine Motor Development: Reaching and Grasping (pp. 190–192)
1. Reaching plays a vital role in infant cognitive development because it opens up a whole new way of exploring the environment.
2. Motor skills, including reaching and grasping, start out as gross, diffuse activities and move toward mastery of fine movements.
3. **Prereaching** refers to the poorly coordinated, primitive reaching movements of newborns.
4. Development of Reaching and Grasping (pp. 190–191)
   a. Voluntary reaching appears at about 3 to 4 months and gradually improves in accuracy.
   b. Early reaching is largely controlled by *proprioception,* our sense of movement and location in space arising from stimuli within the body.
   c. Reaching improves as depth perception advances and as infants gain greater control of body posture and arm and hand movements.
   d. The **ulnar grasp** is a clumsy grasp typical of young infants, in which the fingers close against the palm.
   e. The **pincer grasp** is a well-coordinated grasp that emerges by the end of the first year, involving the oppositional use of the index finger and thumb.
   f. Between 8 and 11 months, attention begins to shift from the reaching and grasping motor skill to the events that occur before and after obtaining the object.

5. Early Experience and Reaching (p. 192)
    a. Trying to push infants beyond their current readiness to handle stimulation can undermine the development of important motor skills.
    b. As infants' and toddlers' motor skills develop, their caregivers must devote more energies to protecting them from harm.
F. Bowel and Bladder Control (pp. 192–193)
    1. Toilet training is best delayed until the months following the second birthday, when children can consistently identify the signals from a full bladder or rectum and can control those muscles until they get to the toilet.
    2. Effective training techniques include establishing regular toileting routines, using gentle encouragement, and praising children for their efforts.

VI. PERCEPTUAL DEVELOPMENT (pp. 193–203)
A. Hearing (pp. 193–195)
    1. During the first year, babies start to organize sounds into complex patterns.
    2. Between 4 and 7 months, babies develop a sense of musical phrasing, preferring Mozart minuets with pauses between phrases to those with awkward breaks.
    3. Speech Perception (pp. 194, 195)
        a. Newborns prefer listening to human speech over nonspeech sounds and prefer the sounds of their native tongue over those of a rhythmically distinct foreign language.
        b. Around 5 months, infants become sensitive to syllable stress patterns in their own language.
        c. Between 6 and 8 months, they start to screen out sounds not used in their own language.
        d. Focus on the larger speech units crucial for figuring out meaning. Older infants can also detect clauses and phrases in sentences.
        e. Around 7 to 9 months, infants begin to divide the speech stream into wordlike units.
    4. Analyzing the Speech Stream (p. 194)
        a. Research reveals that infants are remarkable *statistical analyzers* of sound patterns, detecting patterns of syllables in word sequences.
        b. Babies' ability to extract regularities from complex, continuous speech allows them to acquire a great deal of language-specific knowledge before beginning to talk around 12 months of age.
B. Vision (pp. 195–200)
    1. Around 2 months, infants can focus on objects about as well as adults, and by 4 months, their color vision is adultlike.
    2. By 6 months, babies' visual acuity (fineness of discrimination) is about 20/20, a near adult level.
    3. Over the first half-year, the infant's ability to scan and track moving objects improves as eye movements come under voluntary control.
    4. Depth Perception (pp. 196–197)
        a. *Depth perception* is the ability to judge the distance of objects from one another and from ourselves.
        b. The *visual cliff* was used in the earliest studies of depth perception to observe when infants learned to distinguish deep from shallow surfaces and to avoid drop-offs.
        c. Emergence of Depth Perception (pp. 196–197)
            (1) Babies 3 to 4 weeks old blink their eyes defensively when an object moves toward their face as though it is going to hit.
            (2) At 3 months, motion has helped babies figure out that objects are three-dimensional.
            (3) *Motion* is the first type of depth cue to which infants are sensitive.
            (4) *Binocular depth cues* arise because our two eyes have slightly different views of the visual field; sensitivity to these cues emerges between 2 and 3 months.
            (5) Sensitivity to *pictorial depth cues,* such as changes in texture and overlapping objects, develops around 6 to 7 months.
        d. Independent Movement and Depth Perception (pp. 197, 198)
            (1) Infants' sensitivity to depth information is promoted by crawling.
            (2) As they master each new posture, babies undergo new learning about depth.
            (3) Crawling experience also promotes other aspects of three-dimensional understanding, such as finding hidden objects, because it involves independent movement.

5. Pattern Perception (pp. 197, 199)
    a. Newborns prefer to look at patterned rather than plain stimuli, a preference explained by contrast sensitivity.
    b. Around 2 months of age, infants become sensitive to the contrast in complex patterns and spend more time looking at them.
    c. Combining Pattern Elements (p. 199)
        (1) Newborn infants respond to the separate parts of a pattern, staring at single high-contrast features.
        (2) At 2 to 3 months, infants explore a pattern's internal features, as well, and become able to integrate the parts of a pattern into a unified whole.
        (3) By the end of the first year, infants can detect objects represented by incomplete drawings.
    d. Face Perception (pp. 199–200)
        (1) Infants' tendency to look for structure in a patterned stimulus applies to face perception.
        (2) Babies tend to look longer at faces judged by adults as physically attractive.
        (3) From repeated exposure to their mother's face, babies learn to prefer it to that of an unfamiliar woman.
        (4) Around 3 months, babies can distinguish between photographs of two strangers, and at 5 months they perceive emotional expressions as meaningful wholes.

C. Object Perception (pp. 200–201)
    1. Size and Shape Constancy (pp. 200–201)
        a. To accurately perceive objects, we must translate varying retinal images into a single representation.
        b. **Size constancy**— the perception that an object's size is the same, despite changes in the size of its retinal image—is evident in the first week of life, as is **shape constancy,** the perception that an object's shape is stable, despite changes in the shape projected on the retina.
        c. These perceptual capacities appear to be innate and assist babies in detecting a coherent world of objects.
    2. Perception of Object Identity (p. 201)
        a. At first, babies rely heavily on motion and spatial arrangement to identify objects.
        b. As babies visually track moving objects, they pick up additional information about an object's boundaries, such as shape, color, and texture.
        c. As infants become familiar with many types of objects, they rely more on shape, color, and texture and less on motion to identify objects as separate units.
        d. Perception of *object unity* precedes perception of an object's *continuous path of movement*—a more challenging task.

D. Intermodal Perception (p. 202)
    1. **Intermodal perception** combines information from more than one *modality,* or sensory system.
    2. Recent evidence on newborn infants indicates that they perceive the world in an intermodal fashion from the beginning—for example, that they expect sight, sound, and touch to go together.
    3. Detection of *amodal relations,* such as the rhythm in the sight and sound of clapping hands, may provide a basis for detecting other intermodal matches.

E. Understanding Perceptual Development (pp. 202–203)
    1. Eleanor and James Gibson's **differentiation theory** states that perceptual development involves the detection of increasingly fine-grained, invariant features in the environment—those that remain stable in a constantly changing perceptual world.
    2. Perception is guided by the discovery of **affordances**—the action possibilities a situation offers an organism with certain motor capabilities—which infants discover as they act on their world.
    3. Some researchers, disagreeing with the Gibsons, believe that babies also *impose meaning* on what they perceive, constructing categories of objects and events in the surrounding environment.
    4. Many researchers combine viewpoints, regarding infant development as proceeding from a perceptual to a cognitive emphasis over the first year of life.

LECTURE ENHANCEMENTS

LECTURE ENHANCEMENT 5.1
Long-Term Effects of Severe Environmental Deprivation in Infancy and Toddlerhood (pp. 173, 175–176)

Time: 15–20 minutes

Objective: To examine the long-term effects of extreme environmental deprivation in infancy and toddlerhood.

As noted in the text, severe environmental deprivation in infancy and toddlerhood can have a devastating impact on all aspects of development. To extend existing research on the effects of early deprivation on cognitive development, Beckett and colleagues (2006) followed 181 children who were adopted from Romanian and U.K. institutions. The researchers collected the following information:

(1) Duration of depravation. To compare participant outcomes, children were categorized according to the amount of time they were institutionalized—less than six months, 6-24 months, or more than 24 months.
(2) Birth weight and weight at time of adoption were recorded.
(3) The Denver Developmental Quotient was administered at the time of adoption to estimate developmental status (gross and fine motor skills, language, social development).
(4) Head circumference was taken at the time of adoption, as previous studies have found a link between head size, brain weight, and IQ.
(5) When children were 6 years old, they completed the McCarthy Scales of Children's Ability, which provides a general estimate of cognitive functioning (IQ).
(6) When participants were 11 years old, they completed a short form of the Wechsler Intelligence Scale for Children (WISC-III). Scores were computed for vocabulary, understanding of similarities, block design, and object assembly.
(7) Adoptive mothers completed an intelligence test, and both adoptive mothers and fathers provided information about their educational background.

Results indicated that the effects of severe early deprivation were still evident at age 11, but only for children who spent more than six months in an institution. Specifically, for children who spent more than six months in institutionalized care, their IQ scores were, on average, 15 points below children who spent less than six months in an institution. Interestingly, children who showed the greatest impairment at age 6 demonstrated the most catch-up between ages 6 and 11. This finding suggests that intensive intervention and environmental stimulation has the greatest effects on children with the most severe impairments. It also suggests that catch-up growth is possible in school-age children, although cognitive impairments are still evident. In this sample, severe impairment at age 6 predicted impairment at age 11, despite catch-up.

Findings also revealed that institutionalized children tended to be underweight when adopted, although no relationship was found between weight and cognitive outcomes at age 11. Adoptive mothers' IQ and the educational backgrounds of adoptive mothers and fathers had no significant effect on cognitive outcomes at age 6 or 11. It should be noted that most of the adoptive families had above average education and IQ scores, which may explain why there was no relationship between the family variables and child outcomes. Taken together, these findings suggest that (1) duration of deprivation has the greatest impact on cognitive outcomes, and (2) significant catch-up growth is possible even into the school years.

Ask students to reflect on these findings and those presented in the text. Although this study did not reveal a significant relationship between adoptive parents' IQ and educational background and child outcomes, other studies have identified a relationship. How might adoptive parents' IQ and educational background contribute to catch-up growth and psychological well-being in adopted children?

Beckett, C., Maughan, B., Rutter, M., Castle, J., Colvert, E., Groothues, C., Kreppner, J., Stevens, S., O'Connor, T. G., & Sonuga-Barke, E. J. (2006). Do the effects of early severe deprivation on cognition persist into early adolescence? Findings from the English and Romanian adoptees study. *Child Development, 77*, 696–711.

LECTURE ENHANCEMENT 5.2
More on Parent-Infant Cosleeping (p. 177)

Time: 15–20 minutes

Objective: To highlight the various benefits of parent-infant cosleeping.

As noted in the text, expert child-rearing advice often encourages nighttime separation of baby from parent. Research shows that cultural values strongly influence infant sleeping arrangements. Specifically, mothers in collectivist societies are far more likely to sleep with their babies than mothers in individualistic societies. Moreover, Western cultures often regard solitary infant sleeping as normal and healthy. Despite Western parents' belief in solitary infant sleeping, research indicates that parent–infant cosleeping is associated with a number of short- and long-term benefits. According to McKenna and McDade (2005), parents should sleep with their babies for the following reasons:

(1) Parent and infant sleeping in close proximity is associated with increased infant–mother interactions and arousals, more face-to-face body orientations, more breastfeeding, higher infant body temperatures, reduced nighttime crying, and more total sleep for both infants and their mothers.

(2) Significantly more infants and young children suffer from sleep disturbances in cultures that advocate nighttime separation of baby and parent. It is possible that the biological need for nighttime contact results in more crying and protesting by infants who are isolated from their parents during sleep. As a result, these babies may be more likely to experience sleep disturbances than infants who sleep with their parents.

(3) Despite parental fears that cosleeping puts infants at risk for Sudden Infant Death Syndrome (SIDS), research suggests the opposite—that parent-infant sleep actually protects babies from SIDS. In addition, the majority of SIDS deaths associated with cosleeping occur in families where one or both parents have a history of drug use.

In addition to the short-term benefits of parent–infant cosleeping, McKenna and McDade (2005) cite a number of long-term associations with overall adjustment:

(1) Several studies report that children who did not cosleep with their parents during infancy were more fearful than children who regularly slept in their parents' beds.

(2) A study of male college students found that those who had slept with their parents from infancy through age 5 scored higher on measures of self-esteem and were less likely to experience anxiety than students who did not sleep with their parents.

(3) In a large study of adults from Chicago and New York, researchers found that individuals who had slept with their parents during infancy and early childhood reported greater feelings of life satisfaction than individuals who did not cosleep with their parents.

Before discussing parent–infant cosleeping, have students ask several adults whether they think babies should sleep alone or with their parents, and why. Compile the responses and distribute them to the class for discussion. Are the answers consistent with Western beliefs about parent–infant cosleeping? Explain.

McKenna, J. J., & McDade, T. (2005). Why babies should never sleep alone: A review of the co-sleeping controversy in relation to SIDS, bedsharing, and breastfeeding. *Pediatric Respiratory Reviews, 6,* 134–152.

LECTURE ENHANCEMENT 5.3
Are Newborn Chimpanzees Capable of Facial Imitation? (pp. 186–187)

Time: 5–10 minutes

Objective: To examine newborn imitation in chimpanzees.

As noted in the text, newborn imitation, although controversial, is one of the first signs of learning and communication between parents and children. Newborn imitation has also been observed in chimpanzees, our closest evolutionary relatives (Myowa-Yamakoshi, et al., 2004). However, these chimpanzees were at least 4 weeks old and had been cared for by humans shortly after birth. Therefore, it is possible that human socialization contributed to the chimpanzees' behavior.

To further examine the existence of newborn imitation in chimpanzees, Myowa-Yamakoshi and colleagues (2004) studied two sibling chimpanzees, Ayumu (male) and Pal (female), who were less than 1 week old at the time of this study. The researchers were interested both in facial imitation and the longitudinal development of imitation in the first 16 weeks of life. With the infant chimpanzee on its mother's lap, a researcher sat face-to-face with the infant and demonstrated four gestures: a nonreactive passive face (lips closed and a neutral facial expression), tongue protrusion, mouth opening, and lip protrusion. To assess developmental changes in facial imitation, both chimpanzees were tested once a week for 16 weeks. All sessions were videotaped for later coding.

Results indicated that newborn imitation is evident in chimpanzees younger than 1 week of age. Both Ayuma and Pal demonstrated tongue protrusion and mouth opening in the first session, suggesting that infant chimpanzees, like human infants, are born with the ability to match certain facial gestures. Because the study was conducted in the first week of life, it is unlikely that human socialization contributed to imitative behavior. Interestingly, facial imitation disappeared after 9 weeks of age, when the infant chimpanzees engaged in frequent mouth opening, regardless of the facial gesture being presented. Around 2 months of age, human infants often display the social smile when engaged in face-to-face interactions. Therefore, it is possible that frequent mouth opening in young chimpanzees corresponds to the development of the social smile in human babies. Moreover, unlike chimpanzees, human infants continue to imitate facial gestures into the second year of life.

Overall, these findings indicate that newborn chimpanzees are capable of facial imitation, although their imitation is not identical to that of human infants. Specifically, the range of imitation in infant chimpanzees is more limited, in that it does not include lip protrusion. In addition, imitation seems to fade much earlier in chimpanzees than in humans.

Myowa-Yamakoshi, M., Tomonaga, M., Tanaka, M., & Matsuzawa, T. (2004). Imitation in neonatal chimpanzees. *Developmental Science, 7*, 437–442.

LECTURE ENHANCEMENT 5.4
Motor Planning in Infant Reaching Behavior (pp. 190–192)

Time: 5–10 minutes

Objective: To examine the presence of motor planning in infant reaching behavior.

When adults reach for an object, the intended use of the object influences their reaching behavior. For example, when reaching for an object (such as a screw) to be used for a precision task (fitting it into a hole), adults usually reach slowly. In contrast, when the same object is to be used in a nonprecision task (throwing the screw into a bucket), adults tend to reach quickly. In addition, the precision reach usually has a longer deceleration than the nonprecision reach. Although there does not seem to be an obvious advantage for these differences in reaching, it appears that adults anticipate slower actions in precision tasks and, therefore, adjust their approach to reaching and grasping.

Do infants, like adults, adjust their speed and deceleration according to the intended use of objects? To find out, Claxton, Keen, and McCarty (2003) recruited 21 infants, all about 10.5 months of age, and administered two tasks to each:

(1) *Fit trials.* With infants seated in a booster seat across from the adult, a tube was placed within easy reaching distance at the midline. The adult demonstrated the correct fitting action (but did not demonstrate the reach to the ball) by holding up a ball, gaining the infant's attention, releasing the ball into the tube, and catching the ball with the other hand. The adult also presented the ball within reaching distance of the infant until the infant successfully obtained it three times. The demonstration was repeated until infants engaged in the appropriate actions (reaching for the ball and releasing it into the tube).

(2) *Throw trials.* Infants were seated in a booster seat with a plastic bucket placed on the floor in front of the seat. The adult demonstrated the correct throwing action (but did not demonstrate the reach to the ball). The adult then forcefully threw the ball into the plastic bucket. As with the fit trials, the experimenter presented the ball within reaching distance until the infant successfully obtained it three times. The demonstration was repeated until infants engaged in the appropriate actions (reaching for the ball and throwing it into the bucket).

Results indicated that infants demonstrate planning behavior when reaching for objects, although their behavior is not identical to adults'. Infants adjusted their speed of reaching, depending on what they intended to do with the ball after grabbing it. When engaged in the fit task, infants were more likely to reach slowly, presumably because a more precise movement was needed to fit the ball in the tube. Alternatively, when completing the throw task, infants displayed a faster reach, which is consistent with behavior in a nonprecision task. However, although adults often display a longer decelerative phase immediately before grasping an object for a precision task, infants did not demonstrate this behavior. According to Claxton and colleagues (2003), the absence of a decelerative phase probably reflects immature motor control and / or lack of experience with fitting and throwing.

Claxton, L. J., Keen, R., & McCarty, M. E. (2003). Evidence of motor planning in infant reaching behavior. *Psychological Science, 14*, 354–356.

LEARNING ACTIVITIES

LEARNING ACTIVITY 5.1
Creating a Pamphlet for Parents: Supporting Infant and Toddler Brain Development (pp. 168–176)

Have students review research on brain development, carefully focusing on the importance of appropriate stimulation during the first 2 years. Next, ask students to create a pamphlet for parents about supporting their youngster's early physical development. Students should not only focus on what parents should do, but they should also explain the consequences of overstimulating babies and toddlers.

LEARNING ACTIVITY 5.2
Examining the Importance of Nutrition in Infancy and Toddlerhood (pp. 178–182)

Break students into small groups and present them with the following scenario:

> Marque and Eva are the parents of 6-month-old Oliver. They recently read an article about chubby babies becoming overweight children and adults. Friends and family often comment that Oliver is "chubby," and now Marque and Eva are considering putting him on a diet. Using research from the text to support your answer, explain to Marque and Eva why putting Oliver on a diet would be a bad idea. For example, why is nutrition vital for early physical health and development? Be sure to include recommendations for encouraging healthy eating habits in infants and toddlers.

LEARNING ACTIVITY 5.3
Observing Habituation and Recovery in Young Infants (pp. 185–186)

Arrange for parents of a young baby to visit your class. You will need to obtain two toys of different colors ahead of time (large plastic rings available in the infant section of most toy stores work well). Place the baby in an infant seat or ask the parent to hold the baby. Next, present one of the toys to the baby (about 8 to 10 inches from the eyes). Consult text page 221 to determine how long you should wait before removing the toy—the time needed varies with infants' age. Then hold up both toys, side by side. Call students' attention to the baby's tendency to focus on the new, or unfamiliar, toy.

You may want to combine this activity with Learning Activity 5.6, which is also a classroom demonstration.

LEARNING ACTIVITY 5.4
Applying Developmental Theories to Newborn Imitation (pp. 186–187)

Have students form small groups and review the following theories of development: Behaviorism, Social Learning Theory, and Ethology (Chapter 1, pp. 16–18, 23–24). How might each of these theories explain the importance of newborn imitation? For instance, how can both parents and babies reinforce one another's imitation? How might newborn imitation contribute to the development of attachment? Once students have considered each theory, ask them to share their examples with the class.

LEARNING ACTIVITY 5.5
Scramble: Gross and Fine Motor Skills in the First Two Years (p. 188)

As an in-class activity or quiz, present students with the following exercise:

Directions: Below is a list of gross and fine motor milestones that develop during the first two years. Place them in the order in which they typically occur (that is, average age achieved).

Milestones:

1. Rolls from side to back
2. Plays pat-a-cake
3. Grasps a cube
4. When held upright, holds head erect and steady
5. Jumps in place
6. Pulls to a stand
7. Walks alone
8. Rolls from back to side
9. Scribbles vigorously
10. Stands alone
11. Walks on tiptoe
12. Walks up stairs with help
13. Sits alone

Answers:

1. 4
2. 1
3. 3
4. 8
5. 13
6. 6
7. 2
8. 10
9. 7
10. 9
11. 12
12. 5
13. 11

LEARNING ACTIVITY 5.6
Infant Development Demonstration: Gross and Fine Motor Development (pp. 187–192)

Arrange for parents of three or four babies to bring their children to your class for a demonstration of infant development milestones. Ideally, the infants should represent the following age ranges: less than 2 months, 4 to 8 months, and 8 to 14 months. Students may know parents who are willing to participate, or you may have friends or colleagues willing to attend the class for a demonstration. Before the demonstration, ask parents to bring a small selection of toys, or arrange to provide some yourself. This keeps the infants you are not focusing on at the moment occupied, and it also enables students to observe the babies' spontaneous play.

Demonstrate the following capacities discussed in the chapter:

1. 0–2 MONTHS
Gross motor development: Place the baby prone, and see if he or she lifts the head and looks around. From a supine position, pull the infant slowly to a sitting position and observe the ability to support the head. Infants of about 6 to 8 weeks of age, when held vertically, will hold the head erect.
Other milestones: Demonstrate the baby's ability to track an object with the eyes, respond to the sound of the mother's voice, and smile spontaneously (appears during the second month). You may also demonstrate prereaching (in infants under 7 weeks) by presenting a toy and observing how the infant makes poorly coordinated swipes or swings toward the toy. Alternate the toy between the infant's hands and feet to demonstrate foot reaching.

2. 4–8 MONTHS
Gross motor development: The following gross motor accomplishments generally appear between 4 and 8 months of age and can be demonstrated: sitting, first with support and then alone; standing with support; and (at the end of this period) getting into a sitting position and pulling self to a standing position. To demonstrate, place the infant on his or her stomach and observe the infant's attempts to get up on all fours. Some of the older infants may even crawl a short distance.
Fine motor development: Demonstrate the infant's ability to grasp objects using a rattle or other toy. Babies of about 4.5 months should be able to grasp an object presented at the midline and on the same as, or on the opposite side of the body from, the reaching hand (the younger 3-month-old will only grasp an object offered on the same side of the body). Point out the use of the ulnar grasp, a clumsy motion in which the fingers close against the palm. Infants of about 6 months of age can also be seen passing objects from hand to hand, and they will rake a raisin to obtain it.

3. 8–14 MONTHS
Gross motor development: Crawling, standing alone, and walking are gross motor accomplishments that generally appear during this time frame.
Fine motor development: Place a raisin before the infant to show students the well-coordinated pincer grasp. Babies of this age can put objects in and dump them out of containers. Sometimes they will build a tower of two cubes with blocks.

LEARNING ACTIVITY 5.7
Interviewing Parents about Training Infant Motor Skills (pp. 187–190)

Have students pose the following question to several parents they know: Should sitting, crawling, and walking be deliberately encouraged in infants and toddlers? Why or why not? Next, ask students to bring their answers to class for discussion. Based on their responses, did parents believe that motor development should be encouraged, or did they believe that motor skills will develop on their own? Were there any cultural differences in the answers? Are students surprised by any of the answers? Explain.

LEARNING ACTIVITY 5.8
Evaluating a Website Featuring Developmental Toys for Infants and Toddlers (pp. 193–203)

Have students visit a website sponsored by Fisher Price, *http://www.fisherprice.com/us/*, which presents suggested toys and activities for babies according to their age and developmental level. Once they access the website, students should select two age ranges and answer the following questions: What developmental information is presented for each age range? Is this consistent with research presented in the text? How do the recommended toys appeal to infants' and toddlers' developing learning capacities? How about perceptual development? Using what you know about stimulation, are the toys appropriate for the age range? Why or why not?

LEARNING ACTIVITY 5.9
Examining Environmental Influences on Early Physical Growth

Throughout the chapter, there are numerous examples of how the environment contributes to early physical growth. Break students into small groups and have them consider the many developmental milestones of infancy. Next, have them generate a list of examples highlighting how the environment stimulates or undermines early development. For example, parents can support intermodal sensitivity through certain kinds of communication—showing the infant objects, speaking, and moving objects at the same time.

ASK YOURSELF . . .

REVIEW: How does stimulation affect early brain development? Cite evidence at the level of neurons and at the level of the cerebral cortex. (pp. 168–169)

As neurons form connections, stimulation becomes vital to their survival. Neurons that are stimulated by input from the surrounding environment continue to establish new synapses, forming increasingly elaborate systems of communication that lead to more complex abilities.

The cerebral cortex is the largest, most complex brain structure, containing the greatest number of neurons and synapses. Because it is the last brain structure to stop growing, the cerebral cortex is sensitive to environmental influences for longer than any other part of the brain. At birth, the cortex is highly plastic, or not yet committed to specific functions. Research shows that early experience greatly influences brain organization, including specialization of certain regions of the cerebral cortex.

REVIEW: How do overproduction of synapses and synaptic pruning support infants' and children's ability to learn? (pp. 169–170)

At first, stimulation results in a massive overabundance of synapses, many of which serve identical functions, thereby ensuring that the child will acquire the motor, cognitive, and social skills that our species needs to survive. Neurons that are seldom stimulated soon lose their synapses, in a process called synaptic pruning, which returns neurons that are not needed at the moment to an uncommitted state so they can support future development. After this overproduction of neurons and synapses, cell death and synaptic pruning sculpt away excess building material to form the mature brain—a process that is jointly influenced by heredity and environment.

APPLY: Which infant enrichment program would you choose: one that emphasizes gentle talking and touching and social games, or one that includes reading and number drills and classical music lessons? Explain. (pp. 176–177)

Although stimulation of the brain is vital, environments that overwhelm children with expectations beyond their current capacities actually interfere with development of the brain's potential. Trying to prime infants with stimulation for which they are not ready can cause them to withdraw, thereby threatening their interest in learning and creating conditions much like stimulation deprivation. Therefore, the first program is better because it provides age-appropriate stimulation that will facilitate, rather than compromise, brain growth.

REFLECT: What is your attitude toward parent–infant cosleeping? Is it influenced by your cultural background? Explain. (p. 177)

This is an open-ended question with no right or wrong answer.

REVIEW: Explain why breastfeeding can have lifelong consequences for the development of babies born in poverty-stricken regions of the world. (pp. 178–180)

In early infancy, breastfeeding is ideally suited to babies' needs. Breast milk provides the correct balance of fat and protein, includes iron that is easily absorbed by the baby's system, and helps ensure healthy physical growth. Because of these benefits, breastfed babies in poverty-stricken regions of the world are much less likely to be malnourished and 6 to 14 times more likely to survive the first year of life. Even breastfeeding for just a few weeks offers some protection against respiratory and intestinal infections, which are devastating to young children in developing countries. Furthermore, because a nursing mother is less likely to get pregnant, breastfeeding helps increase spacing among siblings, a major factor in reducing infant and childhood deaths in nations with widespread poverty.

Too often, mothers in the developing world do not know about these benefits. As a result, they may give their babies commercial formula or low-grade nutrients, such as rice water or highly-diluted cow or goat milk, in place of breast milk. Contamination of these foods as a result of poor sanitation is common, often leading to illness and infant death.

APPLY: Ten-month-old Shaun is below-average in height and painfully thin. He has one of two serious growth disorders. Name them, and indicate what clues you would look for to tell which one Shaun has. (pp. 180–182)

One possibility is marasmus, a wasted condition of the body caused by a diet low in all essential nutrients. It usually appears in the first year of life when a baby's mother is too malnourished to produce enough breast milk and bottle-feeding is also inadequate. As a result, the baby's body appears painfully thin.

A second possibility is nonorganic failure to thrive, a growth disorder resulting from lack of parental love that is usually present by 18 months of age. Infants who have it show all the signs of marasmus: Their bodies look wasted, and they are withdrawn and apathetic. But no organic (or biological) cause for the baby's failure to grow can be found. The baby is offered enough food and does not have a serious illness.

Family circumstances help distinguish the two disorders. Mothers of babies with nonorganic failure to thrive sometimes act cold and distant, other times impatient and hostile. Often an unhappy marriage and parental psychological disturbance contribute to serious caregiving problems. In response, babies are often irritable and display abnormal feeding behaviors, such as poor sucking or vomiting, which further stress the parent–child relationship.

CONNECT: How are bidirectional influences between parent and child involved in the impact of malnutrition on psychological development? After her adoption, how did those influences change for Grace? (pp. 180–182)

Both parent and child affect the child's psychological development. In marasmus, for example, the body becomes wasted because of a diet low in all essential nutrients. This disease usually appears in the first year of life, when the baby's mother is too malnourished to produce enough breast milk and bottle-feeding is also inadequate. The passivity and irritability of malnourished children worsen the impact of poor diet. Withdrawal and listlessness reduce the nutritionally deprived child's ability to pay attention, explore, and evoke sensitive caregiving from parents, whose lives are already disrupted by poverty and stressful living conditions. For this reason, interventions for malnourished children must improve the family situation as well as the child's nutrition.

Although Grace's early environment was very depleted, her biological mother was loving. As a result, Grace probably did not have the passive, irritable characteristics of most malnourished children. Her adoptive family was able to provide Grace not only with adequate nourishment but also with a stimulating environment. As a result, Grace was able to make rapid gains in intellectual development.

REFLECT: Imagine that you are the parent of a newborn baby. Describe some feeding practices you would use, and some you would avoid, to prevent overweight and obesity. (p. 180)

This is an open-ended question with no right or wrong answer.

REVIEW: Provide an example of classical conditioning, of operant conditioning, and of habituation/recovery in young infants. Why is each type of learning useful? (pp. 183–186)

Newborn reflexes make *classical conditioning* possible in the young infant. For example, as Carolyn settled down in the rocking chair to nurse Caitlin, she often stroked Caitlin's forehead. Soon Carolyn noticed that each time she did this, Caitlin made active sucking movements, indicating that she had been classically conditioned. Classical conditioning is useful to infants because it helps them recognize which events usually occur together in the everyday world, so they can anticipate what is about to happen next. As a result, the environment becomes more orderly and predictable.

In *operant conditioning,* infants act (or *operate*) on the environment, and stimuli that follow their behavior change the probability that the behavior will occur again. For example, researchers have created special laboratory conditions in which the baby's rate of sucking on a nipple produces a variety of interesting sights and sounds. Newborns will suck faster to see the visual designs or hear music and human voices. Operant conditioning allows infants to explore and control their surroundings in an effort to meet their needs for nutrition, stimulation, and social contact.

Habituation refers to a gradual reduction in the strength of a response due to repetitive stimulation. Once this has occurred, a new stimulus—a change in the environment—causes responsiveness to return to a high level, an increase called *recovery.* By studying infants' habituation and recovery, researchers can explore their understanding of the world. For example, a baby who first habituates to a visual pattern (a photo of a baby) and then recovers to a new one (a photo of a bald man) appears to remember the first stimulus and perceive the second one as new and different. Habituation and recovery enable infants to focus their attention on aspects of the environment they know least about, so that learning is more efficient.

APPLY: Nine-month-old Byron has a toy with large, colored push buttons on it. Each time he pushes a button, he hears a nursery tune. Which learning capacity is the manufacturer of this toy taking advantage of? What can Byron's play with the toy reveal about his perception of sound patterns? (p. 184)

The toy's manufacturer is taking advantage of operant conditioning—Byron's capacity to act, or *operate,* on the environment and to repeat a behavior in response to a stimulus called a *reinforcer.* Each time Byron pushes the buttons, he brings about the stimulus of the nursery tune, thereby reinforcing his action and increasing the chances that he will repeat it. Byron's play also reveals that he is able to organize sounds into complex patterns—that he can associate the push buttons of different colors with different sound patterns, that he prefers the sound of music to awkward breaks, and that he may recognize the same nursery tune when it is played in different keys.

CONNECT: Infants with nonorganic failure to thrive rarely smile at friendly adults but, instead, anxiously keep track of nearby people. Using the learning capacities discussed in the previous sections, explain these reactions. (pp. 183–187)

CLASSICAL CONDITIONING: In terms of classical conditioning, infants suffering from failure to thrive have caregivers who are cold and distant rather than warm and reassuring, and who are likely to handle their infants roughly, evoking a fearful response from the child. When food stimuli are paired with the parent's coldness and rough, insensitive handling, babies learn to avoid eating and, consequently, grow poorly.

OPERANT CONDITIONING: In operant conditioning, the infant's actions evoke a response from the caregiver. This response, either reinforcing or punishing, alters further infant–caregiver interactions. In failure to thrive, when infants cry and seek the closeness of others, caregivers respond in an impatient, hostile, or cold fashion. This acts as punishment, making the baby less likely to continue to try to interact with the caregiver.

IMITATION: Newborn babies come into the world with a primitive ability to learn through imitation—by copying the behavior of another person. Using imitation, young infants explore their social world, getting to know people by matching their behavioral states. In failure to thrive, infants imitate the behavioral states of caregivers, which may be cold and distant or, at other times, impatient and hostile. When adults approach them in a friendly way, instead of smiling, these infants are hesitant and anxious—behaviors they have learned from infant–caregiver interactions.

REVIEW: Cite evidence that motor development is not genetically determined but rather is a joint product of biological, psychological, and environmental factors. (pp. 189–190)

According to dynamic systems theory of motor development, mastery of motor skills involves acquiring increasingly complex systems of action. Each new skill is a joint product of four factors: central nervous system development, the body's movement capacities, the goal the child has in mind, and environmental supports for the skill. A change in any one element makes the system less stable, prompting the child to explore and select new, more effective motor patterns. Because motor development is motivated by exploration and the desire to master new tasks, it cannot be genetically determined. Rather, heredity can map out motor development only at a general level. Rather than being *hardwired* into the nervous system, behaviors are *softly assembled,* allowing for different paths to arrive at the same motor skill.

The factors that induce change vary with age. In the early weeks of life, brain and body growth are especially important as infants achieve control over the head, shoulders, and upper torso. Later, the baby's goals (getting a toy or crossing the room) and environmental supports (parental encouragement, objects in the infant's everyday setting) play a greater role. Cultural variations also affect motor development. For example, among the Kipsigis of Kenya and the West Indians of Jamaica, parents deliberately teach motor skill such as holding the head up, sitting alone, and walking—and babies master these skills earlier than in other cultures. In contrast, the current Western practice of having babies sleep on their backs to protect them from sudden infant death syndrome delays gross motor milestones that are promoted by "tummy time." If motor development were hardwired into the brain, these striking cross-cultural differences would not exist.

APPLY: Rosanne hung mobiles and pictures above her newborn baby's crib, hoping that this would stimulate her infant's motor development. Is Rosanne doing the right thing? Why or why not? (p. 192)

In a well-known study, institutionalized infants given a moderate amount of visual stimulation—at first, simple designs and, later, a mobile hung over the crib—reached for objects six weeks earlier than infants given nothing to look at. A third group given massive stimulation—patterned crib bumpers and mobiles at an early age—also reached sooner than unstimulated babies. But this heavy enrichment took a toll: These infants looked away and cried a great deal, and they were less advanced in reaching than the moderately stimulated group. These findings remind us that more stimulation is not necessarily better. Trying to push infants beyond their current readiness to handle stimulation can actually undermine the development of important motor skills. Therefore, Rosanne should provide her baby with only a moderate amount of stimulation.

CONNECT: Provide several examples of how motor development influences infants' and toddlers' social experiences. How do social experiences, in turn, influence motor development? (p. 187)

Babies' motor achievements have a powerful effect on their social relationships. When babies begin to crawl or walk, for instance, parents begin to restrict their movements by saying "no," expressing mild impatience, or picking them up and moving them—strategies that were unnecessary before. At the same time, parents increase their expressions of affection and playful activities as their independently moving baby or toddler seeks them out for greetings, hugs, and games. In addition, babies' expressions of delight as they work on new motor competencies trigger pleasurable reactions in others, which encourages their efforts further. Motor skills, social competencies, cognition, and language not only develop together, but also support one another.

REFLECT: Do you favor early, systematic training of infants in motor skills such as crawling, walking, running, hopping, and stair climbing? Why or why not? (p. 192)

This is an open-ended question with no right or wrong answer.

REVIEW: Using examples, explain why intermodal stimulation is vital for infants' developing understanding of their physical and social worlds. (p. 202)

We receive constant intermodal stimulation—simultaneous input from more than one sensory system, or modality. Intermodal perception is the way we make sense of these streams of sensory information so that we perceive objects and events as integrated wholes. Newborns turn in the general direction of a sound and reach for objects in a primitive way, suggesting that they expect sight, sound, and touch to go together. By 3 to 4 months of age, infants can match faces with voices on the basis of lip–voice synchrony, emotional expression, and even the speaker's age and gender.

By enabling babies to notice meaningful correlations between sensory inputs and to use these to make sense of their surroundings, intermodal perception facilitates social and language processing. Early parent–infant interaction gives the baby a rich context, consisting of many concurrent instances of intermodal stimulation, for expanding intermodal knowledge. And babies presented with intermodal stimulation process more information, learn faster, and show better memory—another example of infants' active efforts to build an orderly, predictable world.

APPLY: After several weeks of crawling, Ben learned to avoid going headfirst down a steep incline. Now he has started to walk. Can his mother trust him not to try walking down a steep surface? Explain, using the concept of affordances. (pp. 202–203)

According to differentiation theory, developed by Eleanor and James Gibson, perception is guided by the discovery of *affordances*—the action possibilities a situation offers an organism with certain motor capabilities. When babies crawl, and again when they walk, they gradually realize that a steeply sloping surface *affords* the possibility of falling. With added weeks of practicing each skill, they hesitate to crawl or walk down a risky incline. Experience in trying to keep their balance on various surfaces seems to make crawlers and walkers more aware of the consequences of their movements. Crawlers come to detect when surface slant places so much body weight on their arms that they will fall forward, walkers when an incline shifts body weight so their legs and feet can no longer hold them upright. Because Ben is just starting to walk, he probably does not yet realize that a steep incline affords the possibility of falling. Therefore, his mother should hold his hand or support him as he walks down the incline.

CONNECT: According to differentiation theory, perceptual development reflects infants' active search for invariant features. Provide examples from research on hearing, pattern perception, and intermodal perception. (pp. 193–203)

During the first year, babies start to organize sounds into complex patterns. Infants as young as 3 days old turn their eyes and head in the general direction of a sound, an ability that improves greatly over the first 6 months. As they listen to the talk of people around them, infants learn to focus on meaningful sound variations in their own language. Around 5 months, they become sensitive to their own language's syllable stress patterns, and between 6 and 8 months, they start to "screen out" sounds not used in their own language. Soon after, infants focus on larger speech units that are critical to figuring out meaning. They recognize familiar words in spoken passages and listen longer to speech with clear clause and phrase boundaries. Around 7 to 9 months, they extend this sensitivity to speech structure to individual words and begin to divide the speech stream into wordlike units.

Even newborns prefer to look at patterned over plain stimuli. At first, they respond to the separate parts of a pattern. But at 2 to 3 months, when scanning ability and contrast sensitivity have improved, infants thoroughly explore a pattern's internal features, pausing briefly to look at each part. Once babies can take in all aspects of a pattern, they integrate the parts into a unified whole. Around 4 months, babies are so good at detecting pattern organization that they even perceive subjective boundaries that are not really present. At 12 months, infants detect objects represented by incomplete drawings, even when as much as two-thirds of the drawing is missing. Finally, infants' tendency to search for a structure in a patterned stimulus applies to face perception. Newborns prefer to look at simple, facelike stimuli with features arranged naturally (upright) rather than unnaturally (upside down or sideways). They also track a facelike pattern moving across their visual field farther than they track other stimuli.

From the start, babies perceive the world in an intermodal fashion—that is, making use of more than one sensory system. For example, newborns turn in the general direction of a sound and reach for objects in a primitive way, suggesting that they expect sight, sound, and touch to go together. Within a few months, infants make impressive intermodal matches. For example, 3- and 4-month-olds can match faces with voices on the basis of lip–voice synchrony, emotional expression, and the speaker's age and gender. In 4- to 6-month-olds, their extensive face–voice intermodal knowledge allows them to pick up more detailed associations, quickly learning and remembering unique face–voice pairings. Research suggests that babies perceive input from different sensory systems in a unified way by detecting amodal sensory properties—information that overlaps two or more sensory systems, such as the sight and sound of a bouncing ball. By making amodal properties (like rhythm) stand out, intermodal stimulation allows inexperienced perceivers to notice the crucial elements of a meaningful unitary event.

REFLECT: Are young infants more competent than you thought they were before you read this chapter? List capacities that most surprised you.

This is an open-ended question with no right or wrong answer.

SUGGESTED STUDENT READINGS

Brazelton, T. B., & Sparrow, J. D. (2006). *Touchpoints: 0 to 3*. Cambridge, MA: Da Capo Press. Written by leading experts in the field of child development, this book examines a variety of topics on infant and toddler development, including brain development, early learning capacities, toilet training, and child health and safety.

Coch, D., Dawson, G., & Fischer, K. W. (Eds.). (2007). *Human behavior, learning, and the developing brain: Typical development*. New York: Guilford Press. An interdisciplinary examination of brain and behavior relations, this book highlights the relationship between brain development, cognition, and social/emotional development. The chapters also reveal insights into the expanding field of cognitive neuroscience.

Zigler, E. F., Finn-Stevenson, M., & Hall, N. W. (2004). *The first three years and beyond: Brain development and social policy*. New Haven, CT: Yale University Press. Taking an interdisciplinary approach to understanding brain development, this book presents up-to-date research on the importance of early experiences for favorable development. Other topics include appropriate stimulation, the importance of breastfeeding and nutrition, and public policies for children and families.

TRANSPARENCIES

T-44   **Diagram of a Long Bone Showing Upper and Lower Epiphyses** Figure 5.2 (p. 167)

T-45   **The Skull at Birth, Showing Fontanels and Sutures** Figure 5.3 (p. 168)

T-46   **Milestones of Brain Development** Figure 5.5 (p. 169)

T-47   **The Left Side of the Brain, Showing the Cerebral Cortex** Figure 5.7 (p. 172)

T-48   **Gross and Fine Motor Skilss Achieved During the First 2 Years (Part One)** Table 5.2 (p. 188)

T-49   **Gross and Fine Motor Skilss Achieved During the First 2 Years (Part Two)** Table 5.2 (p. 188)

T-50   **Gross and Fine Motor Skilss Achieved During the First 2 Years (Part Three)** Table 5.2 (p. 188)

T-51   **Gross and Fine Motor Skilss Achieved During the First 2 Years (Part Four)** Table 5.2 (p. 188)

T-53   **Milestones of Voluntary Reaching** Figure 5.13 (p. 191)

T-54   **The Steps of Classical Conditioning** Figure 5.9 (p. 183)

T-55   **Example of How the Habituation Recovery Sequence Can Be Used to Sudy Infant Perception and Cognition** Figure 5.10 (p. 185)

T-56   **Photographs from Two fo the First Studies of Newborn Imitation** Figure 5.11 (p. 186)

T-57   **The Visual Cliff** Figure 5.15 (p. 196)

T-58   **The Way Two Checkerboards Differing in Complexity Look to Infants in the First Few Weeks of Life** Figure 5.16 (p. 199)

T-60   **Subjective Boundaries In a Visual Pattern** Figure 5.17 (p. 199)

T-61   **Early Face Perception** Figure 5.18 (p. 200)

T-63   **Display Used to Test Infants' Ability to Perceive Object Unity** Figure 5.19 (p. 201)

T-64   **Acting on the Environment Plays a Major Role in Peceptual Differentiation** Figure5.20 (p. 203)

MEDIA MATERIALS

INFANTS, CHILDREN, AND ADOLESCENTS IN ACTION

Infancy and Toddlerhood

This portion of the Observation Program includes segments on physical development, beginning with changes in body size, proportions, and muscle–fat makeup during infancy and toddlerhood. Next, the attainment of motor skills is addressed, along with factors that influence these milestones and their implications for other aspects of development. Early learning—classical and operant conditioning, habituation and recovery, and newborn imitation—is also illustrated, followed by depth perception and its intimate relationship to motor development.

A WINDOW ON INFANTS, CHILDREN, AND ADOLESCENTS

Segment 2: Learning Capacities: Mac, 3 months

This segment opens with Mac and his father playing. The interaction between Mac and his father illustrates how fathers tend to play differently with their babies than mothers do. When presented with a rattle, Mac shows signs of voluntary reaching. Watch as Mac's mother holds up a green and then a yellow ring. Mac habituates to the green ring and then recovers to the yellow ring.

Segment 4: Physical and Cognitive Development: Randy, 8 months, and Ben, 21 months

This segment opens as Randy and Ben are playing with their mother. The differences in fine and gross motor skills are evident as the boys play. Randy illustrates the beginning of crawling by scooting across the floor on his tummy to retrieve a toy and establish contact with his mother. Ben's skills are more advanced, as evidenced when he walks and runs, uses a toy hammer, winds a jack-in-the-box, and plays catch with Professor Berk. Watch as the boys' mother supports their language development by using child-directed speech, commenting on their behavior, labeling toys, and playing with them. Similarly, her style of interaction helps regulate their emotions. The play behaviors of Randy and Ben demonstrate the difference between functional and make-believe play. Whereas Randy simply explores the toys and moves them about, Ben is able to act out real-life situations, such as pretending to feed a doll and to feed Randy.

Segment 5: High-Quality Infant and Toddler Child Care

This segment, profiling Goodwood Child Care Center and McKinnon Parade Child Care Center in Adelaide, Australia, illustrates a number of ingredients of high-quality child care. For example, at Goodwood Child Care Center, the staff support children's developing motor skills by teaching them how to do somersaults and encouraging them as they learn this new activity. In the second clip, infants play with staff members in the sandbox. Notice the positive interactions between the children and staff. As the babies play, staff members describe what is going on and demonstrate how to use the toys in the sandbox. In the final clip, children and staff at McKinnon Parade Child Care Center enjoy a meal. Children are not seated separately from staff, and there is a lot of interaction, such as a staff member feeding a toddler and talking to the others as they eat.

DVDs AND VIDEOTAPES

The Baby Human (2003, Films Media Group; three parts, 52 minutes each). This three-part series focuses on the psychological and motor skill development of infants from birth to age 18 months.

The Child from 1 to 3 (2000, Films Media Group, 20 min.). This program, part of the Beginning the Journey ... series, offers a guided tour through a developing child's early years, illustrating the dramatic transition from infancy to toddlerhood. Parents and caregivers alike can benefit from awareness of the physical, emotional, and social skills the child is developing in these important years, and of their own role in the growth process. Advice from child-care experts provides additional insight into this formative period of human development.

Classical and Operant Conditioning (1996, Films Media Group, 56 min.). This program explains the nature of the behaviorist perspective on human development and its important applications in child rearing, education, and clinical therapy. The program explores the classical and operant conditioning theories of Pavlov and Skinner, with both archival and present-day footage of research as well as numerous examples of conditioning in everyday life.

Developmental Phases Before and After Birth (1993, Films for the Humanities & Sciences, 30 min.). This program, part of the series The Psychological Development of the Child, illustrates how the major milestones of prenatal physical and psychological development in the first year are the same for all children, regardless of culture or family living standard. Differences resulting from the mother–child relationship are highlighted.

Encouraging Motor Development (1995, Films Media Group, 17 min.). The first section of this program provides an overview of the sequence of gross and fine motor skills that typically develop in the first few years of life. The second section looks at ways of encouraging motor development in children with special health needs. Aimed at home health personnel, physical therapists, and other caregivers, the program recommends some basic principles for encouraging motor development in these children, and illustrates techniques for incorporating each principle into caregiving routines.

Exploring and Learning (2002, Magna Systems, 25 min.). This program shows how the trusted caregiver is initially the child's primary mode of learning. Next, the child learns to handle objects in a variety of ways and to arrange objects, such as baskets and blocks, in space. Infants and toddlers are shown exploring problem solving. Cognitive curriculum is revealed through the actions of children and caregivers involved with materials and the environment.

First Adaptations (1992, RMI Media Productions, 30 min.). In this program, experts discuss how the infant brain grows and describe cognitive capacities that begin to function as the nervous system develops. Live footage provides compelling evidence that newborns are already capable of learning critical facts about their environment.

The First 365 Days in the Life of a Child (1993, Films for the Humanities & Sciences; 13 parts, 28 min. each). The segments of this series detail the normal development of five infants during the first year of life. Monthly development is measured using a system of developmental tests created by several pediatricians and the Research Department for Social Pediatrics and Children's Medicine at the University of Munich.

How Children Learn (1997, Davidson Films, 23 min.). This program uses jargon-free narration and animation to illustrate what we know about learning on the basis of brain research, cognitive development research, and educational practice. Animation is used to show the firing of synapses, the growth of dendrites, and the concept of brain plasticity. Designed as an introduction to a discussion of school and teaching practices, this program can also serve as an introduction to children's learning.

Infancy: Landmarks of Development (2003, Magna Systems, 29 min.; available in English and Spanish). This program portrays the norms of physical development, from the infant's ability to lift the head to the toddler's first step. The program includes a discussion of the influence of environment and culture on these milestones. It also provides an overview of early brain development, with a focus on optimal stimulation in the first two years.

Kids and Sleep (2000, Films Media Group, 22 min.). This program explores new discoveries in sleep dynamics, reflecting cutting-edge brain imagery that scientists are using to expand their understanding of how children sleep. The program addresses the safest way to put a baby to bed, as well as the treatment of sleep disorders.

Landmarks of Development (2003, Magna Systems, 29 min.). This program illustrates the orderly progression of brain development, physical growth, locomotion, and fine motor skills throughout infancy. The program shows landmarks of development, identifies their timing, and clarifies the influences of environment and culture, with a focus on what is optimal in relationships and stimulation in the first two years.

Mothers, Fathers, and Babies (1981, Films Media Group, 26 min.). This program, a segment of the eight-part series The Psychological Development of the Child, examines how breastfeeding practices vary in different cultures and the effect on the role of the father in early caregiving.

Nutrition for Infants and Children (2006, Films Media Group, 26 min.). Designed for parents, expectant parents, and caregivers, this program explains the importance of good nutrition for healthy growth and development of newborns, infants, and toddlers. It explores the relative merits of breastfeeding and bottle feeding, potential food allergies, the importance of a balanced diet and exercise even for very young children, and the implications of special dietary preferences such as vegetarianism.

Pediatric Brain Development: The Importance of a Head Start (1995, Films Media Group, 17 min.). In this short program, *ABC News* anchor Diane Sawyer reports on the neurological connections that form in a child's brain during pregnancy and early childhood, and the long-term effects of sensory stimulation or deprivation during these formative periods, using as an example a case study of a woman with a hearing loss that was not diagnosed until she was 31 years old. Sawyer talks with child development expert Penelope Leach and with Dr. Michael Phelps of UCLA, coinventor of the PET scan, who shed light on topics ranging from language acquisition to possible links between premature birth and later development of attention-deficit disorder.

Physical Development: The First Five Years (1997, Films Media Group, 19 min.). This program looks at children's physical development between birth and age 5—a time in which the child moves from physical helplessness to mastery of a range of large and small motor skills. A pediatrician and a child development specialist talk about what is happening during those early formative years.

The Second Year in the Life of a Child (1993, Films for the Humanities & Sciences; four parts, 20–24 min. each). This four-part series follows typically developing toddlers through the second year of life, observing and documenting milestones of development.

Secret Life of the Brain, Part 1: The Baby's Brain: Wider Than the Sky (2002, PBS Home Video, 60 min.). This program looks at the development of the human brain, starting at conception, as human brain cells begin to develop at the rate of 500,000 per minute. This program, the first episode in the five-part Secret Life of the Brain series, looks at the roles played by genetics and environment in brain development. It traces formation of the infant brain through age 1—the period when the brain is most open to molding through external influence and experience.

Shaping Youngest Minds (1999, Insight Media, 24 min.). This program reviews the physical development of the brain from its earliest stages. It contends that the shaping of behavior begins in the womb and stresses the importance of stimulating learning and growth from infancy. It outlines an approach to child development using specific examples that capitalize on current brain research.

Simple Beginnings? Child Development from Birth to Age Five (1994, Films for the Humanities & Sciences, 25 min.). This program explores infants' early abilities to recognize rules, faces, and biological motion. It also discusses the role of parents in structuring infants' learning experiences in the early development of language.

Toddlerhood: Physical and Cognitive Development (2003, Magna Systems, 29 min.). This program examines how the ability to walk changes a child's interaction with the world and, as a result, the child's developing cognitive abilities. The program illustrates the development of exploration and experimentation, along with mental representations and language. It emphasizes the importance of a stimulating environment and support from adults for the child's development of physical skills, intellectual growth, and language.

To Walk (2003, Films Media Group, 52 min.). This program, a Discovery Channel production, looks at experiments conducted by Esther Thelen of Indiana University and Karen Adolph of New York University to assess motor development in infants as they take their first few steps. The program provides evidence that new crawlers are unable to assess danger, that fear of heights is linked to the expansion of peripheral vision, and that babies must learn and relearn lessons to adapt to their environment.

Wonder Years: First Steps in Autonomy (1995, Films for the Humanities & Sciences, 25 min.). This classic program identifies the three factors that shape a child's development and act as stepping stones to adult independence: extreme biological changes, psychological advances, and physical surroundings. Prenatal and postnatal differences are considered, along with the dangers of premature birth; a video experiment shows infants' remarkable sensitivity to communication and their environment. The impact of postnatal depression on mother and child is discussed.

TEST BANK

MULTIPLE CHOICE

1) By the end of the second year, a typical toddler's height is _____ percent greater than at birth.
   A) 25
   B) 50
   C) 75
   D) 100
   Answer: C
   Page Ref: 166
   Skill: Factual
   Objective: 5.1

2) By the end of the second year, a typical child's weight has _____ since birth.
   A) doubled
   B) tripled
   C) quadrupled
   D) quintupled
   Answer: C
   Page Ref: 166
   Skill: Factual
   Objective: 5.1

3) During the first two years of life, infants can gain as much as _____ in height in a 24-hour period.
   A) 1/16 inch
   B) 1/8 inch
   C) 1/4 inch
   D) 1/2 inch
   Answer: D
   Page Ref: 166–167
   Skill: Factual
   Objective: 5.1

4) The increase in body fat during the first 9 months of infancy
   A) insulates the infants' brittle bones until proper cartilage is formed.
   B) hinders the normal progression of fine motor skills.
   C) serves to cushion the infant from bumps and falls.
   D) helps the infant maintain a constant body temperature.
   Answer: D
   Page Ref: 167
   Skill: Conceptual
   Objective: 5.1

5) During infancy, _____. These sex differences will _____ during adolescence.
   A) boys are slightly shorter and lighter; disappear
   B) boys are slightly shorter and lighter; be greatly magnified
   C) girls have a higher ratio of fat to muscle than do boys; disappear
   D) girls have a higher ratio of fat to muscle than do boys; be greatly magnified
   Answer: D
   Page Ref: 167
   Skill: Conceptual
   Objective: 5.1

6) Of the following, which demonstrates the cephalocaudal trend?
   A) During infancy and childhood, the legs and arms grow faster than the trunk.
   B) During the prenatal period, the head develops more rapidly than the lower part of the body.
   C) During the prenatal period, the head, chest, and trunk grow first, then the arms and legs, and then the hands and feet.
   D) During infancy and childhood, the hands and feet grow ahead of the fingers and toes.
   Answer: B
   Page Ref: 167
   Skill: Factual
   Objective: 5.1

7) Of the following, which is consistent with the proximodistal trend of body growth?
   A) During the prenatal period, the head develops more rapidly than the lower part of the body.
   B) During childhood, the arms and legs grow somewhat ahead of the hands and feet.
   C) During the prenatal period, the trunk grows first, followed by the chest and the head.
   D) During childhood, the hands and feet develop more rapidly than the trunk.
   Answer: B
   Page Ref: 167
   Skill: Applied
   Objective: 5.1

8) An X-ray of the long bones of the body can determine _____ and produces the best estimate of physical maturity.
   A) osteoporosis risk
   B) fragility
   C) risk of fractures
   D) skeletal age
   Answer: D
   Page Ref: 167
   Skill: Factual
   Objective: 5.2

9) Skeletal age is measured by determining
   A) the size of the skull.
   B) the length of the long bones of the body.
   C) the extent to which epiphyses are fused.
   D) muscle and bone strength.
   Answer: C
   Page Ref: 167–168
   Skill: Factual
   Objective: 5.2

10) When skeletal ages are examined,
    A) Caucasian-American children tend to be ahead of African-American children.
    B) more physically mature children are at greater risk of bone disease.
    C) the difference between boys and girls decreases over infancy and childhood.
    D) girls are considerably ahead of boys.
    Answer: D
    Page Ref: 168
    Skill: Factual
    Objective: 5.2

11) Of the following, which is true regarding fontanels?
   A) Fontanels that persist into the second year put the child at risk for brain damage.
   B) The largest fontanel measures about 1/8 of an inch across.
   C) The bones of the newborn's skull are separated by gaps that permit the bones to overlap as the baby passes through the birth canal.
   D) All of the fontanels are filled in during the first few months of life.
   Answer: C
   Page Ref: 168
   Skill: Conceptual
   Objective: 5.2

12) Sutures, or seams in the skull,
   A) are special growth centers at the two extreme ends of each bone.
   B) allow the skull bones to overlap as the large head of the baby passes through the narrow birth canal during delivery.
   C) gradually shrink and are filled in during the second year.
   D) permit the skull to expand easily as the brain grows.
   Answer: D
   Page Ref: 168
   Skill: Factual
   Objective: 5.2

13) Research on teething demonstrates that
   A) nearly all teething babies show increased irritability and sleeplessness.
   B) on average, an African-American baby's first tooth appears at about 4 months, and a Caucasian baby's around 6 months.
   C) most infants do not get their first teeth until around 1 year of age.
   D) babies who get their first teeth early are likely to be delayed in physical maturity.
   Answer: B
   Page Ref: 168
   Skill: Conceptual
   Objective: 5.2

14) At birth, the _____ is/are nearer than any other physical structure to its adult size.
   A) heart
   B) lungs
   C) brain
   D) feet
   Answer: C
   Page Ref: 168
   Skill: Factual
   Objective: 5.3

15) Production and migration of neurons are largely complete by
   A) the end of the second trimester of pregnancy.
   B) birth.
   C) an infant's first birthday.
   D) age 5.
   Answer: A
   Page Ref: 169
   Skill: Factual
   Objective: 5.3

16) Of the following, which is supported by research on brain development?
    A) New neurons are produced throughout the lifespan.
    B) Neurons that are seldom stimulated die.
    C) The production and migration of neurons are not complete until early adolescence.
    D) Neurons that are stimulated by input continue to establish new synapses.
    Answer: D
    Page Ref: 169
    Skill: Conceptual
    Objective: 5.3

17) An early overabundance of synapses
    A) is the result of an overproduction of neurons during infancy.
    B) ensures that infants will acquire basic motor, cognitive, and social skills.
    C) occurs when infants receive overstimulating, intrusive care.
    D) takes place when fibers linking the cerebellum to the cerebral cortex begin to myelinate.
    Answer: B
    Page Ref: 169
    Skill: Conceptual
    Objective: 5.3

18) As the result of synaptic pruning,
    A) overstimulated neurons lose their connections with other neurons.
    B) stimulated neurons reproduce themselves at an astounding pace.
    C) nonstimulated neurons establish synapses with stimulated neurons.
    D) neurons that are not needed at the moment are returned to an uncommitted state.
    Answer: D
    Page Ref: 169
    Skill: Conceptual
    Objective: 5.3

19) As neurons form connections, _____ becomes vital to their survival.
    A) migration
    B) recovery
    C) habituation
    D) stimulation
    Answer: D
    Page Ref: 169
    Skill: Conceptual
    Objective: 5.3

20) _____ are responsible for myelination.
    A) Glial cells
    B) Neurotransmitters
    C) Neurons
    D) Synapses
    Answer: A
    Page Ref: 169
    Skill: Factual
    Objective: 5.3

21) Dramatic increases in _____ are responsible for the rapid gain in brain size during the first 2 years.
   A) neurons
   B) neural fibers and myelination
   C) neurotransmitters
   D) synapses
   Answer: B
   Page Ref: 169–170
   Skill: Factual
   Objective: 5.3

22) ERPs are a very useful tool for researchers who study preverbal infants because ERPs
   A) yield three-dimensional computerized pictures of the brain.
   B) detect increases in blood flow and oxygen metabolism throughout the brain.
   C) detect the precise location of brain-wave activity.
   D) yield a colorful, moving picture of parts of the brain used to perform a given activity.
   Answer: C
   Page Ref: 170
   Skill: Factual
   Objective: 5.6

23) Of the following, which is true regarding neurophysiological methods.
   A) PET and fMRI are useful methods for measuring brain functioning in preverbal infants.
   B) Unlike fMRI, PET does not require injection of a radioactive substance.
   C) NIROT works well in infancy because the apparatus consists only of thin, flexible optical fibers attached to the scalp.
   D) Both ERPs and fMRIs detect changes in electrical activity in the brain.
   Answer: C
   Page Ref: 170, 171
   Skill: Factual
   Objective: 5.6

24) The cortical region with the most extended period of development is the _____ lobe.
   A) temporal
   B) frontal
   C) occipital
   D) parietal
   Answer: B
   Page Ref: 172
   Skill: Factual
   Objective: 5.3

25) Brain research demonstrates that
   A) in most people, the left hemisphere controls spatial abilities.
   B) each hemisphere receives sensory information from the same side of the body.
   C) the cerebral cortex of left-handers is often less clearly specialized than that of right-handers.
   D) in most people, the right hemisphere handles verbal abilities.
   Answer: C
   Page Ref: 172
   Skill: Conceptual
   Objective: 5.4

26) A lateralized brain is adaptive because
    A) a person can still fully function if one hemisphere is severely damaged.
    B) neither hemisphere is overburdened with the processing of information.
    C) it can carry out a wider array of functions than if both sides processed the information in the same manner.
    D) the duplicate processing of information reduces the likelihood of performance errors.
Answer: C
Page Ref: 172
Skill: Conceptual
Objective: 5.4

27) Before brain lateralization occurs,
    A) if a part of the cortex is damaged, other parts can take over tasks it would have handled.
    B) each hemisphere of the cortex controls only one side of the body.
    C) the right hemisphere reacts more strongly to speech stimuli than the left hemisphere.
    D) each hemisphere of the cortex receives sensory information from only one side of the body.
Answer: A
Page Ref: 172
Skill: Conceptual
Objective: 5.4

28) In a highly plastic cerebral cortex,
    A) the hemispheres have lateralized into specific functions.
    B) the right side of the body is favored in motor abilities.
    C) the left hemisphere reacts more strongly than the right hemisphere to nonspeech sounds.
    D) many areas are not yet committed to specific functions.
Answer: D
Page Ref: 172
Skill: Conceptual
Objective: 5.4

29) Which of the following provides evidence that brain lateralization is already under way at birth?
    A) Most neonates show greater electrical activity in the left hemisphere when reacting to stimuli that evoke negative emotion.
    B) Most neonates favor the right side of the body in their head position and reflexive responses.
    C) Most neonates show greater electrical activity in the right hemisphere while listening to speech sounds.
    D) Most neonates use the right eye more than the left eye when viewing objects using peripheral vision.
Answer: B
Page Ref: 173
Skill: Conceptual
Objective: 5.4

30) Animal studies confirm that
    A) plasticity declines while forming new synapses.
    B) plasticity increases during synaptic pruning.
    C) early, extreme sensory deprivation results in permanent brain damage.
    D) most newborns use the right eye more than the left eye when using peripheral vision.
Answer: C
Page Ref: 173
Skill: Conceptual
Objective: 5.4

31) Of the following, which provides evidence for early brain plasticity?
   A) In brain-injured adults, cognitive experiences often lead stimulated cortical structures to compensate for the damaged areas.
   B) Adults have a greater capacity than infants and children to recover function following brain injury.
   C) Deaf adults who learned sign language as children depend more than hearing individuals on the right hemisphere for language processing.
   D) Toddlers who are advanced in language development show greater right-hemispheric specialization for language than their more slowly developing agemates.
Answer: C
Page Ref: 173
Skill: Applied
Objective: 5.4

32) The cerebral cortex
   A) begins to lateralize during the second half of the first year of life.
   B) is the first brain structure to complete its growth during childhood.
   C) is highly plastic throughout the lifespan.
   D) is genetically programmed for hemispheric specialization, but experience greatly influences its organization.
Answer: D
Page Ref: 173
Skill: Conceptual
Objective: 5.4

33) When 1-month-old kittens are put in the dark and kept there for two months, damage to visual centers of the brain is permanent. This provides evidence of
   A) brain plasticity.
   B) synaptic pruning.
   C) lateralization of the cerebral cortex.
   D) a sensitive period in brain development.
Answer: D
Page Ref: 173
Skill: Conceptual
Objective: 5.5

34) When cataract surgery is postponed beyond infancy, children born with cataracts in both eyes show less complete recovery in visual skills than if they have corrective surgery within 4 to 6 months. This finding demonstrates the concept of
   A) affordances.
   B) nonorganic failure to thrive.
   C) a sensitive period.
   D) the proximodistal trend.
Answer: C
Page Ref: 173
Skill: Applied
Objective: 5.5

35) Studies of children adopted from extremely deprived Romanian orphanages have demonstrated that
   A) most of the children completely recovered if they were adopted before age 3.
   B) catch up in physical and cognitive growth was dramatic regardless of when the children were adopted.
   C) only those who experienced inadequate nutrition were impaired in physical and cognitive functioning.
   D) cognitive catch-up growth was most impressive for those children who were adopted before 6 months of age.
   Answer: D
   Page Ref: 173, 175
   Skill: Conceptual
   Objective: 5.5

36) A study of children adopted into Canadian homes from extremely deprived Romanian orphanages found that
   A) the longer the children spent in orphanage care, the higher their cortisol levels.
   B) the children did not show an improvement in mental functioning even if adopted within the first six months of life.
   C) children who experienced adequate early nutrition were not negatively affected by early orphanage rearing.
   D) the children attained depressed mental test scores only if they spent two or more years in an orphanage.
   Answer: A
   Page Ref: 175
   Skill: Conceptual
   Objective: 5.5

37) Early learning centers with full curriculums of reading, math, and science
   A) may overwhelm infants and interfere with the brain's potential.
   B) overwhelm infants who are less advanced in these academic areas than their more rapidly developing agemates.
   C) usually yield extremely bright and psychologically healthy infants.
   D) are as effective in promoting cognitive development as are traditional nursery school programs.
   Answer: A
   Page Ref: 175
   Skill: Applied
   Objective: 5.5

38) Experience-expectant brain growth
   A) cannot be threatened by overstimulation.
   B) occurs throughout our lives.
   C) is dependent on the kinds of stimuli that are present in everyday life.
   D) differs widely across individuals and cultures.
   Answer: C
   Page Ref: 176
   Skill: Conceptual
   Objective: 5.5

39) Of the following activities, which would be associated with experience-expectant brain growth?
   A) practicing the piano
   B) hearing language
   C) playing video games
   D) taking tennis lessons
   Answer: B
   Page Ref: 176
   Skill: Applied
   Objective: 5.5

40) Current neuroscience evidence suggests that
    A) heredity is largely responsible for brain development.
    B) stimulation and teaching have only minimal influence on brain growth during the first two years of life.
    C) as the result of millions of years of evolution, young brains expect to encounter certain experiences.
    D) experience merely fine tunes the brain's functioning.
Answer: C
Page Ref: 176
Skill: Conceptual
Objective: 5.5

41) Experience-dependent brain growth
    A) takes place through naturally occurring interactions with the environment.
    B) provides the foundation for later-occurring, experience-expectant development.
    C) occurs during an early sensitive period of brain development.
    D) relies on specific learning experiences that differ widely across individuals.
Answer: D
Page Ref: 176
Skill: Conceptual
Objective: 5.5

42) Of the following, which experience would promote experience-dependent brain growth?
    A) practicing the violin
    B) singing a song
    C) playing with dirt
    D) taking a bath
Answer: A
Page Ref: 176
Skill: Applied
Objective: 5.5

43) Between birth and age 2,
    A) the sleep-wake pattern increasingly conforms to a night-day schedule.
    B) periods of sleep and wakefulness become shorter.
    C) total sleep time declines rapidly.
    D) napping subsides.
Answer: A
Page Ref: 176
Skill: Conceptual
Objective: 5.7

44) Sleep research demonstrates that
    A) most infants no longer wake during the night by 2 to 3 months of age.
    B) when babies begin to crawl and walk, they often show temporary periods of disrupted sleep.
    C) the secretion of melatonin becomes much greater at night than during the day by about 6 weeks of age.
    D) night waking decreases from 1 1/2 to 2 years.
Answer: B
Page Ref: 176
Skill: Applied
Objective: 5.7

45) Which of these situations is the best example of *catch-up growth*?
    A) A small, malnourished infant becomes a normal-sized 6-year-old when given an adequate diet.
    B) Adolescent girls are taller than adolescent boys, but the boys outgrow them in a few years.
    C) Younger siblings can sometimes outgrow their older siblings before adulthood.
    D) Premature babies often gain weight more quickly than do full-term babies.
Answer: A
Page Ref: 178
Skill: Applied
Objective: 5.8

46) Pound for pound, a young infant's energy needs are _____ those of an adult.
    A) half
    B) the same as
    C) twice
    D) 3 times
Answer: C
Page Ref: 178
Skill: Factual
Objective: 5.9

47) Compared to breastfed babies, bottle-fed babies
    A) accept new solid foods more easily.
    B) rarely suffer from constipation or other gastrointestinal problems.
    C) have a lower infant mortality rate.
    D) have more allergic reactions and respiratory and intestinal illnesses.
Answer: D
Page Ref: 179
Skill: Conceptual
Objective: 5.9

48) Babies in poverty-stricken regions of the world who _____ are 6 to 14 times more likely to survive the first year of life.
    A) are given vitamin-enriched commercial formula
    B) are breastfed
    C) receive goat or cow milk
    D) begin solid food before 6 months of age
Answer: B
Page Ref: 179
Skill: Conceptual
Objective: 5.9

49) The World Health Organization recommends that mothers breastfeed until their infants are _____ of age.
    A) 3 months
    B) 6 months
    C) 1 year
    D) 2 years
Answer: D
Page Ref: 179
Skill: Factual
Objective: 5.9

50) Most developing countries
    A) have banned the practice of giving free or subsidized formula to new mothers.
    B) encourage mothers to give their newborns diluted cow or goat milk.
    C) give free or subsidized formula to new mothers.
    D) encourage new breastfeeding mothers to give their newborns an iron supplement.
Answer: A
Page Ref: 179
Skill: Conceptual
Objective: 5.9

51) In the United States and Canada,
    A) nearly 90 percent of new mothers breastfeed their infants.
    B) most breastfeeding mothers continue until the child is at least 6 months old.
    C) breastfeeding has become less common, especially among well-educated women.
    D) national health agencies recommend exclusive breastfeeding for the first 6 months.
Answer: D
Page Ref: 180
Skill: Factual
Objective: 5.9

52) Longitudinal research demonstrates
    A) that television viewing is not associated overweight in children.
    B) that most chubby babies become obese adults.
    C) that breastfeeding is associated with rapid weight gain during infancy.
    D) a link between rapid weight gain in infancy and obesity in adults.
Answer: D
Page Ref: 180
Skill: Conceptual
Objective: 5.9

53) Interviews with more than 3,000 American parents of 4- to 24-month-olds revealed that
    A) most infants and toddlers do not consume enough calories for adequate growth.
    B) the majority of children eat at least one serving of fruit or vegetables a day.
    C) over half of 12-month-olds eat candy at least once a day.
    D) a growing number of parents are promoting healthy eating habits in their young children.
Answer: C
Page Ref: 180
Skill: Conceptual
Objective: 5.9

54) Research indicates that _____ of the world's children suffer from malnutrition before the age of 5.
    A) 5 percent
    B) 10 percent
    C) one-quarter
    D) one-third
Answer: D
Page Ref: 180
Skill: Factual
Objective: 5.10

55) Enrique is 2 months old, painfully thin, and in danger of dying. His mother is too malnourished to produce enough breast milk, and bottle-feeding is inadequate. What is the most likely cause of Enrique's illness?
    A) iron-deficiency anemia
    B) kwashiorkor
    C) nonorganic failure to thrive
    D) marasmus
Answer: D
Page Ref: 181
Skill: Applied
Objective: 5.10

56) Kiana is 2 years old and has an unbalanced diet very low in protein. She has an enlarged belly, swollen feet, a skin rash, and thinning hair. What is the most likely cause of Kiana's condition?
    A) marasmus
    B) kwashiorkor
    C) iron-deficiency anemia
    D) nonorganic failure to thrive
Answer: B
Page Ref: 180
Skill: Applied
Objective: 5.10

57) When the diets of severely malnourished children improve,
    A) they rarely show catch-up growth in height.
    B) their body protects itself by establishing a high basal metabolism rate.
    C) they tend to undereat even when food becomes plentiful.
    D) they often gain excessive weight.
Answer: D
Page Ref: 181
Skill: Conceptual
Objective: 5.10

58) Studies of North American children reveal that
    A) supplementary food programs have eradicated childhood malnutrition in the United States and Canada.
    B) physical growth and school achievement is not negatively affected by mild to moderate malnutrition
    C) malnutrition is a major problem only in developing countries.
    D) over 30 percent of American and Canadian children in single-parent families suffer from uncertain access to enough food for a healthy, active life.
Answer: D
Page Ref: 182
Skill: Conceptual
Objective: 5.10

59) Safiya, a single mother, feels depressed and overwhelmed by her parental duties and rarely holds, cuddles, or talks to her baby. She reports feeding her baby often, but her baby has lost 3 pounds in the past month. Her baby most likely suffers from
    A) marasmus.
    B) kwashiorkor.
    C) deprivation dwarfism.
    D) nonorganic failure to thrive.
Answer: D
Page Ref: 182
Skill: Applied
Objective: 5.11

60) Classical conditioning
  A) helps infants anticipate what is about to happen next.
  B) disappears once reflexive behaviors become voluntary.
  C) has very little impact on early learning.
  D) emerges only after newborn reflexes have begun to wane.
Answer: A
Page Ref: 183
Skill: Applied
Objective: 5.12

61) Baby Marcus begins to suck as soon as he sees his mother with a bottle of formula. Marcus's response to the bottle illustrates
  A) habituation.
  B) recovery.
  C) operant conditioning.
  D) classical conditioning.
Answer: D
Page Ref: 183
Skill: Applied
Objective: 5.12

62) In order for learning to occur, a(n) _____ becomes a(n) _____, and elicits a(n) _____.
  A) conditioned stimulus; neutral stimulus; unconditioned response
  B) unconditioned stimulus; conditioned stimulus; unconditioned response
  C) conditioned stimulus; neutral stimulus; unconditioned response
  D) neutral stimulus; conditioned stimulus; conditioned response
Answer: D
Page Ref: 184
Skill: Factual
Objective: 5.12

63) Right before baby Dominic's mother leaves for work every morning, she takes her car keys off of a hook on the wall. Now, as soon as Dominic's mother unhooks her car keys, Dominic begins to cry. In this example, _____ is/are the conditioned stimulus.
  A) Dominic's mother unhooking the car keys
  B) Dominic's crying
  C) morning time
  D) Dominic's mother's leaving for work
Answer: A
Page Ref: 184
Skill: Applied
Objective: 5.12

64) Baby Melissa always gets her diaper changed before her mother feeds her. Melissa often sucks vigorously on her thumb during her diaper changes. In this example, diaper changing has become a(n) _____ and Melissa's thumb sucking has become a(n) _____.
  A) unconditioned response; conditioned stimulus
  B) conditioned stimulus; conditioned response
  C) conditioned response; unconditioned stimulus
  D) unconditioned stimulus; conditioned response
Answer: B
Page Ref: 184
Skill: Applied
Objective: 5.12

65) David goes outside to play in his tree house. A swarm of bees has nested near his tree house, and he gets stung when he climbs up to the tree house. This happens three times in the same week. David is now afraid to go near the tree and cries when his dad tries to get him to climb up to the tree house. The bee sting is the _____, the tree house is the _____, and fear is the _____.
   A) unconditioned stimulus; conditioned stimulus; conditioned response
   B) conditioned stimulus; neutral stimulus; unconditioned response
   C) neutral stimulus; unconditioned stimulus; unconditioned response
   D) conditioned stimulus; unconditioned stimulus; conditioned response
Answer: A
Page Ref: 184
Skill: Applied
Objective: 5.12

66) When the _____ is repeatedly presented without being paired with the _____, _____ occurs.
   A) neutral stimulus; conditioned stimulus; extinction
   B) conditioned stimulus; unconditioned stimulus; learning
   C) conditioned stimulus; unconditioned stimulus; extinction
   D) neutral stimulus; conditioned stimulus; learning
Answer: C
Page Ref: 184
Skill: Factual
Objective: 5.12

67) _____ is a very difficult response to classically condition in young infants because they
   A) Hunger; are almost always hungry.
   B) Fear; have no biological need to form these associations.
   C) Happiness; express happiness only in familiar contexts.
   D) Anger; do not yet have the capacity to express anger.
Answer: B
Page Ref: 184
Skill: Conceptual
Objective: 5.12

68) Baby Jacob's mother is more likely to pick him up when he smiles than when he is fussy. As a result, the frequency of Jacob's smiles has increased. This is an example of
   A) habituation.
   B) operant conditioning.
   C) recovery.
   D) classical conditioning.
Answer: B
Page Ref: 184
Skill: Applied
Objective: 5.12

69) Baby Hannah's mother gives her a cookie whenever she behaves during trips to the grocery store. The cookie is an example of a(n)
   A) conditioned stimulus.
   B) unconditioned stimulus.
   C) reinforcer.
   D) extinction.
Answer: C
Page Ref: 184
Skill: Applied
Objective: 5.12

70) Baby Jonah's mother refuses to cuddle him when he whines, and the frequency of his whining has declined. Jonah's mother is using a mild form of
    A) habituation.
    B) reinforcement.
    C) recovery.
    D) punishment.
Answer: D
Page Ref: 184
Skill: Applied
Objective: 5.12

71) At first, baby Mario was easily awakened every night by a barking dog in his neighborhood. Several weeks later, Mario's sleep is not interrupted by the barking. This is an example of
    A) classical conditioning.
    B) extinction.
    C) habituation.
    D) recovery.
Answer: C
Page Ref: 185
Skill: Applied
Objective: 5.12

72) Baby Owen's attention to his music box decreased because his mother has played it several times. When Owen's mother played a different music box, his attention increased. Owen's increase demonstrates
    A) habituation.
    B) imitation.
    C) recovery.
    D) reinforcement.
Answer: C
Page Ref: 185
Skill: Applied
Objective: 5.12

73) When infants exhibit recovery in a habituation paradigm, it shows that they
    A) perceive the second stimulus as the same as the original stimulus.
    B) remember the original stimulus.
    C) recall the original stimulus when it is not present.
    D) imitate the original stimulus when produced by others.
Answer: B
Page Ref: 185
Skill: Conceptual
Objective: 5.12

74) A baby who first habituates to a green circle and then recovers to a blue circle
    A) does not remember the first stimulus (the green circle).
    B) believes that both stimuli are identical.
    C) prefers the first stimulus (the green circle).
    D) can distinguish between green and blue.
Answer: D
Page Ref: 185
Skill: Applied
Objective: 5.12

75) Baby Nora's looking decreases when repeatedly presented a 3 × 3 checkerboard pattern. However, when she is shown a new 9 × 9 checkerboard pattern, her looking increases. In this example, Nora exhibits _____ to the 3 × 3 pattern and exhibits _____ to the 9 × 9 pattern, indicating that she _____.
   A) habituation; recovery; perceives the two stimuli as the same
   B) habituation; recovery; perceives the difference between the two stimuli
   C) recovery; habituation; perceives the two stimuli as the same
   D) recovery; habituation; perceives the difference between the two stimuli
Answer: B
Page Ref: 185
Skill: Applied
Objective: 5.12

76) In the first few days of life, newborns can imitate a wide variety of adult
   A) reflexes.
   B) speech sounds.
   C) facial expressions.
   D) fine motor skills, such as grasping and reaching.
Answer: C
Page Ref: 186
Skill: Conceptual
Objective: 5.12

77) Research on imitation shows that
   A) imitation emerges sometime during the second or third month after birth.
   B) humans are the only primates who imitate facial expressions in infancy.
   C) there is undisputable evidence that newborn imitation is a reflex.
   D) imitation is more difficult to induce in babies 2 to 3 months old than just after birth.
Answer: D
Page Ref: 186
Skill: Conceptual
Objective: 5.12

78) Of the following, which is supported by research on imitation?
   A) Baby chimps cannot imitate facial expressions.
   B) Most newborns can imitate adult hand movements.
   C) Imitation declines in humans, but not chimps, during infancy.
   D) Mirror neurons are believed to be the biological basis of imitation.
Answer: D
Page Ref: 186
Skill: Conceptual
Objective: 5.12

79) Of the following, which of these is the best example of a gross motor skill?
   A) drawing
   B) pointing
   C) crawling
   D) grasping
Answer: C
Page Ref: 187
Skill: Applied
Objective: 5.13

80) _____ and _____ are examples of fine motor activities.
    A) Climbing on a jungle gym; blinking
    B) Pointing; drawing
    C) Crawling; standing
    D) Skipping; grasping a raisin between two fingers
Answer: B
Page Ref: 188
Skill: Applied
Objective: 5.13

81) Of the following, which motor activity typically develops first?
    A) sits alone
    B) grasps a cube
    C) plays pat-a-cake
    D) crawls
Answer: B
Page Ref: 188
Skill: Applied
Objective: 5.13

82) At 6 months, Isaac can pull himself to a sitting position and drag himself around by his arms. By 8 months, he can use his legs to move himself forward with his belly off the floor. This demonstrates
    A) habituation.
    B) the cephalocaudal trend.
    C) recovery.
    D) the proximodistal trend.
Answer: B
Page Ref: 188
Skill: Applied
Objective: 5.13

83) At 4 months, baby Sophia uses her whole hand to grasp objects with little finger control. By 6 months, Sophia can reach for a cube with her fingers extended and transfer it from hand to hand. This is an example of
    A) the cephalocaudal trend.
    B) a gross motor skill.
    C) the proximodistal trend.
    D) prereaching.
Answer: C
Page Ref: 188
Skill: Applied
Objective: 5.13

84) Baby Jason has learned how to put together kicking, rocking on all fours, and reaching into crawling. This development reflects the concept of
    A) coordinated trends.
    B) fine motor skill suites.
    C) gross motor skill packages.
    D) dynamic systems of action.
Answer: D
Page Ref: 189
Skill: Applied
Objective: 5.13

85) Dynamic systems theory provides convincing evidence that the development of motor skills
   A) does not lead to new synaptic connections in the brain.
   B) is hardwired into the nervous system.
   C) always follows the cephalocaudal trend.
   D) cannot be genetically determined.
   Answer: D
   Page Ref: 189
   Skill: Conceptual
   Objective: 5.14

86) Dennis' study of infants in Iranian orphanages demonstrates that
   A) overstimulation can be detrimental.
   B) early movement opportunities and a stimulating environment contribute to motor development.
   C) deliberate encouragement of motor skills does not quicken progress.
   D) motor development proceeds according to a genetic timetable.
   Answer: B
   Page Ref: 190
   Skill: Conceptual
   Objective: 5.14

87) Kipsigi infants walk earlier than North American infants because
   A) Kipsigi parents deliberately teach skills that encourage early walking.
   B) Kipsigi babies are smaller at birth, requiring less leg-muscle strength for standing.
   C) North American babies tend to be overstimulated, resulting in less motivation to walk or crawl.
   D) the Kipsigi are a nomadic tribe in which walking is key for survival.
   Answer: A
   Page Ref: 190
   Skill: Conceptual
   Objective: 5.14

88) The Western practice of having babies sleep on their back
   A) delays gross motor milestones of sitting and crawling.
   B) places infants at increased risk of SIDS.
   C) encourages infants to scoot in a sitting position rather than crawl on their hands and knees.
   D) promotes the rapid development of gross motor milestones of rolling and reaching.
   Answer: A
   Page Ref: 190
   Skill: Conceptual
   Objective: 5.14

89) Of the following motor skills, which is believed to play the greatest role in infant cognitive development?
   A) crawling
   B) voluntary reaching
   C) rolling from back to front
   D) holding head steady and upright
   Answer: B
   Page Ref: 190
   Skill: Conceptual
   Objective: 5.15

90) Of the following, which behavior suggests that babies are biologically prepared for eye-hand coordination?
    A) the ulnar grasp
    B) voluntary reaching
    C) the pincer grasp
    D) prereaching
Answer: D
Page Ref: 190
Skill: Conceptual
Objective: 5.15

91) Nine-month-old Jamal can reach for and grasp an object in a room that has been darkened during the reach because
    A) visual guidance is fully developed by 2 months of age.
    B) Jamal has not yet learned to depend on his vision for fine motor activities.
    C) reaching is largely controlled by proprioception rather than by vision.
    D) Jamal has advanced eye-hand coordination.
Answer: C
Page Ref: 191
Skill: Applied
Objective: 5.15

92) Improvements in reaching during infancy are largely the result of gains in
    A) control of body posture and of arm and hand movements.
    B) depth perception and control of arm and hand movements.
    C) control of arm and hand movements and autonomic nervous system development.
    D) depth perception and of control of body posture.
Answer: A
Page Ref: 191
Skill: Conceptual
Objective: 5.15

93) Two-month old Yueh-Wen grasps a rattle and shakes it vigorously. She probably is using
    A) the pincer grasp.
    B) prereaching.
    C) gross motor skills.
    D) the ulnar grasp.
Answer: D
Page Ref: 191
Skill: Applied
Objective: 5.15

94) One-year-old Sally picks up a raisin with her thumb and index finger. She is probably using
    A) the ulnar grasp.
    B) gross motor skills.
    C) the pincer grasp.
    D) prereaching.
Answer: C
Page Ref: 191
Skill: Applied
Objective: 5.15

95) Research on the development of voluntary reaching in infancy suggests that
   A) infants given only a moderate amount of visual stimulation tend to lag in the development of voluntary reaching behind those who are given a large amount of visual stimulation.
   B) it is best to provide infants with the most visual stimulation possible to promote voluntary reaching.
   C) the amount of visual stimulation does not influence the appearance of voluntary reaching.
   D) only a moderate amount of visual stimulation is needed to facilitate voluntary reaching.
   Answer: D
   Page Ref: 192
   Skill: Conceptual
   Objective: 5.15

96) Research suggests that the best time to begin toilet training is
   A) when infants first start to walk unaided.
   B) during the second half of the second year of life.
   C) early in the middle of the third year.
   D) at one year of age.
   Answer: C
   Page Ref: 192–193
   Skill: Applied
   Objective: 5.15

97) Most 12-month-olds
   A) can identify the signals from a full bladder or rectum, but resist being toilet trained because they are preoccupied with playing and practicing motor skills.
   B) are toilet trained quicker than children whose parents delay toilet training until the second year.
   C) can be toilet trained within 2 months.
   D) cannot consistently identify the signals from a full bladder or rectum.
   Answer: D
   Page Ref: 193
   Skill: Conceptual
   Objective: 5.15

98) Over the first year of life, the greatest change in hearing is the ability to
   A) organize sounds into complex patterns.
   B) hear high-frequency sounds.
   C) distinguish differences in intensity.
   D) detect changes in sound frequency.
   Answer: A
   Page Ref: 193
   Skill: Conceptual
   Objective: 5.16

99) Studies of hearing demonstrate that newborns
   A) prefer Mozart's minuets with awkward breaks to those with pauses between phrases.
   B) "screen out" sounds not used in their own language.
   C) can distinguish nearly all sounds in human languages.
   D) prefer listening to non-native languages.
   Answer: C
   Page Ref: 194
   Skill: Conceptual
   Objective: 5.16

100) Research indicates that around 7 months, infants
   A) detect when words are deliberately mispronounced.
   B) attend to regularities in word sequences.
   C) detect grammatical errors in sentences.
   D) detect words that start with weak syllables.
   Answer: B
   Page Ref: 194
   Skill: Conceptual
   Objective: 5.16

101) Of the following, which is supported by research on infant speech perception?
   A) Rules that infants extract from the speech stream do not generalize to nonspeech sounds.
   B) Parents must directly teach word-order rules for infants to understand the basic grammar of their language.
   C) Infants use statistical regularities in the speech stream to recognize words.
   D) Infants do not become sensitive to the speech structure of individual words until after their first birthday.
   Answer: C
   Page Ref: 194
   Skill: Conceptual
   Objective: 5.16

102) Vision reaches a near-adult level of about 20/20 by
   A) 1 month.
   B) 3 months.
   C) 6 months.
   D) 1 year.
   Answer: C
   Page Ref: 195–196
   Skill: Factual
   Objective: 5.17

103) Gibson and Walk used the visual cliff to study
   A) depth perception.
   B) visual acuity.
   C) pattern perception.
   D) vestibular sensitivity.
   Answer: A
   Page Ref: 196
   Skill: Factual
   Objective: 5.17

104) Between 2 to 3 months,
   A) sensitivity to pictorial depth cues develops.
   B) infants develop 20/20 vision.
   C) the ability to blink the eyes defensively when an object moves toward the face emerges.
   D) sensitivity to binocular cues emerges.
   Answer: D
   Page Ref: 196
   Skill: Conceptual
   Objective: 5.17

105) Infants who have experience with _____ are far more likely to refuse to cross the deep side of the visual cliff.
   A) reaching and grasping
   B) crawling
   C) walking
   D) sitting up
   Answer: B
   Page Ref: 196
   Skill: Conceptual
   Objective: 5.17

106) Of the following, which baby would MOST likely refuse to cross the deep side of the visual cliff?
   A) Seven-month-old Samantha, whose spends several hours each day crawling around the house.
   B) Ten-month-old Emanuel, who can pull to stand but has not yet learned to crawl.
   C) Nine-month-old Mia, who learned to crawl 2 months ago but spends most of her day in her playpen or infant swing.
   D) Five-month-old Pedro, who spends most of his day carried around by his mother in an infant sling.
   Answer: A
   Page Ref: 196
   Skill: Applied
   Objective: 5.17

107) Novice crawlers but experienced sitters will avoid leaning out over a drop-off for an attractive toy when in the sitting position. When placed in the crawling position, they will
   A) head over the edge only when the distance is narrow.
   B) avoid leaning out over the drop-off for an attractive toy only when the distance is narrow.
   C) avoid leaning out over the drop-off for an attractive toy only when the distance is extremely wide.
   D) head over the edge even when the distance is extremely wide.
   Answer: D
   Page Ref: 197
   Skill: Conceptual
   Objective: 5.17

108) Research indicates that _____ strengthens neural connections involved in _____.
   A) crawling; pattern perception
   B) sitting; understanding of space
   C) sitting; pattern perception
   D) crawling; understanding of space
   Answer: D
   Page Ref: 197
   Skill: Conceptual
   Objective: 5.17

109) Baby Juno prefers looking at a checkerboard with large black and white squares rather than one with smaller gray and white squares. Juno is demonstrating
   A) contrast sensitivity.
   B) sensitivity to pictorial depth cues.
   C) proprioception.
   D) sensitivity to the visual cliff.
   Answer: A
   Page Ref: 197
   Skill: Applied
   Objective: 5.17

110) Compared to older babies, very young babies prefer to look at large, bold checkerboards over checkerboards with many small squares. This is because
    A) more complex checkerboard patterns overwhelm very young infants.
    B) very young infants prefer the pattern with the least contrast.
    C) very young infants are more sensitive to the greater contrast in complex patterns.
    D) very young infants cannot resolve the more complex patterns in checkerboards with many small squares.
    Answer: D
    Page Ref: 197
    Skill: Conceptual
    Objective: 5.17

111) By 2 to 3 months of age, but not at 1 month of age, infants
    A) can detect objects represented by incomplete drawings.
    B) perceive subjective boundaries that really are not present.
    C) prefer to look at facelike stimuli arranged naturally rather than unnaturally.
    D) explore the internal features of a pattern.
    Answer: D
    Page Ref: 199
    Skill: Conceptual
    Objective: 5.17

112) Which picture is newborn Bjorn most likely to look at?
    A) a facelike drawing with simple features
    B) a facelike drawing with the features arranged upside down
    C) a facelike drawing with the features arranged sideways
    D) a complex drawing of a face
    Answer: A
    Page Ref: 199
    Skill: Applied
    Objective: 5.17

113) Studies of infant face perception demonstrate that newborns will look longer at
    A) photos of faces with eyes closed than photos of faces with eyes open.
    B) faces judged by adults as attractive than those judged as less attractive.
    C) upside-down faces than upright ones.
    D) an unfamiliar face than their mother's face.
    Answer: B
    Page Ref: 200
    Skill: Conceptual
    Objective: 5.17

114) Habituation research reveals that size and shape constancy are present as early as
    A) the first week of life.
    B) 3 months of age.
    C) the third trimester of pregnancy.
    D) 1 year of age.
    Answer: A
    Page Ref: 201
    Skill: Factual
    Objective: 5.18

115) Studies of object identity show that _____ is mastered before _____.
    A) perception of an object's continued path of movement; object unity
    B) shape constancy; size constancy
    C) object unity; perception of an object's continued path of movement
    D) size constancy; shape constancy
Answer: C
Page Ref: 201
Skill: Conceptual
Objective: 5.18

116) _____ is/are necessary for most 2- to 4-month-olds to infer object unity.
    A) Motion
    B) Binocular depth cues
    C) Pictorial depth cues
    D) Invariant features
Answer: A
Page Ref: 201
Skill: Factual
Objective: 5.18

117) Intermodal perception
    A) develops as the result of independent locomotion.
    B) does not emerge until the second half of the first year of life.
    C) interferes with infants' ability to learn the patterns of their native language.
    D) helps infants make sense of simultaneous input from multiple modalities.
Answer: D
Page Ref: 202
Skill: Conceptual
Objective: 5.19

118) Which of the following is an example of an intermodal match?
    A) An infant blinks her eyes defensively when an object is moved toward her face as if was going to hit.
    B) An infant coordinates reaching and grasping to retrieve a desired toy.
    C) An infant links a happy voice with the appropriate face of a speaking person.
    D) An infant uses pictorial depth cues to distinguish deep and shallow surfaces.
Answer: C
Page Ref: 202
Skill: Applied
Objective: 5.19

119) Babies quickly learn that certain sights are linked with certain sounds. This is because babies are sensitive to
    A) amodal sensory properties.
    B) habituation.
    C) contrast sensitivity.
    D) pictorial cues.
Answer: A
Page Ref: 202
Skill: Conceptual
Objective: 5.19

120) According to the Gibsons' differentiation theory, infants actively search for _____ of the environment in a constantly changing world.
    A) binocular depth cues
    B) intermodal perception
    C) contrast sensitivity
    D) invariant features
Answer: D
Page Ref: 202
Skill: Conceptual
Objective: 5.20

121) In the Gibson's differentiation theory, perceptual development reflects an innate tendency to search for _____ relationships between features of among various stimuli.
    A) stable
    B) discontinuous
    C) dynamic
    D) bidirectional
Answer: A
Page Ref: 202
Skill: Conceptual
Objective: 5.20

122) According to differentiation theory, _____ make(s) our actions future-oriented and mostly successful.
    A) sensitivity to affordances
    B) categories of actions, objects, and events
    C) the discovery of variant features in the environment
    D) learning to search for order and stability in the surrounding world
Answer: A
Page Ref: 203
Skill: Conceptual
Objective: 5.20

123) Baby Amanda knows that her red ball can be squeezed, bounced, and rolled. Using the language of differentiation theory, Amanda knows that her red ball _____ the possibility of squeezing, bouncing, and rolling.
    A) engenders
    B) promotes
    C) excites
    D) affords
Answer: D
Page Ref: 203
Skill: Applied
Objective: 5.20

124) Studies of brain plasticity demonstrate that
    A) children with brain injuries show early delays in language development only if the damage occurred to the left cerebral hemisphere.
    B) recovery after early brain injury is greater for spatial skills than for language.
    C) a "crowding effect" occurs in healthy brain regions that take over the functions of damaged areas.
    D) children with early left-hemispheric damage have more trouble with holistic spatial processing than those with early right-hemispheric damage.
Answer: C
Page Ref: 174
Skill: Conceptual
Objective: (B&E Box) Brain Plasticity

125) Animal research reveals that
    A) children with left-hemispheric damage often have trouble with holistic processing of visual stimuli.
    B) language functioning is more lateralized at birth compared to spatial processing.
    C) plasticity declines during synaptic pruning.
    D) recovery from brain injury is greater for spatial skills than language skills.

Answer: C

Page Ref: 174
Skill: Conceptual
Objective: (B&E Box) Brain Plasticity

126) Cross-cultural research shows that
    A) cosleeping is the norm for approximately 90 percent of the world's population.
    B) cosleeping places infants at increased risk of SIDS.
    C) mothers' total sleep time is decreased by cosleeping.
    D) cosleeping children are at risk for later social problems, especially dependency.

Answer: A

Page Ref: 177
Skill: Conceptual
Objective: (CI Box) Cultural Variation in Infant Sleep Arrangements

127) Research shows that infant-parent cosleeping
    A) is associated with a rise in sleep problems.
    B) is common only in nonindustrialized countries.
    C) is safe even with the use of quilts, comforters, and soft mattresses.
    D) may have evolved to protect infants' survival and health.

Answer: D

Page Ref: 177
Skill: Conceptual
Objective: (CI Box) Cultural Variation in Infant Sleep Arrangements

128) One possible explanation for the high frequency of bedtime struggles in American homes is that
    A) American children are much more dependent than children from other cultures.
    B) young children feel stressed when required to fall asleep without assistance.
    C) American children often eat an abundance of sugary foods in the evening.
    D) American parents do not enforce bedtime rules or rituals as firmly as parents from other cultures.

Answer: B

Page Ref: 177
Skill: Conceptual
Objective: (CI Box) Cultural Variation in Infant Sleep Arrangements

129) In countries where parent-child cosleeping is common,
    A) many infants are suffocated due to entrapment in soft covers.
    B) children become dependent on this sleeping arrangement to fall asleep.
    C) parents and infants often sleep on hard surfaces.
    D) infants tend to sleep through the night months earlier than infants in countries where parents put their babies to sleep in quiet, separate rooms.

Answer: C

Page Ref: 177
Skill: Conceptual
Objective: (CI Box) Cultural Variation in Infant Sleep Arrangements

130) Studies of perception demonstrate that
  A) Western adults, but not infants, can detect rhythmic-pattern deviations of non-Western music.
  B) several weeks of daily opportunities to listen to non-Western music restores Western adults' sensitivity to detect rhythmic-pattern deviations in non-Western melodies.
  C) by 12 months of age, Western babies lose their ability to detect rhythmic-pattern deviations in non-Western melodies.
  D) Western children retain the ability to detect rhythmic-pattern deviations in non-Western melodies throughout childhood.
Answer: C
Page Ref: 195
Skill: Conceptual
Objective: (B&E Box) A Sensitive Period for Culture-Specific Learning

131) Infants with severe visual impairments are not motivated to move on their own until
  A) "reaching on sound" is achieved.
  B) their parents push them to do so.
  C) they have received extensive orientation and mobility training.
  D) they receive vision correction through eyeglasses or surgery.
Answer: A
Page Ref: 198
Skill: Conceptual
Objective: (B&E Box) Development of Infants with Severe Visual Impairments

132) Infants with severe visual impairments have difficulty evoking stimulating caregiver interaction because
  A) their emotional expressions are exaggerated.
  B) they do not reach for and manipulate objects until at least 2 years of age.
  C) they cannot make eye contact, imitate, or pick up nonverbal cues.
  D) they have difficulties combining touch and sound in their surroundings.
Answer: C
Page Ref: 198
Skill: Conceptual
Objective: (B&E Box) Development of Infants with Severe Visual Impairments

ESSAY

133) Discuss research on sensitive periods and brain growth in animals, what is currently known about brain growth spurts in humans, and implications of lack of stimulation during sensitive periods of development for humans.
  Answer: The existence of sensitive periods in postnatal development of the cortex has been demonstrated in studies of animals exposed to extreme forms of sensory deprivation. Findings have shown that rich and varied visual experiences must occur for visual centers to develop normally. The visual centers in the brain of a month-old kitten will start to degenerate if deprived of light for three to four days; the damage is permanent if the time is extended to two months. Brains of pets are heavier and thicker than brains of animals reared in isolation.
  Researchers have identified intermittent brain growth spurts from infancy through adolescence in children, based on gains in brain weight and skull size, as well as by using the EEG. These spurts coincide with peaks in children's intelligence test performance and major cognitive changes such as language development. Surges in EEG activity in the frontal lobe at key milestones in an infant's developmental process suggest the link between brain growth and cognitive and motor development.
  Researchers are convinced that experience is the necessary ingredient for the development of synapses and complex neural networks during the childhood years. However, the effects of stimulation, or the lack of stimulation, during growth spurts have yet to be answered. The research on the visual centers of cats, however, could lead to the conclusion that stimulation during the early years, whether visual, auditory, verbal, or cognitive, is absolutely necessary for normal development.
Page Ref: 173–176

134) Explain the benefits of breastfeeding over bottle-feeding in infancy. Why is breastfeeding particularly important in poverty-stricken countries?

Answer: Breast milk is especially suited for infants' nutritional needs, and bottled formulas try to imitate it. Breast milk has a correct balance of fat and protein, it provides complete nutrition until 6 months of age, it offers protection against disease, it helps avoid faulty jaw development, and it protects against tooth decay. Compared to babies who are bottle-fed, those who are breastfed are less likely to become constipated or have diarrhea, and they accept new solid foods more easily.

Because of these benefits, breastfed babies in poverty-stricken regions of the world are much less likely to be malnourished and much more likely to survive the first year of life. Even a few weeks of breastfeeding would offer some protection against respiratory and intestinal infections that are devastating to young children in developing countries. Further, because nursing offers some protection against pregnancy, breast-feeding helps increase spacing among siblings, a major factor in reducing childhood deaths in developing countries.

Page Ref: 178–180

135) Describe the development of voluntary reaching and why it is important for cognitive development.

Answer: Of all the motor skills, voluntary reaching is believed to play the greatest role in infant cognitive development because it opens up a whole new way of exploring the environment. By grasping things, turning them over, and seeing what happens when they are released, infants learn a great deal about the sights, sounds, and feel of objects. Reaching and grasping start out as gross, diffuse activities, but the child moves toward a mastery of fine movements. Newborns make poorly coordinated swipes, called prereaching, toward objects in front of them. At 3 months, voluntary reaching appears and gradually improves in accuracy. Once infants can reach, they modify their grasp. The newborn grasp reflex is replaced by the ulnar grasp, in which the fingers close against the palm. At 4 to 5 months, babies can hold an object in one hand and explore it with the fingertips of the other. By the end of the first year, infants use the thumb and index finger in a well-coordinated pincer grasp, greatly expanding their ability to manipulate objects.

Page Ref: 190–192

136) Explain dynamic systems theory of motor development. Why, according to this view, is motor development not genetically hardwired but rather softly assembled?

Answer: According to a dynamic systems of action approach, mastery of motor skills involves acquiring increasingly complex, dynamic systems of action. When motor skills work as a system, separate abilities blend together, each cooperating with others to produce more effective ways of exploring and controlling the environment. For example, during infancy, control of the head and upper chest are combined into sitting with support. Kicking, rocking on all fours, and reaching are gradually put together into crawling. Then crawling, standing, and stepping are coordinated in walking.

Each new skill is a joint product of central nervous system development, movement possibilities of the body, the task the child has in mind, and environmental supports for the skill. Change in any one of these elements leads to loss of stability in the system, and the child explores and selects new, more effective motor patterns.

According to this theory, motor development cannot be a genetically determined process. Since it is motivated by exploration and the desire to master new tasks, it can only be mapped out by heredity at a very general level. Instead, behaviors are softly assembled. Each skill is acquired by revising and combining earlier accomplishments into a more complex system that permits the child to reach the desired goal. Consequently, different paths to the same motor skill exist.

Page Ref: 189–190

137) Describe the development of depth perception and depth cues during infancy, and cite factors that influence the emergence of sensitivity to depth.

Answer: Early studies of depth perception used the visual cliff — a glass-covered table with a platform resting between a "shallow" side with a checkerboard pattern just under the glass and a "deep" side with a checkerboard several feet below the glass. Crawling babies readily cross the shallow side, but most react with fear to the deep side. However, this research does not tell us how crawling and avoidance of drop-offs are linked or when sensitivity to depth first appears. More recent research that has examined babies' abilities to detect depth cues provides important information about the development of depth perception. This work reveals that responsiveness to motion cues develops first. By about 3 to 4 weeks of age, babies blink their eyes when an object is moved toward their faces. Researchers speculate that sensitivity to motion cues develops as the result of improvements in head control during the first few weeks of life. Next to develop is a sensitivity to binocular cues, which emerges between 2 and 3 months and is thought to be linked to improved focusing ability. Finally, around 6 months, a sensitivity to pictorial cues develops and is believed to be associated with an improved ability to manipulate objects. Additional research shows that the experience of moving about independently creates babies' avoidance of heights. Infants with more crawling experience (regardless of when they started to crawl) were far more likely to refuse to cross the deep side of the visual cliff. Researchers believe that crawling is so important in structuring babies' experience of the world that it promotes a new level of brain organization by strengthening certain neural connections, especially those involved in vision and understanding of space.

Page Ref: 196–197

138) Explain the differentiation theory of perceptual development.

Answer: According to the Gibsons' differentiation theory, infants actively search for invariant features of the environment—those that remain stable—in a constantly changing perceptual world. The Gibsons use the word *differentiation* to describe their theory because over time, babies make finer and finer distinctions among stimuli. In this view, babies are endowed with a natural tendency to search for order and consistency, a capacity that becomes fine-tuned with age. Acting on the environment plays a major role in perceptual differentiation. Infants constantly look for ways in which the environment affords opportunities for action. By moving about and exploring the environment, they figure out appropriate actions for objects and obstacles in the surrounding environment. As a result, they differentiate the world in new ways and act more competently when confronted with diverse perceptual experiences.

Page Ref: 202–203

STUDY QUESTIONS

Body Growth

Changes in Body Size and Muscle–Fat Makeup

1. Infant and toddler growth is marked by (steady gains / little spurts). (p. 166)

2. Summarize changes in muscle–fat makeup during the first two years of life. (p. 167)

   _____

   _____

   _____

3. Describe sex and ethnic differences in body size and muscle–fat makeup during infancy. (p. 167)

   A. _____

   _____

   B. _____

   _____

Changes in Body Proportions

1. According to the two patterns of body growth, the (cephalocaudal / proximodistal) trend refers to growth from "head to tail," while the (cephalocaudal / proximodistal) trend refers to growth from the center of the body outward. (p. 167)

Skeletal Growth

1. The best way of estimating a child's physical maturity is to use _____, a measure of the development of the bones of the body. Explain how this estimate is obtained. (p. 167)

   _____

   _____

   _____

2. True or False: African-American children tend to be slightly behind Caucasian-American children in skeletal age. (p. 168)

3. Describe sex differences in skeletal age and body size during infancy and toddlerhood. (p. 168)

   _____

   _____

   _____

4. At birth, the bones of the skull are separated by six gaps, or soft spots, called _____. Explain their function. (p. 168)

   _____

   _____

   _____

5.   At approximately what age do infants get their first tooth? What does early appearance of teeth reveal about physical maturity? (p. 168)

A. _____

B. _____

Brain Development

Development of Neurons

1.   The human brain has 100 to 200 billion _____, or nerve cells, that store and transmit information. Between them are tiny gaps, or _____, across which messages pass. (p. 168)

2.   Explain the process of *synaptic pruning*. (p. 169)

_____

_____

_____

3.   About one-half the brain's volume is made up of _____, which are responsible for _____, the coating of neural fibers with an insulating fatty sheath that improves the efficiency of message transfer. (pp. 169–170)

Neurophysiological Methods

1.   Match each of the following methods of measuring brain functioning to the appropriate description. (p. 170)

_____ Electroencephalogram (EEG)
_____ Event-related potentials (ERPs)
_____ Functional magnetic resonance imaging (fMRI)
_____ Positron Emission Tomography (PET)
_____ Near-Infrared Optical Topography (NIROT)

1.   Thin, flexible optical fibers are attached to the scalp and infrared light is beamed at the brain. Absorption by areas of the cerebral cortex varies with changes in blood flow and oxygen metabolism.
2.   Using the EEG, the frequency and amplitude of brain waves in response to particular stimuli are recorded in specific areas of the cerebral cortex.
3.   Electrodes are taped to the scalp to record the stability and organization of electrical brain-wave activity in the brain's outer layers—the cerebral cortex.
4.   After injection or inhalation of a radioactive substance, the individual lies inside a tunnel-shaped apparatus with a scanner that emits fine streams of X-rays, which detect increased blood flow and oxygen metabolism in the brain while a person processes particular stimuli.
5.   A scanner magnetically detects increased blood flow and oxygen metabolism in areas of the brain as the individual processes particular stimuli. The result is a computerized moving picture of activity anywhere in the brain.

2.   True or False: Near-Infrared Optical Topography (NIROT) works well in infancy and early childhood because the child can sit on the parent's lap and move during testing, unlike other methods of measuring brain functioning. (p. 171)

Development of the Cerebral Cortex

1. True or False: The cerebral cortex is the largest, most complex brain structure, accounting for 85 percent of the brain's weight and containing the greatest number of neurons and synapses. (p. 171)

2. Name the regions of the cerebral cortex, and describe the function of each. (p. 172)

    A. _____

    B. _____

    C. _____

    D. _____

3. Describe the different functions controlled by the left and right hemispheres of the brain. (p. 172)

    Left: _____

    _____

    Right: _____

    _____

4. Explain the concepts of *lateralization* and *brain plasticity*. (pp. 172–173)

    Lateralization: _____

    _____

    Brain plasticity: _____

    _____

    _____

5. The brain is (more / less) plastic during the first few years than at any later time in life. (p. 173)

Biology and Environment: Brain Plasticity: Insights from Research on Brain-Damaged Children and Adults

1. Adults who suffered brain injuries in infancy and early childhood show (fewer / more) cognitive impairments than adults with later-occurring injuries. (p. 174)

2. Describe the impact of brain injury on childhood language development and spatial skills, noting how this relates to brain plasticity. (p. 174)

    Language: _____

    _____

    Spatial skills: _____

    _____

3. True or False: Recovery after early brain injury is greater for language than for spatial skills. (p. 174)

4. Describe the negative consequences of high brain plasticity. (p. 174)

    _____

    _____

5. True or False: Brain plasticity is restricted to childhood and is no longer evident by the time individuals reach adulthood. Provide research evidence to support your response. (p. 174)

_____

_____

_____

Sensitive Periods in Brain Development

1. Why is it difficult to study the effects of early deprivation in human infants? (p. 175)

_____

2. What is cognitive catch-up? What does research on orphanage children reveal about cognitive catch-up? (p. 175)

A. _____

_____

B. _____

_____

3. Summarize evidence that appropriate stimulation is essential for healthy brain development. (pp. 173, 175)

_____

_____

_____

4. True or False: Overstimulation of infants and toddlers threatens their interest in learning and may create conditions similar to those of stimulus deprivation. (p. 175)

5. Distinguish between *experience-expectant* and *experience-dependent* brain growth, and provide an example of each. (p. 176)

Experience-expectant: _____

_____

_____

Experience-dependent: _____

_____

_____

6. Evidence (does / does not) exist for a sensitive period in the first few years of life for mastering skills that depend on extensive training, such as musical performance or gymnastics. (p. 176)

Changing States of Arousal

1. In general, newborn babies sleep a total of ___ to ___ hours per day. The total sleep time of an infant declines (quickly / slowly); the average 2-year-old sleeps ___ to ___ hours per day. (p. 176)

2. Discuss how the social environment affects infants' changing arousal patterns. (pp. 176, 178)

_____

_____

_____

Cultural Influences: Cultural Variations in Infant Sleeping Arrangements

1. True or False: Parent–infant cosleeping is the norm for approximately 90 percent of the world's population. (p. 177)

2. Explain how cultural values—specifically, collectivism versus individualism—influence infant sleeping arrangements. (p. 177)

   Collectivism: _____

   _____

   Individualism: _____

   _____

3. True or False: Research suggests that cosleeping evolved to protect infants' survival and health. Briefly explain your answer. (p. 177)

   _____

   _____

4. How do infant sleeping practices affect other aspects of family life? (p. 177)

   _____

   _____

   _____

5. Discuss the criticisms and concerns surrounding infant cosleeping. (p. 177)

   _____

   _____

   _____

Influences on Early Physical Growth

Heredity

1. True or False: When diet and health are adequate, height and rate of physical growth are largely determined by heredity. (p. 178)

2. When are children and adolescents likely to show catch-up growth? (p. 178)

   _____

   _____

Nutrition

1. List four nutritional and health benefits of breast milk. (p. 179)

   A. _____

   B. _____

   C. _____

   D. _____

2.   Discuss the benefits of breastfeeding as they relate to mothers and infants in poverty-stricken regions of the world. (p. 179)

_____

_____

_____

3.   Rapid weight gain in infancy (is / is not) related to obesity at older ages. (p. 180)

4.   Cite four ways in which parents can prevent infants and toddlers from becoming overweight at later ages. (p. 180)

   A.   _____

   B.   _____

   C.   _____

   D.   _____

Malnutrition

1.   Describe the causes of *marasmus* and *kwashiorkor,* two dietary diseases associated with severe malnutrition, and summarize the developmental outcomes associated with these extreme forms of malnutrition. (pp. 181–182)

   Marasmus: _____

   _____

   _____

   _____

   Kwashiorkor: _____

   _____

   _____

   _____

   Outcomes: _____

   _____

   _____

   _____

2.   True or False: Inadequate nutrition is largely confined to developing countries and recent surveys indicate that it is almost nonexistent in the United States and Canada. (p. 182)

3.   What is food insecurity, and in what two populations is food insecurity especially high? (p. 182)

   A.   _____

   B.   _____   C.   _____

Emotional Well-Being

1. What is *nonorganic failure to thrive,* and what are some common symptoms? (p. 182)

    A. _____

    _____

    B. _____

    _____

2. Discuss the family circumstances surrounding nonorganic failure to thrive. (p. 182)

    _____

    _____

    _____

Learning Capacities

1. Define *learning,* and identify two basic forms of learning in which infants are equipped. (p. 183)

    A. _____

    B. _____ C. _____

Classical Conditioning

1. Briefly explain how learning takes place through *classical conditioning.* (p. 183)

    _____

    _____

    _____

2. Why is classical conditioning of great value to infants? (p. 183)

    _____

    _____

3. Match the following terms to the appropriate definitions. (pp. 183–184)

    _____ A neutral stimulus that leads to a new response once learning has occurred

    _____ A learned response exhibited toward a previously neutral stimulus

    _____ A reflexive response

    _____ A stimulus that automatically leads to a reflexive response

    1. Unconditioned stimulus (UCS)
    2. Unconditioned response (UCR)
    3. Conditioned stimulus (CS)
    4. Conditioned response (CR)

4. Using the above definitions as a guide (see question 3), outline the three steps involved in classical conditioning. (pp. 183–184)

    A. _____

    _____

    B. _____

    _____

    C. _____

    _____

5. In classical conditioning, if the CS is presented alone enough times, without being paired with the UCS, the CR will no longer occur. This is referred to as _____. (p. 184)

6. Some responses, such as _____, are very difficult to classically condition in young babies. Explain why. (pp. 183–184)

_____

_____

Operant Conditioning

1. Briefly explain how learning takes place through *operant conditioning*. (p. 184)

_____

_____

_____

2. Define the terms *reinforcer* and *punishment* as they relate to operant conditioning. (p. 184)

Reinforcer: _____

_____

_____

Punishment: _____

_____

_____

3. Describe how operant conditioning plays a role in the development of social relationships. (p. 184)

_____

_____

_____

Habituation

1. Define the terms *habituation* and *recovery.* (p. 185)

Habituation: _____

_____

Recovery: _____

_____

2. As infants get older, they habituate to stimuli more (slowly / quickly). What does this indicate about their cognitive development? (p. 185)

_____

Imitation

1. Summarize what infants are able to learn through the process of *imitation.* (p. 186)

   _____

   _____

   _____

2. Explain the role of mirror neurons in relation to imitation and learning. (p. 186)

   _____

   _____

   _____

Motor Development

The Sequence of Motor Development

1. Distinguish between *gross* and *fine motor development,* and provide two examples of each. (pp. 187–188)

   Gross: _____

   _____

   Examples: _____

   Fine: _____

   _____

   Examples: _____

2. True or False: Although the *sequence* of motor development is fairly uniform, large individual differences exist in the *rate* of development. (p. 188)

3. Discuss the organization and direction of motor development in relation to the cephalocaudal and proximodistal trends. (p. 188)

   _____

   _____

   _____

Motor Skills as Dynamic Systems

1. According to the *dynamic systems theory of motor development,* mastery of motor skills involves acquisition of increasingly complex systems of action. Explain what this means. (p. 189)

   _____

   _____

   _____

2. List four factors that contribute to the development of each new motor skill. (p. 189)

    A. _____

    B. _____

    C. _____

    D. _____

3. True or False: Dynamic systems theory regards motor development as a genetically determined process. Briefly explain your response. (p. 189)

    _____

    _____

    _____

Dynamic Motor Systems in Action

1. What did Galloway and Thelen's microgenetic studies reveal about infant motor development? (pp. 189–190)

    _____

    _____

    _____

Cultural Variations in Motor Development

1. In Wayne Dennis's orphanage research, what effects did lying on their backs have on babies' motor development? (p. 190)

    _____

    _____

2. Give at least one example of how cultural variations in infant-rearing practices affect motor development. (p. 190)

    _____

    _____

Fine Motor Development: Reaching and Grasping

1. Match each of the following terms to the appropriate definition. (pp. 190–191)

    _____ Well-coordinated movement in which infants use the thumb and forefinger   1. Prereaching
            opposably   2. Ulnar grasp
    _____ Poorly coordinated swipes or swings toward an object   3. Pincer grasp
    _____ Clumsy motion in which the fingers close against the palm

2. Explain how reaching and depth perception are related. (p. 191)

    _____

    _____

3. Reaching (is / is not) affected by early experience. (p. 192)

4. Does heavy enrichment lead to advanced motor development in infancy? Explain. (p. 192)

_____

_____

Bowel and Bladder Control

1. At what age should parents typically begin toilet training their children, and why is this the case? (pp. 192–193)

Age: _____

Reason: _____

_____

2. Name three effective toilet training techniques. (p. 193)

A. _____

B. _____

C. _____

Perceptual Development

Hearing

1. What is the greatest change in hearing that takes place over the first year of life? (p. 193)

_____

2. Describe the changes in auditory perception over the first year of life that prepare infants for language acquisition. (pp. 193–194)

Around 6 months: _____

_____

_____

6–12 months: _____

_____

_____

3. Research shows that infants are impressive statistical analyzers of sound patterns. Explain what this means. (p. 199)

_____

_____

Biology and Environment: "Tuning in" to Familiar Speech, Faces, and Music: A Sensitive Period for Culture-Specific Learning

1. Describe changes in the ability to perceive familiar speech and familiar faces over the first year of life. (p. 195)

    Familiar speech: _____

    _____

    Familiar faces: _____

    _____

2. How do research findings on musical rhythm perception support the notion of a sensitive period for culture-specific learning? (p. 195)

    _____

    _____

    _____

Vision

1. What is *depth perception,* and why is it important in infant development? (p. 196)

    A. _____

    _____

    B. _____

    _____

2. Describe Gibson and Walk's studies using the visual cliff, and cite the limitations of this approach for studying infant depth perception. (p. 196)

    A. _____

    _____

    B. _____

    _____

3. Name and describe the three cues for depth. (p. 196)

    A. _____

    _____

    B. _____

    _____

    C. _____

    _____

4. Explain what infants learn from crawling that promotes sensitivity to depth information. (p. 197)

_____

_____

_____

_____

5. Provide an example from adult experience that helps to explain why crawling plays such an important role in the infant's knowledge and understanding of the three-dimensional world. (p. 197)

_____

_____

6. The principle of _____, which accounts for early pattern preferences, states that if infants can detect a difference in contrast between two or more patterns, they will prefer the one with more contrast. (p. 197)

7. True or False: By the end of the first year, a suggestive image of a pattern is all that babies need to recognize a familiar form. (p. 199)

8. Summarize the development of face perception across the first year of life. (pp. 199–200)

Birth–1 month: _____

_____

2–4 months: _____

_____

5–12 months: _____

_____

9. Cite factors that contribute to infants' refinement of face perception. (p. 197)

_____

_____

Social Issues: Education: Development of Infants with Severe Visual Impairments

1. True or False: Children with severe visual impairments show delays in motor, cognitive, and social development. (p. 198)

2. Discuss how severe visual impairments impact motor exploration and spatial understanding. (p. 198)

_____

_____

_____

_____

3. How do severe visual impairments affect the caregiver–infant relationship? (p. 198)

    _____

    _____

    _____

4. Cite four intervention techniques that can help infants with severe visual impairments become aware of their physical and social surroundings. (p. 198)

    A. _____

    _____

    B. _____

    _____

    C. _____

    _____

    D. _____

    _____

Object Perception

1. True or False: Size and shape constancy appear to emerge gradually over time as infants acquire more advanced knowledge of objects in the environment. (p. 201)

2. True or False: When two objects are touching, whether moving in unison or standing still, infants younger than 4 months of age do not perceive the boundary between the two objects, and therefore, cannot distinguish them. (p. 201)

Intermodal Perception

1. What is *intermodal perception*? (p. 202)

    _____

    _____

2. Explain the concept of *amodal sensory properties*. (p. 202)

    _____

    _____

    _____

3. True or False: From birth, infants are capable of combining information from multiple sensory systems. Cite research to support your response. (p. 202)

    _____

    _____

    _____

4. Explain how intermodal perception facilitates processing of the infant's social world. (p. 202)

    _____

    _____

    _____

Understanding Perceptual Development

1. Explain Gibsons' *differentiation theory.* (p. 202)

    _____

    _____

    _____

2. Explain how acting on the environment plays a vital role in perceptual differentiation. (p. 203)

    _____

    _____

    _____

PUZZLE 5.1 TERM REVIEW

Across

2. In classical conditioning, an originally reflexive response that is produced by a CS after learning has occurred (abbr.)

7. Experience-_____ brain growth: early organization of the brain depends on ordinary experiences with the environment

9. In operant conditioning, a stimulus that increases the occurrence of a response

10. _____ conditioning: form of learning that involves associating a neutral stimulus with a stimulus that leads to a reflexive response

11. Brain _____: ability of other parts of the brain to take over functions of damaged regions

13. Process in which neural fibers are coated with an insulating fatty sheath that improves the efficiency of message transfer

15. In operant conditioning, a stimulus that decreases the occurrence of a response

18. Cells that serve the function of myelination

19. The gaps between neurons across which messages are sent

21. _____ conditioning: form of learning in which spontaneous behavior is followed by a stimulus that changes the probability that the behavior will occur again

22. In classical conditioning, a neutral stimulus that through pairing with an UCS leads to a new response (abbr.)

Down

1. The largest, most complex brain structure is the _____ cortex

3. In classical conditioning, a reflexive response that is produced by an UCS (abbr.)

4. Specialization of functions of the two hemispheres of the cerebral cortex

5. An increase in responsiveness to a new stimulus following habituation

6. Experience-_____ brain growth: growth and refinement of brain structures result from specific learning experiences

8. In classical conditioning, a stimulus that leads to a reflexive response (abbr.)

12. Soft spots that separate the bones of the skull at birth

14. Growth centers in the bones

16. Nerve cells that store and transmit information

17. _____ age: an estimate of physical maturity based on development of the bones of the body

20. Synaptic _____: loss of connective fibers by seldom-stimulated neurons

PUZZLE 5.2 TERM REVIEW

Across

2. _____ systems theory of motor development: views new motor skills as a reorganization of previously mastered skills that lead to more effective ways of exploring and controlling the environment

3. Well-formed grasp involving thumb and forefinger opposition

7. Learning by copying another person

9. _____ constancy: perception of an object's shape as the same, despite changes in the shape projected on the retina

13. Chemicals released by neurons that cross the synapse to send messages to other neurons

14. Clumsy grasp in which the fingers close against the palm

15. _____ failure to thrive: growth disorder caused by a lack of affection and stimulation

16. _____ constancy: perception of an object's size as the same, despite changes in the sizes of its retinal image

17. Contrast _____: if babies can detect a difference in contrast between two or more patterns, they will prefer the one with more contrast

18. _____ sensory properties: information that overlaps two or more sensory systems, resulting in perception of such input as an integrated whole

19. _____ perception combines information from more than one sensory system

Down

1. A gradual reduction in the strength of a response as a result of a repeated stimulation

4. _____ trend: pattern of physical growth that proceeds from head to tail

5. The poorly coordinated, primitive reaching movements of newborn infants

6. _____ theory: view that perceptual development involves detection of increasingly fine-grained, invariant features of the environment

8. A disease usually appearing in the first year of life that is caused by a diet low in all essential nutrients

10. The action possibilities that a situation offers an organism with certain motor capabilities

11. A disease usually appearing between 1 and 3 years of age that is caused by a diet low in protein

12. _____ trend: pattern of physical growth that proceeds from the center of the body outward

CROSSWORD PUZZLE SOLUTIONS

PUZZLE 5.1

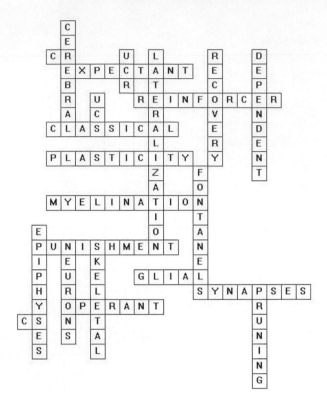

PUZZLE 5.2

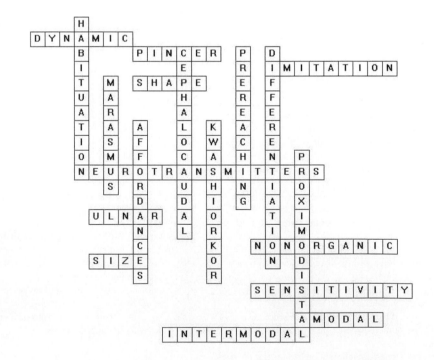

PRACTICE TEST #1

1. During the first 9 months, babies develop "baby fat" in order to (p. 167)
   a. maintain a constant body temperature.
   b. ensure a consistent source of nourishment.
   c. engage adults' affectionate attention.
   d. cushion the vital organs from violent trauma.

2. Examination of the epiphyses can determine the age of a child's skeleton because (pp. 167–168)
   a. the older the skeleton, the more fontanels at the epiphyses.
   b. older epiphyses show a greater proximodistal trend.
   c. the older the skeleton, the thinner the cartilage cells at the plates of the epiphyses.
   d. the younger the epiphyses, the more sutures there are across the plates.

3. Skull growth is especially rapid between birth and age 2 because (p. 168)
   a. the skull is developing many new fontanels.
   b. all of the bones are producing epiphyses.
   c. the birth sutures are disappearing.
   d. brain size is increasing.

4. The major limitation of neurophysiological methods is that they (p. 171)
   a. are unsuitable for infants and young children, since they require that the child remain as motionless as possible.
   b. cannot show that the research participant has processed a stimulus in a certain way.
   c. depend on X-ray photography.
   d. can determine only the stability and organization of brain-wave patterns.

5. The fact that damage to either hemisphere of the young brain affects early language competence indicates that (p. 174)
   a. language and spatial skills develop in the frontal lobes.
   b. the crowding effect slows the processing of verbal stimuli.
   c. the brain is less plastic than researchers once thought.
   d. language functioning is broadly distributed in the brain.

6. Rapid brain growth means that by age 2, most children (p. 176)
   a. no longer nap.
   b. need 12 to 13 hours of sleep.
   c. nap between 16 and 18 hours.
   d. take two daytime naps.

7. Breastfed infants become hungry quite often because (p. 180)
   a. breast milk is so easily digestible.
   b. they tend to be more active than bottle-fed infants.
   c. mothers of such babies tend to introduce them to solid food later.
   d. some of the nutrients in breast milk trigger hunger so that babies will consume more of it.

8. Infants can develop the signs of marasmus from (p. 182)
   a. excessive bottle-feeding.
   b. prolonged kwashiorkor.
   c. nonorganic failure to thrive resulting from lack of parental love.
   d. a diet too heavy in starch.

9. In classical conditioning, for learning to occur, (p. 184)
   a.   a conditioned stimulus must produce an unconditioned response.
   b.   a neutral stimulus that does not lead to the reflex must be presented just before, or at about the same time as, the unconditioned stimulus.
   c.   extinction must cancel out all unconditioned responses.
   d.   the conditioned response must lead to a new reflex.

10. By focusing on how infants shift from a novelty preference to a familiarity preference, researchers use habituation to assess infants' (p. 185)
   a.   recent memory.
   b.   recall.
   c.   remote memory.
   d.   attention.

11. Ninety percent of infants achieve the motor skill of scribbling vigorously at about age _____ months. (p. 188)
   a.   9-16
   b.   9-17
   c.   10-19
   d.   10-21

12. According to dynamic systems theory, motor development cannot be genetically determined because it (p. 189)
   a.   is motivated by exploration and the desire to master new tasks.
   b.   results from instabilities in the system.
   c.   is too complex for human genetic patterning to encode.
   d.   is hardwired.

13. Among the Kipsigis of Kenya, babies tend to hold their heads up, sit alone, and walk earlier than North American babies because Kipsigi mothers (p. 190)
   a.   give babies more tummy time than North American mothers do.
   b.   deliberately teach these skills by seating very young babies in holes in the ground, with rolled blankets to keep them upright.
   c.   leave babies lying on their backs in cribs for long hours, while the mothers are doing their work.
   d.   encourage babies to scoot on their bottoms rather than crawl.

14. By 5 to 6 months, infants can reach for and grasp objects in a room that has been darkened during the reach. This skill suggests that (p. 191)
   a.   infants aim their reaching motions at an object through prereaching.
   b.   reaching is largely controlled by proprioception.
   c.   infants of that age have reached a higher level of cephalocaudal development.
   d.   reaching is a softly assembled skill.

15. Toilet training should be delayed until the months following the second birthday because (p. 192)
   a.   prior to that time, the stimulation of training could undermine the development of motor skills.
   b.   younger children are generally uninterested in bowel and bladder control.
   c.   after age 2, children have the motor development to manipulate their own diapers.
   d.   at that time, children can consistently identify signals from a full bladder and rectum.

16. ERP brain-wave recordings indicate that around 5 months, infants (p. 194)
   a.   prefer rhythmically distinct foreign languages as much as sounds of their native tongue.
   b.   become sensitive to syllable stress patterns in their own language.
   c.   start to screen out sounds not used in their native language.
   d.   cannot yet distinguish most sounds in their own language.

17. Statistical analysis helps babies learn language by enabling them to (p. 194)
    a. **extract regularities from complex, continuous speech.**
    b. learn rules of grammar.
    c. detect words that start with strong syllables.
    d. distinguish between their own language and a foreign one.

18. Motion provides important information about depth because it (p. 196)
    a. gives children binocular depth cues.
    b. enhances children's sensitivity to pictorial depth.
    c. **helps children learn that objects are not flat but three-dimensional.**
    d. enables children to perceive the visual cliff.

19. Not until around the middle of the first year can blind infants (p. 198)
    a. initiate meaningful contact with peers and caregivers.
    b. **use sound as a precise clue to object location.**
    c. explore their world through reaching and crawling.
    d. produce definite emotional expressions.

20. At 12 months, infants' pattern perception has developed to the point that they (p. 199)
    a. are more contrast sensitive than they were at 6 months.
    b. stare at a single, high-contrast feature in a pattern.
    c. can perceive subjective boundaries in patterns that are not really present.
    d. **detect objects represented by incomplete drawings.**

21. Habituation research has revealed that young infants (p. 201)
    a. possess only size constancy.
    b. see only two-dimensional objects.
    c. **have both size and shape constancy at birth.**
    d. perceive only the constantly shifting images that objects cast on their retina.

22. Intermodal perception engages our capacity for (p. 202)
    a. **assembling varied sensory information into integrated wholes.**
    b. object unity.
    c. size and shape constancy.
    d. depth perception.

23. Intermodal sensitivity advances perceptual development by (p. 202)
    a. helping infants to develop contrast sensitivity.
    b. **making amodal properties stand out.**
    c. enabling children to ignore distracting social cues.
    d. making infants' statistical speech analysis more precise.

24. According to the Gibsons' differentiation theory, infants search for invariant features because those (p. 202)
    a. have the greatest object unity.
    b. offer the richest array of intermodal relationships.
    c. have the simplest patterns.
    d. **are the stable features in a constantly shifting perceptual world.**

25. A baby's sensitivity to affordances makes his or her exploratory actions (p. 203)
    a. **future oriented and largely successful.**
    b. less likely to be overwhelmed by complex intermodal stimuli.
    c. more sensitive to invariant features.
    d. reactive and blundering until around age 18 months.

PRACTICE TEST #2

1. After birth, the cephalocaudal trend changes, so that by age 2 the (p. 167)
   a. arms and legs have grown faster than the hands and feet.
   b. head accounts for one-fifth of total body length.
   c. chest and trunk have grown faster than any other part of the body.
   d. legs account for one-third of total body length.

2. Beginning in the sixth week of pregnancy, (p. 167)
   a. the embryonic skeleton forms out of cartilage.
   b. epiphyses develop on the ends of the fetus' long bones.
   c. cartilage cells harden into bone.
   d. the growth of the skeleton gradually slows and does not begin again until after birth.

3. During the prenatal period, the neural tube produces more neurons than the brain will need because (p. 169)
   a. when synapses are formed, many surrounding neurons die to make room for the final structure.
   b. stimulation kills off many of the delicate fetal neurons.
   c. synaptic pruning returns many neurons to undifferentiated brain tissue.
   d. neurons not coated during the myelination process die.

4. The frontal lobes undergo the most extended period of development because they (p. 172)
   a. specialize through lateralization.
   b. are the least plastic areas of the cerebral cortex.
   c. become the region of the "left-brained" functions.
   d. are responsible for consciousness, reasoning, and other thought.

5. fMRI studies reveal that the left hemisphere of the cerebral cortex is better at (p. 172)
   a. composing complex speech.
   b. processing information in a holistic, integrative manner.
   c. dealing with information in a sequential, analytic way.
   d. recovering from severe trauma.

6. Researchers speculate that attempts to hasten experience-dependent brain growth with intensive early learning (p. 176)
   a. can, in some instances, produce smarter babies.
   b. may accelerate experience-expected brain growth.
   c. could overwhelm neural circuits, thereby reducing the brain's sensitivity to everyday experiences.
   d. would do little to change patterns of development established by millions of years of evolution.

7. Studies of cosleeping have revealed that the practice (p. 177)
   a. often leads to emotional dependence in children.
   b. does not reduce mothers' total sleep time.
   c. has declined dramatically in North America.
   d. is largely unrelated to culture.

8. When diet and health are adequate, rate of physical growth is largely determined by (p. 178)
   a. heredity.
   b. the pace of catch-up growth.
   c. cultural variations.
   d. environment.

9. Marasmus usually appears in the first year of life when (p. 181)
   a. the baby's diet is very low in protein.
   b. too much starch is introduced too early.
   c. a baby's mother is too malnourished to produce enough breast milk and bottle-feeding is also inadequate.
   d. the baby suffers prolonged iron-deficiency anemia.

10. In newborns, reinforcement of the sucking response occurs (p. 184)
   a. only in response to milk or another sweet liquid.
   b. in response to stimuli that produce interesting sights and sounds, as well as to food.
   c. in response to loud, sudden noises.
   d. in response to deprivation of food.

11. Many scientists believe that mirror neurons (p. 186)
   a. are the biological basis of certain complex social abilities, including imitation.
   b. produce automatic responses that decline with age.
   c. are what distinguishes humans from other primates, such as chimpanzees.
   d. cause infants to turn their heads in response to sounds.

12. In the acquisition of motor skills, large individual differences exist in the (p. 188)
   a. cephalocaudal trend.
   b. rate of progress.
   c. proximodistal trend.
   d. sequence of development.

13. The research of James Galloway and Esther Thelen confirms that the order in which motor skills develop depends on (p. 190)
   a. a predetermined proximodistal pattern.
   b. each baby's inherited traits.
   c. the rate of early gross motor development.
   d. the anatomy of the body part used, the surrounding environment, and the baby's efforts.

14. Infants' prereaching declines around age 7 weeks because at that point, (p. 190)
   a. experience teaches babies how to control their hand movements.
   b. the mirror neurons necessary for finer reaching have grown.
   c. babies begin to improve the eye movements involved in tracking and fixing on objects.
   d. babies gain greater control over their fingers.

15. By the end of the first year, infants shift from ulnar grasp to pincer grasp when they (p. 191)
   a. begin to coordinate their thumbs and index fingers.
   b. can reach for objects in a darkened room.
   c. close their fingers against their palms.
   d. start coordinating both hands to explore objects.

16. Around 6 to 7 months, infants (p. 193)
   a. develop a sense of musical phrasing.
   b. recognize the same melody when it is played in different keys.
   c. can make more discriminations in music than in human speech.
   d. can distinguish musical tunes on the basis of rhythmic patterns.

17. Studies of infants' discriminations of speech, faces, and music suggest that between 6 and 12 months, (p. 195)
   a. babies retain their sensitivity to virtually all speech sounds but narrow their focus to familiar faces and music.
   b. babies experience a sensitive period during which they are biologically prepared to focus on socially meaningful perceptual distinctions.
   c. learning slows across the domains of vision and hearing.
   d. these areas of perception are largely unaffected by experience or other environmental factors.

18. Depth perception is especially important for (p. 196)
   a. enhancing scanning.
   b. tracking moving objects.
   c. understanding the layout of the environment and guiding motor activity.
   d. developing mature color vision.

19. Crawling promotes sensitivity to depth information because (p. 197)
    a.   it keeps babies in a single posture so that they can master particular spatial relations.
    b.   it enhances babies' confidence and, therefore, further exploration of their world.
    c.   babies quickly learn that the visual cliff is an illusion.
    d.   babies gradually figure out how to use depth cues to detect the danger of falling.

20. Children with limited or no vision show impressive developmental rebounds when (p. 198)
    a.   language emerges.
    b.   they achieve "reaching on sound."
    c.   their gross motor skills permit crawling.
    d.   they learn to interpret the meaning of others' reactions through touch.

21. Between 2 and 4 months, infants' face perception develops to the point that they (p. 200)
    a.   can perceive emotional expressions as meaningful wholes.
    b.   become sensitive to pictorial cues.
    c.   prefer a complex facial pattern over other, equally complex patterns.
    d.   prefer photos of faces with eyes open and a direct gaze.

22. Infants master object unity before perception of an object's continuous path because (p. 200)
    a.   the former requires only size constancy.
    b.   the latter is a more challenging task.
    c.   to achieve the latter, the child must have achieved a high level of pattern perception.
    d.   infants' contrast sensitivity improves with age.

23. When babies detect amodal sensory properties, they (p. 202)
    a.   acquire information that overlaps two or more sensory systems.
    b.   focus on information from a single modality.
    c.   succeed in perceiving an object's continuous path of movement.
    d.   take in scattered sensory information that is difficult to assemble into a whole.

24. At 3 to 4 months, infants' intermodal perception is such that they can (p. 202)
    a.   make sense of complex amodal relationships.
    b.   reach for an object in a room that has been darkened during their reach.
    c.   reach for a sounding object in the dark.
    d.   match faces with voices on the basis of lip-voice synchrony.

25. According to the Gibsons' differentiation theory, babies detect complex patterns when they (p. 202)
    a.   focus on invariant features.
    b.   explore internal features by noticing stable relationships.
    c.   assemble amodal properties into coherent wholes.
    d.   achieve both size and shape constancy.

POWERPOINT SLIDES

Infants, Children, and Adolescents
Laura E. Berk 6th edition

Chapter 5

Physical
Development
in Infancy and
Toddlerhood

This multimedia product and its contents are
protected under copyright law. The following are
prohibited by law:
- Any public performance or display, including
  transmission of any image over a network;
- Preparation of any derivative work, including the
  extraction, in whole or in part of any images;
- Any rental, lease, or lending of the program.

Body Growth

- Gain 50% in height from birth to age 1; 75% by age 2
- Grow in spurts
- Gain "baby fat" until about 9 months, then get slimmer
- Girls slightly shorter and lighter than boys

Growth Trends

Cephalocaudal

- "Head to Tail"
- Lower part of body grows later than the head

Proximodistal

- "Near to far"
- Extremities grow later than head, chest, and trunk

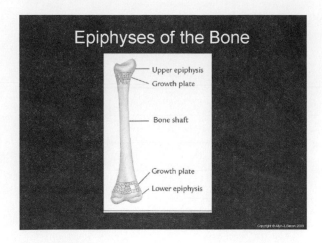

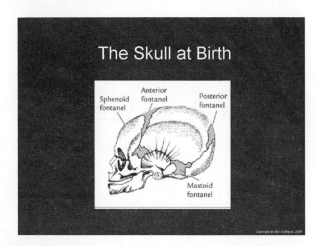

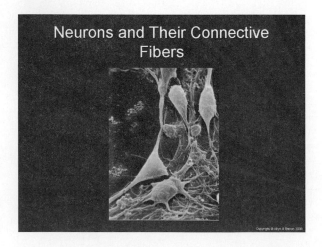

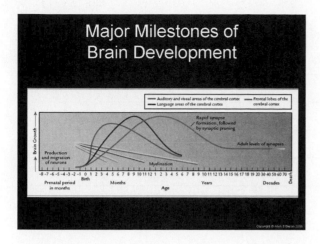

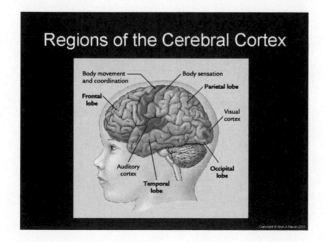

Lateralization and Plasticity of the Cerebral Cortex

- The left and right hemispheres of the brain control different functions.
- Specialization of the two hemispheres is called lateralization.
  - Left hemisphere: best at processing information in a sequential, analytic way.
  - Right hemisphere: best at processing information in a holistic, integrative manner.
- In a highly *plastic* cerebral cortex, many areas are not yet committed to one function, consequently, the cortex has a high capacity for learning.

Copyright © Allyn & Bacon 2008

Brain Plasticity Insights

- In children with injuries to the cerebral cortex that occurred before birth or in the first 6 months of life, language delays persisted to about 3½ years of age.
- Yet, by age 5, the children caught up in grammatical and vocabulary skills, showing that the undamaged area of the brain—either hemisphere—had taken over the language function.
- Spatial skills showed more impairment after a brain injury. Researchers speculate that spatial processing is more lateralized at birth.
- Brain plasticity can occur later in adulthood, for example, in stroke victims.

Copyright © Allyn & Bacon 2008

Sensitive Periods in Brain Development

- Early, extreme sensory deprivation results in permanent brain damage and loss of function.
- Babies born with cataracts in both eyes who have corrective surgery within 4 to 6 months show rapid improvement in vision.
- The longer the surgery is postponed, the less complete the recovery of visual skills.

Copyright © Allyn & Bacon 2008

Brain Development in Orphanage Children

- Children adopted from Romanian orphanages before 6 months of age showed dramatic cognitive and physical gains.
- Those adopted after 6 months, however, showed serious intellectual deficits.
- The chronic stress of early, deprived orphanage rearing disrupts the brain's ability to manage stress, with long-term consequences.

Relationship of Age at Adoption to Mental Test Scores

Romanian children adopted after 6 months of age showed increasing cognitive impairment the longer they were institutionalized.

Early-adopted Romanian children fared as well as early-adopted British children.

Sensitive Periods in Brain Development

- Experience-expectant growth
  - Ordinary experiences "expected" by brain to grow normally
- Experience-dependent growth
  - Specific experience, varies widely

Appropriate Stimulation

- Experience-expectant brain development takes place early and naturally as part of a preschooler's daily routine.
- No evidence exists to support a sensitive period in early life when mastering skills that depend on extensive training can occur. In fact, rushing early learning can overwhelm young brains.

Copyright © Allyn & Bacon 2008

Sleep Patterns

- Sleep moves to an adult-like night-day schedule during the first year.
- Sleep needs decline from 18 to 12 hours a day by age 2.
- Night wakings often increase between the ages of 1½ and 2 years, and then decline.

Copyright © Allyn & Bacon 2008

Cultural Variations in Infant Sleeping Arrangements

- Cosleeping is the norm for 90% of the world's population.
- Cultural values of collectivism versus individualism strongly influence infant sleeping arrangements.
- Cosleeping is increasing in North America, perhaps because more mothers are breastfeeding.

Copyright © Allyn & Bacon 2008

Influences on Early Growth

- Heredity
- Nutrition
  - Breast v. Bottle Feeding
  - Malnutrition
- Emotional Well-Being
  - Problems Can Cause Failure to Thrive

Copyright © Allyn & Bacon 2009

Benefits of Breastfeeding

- Correct fat-protein balance
- Nutritionally complete
- More digestible
- Better growth
- Disease protection
- Better jaw and tooth development
- Easier transition to solid food

Copyright © Allyn & Bacon 2009

Are Chubby Babies At Risk for Later Obesity?

- Recent research shows that there is a relationship between rapid weight gain in infancy and later obesity.
- What to do?
  - Breastfeed for six months.
  - Avoid foods loaded with sugar, salt, and saturated fats.
  - Promote physical exercise.
  - Limit TV viewing time.

Copyright © Allyn & Bacon 2009

Malnutrition

Types	▪Marasmus ▪Kwashiorkor ▪Iron-deficiency anemia ▪Food insecurity
Consequences	▪Physical symptoms ▪Growth and weight problems ▪Poor motor development ▪Learning, attention problems ▪Passivity, irritability, anxiety

Nonorganic Failure to Thrive

- The baby is offered enough food and has no serious illness, but still has a wasted body and is withdrawn and apathetic.
- Family circumstances surrounding failure to thrive often help explain the problem.
- When treated early, by helping the parents or placing the baby in a caring foster home, failure-to-thrive infants show quick catch-up growth. Left untreated, most will remain small and have lasting difficulties.

The Steps of Classical Conditioning

Operant Conditioning Terms

Reinforcer

- *Increases* probability of behavior occurring again
- Presenting desirable stimulus
- Removing unpleasant stimulus

Punishment

- *Reduces* probability of behavior occurring again
- Presenting unpleasant stimulus
- Removing desirable stimulus

Copyright © Allyn & Bacon 2003

Using Habituation to Study Infants

Habituation phase

Immediate test phase

Delayed test phase

(a) Novelty Preference
(Recovery to a new stimulus)
Assesses Recent Memory

(b) Familiarity Preference
(Recovery to the familiar stimulus)
Assesses Remote Memory

Copyright © Allyn & Bacon 2003

Imitation

- Imitation is a powerful method of learning.
- It is more difficult to induce in babies 2 to 3 months old than right after birth.
- Andrew Meltzoff: newborns imitate as much as older children and adults do.
- Mirror neurons enable us to observe another person's behavior while simulating that behavior in our own brain.
- Meltzoff's theory of newborn imitation as a voluntary capacity is controversial.

Copyright © Allyn & Bacon 2003

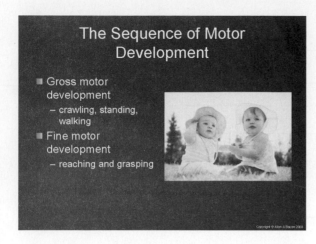

The Sequence of Motor Development

- Gross motor development
  - crawling, standing, walking
- Fine motor development
  - reaching and grasping

Copyright © Allyn & Bacon 2008

Gross and Motor Development in the First Two Years

MOTOR SKILL	AVERAGE AGE ACHIEVED	AGE RANGE IN WHICH 90 PERCENT OF INFANTS ACHIEVE THE SKILL
When held upright, holds head erect and steady	6 weeks	3 weeks–4 months
When prone, lifts self by arms	2 months	3 weeks–4 months
Rolls from side to back	2 months	3 weeks–5 months
Grasps cube	3 months, 3 weeks	2–7 months
Rolls from back to side	4½ months	2–7 months
Sits alone	7 months	5–9 months
Crawls	7 months	5–11 months
Pulls to stand	8 months	5–12 months
Plays pat-a-cake	9 months, 3 weeks	7–15 months
Stands alone	11 months	9–16 months
Walks alone	11 months, 3 weeks	9–17 months
Builds tower of two cubes	11 months, 3 weeks	10–19 months
Scribbles vigorously	14 months	10–21 months
Walks up stairs with help	16 months	12–23 months
Jumps in place	23 months, 2 weeks	17–30 months
Walks on tiptoe	25 months	16–30 months

n 2008

Motor Skills as Dynamic Systems

- Increasingly complex *systems* of action with each skill
- 4 factors in each new skill:
  1. CNS development
  2. Body's movement capacity
  3. Child's goals
  4. Environmental supports

Copyright © Allyn & Bacon 2008

Steps in Reaching and Grasping

- Prereaching
- Reaching
  - With two hands, then one
- Ulnar Grasp
  - Adjust grip to object
  - Move objects from hand to hand
- Pincer Grasp

_____

_____

_____

_____

_____

_____

_____

Keeping Infants and Toddlers Safe

- Provide safe toys
- Child-proof all rooms
- Continuously monitor the infant or toddler
- Use a car seat, following government regulations
- Report any unsafe toys and equipment

_____

_____

_____

_____

_____

_____

Bowel and Bladder Control

- Toilet training is best delayed until the months following the second birthday.
- Effective training techniques include:
  - establishing regular toileting routines
  - using gentle encouragement
  - praising children for their effort

_____

_____

_____

_____

_____

_____

Developments in Hearing

4 – 7 months	Sense of musical phrasing
6- 8 months	"Screen out" sounds from non-native languages
7 – 9 months	Divide the speech stream into word-like units
10 months	Can detect words that start with weak syllables

Copyright © Allyn & Bacon 2008

Improvements in Vision

Brain development helps infants reach adult levels of vision skills:
- 2–4 months: focus and color vision
- 6 months: acuity, scanning & tracking
- 6–7 months: depth perception

Copyright © Allyn & Bacon 2008

Steps in Depth Perception

Birth – 1 month	Sensitivity to motion cues.
2 – 3 months	Sensitivity to binocular cues.
6 –7 months	Sensitivity to pictorial cues. Wariness of heights.

Copyright © Allyn & Bacon 2008

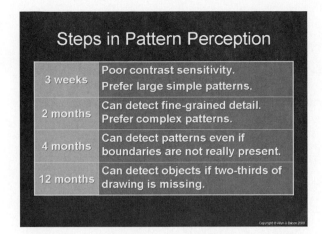

Steps in Pattern Perception

3 weeks	Poor contrast sensitivity. Prefer large simple patterns.
2 months	Can detect fine-grained detail. Prefer complex patterns.
4 months	Can detect patterns even if boundaries are not really present.
12 months	Can detect objects if two-thirds of drawing is missing.

Appearance of Checkerboards to Very Young Infants

Bold checkerboard   Complex checkerboard

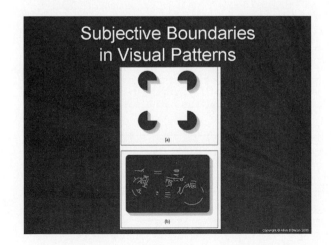

Subjective Boundaries in Visual Patterns

(a)

(b)

419

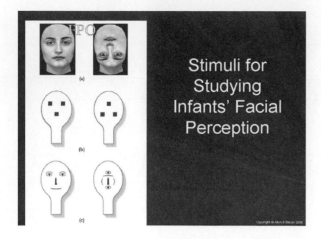

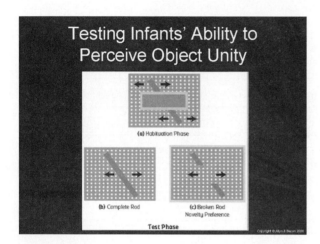

Differentiation Theory of Infant Perception

■ Infants actively search for *invariant*, unchanging features of the environment.
   − Borders of stimuli, faces

■ They note stable relationships between features.
   − Complex visual patterns, *intermodal* relationships

■ Perception gets more and more sensitive—*differentiation*

■ Acting on the environment helps this process—*affordances*

Copyright © Allyn & Bacon 2006

CHAPTER 6
COGNITIVE DEVELOPMENT
IN INFANCY AND TODDLERHOOD

CHAPTER-AT-A-GLANCE

Chapter Outline	Instruction Ideas	Supplements
Piaget's Cognitive-Developmental Theory pp. 208–219 Piaget's Ideas about Cognitive Change • The Sensorimotor Stage • Follow-Up Research on Infant Cognitive Development • Evaluation of the Sensorimotor Stage	Learning Objectives 6.1– 6.4 Learning Activities 6.1–6.2 Ask Yourself p. 219	Transparencies 67–69 Test Bank Items 1–42, 124–125, 132 Please contact your Allyn and Bacon publisher's representative for a wide range of video offerings available to adopters.
Information Processing pp. 220–226 Structure of the Information-Processing System • Attention • Memory • Categorization • Evaluation of Information-Processing Findings	Learning Objectives 6.5–6.6 Learning Activities 6.3–6.4	Transparencies 70–72 Test Bank Items 43–58, 126–127, 133–134
The Social Context of Early Cognitive Development pp. 227-228	Learning Objective 6.7 Lecture Enhancement 6.1 Ask Yourself p. 228	Test Bank Items 59–64, 128–129, 135
Individual Differences in Early Mental Development pp. 228–236 Infant Intelligence Tests • Early Environment and Mental Development • Early Intervention for At-Risk Infants and Toddlers	Learning Objectives 6.8–6.9 Lecture Enhancement 6.2 Learning Activity 6.5 Ask Yourself p. 236	Transparency 74 Test Bank Items 65–89, 136
Language Development pp. 236–247 Three Theories of Language Development • Getting Ready to Talk • First Words • The Two-Word Utterance Phase • Comprehension versus Production • Individual and Cultural Differences • Supporting Early Language Development	Learning Objectives 6.10–6.14 Lecture Enhancements 6.3–6.4 Learning Activities 6.6–6.8 Ask Yourself p. 247	Transparency 75 Test Bank Items 90–123, 130–131, 137–138

BRIEF CHAPTER SUMMARY

According to Piaget, from earliest infancy, children actively build psychological structures, or schemes, as they manipulate and explore their world. The vast changes that take place in Piaget's sensorimotor stage are divided into six substages. By acting on the world, infants make strides in intentional behavior, mastery of object permanence, and physical reasoning. In the final substage, they transfer their action-based schemes to a mental level, and representation appears.

Alternative explanations for babies' amazing cognitive accomplishments include the core knowledge perspective, which holds that babies are born with a set of innate knowledge systems, or core domains of thought—"prewired" understandings that permit a ready grasp of new, related information and therefore support early, rapid development. However, this approach has not offered greater clarity than Piaget's theory on how biology and environment jointly produce cognitive change.

Research findings have yielded broad agreement that many cognitive changes of infancy are gradual and continuous, not abrupt and stagelike, and that various aspects of infant cognition change unevenly. These ideas form the basis for another major approach to cognitive development—information processing, which focuses on the development of mental strategies for storing and interpreting information. With age, infants' attention becomes more efficient and flexible, and memory improves and is supported by a capacity for mental representation. Findings on infant categorization indicate that young babies structure experience in adultlike ways.

Vygotsky's sociocultural theory emphasizes that cognitive development is socially mediated as adults help infants and toddlers master challenging tasks. More specifically, skilled partners aid the child in carrying out tasks within their zone of proximal development.

A variety of infant intelligence tests have been devised to measure individual differences in early mental development. Most predict later performance poorly, but tests that focus on speed of habituation and recovery to visual stimuli and on object permanence are better predictors because they assess factors, such as memory and quickness and flexibility of thinking, that underlie intelligent behavior at any age. Other powerful influences on intellectual progress are the home environment, child care, and early intervention for at-risk infants and toddlers.

Behaviorist and nativist theories provide sharply contrasting accounts of language development. The interactionist view emphasizes that innate abilities and environmental influences combine to produce children's extraordinary language achievements. During the first year, infants prepare for language in many ways. First words appear around 12 months, two-word utterances between 18 and 24 months. Substantial individual differences exist in rate and style of early language progress. Conversational give-and-take and the use of child-directed speech (a simplified form of parental language) support infants' and toddlers' efforts to become competent speakers.

LEARNING OBJECTIVES

After reading this chapter, you should be able to:

6.1   Describe Piaget's view of development, noting how schemes change over the course of development. (pp. 208–209)

6.2   Describe the major cognitive achievements of Piaget's sensorimotor stage. (pp. 209–212)

6.3   Discuss follow-up research on sensorimotor development and its implications for the accuracy of Piaget's theory. (pp. 212–216)

6.4   Describe the alternate views of cognitive development, including the core knowledge perspective. (pp. 216–219)

6.5   Describe the general structure of the information-processing system, explain how this approach differs from Piaget's perspective, and review the strengths and limitations of the information-processing theory of cognitive development. (pp. 220–221)

6.6   Discuss changes in attention, memory, and categorization that take place over the first two years. (pp. 221–226)

6.7   Explain how Vygotsky's concept of the zone of proximal development expands our understanding of early cognitive development. (pp. 227–228)

6.8   Describe the mental testing approach, the meaning of intelligence test scores, and the extent to which infant tests predict later performance. (pp. 228–231)

6.9   Discuss environmental influences on early mental development, including home, child care, and early interventions for at-risk infants and toddlers. (pp. 231–235)

6.10 Describe three theories of language development, indicating the emphasis each places on innate and environmental influences. (pp. 236–240)

6.11 Describe major milestones of language development in the first two years, individual differences, and ways adults can support infants' and toddlers' emerging capacities. (pp. 240–242)

6.12 Describe the characteristics of infants' first words and two-word phrases, and explain why language comprehension develops ahead of language production. (pp. 242–243)

6.13 Describe individual and cultural differences in early language development, including factors that influence these differences. (p. 244)

6.14 Explain how child-directed speech and conversation support early language development. (pp. 244–246)

LECTURE OUTLINE

I.   PIAGET'S COGNITIVE-DEVELOPMENTAL THEORY (pp. 208–219)
  A. Piaget believed children move through four stages of development between infancy and adolescence, during which all aspects of cognition develop in an integrated fashion.
  B. During Piaget's first stage, the **sensorimotor stage,** infants and toddlers in the first two years of life "think" with their eyes, ears, hands, and other sensorimotor equipment but cannot yet carry out many activities inside their heads.
  C. Piaget's Ideas about Cognitive Change (pp. 208–209)
    1. Piaget believed a child's **schemes,** or organized ways of making sense of experience, change with age, progressing from sensorimotor action patterns to deliberate, creative actions as a result of adaptation and organization.
    2. Adaptation (p. 208)
      a. **Adaptation** involves building schemes through direct interaction with the environment.
        (1) **Assimilation** is the aspect of adaptation in which the external world is interpreted through existing schemes.
        (2) **Accommodation** is the aspect of adaptation in which new schemes are created or old ones adjusted to produce a better fit with the environment.
      b. When children are not changing very much and they are in a steady, comfortable cognitive state, they use assimilation more than accommodation, a state Piaget called cognitive *equilibrium.*
      c. During rapid cognitive change, children are in a state of *disequilibrium,* or cognitive discomfort, and make use of accommodation more than assimilation.
      d. Back-and-forth movement between equilibrium and disequilibrium leads to the development of more effective schemes.
    3. Organization (pp. 208–209)
      a. **Organization** is an internal process of rearranging and linking together schemes to form an interconnected cognitive system.
      b. Schemes reach a true state of equilibrium when they become part of a broad network of structures that can be jointly applied to the surrounding world.
  D. The Sensorimotor Stage (pp. 209–212)
    1. Piaget, basing his ideas about the sensorimotor stage on observations of his own children, divided the stage into six substages.
    2. The **circular reaction** is the means by which infants explore the environment and build schemes by trying to repeat chance events caused by their own motor activity.
      a. The reaction is first centered on the infant's own body.
      b. Subsequently, the baby shifts to manipulating objects, and then, in the second year, to producing novel effects in the environment.

423

3.   Repeating Chance Behaviors (p. 210)
   a.   Piaget saw newborn reflexes as the building blocks of sensorimotor intelligence.
   b.   Substage 1: Babies suck, grasp, and look in much the same way, no matter what the circumstances.
   c.   Substage 2: Around 1 month, babies start to gain voluntary control over their actions through the *primary circular reaction,* by repeating chance behaviors motivated by basic needs. They develop some simple motor habits and begin to vary their behavior in response to environmental demands.
   d.   Substage 3: From 4 to 8 months, infants sit up and become skilled at reaching for and manipulating objects—motor achievements that encourage them to turn their attention outward toward the environment. Using the *secondary circular reaction,* babies try to repeat interesting events caused by their own actions, but they cannot yet initiate novel behaviors.
4.   Intentional Behavior (pp. 210–211)
   a.   Substage 4: From 8 to 12 months, babies combine schemes into new, more complex action sequences.
      (1)   They are able to engage in **intentional,** or **goal-directed, behavior,** deliberately coordinating schemes to solve simple problems such as Piaget's object-hiding task, in which infants must coordinate two schemes (pushing aside the obstacle and then grasping the toy) to find the hidden object.
      (2)   Piaget regarded these *means–end action sequences* as the foundation for all later problem solving.
      (3)   Retrieving hidden objects shows mastery of **object permanence,** the understanding that objects continue to exist when they are out of sight
      (4)   However, babies in this substage still make the **A-not-B search error,** looking for an object in hiding place A after it has been moved to hiding place B—evidence that they do not yet have a clear image of the object as persisting when they cannot see it.
      (5)   Infants of Substage 4 sometimes use their capacity for intentional behavior to try to change events—for example, trying to stir with a spoon or push a toy car after seeing someone else do this.
   b.   Substage 5: From 12 to 18 months, the *tertiary circular reaction* emerges as toddlers repeat behaviors with variation.
      (1)   Because they approach the world in this deliberately exploratory way, 12- to 18-month-olds become better problem solvers.
      (2)   Experimentation leads to a more advanced understanding of object permanence, so that toddlers no longer make the A-not-B search error.
5.   Mental Representation (pp. 211–212)
   a.   Substage 6: This substage, from 18 to 24 months, brings the ability to create **mental representations**—internal depictions of information that the mind can manipulate.
      (1)   The most powerful mental representations are *images* and *concepts.*
      (2)   Toddlers now arrive at solutions suddenly instead of through trial-and-error behavior, indicating that they are experimenting with actions inside their heads.
      (3)   Representation enables older toddlers to solve object permanence problems involving *invisible displacement* (when a toy is moved while out of sight) and also permits **deferred imitation**—the ability to remember and copy the behavior of models who are not present.
      (4)   Representation also makes possible **make-believe play,** in which children act out everyday and imaginary activities.
E.   Follow-Up Research on Infant Cognitive Development (pp. 212–216)
   1.   Many studies suggest that infants display a wide array of understandings earlier than Piaget believed.
   2.   A major method used to find out what infants know about hidden objects and other aspects of physical reality capitalizes on habituation/recovery.
      a.   Researchers often use a **violation-of-expectation method,** in which they *habituate* babies to a physical event and then determine whether infants *recover* responsiveness to an *expected event* or an *unexpected event.*

       b.   Recovery to an unexpected event (a variation that violates physical laws) suggests that the infant is aware of that aspect of the physical world and is "surprised" by a deviation from it.

       c.   Some researchers claim that the violation-of-expectation method indicates limited awareness of physical events, not the conscious understanding that was Piaget's focus, while others believe that the method reveals only babies' perceptual preference for novelty, not their understanding of experience.

   3.   Object Permanence (pp. 212–213)

       a.   Research by Renée Baillargeon and her collaborators indicates that babies as young as 2½ to 3½ months of age understand object permanence; other violation-of-expectation studies have yielded similar results.

       b.   Although young infants have some notion of object permanence, searching for hidden objects is a true cognitive advance, as Piaget suggested, because babies solve some object-hiding tasks before others.

       c.   By 14 months, toddlers understand that objects continue to exist in their hidden locations even after the infants have left the location.

   4.   Searching for Objects Hidden in More than One Location (pp. 213–214)

       a.   Recent findings reveal that poor memory cannot fully account for infants' unsuccessful performance on the A-not-B task.

       b.   Mastery of object permanence is a gradual achievement, and success at simple object search and A–B search tasks coincides with rapid development of the frontal lobes of the cerebral cortex, along with experiences perceiving, acting on, and remembering objects.

   5.   Mental Representation (pp. 214–216)

       a.   Piaget viewed infants as leading purely sensorimotor lives, unable to represent experience until about 18 months of age.

       b.   But research reveals that babies do construct mental representations of objects and their whereabouts, and that representational thought is evident earlier than Piaget believed.

       c.   Deferred Imitation (pp. 214–215)

           (1)   Research reveals that 6-week-old infants demonstrate deferred imitation of facial expressions.

           (2)   Between 12 and 18 months, toddlers use deferred imitation skillfully to enrich their range of schemes, copying the actions of peers and adults and imitating actions across a change in context.

       d.   Problem Solving (pp. 215–216)

           (1)   Around 7 to 8 months, infants develop intentional means–end action sequences, which they use to solve simple problems.

           (2)   By 10 to 12 months, babies can *solve problems by analogy*—an ability that increases with age.

           (3)   Even in the first year, infants have some ability to move beyond trial-and-error experimentation, represent a solution mentally, and use it in new contexts.

F.   Evaluation of the Sensorimotor Stage (pp. 216–219)

   1.   Some capacities, such as first signs of object permanence and deferred imitation, emerge much earlier than Piaget believed, while others develop within Piaget's time frame.

   2.   In contrast to Piaget's ideas, infants appear to develop in a gradual, continuous manner, not in a neat, stepwise fashion.

   3.   Consistent with Piaget's views, sensorimotor action helps infants construct some forms of knowledge. But evidence suggests that infants comprehend a great deal before they are capable of the motor behaviors that Piaget assumed were necessary for leading to these understandings.

   4.   Alternative Explanations (pp. 216–217, 218)

       a.   Most researchers now believe that young babies have some built-in cognitive equipment, but intense disagreement exists over the extent of infants' initial understanding.

       b.   Some researchers argue that babies' cognitive starting point is limited.

      c.   Others believe that infants begin with impressive understandings. In this **core knowledge perspective**—the view that babies are born with a set of innate knowledge systems, or *core domains of thought,* permitting a ready grasp of new, related information and supporting rapid development.

         (1) Findings suggest that infants demonstrate *physical knowledge,* including object permanence, object solidity, and gravity, to some extent, in the first few months.

         (2) Researchers have investigated infants' *numerical knowledge,* or ability to distinguish small quantities.

         (3) Core knowledge theorists assume that *linguistic knowledge* is innate.

         (4) Infants' early orientation toward people initiates swift development of *psychological knowledge.*

         (5) Although the core knowledge perspective emphasizes native endowment, it acknowledges that experience is essential for children to extend this initial knowledge.

         (6) So far, studies of young infants' knowledge have yielded mixed results.

    5. Piaget's Legacy (pp. 217, 219)

      a.   Follow-up research on Piaget's sensorimotor stage yields agreement on two issues:

         (1) Many cognitive changes of infancy are gradual and continuous, rather than abrupt and stagelike.

         (2) Rather than developing together, various aspects of infant cognition change unevenly because of the challenges posed by different types of tasks and infants' varying experiences with them.

      b.   These ideas serve as the basis for the *information-processing* approach to cognitive development.

      c.   Piaget's work inspired a wealth of research on infant cognition.

      d.   Piaget's observations have been of great practical value, particularly for teachers and caregivers.

II.   INFORMATION PROCESSING (pp. 220–226)

    A. Information processing focuses on many different aspects of thinking, from attention, memory, and categorization skills to complex problem solving.

    B. Structure of the Information-Processing System (pp. 220–221)

      1. Information-processing researchers assume that we hold information in three parts of the mental system for processing: the *sensory register; working,* or *short-term, memory;* and *long-term memory.*

      2. **Mental strategies** operate on and transform information as it flows through the system, increasing the efficiency of thinking and the likelihood that information will be retained.

      3. Information first enters the **sensory register,** where sights and sounds are stored briefly before they decay or are transferred to short-term memory.

      4. In **working,** or **short-term, memory,** we actively applying mental strategies, "working" on information to ensure that it will be retained.

      5. A special part of working memory, the **central executive,** directs the flow of information; this is the conscious, reflective part of our mental system.

      6. **Long-term memory** is the third and largest storage area for information—our permanent, unlimited knowledge base.

      7. Categorization of information in long-term memory aids *retrieval* from long-term memory.

      8. The *capacity* of the mental system—the amount of information that can be processed at once and the speed with which it can be processed—expands with age as a result of brain development and improvements in strategies.

    C. Attention (pp. 221–222)

      1. Infants gradually become more efficient at managing their attention, taking information in more quickly with age.

      2. Research reveals that preterm and newborn infants need more time to habituate and recover to novel stimuli.

      3. By 4 months, infants' attention becomes more flexible, and they are better able to disengage or shift attention from one stimulus to another.

4. Sustained attention improves with the transition to toddlerhood and increasing capacity for intentional behavior.

5. Adults can foster sustained attention through joint attention, which is important for language development.

D. Memory (pp. 222–223, 224–225)

1. Operant Conditioning Research (pp. 222–223)

a. Researchers use operant conditioning to study infant memory by teaching 2- to 6-month-olds to move a mobile by kicking a foot tied to it with a long cord and observing how long babies remember how to activate the mobile.

b. Duration of memory for operant responses rises over the first 18 months, but even 2- to 6-month-olds need only a brief prompt to reinstate the memory.

c. At first, memory is *context-dependent,* and infants remember poorly when tested in a new situation, but after 9 months, the importance of context declines.

2. Habituation/Recovery Research (p. 223)

a. Infants learn and retain much information simply by watching objects and events, without being physically active—sometimes for longer time spans than in operant conditioning studies.

b. Babies are especially attentive to the movements of objects and people.

c. Although infants need not be physically active to acquire new information, research indicates that motor activity, such as crawling to find a hidden object, does promote some aspects of learning and memory.

3. Recall Memory (p. 223, 224–225)

a. **Recognition**, which involves noticing whether a stimulus is identical or similar to one previously experienced, is the simplest form of memory.

b. By the end of the first year, babies can also engage in **recall**, a more complex type of memory, which involves remembering a stimulus without perceptual support, by generating a mental image of the past experience.

c. Long-term recall depends on connections among multiple regions of the cerebral cortex—neural circuits that develop rapidly in the second year.

4. **Infantile amnesia** describes the inability of most people to retrieve events that happened to them before age 3, despite the remarkable memory skills of infants and toddlers.

5. Both biology and social experience contribute to the decline of infantile amnesia and the development of **autobiographical memory**—recollections of significant one-time events that are imbued with personal meaning.

E. Categorization (pp. 224–226)

1. Evidence indicates that even very young infants organize their physical, emotional, and social worlds by categorizing similar objects and events into a single representation.

2. The earliest categories are *perceptual*—based on shape, size, and other physical properties and, starting at 6 months of age, on the basis of two correlated features such as shape and color.

3. By the second half of the first year, more categories are *conceptual*—based on common function and behavior.

4. In the second year, children actively categorize items during their play.

5. Exploration of objects and expanding knowledge of the world contribute to older infants' capacity to move beyond physical features and group objects by their functions and behaviors.

6. Language both builds on and facilitates categorization; variations among languages lead to cultural differences in conceptual development.

F. Evaluation of Information-Processing Findings (p. 226)

1. Information-processing research underscores the continuity of thinking from infancy into adulthood and has contributed greatly to our view of infants and toddlers as sophisticated cognitive beings.

2. One drawback to this approach is that, whereas its greatest strength is in separating the different components of cognition (perception, attention, memory), it has difficulty putting these components back together into a broad, comprehensive theory of cognitive development.

3. Recent theorists have attempted to overcome this weakness by combining Piaget's theory with the information-processing approach or applying a *dynamic systems view* to early cognition.

III. THE SOCIAL CONTEXT OF EARLY COGNITIVE DEVELOPMENT (pp. 227–228, 229)
    A. Vygotsky believed that complex mental activities originate in social interaction.
    B. Vygotsky's concept of the **zone of proximal development** refers to a range of tasks that a child cannot yet handle alone but can do with the help of more skilled partners.
    C. Research indicates that adult guidance and support within the zone of proximal development, a form of teaching known as *scaffolding,* promotes learning at all ages.
    D. Cultural variations in social experiences affect mental strategies as early as the first year.

IV. INDIVIDUAL DIFFERENCES IN EARLY MENTAL DEVELOPMENT (pp. 228, 230–236)
    A. Whereas cognitive theories try to explain the *process of development,* mental tests measure cognitive *products* reflecting mental development, with the aim of *predicting* future performance.
    B. Infant Intelligence Tests (pp. 228, 230)
        1. Most infant tests emphasize perceptual and motor responses, and some newer tests also tap early language, cognition, and social behavior.
        2. The Bayley Scales of Infant Development is a commonly used test suitable for children between 1 month and 3½ years. It has three main subsets:
           a. The Cognitive Scale includes such items as attention to familiar and unfamiliar objects, looking for a fallen object, and pretend play.
           b. The Language Scale taps understanding and expressions of language, including recognition of objects and people.
           c. The Motor Scale assesses gross and fine motor skills, such as grasping, sitting, stacking blocks, and climbing stairs.
        3. Computing Intelligence Test Scores (p. 230)
           a. Intelligence tests are scored by computing an **intelligence quotient (IQ),** which indicates the extent to which the raw score deviates from the typical performance of same-age individuals.
           b. In constructing a test, designers engage in **standardization**—giving the test to a large, representative sample and using the results as a *standard* for interpreting scores.
           c. Within the standardization sample, performances at each age level form a **normal distribution,** with most scores clustering around the mean in a *bell-shaped distribution* that results whenever researchers measure individual differences in large samples.
        4. Predicting Later Performance from Infant Tests (pp. 230–231)
           a. Despite careful construction, most infant tests are poor predictors of later intelligence.
           b. Longitudinal research reveals that the majority of children show substantial fluctuations in IQ between toddlerhood and adolescence—typically 10 to 20 points or more.
           c. Infant test scores may not accurately reflect abilities because the babies are likely to become distracted, tired, or bored during test administration, and because infant test items differ from the tasks given to older children.
           d. Reflecting these concerns, infant test scores are conservatively labeled **developmental quotients (DQs),** rather than IQs.
           e. Infant test scores are somewhat better at making long-term prediction for extremely low-scoring babies, and are used largely for *screening* of such babies for further observation and intervention.
           f. Information-processing measures like the habituation–recovery sequence, as well as Piagetian object permanence tasks, predict later IQ more effectively than traditional infant measures.
    C. Early Environment and Mental Development (pp. 231–233)
        1. Home Environment (pp. 231–232)
           a. The **Home Observation for Measurement of the Environment (HOME)** is a checklist for gathering information about the quality of children's home lives through observation and parental interviews.
           b. An organized, stimulating physical setting and parental encouragement, involvement, and affection repeatedly predict infant and early childhood IQ, regardless of SES and ethnicity.

      c.   Although genetically more intelligent parents may provide a better home environment and also have more intelligent children, heredity does not account for all of the correlation between HOME and mental test scores; family living conditions contribute substantially.

   2.   Infant and Toddler Child Care (pp. 232–233)

      a.   Today, over 60 percent of North American mothers with a child under age 2 are employed, and child care for infants and toddlers has become common.

      b.   Quality of child care has an impact on children's mental development and social skills.

      c.   Good child care can reduce the negative impact of a stressed, poverty-stricken home life, and it sustains the benefits of growing up in an economically advantaged family.

      d.   **Developmentally appropriate practice** is a set of standards specifying program characteristics that meet the developmental and individual needs of young children of varying ages, based on current research and consensus of experts.

      e.   Child care in the United States and Canada is affected by a macrosystem of individualistic values and weak government regulation and funding.

      f.   High-quality child care is a cost-effective means of protecting children's well-being, and can serve as effective early intervention for children whose development is at risk.

  D. Early Intervention for At-Risk Infants and Toddlers (pp. 233–236)

   1.   Children living in poverty are likely to show gradual declines in intelligence test scores and to achieve poorly when they reach school age, largely as a result of living in disorganized, stressful home environments that undermine their ability to learn.

   2.   Children who participate in both center-based and home-based interventions show gains in cognitive and academic performance; the earlier intervention begins, the longer it lasts, and the greater its scope and intensity, the better participants' performance is throughout childhood and adolescence.

   3.   The Carolina Abecedarian Project is a center-based intervention that demonstrates the benefits of continuous, high-quality enrichment from infancy through the preschool years.

   4.   Recognition of the benefits of early intervention has led the U.S. Congress to provide limited funding for intervention services for at-risk infants and toddlers. An evaluation of Early Head Start in the United States shows that intervention led to warmer, more stimulating parenting, gains in cognitive and language development, and lessening of child aggression.

V. LANGUAGE DEVELOPMENT (pp. 236–247)

  A. Young children typically say their first word at around 12 months of age and combine two words between 1½ and 2 years; by age 6, children are skilled conversationalists with a vocabulary of about 10,000 words.

  B. Three Theories of Language Development (pp. 236–240)

   1.   The Behaviorist Perspective (p. 237)

      a.   This perspective regards language development as entirely due to environmental influences.

      b.   In this view, language is acquired through *operant conditioning,* as parents reinforce the sounds their baby makes that are most like words.

      c.   Some behaviorists believe that *imitation* combines with reinforcement to promote language development.

   2.   The Nativist Perspective (pp. 237–239)

      a.   This view assumes that children are born with an innate system for acquiring language, the **language acquisition device (LAD),** which contains a *universal grammar,* or set of rules common to all languages.

      b.   Linguist Noam Chomsky maintained that the LAD allows children to speak in a rule-oriented way from the beginning.

      c.   Children all over the world tend to master language milestones in a similar sequence—evidence that fits with a biologically based view of language development.

      d.   Studies with chimpanzees show that they can master only a basic vocabulary and do not acquire complex grammatical forms—findings consistent with Chomsky's view that humans are uniquely prepared for language.

  e. Language Areas in the Brain (pp. 237–238)

   (1) For most people, language is housed in the left hemisphere of the cerebral cortex, where there are two important language-related structures.

   (2) **Broca's area,** located in the left frontal lobe, supports grammatical processing and language production.

   (3) **Wernicke's area,** located in the left temporal lobe, plays a role in comprehending word meaning.

   (4) PET and fMRI brain-imaging research suggests complex relationships between language functions and brain structures.

   (5) Rather than the brain being innately programmed for language, language-learning experiences seem to lead certain brain areas to become dedicated to language.

  f. A Sensitive Period for Language Development (pp. 238–239)

   (1) Evidence for a sensitive period that coincides with brain lateralization would support the view that language development has unique biological properties.

   (2) To test this idea, researchers have examined the language competence of deaf adults who acquired their first language, American Sign Language (ASL), at different ages, and have found evidence that childhood is a sensitive period for language learning.

   (3) In studies of second-language learners, ERP and fMRI measures of brain activity indicate that second-language processing is less lateralized in older than in younger learners, and that the capacity to acquire a second language declines in gradual, continuous fashion, not abruptly.

 3. Limitations of the Nativist Perspective (p. 239)

  a. Researchers have had difficulty identifying the single system of grammar believed to underlie all languages.

  b. Research indicates that language acquisition occurs gradually, which does not fit with Chomsky's idea that grammatical knowledge is innately determined.

 4. The Interactionist Perspective (pp. 239–240)

  a. This view emphasizes that language achievements emerge through the *interactions* between inner capacities and environmental influences.

  b. One type of interactionist theory is based on *information processing;* a second type emphasizes *social interaction.*

  c. Much support exists for the central premise of the social interactionist view, that children's social competencies and language experiences greatly influence their language progress.

C. Getting Ready to Talk (pp. 240–242)

 1. Cooing and Babbling (pp. 240–241)

  a. Around 2 months, babies make vowel-like noises called **cooing.**

  b. At about 6 months, infants begin **babbling**—combining consonants with vowels in long strings.

  c. Babies must hear human speech for babbling to develop further.

  d. As adults interact with infants and the infants listen to spoken language, babbling increases.

  e. Deaf infants exposed to sign language from birth babble with their hands much as hearing infants do through speech.

 2. Becoming a Communicator (pp. 241–242)

  a. By 3 to 4 months, infants start to gaze in the same general direction as adults are looking.

  b. Around 10 to 11 months, babies become sensitive to adults' precise direction of gaze.

  c. Experiencing this **joint attention** contributes greatly to early language development.

  d. Around 4 to 6 months, caregivers' interactions with babies begin to include *give-and-take,* as in pat-a-cake and peekaboo games.

  e. By 12 months, babies participate actively in these games, practicing the turn-taking pattern of human conversation—a vital context for acquiring communication skills.

  f. At the end of the first year, infants use *preverbal gestures* to attract adults' attention and interest and to influence their behavior.

D. First Words (p. 242)
1. Children's first spoken words, around 1 year, usually refer to important people, objects that move, familiar actions, or outcomes of familiar actions.
2. Children seem to be motivated to acquire words that are relevant to the particular cognitive problems they are working on at the moment.
3. Emotion also influences early word learning.
4. Young children sometimes apply words to narrowly, an error called **underextension.**
5. A more common error is **overextension,** which occurs when a word is applied to a wider collection of objects and events than is appropriate.

E. The Two-Word Utterance Phase (pp. 242–243)
1. Young toddlers add to their vocabularies slowly, at a rate of one to three words a week. Between 18 and 24 months, a *spurt in vocabulary* often occurs, with children adding from 10 to 20 new words a week.
2. An improved ability to categorize experience, recall words, and pick up on social cues, including others' intentions, supports a spurt in vocabulary growth in the second half of the second year.
3. **Telegraphic speech** refers to the two-word utterances of toddlers, which leave out smaller and less important words.
4. Many early word combinations do not follow adult grammatical rules.

F. Comprehension versus Production (p. 243)
1. Language **production** refers to the words and word combinations that children use, while **comprehension** refers to the language they understand, which develops ahead of production at all ages.
2. Comprehension only necessitates recognition of word meaning, whereas production requires active recall of the word and its meaning.

G. Individual and Cultural Differences (p. 244)
1. Many studies show that girls are slightly ahead of boys in early vocabulary growth. Temperament and life circumstances also play a role.
2. Toddlers with a **referential style** of early language learning primarily use language to label objects.
3. Those with an **expressive style** use language primarily to talk about their own feelings and needs and those of other people, producing social formulas and pronouns such as "Stop it" or "Thank you."
4. Referential-style children's vocabularies grow faster than those of expressive-style children because all languages contain more object labels than social phrases.
5. Both biological and environmental factors influence a toddler's choice of a particular language style.
6. A problem with language development may exist if a child is greatly delayed when compared to language norms, cannot follow simple directions, or has problems putting thoughts into words.

H. Supporting Early Language Development (pp. 244–247)
1. Caregivers can consciously support early language learning through a special style of speech known as **child-directed speech (CDS),** consisting of short sentences with high-pitched, exaggerated expression and very clear pronunciation.
2. From birth on, children prefer CDS to other kinds of adult talk, and the use of CDS supports early language development.
3. Conversational give-and-take between parent and toddler strongly predicts early language development and later academic success.
4. CDS and parent–child conversations create a *zone of proximal development* in which children's language expands.

LECTURE ENHANCEMENTS

LECTURE ENHANCEMENT 6.1
The Social Context of Early Cognitive Development: Do Cultural Beliefs about Make-Believe Play Matter?
(pp. 227–228)

Time: 5–10 minutes

Objective: To examine cross-cultural differences in beliefs about make-believe play.

As noted in the text, make-believe play not only reflects but also contributes to children's cognitive and emotional/social development. At the same time, the nature of play varies considerably across cultures. Furthermore, although the majority of North American parents acknowledge the importance of play, not all cultures value children's make-believe.

To examine cross-cultural beliefs about play, Parmar, Harkness, and Super (2004) recruited 24 Caucasian-American parents and 24 Asian parents from China, Korea, Pakistan, Nepal, and India. Their children ranged in age from 3 to 6 years. The researchers collected information on parents' history and background, beliefs and practices related to play and learning, and expectations and values related to child development during the preschool years. The parents were also asked to complete a weeklong daily activities checklist that focused on play and learning activities, including who was with the child, where the activities took place, and how long the activities lasted.

Results indicated that Caucasian-American parents perceived play to be important for the early development of their children. Asian parents, in contrast, believed that early exposure to academics was more important than play. Parents' beliefs about play contributed to differences in home activities. Caucasian-American parents provided their children with a greater number of toys than Asian parents. In addition, the types of toys provided were different: Asian parents provided more educational toys than Caucasian-American parents. They also spent less time in adult–child play.

These findings illustrate how cultural beliefs about child development influence child-rearing behaviors. As discussed throughout the text, it is critical for researchers to consider cultural experiences when assessing and drawing conclusion about child development. Evaluating children from different backgrounds and cultures on the basis of cultural majority beliefs and values can be very misleading.

Ask students from minority backgrounds to describe their parents' views on early childhood play and to recall how much time they spent playing with their parents as young children. With the class, discuss cultural values and family conditions that might influence parental attitudes and children's play experiences.

Parmar, P., Harkness, S., & Super, C. M. (2004). Asian and Euro-American parents' ethnotheories of play and learning: Effects on preschool children's home routines and school behavior. *International Journal of Behavioral Development, 28*, 97–104.

LECTURE ENHANCEMENT 6.2
More on Early Intervention for At-Risk Infants and Toddlers (pp. 233–235)

Time: 15–20 minutes

Objective: To examine the effectiveness of Early Head Start on low-income children and their families.

Early Head Start is a comprehensive federal program that provides early intervention services to low-income pregnant women and their infants and toddlers. To examine the effectiveness of Early Head Start on children and their parents, Love and colleagues (2005) conducted a randomized trial of 3,001 families in 17 programs across the United States. Half of the participants were assigned to the Early Head Start group, and the other half were assigned to a control group. Although control group families could not participate in Early Head Start, they did have access to community resources.

To determine if Early Head Start resulted in improvements in child and parent outcomes, the researchers collected the following data at three separate intervals: 7 months, 16 months, and 24 months after enrollment / random assignment:

(1) *Child cognitive and language development.* To evaluate gains in cognitive and language development, the researchers administered two standardized assessments: the Mental Development Index and the Peabody Picture Vocabulary test, which assesses receptive vocabulary.

(2) *Child social-emotional development.* Using videotaped observations of parents and children during a semi-structured play task, the researchers rated the duration and quality of children's play with toys and the extent to which parents and children interacted during joint play. Parents were also asked to complete a questionnaire about their child's aggressive behavior.

(3) *Child health.* The researchers gathered information on child health through parent interviews. They were primarily interested in immunization records and global ratings of child health status.

(4) *Parenting.* The following measures were used to assess quality of parenting:
- The Home Observation for Measurement of the Environment (HOME) was used to assess the quality of stimulation and support in the child's home environment.
- Using videotaped observations of parents and children during a semi-structured play task, the researchers rated parent supportiveness (sensitivity, positive regard, and cognitive stimulation) and parent detachment (the degree to which parents were emotionally unavailable during play).
- Parents were asked to rate the frequency of parent-child reading: every day, once a week, once a month, or never.
- Parents were asked to rate their use of physical punishment during the previous week.

Findings revealed a number of positive outcomes for Early Head Start children and their families. Specifically, compared to the control group, Early Head Start children demonstrated greater gains in cognitive and language development and a reduction in aggressive behavior. During the semi-structured play task, Early Head Start children engaged their parents more than children in the control group, and they demonstrated greater gains in sustained attention to objects. Over the course of the study, Early Head Start parents provided more supportive and stimulating home environments than parents in the control group, and they were more likely to read to their children every day. They were also less likely to spank their children. These findings were especially strong at Early Head Start centers offering a mix of center- and home-based services. Taken together, the results of this study indicate that Early Head Start contributes to a diverse range of positive child development and parenting outcomes.

Using research from this study and the text discussion of sensitive periods in brain development (Chapter 5, pp. 173–176), ask students to explain why early intervention works best when it begins in infancy and toddlerhood. Why is it important to include parents in early intervention?

Love, J. M., Kisker, E. E., Ross, C., Raikes, H., Constantine, J., Boller, K., Brooks-Gunn, J., Chazan-Cohen, R., Turullo, L. B., Brady-Smith, C., Fuligni, A. S., Schochet, P. Z., Paulsell, D., & Vogel, C. (2005). The effectiveness of Early Head Start for 3-year-old children and their parents: Lessons for policy and programs. *Developmental Psychology, 41,* 885–901.

LECTURE ENHANCEMENT 6.3
More on the Importance of Gestures for Early Language Development (pp. 240–242)

Time: 15–20 minutes

Objective: To further examine the developmental importance of gestures for early language development.

As discussed in the text, young children use gestures long before they are able to speak. Between 9 and 12 months, babies often point at objects in their environment. Even as they develop the ability to communicate with language, toddlers continue to use gestures, as when they point to a cup and say, "Cup!" According to Iverson and Goldin-Meadow (2005), gestures permit young children to communicate meanings that may be difficult to express in words. Therefore, it is possible that gestures not only help children to learn verbal language but also predict changes in language.

To further examine the relationship between gestures and language development, Iverson and Goldin-Meadow (2005) recruited 10 children between the ages of 10 and 24 months. Each child was observed and videotaped approximately eight times during parent–child play and during snacks or at mealtime. Researchers watched the gestures and speech the children used during communication. For a child's behavior to be considered communicative, he or she had to attempt to direct the adult's attention. Communicative behavior could be a gesture, speech, or a combination of both. To ensure that gestures were being used as communicative symbols, researchers did not code acts performed on objects unless they were used to get an adult's attention. In addition, gestures could not be ritual acts, such as blowing kisses or playing games (for example, pat-a-cake). Researchers classified gestures into one of three categories:

(1) *Deictic gestures*—showing, (for example, by holding up an object so the adult can see it), index pointing, or palm pointing.
(2) *Conventional gestures*—gestures with a cultural meaning, as in nodding the head "yes" or running the hands over the hair to mean "pretty."
(3) *Ritualized reaches*—extending the arm toward an object, usually with repeated opening and closing of the palm.

Communicative vocalizations were also coded. These consisted of either English words (for example, "dog," "hot") or meaningful patterns of speech sounds (for example, "ba ba" for "bottle"). When gestures and speech were used together, researchers classified them as gesture-plus-word combinations and divided them into two categories: gestures that complemented speech (for example, a child pointed to flowers while saying "flowers") and gestures that supplemented speech (for example, a child pointed to a picture of a bird and said "nap" because the bird was sleeping).

Results indicated that children's gestures both precede and contribute to language development. Children who used gestures for certain objects (for example, pointing at a favorite toy) subsequently used words to label those objects once they were capable of speaking. In addition, the onset of gesture-plus-word combinations predicted the onset of two-word combinations, indicating that gestures do indeed facilitate early language development.

To further explain these findings, Iverson and Goldin-Meadow (2005) suggest that gestures may facilitate language development by signaling to caregivers that the child is ready for verbal input. For instance, a young child may point at her father's hat while saying, "Dada." The father, in turn, says, "Yes, that's daddy's hat," which essentially translates the child's gesture-plus-word combination into a two-word phrase. Gestures also have an important developmental function: they reduce demands on a young child's memory. Producing a word for an object requires more effort than simply pointing at the object. Similarly, combining a gesture with a word is probably less demanding than producing two words.

Using these findings and research presented in the text, ask students their reactions to a mother's refusing to acknowledge her toddler's gestures, fearing that it will delay the child's language development. For example, instead of translating the gestures into words, the mother insists that the child use verbal labels. How might the mother's approach actually impede her child's language development?

Iverson, J. M., & Goldin-Meadow, S. (2005). Gesture paves the way for language development. *Psychological Science, 16,* 367–371.

LECTURE ENHANCEMENT 6.4
Early Language Development: Mother–Child and Father–Child Interactions in Low-Income Homes (pp. 244–247)

Time: 10–15 minutes

Objective: To examine differences in mother–child and father–child interactions in low-income homes.

Many researchers agree that language development emerges within the context of adult–child interactions. However, few studies have focused on the importance of father–child interactions. Even fewer studies have investigated father–child interactions in low-income families. To extend existing research on the importance of adult–child interactions for language development, Rowe, Coker, and Pan (2004) recruited 33 father–child and mother–child dyads who were participating in an evaluation study of Early Head Start. Each father–child and mother–child pair came from the same family. All families qualified for welfare services, and their children were toddlers at the time of the study. Eighty-two percent of the fathers lived with the mother and the child.

The researchers interviewed mothers and fathers about family composition, parenting practices, child-rearing beliefs, and the family's financial and social situation. Mothers and fathers were also asked to describe how they spend time when interacting with their child (for example, preferred activities, where they go). The researchers visited each home and videotaped parent–child interactions during book reading and free play. Mother–child and father–child interactions were recorded separately. To compare differences in parent–child interactions, the researchers provided the same materials to all dyads: a book and several small bags of age-appropriate toys.

The researchers coded and analyzed parent–child interactions using the Child Language Data Exchange System (CHILDES). They were specifically interested in the following:

(1) Parent word tokens—the total number words spoken by each parent
(2) Child word tokens—the total number of words spoken by each child
(3) Parent and child word types—the diversity of vocabulary, or the number of different words used by mothers, fathers, and children
(4) Parent and child mean length of utterance (MLU)—the average utterance length for fathers, mothers, and children

Pragmatic features in parental speech were also analyzed. These included *wh*-questions (who, what, where, when, why, and how), explicit clarification requests, direct and indirect directives, and direct and indirect prohibitions. Results indicated that the mothers and fathers did not differ in amount of talk, in diversity of vocabulary, or in MLU. However, they did differ in the association between amount of talk and use of prohibitions. Mothers who talked more used fewer prohibitions, whereas fathers who talked more used more prohibitions. Regarding pragmatics, fathers produced substantially more *wh*-questions and requests for clarification than mothers. Mothers and fathers engaged in similar frequencies of both direct and indirect directives, and they also used directives more often than middle-SES parents do. Although the researchers speculated that fathers' residential status would affect the quality of father–child interactions, the only difference between residential and nonresidential fathers was in the use of prohibitions. Nonresidential fathers used more prohibitions than residential fathers.

Because *wh*-questions and requests for clarification require children to assume more communicative responsibility, it seems that fathers are more challenging communicative partners than mothers. However, the sample was relatively small, so this finding must be viewed with caution. In fact, in studies of older children, the reverse has been found. Future research might focus on longitudinal differences between mother–child and father–child speech in families from different economic backgrounds.

Rowe, M. L., Coker, D., & Pan, B. A. (2004). A comparison of fathers' and mothers' talk to toddlers in low-income families. *Social Development, 13,* 278–291.

LEARNING ACTIVITIES

LEARNING ACTIVITY 6.1
Applying Piaget's Concepts of Assimilation and Accommodation (pp. 208–209)

Piagetian concepts can be complex and challenging to grasp. Often, new ideas are best understood when they are applied to one's personal experiences. Ask students to consider their own learning in relation to Piaget's theory. For example, each semester students find themselves in a challenging state of *disequilibrium* as they enroll in new courses. They have to *accommodate* quickly, creating new *schemes* so they can make sense of new realms of knowledge (that is, course material). Once they do so, their new cognitive structures enable them to *assimilate*, or see the world in a different light, and they experience the thrill of mastery. And when students combine new concepts into *organized* wholes, their sense of equilibrium is enhanced. Under these conditions, they probably do best on exams.

Suggest that students illustrate Piaget's concepts of cognitive change through one of their own learning experiences. Then ask them to imagine themselves in the place of the young infant, for whom creating and organizing schemes are awesome tasks. The baby does not just enroll in a new course of study that is similar to ones he has taken before. Instead, many aspects of the environment are strange and mysterious, and thousands of schemes must be created, revised, and put together.

LEARNING ACTIVITY 6.2
Testing Infants for Object Permanence (pp. 212–213)

Arrange for several infants to visit your class for a demonstration of object permanence. If possible, infants should range in age from 6 to 24 months of age.

(1) *Successive Object-Hiding Task.* After attracting the baby's attention, hide a rattle or other attractive toy beneath a cup or under a cloth. See if the baby will set aside the obstacle and retrieve the object. Infants between 8 and 12 months generally succeed at this task; younger ones have difficulty.

(2) *Hiding-by-Cloth and Hiding-by-Hand Task.* Place the toy on a table or desk, next to a folded cloth. Then unfold the cloth over the toy. By 10 months, babies will usually retrieve the toy. Next, using your hand, carry the toy toward and under the cloth, and bring your hand out without the toy (leave the toy under the cloth). Not until age 14 months will most babies search for the toy. In the second, more difficult task, younger infants seem to expect the object to appear in the hand because that is where the object initially disappeared.

(3) *Successive Object-Hiding Task.* This time, set two cups on the table. Place the toy under one cup (A) and then move it beneath the other (B). Infants between 12 and 18 months of age easily find the object in the second location; younger ones frequently make the well-known A-not-B search error by looking in the first hiding place.

(4) *Invisible Object-Hiding Task.* Hide the toy in a small box, place the box under a cover, and, while out of the baby's sight, dump the toy out of the box. Then show the baby the empty box. With the capacity to represent sensorimotor actions internally, infants between 18 months and 2 years of age can solve this problem.

LEARNING ACTIVITY 6.3
True or False: Information Processing (pp. 220–226)

Present the following exercise to students as a quiz or in-class activity:

Directions: Read each of the following statements and indicate whether it is *True* (T) or *False* (F).

Statements:

_____ 1. Like Piaget, information-processing theorists are interested in general concepts, such as assimilation and accommodation, to describe how children think.

_____ 2. Information first enters the sensory register, where sights and sounds are represented directly and stored briefly.

_____ 3. The central executive is the conscious, reflective part of our mental system.

_____ 4. Research shows that even long-term memory is limited, which is why we sometimes have problems with retrieval.

_____ 5. With the transition to toddlerhood, attraction to novelty increases and sustained attention decreases.

_____ 6.   Habituation / recovery research shows that infants learn and retain a wide variety of information just by watching objects and events, without being physically active.

_____ 7. Recall is the simplest form of memory.

_____ 8. Not until 10 months can infants categorize similar objects and events into a single representation.

_____ 9. Critics argue that the information-processing perspective underscores the continuity of human thinking from infancy into adult life.

_____ 10. The central strength of information-processing research—analyzing cognition into its components, such as perception, attention, and memory—is also its greatest drawback.

Answers:

1. F
2. T
3. T
4. F
5. F
6. T
7. F
8. F
9. T
10. T

LEARNING ACTIVITY 6.4
Observing Early Categorization Skills (pp. 224–226)

This demonstration can be combined with Learning Activity 6.2, or you can suggest that students locate a toddler for observation. Place a set of objects, such as four boxes and four balls, in front of the child. Research indicates that 12-month-olds will touch objects that belong together, but they do not yet group them. A little later, single-category grouping can be seen. For example, 16-month-olds are likely to put all the balls together but not the boxes. Finally, around 18 months, children sort the objects exhaustively into two classes. Advanced categorization skills are believed to contribute to the vocabulary spurt that typically occurs between 18 months and 2 years.

LEARNING ACTIVITY 6.5
Supporting Early Mental Development (pp. 231–233)

Tell students to pretend that they have been asked to speak to a group of parents with very young children. Using research in the text as a guide, have students describe environmental factors that promote favorable mental development in infants and toddlers. What environmental factors tend to undermine mental development? Why are high-quality child care and / or early intervention especially important for low-income infants and toddlers?

LEARNING ACTIVITY 6.6
Matching: Language Development (pp. 236–246)

Present the following exercise as an in-class activity or quiz:

Directions: Match each of the following terms with its correct description.

Terms:

1. Language acquisition device
2. Cooing
3. Babbling
4. Joint attention
5. Underextension
6. Overextension
7. Telegraphic speech
8. Referential style
9. Expressive style
10. Child-directed speech

Descriptions:

A.   When toddlers apply a word to a wider collection of objects and events than is appropriate.
B.   Two-word utterances that, like a telegram, focus on high-content words and leave out smaller and less important words.
C.   Around 6 months, infants repeat consonant-vowel combinations in long strings, such as "babababababa" or "nanananana."
D.   An innate system that contains a set of rules common to all languages.
E.   A style of language where vocabularies consist mainly of words that refer to objects.
F.   Around 4 months, infants gaze in the same direction adults are looking, a skill that becomes more accurate around 10 to 11 months.
G.   A style of language in which toddlers produce many more pronouns and social formulas.
H.   Around 2 months, babies begin to make vowel-like noises.
I.   When toddlers first learn new words, they sometimes apply them too narrowly.
J.   A form of communication made up of short sentences with high-pitched, exaggerated expression, clear pronunciation, distinct pauses between speech segments, clear gestures to support verbal meaning, and repetition of new words in a variety of contexts.

Answers:

1.   D
2.   H
3.   C
4.   F
5.   I
6.   A
7.   B
8.   E
9.   G
10. J

LEARNING ACTIVITY 6.7
Comprehension versus Production (p. 243)

At all ages, language comprehension develops ahead of language production. To illustrate this concept, have students discuss their own learning experiences. For example, when acquiring a second language, students comprehend words, phrases, and conversations with greater ease and accuracy than when asked to produce the same words, phrases, and conversations. In addition, although students may comprehend the key elements in a lecture or assigned reading, they may have difficulty reproducing these elements in a testing situation. Furthermore, as pointed out in the text, recall is more difficult than recognition. Therefore, if we rely solely on what children or students produce or recall, we may greatly underestimate what they actually know or comprehend.

LEARNING ACTIVITY 6.8
Interviewing Parents About Their Toddler's Early Vocabulary (pp. 242–246)

Ask students to interview the parent of a toddler about early vocabulary development. During the interview, parents can be asked to list the words their child produces and the contexts in which the child uses them. Students should note examples of object words, action words, and state words and of early two-word combinations. Once students have completed the activity, ask them to share their findings with the class. Use their findings to discuss individual differences in early language development.

ASK YOURSELF...

REVIEW: Using the text discussion on pages 209–212, construct your own table providing an overview of infant and toddler cognitive development. Which entries in your table are consistent with Piaget's sensorimotor stage? Which ones develop earlier than Piaget anticipated? (pp. 208–216)

This is an open-ended question with no right or wrong answer.

APPLY: Mimi's father holds up her favorite teething biscuit, deposits it under a napkin, and shows Mimi his empty hand. Ten-month-old Mimi, looking puzzled, fails to search for the biscuit. Why does Mimi find this object-hiding task difficult? (pp. 211–212)

Research suggests that searching for hidden objects represents a true advance in understanding of object permanence because infants solve some object-hiding tasks before others. Ten-month-olds like Mimi search for an object placed on a table and covered by a cloth before they search for an object that a hand deposits under a cloth. In the second, more difficult task, infants seem to expect the object to reappear in the hand because that is where the object initially disappeared. When the hand emerges without the object, they conclude that there is no other place the object could be. This explains why Mimi fails to search for the biscuit.

CONNECT: Recall from Chapter 5 (page 201) that around the middle of the first year, infants become adept at identifying objects by their features (shape, color, and texture) and by their paths of movement, even when they cannot observe the entire path. How might these capacities contribute to infants' understanding of object permanence? (pp. 212–213)

When infants appreciate that features distinguish objects, they realize that two objects (each with distinctive features) can be in the same place, one on top of or next to the other. These understandings increase the likelihood that a baby who sees an adult cover an object with a cloth will realize that the object has not disappeared (been replaced by the cloth) but, rather, is merely concealed.

REFLECT: Which explanation of infants' cognitive competencies do you prefer, and why? (pp. 208–219)

This is an open-ended question with no right or wrong answer.

REVIEW: Cite evidence that categorization becomes less perceptual and more conceptual with age. What factors support this shift? How can adults promote the development of categorization? (pp. 224–226)

Babies' earliest categories are *perceptual*—based on similar overall appearance or prominent object parts, such as legs for animals or wheels for vehicles. By the end of the first year, more categories are *conceptual*—based on common function and behavior. Older infants can even make categorical distinctions when the perceptual contrast between two categories—animals and vehicles—is minimal. For instance, around 12 months, toddlers touch objects that go together, without grouping them. At 16 months, they can group objects into a single category, and around 18 months, toddlers can sort objects into two classes.

Several factors support the shift from perceptual to conceptual categorization. Most researchers acknowledge that exploration of objects and expanding knowledge of the world contribute to older infants' capacity to move beyond physical features and group objects by their functions and behaviors. In addition, language both builds on and facilitates categorization. Therefore, adults can facilitate the development of categorization by labeling objects, which calls infants' attention to commonalities among objects and also promotes vocabulary growth. Toddlers' advancing vocabulary, in turn, is associated with advanced object-grouping behavior.

APPLY: Rosa, who is growing up in a rural Mexican village, played with toys in a more intentional, goal-directed way as a toddler than as an infant. What impact is her more advanced toy play likely to have on her development of attention? How is Rosa's cultural background likely to affect her attention? (pp. 221–222, 227–228)

Rosa's advanced play with toys indicates that her attraction to novelty has declined while her ability to sustain attention has improved. When a toddler engages in goal-directed behavior even in a limited way, such as stacking blocks or putting them in a container, attention must be maintained to reach the goal. As plans and activities gradually become more complex, so does the duration of attention. As early as the first year, cultural variations in social experiences affect mental strategies. For example, in a rural Mexican village such as Rosa's, adults and children often focus their attention on several events at once—a strategy that may be vital in cultures where children primarily learn not through formal lessons but, rather, through keen observation of others' ongoing activities at home, at work, and in public life.

CONNECT: Review the research on page 215, indicating that by age 10 to 12 months, infants can solve problems by analogy. How might this capacity be related to a context-free memory, which develops about the same time? (pp. 215, 222–223)

By 10 to 12 months, infants can solve problems by analogy—take a strategy from one problem and apply it to other relevant problems. With age, children become better at reasoning by analogy, applying relevant strategies across increasingly dissimilar situations. Similarly, around 9 months, as babies move on their own and experience frequent changes in context, their memory becomes increasingly context free. They can apply learned responses more flexibly, generalizing them to relevant new situations.

REFLECT: Describe your earliest autobiographical memory. How old were you when the event occurred? Do your responses fit with research on infantile amnesia? (pp. 224–225)

This is an open-ended question with no right or wrong answer.

REVIEW: What probably accounts for the finding that speed of habituation and recovery to visual stimuli predicts later IQ better than an infant mental test score? (pp. 228, 230–231)

Habituation and recovery seem to be an especially effective early index of intelligence because they assess memory as well as quickness and flexibility of thinking, characteristics that underlie intelligent behavior at all ages. In contrast, infant intelligence tests involve presenting infants with stimuli, coaxing them to respond, and observing their behavior. Most infant tests measure perceptual and motor responses, with just a few tasks that tap early cognition. In addition, infants and toddlers are especially likely to become distracted, fatigued, or bored during testing, and their scores do not reflect their true abilities. Furthermore, the perceptual and motor items typical of infant tests differ from the test questions given to older children, which emphasize verbal, conceptual, and problem-solving skills. As a result, infant test scores do not tap the same dimensions of intelligence measured at older ages and are poor predictors of later IQ.

APPLY: Fifteen-month-old Joey's developmental quotient (DQ) is 115. His mother wants to know exactly what this means and what she should do at home to support his mental development. How would you respond? (pp. 230–232)

Joey's DQ of 115 indicates that he did better than 84 percent of same-aged children on a test of early mental development. However, most infant/toddler tests do a poor job of predicting later intelligence test scores. Therefore, to support his ongoing mental development, Joey's mother should focus on providing an organized, stimulating physical setting, being emotionally and verbally responsive, and encouraging and accepting his development. As research with the Home Observation for Measurement of the Environment (HOME) checklist indicates, these characteristics are positively related to mental development.

CONNECT: Using what you learned about brain development in Chapter 5, explain why it is best to initiate intervention for poverty-stricken children in the first two years, rather than later. (pp. 233–235)

As neurons form connections, stimulation becomes vital to their survival. Neurons that are stimulated by input from the surrounding environment continue to establish new synapses, forming increasingly elaborate systems of communication that lead to more complex abilities. At first, stimulation results in massive overproduction of synapses, many of which serve identical functions, thereby ensuring that the child will acquire the motor, cognitive, and social skills that our species needs to survive. Neurons that are seldom stimulated soon lose their synapses, a process called *synaptic pruning,* which returns neurons that are not needed at the moment to an uncommitted state so they can support future development. For this process to proceed, appropriate stimulation of the child's brain is vital during periods in which the formation of synapses is at its peak—a prime reason that very early intervention is necessary to help poverty-stricken children reach their cognitive potential.

REFLECT: Suppose you were seeking a child-care setting for your baby. What would you want it to be like, and why? (p. 234)

This is an open-ended question with no right or wrong answer.

REVIEW: Why is the social interactionist perspective attractive to many investigators of language development? Cite evidence that supports it. (pp. 239–240)

Because early researchers did not take seriously the idea that very young children might be able to figure out important properties of the language they hear, the first two theories of how children acquire language were extreme views. One, *behaviorism,* regards language development as entirely due to environmental influences. The second, *nativism,* assumes that children are "prewired" to master the intricate rules of their language. The social interactionist perspective, in contrast, takes a middle position, emphasizing interactions between inner capacities and environmental influences. According to this perspective, native endowment, a strong desire to communicate with others, and a rich language and social environment combine to help build a communicative system. And because genetic and environmental contributions vary across children, the social interactionist perspective predicts individual differences in language learning.

APPLY: Prepare a list of research-based recommendations on how to support language development during the first two years. (pp. 244–246)

1. Respond to coos and babbles with speech sounds and words.
2. Establish joint attention and comment on what the child sees.
3. Play social games, such as pat-a-cake and peekaboo.
4. Engage toddlers in joint make-believe play.
5. Engage toddlers in frequent conversations.
6. Read to toddlers often, engaging them in dialogues about picture books.

CONNECT: Cognition and language are interrelated. List examples of how cognition fosters language development. Next, list examples of how language fosters cognitive development. (pp. 242–244)

Research indicates that first spoken words, around 1 year, build on the sensorimotor foundations Piaget described and on categories children form during infancy and toddlerhood. Earliest words usually refer to important people ("Mama," "Dada"), objects that move ("ball," "car," "cat," "shoe"), familiar actions ("bye-bye," "up," "more"), or outcomes of familiar actions ("dirty," "hot," "wet"). Some early words are linked to specific cognitive achievements. For example, about the time toddlers master advanced object permanence problems, they use disappearance words, such as "all gone." And success and failure expressions ("There!" "Uh-oh!") appear when toddlers can solve sensorimotor problems suddenly rather than through trial and error.

Emerging language also fosters cognitive development. Between 18 and 24 months, the speed of identifying words in spoken sentences picks up, and memory, categorization, and ability to detect a speaking partner's intentions also improve. As a result, many children add 10 to 20 new words a week. When vocabulary approaches 200 words, toddlers start to combine two words: "Mommy shoe," "go car," "my truck." Toddlers are absorbed in figuring out word meanings and using their limited vocabularies in whatever ways possible to get their thoughts across.

REFLECT: Find an opportunity to speak to an infant or toddler. How did your manner of speaking differ from the way you typically speak to an adult? What features of your speech are likely to promote early language development, and why? (pp. 244–246)

This is an open-ended question with no right or wrong answer.

SUGGESTED STUDENT READINGS

Goldin-Meadow, S. (2005). *Hearing gesture: How our hands help us think.* Cambridge, MA: Harvard University Press. Presents up-to-date research on the meaning and importance of nonverbal behaviors in learning and communication. The author maintains that understanding children's gestures has significant implications for supporting their language development and other aspects of learning.

Lombardi, J., & Bogle, M. M. (Eds.). (2004). *The promise of Early Head Start for American's youngest children.* Washington, DC: Zero to Three. Provides a thorough overview of Early Head Start, including services offered to children and families, the importance of early learning experiences for infants and toddlers, and current research on early intervention.

Posner, M. I., & Rothbart, M. K. (2006). *Educating the human brain.* Washington, DC: American Psychological Association. Presents 25 years of research on early cognitive development, including attention, self-regulation, the relationship between emotion and cognition, and ways parents and educators can foster early learning.

TRANSPARENCIES

T-67   Testing Infants for Understanding of Object Permanence Using the Violation-of-Expectation Method Figure 6.1 (p. 213)

T-68   Analogical Problem Solving by 10- to 12-Month-Olds Figure 6.2 (p. 215)

T- 69   Testing Infants for Basic Number Concepts Figure 6.3 (p. 218)

T-70   Store Model of the Human Information-Processing System Figure 6.4 (p. 220)

T-71   Investigating Infant Categorization Using Operant Conditioning Figure 6.7 (p. 225)

T-72   Categorical Distinction Made by 9- to 11-Month-Olds Figure 6.8 (p. 226)

T-74   IQ Scores of Treatment and Control Children from Infancy to 21 Years in the Carolina Abecedarian Project Figure 6.10 (p. 235)

T-75   Language-Specific Structures in the Left Hemisphere of the Cerebral Cortex Figure 6.11 (p. 238)

MEDIA MATERIALS

INFANTS, CHILDREN, AND ADOLESCENTS IN ACTION

Infancy and Toddlerhood

The segments of the Observation Program on infant cognitive development trace mastery of object permanence during Piaget's sensorimotor stage, along with advances in mental representation during the second year, as illustrated by make-believe play and categorization. Then the Observation Program turns to early language development. Prelinguistic milestones are depicted, with emphasis on infant receptivity to language and characteristics of parental communication that help infants make sense of a complex speech stream. Alex, Hannah, Zachary, Katherine, and Nicole demonstrate early communicative capacities, first words, and the distinction between language comprehension and production. Zachary and Ben highlight individual differences in early styles of language learning. The section ends with examples of how storybook reading and make-believe play foster early language development.

A WINDOW ON INFANTS, CHILDREN, AND ADOLESCENTS

Segment 1: The Newborn Baby's Capacities: Anna, 2 weeks

In this segment, 2-week-old Anna exhibits a variety of newborn reflexes and capacities. Anna's mother carefully attends to the newborn, responding to Anna's signals by speaking softly and asking if she is hungry when she begins to suck on her fingers. Next, Professor Berk holds Anna while her mother shakes a rattle, illustrating the newborn's responsiveness to sound and visual stimulation. The segment concludes with Anna demonstrating the crawling motion, Moro reflex, and stepping reflex.

Segment 2: Learning Capacities: Mac, 3 months

This segment opens with Mac and his father playing. The interaction between Mac and his father illustrates how fathers tend to play differently with their babies than mothers do. When presented with a rattle, Mac shows signs of voluntary reaching. Watch as Mac's mother holds up a green and then a yellow ring. Mac habituates to the green ring and then recovers to the yellow ring.

Segment 3: Object Permanence and Parent–Infant Interaction: Hannah, 7 months

This segment begins with Hannah handling two rattles. Professor Berk uses one of the rattles for several object-hiding tasks. Notice how Hannah successfully searches for the rattle when it is partially covered by a cloth diaper. When the rattle is completely covered, however, Hannah fails to search for it. Finally, Hannah plays with her mother. As mother and baby interact, their mutual gaze and exchange of emotional signals illustrate Vygotsky's concept of intersubjectivity.

Segment 4: Physical and Cognitive Development: Randy, 8 months, and Ben, 21 months

This segment opens as Randy and Ben are playing with their mother. The differences in fine and gross motor skills are evident as the boys play. Randy illustrates the beginning of crawling by scooting across the floor on his tummy to retrieve a toy and establish contact with his mother. Ben's skills are more advanced, as evidenced when he walks and runs, uses a toy hammer, winds a jack-in-the-box, and plays catch with Professor Berk. Watch as the boys' mother supports their language development by using child-directed speech, commenting on their behavior, labeling toys, and playing with them. Similarly, her style of interaction helps regulate their emotions. The play behaviors of Randy and Ben demonstrate the difference between functional and make-believe play. Whereas Randy simply explores the toys and moves them about, Ben is able to act out real-life situations, such as pretending to feed a doll and to feed Randy.

Segment 5: High-Quality Infant and Toddler Child Care

This segment, profiling Goodwood Child Care Center and McKinnon Parade Child Care Center in Adelaide, Australia, illustrates a number of ingredients of high-quality child care. For example, at Goodwood Child Care Center, the staff support children's developing motor skills by teaching them how to do somersaults and encouraging them as they learn this new activity. In the second clip, infants play with staff members in the sandbox. Notice the positive interactions between the children and staff. As the babies play, staff members describe what is going on and demonstrate how to use the toys in the sandbox. In the final clip, children and staff at McKinnon Parade Child Care Center enjoy a meal. Children are not seated separately from staff, and there is a lot of interaction, such as a staff member feeding a toddler and talking to the others as they eat.

Segment 6: Supporting Early Language Learning: Luke 1½ years, Sophie and Elena, 2½ years

This segment opens with 1½-year-old Luke reading a book with his mother. Next, 2½-year-old twins, Sophie and Elena, read a storybook with their mother. Notice the rich dialogue between these toddlers and their mothers. Next, Sophie and Elena engage in make-believe play. Their mother comments on their activities, which helps sustain the play session and fosters language learning.

DVDs AND VIDEOTAPES

Acquiring the Human Language (Ways of Knowing/Equinox Films, 55 min.). Part Two of The Human Language series. How do children "acquire" language—seemingly without being taught? Do they "inherit grammar"? Myths about language are shattered and new, counterintuitive theories advanced.

Animals: How Smart Are They? (1990, Films for the Humanities & Sciences, 26 min.). This program looks at some of the present research on whether or not higher intelligence exists in animals. Studies examined include work at Rutgers University with chimps, who can use tools and logic at the same level as a human toddler; research at the San Francisco Gorilla Foundation with Koko, who asks for food and expresses emotions through sign language; and work at the University of Hawaii with dolphins, who are being taught not only words, but syntax.

Classical and Operant Conditioning (1996, Films Media Group, 56 min.). This program explores the principles of behaviorism and their applications in child rearing, education, and clinical therapy. The program looks at the complex classical and operant conditioning theories of Pavlov and Skinner, with examples of conditioning drawn from archival footage, present-day research, and situations in everyday life.

Cognition and Language (2001, RMI Media, 30 min.). This program explores animal communication and makes the point that although most animals do have the ability to communicate, only humans have language—symbols for objects, actions, ideas, and feelings.

Cognitive Development (1995, Films Media Group, 58 min.). This program evaluates Piaget's theory of cognitive development in light of current research. It presents Piaget's central themes, covering the cognitive stages of development from birth to age 12, with examples of children's behavior at each level. For each stage, recent research is examined, and comparisons are drawn between Piaget's theories and those of Jerome Bruner. The conclusion is that children's cognitive capabilities develop earlier than Piaget suggested. The program also outlines other theoretical developments, including research findings on metacognition and theory of mind.

The Developing Child: The Crucial Early Years (1990, Films for the Humanities & Sciences, 26 min.). Examines mental development in infants and how it can be assisted. Looks at aspects of learning, IQ testing, and group behavior.

Developing Language: Learning to Question, Inform, and Entertain (1994, Films Media Group, 25 min.). This program reviews the development of language during early childhood. It describes how basic language is acquired through interactions between the child and caregivers. The program also looks at aspects of language competence that go beyond the purpose of simple communication—for example, the skill of using conversation to establish and advance social relationships, the use of language in games and jokes, and the awareness of what other people know and understand.

The Development of the Human Brain (Films for the Humanities & Sciences, 40 min.). This program follows the physiological development of the human brain, starting at conception and moving through the growth of the neurological system in utero to the moment of birth, when a wide variety of brain functions are already apparent. It continues to follow a child to the age of 8, as a whole range of motor and cognitive skills appears.

Discovering the Human Language: "Colorless Green Ideas" (1997, Transit Media, 55 min.). This program, Part I of the PBS Human Language series, explains how the Chomskyan revolution transformed language study into a search for what goes on inside the brain. The program compares the ground plans of diverse human languages and evaluates the effectiveness of human language at what it does.

The First 2½ Years: Cognitive Development (1991, Concept Media, 25 min.). Studies the process by which infants from birth to 2½ years acquire and use knowledge. Discussion topics include habituation, perception, memory, and problem solving. Observations by Piaget and Kagan are reviewed and suggestions for optimizing cognitive development are given.

The First 2½ Years: Language Development (1991, Concept Media, 25 min.). Presents the stages and sequences infants and toddlers display in developing language. Looks at child-directed speech, nonverbal communication, semantics, and syntax. Offers advice for facilitating language development.

Individual Differences and Developmental Milestones (1993, GPN, 30 min.). This program, part of the Worlds of Childhood series, looks at the perceptual capacities that newborn infants bring into the world and how their abilities develop in the first few hours, days, and weeks after birth. Through observations of two infants, the program shows how the capacity to learn, to act, and to remember begins developing from the moment of birth.

Infancy: Beginnings in Cognition & Language (1991, Magna Systems, 29 min.). This program addresses current theories of the sensory and perceptual capabilities involved in early learning, and how the baby uses these, along with innate reflexes, to discover the world. The program illustrates how the child continues learning by adapting new skills of looking, mouthing, and manipulation, as well as other means of interacting with people and objects. The child's behaviors are viewed in terms of stages within the sensorimotor period. The program shows how the infant comes to understand words and phrases within the first year, while also beginning to speak a few words.

Infant and Child Development (2001, RMI Media, 30 min.). This program provides an overview of Piaget's four stages of cognitive development: sensorimotor, preoperational, concrete operational, and formal operational.

The Infant Mind (1992, Insight Media, 30 min.). Piaget's stage theory is reviewed and challenged as infant learning is investigated. New evidence shows that infants understand basic cause and effect and object permanence and have a primitive knowledge of number. Furthermore, memory skills and concept formation are present much earlier than Piaget believed.

Intellectual Growth and Achievement (1994, Concept Media, 27 min.). Illustrates common factors that may limit intellectual development, such as lead poisoning and hearing loss. Also reviews cultural factors that may influence achievement. The roles of both heredity and environment in developmental outcomes are discussed.

Intelligence (1990, RMI Media, 30 min.). This program explores the significant differences between intellectually gifted individuals and those who are developmentally disabled. It also examines the lack of agreement among experts about what intelligence tests can and can't measure. Historical film footage is used to review the origins of IQ tests, including some of the testing movement's embarrassing failures. The program also looks at the debate over whether IQ tests measure aptitude (as their advocates claim) or achievement (as their critics assert). Strong arguments are presented for the idea that IQ tests primarily measure the knowledge individuals already possess, rather than their potential to learn.

Intelligence (2001, RMI Media Productions, 30 min.). Explores what intelligence means in different environments and cultures and discusses nature versus nurture and the history and biases of intelligence testing.

Intelligence and Creativity (2001, RMI Media, 30 min.). This program considers the ways in which the definition of intelligence varies in different environments and cultures. It looks at ideas about the effects of nature and nurture on intelligence, and probes the history of intelligence testing and criticisms of various mental tests.

Language (1990, Insight Media, 30 min.). This program explores how both innate biological makeup and experience affect language development. Considers language ability in animals, details the sequences of language development in humans, and looks at how language disorders resulting from brain damage can assist researchers in learning about human language capacities.

Language Development (1996, Films Media Group, 40 min.). This program emphasizes language development in infancy and early childhood, starting with an infant's first cry in the delivery room and continuing to age 7, when language development is almost complete. The program illustrates how babies and children attempt to communicate, starting with infant crying and babbling and following the development of speech until children attain fluency. Topics covered include the nature–nurture debate, the interactionist approach, and questions about whether nonhuman animals can use language.

Language Development (1993, Magna Systems, 32 min.). Describes the functions of language and literacy from infancy through adolescence. Explores the role of the adult in supporting language and literacy development, as well as social and cultural factors in language learning and usage.

Language and Thinking (1992, RMI Media Productions, 30 min.). This program observes toddlers in an effort to explore where and how language originates. Experts present theories about the brain and its role in language development.

Learning to Communicate: Doing What Comes Naturally (1991, RMI Media Productions, 60 min.). Part 4 of the series Developmental Psychology. First distinguishes human language from the communication systems of other animals and then examines the sequence of language development. Provides an overview of various theories on language acquisition. Includes a discussion of bilingual, learning disabled, and deaf children. Robbie Case, Professor of Applied Cognitive Science, Ontario Institute for Studies in Education, offers his views on the relationship between cognitive and language development.

Memory (2001, Insight Media, 30 min.). What is memory? How are events encoded as memories? Explaining that a sense of identity is based upon memories of personal history, this program examines how memories are formed, stored, and recalled.

Memory: Fabric of the Mind (Films Media Group, 28 min.). This program looks at aspects of memory that researchers are now exploring, including how brain chemistry can help explain memory, the structural changes that take place in the brain as memory develops, and how the process of forgetting occurs. The program reviews the research under way at several internationally renowned memory research labs, including the work of Gary Lynch, James McGaugh, Richard Thompson, and John Hopfield. Also illustrated are examples of prodigious feats of memory, as well as the advice of a memory teacher.

The Mind's Eye: How the Brain Sees the World (2000, Films Media Group/BBC, 50 min.). This program, featuring British neuroscientist Susan Greenfield, explores the tricks and shortcuts that the brain uses to construct its version of reality. Examples are drawn from the experiences of people with rare forms of brain damage, including a patient who cannot recognize anyone's face, including his own, and another who cannot see anything that is moving.

The Mind's I (Films for the Humanities & Sciences, 58 min.). Examines what makes a brain give rise to a unique individual. Through the examples of memory and language, shows that although the brain can be divided into regions, these regions are not independent mini-brains but vast banks of neuronal circuits that work together as a cohesive whole. Although we know a great deal about how different brain regions function, understanding how these regions work together to generate a cohesive individual consciousness remains a tantalizing puzzle.

Perception (1999, Films Media Group, 53 min.; not available in French-speaking Canada). In this program, parents and experts offer insights into the stage of perception that children experience from birth to age 3. Specific topics related to perception include the role of parents in child rearing; how daily interactions mold the physiology of the infant brain; the effect of a child's sex on the expectations of parents and society; and how children become part of their culture through naming and other ceremonies.

Piaget's Developmental Theory: An Overview (1989, Davidson Films, 25 min.). In this video David Elkind explores the roots of Piaget's work and outlines important vocabulary and concepts that structure much of the study of child development. Presents an overview of Piaget's developmental theory, its scope and content.

Promoting Language and Literacy (2003, Magna Systems, 29 min.). This program shows caregivers of an infant, a toddler, and several 2-year-olds as they follow the children's initial steps in language learning and preparation for literacy. The program illustrates how skilled caregivers listen to a child's communication and respond with nonverbal expressions, words, phrases, and sentences. Caregivers talk about ways to facilitate language in children who show delays and in those whose home language is not English. The program depicts caregivers sharing books and other materials with children to encourage literacy development.

The Psychology of Learning (Films Media Group, 7-part series). This seven-part series provides a comprehensive analysis of how people learn, with a focus on attention, cognitive development, memory, language development, classical and operant conditioning, different approaches to learning, and perception.

A Question of Quality (Films for the Humanities & Sciences, 26 min.). Presents a general overview of the benefits children get from child care, and ways parents can ensure suitable placement. Also describes children's needs and the components of good child care.

Simple Beginnings? Child Development from Birth to Age Five (1994, Films Media Group, 25 min.). This program provides an overview of key topics in developmental psychology through an exploration of the period from birth through age 4 or 5. The program features several experiments illustrating infants' early abilities—face recognition, short-term memory, and the ability to distinguish between biodynamic and non-biodynamic motion. The program also looks at the role of parents in structuring infants' early language development experiences.

Simple Beginnings? Child Development from Birth to Age Five (1997, Films for the Humanities & Sciences, 24 min.). Explores infant capacities, such as face recognition, short-term memory, and motion discrimination. Also discusses parents' role in scaffolding infants' early learning experiences.

Symbol Formation and the Acquisition of Language (1993, GPN, 30 min.). Program 9 of the Worlds of Childhood series. From observations in a deaf couple's home during the time when their child develops signing skills to observations of a second child learning to speak, the universal function of language as a form of symbolic communication is demonstrated.

Talking (1999, Films Media Group, 55 min.; not available in French-speaking Canada). This program demonstrates how newborn crying is the beginning of coexistence—infants' realization that there are others in their world with whom they can communicate. Child development experts and parents discuss the steps children follow in mastering their native language. Additional topics include the baby's use of body language and semiotic gestures, babbling, time frames for learning to speak, and the experience of growing up in a multilingual home.

Theories of Development (1997, Insight Media, 29 min.). This program reviews several theories of child development, including the work of Piaget, Skinner, and Vygotsky. It discusses the concept of the "whole child" and illustrates how, in contrast, many developmental theories adopt a one-dimensional focus.

To Talk (2003, Films Media Group/A Discovery Channel Production, 52 min.). This program, part of the series The Baby Human, explores several provocative questions about language: Why do newborn babies prefer the sound of the human voice to other sounds? Is language learned in the womb? How are infants able to distinguish sounds of other languages from those of their native tongue? Andrew Meltzoff and other leading psychologists specializing in infant communication provide current research on babies' linguistic journey, from the importance of child-directed speech in the early months to the language explosion of the second year.

To Think (2003, Films Media Group/A Discovery Channel Production, 52 min.). This program, part of the series The Baby Human, features more than a dozen short experiments designed to demonstrate how infants learn to grasp the rules of logic. The program illustrates how the baby's mind is continually expanding—for example, in perceiving the patterns of light and darkness that make up a parent's face, or in developing an understanding of object permanence. It also addresses how babies develop their consciousness and sense of place in the world.

Unlocking Language (1998, Films Media Group, 29 min.). In this program, a diverse group of experts, including an evolutionary linguist, a neurologist, a geneticist, a neuropsychologist, a developmental cognitive neuroscientist, and a professor of communication, talk about the origins and development of language. Topics include how language expresses abstractions; language as an innately guided behavior, both prenatally and in infants and toddlers; the parts of the brain involved in language; and the relationship between genes and language disorders.

TEST BANK

MULTIPLE CHOICE

1) In Piaget's theory of cognitive development, infants
   A) "think" with their eyes, ears, and hands.
   B) assimilate more than they accommodate.
   C) represent their experiences in speech, gesture, and play.
   D) do not yet use schemes to make sense of experience.
   Answer: A
   Page Ref: 208
   Skill: Conceptual
   Objective: 6.1

2) According to Piaget, infants' very first schemes
   A) are deliberate and creative.
   B) are based on internal representations of experience.
   C) show evidence that young infants think before they act.
   D) are sensorimotor action patterns.
   Answer: D
   Page Ref: 208
   Skill: Conceptual
   Objective: 6.1

3) In Piaget's theory, adaptation refers to
   A) the back-and-forth movement between equilibration and disequilibration.
   B) the process of building schemes through direct interaction with the environment.
   C) a steady, comfortable cognitive state.
   D) a rearrangement and linking together of schemes.
   Answer: B
   Page Ref: 208
   Skill: Factual
   Objective: 6.1

4) In Piaget's theory, the process of _____ is made up of two complementary activities: _____ and
   _____.
   A) equilibration; assimilation; accommodation
   B) equilibration; adaptation; organization
   C) adaptation; assimilation; accommodation
   D) adaptation; equilibration; organization
   Answer: C
   Page Ref: 208
   Skill: Conceptual
   Objective: 6.1

5) According to Piaget, during _____, children interpret experiences in terms of existing schemes, whereas in
   _____, old schemes are adjusted and new ones created to make sense of the environment.
   A) assimilation; accommodation
   B) equilibration; disequilibration
   C) adaptation; organization
   D) accommodation; assimilation
   Answer: A
   Page Ref: 208
   Skill: Conceptual
   Objective: 6.1

6) When 1-year-old James is given peas for the first time, he picks one up, throws it off the high chair tray, and says, "Ball." According to Piaget's theory, James is most likely _____ the pea into his ball scheme.
   A) accommodating
   B) equilibrating
   C) organizing
   D) assimilating

Answer: D
Page Ref: 208
Skill: Applied
Objective: 6.1

7) One-year-old Abbie is dropping various toys from her toybox in different ways. According to Piaget's theory, Abbie's modifications of her dropping scheme most likely reflects
   A) accommodation.
   B) organization.
   C) equilibration.
   D) assimilation.

Answer: A
Page Ref: 208
Skill: Applied
Objective: 6.1

8) According to Piaget's theory, during periods of rapid cognitive change,
   A) assimilation predominates over accommodation.
   B) accommodation predominates over assimilation.
   C) assimilation and accommodation are balanced.
   D) assimilation and accommodation are in a state of equilibrium.

Answer: B
Page Ref: 208
Skill: Conceptual
Objective: 6.1

9) In Piaget's theory, when children are in a state of disequilibrium,
   A) they shift away from accommodation toward assimilation.
   B) they realize that new information does not match their current schemes.
   C) they are likely to construct inefficient schemes.
   D) their existing schemes are not likely to change much.

Answer: B
Page Ref: 208
Skill: Conceptual
Objective: 6.1

10) Four-year-old Vanessa believes that all birds fly, but her father has just read her a book about penguins who are birds but cannot fly. This new information likely
   A) brings about a state of disequilibrium.
   B) results in a circular reaction.
   C) leads to assimilation.
   D) brings about a state of equilibrium.

Answer: A
Page Ref: 208
Skill: Applied
Objective: 6.1

11) Baby Lindsay has combined her reaching, grasping, and sucking schemes into a higher-order scheme that allows her, in a coordinated manner, to reach for her pacifier and put it into her mouth to suck. This achievement is an example of
   A) organization.
   B) accommodation.
   C) equilibrium.
   D) assimilation.
Answer: A
Page Ref: 208–209
Skill: Applied
Objective: 6.1

12) Piaget based his sequence of sensorimotor development on
   A) observations of his own children.
   B) children who were patients in his pediatric practice.
   C) experimental studies of children at various ages.
   D) interviews with children and their parents.
Answer: A
Page Ref: 209
Skill: Factual
Objective: 6.2

13) In Piaget's theory, a circular reaction is a means of building schemes in which infants
   A) attempt to form mental symbols of the world.
   B) try to repeat chance behaviors again and again.
   C) try to imitate the behaviors of others around them.
   D) act out imaginary activities.
Answer: B
Page Ref: 209
Skill: Conceptual
Objective: 6.2

14) Infants' difficulty _____ may underlie the circular reaction by ensuring that new skills will not be interrupted before they strengthen.
   A) inhibiting new and interesting behaviors
   B) anticipating events
   C) producing novel effects in the environment
   D) repeating chance behaviors
Answer: A
Page Ref: 209
Skill: Conceptual
Objective: 6.2

15) In Piaget's theory, a circular reaction is a means of building schemes in which infants
   A) construct mental representations of sights and sounds encountered during their interactions with the environment.
   B) try to repeat chance motor behaviors again and again.
   C) make use of operant conditioning to make sense of their everyday experiences.
   D) attempt to imitate the behaviors of others around them.
Answer: B
Page Ref: 209
Skill: Conceptual
Objective: 6.2

16) During Substage 1 of the sensorimotor period,
    A) infants apply reflexive behaviors rather indiscriminately.
    B) simple motor habits center around the infant's own body.
    C) behaviors are aimed at producing novel effects in the environment.
    D) babies begin to vary their behaviors in response to environmental demands.
    Answer: A
    Page Ref: 210
    Skill: Factual
    Objective: 6.2

17) Baby Victor accidentally puts his fist in his mouth and begins to suck on it. Later, he tries to repeat this behavior again and again. In Piaget's theory, this is an example of a _____ circular reaction.
    A) reflexive
    B) primary
    C) secondary
    D) tertiary
    Answer: B
    Page Ref: 210
    Skill: Applied
    Objective: 6.2

18) Baby Tom accidentally pushes over a tower of blocks. Each time his sister rebuilds the tower, Tom tries to push it over again and again. In Piaget's theory, this is an example of a _____ circular reaction.
    A) reflexive
    B) primary
    C) secondary
    D) tertiary
    Answer: C
    Page Ref: 210
    Skill: Applied
    Objective: 6.2

19) Primary circular reactions are oriented toward _____, whereas secondary circular reactions are aimed toward _____.
    A) involuntary actions; voluntary actions
    B) the infant's own body; the environment
    C) external actions; internal representations
    D) concrete thought; abstract thought
    Answer: B
    Page Ref: 210
    Skill: Conceptual
    Objective: 6.2

20) Compared to schemes in Substage 3 of the sensorimotor period, schemes in Substage 4
    A) are coordinated deliberately to solve problems.
    B) are directed toward the infant's body.
    C) represent sudden solutions rather than trial-and-error solutions.
    D) are repeated with variation to produce new outcomes.
    Answer: A
    Page Ref: 210
    Skill: Conceptual
    Objective: 6.2

21) Two landmark cognitive changes that take place in Substage 4 of the sensorimotor period of Piaget's theory are
    _____ and _____.
    A) deferred imitation; animistic thinking
    B) deferred imitation; object permanence
    C) dual representation; analogical problem solving
    D) intentional behavior; object permanence
Answer: D
Page Ref: 210
Skill: Conceptual
Objective: 6.2

22) When baby Radsheda reaches for her pacifier, she accidentally pushes it under her pillow. Rather than searching for the pacifier under the pillow, Radsheda cries. One possibility why Radsheda does not search for the pacifier under the pillow is because she has not yet developed
    A) dual representation.
    B) conservation.
    C) object permanence.
    D) animistic thinking.
Answer: C
Page Ref: 210
Skill: Applied
Objective: 6.2

23) Baby Sheila drops her toy keys off of the right side of her high chair three times in a row. Each time, Sheila's father picks them up and gives them back to her. Next, Sheila drops her keys off of the left side but looks for them on the right side. This is most likely because Sheila
    A) has not yet attained even rudimentary object permanence.
    B) does not yet appreciate physical causality.
    C) is not yet able to make an accurate A-B search.
    D) cannot yet engage in goal-directed behavior.
Answer: C
Page Ref: 211
Skill: Applied
Objective: 6.2

24) Piaget argued that babies make the A-not-B search error because
    A) awareness of object permanence is not yet complete.
    B) the ability to engage in goal-directed behavior has not yet developed.
    C) appreciation of physical causality has not yet been attained.
    D) they cannot yet coordinate means-end action sequences.
Answer: A
Page Ref: 211
Skill: Conceptual
Objective: 6.2

25) Tertiary circular reactions differ from primary and secondary circular reactions in that they are
    A) experimental.
    B) directed toward the environment.
    C) centered around the infant's own body.
    D) deliberate.
Answer: A
Page Ref: 211
Skill: Conceptual
Objective: 6.2

26) Baby Marisa is twisting and turning triangles, circles, and squares to fit them into her shape-sorter. According to Piaget, this behavior would best be described as a _____ circular reaction.
   A) reflexive
   B) primary
   C) secondary
   D) tertiary

Answer: D
Page Ref: 211
Skill: Applied
Objective: 6.2

27) Children in Substage 6 of the sensorimotor period often can solve object-permanence problems involving invisible displacement because they have developed the capacity to
   A) engage in goal-directed behavior.
   B) construct mental representations.
   C) display an accurate A-B search.
   D) understand dual representation.

Answer: B
Page Ref: 211
Skill: Conceptual
Objective: 6.2

28) According to Piaget, children's ability to experiment with actions inside their heads in Substage 6 of the sensorimotor period makes _____ and _____ possible.
   A) conservation; centration
   B) deferred imitation; make-believe play
   C) object permanence; conservation
   D) problem solving by analogy; deferred imitation

Answer: B
Page Ref: 212
Skill: Conceptual
Objective: 6.2

29) In the violation-of-expectation method, _____ suggests that the infant is surprised at a deviation from physical reality.
   A) habituation to the expected event
   B) recovery to the expected event
   C) habituation to the unexpected event
   D) recovery to the unexpected event

Answer: D
Page Ref: 212
Skill: Conceptual
Objective: 6.3

30) Some critics argue that the violation-of-expectation method is flawed because
   A) it is difficult for observers to discern when babies have habituated to the familiar event.
   B) this method cannot be used with very young babies.
   C) babies make only very subtle changes to their behaviors when they recover to a new stimulus.
   D) it reveals only babies' perceptual preference for novelty, not their understanding of experience.

Answer: D
Page Ref: 212
Skill: Conceptual
Objective: 6.3

31) Studies using the violation-of-expectation method provide evidence that infants have some knowledge of object permanence as early as _____, whereas Piaget argued that this ability emerges _____.
    A) 6 months; by 12 months
    B) 4 months; by 8 months
    C) 2 1/2 months; between 6 and 8 months
    D) 2 1/2 months; between 8 and 12 months
Answer: D
Page Ref: 212, 213
Skill: Conceptual
Objective: 6.3

32) Sabine is shown a doll and then it is hidden under a cover. Which of the following statements is true?
    A) Sabine must coordinate a "pushing aside" and a "grasping" scheme to retrieve the doll.
    B) Deliberately retrieving the doll is an example of a secondary circular reaction.
    C) Sabine will not be able to retrieve the doll until she is in Substage 4 of the sensorimotor period.
    D) Sabine will have trouble retrieving the doll until she masters the violation-of-expectation method.
Answer: A
Page Ref: 210
Skill: Applied
Objective: 6.3

33) Follow-up research suggests that 8- to 12-month-olds may make the A-not-B search error because they
    A) do not attend closely when the object is hidden at A.
    B) have trouble remembering an object's new locations after it was hidden in more than one place.
    C) have not yet developed the motor skills necessary for intentional reaching and grasping.
    D) have trouble inhibiting a previously rewarded motor response.
Answer: D
Page Ref: 213–214
Skill: Conceptual
Objective: 6.3

34) Piaget believed that the capacity to engage in deferred imitation emerges between _____. However, follow-up research indicates that deferred imitation is present as early as _____.
    A) 18 and 24 months; 6 weeks
    B) 8 to 12 months; 4 months
    C) 8 to 12 months; 6 weeks
    D) 18 and 24 months; 4 months
Answer: A
Page Ref: 214
Skill: Factual
Objective: 6.3

35) Follow-up research on deferred imitation demonstrates that by 14 months of age, children
    A) are more likely to imitate accidental behaviors than purposeful behaviors.
    B) adapt their imitative acts to a model's goals.
    C) mimic entire social roles, such as mommy and daddy, during make-believe play.
    D) can imitate actions an adult tries to produce, even if they are not fully realized.
Answer: B
Page Ref: 215
Skill: Conceptual
Objective: 6.3

36) Follow-up research on analogical problem solving demonstrates that the capacity to _____ emerges earlier than Piaget expected.
   A) imitate the behavior of models not present
   B) form flexible mental representations
   C) seriate items mentally
   D) master A-B object search
Answer: B
Page Ref: 215
Skill: Conceptual
Objective: 6.3

37) Marcus's mother showed him how to obtain an out-of-reach toy by pulling a string. When encouraged to imitate his mother with a different looking toy, Marcus successfully retrieved the toy. Marcus's behavior demonstrates that he
   A) can solve problems by analogy.
   B) has attained hypothetical thought.
   C) no longer exhibits the A-not-B error.
   D) can engage in make-believe play.
Answer: A
Page Ref: 215
Skill: Applied
Objective: 6.3

38) Follow-up research on the sensorimotor period indicates that
   A) the cognitive attainments of infancy develop in the stepwise fashion Piaget predicted.
   B) make-believe play emerges later than Piaget expected.
   C) infants comprehend a great deal before they are capable of the motor behaviors Piaget assumed led to those understandings.
   D) young babies have less built-in cognitive equipment for making sense of experience than granted by Piaget.
Answer: C
Page Ref: 216
Skill: Conceptual
Objective: 6.3

39) According to the core knowledge perspective, infants
   A) construct knowledge through independent exploration of their world.
   B) internalize knowledge though social interaction with others.
   C) achieve new mental abilities through schedules of reinforcement and punishment.
   D) begin life with innate, special-purpose knowledge systems.
Answer: D
Page Ref: 217
Skill: Conceptual
Objective: 6.4

40) According to core knowledge theorists,
   A) infants could not make sense of the varied stimulation around them without having been genetically "set up" in the course of evolution to comprehend its crucial aspects.
   B) older children's verbal and motor behaviors are more reliable indicators of understanding than infants' looking behaviors.
   C) infants are endowed with very little innate understanding and must rely on their interactions with the environment to construct knowledge.
   D) infants are not born with knowledge of concepts or reasoning because such ready-made knowledge would limit their ability to adapt to environmental changes.

Answer: A
Page Ref: 217
Skill: Conceptual
Objective: 6.4

41) Of the following, which provides support for the core knowledge perspective?
   A) Infants will look longer at an unexpected physical event than an expected physical event.
   B) Before 14 months, toddlers have difficulty with less-than and greater-than relationships between small sets.
   C) Young infants have the ability to distinguish small numerical quantities.
   D) Not until the preschool years do children add and subtract small numbers of objects correctly.

Answer: C
Page Ref: 217
Skill: Conceptual
Objective: 6.4

42) Investigations of brain development
   A) indicate that infants' looking behavior indicates the existence of concepts and reasoning.
   B) show that young children's cerebral cortex specializes rapidly as the result of a genetic blueprint.
   C) provide little support for the prewiring of complex cognitive functions in the brain.
   D) demonstrate that the young brain is less plastic than the mature brain.

Answer: C
Page Ref: 217
Skill: Conceptual
Objective: 6.4

43) Input in the information-processing system
   A) is held in the sensory register until it is attended to.
   B) simply flows on its own through the various stores.
   C) is automatically transferred into long-term memory.
   D) is channeled through the parts of the mental system using mental strategies.

Answer: D
Page Ref: 220
Skill: Conceptual
Objective: 6.5

44) In the information-processing system,
   A) the long-term memory store is limited in capacity.
   B) the longer information is retained in working memory, the greater the likelihood that it will drop out of the information-processing system.
   C) the capacity of the sensory register is more restricted than that of working memory.
   D) automatic cognitive processing expands working memory.

Answer: D
Page Ref: 221
Skill: Conceptual
Objective: 6.5

45) In the information-processing system, the central executive _____ the mental system.
   A) directs the flow of information in
   B) is the unconscious part of
   C) operates on and transforms information in
   D) is the initial storage site of information in
   Answer: A
   Page Ref: 221
   Skill: Factual
   Objective: 6.5

46) In the information-processing system, long-term memory
   A) is the conscious part of the cognitive system.
   B) stores information temporarily.
   C) is unlimited in capacity.
   D) directs the flow of information in the cognitive system.
   Answer: C
   Page Ref: 221
   Skill: Factual
   Objective: 6.5

47) According to the information-processing framework, _____ make(s) complex forms of thinking possible with age.
   A) increases in the size of short-term memory
   B) changes in the structure of the mental system
   C) increases in the capacity of the system
   D) goal-directed behavior
   Answer: C
   Page Ref: 221
   Skill: Conceptual
   Objective: 6.5

48) Research on infant attention demonstrates that _____ between birth and 4 to 5 months of age.
   A) attraction to novelty increases
   B) sustained attention declines
   C) habituation time decreases
   D) the ability to shift attention declines
   Answer: C
   Page Ref: 221
   Skill: Conceptual
   Objective: 6.6

49) By 4 months of age,
   A) infants' attention becomes more flexible.
   B) infants require about 3 or 4 minutes to habituate and recover to novel visual stimuli.
   C) infants begin to have trouble shifting attention.
   D) attraction to novelty disappears.
   Answer: A
   Page Ref: 221
   Skill: Conceptual
   Objective: 6.6

50) Rovee-Collier's operant conditioning research, in which infants kick to move mobiles attached to their feet by a long cord, provides evidence that
    A) the ability to remember visual stimuli does not emerge until the end of the sensorimotor stage.
    B) infants as young as 2 to 3 months have the ability to remember visual stimuli.
    C) the capacity to remember visual stimuli is present at birth.
    D) infants begin to communicate with gestures indicative of memory beginning around 6 weeks of age.
Answer: B
Page Ref: 222
Skill: Conceptual
Objective: 6.6

51) Studies of memory development show that
    A) infants are capable of recall by at least 6 months of age.
    B) memory becomes increasingly context free during toddlerhood.
    C) toddlers cannot engage in recall until about the age of 2 years.
    D) recognition is much more challenging for toddlers than is recall.
Answer: B
Page Ref: 223
Skill: Conceptual
Objective: 6.6

52) Of the following, which provides the best evidence of infants' ability to engage in recall by the end of the first year?
    A) Following training, infants remember for weeks how to rotate a mobile by kicking a foot tied to the mobile with a cord.
    B) Infants can find hidden objects hours or days after observing the behavior.
    C) Infants remember for weeks how to make a toy train move around a track by pressing a level.
    D) After habituating to a visual stimulus, infants' responsiveness increases when the stimulus is changed slightly.
Answer: B
Page Ref: 223
Skill: Conceptual
Objective: 6.6

53) _____ research indicates that young infants are capable of _____.
    A) Operant conditioning; rehearsal
    B) Habituation/recovery; recall
    C) Operant conditioning; recall
    D) Habituation/recovery; recognition
Answer: D
Page Ref: 223
Skill: Conceptual
Objective: 6.6

54) Recall is more challenging than recognition because it
    A) requires looking, kicking, or pressing a lever to indicate whether a new experience is identical or similar to a previous one.
    B) involves remembering a stimulus without perceptual support.
    C) does not involve a deliberate search of long-term memory.
    D) involves noticing that a stimulus is identical or similar to one previously experienced.
Answer: B
Page Ref: 223
Skill: Factual
Objective: 6.6

55) Categorization research demonstrates that
    A) infants' earliest categories are conceptual.
    B) by 6 months, babies can categorize stimuli on the basis of two correlated features, such as shape and color.
    C) 1-year-olds are not yet sensitive to common adultlike categories, such as furniture, food, and animals.
    D) not until the early preschool years can children sort people and their voices by gender and age.
Answer: B
Page Ref: 224
Skill: Conceptual
Objective: 6.6

56) Of the following, which is MOST likely be among an infant's first categories?
    A) furniture
    B) vehicles
    C) toys
    D) tools
Answer: B
Page Ref: 224, 225
Skill: Applied
Objective: 6.6

57) Information-processing research indicates that by 3 months, infants can remember events for as long as 3 months and categorize stimuli. These findings challenge Piaget's assumption that
    A) the emergence of language brings about representational ability.
    B) infants are unable to distinguish fantasy from reality until at least 2 years of age.
    C) infants are unable to mentally represent experience until at least 18 months of age.
    D) object permanence emerges towa the end of the first year.
Answer: C
Page Ref: 223
Skill: Conceptual
Objective: 6.6

58) Compared with Piaget's theory, the information-processing approach to development has more difficulty with
    A) breaking down children's thoughts into precise procedures.
    B) integrating information into a broad, comprehensive theory.
    C) reducing changes in thoughts into manageable proportions.
    D) counting the number of stages children's thoughts go through.
Answer: B
Page Ref: 226
Skill: Conceptual
Objective: 6.6

59) One major difference between Piaget's and Vygotsky's theories is that Vygotsky emphasized that
    A) children are born with prewired understandings that permit a ready grasp of new information.
    B) children learn best when tasks are outside of the zone of proximal development.
    C) complex mental activities have their origins in social interaction.
    D) children discover virtually all knowledge about the world through their own activity.
Answer: C
Page Ref: 227
Skill: Conceptual
Objective: 6.7

60) According to Vygotsky, the force that drives children's cognitive development is
   A) the physical world acting on children.
   B) independent interaction with the physical environment.
   C) the biological unfolding of genetic structures.
   D) joint activities with more mature members of their society.
   Answer: D
   Page Ref: 227
   Skill: Conceptual
   Objective: 6.7

61) Of the following, which would be within a child's zone of proximal development?
   A) a task that a child cannot accomplish alone or with the help of an adult
   B) a task that a child has recently mastered independently following the assistance of an adult
   C) a task that a child cannot yet handle on her own but can do with the help of an adult
   D) a task that a child accomplishes through her independent activity
   Answer: C
   Page Ref: 227
   Skill: Applied
   Objective: 6.7

62) One-year-old Maya is building a block tower. Maya's father begins by pointing to where each block needs to go and then straightening out each block as Maya piles them up. As Maya's competence with the task increases, her father gradually withdraws support. This is an example of
   A) transitive inference.
   B) cooperative learning.
   C) reciprocal teaching.
   D) scaffolding.
   Answer: D
   Page Ref: 227
   Skill: Applied
   Objective: 6.7

63) Findings that _____ provide support for Vygotsky's ideas.
   A) infants' earliest categories are perceptual
   B) attraction to novelty declines during the first year
   C) infants can perform simple arithmetic by the end of the first year
   D) fine-tuned support from parents is related to advanced play, language, and problem solving during the second year
   Answer: D
   Page Ref: 227
   Skill: Conceptual
   Objective: 6.7

64) Vygotsky's theory emphasizes that societal variations in complex mental activities are mainly due to
   A) genetic differences between cultures.
   B) cultural differences in social experiences.
   C) differences in the economic resources of various cultures.
   D) cultural differences in formal schooling.
   Answer: B
   Page Ref: 227
   Skill: Conceptual
   Objective: 6.7

65) Compared with Piagetian and information-processing views of intelligence, the mental testing approach
    A) focuses on the products of cognitive development rather than on the processes of cognitive development.
    B) views the child as a passive processor of information rather than as an active processor of information.
    C) emphasizes the biological bases of cognitive development rather than environmental influences.
    D) focuses on the child's independent efforts in advancing cognitive development rather than the influences of interactions with others.
Answer: A
Page Ref: 228
Skill: Conceptual
Objective: 6.8

66) An intelligence quotient (IQ)
    A) is expressed as the ratio of an individual's chronological age to his or her mental age.
    B) indicates the extent to which the raw score deviates from the typical performance of same-age individuals.
    C) represents the number of test items passed as a function of individuals of the same mental age in the standardization sample.
    D) reflects the number of items passed divided by the number of items passed by an average child of the same age.
Answer: B
Page Ref: 230
Skill: Conceptual
Objective: 6.8

67) In constructing a mental test, designers engage in standardization by giving the test to a large sample of individuals who
    A) have no previous exposure to intelligence tests.
    B) are more diverse in terms of ethnicity and SES than the population for which the test is being normed.
    C) perform at or near the test mean.
    D) are representative of the population.
Answer: D
Page Ref: 230
Skill: Conceptual
Objective: 6.8

68) Within a standardization sample for an IQ test, performances at each level
    A) are distributed equally among all scores.
    B) cluster around the extreme scores.
    C) form a normal distribution.
    D) infrequently fall around the mean.
Answer: C
Page Ref: 230
Skill: Conceptual
Objective: 6.8

69) By knowing a child's IQ score, one
    A) can calculate the mental and chronological age of the child.
    B) knows whether the child is ahead, behind, or average in mental development compared to agemates.
    C) can determine the percentage of younger and older children who fall above or below the child's score.
    D) knows how he or she compares in mental development to younger and older children.
Answer: B
Page Ref: 230
Skill: Conceptual
Objective: 6.8

70) Nsia has an IQ of 85. She did better than _____ percent of her agemates.
    A) 16
    B) 34
    C) 50
    D) 85
Answer: A
Page Ref: 230
Skill: Applied
Objective: 6.8

71) Edgardo has an IQ of 130. This means that he
    A) performed better than 98 percent of children at any age.
    B) outperformed 84 percent of his same-age peers.
    C) scored better than 30 percent of his same-age peers.
    D) performed better than 98 percent of his same-age peers.
Answer: D
Page Ref: 230
Skill: Applied
Objective: 6.8

72) Studies using mental tests demonstrate that
    A) IQ scores become stable by about age 6.
    B) most infants' IQ tests are strong predictors of later intelligence.
    C) the majority of children show substantial fluctuation in IQ between toddlerhood and adolescence.
    D) IQ is a measure of inborn ability that does not change with age.
Answer: C
Page Ref: 230–231
Skill: Conceptual
Objective: 6.8

73) The Bayley Scales of Infant Development
    A) emphasize higher-order cognitive skills like memory and problem solving.
    B) are helpful in assessing the newborn's adjustment to life outside the womb.
    C) show good long-term prediction of childhood intellectual functioning.
    D) do not tap the same dimensions of intelligence measured at older ages.
Answer: D
Page Ref: 230–231
Skill: Conceptual
Objective: 6.8

74) Many infant test scores are conservatively labeled _____ because _____.
    A) intelligence quotients; they compare performance among infants and children within certain age levels
    B) developmental quotients; they compare performance among infants and children within certain age levels
    C) intelligence quotients; they tap different skills than those measured at later ages
    D) developmental quotients; they tap different skills than those measured at later ages
Answer: D
Page Ref: 231
Skill: Conceptual
Objective: 6.8

75) Infant intelligence tests
    A) show better long-term prediction for high-scoring than low-scoring babies.
    B) are helpful in identifying infants who are likely to have developmental problems in the future.
    C) accurately predict childhood intelligence tests scores.
    D) can be used to identify infants who are likely to be intellectually gifted as children.
Answer: B
Page Ref: 231
Skill: Conceptual
Objective: 6.8

76) Of the following, which is the BEST available infant predictor of childhood and adolescent IQ?
    A) perceptual and motor responses
    B) reaction time to auditory and tactile stimuli
    C) infant memory, problem solving, categorization, and other complex cognitive skills
    D) speed of habituation and recovery to novel visual stimuli
Answer: D
Page Ref: 231
Skill: Factual
Objective: 6.8

77) Researchers believe that habituation and recovery are an especially effective early index of intelligence because they
    A) are an index of an important sensorimotor milestone.
    B) measure a higher-order cognitive skill.
    C) assess skills that underlie intelligent behavior at all ages.
    D) reveal infants' ability to process complex stimuli.
Answer: C
Page Ref: 231
Skill: Conceptual
Objective: 6.8

78) Of the following, which is supported by research on intelligence tests?
    A) Piagetian object permanence tasks predict later IQ better than traditional infant intelligence tests.
    B) Infant intelligence tests are used largely for identifying those infants who are likely to be intellectual gifted and in need of advanced cognitive support.
    C) Traditional infant intelligence tests predict later IQ better than speed of habituation and recovery.
    D) Intelligence test scores become relatively stable beginning at about age 2 years.
Answer: A
Page Ref: 231
Skill: Conceptual
Objective: 6.8

79) Research using the HOME has revealed that the extent to which parents _____ is especially important in facilitating toddlers' intelligence test performance.
    A) engage their children in physical activity
    B) watch educational television with their children
    C) talk to their children
    D) teach their children specific literacy and math skills
Answer: C
Page Ref: 231
Skill: Conceptual
Objective: 6.9

80) Research has shown that family living conditions, such as those measured by the HOME,
    A) predict children's IQ scores beyond the contribution of parental IQ and education
    B) show equally strong correlations with IQ for both adopted and biological children.
    C) are not associated with IQ for children living in poverty.
    D) predict children's school performance better than their IQ scores.
Answer: A
Page Ref: 232
Skill: Conceptual
Objective: 6.9

81) Studies on infant and toddler child care in the United States and Canada show that
    A) settings providing the very worst care tend to serve high-SES families.
    B) the vast majority of children receive high-quality child care.
    C) good child care can reduce the negative impact of a stressed, poverty-stricken home life.
    D) infants exposed to poor-quality child care rarely experience a drop in cognitive performance unless they
       come from low-SES homes.
Answer: C
Page Ref: 233
Skill: Conceptual
Objective: 6.9

82) In North America,
    A) only 20 to 25 percent of child-care settings provide a level of care sufficient to promote healthy
       development.
    B) child care is nationally regulated to ensure high standards.
    C) caregivers are required by law to have special training in infant and child care.
    D) the government offers subsidized child care to all families.
Answer: A
Page Ref: 233
Skill: Factual
Objective: 6.9

83) In contrast to the United States and Canada, most European countries
    A) do not require that caregivers have special training in child development.
    B) nationally regulate child care to ensure its quality.
    C) offer government-subsidized child care only to poverty-stricken families.
    D) provide child-care benefits only when both parents are working in the labor market.
Answer: B
Page Ref: 233
Skill: Factual
Objective: 6.9

84) In the United States, settings that provide the very worst care tend to serve _____ families.
    A) middle-SES
    B) low-SES
    C) high-SES
    D) single-parent
Answer: A
Page Ref: 233
Skill: Factual
Objective: 6.9

85) Which of the following is supported by research on child care?
   A) In contrast to conditions of American and Canadian children, large numbers of European children attend unlicensed child-care homes, where no one checks to see that minimum health and safety standards are met.
   B) Recent increases in federal funds to subsidize the cost of child care in the United States and Canada have had a positive impact on child-care quality.
   C) In contrast to the public child-care system in most European countries, the private child-care systems in the United States and Canada ensure high-quality care.
   D) In the United States and Canada, early child care is viewed as a public responsibility and a public good, like elementary and secondary education.

Answer: B
Page Ref: 233
Skill: Conceptual
Objective: 6.9

86) Research on early intervention for at-risk infants and toddlers demonstrates that
   A) home-based programs are inferior to center-based programs.
   B) there is usually no need to begin programs until the child is at least 3 years of age and old enough to benefit from educational supports.
   C) gains in cognitive performance persist as long as the program lasts and occasionally longer.
   D) most poverty-stricken children do not evidence gains in IQ as the result of early intervention.

Answer: C
Page Ref: 234
Skill: Conceptual
Objective: 6.9

87) The Carolina Abecedarian Project shows that _____ is an effective way to reduce the negative effects of poverty on children's mental development.
   A) furnishing free nutrition and health services
   B) providing children a special resource teacher during the early elementary school years
   C) an early intervention approach that focuses on parental involvement
   D) continuous high-quality child care from infancy throughout the preschool years

Answer: D
Page Ref: 235
Skill: Conceptual
Objective: 6.9

88) Findings from the Carolina Abecedarian Project suggest that _____ is/are key for fostering the mental development of children born into extreme poverty.
   A) beginning enrichment programs during infancy
   B) intervention during the middle- and high-school years
   C) nutrition and health services
   D) parental involvement

Answer: A
Page Ref: 235
Skill: Conceptual
Objective: 6.9

89) Research shows that by age 3, children in *Early Head Start*
    A) had warmer, more stimulating parenting.
    B) showed an increase in aggression.
    C) lost gains in IQ that they had acquired while enrolled in the program as infants and toddlers.
    D) evidenced gains in IQ only among middle-SES children.
Answer: A
Page Ref: 235
Skill: Conceptual
Objective: 6.9

90) Behaviorist B. F. Skinner proposed that language is acquired
    A) as children's inborn language capacity unfolds.
    B) through imitation.
    C) as the result of a language acquisition device.
    D) through operant conditioning.
Answer: D
Page Ref: 237
Skill: Conceptual
Objective: 6.10

91) Two-year-old Abigail calls the toaster a "breadbaker." Abigail's coining of this original term shows that
    _____ alone cannot fully explain language acquisition.
    A) a language acquisition device
    B) reinforcement and imitation
    C) a speech-analyzing brain mechanism
    D) a built-in universal grammar
Answer: B
Page Ref: 237
Skill: Applied
Objective: 6.10

92) Nativist Noam Chomsky believed that
    A) children are born with a series of modules that are specialized for different aspects of language
       acquisition.
    B) children's innate desire to verbally interact with others promotes language development.
    C) children rely largely on imitation to acquire grammatical rules and vocabulary.
    D) the rules of sentence organization are too complex to be directly taught or discovered by a young child.
Answer: D
Page Ref: 237
Skill: Factual
Objective: 6.10

93) Chomsky's LAD
    A) involves language acquisition drills that are used to foster young children's vocabulary acquisition.
    B) refers to linguistic tutoring processes by which parents assist children in learning grammatical rules.
    C) is made up of computer programs that attempt to generate the linguistic rules that are needed for
       language acquisition.
    D) is an innate system that permits children to master the structure of language spontaneously and swiftly.
Answer: D
Page Ref: 237
Skill: Conceptual
Objective: 6.10

94) The finding that children everywhere reach major language milestones in a similar sequence is consistent with
    A) Chomsky's account of language acquisition.
    B) a behaviorist account of language acquisition.
    C) the notion that language acquisition is entirely due to environmental influences.
    D) Skinner's account of language acquisition.
Answer: A
Page Ref: 237
Skill: Conceptual
Objective: 6.10

95) Animal studies demonstrate that
    A) chimpanzees with extensive training produce words and word combinations with much more consistency compared to human preschoolers.
    B) nonhuman primates cannot learn even a very basic vocabulary.
    C) chimpanzees can master extensive vocabularies and complex sentences.
    D) the capacity for an elaborate grammar is unique to humans.
Answer: D
Page Ref: 237
Skill: Conceptual
Objective: 6.10

96) Which statement about the brain and language functions is correct?
    A) Broca's area is responsible for language production and grammatical processing.
    B) Language functions are typically associated with the right hemisphere of the brain.
    C) Wernicke's area is responsible for language comprehension.
    D) Left-hemispheric localization is not necessary for effective language processing.
Answer: D
Page Ref: 238
Skill: Conceptual
Objective: 6.10

97) Research on acquiring a first language demonstrate that
    A) no precise age cutoff has been established for a decline in first-language competence.
    B) as the brain becomes increasingly specialized for language, it becomes easier to learn a first language
    C) first-language competence drops sharply at adolescence.
    D) individuals who acquire a first language in adulthood usually become as proficient as those who learned in childhood.
Answer: A
Page Ref: 238
Skill: Conceptual
Objective: 6.10

98) Mr. Li is a 60-year-old college graduate from China who has just immigrated to the United States and is learning English. Jet is 3 years old and has just immigrated to the United States from China and is also learning English. Jet will eventually complete high school, but not college. What can we ascertain about the second-language acquisition of these two individuals?
    A) There is not enough information provided to determine anything about their second-language acquisition.
    B) By the time Jet is an adult, he and Mr. Li will have comparable English-speaking skills.
    C) Mr. Li will have greater English proficiency than Jet.
    D) Jet will have greater English proficiency than Mr. Li.
Answer: D
Page Ref: 239
Skill: Applied
Objective: 6.10

99) Which of the following is a limitation of Chomsky's nativist perspective?
    A) Chomsky's theory is inconsistent with research on efforts to teach nonhuman primates language systems.
    B) Chomsky's theory cannot explain why children refine and generalize many grammatical forms gradually.
    C) Chomsky's theory overemphasizes the role of social experience in language development.
    D) Chomsky's theory is inconsistent with findings that have demonstrated that humans have evolved specialized regions in the brain that support language skills.
Answer: B
Page Ref: 239
Skill: Conceptual
Objective: 6.10

100) All interactionist theories of language learning emphasize
    A) that language competence is an outgrowth of cognitive strategies rather than ones specifically tuned to language.
    B) an inborn universal grammar.
    C) interactions between inner capacities and environmental influences.
    D) the child as a passive communicative partner.
Answer: C
Page Ref: 239
Skill: Factual
Objective: 6.10

101) Information-processing theorists
    A) assume that children make sense of language by applying powerful cognitive capacities of a general kind.
    B) argue that children are born with an innate mechanism that permits the rapid learning of language.
    C) regions of the brain housing language govern only language abilities and do not play a role in other skills.
    D) emphasize children's social skills and language experiences as centrally involved in language development.
Answer: A
Page Ref: 239
Skill: Factual
Objective: 6.10

102) Which of the following sounds is the BEST example of babbling?
    A) "oooo"
    B) "mae-do" (for "tomato")
    C) "go car"
    D) "dadadadada"
Answer: D
Page Ref: 240
Skill: Applied
Objective: 6.11

103) Research on babbling shows that
    A) infants must be able to hear language in order for the brain to develop the necessary organization for normal speech processing.
    B) babies in industrialized countries begin babbling earlier than babies in developing countries.
    C) the babbling of infants with different native languages sounds very different from one another.
    D) deaf babies begin babbling later than hearing babies.
Answer: A
Page Ref: 240
Skill: Conceptual
Objective: 6.11

104) Of the following, which is supported by research on babbling?
   A) Deaf infants exposed to sign language from birth babble with their hands.
   B) Babies of different native languages differ widely in the range of early sounds that they produce.
   C) Most babies say their first word within days after the onset of babbling.
   D) Deaf infants start babbling much later than hearing infants.

Answer: A
Page Ref: 241
Skill: Conceptual
Objective: 6.11

105) Eight-month-old Thea and her mother watch a grasshopper in their yard. Thea looks at the grasshopper and then looks at her mother to ensure that her mother is also watching the insect. Thea's mother then labels the grasshopper and describes what it is doing. Thea and her mother are engaged in
   A) expressive speech.
   B) telegraphic speech.
   C) child-directed speech.
   D) joint attention.

Answer: D
Page Ref: 241
Skill: Applied
Objective: 6.11

106) Games like pat-a-cake and peekaboo
   A) help children learn how to overextend and underextend.
   B) foster infants' understanding of the turn-taking pattern of human conversation.
   C) support the development of a referential style of communication.
   D) facilitate children's understanding of telegraphic speech.

Answer: B
Page Ref: 241
Skill: Applied
Objective: 6.11

107) When adults respond to babies' gestures, such as pointing to a cookie, by labeling them ("Oh, you want a cookie!") and complying with them (giving a cookie), the infants learn that
   A) using gestures is as effective as speech.
   B) using language leads to desired results.
   C) parents will not respond to language.
   D) parents are unresponsive to their needs.

Answer: B
Page Ref: 242
Skill: Conceptual
Objective: 6.11

108) When 6-month-olds listened to the words "Mommy" and "Daddy" while looking at side-by-side videos of their parents, they looked longer at the video of
   A) the mother.
   B) whichever parent was their primary caregiver.
   C) the named parent.
   D) the unnamed parent.

Answer: C
Page Ref: 242
Skill: Conceptual
Objective: 6.12

109) Sun is learning her first words. Of the following, which is MOST likely to be one of her first words.
    A) "hop"
    B) "ball"
    C) "vase"
    D) "table"
Answer: B
Page Ref: 242
Skill: Applied
Objective: 6.12

110) Children start to use disappearance terms like *all gone* about the same time they master
    A) child-directed speech.
    B) joint attention.
    C) deferred imitation.
    D) advanced object permanence problems.
Answer: D
Page Ref: 242
Skill: Conceptual
Objective: 6.12

111) One-year-old Dominic uses the word "train" to refer only to his favorite toy train. This is an example of
    A) an underextension.
    B) an overextension.
    C) telegraphic speech.
    D) child-directed speech.
Answer: A
Page Ref: 242
Skill: Applied
Objective: 6.12

112) Which of the following is an example of overextension?
    A) Jonah uses the word "cat" to refer to all four-legged, furry animals.
    B) Ali uses the word "car" only when referring to her family's car.
    C) Gabriel uses the word "waterglasses" to refer to swimming goggles.
    D) Jasmin uses the word "soupcase" to refer to a suitcase.
Answer: A
Page Ref: 242
Skill: Applied
Objective: 6.12

113) Two-year-old Serena refers to a gazelle as a "deer" when she sees one at the zoo. But Serena can point to a picture of a gazelle correctly when given its name. Serena MOST likely
    A) has trouble distinguishing between deer and gazelles.
    B) thinks that a gazelle is a type of deer.
    C) has difficulty recalling the word "gazelle."
    D) is visually impaired.
Answer: C
Page Ref: 242
Skill: Applied
Objective: 6.12

114) Two-year-old Roshan said "kiss booboo" to indicate to his mother that he wanted her to kiss the finger that he just pinched in the door. Roshan's utterance is an example of
    A) an underextension.
    B) babbling.
    C) telegraphic speech.
    D) referential style.
Answer: C
Page Ref: 243
Skill: Applied
Objective: 6.12

115) Children's telegraphic speech
    A) usually copies adult word pairings.
    B) emerges when toddlers' vocabulary approaches about 50 words.
    C) often violates grammatical rules.
    D) typically emphasizes smaller and less important words.
Answer: A
Page Ref: 243
Skill: Conceptual
Objective: 6.12

116) One reason that children's language comprehension is ahead of production is because
    A) production requires recognition, whereas comprehension demands recall.
    B) production requires active retrieval, whereas comprehension demands recall.
    C) comprehension requires recognition, whereas production demands recall.
    D) comprehension requires active retrieval, whereas production demands recall.
Answer: C
Page Ref: 243
Skill: Factual
Objective: 6.12

117) Research demonstrates that referential-style children often have
    A) an especially active interest in exploring objects.
    B) highly sociable personalities.
    C) parents who use verbal routines designed to support personal relationships.
    D) to spend a lot of time watching people.
Answer: A
Page Ref: 244
Skill: Conceptual
Objective: 6.13

118) Studies show that children with an expressive style of language learning
    A) tend to be highly sociable.
    B) eagerly imitate their parents' frequent naming of objects, and their parents imitate back.
    C) believe that words are for naming objects.
    D) have a faster growing vocabulary than children with a referential style.
Answer: A
Page Ref: 244
Skill: Conceptual
Objective: 6.13

119) Of the following, in which case should parents be concerned about their child's language development?
    A) a 6-month-old infant who has not yet begun to coo
    B) a 12-month-old who has not yet said her first recognizable word
    C) an 18-month-old who has a vocabulary of about 50 words
    D) a 20-month-old who has not yet combined two words
Answer: A
Page Ref: 244
Skill: Applied
Objective: 6.13

120) Of the following, which is supported by research on child-directed speech?
    A) When signing to their babies, deaf mothers show a style of communication similar to child-directed speech.
    B) Child-directed speech refers to a deliberate form of language instruction used by adults when talking to infants and toddlers.
    C) Infants begin to prefer child-directed speech over other kinds of adult talk during the second half of the first year.
    D) Child-directed speech becomes less information-laden and more emotion-laden over the first year of life.
Answer: A
Page Ref: 245
Skill: Conceptual
Objective: 6.14

121) Children prefer to listen to child-directed speech over other kinds of adult talk beginning at
    A) birth.
    B) 2 months of age.
    C) 4 months of age.
    D) 6 months of age.
Answer: A
Page Ref: 245
Skill: Factual
Objective: 6.14

122) The degree to which _____ promotes language comprehension.
    A) parents' child-directed speech is emotion-laden
    B) parents deliberately teach infants to talk using child-directed speech
    C) parents fine-tune their child-directed speech to fit with their children's needs
    D) parents' child-directed speech repeats new words in a variety of contexts
Answer: C
Page Ref: 245
Skill: Conceptual
Objective: 6.14

123) The most effective child-directed speech
    A) creates a zone of proximal development.
    B) promotes a referential style.
    C) uses telegraphic speech.
    D) promotes an expressive style.
Answer: A
Page Ref: 246
Skill: Conceptual
Objective: 6.14

124) Critics of the core knowledge perspective question findings of infants' numerical knowledge from violation-of-expectation studies because
  A) this method is not an accurate indicator of cognitive performance until at least 6 months of age.
  B) ample evidence indicates that young infants cannot form mental representations.
  C) not until the preschool years do children add and subtract small sets correctly.
  D) most infants are not exposed to number concepts during the first half year of life.
Answer: C
Page Ref: 218
Skill: Conceptual
Objective: (B&E Box) Do Infants Have Built-In Numerical Knowledge?

125) Core knowledge theorists respond to skeptics by arguing that
  A) human evolution did not equip infants with ready-made knowledge because such knowledge would limit their ability to adapt to change.
  B) infants' understanding of number concepts is surprising because toddlers do not show these understandings.
  C) infant looking preferences provide little information about their true understandings.
  D) violation-of-expectation methods may be more reliable indicators of understanding than later verbal and motor behaviors.
Answer: D
Page Ref: 218
Skill: Conceptual
Objective: (B&E Box) Do Infants Have Built-In Numerical Knowledge?

126) The literature on infantile amnesia suggests that adults typically cannot remember events that happened during the first few years of life because
  A) early memories are placed into an explicit memory system that is inaccessible once implicit memory develops.
  B) most adults have forgotten these early memories due to the passage of time.
  C) memories are not formed during this time period.
  D) adults cannot translate early preverbal memories into language.
Answer: D
Page Ref: 224
Skill: Conceptual
Objective: (B&E Box) Infantile Amnesia

127) Studies of infantile amnesia suggest that _____ is needed for the offset of infantile amnesia.
  A) an implicit memory system
  B) a variety of mnemonic strategies
  C) object permanence
  D) a clear self-image
Answer: D
Page Ref: 224
Skill: Conceptual
Objective: (B&E Box) Infantile Amnesia

128) Of the following, which is supported by research on make-believe play?
 A) When adults participate in toddlers' make-believe play, it is more elaborate than when toddlers pretend alone.
 B) In cultures where make-believe play is more frequent with older siblings than with mothers, the pretend play of toddlers is hindered.
 C) Most episodes of make-believe play during toddlerhood occur when children are playing with same-aged children.
 D) Children are more likely to combine play schemes into complex sequences when they are playing with agemates than when they are playing with caregivers.

Answer: A
Page Ref: 229
Skill: Conceptual
Objective: (CI Box) Social Origins of Make-Believe Play

129) Research demonstrates that make-believe play is
 A) less frequent and rich in collectivists cultures than in individualistic cultures.
 B) a major means through which children extend their cognitive skills.
 C) usually initiated by toddlers rather than their parents or older siblings.
 D) discovered by toddlers independently, once they are capable of representational schemes.

Answer: B
Page Ref: 229
Skill: Conceptual
Objective: (CI Box) Social Origins of Make-Believe Play

130) Research on deaf children shows that
 A) deaf children of deaf parents show language and social skills that are on par with hearing children.
 B) deaf children typically lag behind their hearing agemates in school, regardless of whether their parents are hearing or deaf.
 C) about 10 percent of deaf children have hearing parents.
 D) deaf children of hearing parents are more cognitively advanced than deaf children of deaf parents.

Answer: A
Page Ref: 246
Skill: Conceptual
Objective: (SI Box) Impact on Language and Cognitive Development of Deaf Children

131) Studies show that
 A) deafness cannot be diagnosed until at least the third postnatal month.
 B) deaf children do not need access to deaf adults or peers to experience natural language learning.
 C) deaf children of hearing parents frequently are delayed in the development of make-believe play and show impulse control problems.
 D) deaf children exhibit more favorable developmental outcomes if they have hearing parents than if they have deaf parents.

Answer: C
Page Ref: 246
Skill: Conceptual
Objective: (SI Box) Impact on Language and Cognitive Development of Deaf Children

ESSAY

132) Discuss Piaget's ideas about cognitive change. Use the following concepts in your answer: scheme, adaptation, assimilation, accommodation, organization, equilibrium, and disequilibrium.

Answer: According to Piaget, specific psychological structures, or schemes, change with age. At first, schemes are sensorimotor action patterns. With age and experience, schemes move from an action-based level to a mental level. Adaptation and organization are two processes that account for changes in schemes. Adaptation involves building schemes through direct interaction with the environment. It consists of two complementary activities: assimilation and accommodation. During assimilation, the world is interpreted in terms of current schemes. In accommodation, old schemes are adjusted or new ones are created to produce a better fit with the environment. Piaget regarded assimilation and accommodation as always working together, but the balance between these two processes varies over time. When children are not changing very much, they assimilate more than they accommodate. Piaget called this a state of cognitive equilibrium, implying a steady, comfortable condition. During times of rapid cognitive change, children are in a state of disequilibrium, or cognitive discomfort. They realize that new information does not match their current schemes, so they shift away from assimilation toward accommodation. Each time this back-and-forth movement between equilibrium and disequilibrium occurs, more effective schemes are produced.

Organization refers to the internal rearrangement and linking together of schemes so they form a strongly interconnected system. According to Piaget, schemes reach a true state of equilibrium when they become part of a broad network of structures that can be jointly applied to the surrounding world.

Page Ref: 208

133) Describe the information-processing view of cognitive development and the general structure of the information-processing system.

Answer: The information-processing approach relies on flowcharts to describe the human information-processing system. Information-processing investigators want to know exactly what individuals of different ages do when faced with a task or problem. Most information-processing models divide the mind into three basic components: the sensory register, short-term memory, and long-term memory. As information flows through each, we operate on and transform it using mental strategies, increasing the efficiency of thinking and the chances we will retain information for later use. First, information enters the sensory register where sights and sounds are directly represented but are held only briefly. Working, or short-term memory, is the conscious part of the mental system where we actively "work" on a limited amount of information. Once the limited space in working memory is occupied, either new information cannot enter the system or, if it does, it will push out existing information. Long-term memory contains our permanent knowledge base and is not limited in capacity.

Page Ref: 220–221

134) Explain the core knowledge perspective on cognitive development, noting research that both supports and challenges its assumptions.

Answer: According to the core knowledge perspective, infants begin life with an innate foundation of knowledge that supports early, rapid cognitive development. These prewired understandings allow infants to make sense of the complex stimulation that surrounds them.

Some violation-of-expectation research suggests that young infants have impressive physical and numerical understanding. In the best-known of these investigations, 5-month-olds saw a screen raised to hide a single toy. They then watched a hand place a second toy behind the screen. When the screen was removed, infants looked longer at a one-toy display than a two-toy display, indicating that they were able to keep track of the two objects. Similar studies indicate that babies can use their knowledge of quantities up to three to perform simple arithmetic.

Critics argue that such findings may simply reflect infants' looking preferences rather than an innate understanding of number concepts. And some attempts to replicate the original studies have not been successful. Further, toddlers do not show understanding of the numerical concepts displayed by 5-month-olds. Core knowledge theorists counter these arguments by suggesting that infant looking behavior may be a more reliable indicator of understanding than older children's verbal and motor behaviors.

Page Ref: 217

135) How does Vygotsky's concept of the zone of proximal development expand our understanding of early cognitive development?

Answer: Vygotsky's sociocultural theory has brought researchers to the realization that children live in rich social contexts that affect the way their cognitive world is structured. According to Vygotsky, complex mental activities, such as voluntary attention, deliberate memory, and problem solving, originate in social interaction. Through joint activities with more mature members of their society, children come to master activities and think in ways that have meaning in their culture. The concept of zone of proximal development explains how this happens. It refers to a range of tasks that the child cannot yet handle alone but can do with the help of more skilled partners.

Page Ref: 227

136) Discuss the extent to which traditional and nontraditional tests of infant intelligence predict childhood IQ.

Answer: Traditional infant tests, such as the Bayley Scales of Infant Development, include measures of perceptual and motor responses, and infant memory, problem solving, and other complex cognitive skills. These tests are poor predictors of intelligence during the childhood years, at least for samples of normal babies. This finding has been attributed to the fact that tests of infant behavior do not tap the same aspects of intelligence measured in childhood. However, traditional infant tests show somewhat better long-term prediction for very low-scoring babies. As a result, they are largely used for screening infants who are likely to have developmental problems for further observation and intervention. In contrast to traditional infant tests, speed of habituation and recovery to visual stimuli is an effective infant correlate of childhood intelligence. Unlike typical test items, the habituation-recovery response seems to tap aspects of cognitive processing (speed of thinking and attention, memory, and response to novelty) that are important in the verbal, conceptual, and problem-solving skills assessed at later ages.

Page Ref: 228, 230–231

137) Compare and contrast three major theories of language development.

    Answer: According to behaviorists, language is learned through operant conditioning and imitation. Although reinforcement and modeling contribute to language learning, these principles cannot account for the speed of early language development or children's novel, rule-based utterances.

        In contrast, Chomsky's nativist view regards children as biologically equipped with a language acquisition device (LAD) that supports rapid mastery of the structure of language. Within the LAD is a universal grammar, which refers to a built-in storehouse of rules that apply to all human languages. Children's ability to invent new language systems, efforts to teach language to apes, and the notion of a sensitive period for language development support a biological contribution to language development. However, Chomsky's theory cannot explain many aspects of language learning. For example, comparisons among different languages reveal vastly different grammatical systems. Also, Chomsky's assumption that grammatical knowledge is innate does not fit with the gradual and steady growth of children's acquisition of sentence structure.

        Interactionist theories offer a compromise between these two views, emphasizing the interactions between inner predispositions and environmental influences. Information-processing theorists focus on biological abilities of the human brain to detect patterns in language, while social interactionists propose that native capacity, a strong desire to understand others and to be understood by them, and a rich language environment combine to help children discover the functions and regularities of language.

    Page Ref: 236–240

138) Describe factors believed to bring about the offset of infantile amnesia and the onset of autobiographical memory.

    Answer: Some researchers speculate that brain development, especially the growth of the frontal lobes of the cerebral cortex, leads to gains in explicit, conscious memory during toddlerhood.

        Others believe that for memories to become autobiographical, children must have a well-developed sense of self so that memories can become personally relevant. In the first few years of life, the sense of self is not yet mature enough to serve as an anchor for one-time events.

        Further, autobiographical memory requires that children organize their experiences into a meaningful, time-organized life story. Young children learn to structure their memories into the conventional narrative form by talking about their experiences with others.

    Page Ref: 224

STUDY QUESTIONS

Piaget's Cognitive-Developmental Theory

1. During Piaget's _____ stage, which spans the first 2 years of life, infants and toddlers "think" with their eyes, ears, and hands. (p. 208)

Piaget's Ideas About Cognitive Change

1. According to Piaget, specific psychological structures, or organized ways of making sense of experience called _____, change with age. (p. 208)

2. Match the following terms with the appropriate description. (pp. 208–209)

   _____ Creating new schemes or adjusting old ones to produce a better fit with the environment

   _____ Taking new schemes, rearranging them, and linking them with other schemes to create an interconnected cognitive system

   _____ Using current schemes to interpret the external world

   _____ Building schemes through direct interaction with the environment

   1. Adaptation
   2. Assimilation
   3. Accommodation
   4. Organization

The Sensorimotor Stage

1. True or False: Piaget believed that infants already know a great deal about their world from the time they are born. (p. 209)

2. Match each of the following sensorimotor substages with its appropriate description. (pp. 209–212)

   _____ Infants' primary means of adapting to the environment is through reflexes

   _____ Infants engage in goal-directed behavior and begin to attain object permanence

   _____ Toddlers repeat behaviors with variation, producing new effects

   _____ Infants' adaptations are oriented toward their own bodies

   _____ Infants' attention begins to turn outward toward the environment

   _____ Toddlers gain the ability to create mental representations

   1. Substage 1
   2. Substage 2
   3. Substage 3
   4. Substage 4
   5. Substage 5
   6. Substage 6

3. Explain the differences between primary, secondary, and tertiary circular reactions. (pp. 210–211)

   Primary: _____

   _____

   Secondary: _____

   _____

   Tertiary: _____

   _____

4. The ability to coordinate schemes deliberately to solve simple problems is called _____. (p. 210)

5. The understanding that objects continue to exist when out of sight is called _____. (p. 210)

6. Describe the *A-not-B search error*. (p. 211)

   _____

   _____

7. Our most powerful mental representations are of two kinds: (p. 211)

   A. _____

   B. _____

8. Describe three new capacities that result from the ability to create mental representations. (pp. 211–212)

   A. _____

   _____

   B. _____

   _____

   C. _____

   _____

Follow-Up Research on Infant Cognitive Development

1. Many studies show that infants understand concepts (earlier / later) than Piaget believed. (p. 211)

2. Explain the *violation-of-expectation method,* which is often used by researchers to identify infants' grasp of object permanence and other aspects of physical reasoning. (p. 212)

   _____

   _____

   _____

   _____

3. Explain why the violation-of-expectation method is controversial. (p. 212)

   _____

   _____

   _____

4. Briefly summarize the controversial new evidence on object permanence in infancy, including Renée Baillageon's studies, as well as those seeking to confirm or refute her findings. (pp. 212–213)

   _____

   _____

   _____

   _____

5. True or False: Around 14 months, toddlers demonstrate a thorough understanding of hidden objects. (p. 213)

6. True or False: Infants demonstrate the A-not-B search error because of memory deficits; that is, they cannot remember an object's new location after it has been hidden in more than one place. (pp. 213–214)

7. Mastery of object permanence is a (gradual / sudden) achievement. (p. 214)

8. True or False: Laboratory research on deferred imitation supports Piaget's conclusion that infants cannot mentally represent experience until about 18 months of age. Provide evidence to support your response. (pp. 214–215)

     _____

     _____

     _____

9. By 10 to 12 months of age, infants can solve problems by _____, meaning that they take a strategy from one problem and apply it to other relevant problems. (p. 215)

Evaluation of the Sensorimotor Stage

1. True or False: Recent research indicates that the cognitive attainments of infancy do, in fact, follow the neat, stepwise progression that Piaget postulated. (p. 216)

2. According to the _____ perspective, babies are born with a set of innate knowledge systems, or core domains of thought. (p. 217)

3. Cite four domains of thought studied by core knowledge theorists. (p. 217)

     A. _____   B. _____

     C. _____   D. _____

4. Summarize criticisms of the core knowledge perspective. (p. 217)

     _____

     _____

     _____

5. True or False: The core knowledge perspective acknowledges that experience is essential for children to extend their initial knowledge. (p. 217)

6. Follow-up research on Piaget's sensorimotor stage yields broad agreement on two issues. Describe them. (p. 217)

     A. _____

     _____

     B. _____

     _____

Biology and Environment: Do Infants Have Built-In Numerical Knowledge?

1. According to the core knowledge perspective, what factors help infants advance their inherited foundation of knowledge? (p. 218)

     _____

     _____

2. What do research findings on infants' knowledge of numbers reveal? Why are these findings controversial? (p. 218)

     A. _____

     _____

     B. _____

     _____

Information Processing

1. In what ways do *information-processing* researchers agree with Piaget's theory? (p. 220)

_____

Structure of the Information-Processing System

1. Describe the three basic parts of the information-processing system, noting ways in which mental strategies can facilitate storage and retrieval at each level. (pp. 220–221)

   Sensory Register: _____

   _____

   _____

   Working Memory: _____

   _____

   _____

   Long-term Memory: _____

   _____

   _____

2. Explain the role of the *central executive* in managing the complex activities of the working memory system. (p. 221)

   _____

   _____

3. *Long-term memory* has a(n) (limited / unlimited) capacity. (p. 221)

4. Information-processing researchers believe that the (structure / capacity) of the human mental system is similar throughout life. (p. 221)

Attention

1. List three ways in which attention improves during infancy. (pp. 221–222)

   A. _____

   B. _____

   C. _____

2. Cite one change in attention that occurs during the toddler years. (p. 222)

   _____

3. Explain how adults can foster sustained attention during infancy and toddlerhood. (p. 222)

   _____

   _____

Memory

1. Explain how researchers use operant conditioning to study infant memory. (p. 222)

    _____

    _____

    _____

2. True or False: From the first few months of life, infant memory for operant responses is independent of context, meaning that infants apply learned responses to relevant new situations. (p. 222)

3. True or False: Habituation/recovery research confirms that infants need to be physically active to acquire new information. Briefly explain your response. (p. 223)

    _____

    _____

4. Distinguish between *recognition* and *recall* memory. (p. 223)

    Recognition: _____

    Recall: _____

5. Can infants engage in recall? Explain, citing at least one example. (p. 223)

    A. _____

    B. _____

Biology and Environment: Infantile Amnesia

1. What is *infantile amnesia*? (p. 224)

    _____

    _____

2. Recall of personally meaningful one-time events from both the recent and distant past is called _____ *memory*. (pp. 224)

3. Provide two explanations for infantile amnesia. (p. 224)

    A. _____

    _____

    B. _____

    _____

4. Explain how the phenomenon of infantile amnesia can be reconciled with infants' and toddlers' remarkable memory skills. (p. 224)

    _____

    _____

    _____

5. Discuss two developments that contribute to the end of infantile amnesia. (pp. 224–225)

A. _____

_____

B. _____

_____

Categorization

1. Explain how categorization helps infants make sense of experience. (p. 224)

_____

_____

2. The earliest categories are _____, or based on similar overall appearance or prominent object part. By the second half of the first year, more categories are _____, or based on common function and behavior. (p. 225)

3. Briefly explain how the perceptual-to-conceptual change takes place. (pp. 225–226)

_____

_____

_____

Evaluation of Information-Processing Findings

1. Information-processing research underscores the (continuity / discontinuity) of human thinking from infancy into adulthood. (p. 226)

2. In what way does information-processing research challenge Piaget's view of early cognitive development? (p. 226)

_____

_____

3. What is the greatest drawback of the information-processing approach to cognitive development? (p. 226)

_____

_____

The Social Context of Early Cognitive Development

1. According to Vygotsky's sociocultural theory, how do children learn to master activities and think in culturally meaningful ways? (p. 227)

_____

_____

2. Explain Vygotsky's concept of the *zone of proximal development,* emphasizing the role of adults in fostering children's cognitive development. (p. 227)

_____

_____

_____

3. Explain how cultural variations in social experiences influence children's mental strategies. (pp. 227–228)

_____

_____

_____

Cultural Influences: Social Origins of Make-Believe Play

1. Briefly summarize Vygotsky's view of make-believe play. (p. 229)

_____

_____

2. Explain why adults' participation in toddlers' make-believe play is so important. (p. 229)

_____

_____

_____

3. True or False: In some cultures, such as Indonesia and Mexico, make-believe play is more frequent and complex with older siblings than with mothers. (p. 229)

Individual Differences in Early Mental Development

1. How does the mental testing approach differ from the cognitive theories discussed earlier in this chapter? (p. 228)

_____

_____

_____

Infant Intelligence Tests

1. What types of responses are tapped by most infant intelligence tests? (pp. 228–229)

_____

_____

_____

2. One commonly used infant test is the _____ *Scales of Infant Development,* designed for children between 1 month and 3 ½ years. (p. 230)

3. Intelligence tests are scored by computing a(n) _____, which indicates the extent to which the raw score deviates from the typical performance of same-age individuals. (p. 230)

4. In constructing intelligence tests, designers engage in _____, giving the tests to a large, representative sample and using the results as the standard for interpreting scores. (p. 230)

5. What is a *normal distribution*? (p. 230)

_____

_____

6. When intelligence tests are standardized, the mean IQ is set at _____. (p. 230)

7. True or False: Scores on infant intelligence tests are excellent predictors of later intelligence. Why or why not? (pp. 230–231)

_____

_____

_____

8. Due to concerns that infant test scores do not tap the same dimensions of intelligence measured at older ages, they are labeled _____, or _____, rather than IQs. (p. 231)

9. For what purpose are infant intelligence tests largely used? (p. 231)

_____

_____

10. Why do habituation and recovery and Piagetian object-permanence tasks predict later IQ more effectively than traditional infant intelligence tests? (p. 231)

_____

_____

Early Environment and Mental Development

1. What is the *Home Observation for Measurement of the Environment* (HOME)? What factors does the HOME measure? (pp. 231–232)

   A. _____

   _____

   B. _____

   _____

2. Regardless of SES and ethnicity, what aspects measured by HOME predict better language and IQ scores in toddlerhood and early childhood? (p. 231)

   _____

   _____

   _____

3. Cite ways in which both heredity and home environment contribute to mental test scores. (pp. 231–232)

   Heredity: _____

   _____

   Home environment: _____

   _____

4. Today, more than _____ percent of North American mothers with children under age 2 are employed. (p. 232)

5. Discuss the impact of low- versus high-quality child care on mental development. (pp. 232–233)

    Low-quality: _____

    _____

    High-quality: _____

    _____

6. Describe the overall condition of child care for infants and toddlers in the United States and Canada. (p. 233)

    _____

    _____

    _____

7. In the United States, child-care settings that serve (low-SES / middle-SES) families provide the very worst care. Briefly explain your response. (p. 233)

    _____

    _____

8. List and briefly describe at least four signs of *developmentally appropriate practice* in infant and toddler child care. (p. 234)

    A. _____

    B. _____

    C. _____

    D. _____

Early Intervention for At-Risk Infants and Toddlers

1. Describe center- and home-based interventions for infants and toddlers. (p. 234)

    Center-based: _____

    _____

    _____

    Home-based: _____

    _____

    _____

2. Discuss the effectiveness of early intervention programs with relation to infant and toddler mental development. (pp. 234–235)

    _____

    _____

3. Briefly describe the Carolina Abecedarian Project, and summarize the outcomes of this program. (p. 235)

A. _____

_____

B. _____

_____

4. What is Early Head Start? Cite three services available through Early Head Start. (p. 235)

A. _____

B. _____

C. _____

D. _____

Language Development

1. On average, children say their first word at _____ months of age. (p. 236)

Three Theories of Language Development

1. According to the behaviorist perspective, what two processes account for early language acquisition, and how do they do so? (pp. 236–237)

A. _____

_____

B. _____

_____

2. Why is the behaviorist perspective an incomplete explanation of early language development? (p. 237)

_____

_____

3. Discuss Chomsky's nativist perspective of language acquisition, noting how this approach differs from the behaviorist perspective. Be sure to explain the *language acquisition device* (LAD) in your response. (p. 237)

_____

_____

_____

_____

4. Provide evidence supporting Chomsky's view that human infants are biologically primed to acquire language. (p. 237)

_____

_____

_____

5. Name the two language-specific areas of the brain, and cite the function of each. (pp. 237–238)

A. _____

_____

B. _____

_____

6. True or False: If the left-hemispheric region is injured in the early years, other regions of the brain take over its language function. Briefly explain your response. (p. 238)

_____

_____

7. True or False: Research supports the idea that there is a biologically based sensitive period for language development. (p. 238)

8. Is acquiring a second language harder after a sensitive period has passed? Explain. (p. 239)

_____

_____

_____

9. List two challenges to Chomsky's theory. (p. 239)

A. _____

B. _____

10. Summarize two views of the interactionist perspective of language development. (pp. 239–240)

Information-processing perspective: _____

_____

Social-interaction perspective: _____

_____

Getting Ready to Talk

1. At around 2 months of age, infants begin to make vowel-like noises called _____. At around 4 months of age, _____ appears, in which infants repeat consonant–vowel combinations in long strings. (p. 240)

2. What does research on deaf-born infants reveal about an early sensitive period for language development? (pp. 240–241)

_____

_____

_____

3. Describe *joint attention,* and indicate how it contributes to early language development. (p. 241)

A. _____

_____

B. _____

_____

4.   Explain how caregivers can support conversational give-and-take in babies. (p. 241)

_____

_____

5.   At the end of the first year, infants use _____ gestures to attract attention and interest of adults and to influence their behavior. How do these gestures contribute to language development? (p. 242)

_____

_____

First Words

1.   Briefly describe the nature of toddlers' first words (for example, to which subjects do these words commonly refer?) (p. 242)

_____

_____

_____

2.   True or False: Emotion influences early word learning. (p. 242)

3.   When young children learn new words, they tend to make two types of errors. Name and describe each error, and provide an example of each. (p. 242)

   A.   _____

   _____

   _____

   B.   _____

   _____

   _____

The Two-Word Utterance Phase

1.   List three developments that support rapid vocabulary growth during toddlerhood. (pp. 242–243)

   A.   _____

   B.   _____

   C.   _____

2.   Explain the nature of *telegraphic speech.* (p. 243)

_____

_____

_____

Comprehension versus Production

1.   Distinguish between language *comprehension* and language *production*. (p. 243)

Comprehension: _____

_____

Production: _____

_____

2.   (Comprehension / Production) requires that children *recognize* only the meaning of a word, but for (comprehension / production) children must *recall* not only the word, but also the concept for which it stands. (p. 243)

Individual and Cultural Differences

1.   True or False: Early vocabulary development proceeds at about the same rate for boys and girls. (p. 244)

2.   Explain how a child's environment influences language development. (p. 244)

_____

_____

_____

3.   Distinguish between *referential* and *expressive* styles of early language learning. (p. 244)

Referential: _____

_____

Expressive: _____

_____

4.   (Expressive / Referential) style is associated with faster vocabulary development. (p. 244)

5.   Cite factors that influence the development of referential and expressive styles. (p. 244)

_____

_____

Supporting Early Language Development

1.   Describe three ways in which caregivers can support early language learning. (p. 245)

A.   _____

B.   _____

C.   _____

2. Describe the characteristics of *child-directed speech*, noting how it promotes language development. (p. 245)

_____

_____

_____

3. True or False: Parent–toddler conversation strongly predicts early language development and academic success during the school years. (p. 245)

Social Issues: Education: Parent–Child Interaction: Impact on Language and Cognitive Development of Deaf Children

1. True or False: Over 90 percent of deaf children have hearing parents who are fluent in sign language. (p. 246)

2. Describe outcomes for children who have hearing parents not fluent in sign language. (p. 246)

_____

_____

_____

3. Discuss differences in parent–child communication experienced by deaf children of hearing parents and deaf children of deaf parents. (p. 246)

_____

_____

_____

PUZZLE 6.1 TERM REVIEW

Across

1. _____ distribution: a bell-shaped distribution that results when individual differences are measured in large samples
4. Mental _____: procedures that operate on and transform information, thereby increasing the efficiency of thinking and the chances that information will be retained
5. _____, or short-term, memory: conscious part of memory where we actively work on a limited amount of information
6. _____, or goal-directed, behavior is a sequence of actions in which schemes are deliberately combined to solve a problem
7. The _____ register is the part of the mental system in which sights and sounds are held until they decay or are transferred to short-term memory
8. In Piaget's theory, a specific structure, or organized way of making sense of experience, that changes with age
11. The ability to remember and copy the behavior of a model who is not immediately present is known as _____ imitation
12. Object _____: understanding that objects still exist even when they are out of sight
16. A special part of working memory that directs the flow of information (2 words)
17. When infants stumble onto a new experience caused by their own motor activity and then try to repeat the event again and again, they are exhibiting a _____ reaction
18. Process of building new schemes through direct contact with the environment
19. _____-_____ memory: contains our permanent knowledge base

20. Infantile _____: the inability of most people to recall events that happened to them before age 3
21. Type of memory that involves noticing whether a new experience is identical to or similar to a previous one
22. _____-_____-_____ search error: if an object is moved from hiding place A to hiding place B, 8- to 12- month-old infants will search only in the first hiding place
23. _____ knowledge perspective: babies are born with a set of innate knowledge systems

Down

2. The external world is represented in terms of current schemes
3. The practice of giving an intelligence test to a large, representative sample, which serves as the standard for interpreting individual scores
9. Violation-of-_____ method: researchers habituate infants to an event and then determine whether they recover to a possible event or an impossible event
10. Mental _____: internal image of an absent object or past event
13. The internal arrangement and linking together of schemes so that they form a strongly interconnected cognitive system
14. New schemes are created and old ones adjusted to produce a better fit with the environment
15. Piaget's first stage, during which infants and toddlers "think" with their eyes, ears, and hands
21. Type of memory that involves remembering something in the absence of perceptual support

PUZZLE 6.2 TERM REVIEW

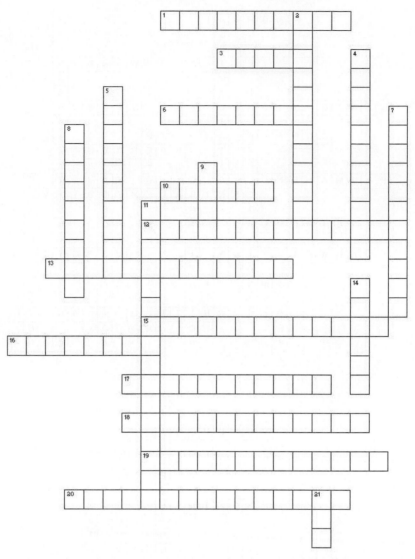

Across

1. In language development, the words and word combinations that children use

3. _____ attention: the child attends to the same object or event as the caregiver, who offers verbal information

6. Zone of _____ development: range of tasks that a child cannot yet handle independently but can accomplish with the help of more skilled partners

10. Pleasant vowel-like noises made by infants

12. Early language error in which words are applied too narrowly

13. _____ quotient: a score on an infant intelligence test; based primarily on perceptual and motor responses

15. Early language error in which words are applied too narrowly, to a wider collection of objects and events than is appropriate

16. Repetition of consonant-vowel combinations in long strings

17. Type of play in which children pretend, acting out everyday and imaginary images

18. Form of speech marked by high-pitched, exaggerated expression, clear pronunciations, and distinct pauses between speech segments (2 words, hyph.)

19. In language development, the words and word combinations that children understand

20. Standards devised by NAEYC that specify program characteristics that meet the developmental and individual needs of young children are called _____ appropriate practice

Down

2. _____ quotient: a score that permits an individual's performance on an intelligence test to be compared to the performances of other same-age individuals

4. _____ speech: toddlers' two-word utterances that leave out smaller and less important words

5. Style of early language learning in which toddlers use language mainly to talk about feelings and needs

7. Style of early language learning in which toddlers use language mainly to label objects

8. Area of the brain responsible for interpreting language

9. Checklist for gathering information about the quality of children's home lives (abbr.)

11. _____ memory: narrative accounts of significant, one-time events that are long-lasting because they are imbued with personal meaning

14. Area of the brain that controls language production

21. Innate system that permits children to speak in a rule-oriented fashion as soon as they learn enough words (abbr.)

CROSSWORD PUZZLE SOLUTIONS

PUZZLE 6.1

PUZZLE 6.2

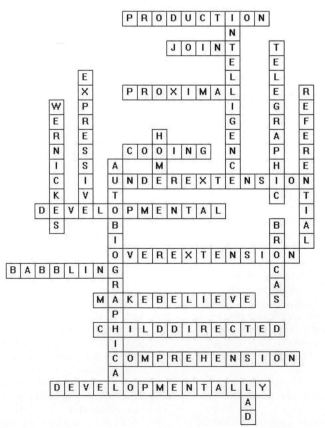

PRACTICE TEST #1

1. According to Piaget, at times when children are not changing much, they (p. 208)
   a. adapt through equilibrium.
   b. assimilate more than they accommodate.
   c. shift from assimilation to accommodation.
   d. accommodate to disequilibrium.

2. According to Piaget, in the second year, the circular reaction (p. 209)
   a. enters the tertiary substage.
   b. centers around the child's body.
   c. declines because it is no longer adaptive.
   d. becomes experimental and creative.

3. Because infants in Piaget's Substage 4 can better anticipate events, they (p. 211)
   a. try to use their capacity for intentional behavior to change those events.
   b. no longer make the A-not-B search error.
   c. repeat events caused by their own behaviors.
   d. repeat behaviors with variation.

4. Some critics of the violation-of-expectation method of research believe that it (p. 212)
   a. does not take make-believe play into account.
   b. reveals babies' limited capacity to assimilate many new experiences.
   c. indicates only limited awareness of physical events.
   d. merely confirms the effects of deferred imitation.

5. Recent studies of deferred imitation and problem solving reveal that (p. 214)
   a. toddlers do not imitate rationally until about 18 months.
   b. deferred imitation is present as early as 6 weeks of age.
   c. infants lead purely sensorimotor lives.
   d. babies use representational thought at birth.

6. Contrary to Piaget, core knowledge theorists argue that (p. 217)
   a. babies construct all mental representations through sensorimotor activity.
   b. the violation-of-expectation method reveals very little about babies' cognitive abilities.
   c. babies begin life with a limited set of biases for attending to certain information.
   d. babies are born with a set of innate knowledge systems that permit a ready grasp of new, related information.

7. Follow-up studies of Piaget's sensorimotor stage have led researchers to (p. 217)
   a. reaffirm Piaget's basic model.
   b. agree that many cognitive changes in infancy are gradual and continuous.
   c. reject Piaget's description of the later sensorimotor substages.
   d. propose that various aspects of infant cognition develop together.

8. To aid retrieval of information from long-term memory, we (p. 221)
   a. categorize information as it is taken in.
   b. use the central executive to direct the flow of information.
   c. practice using it.
   d. associate it with particular mental strategies.

9. Information-processing researchers believe that the human mental system (p. 221)
   a. changes its structure through each stage of life.
   b. gradually comes to prefer long-term memory to working memory.
   c. enlarges its capacity throughout life.
   d. is due almost entirely to brain development.

10. In toddlerhood, sustained attention typically improves because (p. 222)
    a.   attraction to novelty declines.
    b.   children attend to more aspects of the environment.
    c.   habituation time rises to 3 or 4 minutes.
    d.   children become long lookers.

11. Habituation research on infants' memory of actions confirms that (p. 223)
    a.   novelty preference is stronger than familiarity preference.
    b.   Piaget's model of sensorimotor development is essentially correct.
    c.   memory is context dependent.
    d.   infants need not be physically active to acquire new information.

12. Categorization allows infants to (p. 224)
    a.   reduce the huge amount of new information they encounter and thus make sense of experience.
    b.   successfully solve object permanence tasks.
    c.   increase the huge amount of new information they encounter and thus make sense of experience.
    d.   accurately sort objects by name, color, size, and function.

13. Vygotsky believed that complex mental activities, such as voluntary attention and deliberate memory, originate in (p. 227)
    a.   conditioning.
    b.   dynamic systems.
    c.   social interaction.
    d.   conceptual categories.

14. Of the following Bayley-III scales, which depends on parental report? (p. 230)
    a.   Adaptive Behavior
    b.   Cognitive
    c.   Language
    d.   Motor

15. Intelligence test designers reach the standard for interpreting scores by (p. 230)
    a.   computing how much the raw score deviates from the typical performance.
    b.   determining how scores cluster around the mean.
    c.   establishing the number of scales to be measured.
    d.   giving the test to a large, representative sample and using the results.

16. According to research findings, one of the best infant predictors of IQ from early childhood into adolescence is (p. 231)
    a.   developmental quotients.
    b.   habituation and recovery to novel visual stimuli.
    c.   the rate at which the infant becomes fatigued during testing.
    d.   the amount of fluctuation in IQ between infancy and toddlerhood.

17. The HOME correlational findings must be treated with caution because they (p. 231)
    a.   make too little of the genetic-environment correlation.
    b.   are based on too narrow of a sample.
    c.   do not account sufficiently for the association between home environment and mental test scores.
    d.   rely on developmental quotients that are too vague to be useful.

18. In the United States, children of middle-SES families tend to receive the poorest quality child care because (p. 233)
    a. **their parents are especially likely to place them in for-profit centers where the quality of care is often low.**
    b. very few U.S. child-care centers offer high-quality care.
    c. most of the families that use child care are in that socioeconomic category.
    d. these families are most likely to take advantage of underfunded public centers.

19. Children who participate in center-based interventions and home-based interventions (p. 234)
    a. showed greater intelligence gains in Canada than in the United States.
    b. tend to come from more organized homes than children who do not participate.
    c. mostly remain in the same SES as their parents.
    d. **score higher on mental tests by age 2 than children who do not participate.**

20. According to the behaviorist perspective, children acquire language (p. 237)
    a. through application of the universal grammar.
    b. **by imitation and reinforcement.**
    c. through the work of specialized language areas in the brain.
    d. at a sensitive period during childhood.

21. Social-interactionist theorists of language development argue that children (p. 240)
    a. **learn language as their efforts to communicate cue caregivers to provide appropriate language experiences.**
    b. make sense of complex language environments by applying general cognitive capacities.
    c. master intricate grammatical structures with little experimentation.
    d. learn language with the brain regions that also control social interaction.

22. Young children sometimes overextend words to groups of similar experiences because (p. 242)
    a. they are still learning to assimilate adults' intermodal perceptual cues.
    b. their understanding of word meanings is too narrow.
    c. **they have difficulty recalling, or have not acquired, a suitable word.**
    d. emotion still influences their word learning more than cognitive achievements.

23. Young children's comprehension of language precedes production because (p. 243)
    a. they can retrieve from their memories either the word or the concept for which it stands, but not both.
    b. they still rely on adults' perceptual cues.
    c. until about 18 months, underextension limits production.
    d. **comprehension requires only that they recognize the meanings of words.**

24. Effective CDS can stimulate children's language development by (p. 245)
    a. **employing utterance length just ahead of the of the child's.**
    b. urging the child to overextend and thus learn by error.
    c. moving the child beyond his or her zone of proximal development.
    d. discouraging joint attention while encouraging use of more complex sentences.

25. Ninety percent of deaf children experience delayed language development and have poor social skills in toddlerhood through middle childhood because (p. 246)
    a. schools are not sensitive to their needs.
    b. **their parents are not fluent in sign language.**
    c. they tend to develop extremely expressive styles to compensate for communication difficulties.
    d. caregivers tend to only communicate with them visually.

PRACTICE TEST #2

1. According to Piaget, schemes reach true equilibrium when they (p. 209)
   a. enter a period of rest, during which they do not adapt to the environment.
   d. shift from organization to accommodation.
   c. become part of a network of structures applicable to the surrounding world.
   d. connect with sensorimotor functions.

2. In Piaget's model, children move from primary circular reaction to secondary circular reaction when they (p. 210)
   a. begin trying to repeat interesting events caused by their own actions.
   b. move from actions unrelated to experience to repeating chance behaviors largely motivated by their basic needs.
   c. start forming goal-directed schemes.
   d. learn to master object permanence.

3. According to Piaget, children in Substage 6 (p. 211)
   a. repeat behaviors with variation.
   b. arrive at solutions suddenly through apparent mental representation.
   c. use invisible displacement to solve problems of deferred imitation.
   d. fully grasp everyday activities so that they no longer need to act them out.

4. Recent studies of infants and object permanence suggest that mastery of the skill (p. 214)
   a. occurs suddenly at Substage 3.
   b. is not clearly linked to physical changes in the brain.
   c. happens at a rate determined by the frequency of external stimulation.
   d. is a gradual achievement.

5. Recent studies of babies' problem solving (p. 215)
   a. suggest that children form flexible mental representations by the middle of the second year.
   b. confirm Piaget's argument that infants develop intentional means-end sequences around 7 to 8 months.
   c. reveal that by 10 to 12 months, infants can solve problems by analogy.
   d. indicate that children do not move beyond trial-and-error experimentation until the end of the second year.

6. Core knowledge theorists base their conclusions about built-in numerical knowledge on babies' (p. 218)
   a. ability to deal with less-than and greater-than relationships.
   b. looking preferences.
   c. sensorimotor responses to quantities of toys.
   d. cerebral cortex development.

7. Because the capacity of working memory is relatively restricted, (p. 221)
   a. we must use mental strategies to increase our chances of retaining information.
   b. it can process only limited amounts of information from the sensory register.
   c. it cannot connect more than a few pieces of information.
   d. we cannot automatically use information gathered through it.

8. Very young babies have long habituation times because they (p. 221)
   a. take in information almost exclusively through the sensory register.
   b. thoroughly scan complex designs.
   c. cannot yet anticipate events.
   d. have difficulty disengaging their attention from interesting stimuli.

9. Operant conditioning research has revealed that as babies grow older, their memory becomes increasingly (p. 223)
   a. linked to novel experience.
   b. free of the central executive.
   c. context free.
   d. dependent on the ability to repeat previously learned behavior.

10. During the second year, children become capable of long-term recall because (p. 223)
   a. they have achieved the capacity for recognition.
   b. new neural connections have grown among multiple regions of the cerebral cortex.
   c. their memory has become increasingly context dependent.
   d. they have acquired so much information through physical engagement with their environment.

11. Nearly all studies of infantile amnesia agree that the acquisition of autobiographical memory depends on the child's (p. 224)
   a. implicit memory.
   b. self-image.
   c. social experience.
   d. language development.

12. Language both builds on and fosters categorization by (p. 226)
   a. enlarging the infants' store of perceptual categories.
   b. making the process largely context-free.
   c. calling infants' attention to commonalities among objects.
   d. expanding infants' recognition of familiar experiences.

13. To overcome the weakness of the information-processing approach, researchers have (p. 226)
   a. applied the dynamic systems view to early cognition.
   b. detached it from Piaget's system of sensorimotor stages.
   c. analyzed recall into even smaller components.
   d. tried to trace stronger links between perception and attention.

14. A child approaching a task within his or her zone of proximal development needs (p. 227)
   a. fewer perceptual categories than a child not working within that zone.
   b. to create new schemes by acting on the physical world.
   c. the help of a more skilled partner.
   d. to represent his or her experiences as efficiently and meaningfully as possible.

15. Vygotsky's theory suggests that to promote children's make-believe play, parents and teachers should (p. 229)
   a. provide a stimulating environment.
   b. emulate the practices of collectivist societies.
   c. allow children complete freedom to pursue their inclinations.
   d. participate with children and guide them through such play.

16. Which of the following items would be included in the Bayley-III Cognitive Scale? (p. 230)
   a. Attention to familiar and unfamiliar objects
   b. Recognition of objects and people following simple directions
   c. Naming of objects and pictures
   d. Grasping, sitting, and stacking blocks

17. A child who does better than 50 percent of his or her agemates on an intelligence test has an IQ of (p. 230)
   a. 60.
   b. 85.
   c. 100.
   d. 130.

18. The quality of child care in the United States and Canada is affected by a macrosystem of (p. 233)
    a. high taxation and poor financial management.
    b. individualistic values and weak regulation.
    c. excessive government oversight.
    d. an overemphasis on the needs of immigrant children.

19. One criticism of Chomsky's nativist theory is that (p. 239)
    a. the assumption of innate grammatical knowledge does not fit with some important observations of actual language development.
    b. it does not take sufficient account of the effects of reinforcement.
    c. the idea of a universal grammar is based on the structures of Western languages so it does not actually apply universally.
    d. the grammatical rules are too general to provide sufficient explanations.

20. Interactionist theories of language development emphasize both (p. 239)
    a. brain development and Piaget's idea of deferred imitation.
    b. imitation and reinforcement.
    c. language areas in the brain and a sensitive period for language development.
    d. inner capacities and environmental influences.

21. Babies move from cooing to babbling when they (p. 240)
    a. recognize that adults respond favorably.
    b. want to make more unpleasant sounds.
    c. add consonants to vowels.
    d. reach age 2 months.

22. By the end of the first year, infants use preverbal gestures to (p. 242)
    a. establish joint attention with adults.
    b. attract adults' attention and interest and influence their behavior.
    c. make greater sense of babbling.
    d. avoid give-and-take with adults.

23. When children's vocabulary permits telegraphic speech, they (p. 243)
    a. focus on high-content words and omit smaller, less important ones.
    b. display a remarkable grasp of subtle grammatical rules.
    c. organize experience into simple categories.
    d. tend to use nouns more than verbs.

24. Children who develop referential-style language tend to (p. 244)
    a. be unusually shy.
    b. utter compressed phrases that sound like single words.
    c. have an especially active interest in exploring objects.
    d. be speakers of Asian languages.

25. Young children tend to prefer CDS over other kinds of adult talk because it (p. 245)
    a. helps them to develop expressive-style language.
    b. involves pleasant cooing and babbling.
    c. holds their interests with long sentences.
    d. builds on communication strategies such as joint attention, to which they already respond.

POWERPOINT SLIDES

Infants, Children and Adolescents
Laura E. Berk 6th edition

Chapter 6

Cognitive
Development
in Infancy and
Toddlerhood

This multimedia product and its contents are
protected under copyright law. The following are
prohibited by law:
- Any public performance or display, including
  transmission of any image over a network;
- Preparation of any derivative work, including the
  extraction, in whole or in part of any images;
- Any rental, lease, or lending of the program.

INFANTS,
CHILDREN,
AND
ADOLESCENTS
SIXTH EDITION

LAURA E. BERK

Copyright © Allyn & Bacon 2008

Piaget's Cognitive-Development Theory

■ **The sensorimotor stage spans the first two years of life.**

■ **Organized ways of making sense of experience called schemes change with age:**
  - **Action-based (motor patterns) at first**
  - **Later move to a mental (thinking) level**

Copyright © Allyn & Bacon 2008

Building Schemes

■ **Adaptation**
  - Building schemes
■ **Assimilation**
  - Using current schemes to interpret external world
■ **Accommodation**
  - Adjusting old schemes and creating new ones to better fit environment

Copyright © Allyn & Bacon 2008

Using Assimilation and Accommodation

- **Equilibrium and Disequilibrium**
  - Use assimilation during equilibrium
  - Disequilibrium prompts accommodation
- **Organization**
  - Internal rearranging and linking schemes

Copyright © Allyn & Bacon 2008

Sensorimotor Stage

- Birth to 2 years, divided into six substages
- Building schemes through sensory and motor exploration
- Circular reactions— stumbling upon a new experience caused by the baby's own motor activity.

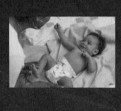

Copyright © Allyn & Bacon 2008

Piaget's Sensorimotor Substages

SENSORIMOTOR SUBSTAGE	TYPICAL ADAPTIVE BEHAVIORS
1. Reflexive schemes (birth–1 month)	Newborn reflexes (see Chapter 4, page 000)
2. Primary circular reactions (1–4 months)	Simple motor habits centered around the infant's own body; limited anticipation of events
3. Secondary circular reactions (4–8 months)	Actions aimed at repeating interesting effects in the surrounding world; imitation of familiar behaviors
4. Coordination of secondary circular reactions (8–12 months)	Intentional, or goal-directed, behavior; ability to find a hidden object in the first location in which it is hidden (object permanence); improved anticipation of events; imitation of behaviors slightly different from those the infant usually performs
5. Tertiary circular reactions (12–18 months)	Exploration of the properties of objects by acting on them in novel ways; imitation of unfamiliar behaviors; ability to search in several locations for a hidden object (accurate A–B search)
6. Mental representation (18 months–2 years)	Internal depictions of objects and events, as indicated by sudden solutions to problems; ability to find an object that has been moved while out of sight (invisible displacement); deferred imitation; and make-believe play

Copyright © Allyn & Bacon 2008

Object Permanence

- Understanding that objects continue to exist when out of sight
- According to Piaget, develops in Substage 4
- Incomplete at first: A-not-B search error

Object Permanence (cont.)

- Renée Baillargeon and her collaborators claim to have found evidence for object permanence in the first few months of life.
- Some critics question whether babies' looking preferences tell us what they really know.
- Mastery of object permanence is a gradual achievement.

Violation of Expectation Method

Habituation Events
Short-carrot event | Tall-carrot event
(a)
Test Events
Expected event | Unexpected event
(b) | (c)

Mental Representations

- Internal, mental depictions of objects, people, events, information
  - Can manipulate with mind
  - Allow *deferred imitation* and *make-believe play*

Copyright © Allyn & Bacon 2008

Deferred Imitation

- **Piaget**: Develops at about 18 months
- **Newer research:**
  - Present at 6 weeks – facial imitation
  - 6 – 9 months – copy actions
  - 14 months – imitate rationally
  - 18 months – imitate intended, but not completed, actions

Copyright © Allyn & Bacon 2008

Problem Solving

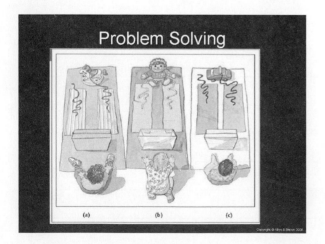

(a)   (b)   (c)

Copyright © Allyn & Bacon 2008

Some Cognitive Attainments of Infancy and Toddlerhood

AGE	COGNITIVE ATTAINMENTS
Birth–1 month	Secondary circular reactions using limited motor skills, such as sucking a nipple to gain access to interesting sights and sounds
1–4 months	Awareness of many object properties, including object permanence, object solidity, and gravity, as suggested by violation-of-expectation findings; deferred imitation of an adult's facial expression after a short delay (1 day)
4–8 months	Improved physical knowledge and basic numerical knowledge, as suggested by violation-of-expectation findings; deferred imitation of an adult's novel actions on objects over a short delay (1 day)
8–12 months	Ability to search for a hidden object in diverse situations—when covered by a cloth, when a hand deposits it under a cloth, and when it is moved from one location to another (accurate A–B search); ability to solve sensorimotor problems by analogy to a previous problem
12–18 months	Deferred imitation of an adult's novel actions on an object over a long delay (at least several months) and across a change in situation (from child care to home, from TV to everyday life); rational imitation, taking into account the model's intentions
18 months–2 years	Deferred imitation of actions an adult tries to produce, even if these are not fully realized, again indicating a capacity to infer others' intentions; imitation of everyday behaviors in make-believe play

Copyright © Allyn & Bacon 2006

Evaluation of Sensorimotor Stage

- **Some developments happen at time Piaget described:**
  - Object search, A-not-B, make-believe play
- **Many appear to happen sooner than Piaget thought:**
  - Object permanence, secondary circular reactions, deferred imitation, problem solving by analogy
- **Some have suggested that infants are born with *core knowledge* in several domains of thought.**

Copyright © Allyn & Bacon 2006

Store Model of Information Processing System

Copyright © Allyn & Bacon 2006

Attention

- During the first year, infants pay attention to novel events.
- During toddlerhood, children become capable of intentional behavior and sustained attention improves.

Memory

- Operant conditioning research shows that infants' memories increase dramatically during infancy and toddlerhood—moving from highly context-dependent to increasingly context-free.
- Habituation/recovery research confirms that infants do not need to be physically active to acquire and retain new information.
- Infants can engage in recall by the end of the first year.

Increase in Retention in Two Operant Conditioning Tasks from 2 to 18 Months

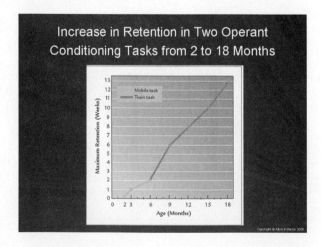

Categorization

- By 6 months, infants can categorize based on two features (ex. shape and color).
- Earliest categories are perceptual, but by the second half of the first year, more categories are conceptual.

Copyright © Allyn & Bacon 2008

Vygotsky's Sociocultural Theory

- **Social contexts** (other people) contribute to cognitive development.

- **Zone of Proximal Development** – tasks child cannot do alone but can learn to do with help

Copyright © Allyn & Bacon 2008

Infant Intelligence Tests

- Bayley Scales of Infant Development: suitable for children between 1 month and 3½ years.
- ❖ The Bayley-III
  1. The Cognitive Scale
  2. The Language Scale
  3. The Motor Scale
  4. The Social-Emotional Scale *
  5. The Adaptive Behavior Scale *
     * Rely on parental report.

Copyright © Allyn & Bacon 2008

Normal Distribution of Intelligence Test Scores

Mean

| 0.1% | 2% | 14% | 34% | 34% | 14% | 2% | 0.1% |

55 70 85 100 115 130 145

IQ Score

Copyright © Allyn & Bacon 2008

High Quality HOME Environment

- Parent emotional and verbal responsiveness
- Parental acceptance
- Safe physical environment
- Appropriate play materials
- Parental involvement
- Variety, daily stimulation

Copyright © Allyn & Bacon 2008

Elements of Developmentally Appropriate Child Care

- Responsive, interactive, well-trained caregivers
- Clean, safe, uncrowded indoor spaces
- Appropriate toys, stored within reach
- Safe equipment
- Low teacher-child ratios
- Flexible daily schedule
- Warm atmosphere
- Parents welcome anytime
- Accredited

Copyright © Allyn & Bacon 2008

IQ Improvement from Early Intervention Programs

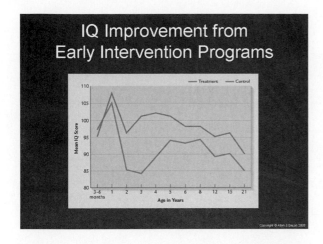

Early Head Start

- Begun in 1995, currently has 700 sites serving 62,000 low-income families.
- Intervention leads to warmer, more stimulating parenting, and gains in children's cognitive and language development.

Three Theories of Language Development

Behaviorist (B.F. Skinner)	Learned through operant conditioning (reinforcement) and imitation.
Nativist (Noam Chomsky)	Inborn Language Acquisition Device (LAD) biologically prepares infants to learn rules of language.
Interactionist	Inner capacities and environment work together; social context is important.

Language Areas in the Brain

- Broca's Area: located in the left frontal lobe, supports grammatical processing and language production.
- Wernicke's Area: located in the left temporal lobe, plays a role in comprehending word meaning.

Copyright © Allyn & Bacon 2008

Broca's and Wernicke's Areas in the Left Hemisphere of the Cerebral Cortex

Copyright © Allyn & Bacon 2008

Recent Developments in the Interactionist Perspective

- Recent ideas about language development emphasize interactions between inner capacities and environmental influences.
- Two theories:
  - Information-processing perspective
  - Social interaction

Copyright © Allyn & Bacon 2008

Milestones of Language Development During the First Two Years

APPROXIMATE AGE	MILESTONE
2 months	Infants coo, making pleasant vowel sounds.
6 months on	Infants babble, adding consonants to their cooing sounds and repeating syllables. By 7 months, babbling starts to include many sounds of spoken languages.
	Infants observe with interest as the caregiver plays turn-taking games, such as pat-a-cake and peekaboo.
8–12 months	Infants comprehend some words.
	Infants become more accurate at establishing joint attention with the caregiver, who often verbally labels what the baby is looking at.
	Infants actively participate in turn-taking games, trading roles with the caregiver.
	Infants use preverbal gestures, such as showing and pointing, to influence the behavior of others.
12 months	Babbling includes sound and intonation patterns of the child's language community.
	Toddlers say their first recognizable word.
18–24 months	Vocabulary expands from about 50 to 200 spoken words.
	Toddlers combine two words.

Copyright © Allyn & Bacon 2008

Getting Ready to Talk

- **First speech sounds**
  - Cooing
  - Babbling
- **Becoming a communicator**
  - Joint attention
  - Give-and-take
  - Preverbal gestures

Copyright © Allyn & Bacon 2008

Sensitive Period for Language Development

- A deaf-born 5-month-old given a cochlear implant showed typical infant babbling and resembled her hearing agemates in language development at 3 to 4 years.
- If hearing is not restored until after age 2, children remain behind in language development.
- If implantation occurs after age 4, language delays are severe and persistent.

Copyright © Allyn & Bacon 2008

Starting to Talk

- First Words
  - Underextension
  - Overextension
- Two-Word Utterances
  - Most children show a steady, continuous increase in the rate of word learning through the preschool years
  - Telegraphic speech

Copyright © Allyn & Bacon 2008

Building Blocks of Language

Toddlers first acquire "concrete pieces of language," gradually generalizing to construct the word order and grammatical rules of their native tongue.

Copyright © Allyn & Bacon 2008

Comprehension versus Production

- Toddlers' comprehension of the spoken language increases dramatically over the second year.
- Quick comprehension frees space in working memory for picking up new words and for the more demanding task of using them to communicate.

Copyright © Allyn & Bacon 2008

Individual Differences in Language Development

- **Gender**
- **Temperament**
- **Environment**
  - SES
  - Child Directed Speech
- **Language Style**
  - Referential
  - Expressive
- **Language Delay**

Copyright © Allyn & Bacon 2008

Supporting Early Language Development

Infants	▪Respond to coos and babbles ▪Establish and respond to joint attention ▪Play social games
Toddlers	▪Play make-believe together ▪Have frequent conversations ▪Read to toddlers often and talk about the books

Copyright © Allyn & Bacon 2008

Parent-Child Interaction: Impact on Language and Cognitive Development of Deaf Children

- About one in every 1,000 infants in North America is born deaf. Over 90% of these children have hearing parents who are not fluent in sign language.
- Deaf children of hearing parents are often delayed in development of language and make-believe play and have deficient social skills. Yet, children of deaf parents do not have these problems.
- Intervention within the first year of life can have a positive impact on language, cognitive, and social outcomes for deaf children of hearing parents.

Copyright © Allyn & Bacon 2008

CHAPTER 7
EMOTIONAL AND SOCIAL DEVELOPMENT
IN INFANCY AND TODDLERHOOD

CHAPTER-AT-A-GLANCE

Chapter Outline	Instruction Ideas	Supplements
Erikson's Theory of Infant and Toddler Personality pp. 252–253 Basic Trust versus Mistrust • Autonomy versus Shame and Doubt	Learning Objective 7.1 Ask Yourself p. 253	Test Bank Items 1–4 Please contact your Allyn and Bacon publisher's representative for a wide range of video offerings available to adopters.
Emotional Development pp. 253–259 Development of Basic Emotions • Understanding and Responding to the Emotions of Others • Emergence of Self–Conscious Emotions • Beginnings of Emotional Self-Regulation	Learning Objectives 7.2–7.5 Lecture Enhancements 7.1, 7.4 Learning Activities 7.1–7.2 Ask Yourself p. 259	Test Bank Items 5–32 Transparencies 76, 108–109
Development of Temperament pp. 260–268 The Structure of Temperament • Measuring Temperament • Stability of Temperament • Genetic Influences • Environmental Influences • Temperament and Child Rearing: The Goodness-of-Fit Model	Learning Objectives 7.6–7.8 Learning Activities 7.3–7.4 Ask Yourself p. 268	Test Bank Items 33–52, 101–102, 110–111
Development of Attachment pp. 268–283 Bowlby's Ethological Theory • Measuring the Security of Attachment • Stability of Attachment • Cultural Variations • Factors That Affect Attachment Security • Multiple Attachments • From Attachment to Peer Sociability • Attachment and Later Development	Learning Objectives 7.9–7.13 Lecture Enhancements 7.2–7.4 Learning Activities 7.5–7.8 Ask Yourself p. 282	Test Bank Items 53–93, 103–107, 112–114 Transparency 79
Sef-Understanding pp. 283–287 Self-Awareness • Categorizing the Self • Self-Control	Learning Objective 7.14 Learning Activities 7.9–7.10 Ask Yourself p. 286	Test Bank Items 94–100 Transparency 82

BRIEF CHAPTER SUMMARY

Erikson's psychosocial theory, which builds on Freud's psychoanalytic theory, provides an overview of the emotional and social tasks of infancy and toddlerhood. For Erikson, trust and autonomy grow out of warm, supportive parenting in the first year, followed by reasonable expectations for impulse control during the second year.

Emotions play an important role in the organization of relationships with caregivers, exploration of the environment, and discovery of the self. Infants' ability to express basic emotions, such as happiness, anger, sadness, and fear, and respond to the emotions of others expands over the first year. As toddlers become more self-aware, self-conscious emotions, such as shame, embarrassment, and pride, begin to emerge. Emotional self-regulation improves as a result of brain maturation, gains in cognition and language, and sensitive child rearing.

Children's unique temperaments, or styles of emotional responding, are already apparent in early infancy. Heredity influences early temperament, but child-rearing and other experiences determine whether a child's temperament is sustained or modified over time. The goodness-of-fit model helps explain the bidirectional relationship between children's temperaments and parents' child-rearing styles.

Ethological theory is the most widely accepted view of the development of attachment—the strong affectionate tie that develops between infants and caregivers. According to this perspective, attachment evolved over the history of our species to promote survival. Research shows that responding promptly, consistently, and appropriately to infant signals supports secure attachment, whereas insensitive caregiving is linked to attachment insecurity. Because children and parents are embedded in larger contexts, family circumstances and cultural factors influence attachment patterns. Parents' internal working models—their view of their own attachment experiences—also play a role. Infants form attachment bonds not only with their mothers but also with other familiar people, including fathers, and siblings. When grandparents serve as primary caregivers for children, strong attachment ties develop between them.

Though limited, peer sociability is already present in the first two years, and it is fostered by the early caregiver–child bond. Continuity of caregiving seems to play a role in the relationship between early attachment security or insecurity and later development.

Once self-awareness develops over the first and second year, it supports a diverse array of social and emotional achievements. Empathy, the ability to categorize the self, compliance, and self-control are all by-products of toddlers' emerging sense of self.

LEARNING OBJECTIVES

After reading this chapter, you should be able to:

7.1   Discuss the first two stages of Erikson's psychosocial theory, noting the personality changes that take place at each stage. (pp. 252–253)

7.2   Describe the development of basic emotions, including happiness, anger, sadness, and fear, over the first year, noting the adaptive function of each. (pp. 253–256)

7.3   Summarize changes that occur during the first two years in understanding others' emotions. (pp. 256–257)

7.4   Discuss the nature of self-conscious emotions, explaining why they emerge during the second year and indicating their role in development. (pp. 257–258)

7.5   Trace the development of emotional self-regulation during the first two years. (pp. 258–259)

7.6   Discuss the three underlying components of temperament, and identify three types of children described by Thomas and Chess. (pp. 260–261)

7.7   Explain how temperament is measured. (p. 262)

7.8   Summarize the role of heredity and environment in the stability of temperament, including the goodness-of-fit model. (pp. 262–267)

7.9   Describe the unique features of ethological theory of attachment. (pp. 268–270)

7.10 Describe the Strange Situation and the Attachment Q-sort procedures for measuring attachment, and cite the four patterns of attachment assessed by the Strange Situation. (pp. 270–272)

7.11 Discuss the factors that affect attachment security. (pp. 273–276)

7.12 Discuss infants' formation of multiple attachments, and indicate how attachment paves the way for early peer sociability. (pp. 276–281)

7.13 Describe and interpret the relationship between secure attachment in infancy and cognitive, emotional, and social competence in childhood. (pp. 281–283)

7.14 Trace the emergence of self-awareness in infancy and toddlerhood, along with the emotional and social capacities it supports. (pp. 283–287)

LECTURE OUTLINE

I. ERIKSON'S THEORY OF INFANT AND TODDLER PERSONALITY (pp. 252–253)
   A. Although Freud's psychoanalytic theory is no longer in the mainstream of child development research, it does capture the essence of personality development during each stage of life.
   B. The most influential approach that accepts and elaborates the basic outlines of Freud's is Erik Erikson's *psychosocial theory.*
   C. Basic Trust versus Mistrust (p. 252)
      1. Erikson believed that a healthy outcome during infancy depended on the *quality* of caregiving during feeding, not the *amount* of food or oral stimulation offered.
      2. Erikson defined the psychological conflict of the first year as **basic trust versus mistrust,** which is resolved positively when the *balance of care* is sympathetic and loving.
   D. Autonomy versus Shame and Doubt (pp. 252–253)
      1. Erikson's theory identifies the conflict of toddlerhood as **autonomy versus shame and doubt.** It is resolved positively if parents provide suitable guidance and reasonable choices during this period of budding selfhood.
      2. If children emerge from the first few years without sufficient trust in caregivers and without a healthy sense of individuality, the seeds are sown for later adjustment problems.

II. EMOTIONAL DEVELOPMENT (pp. 253–259)
   A. Emotions are an integral part of young children's dynamic systems of action, and play powerful roles in organizing the attainments that Erikson regarded as vitally important: social relationships, exploration of the environment, and discovery of the self.
   B. Development of Basic Emotions (pp. 254–256)
      1. **Basic emotions**—happiness, interest, surprise, fear, anger, sadness, and disgust—are universal in humans and other primates and have a long evolutionary history of promoting survival.
      2. At first, a baby's emotional life consists of little more than two global arousal states: attraction to pleasant stimulation and withdrawal from unpleasant stimulation. Gradually, emotions become clear, well-organized signals.
      3. Children coordinate separate skills into more effective systems as the central nervous system develops and the child's goals and experiences change.
      4. Sensitive, contingent caregiver communication helps infants construct emotional expressions that closely resemble those of adults.
      5. Happiness (pp. 254–255)
         a. Happiness binds parent and baby into a warm, supportive relationship that fosters the infant's developing competence.
         b. The **social smile,** which is evoked by the parent's communication, first appears between 6 and 10 weeks.
         c. Laughter first occurs around 3 to 4 months in response to active stimuli. It reflects faster processing of information than does smiling.
         d. Like adults, 10- to 12-month-olds have several smiles, which vary with context, and at the end of the first year, the smile becomes a deliberate social signal.

6. Anger and Sadness (pp. 255–256)
    a. From 4 to 6 months into the second year, angry expressions increase in frequency and intensity.
    b. As infants become capable of intentional behavior and develop new motor capacities, anger rises, motivating caregivers to relieve the infant's distress.
    c. Sadness is common when the infant is deprived of a familiar loving caregiver, especially when parent–infant interaction is seriously disrupted.
7. Fear (p. 256)
    a. Like anger, fear rises during the second half of the first year.
    b. The most frequent expression of fear is to unfamiliar adults, a response called **stranger anxiety.**
    c. Stranger anxiety depends on several factors: temperament, past experiences with strangers, the situation in which baby and stranger meet, and culturally determined infant-rearing practices.
    d. The rise in fear after 6 months of age helps protect newly crawling and walking babies by keeping them close to caregivers and careful about approaching unfamiliar people and objects.
    e. Once wariness develops, infants use the familiar caregiver as a **secure base** from which to explore, and encounters with strangers lead to a balance between approach and avoidance.
    f. Fear wanes as children acquire a wider array of strategies for coping with it.
C. Understanding and Responding to the Emotions of Others (pp. 256–257)
    1. Early on, babies match the feeling tone of the caregiver in face-to-face communication. Researchers disagree on whether this result from an automatic process of *emotional contagion* or from operant conditioning.
    2. Around 3 to 4 months, infants are sensitive to the structure and timing of face-to-face interactions and become increasingly aware of the range of emotional expressions.
    3. From 5 months on, infants perceive facial expressions as organized patterns and respond to emotional expressions as organized wholes.
    4. **Social referencing** begins at 8 to 10 months, when infants start to evaluate unfamiliar people, objects, and events in terms of their safety and security, relying on a trusted person's emotional reaction to decide how to respond in an uncertain situation.
    5. By toddlerhood, children use emotional signals to infer others' internal states and guide their own actions.
D. Emergence of Self-Conscious Emotions (pp. 257–258)
    1. **Self-conscious emotions** are those that involve injury to or enhancement of the sense of self. They include shame, embarrassment, guilt, envy, and pride.
    2. Self-conscious emotions appear in the middle of the second year, as 18- to 24-month-olds develop a sense of the self as a separate, unique individual. Adult instruction, as well as self-awareness, plays a role in development of these emotions.
    3. Self-conscious emotions play an important role in children's achievement-related and moral behaviors.
E. Beginnings of Emotional Self-Regulation (pp. 258–259)
    1. Emotional self-regulation refers to the strategies used to adjust an emotional state to a comfortable level of intensity so we can accomplish our goals. It requires *effortful control,* which improves gradually through development of the cerebral cortex and through the help caregivers provide to children in managing intense emotion.
    2. In the early months, infants have only limited capacity to regulate their emotional states; they depend on caregivers to soothe them.
    3. Rapid development of the cerebral cortex increases the baby's tolerance for stimulation, and caregivers build on this capacity through face-to-face play.
    4. By 4 to 6 months, infants have some ability to shift attention and engage in self-soothing.
    5. By the end of the first year, babies' ability to move around permits them to regulate feelings more effectively by approaching or retreating from various stimuli.
    6. As caregivers help infants regulate their emotional states, they contribute to the child's style of emotional self-regulation.
        a. When parents respond contingently and sympathetically to babies' emotional cues, infants tend to be less fussy and easier to soothe.
        b. Caregivers also provide lessons in socially approved ways of expressing feelings, which reflect cultural ideas of what is appropriate.

7. In the second year, growth in representation and language leads to new ways of regulating emotions as children become able to label emotions and describe their internal states.

III. DEVELOPMENT OF TEMPERAMENT (pp. 260–268)
   A. **Temperament** refers to early-appearing, stable individual differences in reactivity and self-regulation.
      1. *Reactivity* refers to quickness and intensity of emotional arousal, attention, and motor activity.
      2. *Self-regulation* refers to strategies that modify reactivity.
   B. In 1956, Thomas and Chess initiated the New York Longitudinal Study, a comprehensive examination of the development of temperament. Results indicated the following:
      1. Temperament is predictive of psychological adjustment.
      2. Parenting practices can modify children's emotional styles.
   C. The Structure of Temperament (pp. 260–261)
      1. The majority of the Thomas and Chess sample fell into one of three types of children:
         a. **Easy children** (40 percent of the sample) quickly establish regular routines, are cheerful, and adapt easily to new experiences.
         b. **Difficult children** (10 percent of the sample) are irregular in daily routines, slow to accept new experiences, and tend to react negatively and intensely.
         c. **Slow-to-warm-up children** (15 percent of the sample) are inactive, have mild, low-key reactions to stimuli, and adjust slowly to new experiences.
      2. An additional 35 percent of children did not fit any of these categories but showed blends of characteristics.
      3. The "difficult" pattern places children at risk for adjustment problems, both anxious withdrawal and aggressive behavior.
      4. A second model of temperament, developed by Mary Rothbart (1981), combines overlapping dimensions of Thomas and Chess and other researchers to yield six dimensions representing three underlying components of temperament.
         a. Emotion includes "fearful distress," "irritable distress," "positive affect," and "soothability."
         b. Attention measures "attention span/persistence."
         c. Action looks at "activity level."
      5. Rothbart also considers **effortful control,** the self-regulatory dimension of temperament, which identifies how effectively a child can focus and shift attention, inhibit impulses, and manage negative emotions.
   D. Measuring Temperament (pp. 262, 263)
      1. Temperament is often assessed through parent interviews and questionnaires, behavior ratings by medical professionals or caregivers, and direct researcher observation.
      2. Parental reports, though convenient, have been criticized as being biased but are moderately related to researchers' observations of children's behavior and are vital for understanding how parents view and respond to their child.
      3. Laboratory observations can lead to inaccuracies because they may not capture all relevant information, but they allow researchers to combine observations with physiological measures to study the biological basis of temperament.
      4. Most physiological assessments have focused on children at the extremes: **inhibited, or shy, children,** who react negatively to and withdraw from novel stimuli, and **uninhibited, or sociable, children,** who display positive emotion to and approach novel stimuli.
      5. Heart rate, hormone levels, and EEG waves in the frontal region of the cerebral cortex differentiate children with inhibited and uninhibited temperaments.
   E. Stability of Temperament (pp. 262, 264)
      1. The overall stability of temperament is low in infancy and toddlerhood and only moderate from the preschool years on, in part because temperament itself develops with age.
      2. Long-term prediction from early temperament is best achieved after age 3, when the child's system of emotion, attention, and action is better established.
      3. Child rearing and other experiences play an important role in modifying biologically based temperamental traits, but children rarely change from one extreme to the other.

F.   Genetic Influences (pp. 264-265)
   1.   Findings of twin studies reveal that identical twins are more similar than fraternal twins across a wide range of temperamental traits and personality measures.
   2.   Heritability estimates derived from twin studies suggest that about half of individual differences in temperament and personality can be traced to differences in our genetic makeup.
   3.   Consistent ethnic and sex differences in early temperament also exist, supporting a role for heredity.
      a.   Asian infants tend to be less active, irritable, and vocal than Caucasian infants.
      b.   Boys tend to be more active and daring than girls.
   4.   However, heritability estimates are much higher for expressions of negative than of positive emotion.
G.   Environmental Influences (pp. 265–266)
   1.   Persistent nutritional and emotional deprivation are among the environmental influences that profoundly alter temperament, resulting in maladaptive emotional reactivity, as seen in children exposed to severe malnutrition in infancy or reared in deprived orphanages.
   2.   Heredity and environment often jointly contribute to temperament, since a child's approach to the world affects the experiences to which he or she is exposed.
   3.   Cultural and sex differences in temperament reflect this interaction between heredity and environment.
      a.   For example, Asian mothers do more comforting and Caucasian mothers more stimulating.
      b.   Parents more often encourage infant sons to be physically active and daughters to seek help and physical closeness.
   4.   In families with more than one child, parents' tendency to emphasize differences between siblings also influences temperament by affecting parents' child-rearing practices.
   5.   Children's unique experiences with people outside the family also contribute to the tendency of siblings to become increasingly dissimilar in personality with age.
H.   Temperament and Child Rearing: The Goodness-of-Fit Model (pp. 266–267)
   1.   The **goodness-of-fit model** explains how temperament and environment work together to produce favorable outcomes. Goodness of fit involves creating child-rearing environments that recognize each child's temperament while simultaneously encouraging more adaptive functioning.
   2.   For example, difficult infants are less likely than easy babies to receive sensitive care, and the parents' response is likely to sustain and even increase the child's irritable, conflict-ridden style.
   3.   Caregiving is affected by other factors in addition to the child's temperament, including life conditions and cultural values.

IV.   DEVELOPMENT OF ATTACHMENT (pp. 268–283)
   A.   **Attachment** is the strong affectionate tie we feel toward special people in our lives that leads us to experience pleasure and joy when we interact with them and to be comforted by their nearness during times of stress.
   B.   The psychoanalytic perspective and behaviorism both viewed feeding as the central context for attachment, but for different reasons.
   C.   Research indicates that although feeding is an important context for building attachment, hunger satisfaction is not the only factor in development of a close relationship with the caregiver. Human infants can also become attached to people who do not feed them, as well as to soft, cuddly objects.
   D.   Bowlby's Ethological Theory (pp. 269–270)
      1.   Today, **ethological theory of attachment** is the most widely accepted view of attachment. This theory, which John Bowlby (inspired by Konrad Lorenz's studies of imprinting in baby geese) first applied to the infant–caregiver bond, recognizes the infant's emotional tie to the caregiver as an evolved response that promotes survival.
      2.   The human infant is endowed with a set of built-in behaviors that keep the parent nearby, increasing the chances that the infant will be protected from danger.
      3.   Attachment develops in four phases:
         a.   *Preattachment phase* (birth to 6 weeks): Built-in signals such as smiling and crying help bring the newborn into close contact with other humans.

      b.   *"Attachment in the making" phase* (6 weeks to 6 to 8 months): Infants begin to respond differently to a familiar caregiver than to a stranger and develop a sense of trust, expecting the caregiver to respond when signaled.

      c.   *"Clear-cut" attachment phase* (6 to 8 months to 18 months to 2 years): Attachment to the familiar caregiver is evident. Babies exhibit **separation anxiety** when they become upset at the departure of a familiar caregiver. They use caregivers as a secure base from which to explore the environment, returning periodically for emotional support.

      d.   *Formation of a reciprocal relationship* (18 months to 2 years and on): Separation anxiety decreases; instead, toddlers try to persuade caregivers not to leave.

   4.   Through their experiences in these four phases, children construct an **internal working model**—a set of expectations derived from early caregiving experiences concerning the availability of attachment figures, their likelihood of providing support during times of stress, and the self's interaction with those figures—which becomes a guide for all future close relationships.

E.   Measuring the Security of Attachment (pp. 270–271)

   1.   The **Strange Situation** is a procedure for measuring the quality of attachment between 1 and 2 years of age. It involves short separations from and reunions with the parent.

      a.   **Secure attachment** characterizes infants who may or may not cry at parental separation but are easily comforted by the parent when she returns.

      b.   **Avoidant attachment** describes infants who are usually not distressed by parental separation and who avoid the parent when she returns.

      c.   **Resistant attachment** identifies infants who remain close to the parent before departure and display angry, resistive behavior when she returns.

      d.   **Disorganized/disoriented attachment** characterizes infants who respond in a confused, contradictory way when reunited with parents. This pattern seems to reflect the greatest insecurity.

   2.   The **Attachment Q-Sort** is an alternative assessment method suitable for children between 1 and 5 years of age, which taps a wider array of attachment-related behaviors than the Strange Situation.

      a.   Descriptors regarding attachment-related behaviors are sorted into categories ranging from "highly descriptive" to "not at all descriptive" of the child.

      b.   Then, a score is computed, ranging from high to low in security.

F.   Stability of Attachment (p. 272)

   1.   Quality of attachment is usually secure and stable for middle-SES babies experiencing favorable life conditions.

   2.   Infants who move from insecurity to security typically have well-adjusted mothers with positive family and friendship ties.

   3.   For low-SES families with many stresses and little support, attachment status usually moves away from security or changes from one insecure pattern to another.

   4.   Many children show short-term instability in attachment quality. Those with high long-term stability usually come from middle-SES homes with stable family lives.

G.   Cultural Variations (p. 272)

   1.   Cross-cultural evidence indicates that attachment patterns may have to be interpreted differently in certain cultures.

      a.   German parents encourage their infants to be independent, which may explain why more German infants show avoidant attachment than American babies.

      b.   Japanese infants rarely show avoidance attachment; they are more likely to display resistant attachment responses. Because Japanese mothers rarely leave their babies in the care of strange people, the Strange Situation may be more stressful for these infants.

   2.   The secure attachment pattern is the most common in all societies studied.

H.   Factors That Affect Attachment Security (pp. 273–276)

   1.   Opportunity for Attachment (p. 273)

      a.   In a series of studies, René Spitz observed that institutionalized infants experienced emotional difficulties, wept and withdrew from their surroundings, lost weight, and had difficulty sleeping.

     b.   Institutionalized babies had emotional difficulties not because they were separated from their mothers, but because they were prevented from forming a bond with one or a few adults.

     c.   The evidence indicates that fully normal attachment development depends on establishing close bonds with caregivers during the first few years of life.

2.   Quality of Caregiving (pp. 273–274)

     a.   Research findings indicate that securely attached infants have mothers who engage in **sensitive caregiving**—responding promptly, consistently, and appropriately to infants and handling them tenderly and carefully.

     b.   Insecurely attached infants have mothers who engage in less physical contact, handle them awkwardly, and behave in a "routine" manner when meeting the baby's needs.

     c.   **Interactional synchrony** refers to the sensitively tuned "emotional dance" in which the caregiver responds to infant signals in a well-timed, rhythmic, appropriate fashion and both partners match emotional states, especially the positive ones.

     d.   Although secure attachment depends on attentive caregiving, its association with immediate contingent interaction is probably limited to certain cultures.

     e.   Avoidant infants tend to receive caregiving that is overstimulating and intrusive.

     f.   Highly inadequate caregiving, including child abuse and neglect, is a powerful predictor of disruptions in attachment.

3.   Infant Characteristics (pp. 274–275)

     a.   Prematurity, birth complications, and newborn illness make caregiving more taxing and are linked to attachment insecurity in poverty-stricken, stressed families, though not in infants whose parents have adequate time and patience to care for them.

     b.   The role of infant temperament in attachment security has been intensely debated, with varying evidence on the importance of the parent's response to the baby.

     c.   The heritability of attachment is virtually nil, and siblings differing in temperament are nevertheless likely to establish similar attachment patterns with their parents, suggesting that the parents are adjusting their caregiving styles to each individual child's needs.

     d.   Some evidence indicates that sensitive caregiving can override the impact of infant characteristics on attachment security.

     e.   A major reason that temperament and other infant characteristics do not show strong relationships with attachment security may be that their influence depends on goodness of fit.

4.   Family Circumstances (pp. 275–276)

     a.   In families where there is stress and instability, insecure attachment is especially high, but parents can protect the child's development by sustaining a favorable relationship with their baby in spite of these stressors.

     b.   Availability of social supports reduces parental stress and thereby fosters attachment security.

5.   Parents' Internal Working Models (p. 276)

     a.   Parents bring to the family context their own history of attachment experiences, from which they construct internal working models that they apply to the bonds they establish with their babies.

     b.   Parents who discuss their own childhoods with objectivity and balance tend to have securely attached infants, regardless of whether their experiences were positive or negative. In contrast, parents who dismiss the importance of early relationships or describe them in angry, confused ways usually have insecurely attached babies.

     c.   Internal working models are *reconstructed memories* affected by many factors besides early attachment experiences, including other close relationships, personality, and current life satisfaction. As a result, our own early rearing experiences do not destine us to become sensitive or insensitive parents.

6.   Attachment in Context (pp. 276, 277)

     a.   Many factors influence the development of attachment—infant and parent characteristics, the parents' relationship with each other, family stressors, social support, parents' internal working models, and child-care arrangements.

     b.   As a result, attachment can only be fully understood within an ecological systems perspective.

I. Multiple Attachments (pp. 276, 278–280)
1. Bowlby believed that infants are predisposed to direct their attachment behaviors to a single attachment figure, especially when they are distressed, but that multiple attachments are possible.
2. Fathers (pp. 278, 279)
   a. Fathers' sensitive caregiving and interactional synchrony with infants predict attachment security.
   b. Mothers and fathers interact differently with their babies, with mothers spending more time in physical care and gentle play, fathers in highly arousing physical play.
      (1) Cultural differences affect the division of parental roles.
      (2) Mothers in dual-earner families tend to engage in more playful stimulation of their babies than those who are at home full-time, but fathers who are primary caregivers retain their arousing play style.
      (3) Highly involved fathers are less gender-stereotyped in their beliefs, have sympathetic, friendly personalities, and regard parenthood as an especially enriching experience.
   c. A warm marital bond supports both parents' involvement with babies, but it is particularly important for fathers.
3. Grandparent Primary Caregivers (pp. 278–280)
   a. Primary caregiving by children's grandparents has become increasingly common in the past decade, with 4 to 5 percent of the North American child population living apart from their parents and with their grandparents.
   b. This arrangement is more common in African-American, Hispanic, and Canadian-Aboriginal families than in Caucasian families.
   c. Grandparents tend to assume the parenting role under stressful circumstances, and also take on financial burdens that may leave them feeling emotionally drained.
   d. Nevertheless, these grandparent caregivers form significant attachment relationships with their grandchildren—bonds that help protect children from adjustment problems.
4. Siblings (p. 280)
   a. Eighty percent of North American children grow up with at least one sibling.
   b. Conflict between siblings increases when one member of a sibling pair is emotionally intense or highly active.
   c. Secure infant–mother attachment and warmth toward both children are related to positive sibling interaction, whereas maternal harshness and lack of involvement are associated with sibling friction.

J. From Attachment to Peer Sociability (pp. 280–281)
1. Between 1 and 2 years, coordinated peer interaction occurs more often, typically in the form of mutual physical play and imitation.
2. Reciprocal play and positive emotion are especially frequent in toddlers' interactions with familiar agemates, suggesting that they are building true peer relationships.
3. Peer sociability is present in the first two years, and it is fostered by the early caregiver–child bond, through which babies learn how to send and interpret emotional signals in their first peer associations.

K. Attachment and Later Development (pp. 281–283)
1. Research indicates that *continuity of caregiving* determines whether early attachment security is linked to later development.
2. A child whose parental caregiving improves or who has compensating affectionate ties outside the immediate family can bounce back from adversity.

V. SELF-UNDERSTANDING (pp. 283–287)
A. Self-Awareness (pp. 283–285)
1. Beginnings of Self-Awareness (p. 283)
   a. At birth, infants sense that they are physically distinct from their surroundings.
   b. Over the first few months, infants distinguish their own visual image from other stimuli but have limited self-awareness, expressed only in perception and action.
   c. By 4 months, infants look and smile more at video images of others than images of themselves, indicating that they view another person (as opposed to the self) as a potential social partner.

2. Self-Recognition (pp. 283–284)
    a. Around age 2, self-recognition, or identification of the self as a physically unique being, is well under way.
    b. As infants act on the environment, they notice effects that help them sort out self, other people, and objects.
    c. Sensitive caregiving promotes early self-development. Securely attached toddlers display more complex self-related actions during play.
3. Self-Awareness and Early Emotional and Social Development (pp. 284–285)
    a. At the end of the first year, babies realize that the self can be the focus of others' intentions and emotional reactions, and they become increasingly sensitive to variations in caregivers' emotional messages, setting the stage for social referencing.
    b. Self-awareness leads to the child's first efforts to appreciate another's perspective.
    c. Toddlers also show early signs of **empathy**—the ability to understand another's emotional state and *feel with* that person, or respond emotionally in a similar way. Going along with empathy is a clearer understanding of how to upset others.
B. Categorizing the Self (p. 285)
    1. Between 18 and 30 months, children develop a **categorical self** based on age, physical characteristics, and even goodness or badness, and they begin to refer to the self's competencies.
    2. Toddlers use their limited understanding of these social categories to organize their own behavior, as seen in a sharp rise in gender-stereotyped responses starting as early as 18 months.
C. Self-Control (pp. 285–287)
    1. Self-awareness contributes to *effortful control,* the ability to inhibit impulses, manage negative emotions, and behave in socially acceptable ways.
    2. The first signs of self-control appear between 12 and 18 months as **compliance**—clear awareness of and voluntary obedience to simple requests and commands.
    3. Researchers study self-control by giving children tasks that require **delay of gratification**—waiting for an appropriate time and place to engage in a tempting act. Children show an increasing ability to delay gratification between ages 1½ and 3 years.
    4. Toddlers who experience parental warmth and gentle encouragement are more likely to be cooperative and advanced in self-control.
    5. Toddlers' control over their own actions is dependent upon constant parental oversight and reminders.

LECTURE ENHANCEMENTS

LECTURE ENHANCEMENT 7.1
Age-Related Differences in Social Referencing: Mothers versus Strangers (pp. 256–257)

Time: 5-10 minutes

Objective: To examine age-related differences in infants' use of social referencing.

As noted in the text, infants use social referencing to appraise novel or uncertain events. To examine infants' use of social referencing with parents versus strangers, Walden and Kim (2005) recruited 61 infant-mother pairs and observed them at 18 and 24 months of age.

During a free play trial, infants and mothers interacted in a room that contained a variety of toys and books. A "stranger" (one of several graduate students) was also present. Prior to the free play trial, parents and strangers were instructed to give positive or negative vocal messages and facial expressions, such as "Nice toy!" or "Scary toy!" Once infants became accustomed to their surroundings, they were placed in the middle of the room with their mother and the stranger behind them. They were then presented with three remote-controlled toys—a robot with a foam ball for a head, a white robot with red eyes, and a red furry toy with black button eyes. The toys were chosen because they had a curious appearance and did not naturally elicit a positive or negative reaction. When each toy was presented, parents and strangers showed a neutral expression and then changed to a positive or negative expression. The researchers coded the amount of time infants looked at their mother and the stranger. They also coded whether or not infants had a positive or negative reaction to each of the toys.

Results indicated that 24 month olds were more likely than 18 month olds to seek social information from a stranger than their mother. That is, 24 month olds relied more on the stranger's reaction toward the remote-controlled toys, whereas 18 month olds relied more on their mother's reaction. Walden and Kim (2005) suggest that younger infants may be more oriented to emotional comfort in an unfamiliar situation, which is why they primarily look to their mother for social information. Older infants, in contrast, may view a stranger as having more expertise than their mother. However, since infants cannot explain their motivations for looking to caregivers versus strangers, this interpretation must be considered with caution. Nevertheless, these findings highlight a developmental change in social referencing that occurs between 18 and 24 months of age.

Ask students to briefly reflect on these findings. What milestones of early cognitive development and social understanding might contribute to age-related differences in social referencing?

Walden, T. A., & Kim, G. (2005). Infants' social looking toward mothers and strangers. *International Journal of Behavioral Development, 29,* 356–360.

LECTURE ENHANCEMENT 7.2
Do Early Temperament and Attachment Styles Predict Personality at Age 9? (pp. 268–272)

Time: 10–15 minutes

Objective: To examine whether early temperament and attachment styles predict certain aspects of personality at age 9.

The text notes that the overall stability of early temperament is low to moderate, and attachment research reveals that securely attached babies more often maintain their attachment status than insecure babies. However, no empirical studies have been conducted on early temperament and attachment as predictors of the Five Factor Model of personality (Hagekull & Bohlin, 2003). The Five Factor Model includes the following scales:

(1) Extraversion—energetic, talkative, bold, enthusiastic, cheerful, happy, shy, timid, quiet
(2) Agreeableness—cooperative, modest, sensitive, trusting, sincere, polite, patient, stubborn, selfish, dishonest, bossy, quarrelsome, rebellious
(3) Conscientiousness—organized, dependable, responsible, careful, neat, disorganized, messy, lazy, forgetful, careless
(4) Neuroticism—nervous, tense, anxious, worries about things, fearful, relaxed, content, self-confident, oversensitive, calm, stable
(5) Openness—imaginative, curious, creative, tries new activities

To further examine the relationship between early temperament, attachment, and personality development, Hagekull and Bohlin (2003) recruited 93 children from middle-income families and followed them from 6 weeks to 9 years of age. At 15 months, parents and children completed Ainsworth's Strange Situation, and researchers classified attachment as secure, avoidant, or resistant. When children were 20 months old, both mothers and fathers completed a standardized temperament questionnaire. When children were in the second grade, parents and teachers completed a personality questionnaire based on the Five Factor Model.

Results indicated that early temperament and attachment security predicted certain aspects of personality. Children who were described as having an easy temperament at 20 months scored higher on extraversion at age 9. Children who were securely attached at 15 months were also more likely to be described by teachers and parents as extraverted than children with an avoidant or resistant attachment style. In addition, the researchers found that early attachment security predicted neuroticism and openness. That is, securely attached infants were less neurotic and more open to experience at age 9 than infants with an insecure attachment style. Interestingly, neither temperament nor attachment style predicted agreeableness or conscientiousness.

These findings support those presented in the text; Securely attached infants with an easy temperament develop more favorably than insecure infants with a difficult temperament. However, it is important to note that temperament and attachment status were not reassessed throughout the study. Therefore, we do not know if these patterns were stable over time. Instead, the findings suggest that early assessments of temperament and attachment can predict certain aspects of personality in middle childhood.

In small groups, have students list environmental factors that contribute to temperament and attachment security in infancy and toddlerhood. How can adults help modify a difficult temperament or insecure attachment style?

Hagekull, B., & Bohlin, G. (2003). Early temperament and attachment as predictors of the Five Factor Model of personality. *Attachment & Human Development, 5,* 2–18.

LECTURE ENHANCEMENT 7.3
More on the Link Between Paternal Depression and Child Development (p. 278)

Time: 5–10 minutes

Objective: To examine the effects of paternal depression on young children's emotional and social development.

Mental health problems like depression can have a profound impact on father involvement and child development. In one study, Ramchandani and colleagues (2005) investigated the effects of paternal depression on young children's social and emotional development. The researchers sent questionnaires to 13,351 expectant mothers and 12,884 expectant fathers at regular intervals during and after pregnancy. The questionnaires focused on a diverse range of factors, including exposure to environmental toxins, psychosocial risk, and physical and psychological development. At 8 weeks after the baby's birth, mothers and fathers completed a standardized depression scale. Fathers completed a second depression scale at 21 months. When children were 3½ years old, their mothers completed a standardized measure of children's emotional and behavioral development. The questionnaire provided an assessment of conduct disorder, emotional problems, hyperactivity, and prosocial behavior.

Results indicated that children of depressed fathers were more likely to experience emotional and behavioral problems at 3½ years, even after controlling for maternal depression. This finding was particularly strong for children whose fathers reported depression in the first few months following the birth. That is, early paternal depression seemed to put children at greater risk for emotional and behavioral problems than later paternal depression. The researchers also found that paternal depression affected boys more adversely than girls. Interestingly, maternal depression affected boys and girls similarly. Ramchandani and his colleagues (2005) speculated that boys may be especially sensitive to their fathers' parenting behaviors, making them more vulnerable to the effects of paternal depression.

Taken together, these findings highlight the importance of fathers in early child development. Even after controlling for maternal depression, paternal depression can have a profound impact children's social and emotional development.

In small groups, have students list stressors associated with the birth of a new baby (see Chapter 4, pp. 157–161). According to the text, why can parenthood be an especially stressful time for some parents? Based on these findings and research presented in the text, do students think both mothers and fathers should be assessed for depression following the birth of a baby? Why or why not?

Ramchandani, P., Stein, A., Evans, J., & O'Connor, T. G. (2005). Paternal depression in the postnatal period and child development: A prospective population study. *Lancet, 365,* 2201–2205.

LECTURE ENHANCEMENT 7.4
Developmental Differences in Infants' Sensitivity to Social Contingencies (pp. 256–257)

Time: 5–10 minutes

Objective: To examine developmental differences in young infants' sensitivity to social contingencies.

As noted in the text, infant–caregiver interactions are particularly important for the development of social understanding. During the first few months of life, young babies become sensitive to differences in social contingencies, which affects how they interact with caregivers. To further examine infants' sensitivity to social contingencies, Striano, Henning, and Stahl (2005) conducted two studies. In the first, 68 1-month-old infants and their mothers were videotaped during normal face-to-face interaction. The mothers were not given any instructions on how to interact with their babies. One week later, the mothers and infants returned for a second videotaped observation. The mothers were asked to put on a pair of headphones attached to an audio recorder. With their infants seated across from them, the mothers participated in the following conditions:

(1) *Normal interaction.* Mothers were simply asked to interact with their babies as they normally do.
(2) *Noncontingent interaction.* Mothers were asked to play the audio recorder, which contained a recording of what they had said to their infant during the first visit. They were instructed to listen through the headphones and repeat what was on the tape, using the exact same voice inflection. Therefore, the mother's behavior did not necessarily match their baby's actions. Regardless of what the baby was doing, the mothers repeated what was on the tape.
(3) *Imitation interaction.* Mothers were instructed to imitate their infant's behavior, including facial expressions, hand and arm gestures, and vocalizations.

The second study was identical to the first, except the infants were approximately 3 months old. A total of 66 infants and their mothers participated in the second study.

Results indicated that 3-month-olds are highly sensitive to social contingencies. Specifically, 3-month-olds smiled more at their mothers in the normal interaction condition than in the other two conditions. They also gazed more in the imitation condition than in the normal or noncontingent interaction conditions. In contrast, 1-month-olds engaged in similar amounts of gazing and smiling across all three conditions, suggesting that very young babies are not yet sensitive to social contingencies. One explanation for 3-month-olds' increasing gazing during imitation was that their mothers' imitation was surprising or novel, which resulted in greater interest. One-month-olds did not seem to notice differences in their mother's behavior, since they responded similarly across the conditions.

Taken together, these findings highlight a developmental transition in young infants' sensitivity to social contingencies. By 3 months, infants seem to detect a difference between everyday, normal interactions with their mothers and unusual or imperfect social interactions, which were created in the noncontingent and imitation conditions.

Striano, T., Henning, A., & Stahl, D. (2005). Sensitivity to social contingencies between 1 and 3 months of age. *Developmental Science, 8,* 509–518.

LEARNING ACTIVITIES

LEARNING ACTIVITY 7.1
Classroom Demonstration: Development of Emotional Expression (pp. 253–256)

Arrange for a group of babies, ranging in age from several weeks to 18 months, to visit your classroom for a demonstration of emotional expression during infancy. Students may have friends or family members who are willing to participate in the demonstration. Alternatively, you may have friends or colleagues who are available for a class period.

During the demonstration, have students carefully observe the infants' facial, body, and vocal expressions and record any examples of basic emotions, including events that may have elicited these emotions. For example, a baby may smile in response to his or her parent's facial expression and / or voice. In addition, interview parents about their infants' range of emotional expressions (happiness, interest, surprise, fear, anger, sadness, and disgust). Are their answers consistent with research in the text—that infants' precise emotions are difficult to detect in the early months but become more recognizable with age?

Using a baby between 2 and 4 months of age, demonstrate the social smile by nodding, smiling, and talking softly to the infant. Also, illustrate parental responsiveness to infant smiling to underscore the adaptive role of the smile in promoting positive interactions between parent and child. For babies 3 months of age and older, have parents describe and, if possible, demonstrate, stimuli that elicit laughter, and note their dynamic and intrusive quality (for example, kissing the baby's tummy). For infants over 7 months of age, point out the rise in fear reactions that generally occurs around this time and that is reflected in the baby's hesitancy to reach for novel objects, wariness of strange adults, and tendency to keep track of the parent's whereabouts in an unfamiliar environment. Finally, ask students to look for instances of social referencing and use of the secure base in older infants. Point out that after 10 months of age, babies often rely on the caregiver's emotional response to form an appraisal of an uncertain situation.

LEARNING ACTIVITY 7.2
Supporting Emotional Self-Regulation in Infants and Toddlers (pp. 258–259)

Ask students to pretend that they have been asked to speak to a group of parents on the importance of helping young children manage their emotional experiences. Using research in the text as a guide, have students list the information they would include in their presentation. For example, why is emotional self-regulation important? What infant and toddler behaviors reflect the beginnings of effortful control and emotional self-regulation? How can parents help their infants and toddlers regulate emotion? What caregiving behaviors should parents avoid, and why?

LEARNING ACTIVITY 7.3
Matching: The Thomas and Chess Model of Temperament (p. 261)

Present the following exercise as an in-class activity or quiz:

Directions: Match each of the following terms with its correct description.

Terms:

1. Activity level
2. Rhythmicity
3. Distractibility
4. Approach / withdrawal
5. Adaptability
6. Attention span and persistence
7. Intensity of reaction
8. Threshold of responsiveness
9. Quality of mood

Descriptions:

    A. Response to a new object, food, or person
    B. Energy level of response, such as laughing, crying, talking, or gross motor activity
    C. Ratio of active periods to inactive ones
    D. Intensity of stimulation required to evoke a response
    E. Amount of time devoted to an activity, such as watching a mobile or playing with a toy
    F. Degree to which stimulation from the environment alters behavior—for example, whether crying stops when a toy is offered
    G. Amount of friendly, joyful behavior as opposed to unpleasant, unfriendly behavior
    H. Regularity of body functions, such as sleep, wakefulness, hunger, and excretion
    I. Ease with which child adapts to changes in the environment, such as sleeping or eating in a new place

Answers:

    1. C
    2. H
    3. F
    4. A
    5. I
    6. E
    7. B
    8. D
    9. G

LEARNING ACTIVITY 7.4
Examining Student Temperament (pp. 260–267)

Have students visit the Keirsey Temperament and Character website, *http://www.keirsey.com*, and complete the online personality questionnaire. After completing the questionnaire, students should answer the following questions: What did the questionnaire reveal about your temperament? Do you agree with the results? Based on the results and on research in the text, explain how your temperament may have affected, and been affected by, relationships with parents and caregivers. Next, click on *Parenting and Temperament*. What problems can arise when parent and child have different temperaments?

LEARNING ACTIVITY 7.5
Observing the Attachment Relationship During the First Two Years (pp. 268–271)

This activity can be included as an extension of Learning Activity 7.1. If you have access to a baby 6 weeks of age or younger, demonstrate and / or describe the built-in signals of the preattachment phase—grasping, smiling, crying, and gazing into the adult's eyes. Next, show students that babies under 6 months are generally willing to be held and soothed by unfamiliar adults, although from 2 to 8 months, they respond preferentially to familiar caregivers. For example, when held by familiar adults, babies smile and vocalize more consistently and quiet more readily when picked up. Around 6 to 8 months, "clear-cut" attachment is evident. To illustrate, ask the parent of a baby between 8 and 18 months old to leave the room briefly, as is done in Ainsworth's Strange Situation. Securely attached infants generally try to follow; if they cannot, they become distressed at the parent's departure but are quickly comforted by physical proximity when he or she returns. By the end of the second year, growth in mental representation and language enables children to tolerate parental absences more easily. After participants have had sufficient time to become comfortable in the classroom, ask the parent of an 18- to 24-month-old to explain to the child that he or she is going to leave the room for a moment but will be back shortly. Students should note the reaction of the child and compare it to research in the text.

*For demonstrations in which the parent leaves the room, make sure the parent immediately returns if the child becomes distressed.

LEARNING ACTIVITY 7.6
Exploring Security of Attachment from an Ecological Systems Perspective (pp. 273–276)

Ask students to complete the following activity in small groups: List as many factors as you can that might affect attachment security. Next, return to Chapter 1 and review Bronfenbrenner's ecological systems theory (pp. 25–27). For each factor you listed, determine the level of the environment (microsystem, mesosystem, exosystem, or macrosystem) with which it is associated. In addition, provide examples of bidirectional influences that contribute to attachment security. Under what circumstances do third parties foster attachment security? How might third parties compromise attachment security? Explain.

LEARNING ACTIVITY 7.7
Investigating Threats to Attachment Security (p. 277)

Indicate to students that they have been asked to conduct home visits for infants and toddlers who may be at risk for insecure attachment. What clues would students look for to distinguish among avoidant, resistant, and disorganized–disoriented attachment? What caregiving behaviors might signal a threat to attachment security? How about infant characteristics? What questions would students ask to identify important contextual influences on the infant–parent relationship (for example, recent divorce, financial difficulties)?

LEARNING ACTIVITY 7.8
Researching Laws Regulating Child Care (pp. 273–274)

As discussed in the text, quality of care, both at home and in the child-care setting, is vital for fostering the emotional security of young children. As noted in Chapter 1, the quality of American and Canadian child care is cause for deep concern. Standards are set by states or provinces, and they vary greatly across each nation. In some places, caregivers need no special training in child development, and one adult is permitted to care for as many as 6 to 12 infants and toddlers at once. Have students research information about standards of child care in their home state (American students) or province or territory (Canadian students). The websites sponsored by the National Association for the Education of Young Children, *http://www.naeyc.org* and Child & Family Canada, *http://www.cfc-efc.ca* may be helpful.

While conducting their research, students should try to locate licensure information about (1) child-care staff (for example, minimum age for center director, required education, and / or training); (2) caregiver–child ratios and maximum group size (including variations by children's age); (3) space and equipment; (4) curriculum requirements; (5) health and safety requirements (for example, immunizations, nutrition); (6) transportation; (7) child records; (8) discipline (for example, written policy); and (9) parental rights. After students have gathered the relevant information, ask them to compare their findings with the standards for developmentally appropriate practice presented on page 234 of the text. Finally, have students use this information to rate the quality of child care in their state, province, or territory, and discuss the findings in class.

LEARNING ACTIVITY 7.9
True or False: Self-Understanding During the First Two Years (pp. 283–286)

Present the following exercise to students as a quiz or in-class activity:

Directions: Read each of the following statements and indicate whether it is *True* (T) or *False* (F).

Statements:

_____ 1. Newborns' capacity for intermodal perception supports the beginnings of self-awareness.
_____ 2. During the second month, infants become consciously aware of the self's physical features.
_____ 3. Around age 2, children point to themselves in photos and refer to themselves by name or personal pronoun.
_____ 4. Self-awareness is associated with the beginnings of empathy—the ability to understand another's emotional state and feel with that person, or respond emotionally in a similar way.
_____ 5. Between 10 and 12 months, children develop a categorical self as they categorize themselves and others on the basis of age, sex, physical characteristics, and goodness versus badness.
_____ 6. Effortful control refers to toddlers' awareness of caregivers' wishes and expectations.
_____ 7. For most toddlers, opposition is far less common than compliance.
_____ 8. Delay-of-gratification tasks reveal that boys are typically more self-controlled than girls.
_____ 9. When toddlers fail to comply with adult directives, parents should resort to harsh and forceful tactics to ensure obedience.
_____ 10. Parents should respond to self-controlled behavior with verbal and physical approval, increasing its likelihood of occurring again.

Answers:

1. T
2. F
3. T
4. T
5. F
6. F
7. T
8. F
9. F
10. T

LEARNING ACTIVITY 7.10
Observing Toddlers for Compliance and Self-Control (pp. 285–286)

Invite two or three toddlers and parents to your classroom for a demonstration of compliance and self-control. Prior to the demonstration, gather several age-appropriate toys and several boxes of raisins. If you do not have access to these materials, ask parents to bring toys from home and / or raisins.

Present the following activities: Ask the child (or have the parent ask the child) not to touch an interesting toy within arm's reach. Alternatively, hide some raisins under cups, and instruct the child to wait until you (or the parent) say it is all right to pick up a cup and eat a raisin. Have students note how easily each child is able to resist temptation. Then give the children several directions (for example, to bring you an object or to clean up some toys). Did older children exhibit more compliance and self-control? Did they also try to exert more independence and not comply with directives? How did parents respond to their child's behavior?

ASK YOURSELF . . .

APPLY: Derek's mother fed him in a warm and loving manner during the first year. But when he became a toddler, she kept him in a playpen for many hours because he got into too much mischief while exploring freely. Use Erikson's theory to evaluate Derek's early experiences. (pp. 252–253)

Because of the warm and loving care Derek experienced during the first year, he developed a sense of basic trust—a positive outcome in Erikson's first stage. As a result, Derek enters his second year as a trusting child who expects the world to be good and gratifying, and he feels confident about venturing out and exploring it. As a toddler, Derek is now in Erikson's second stage, in which the essential conflict is autonomy versus shame and doubt. Because his mother has placed such drastic limitations on his freedom to explore, Derek's opportunities to develop self-confidence and self-control are severely restricted. A sense of autonomy depends on access to the environment and a careful balance of suitable guidance and reasonable choices. It cannot be built through confinement. Unless his mother increases his opportunities to explore, Derek may have an unfavorable resolution of the conflict of this stage.

CONNECT: Do Erikson's recommendations for fostering autonomy in toddlerhood fit with Vygotsky's concept of the zone of proximal development, described on page 227 in Chapter 6? Explain. (pp. 252–253)

Erikson maintained that the conflict of toddlerhood, autonomy versus shame and doubt, is resolved favorably when parents provide young children with suitable guidance and reasonable choices. Warm, sensitive parenting and reasonable expectations are essential ingredients for fostering autonomy in toddlerhood. Vygotsky defines the zone of proximal development as a range of tasks the child cannot yet handle alone but can do with help from more skilled partners. When parents give children the combination of appropriate choices and suitable guidance that foster autonomy and a sense of competence in toddlerhood, they are also providing the kind of support that Vygotsky described as *scaffolding,* which promotes learning within children's zone of proximal development.

REVIEW: Why do many infants show stranger anxiety in the second half of the first year? What factors can increase or decrease wariness of strangers? (p. 256)

Like anger, fear rises during the second half of the first year. Older infants hesitate before playing with a new toy, and crawling infants soon show fear of heights. But the most frequent expression of fear is *stranger anxiety* in response to unfamiliar adults. Many, though not all, infants and toddlers are quite wary of strangers. The response depends on several factors: temperament (some babies are generally more fearful), past experiences with strangers, and the current situation. When an unfamiliar adult picks up the infant in a new situation, stranger anxiety is likely. But if the adult sits still while the baby moves around and a parent is nearby, infants often show positive and curious behavior. The stranger's style of interaction—expressing warmth, holding out an attractive toy, playing a familiar game, and approaching slowly rather than abruptly—reduces the baby's fear. In addition, culture plays a role: Infant-rearing practices can modify stranger anxiety. For example, among the Efe hunters and gatherers of Congo, West Africa, where the maternal death rate is high, infant survival is safeguarded by a collective caregiving system in which, starting at birth, Efe babies are passed from one adult to another. Consequently, Efe infants show little stranger anxiety.

APPLY: At 14 months, Reggie built a block tower and gleefully knocked it down. But at age 2, he called to his mother and pointed proudly at his tall block tower. What explains this change in Reggie's emotional behavior? (pp. 257–258)

In the second half of the first year, as 18- to 24-month olds become firmly aware of the self as a separate, unique individual, self-conscious emotions appear. These emotions, which involve injury to or enhancement of our sense of self, include guilt, shame, embarrassment, envy, and pride. At 14 months, Reggie had not yet developed a clear sense of himself as a separate person, so he simply enjoyed the experience of building the block tower and then knocking it down. But by the time he was 2, he had developed a sense of pride in his achievement at stacking the blocks into a tower, and wanted to share his accomplishment with his mother.

In addition to self-awareness, development of pride and other self-conscious emotions depends on adult instruction in *when* to feel proud, ashamed, or guilty. The situations in which adults encourage these feelings vary from culture to culture, but in individualistic cultures, like that of the United States, children are generally taught to feel pride in personal achievement, as Reggie is expressing.

CONNECT: Why do children of depressed parents have difficulty regulating emotion (see page 160)? What implications do their weak self-regulatory skills have for their response to cognitive and social challenges? (pp. 258–259)

Depressed parents rarely smile at, comfort, or talk to their babies, who respond to the parent's sad, vacant gaze by turning away, crying, and often looking sad or angry themselves. As a result, depressed parents fail to effectively regulate their infant's emotional states. Over time, these babies begin to exhibit mental and emotional symptoms, including developmental delays, an irritable mood, and attachment difficulties.

When maternal or paternal depression persists, the parent–child relationship worsens. Depressed parents view their infants more negatively than do independent observers, and they use inconsistent discipline. Children who experience these maladaptive parenting practices often have serious adjustment problems. To avoid their parents' insensitivity, some withdraw into a depressive mood themselves. Others mimic their parents' anger, becoming impulsive and aggressive. Further, these parenting behaviors can lead children to develop a negative worldview—one in which they lack confidence in themselves and perceive their parents and other people as threatening to their well-being. Children who constantly feel in danger are likely to become overly aroused in stressful situations, easily losing control in the face of cognitive and social challenges.

REFLECT: Describe several recent events in your own life that required you to manage negative emotion. How did you react in each case? How might your early experiences, gender, and cultural background have influenced your style of emotional self-regulation? (pp. 258–259)

This is an open-ended question with no right or wrong answer.

REVIEW: How do genetic and environmental factors work together to influence temperament? Cite several examples. (pp. 264–266)

The concept of genetic–environmental correlation states that our genes influence the environments to which we are exposed. For example, research shows that identical twins are more similar than fraternal twins across a wide range of temperamental and personality traits. Consistent ethnic and sex differences in early temperament also exist, again implying a role for heredity. Compared with Caucasian infants, Asian babies tend to be less active, irritable, and vocal, more easily soothed when upset, and better at quieting themselves. Similarly, sex differences are apparent from an early age. Boys tend to be more active and daring and girls more anxious and timid—a difference reflected in boys' higher injury rates throughout childhood and adolescence.

Environment also has a powerful influence on temperament. For example, persistent nutritional and emotional deprivation profoundly alters temperament, leading to poor regulation of emotion. And research shows that heredity and environment combine to influence temperament, since a child's approach to the world affects the experiences to which he or she is exposed. For example, research on ethnic differences in temperament reveals that Japanese mothers usually describe newborn babies as independent beings who must learn to rely on their mothers through close physical contact. North American mothers are likely to believe just the opposite—that they must wean babies away from dependence to autonomy. Consistent with these beliefs, Asian mothers interact gently and soothingly, relying heavily on gestures and discouraging strong emotion in their babies. In contrast, Caucasian mothers use a more active, stimulating, verbal approach. These differences enhance early ethnic differences in temperament.

A similar process seems to contribute to sex differences in temperament. Within 24 hours after birth, parents perceive boys and girls differently, and gender-stereotyped beliefs influence parents' treatment of infants and toddlers. Finally, experiences outside the family, such as unique experiences with teachers, peers, and others in the community, also contribute to personality development.

APPLY: At 18 months, highly active Jake climbed out of his highchair and had a tantrum when his father insisted that he sit at the table until the meal was finished. Using the concept of goodness of fit, suggest another way of handling Jake. (pp. 266–267)

The goodness-of-fit model describes how temperament and environment can work together to produce favorable outcomes. Goodness of fit involves creating child-rearing environments that recognize each child's temperament while simultaneously encouraging more adaptive functioning. In Jake's case, his father needs to recognize Jake's active temperamental style and respond in patient, consistent ways that help Jake achieve more adaptive functioning. Requiring Jake to sit for only a short period of time and to eat a small amount is far more consistent with his capacities as a toddler and with his temperamental disposition. When parents are warm and responsive and make reasonable demands that fit with toddlers' developing capacities, they can transform an environment that exaggerates a child's problems into one that builds on the child's strengths. By readjusting his demands for better goodness of fit, Jake's father can expect his son's difficult behavior to subside.

CONNECT: Do findings on ethnic and sex differences in temperament illustrate genetic–environmental correlation, discussed on pages 86–87 in Chapter 2? Explain. (pp. 264–266)

The concept of genetic–environmental correlation tells us that our genes influence the environments to which we are exposed. This helps to explain ethnic and sex differences in temperament, because children of different genders and different ethnic groups are exposed to different experiences. For instance, Japanese mothers view their infants as independent beings who must learn to rely on their mothers through close physical contact. As a result, they interact differently with their infants than do North American mothers, who tend to believe that babies are naturally dependent and must be weaned away from dependence to autonomy. These differences in parenting practices help explain why Asian babies tend to be less active, irritable, and vocal, more easily soothed when upset, and better at quieting themselves than Caucasian babies.

A similar process seems to contribute to sex differences in temperament. Parents of newborns almost immediately perceive male and female infants differently and, as a result, treat them differently. And from an early age, boys tend to be more active and daring and girls more anxious and timid, again reflecting genetic–environmental correlation.

REFLECT: How would you describe your temperament as a young child? Do you think your temperament has remained stable, or has it changed? What factors might be involved? (pp. 260–261)

This is an open-ended question with no right or wrong answer.

REVIEW: What factors explain stability in attachment pattern for some children and change for others? Are these factors also involved in the link between attachment in infancy and later development? Explain. (p. 272)

Quality of attachment is usually secure and stable for middle-SES babies experiencing favorable life conditions. And infants who move from insecurity to security typically have well-adjusted mothers with positive family and friendship ties. These mothers may have become parents before they were psychologically ready, but grow into the role with social support. In contrast, in low-SES families with many daily stresses, attachment usually moves away from security or changes from one insecure pattern to another. Research shows that securely attached babies more often maintain their attachment status than do insecure babies—a trend that is also evident in long-term assessments of attachment stability based on follow-up interviews with adolescents and young adults. The exception is disorganized/disoriented attachment—an insecure pattern that remains highly stable.

Research suggests that continuity of caregiving determines whether attachment is linked to later development. When parents respond sensitively, not just in infancy but during later years as well, children are likely to develop favorably. In contrast, children of parents who react insensitively over a long period tend to establish lasting patterns of avoidant, resistant, or disorganized attachment and are at greater risk for later academic, emotional, and social difficulties. However, a child whose parental caregiving improves or who has compensating, affectionate ties outside the family is likely to fare well.

APPLY: What attachment pattern did Timmy display when Vanessa arrived home from work, and what factors probably contributed to it? (pp. 275–276)

On the days that Vanessa worked late and a babysitter picked Timmy up at child care, Timmy displayed an avoidant attachment to Vanessa when she came home. Instead of reaching out, crawling, or running to her, he ignored her. Timmy's behavior reflects a repeated finding: Job loss, a failing marriage, financial strain, and other stressors can undermine attachment indirectly, by interfering with the sensitivity of parental care. However, Timmy's insecurity does not have to compromise his development. The availability of social supports, especially assistance in caregiving, reduces parental stress and fosters attachment security. Ginette's sensitivity toward Timmy while he was at child care was helpful, as was the parenting advice Vanessa received from a psychologist.

CONNECT: Review research on emotional self-regulation on pages 258–259. How do the caregiving experiences of securely attached infants promote the development of emotional self-regulation? (pp. 273–274)

Sensitive caregiving is at the heart of secure attachment. It is essential for the parent or caregiver to respond to infant signals in a well-timed, appropriate fashion. Infants whose parents "read" and respond sympathetically to their emotional cues tend to be less fussy, more easily soothed, and more interested in exploration. A special form of communication called *interactional synchrony,* in which the infant and adult are able to match emotional states, helps the baby regulate emotion.

REFLECT: How would you characterize your internal working model? What factors, in addition to your early relationship with your parents, might have influenced it? (p. 276)

This is an open-ended question with no right or wrong answer.

REVIEW: Why is insisting that infants comply with parental directives inappropriate? What competencies are necessary for the emergence of compliance and self-control? (pp. 285–286)

To behave in a self-controlled fashion, children must have some ability to think of themselves as separate, autonomous beings who can direct their own actions. They must also have the representational and memory capacities to recall a caregiver's directives and apply them to their own behavior. The ability to shift attention from a captivating stimulus and focus on a less attractive alternative, which is supported by the development of the frontal lobes of the cerebral cortex, is also essential. Therefore, insisting that infants comply with parental directives is not only inappropriate but actually beyond their developmental capacities.

To comply with parental directives, toddlers must show a clear awareness of caregivers' wishes and expectations and be able to obey simple requests and commands. This ability appears between 12 and 18 months. However, one way toddlers assert their autonomy is by resisting adult directives. But among toddlers who experience warm parenting, opposition is far less common than compliance with an eager, willing spirit, suggesting that the child is beginning to adopt the adult's directive as his own.

APPLY: Len, a caregiver of 1- and 2-year-olds, wonders whether toddlers recognize themselves. List signs of self-recognition in the second year that Len can observe. (pp. 283–284)

1. Toddlers seeing their own image in a mirror may act silly or coy, playfully experimenting with the way the self looks.
2. Around age 2, children show self-recognition when they point to themselves in photos.
3. Children of this age begin referring to themselves by name or with a personal pronoun ("I" or "me").

CONNECT: What type of early parenting fosters the development of emotional self-regulation, secure attachment, and self-control? Why, in each instance, is it effective? (pp. 285–286)

Infants whose parents "read" and respond sympathetically to their emotional cues tend to be less fussy, more easily soothed, and more interested in exploration. As parents adjust the pace of their interactions so the infant does not become overwhelmed and distressed, the baby's tolerance for stimulation increases. By 4 months, the baby develops the ability to shift attention, which is helpful in controlling emotion. As parents help the infant regulate her emotional states, they contribute to the child's style of emotional self-regulation. Similarly, secure attachment evolves from warm, sensitive interactions between the baby and her parents.

Finally, between 12 and 18 months, self-control begins to emerge. Children start to show clear awareness of parents' wishes and expectations and can voluntarily obey simple requests and commands. Of course, they can also decide to do the opposite: One way toddlers assert their autonomy is by resisting adult directives. Among toddlers who experience warm parenting, however, eager, willing compliance is far more common than opposition.

SUGGESTED STUDENT READINGS

Grossmann, K. E., Grossmann, K., & Walters, E. (Eds.). (2006). *Attachment from infancy to adulthood: The major longitudinal studies*. New York: Guilford. Presents findings from some of the most well-known longitudinal studies of attachment. Each chapter highlights the importance of early relationships for favorable development throughout the lifespan.

Kagan, J., & Snidman, N. (2004). *The long shadow of temperament*. Cambridge, MA: Harvard University Press. Using results from over two decades of longitudinal research, this book explores the relationship between temperament and psychological development.

Lamb, M. E. (Ed.). (2004). *The role of the father in child development* (4th ed.). Hoboken, NJ: Wiley. Examines the diverse and enduring contributions of father involvement to child development. An excellent resource for students, educators, mental health professionals, and anyone interested in working with children and families.

TRANSPARENCIES

T-76   **Which Emotions are These Babies Displaying** Figure 7.1 (p. 254)

T-79   **A Cross-Cultural Comparison of Infants' Reactions in the Strange Situation** Figure 7.4 (p. 273)

T-82   **Three-Month-Olds' Emerging Self-Awareness, As Indicated by Reactions to Video Images** Figure 7.6 (p. 283)

MEDIA MATERIALS

INFANTS, CHILDREN, AND ADOLESCENTS IN ACTION

Infancy and Toddlerhood

Emotional milestones of infancy—the social smile, laughter, fear (including stranger anxiety), use of the caregiver as a secure base, and social referencing—are illustrated in this portion of the Observation Program. Variations in temperament are explored by examining individual differences in sociability, attention span, activity level, and persistence, as well as the importance of adapting parenting to children's temperaments. Next, the development of infant–caregiver attachment is considered. Among the milestones depicted are newborn capacities that evoke loving care; emotional responsiveness to the familiar caregiver in the first half-year; appearance of clear-cut attachment (including separation anxiety) around 6 to 8 months; and the capacity to tolerate short absences of the parent by the end of the second year. The vital role of sensitive, responsive caregiving in the development of a secure attachment bond is explained. Similarities and differences in mothers' and fathers' styles of interacting with their babies are also shown.

Finally, a secure attachment bond fosters a sturdy sense of self. Emergence of self-recognition is explored by dabbing red dye on toddlers' noses and observing reactions to their changed appearance using a mirror. Early self-development provides the foundation for compliance and self-control, which emerge during the second year of life. First, 1½-year-old Luke illustrates the toddler's ability to comply with adult directives, followed by 2½-year-old Sophie and Elena, who demonstrate self-control during a delay–of–gratification task.

A WINDOW ON INFANTS, CHILDREN, AND ADOLESCENTS

Segment 1: The Newborn Baby's Capacities: Anna, 2 weeks

In this segment, 2-week-old Anna exhibits a variety of newborn reflexes and capacities. Anna's mother carefully attends to the newborn, responding to Anna's signals by speaking softly and asking if she is hungry when she begins to suck on her fingers. Next, Professor Berk holds Anna while her mother shakes a rattle, illustrating the newborn's responsiveness to sound and visual stimulation. The segment concludes with Anna demonstrating the crawling motion, Moro reflex, and stepping reflex.

Segment 2: Learning Capacities: Mac, 3 months

This segment opens with Mac and his father playing. The interaction between Mac and his father illustrates how fathers tend to play differently with their babies than mothers do. When presented with a rattle, Mac shows signs of voluntary reaching. Watch as Mac's mother holds up a green and then a yellow ring. Mac habituates to the green ring and then recovers to the yellow ring.

Segment 3: Object Permanence and Parent–Infant Interaction: Hannah, 7 months

This segment begins with Hannah handling two rattles. Professor Berk uses one of the rattles for several object-hiding tasks. Notice how Hannah successfully searches for the rattle when it is partially covered by a cloth diaper. When the rattle is completely covered, however, Hannah fails to search for it. Finally, Hannah plays with her mother. As mother and baby interact, their mutual gaze and exchange of emotional signals illustrate Vygotsky's concept of intersubjectivity.

Segment 4: Physical and Cognitive Development: Randy, 8 months and Ben, 21 months

This segment opens as Randy and Ben are playing with their mother. The differences in fine and gross motor skills are evident as the boys play. Randy illustrates the beginning of crawling by scooting across the floor on his tummy to retrieve a toy and establish contact with his mother. Ben's skills are more advanced, as evidenced when he walks and runs, uses a toy hammer, winds a jack-in-the-box, and plays catch with Professor Berk. Watch as the boys' mother supports their language development by using child-directed speech, commenting on their behavior, labeling toys, and playing with them. Similarly, her style of interaction helps regulate their emotions. The play behaviors of Randy and Ben demonstrate the difference between functional and make-believe play. Whereas Randy simply explores the toys and moves them about, Ben is able to act out real-life situations, such as pretending to feed a doll and to feed Randy.

Segment 5: High-Quality Infant and Toddler Child Care

This segment, profiling Goodwood Child Care Center and McKinnon Parade Child Care Center in Adelaide, Australia, illustrates a number of ingredients of high-quality child care. For example, at Goodwood Child Care Center, the staff support children's developing motor skills by teaching them how to do somersaults and encouraging them as they learn this new activity. In the second clip, infants play with staff members in the sandbox. Notice the positive interactions between the children and staff. As the babies play, staff members describe what is going on and demonstrate how to use the toys in the sandbox. In the final clip, children and staff at McKinnon Parade Child Care Center enjoy a meal. Children are not seated separately from staff, and there is a lot of interaction, such as a staff member feeding a toddler and talking to the others as they eat.

Segment 7: Compliance and Self-Control: Luke, 1½ years, Peter, 2 years, and Sophie and Elena, 2½ years

In this segment, 1½-year-old Luke and 2½-year-old twins Sophie and Elena demonstrate the ability of toddlers to comply with adult directives as they retrieve various objects. Next, Professor Berk presents a delay-of-gratification task to 2-year-old Peter and to Sophie and Elena. Notice how Peter immediately eats the M&Ms, whereas Sophie and Elena are able to wait until Professor Berk returns before eating the candy. In a second delay-of-gratification task, Sophie and Elena again demonstrate self-control by waiting for Professor Berk to return before they look into a bag for presents. Notice the strategies they use to delay gratification.

DVDs AND VIDEOTAPES

Attachment (1996, Insight Media, 24 min.). This video examines some of the research on the development of relationships with caregivers, focusing on a laboratory procedure that provides insights into a young child's state of mind about an attachment.

The Bonds of Family (2000, Films Media Group, 22 min.). This program, Section 2 of the Brazelton on Parenting series, examines changing concepts of the ingredients that make up a family unit, reflecting new ways of looking at families and their members.

Brothers and Sisters: Sibling Relationships (1997, Films Media Group, 55 min.). This probing documentary, based on *Brothers and Sisters* by Joan Sauers, explores the emotional dynamics of the sibling bond. Groups of siblings talk about their love–hate feelings for one another, while an only child provides additional insights into growing up without siblings. The program also includes commentary by MIT professor Frank Sulloway, author of the best-selling book *Born to Rebel,* whose controversial conclusion is that birth order has more of an impact on personality than gender, race, nationality, or social class.

Compliance, Self-Control, and Prosocial Behavior (1994, Concept Media, 27 min.). This program, designed for caregivers who want to instill positive behaviors in children, discusses factors that influence compliance, self-control, and prosocial behavior, including temperament, attachment, and the normal cognitive-developmental changes that occur around age 2. The program presents techniques that have been shown to help children delay gratification. It describes inductive and power-assertive discipline and the role of empathy in the development of prosocial behavior. Parenting styles—permissive, authoritarian, authoritative, and rejecting/neglecting—are also illustrated.

Daddy & Me (2001, Aquarius Health Care Videos, 27 min.). This program addresses the significant role of a father in a child's life, as seen through the eyes of both children and adults. Noting that 27 million children in America currently live apart from their fathers, the program considers the issue of father absence and its effects on individuals and society. It offers advice from experts on the father's role in the family, including those from the National Center on Fathering.

Developing the Sense of Family (1993, Films Media Group, 21 min.). This program, from the eight-part series The Psychological Development of the Child, focuses on infants who are about 6 months old—the age at which stranger anxiety typically appears as children develop the ability to differentiate family members from strangers. The programs in this series were filmed in 14 countries and five continents, in consultation with many scientists.

The Development of Self (1981, Films Media Group, 23 min.). Part of the series The Psychological Development of the Child, this program examines how, in the first 12 months of life, infants develop mobility and the ability to send and receive messages; how the family accommodates itself to the infant's emotional "weapons" of anger and fury; and how babies gradually learn to deal with the social world and to work their way through and beyond conflict.

Fatherhood (2000, Films Media Group, 22 min.). This program presents new research pointing to the importance of the father's role in promoting a child's intellectual development, social adaptation, and even future marriage stability.

How Relationships Are Formed (1993, Films for the Humanities and Sciences, 30 min.). Part of the Psychological Development of the Child series. This program focuses on the first 3 months after birth. During this time, the relationship between the infant and the mother is developing and the infant has learned that smiling is a social act comprised of recognition and pleasure.

Infancy: Early Relationships (2003, Magna Systems, 19 min.; available in English and Spanish). This program examines the establishment of trust and how it depends on the child's significant early relationships. The program presents early bonding and the signs of unfolding attachment between parent and child. It highlights influences on security of attachment, including cultural values, temperament, and the parent's sensitivity to the child's needs. It also examines the development of stranger anxiety and separation anxiety from the perspective of attachment, with an emphasis on the qualities that are essential for infant care in order to ensure that it promotes strong attachment relationships. The program explores current thinking on the long-term impact of early attachment relationships as they affect children's eagerness to explore the world and their close relationships with others throughout life.

Infancy: Emotional & Social World (2003, Magna Systems, 15 min.; available in English and Spanish). This program illustrates suitable adult responses to infants' strong emotions of crying and anger. Other topics addressed include how infants learn self-regulation and how significant interchanges with an adult can guide early behavior. The program marks four stages of emotional milestones in infancy and illustrates how emotional closeness is experienced through synchrony, social referencing, and later separation–individuation. Emphasis is placed on the implications of early experience for lifelong awareness of nonverbal cues from others, and on the importance of this awareness in developing social abilities.

In the Heat of the Moment: The Biochemistry of Feelings (2000, Films Media Group/A BBC Production, 50 min.). Through an interview with British neuroscientist Susan Greenfield, this program focuses on past research that attempted to explain emotions in terms of specific brain areas, as well as more current research emphasizing the role of neurotransmitters. The program includes a discussion of a landmark study of facial expressions among natives of Papua New Guinea, which suggests that all human beings share six basic emotions. It also provides an overview of how emotional responses vary according to age and experience, including a segment on how battlefield terror can actually alter the structure of the brain.

Pediatric Neuroscience: Rage of Innocents (1999, Films Media Group, 47 min.). This program looks at the results of recent laboratory research indicating that emotional neglect of children in the first few years of life can have long-term biochemical consequences. Anthropologists from Cornell and Emory Universities and other experts share their findings on the subtle biochemical link between parental attentiveness and the proper development of the regions of a child's brain that control responses to stress. The program also investigates approaches to caregiving from the perspectives of social science and evolutionary biology. Some language may be objectionable.

Play and the Social World: Acquiring Social Intelligence (1994, Films Media Group, 25 min.). This program explores the educational value and social dynamics of play. It emphasizes the importance of the presence of a supportive adult on the playground. The program includes information about playground design as well as examples of games and techniques that teachers and psychologists can use to help children develop interpersonal skills, articulate their feelings, and reflect on their behavior.

Secure Attachments: The Foundation of Relationships in Child Care Programs (2005, Child Development Media, 21 min.). This program is designed to give child-care professionals an understanding of attachment theory, with links to research. The components of a secure attachment relationship are explored, along with examples of behaviors that indicate insecure attachment. Set in a busy infant room, the program highlights practical steps that caregivers can take to create links between home and child-care center that will facilitate secure attachment relationships. This program is also useful for communicating with parents about the importance of attachment relationships and the role of the professional caregiver.

Steps and Stages: A Caregiver's Guide to Child Development (2002, Films Media Group/A Cambridge Educational Production, 20 min.). This program provides essential information about the developmental milestones of a child's first 15 months. It looks at the importance of communication, ways of recognizing cognitive and motor development, and the standards of the National Coalition for Family and Consumer Sciences Education.

The Temperament Program (2005, Child Development Media; 4 programs, each 20–22 min.). This series of four programs is based on the research of Stella Chess and Alexander Thomas and the work of the Temperament Program at Kaiser Permanente Northern California. It provides a general introduction to temperament concepts, as well as detailed presentations of three clusters of temperament traits associated with the development of behavioral problems. Originally designed to present temperament concerns to health care providers, the series has also been edited for parents, who, in interviews, discuss their concerns about their children's behavior, while pediatricians and pediatric nurse practitioners talk about the use of temperament concepts in professional practice. The program describes practical strategies that can be used by parents whose children pose various challenges related to temperament.

TEST BANK

MULTIPLE CHOICE

1) In Erikson's theory, _____ is associated with a positive outcome of infancy.
   A) the amount of oral stimulation provided
   B) whether the child is breastfed or bottle-fed
   C) the quality of caregiving
   D) the amount of food given
   Answer: C
   Page Ref: 252
   Skill: Factual
   Objective: 7.1

2) According to Erikson's theory, a mother who is sympathetic and loving is fostering her baby's sense of
   A) attachment.
   B) autonomy.
   C) trust.
   D) self-regulation.
   Answer: C
   Page Ref: 252
   Skill: Factual
   Objective: 7.1

3) In Erikson's theory, the conflicts of toddlerhood are resolved favorably when parents
   A) provide suitable guidance and reasonable choices.
   B) use appropriate and warm toilet-training techniques.
   C) employ an authoritarian child-rearing style.
   D) engage their children in democratic decision making.
   Answer: A
   Page Ref: 252–253
   Skill: Factual
   Objective: 7.1

4) According to Erikson, a mother who _____ is likely to promote autonomy in toddlerhood.
   A) waits patiently while her son puts on his socks and shoes
   B) makes her son quit playing immediately whenever she needs to run an errand
   C) picks up her son's toys, puts away his books, and makes his bed on a daily basis
   D) quickly corrects her son whenever he incorrectly uses his fork or spoon.
   Answer: A
   Page Ref: 253
   Skill: Applied
   Objective: 7.1

5) Of the following, which is supported by research on emotional development?
   A) Infants and children display the same facial pattern each time they experience a particular emotion.
   B) The emotional expressions of blind infants are exaggerated compared to infants with normal vision.
   C) Depending on the situation, the same general response can express several emotions.
   D) Wide cultural differences exist in the facial expressions that people associate with different emotions.
   Answer: C
   Page Ref: 254
   Skill: Conceptual
   Objective: 7.2

6) Basic emotions
    A) are not evident in non-human primates.
    B) can be inferred correctly from only facial expressions.
    C) are universal in humans.
    D) have no evolutionary history of adaptation.
Answer: C
Page Ref: 254
Skill: Conceptual
Objective: 7.2

7) Babies' earliest emotional life consists of the two following arousal states:
    A) happiness and sadness.
    B) fullness and hunger.
    C) attraction to pleasant stimuli and withdrawal from unpleasant stimuli.
    D) happiness and fear.
Answer: C
Page Ref: 254
Skill: Conceptual
Objective: 7.2

8) According to the dynamic systems perspective, basic emotions emerge
    A) through the unfolding of a genetic blueprint for emotional reactions.
    B) as babies model adult facial gestures during social events that are associated with various emotions.
    C) during a sensitive period in which infants are especially responsive to adults' emotional expressions.
    D) as infants coordinate separate skills into more effective capacities.
Answer: D
Page Ref: 254
Skill: Conceptual
Objective: 7.2

9) _____ is evoked by the human face and first appears between _____ of age.
    A) The social smile; 6 and 10 weeks
    B) Laughter; 6 and 10 weeks
    C) The social smile; 2 and 3 months
    D) Laughter; 2 and 3 months
Answer: A
Page Ref: 255
Skill: Factual
Objective: 7.2

10) Laughter first appears around _____ of age.
    A) 6 to 10 weeks
    B) 3 to 4 months
    C) 10 to 12 months
    D) 18 months
Answer: B
Page Ref: 255
Skill: Factual
Objective: 7.2

11) Of the following, which is MOST likely to make 4-month-old Zoe laugh out loud?
   A) a silent game of peekaboo
   B) a funny cartoon on TV
   C) a funny face
   D) a playful, "I'm gonna get you!" and a kiss on the tummy
Answer: D
Page Ref: 255
Skill: Applied
Objective: 7.2

12) One-year-old Gil will most likely display a _____ smile during stimulating play with his father.
   A) brief, fleeting
   B) broad, "cheek-raised"
   C) reserved, muted
   D) "mouth-open"
Answer: D
Page Ref: 255
Skill: Applied
Objective: 7.2

13) Studies of emotional development demonstrate that
   A) among older infants, loss of contingent control evokes especially strong angry responses.
   B) older infants display anger less frequently than younger infants.
   C) compared to older infants, younger infants react with anger in a wider range of situations.
   D) as infants become capable of intentional behavior, they display less intense angry responses.
Answer: A
Page Ref: 255
Skill: Conceptual
Objective: 7.2

14) Older infants' most frequent expression of fear is
   A) overstimulation.
   B) stranger anxiety.
   C) wariness of heights.
   D) separation anxiety.
Answer: B
Page Ref: 256
Skill: Conceptual
Objective: 7.2

15) At 8 months, Etta, who had always been a friendly baby, began showing signs of fear when an unfamiliar person entered the room. Etta was exhibiting
   A) insecure attachment.
   B) avoidant attachment.
   C) stranger anxiety.
   D) separation anxiety.
Answer: C
Page Ref: 256
Skill: Applied
Objective: 7.2

16) Infants raised among the Efe hunters and gathers of Zaire, Africa, show little stranger anxiety because
   A) they are discouraged from developing a strong emotional bond with their mother.
   B) a collective caregiving system exists.
   C) they are discouraged from developing a strong emotional bond with anyone in the tribe.
   D) an individualistic caregiving system exists.
   Answer: B
   Page Ref: 256
   Skill: Conceptual
   Objective: 7.2

17) Infants raised in Israeli kibbutzim
   A) show little stranger anxiety because of a collective caregiving system in which babies are passed from one adult to another.
   B) exhibit a great deal of stranger anxiety because they are discouraged from interacting with nonrelatives in infancy.
   C) show little stranger anxiety because they are carried around in cloth sacks harnessed to their mothers.
   D) display far greater stranger anxiety than do their city-reared counterparts as a result of widespread wariness of strangers among adults, a consequence of frequent terrorist attacks.
   Answer: D
   Page Ref: 256
   Skill: Conceptual
   Objective: 7.2

18) The rise in fear after 6 months of age
   A) hinders infants' ability to use their new motor skills to explore the environment.
   B) occurs only in infants who do not have a warm relationship with a primary caregiver.
   C) is adaptive because it keeps newly mobile babies' enthusiasm for exploration in check.
   D) occurs only among children who are raised in cultures with some degree of regular violence.
   Answer: C
   Page Ref: 256
   Skill: Conceptual
   Objective: 7.2

19) One-year-old Brinna who wanders to her aunt, returns to her mother, interacts briefly with her uncle, and then returns to her mother again is demonstrating the concept of
   A) stranger anxiety.
   B) self-consciousness.
   C) a secure base.
   D) emotional self-regulation.
   Answer: C
   Page Ref: 256
   Skill: Applied
   Objective: 7.2

20) During toddlerhood, _____ lead(s) to the decline in stranger anxiety and other fears.
   A) improved memory
   B) advanced emotional self-regulation
   C) new motor capacities to explore the environment
   D) a more effective ability to discriminate between threatening and nonthreatening people and situations
   Answer: D
   Page Ref: 256
   Skill: Conceptual
   Objective: 7.2

21) Around 3 to 4 months of age,
    A) babies begin to respond in kind to others' emotions through a built-in process of emotional contagion.
    B) when infants gaze, smile, or vocalize, they now expect their social partner to respond in kind.
    C) babies perceive facial expressions as organized patterns.
    D) babies use social referencing to actively seek emotional information from a trusted person in an uncertain situation.
Answer: B
Page Ref: 256–257
Skill: Conceptual
Objective: 7.3

22) One-year-old Dalila is learning how to walk. Each time she falls, she looks looks up at her mother. If her mother looks upset, Dalila cries. But if he mother is smiling, Dalila gets up and tries again. Dalila is using
    A) effortful control.
    B) an internal working model.
    C) emotional self-regulation.
    D) social referencing.
Answer: D
Page Ref: 257
Skill: Applied
Objective: 7.3

23) From 5 months on, infants perceive _____ as organized patterns.
    A) facial expressions
    B) color
    C) numbers
    D) basic shapes
Answer: A
Page Ref: 257
Skill: Conceptual
Objective: 7.3

24) _____ are examples of self-conscious emotions.
    A) Anger and fear
    B) Happiness and pride
    C) Shame and embarrassment
    D) Envy and anger
Answer: C
Page Ref: 257
Skill: Conceptual
Objective: 7.4

25) The appearance of emotions, such as embarrassment, pride, guilt, and envy is linked with the development of
    A) self-awareness.
    B) emotional self-regulation.
    C) an internal working model.
    D) social referencing.
Answer: A
Page Ref: 257
Skill: Conceptual
Objective: 7.4

26) Self-conscious emotions differ from basic emotions in that self-conscious emotions
   A) are present at birth.
   B) involve distinct facial expressions.
   C) require adult instruction in when to feel them.
   D) are universally experienced in response to the same types of situations.
   Answer: C
   Page Ref: 257
   Skill: Conceptual
   Objective: 7.4

27) Cross-cultural research indicates that
   A) the situations in which adults encourage various self-conscious emotions vary from culture to culture.
   B) humans have a universal, built-in set of emotions that express all types of reactions.
   C) nonverbal expressions of basic emotions differ widely from culture to culture.
   D) people from nonindustrialized cultures have trouble distinguishing the facial expressions common to people in industrialized cultures.
   Answer: A
   Page Ref: 258
   Skill: Conceptual
   Objective: 7.4

28) _____ is an example of emotional self-regulation.
   A) Suppressing a laugh when seeing someone trip
   B) Covering one's eyes during a scary movie
   C) Blaming someone else for a broken vase
   D) Hugging a playmate who is upset
   Answer: B
   Page Ref: 258
   Skill: Applied
   Objective: 7.5

29) Infants who more readily turn away or suck their fingers when faced with a highly stimulating novel event
   A) have less well developed self-regulatory skills than other infants.
   B) tend to have an anxious, reactive temperament.
   C) are less prone to distress than other infants.
   D) often have parents who fail to regulate stressful experiences.
   Answer: C
   Page Ref: 258
   Skill: Conceptual
   Objective: 7.5

30) By the end of the first year, infants become increasingly better at regulating emotions because they are better able to
   A) express their feelings more accurately in words.
   B) move about to approach or avoid situations.
   C) understand others' emotions.
   D) think about how others would feel in the same situation.
   Answer: B
   Page Ref: 258
   Skill: Conceptual
   Objective: 7.5

31) Of the following, which is supported by research on emotion in infancy?
    A) Infant girls get more training than infant boys in socially approved ways of expressing feelings.
    B) When caregivers fail to regulate distress for young infants, brain structures that buffer stress may fail to develop properly.
    C) One-year-old American infants smile and cry less than same-age Chinese and Japanese infants.
    D) Babies who readily turn away from unpleasant events are more prone to distress.
Answer: B
Page Ref: 259
Skill: Conceptual
Objective: 7.5

32) Of the following, which is supported by research on emotional self-regulation?
    A) Collectivist cultures usually discourage the expression of strong emotion in infants.
    B) Beginning in infancy, girls find it harder to regulate negative emotion than boys.
    C) By the second year, toddlers are quite skilled at using language to comfort themselves.
    D) Beginning in the first few months, mothers imitate their babies' negative feelings far more often than their positive ones.
Answer: A
Page Ref: 259
Skill: Conceptual
Objective: 7.5

33) Thomas and Chess's New York Longitudinal Study demonstrated that
    A) parenting practices have little effect on children's temperaments.
    B) the stability of temperament across childhood is high.
    C) temperament is largely genetically determined.
    D) temperament can protect a child from the negative effects of a highly stressful home life.
Answer: D
Page Ref: 260
Skill: Conceptual
Objective: 7.6

34) In the Thomas and Chess model for classifying children's temperaments, the most frequently observed category was the _____ child.
    A) difficult
    B) easy
    C) slow-to-warm-up
    D) uninhibited
Answer: B
Page Ref: 260
Skill: Conceptual
Objective: 7.6

35) Josh is irregular in daily routines, is slow to accept new experiences, and tends to react negatively and intensely. In Thomas and Chess's research, Josh would be classified as
    A) slow-to-warm-up.
    B) uninhibited.
    C) difficult.
    D) inhibited.
Answer: C
Page Ref: 260
Skill: Applied
Objective: 7.6

36) Sadira is inactive, shows mild, low-key reactions to environmental stimuli, is negative in mood, and adjusts slowly to new experiences. Sadira would be classified by Thomas and Chess as
   A) easy.
   B) slow-to-warm-up.
   C) difficult.
   D) uninhibited.
   Answer: B
   Page Ref: 260
   Skill: Applied
   Objective: 7.6

37) Thirty-five percent of children do not fit into any of the Thomas and Chess temperament categories. Instead, these children
   A) exhibit emotional behaviors that researchers are still struggling to classify.
   B) often have temperamental traits that change on the basis of family influences.
   C) show unique blends of temperamental characteristics.
   D) display no identifiable temperamental traits.
   Answer: C
   Page Ref: 260
   Skill: Factual
   Objective: 7.6

38) In Thomas and Chess's research, _____ children are at high risk for anxious withdrawal and aggressive behavior in early and middle childhood.
   A) inhibited
   B) difficult
   C) slow-to-warm-up
   D) uninhibited
   Answer: B
   Page Ref: 260
   Skill: Conceptual
   Objective: 7.6

39) Which dimension in Rothbart's model of temperament was not identified by Thomas and Chess?
   A) rhythmicity
   B) attention span/persistence
   C) irritable distress
   D) distractibility
   Answer: C
   Page Ref: 261
   Skill: Conceptual
   Objective: 7.6

40) A key concept in Mary Rothbart's model of infant temperament is
   A) effortful control.
   B) internal working model.
   C) goodness of fit.
   D) interactional synchrony.
   Answer: A
   Page Ref: 261
   Skill: Conceptual
   Objective: 7.6

41) One criticism of parental reports for measuring temperament is that
    A) parental perceptions provide little information about the way parents view and respond to their babies.
    B) mothers with depression and low self-esteem regard their babies as less difficult than they really are.
    C) parents' prebirth expectations of infant temperament impact their reports.
    D) they are inconvenient for researchers to administer.
Answer: C
Page Ref: 262
Skill: Conceptual
Objective: 7.7

42) Long-term prediction from early temperament is best achieved after age 3 because
    A) researchers lack adequate techniques to measure temperament in infants.
    B) experience has little effect on temperament until after age 3.
    C) the child's system of emotion, attention, and action is better established between 2 1/2 and 3.
    D) biologically-based temperamental traits begin to unfold during the third year of life.
Answer: C
Page Ref: 262
Skill: Conceptual
Objective: 7.8

43) Research on temperament demonstrates that
    A) beginning in the preschool years, effortful control predicts cognitive and social competence.
    B) during the first year of life, areas in frontal lobes involved in suppressing impulses develop rapidly.
    C) child rearing cannot modify biologically-based temperamental traits.
    D) long-term prediction from early temperament is achieved by the end of the first year.
Answer: A
Page Ref: 262
Skill: Conceptual
Objective: 7.8

44) Of the following, which is supported by research on the stability of temperament?
    A) Children's temperaments rarely change from one extreme to another when assessed at different points in time.
    B) The overall stability of temperament is moderate in infancy and toddlerhood.
    C) Most irritable infants become difficult children.
    D) Childhood temperament is a fairly good predictor of personality in adulthood.
Answer: A
Page Ref: 264
Skill: Conceptual
Objective: 7.8

45) Research on the role of heredity in temperament indicates that
    A) even persistent emotional deprivation has little effect on modifying children's temperament.
    B) identical twins are more similar than fraternal twins across a wide range of temperamental traits and personality measures.
    C) only 5 to 10 percent of individual differences in temperament have been attributed to differences in genetic makeup.
    D) heritability estimates are much higher for expressions of positive emotion than for negative emotion.
Answer: B
Page Ref: 264
Skill: Conceptual
Objective: 7.8

46) Research on cultural influences on temperament shows that
    A) Japanese mothers usually believe that they must wean their infants away from dependence into autonomy.
    B) Chinese and Japanese mothers contribute to their infants' tranquility by discouraging them from expressing strong emotion.
    C) compared to Japanese mothers, North American mothers interact more gently and soothingly with their infants.
    D) North American mothers typically say that babies come into the world as independent beings who must learn to rely on their parents through close physical contact.
Answer: B
Page Ref: 265
Skill: Conceptual
Objective: 7.8

47) Studies on the environmental effects of temperament demonstrate that
    A) parents often regard siblings as more alike than other observers do.
    B) mothers' differential treatment of twins predicts differences between twins in psychological adjustment.
    C) parents do not perceive male and female infants differently until they begin to act in line with gender-stereotyped traits.
    D) twins tend to become increasingly similar in personality with age.
Answer: B
Page Ref: 265
Skill: Conceptual
Objective: 7.8

48) According to the goodness-of-fit model, infants with difficult temperaments often
    A) have parents who tend to resort to a lax, indifferent style of parenting.
    B) have neurological deficits that are difficult to correct even with positive, warm parenting.
    C) suffer from a range of behavioral disorders that are resistant to effective parenting.
    D) experience parenting that fits poorly with their dispositions.
Answer: D
Page Ref: 266
Skill: Conceptual
Objective: 7.8

49) Research on temperament has shown that
    A) since at least 1990, shyness in China, but not the United States, has been positively correlated with academic achievement.
    B) highly stimulating parental behavior fosters exploration among reserved toddlers but not highly active toddlers.
    C) shy, but not difficult, children benefit from warm, accepting parenting.
    D) Russian infants are less reactive and fearful than Western infants.
Answer: B
Page Ref: 267
Skill: Conceptual
Objective: 7.8

50) Two-year-old Jonathan is a difficult child. What would be the probable outcome if Jonathan's parents responded with angry and punitive discipline?
    A) His difficult behavior will decrease with age.
    B) He will maintain his difficult behavior throughout childhood, but it will not increase.
    C) His difficult behavior will be maintained and even increase over time.
    D) His defiant and irritable behavior will be extinguished before he reaches school-age.
    Answer: C
    Page Ref: 267
    Skill: Applied
    Objective: 7.8

51) The strongest criticism of the psychoanalytic theory of attachment is that it
    A) overemphasizes the importance of the mother-infant bond.
    B) views attachment as a "secure base" from which to explore.
    C) ignores the internal representation of the attachment figure.
    D) overemphasizes the importance of feeding in attachment.
    Answer: D
    Page Ref: 268
    Skill: Conceptual
    Objective: 7.9

52) In the 1950s, a famous experiment of rhesus monkeys reared with terry-cloth and wire-mesh "surrogate mothers" provided evidence that
    A) the development of emotional ties between infant and mother does not depend on hunger satisfaction.
    B) the infant's characteristics play a larger role in the attachment relationship than the caregiver's contributions.
    C) sensitive caregiving is key to the development of a secure attachment pattern.
    D) infants are born with a set of innate signals that call the adult to the baby's side.
    Answer: A
    Page Ref: 268
    Skill: Conceptual
    Objective: 7.9

53) John Bowlby advocated which of the following explanations of human mother-infant attachment?
    A) Mothers and infants are instinctively attached to each other at birth.
    B) Mothers' behaviors, such as smiling, hugging, and vocalizing reinforce their infants' social engagement.
    C) Infant behaviors, such as smiling, babbling, and crying are innate social signals that encourage mothers to protect and provide support for their infants.
    D) Infants become attached to their mothers because mothers are associated with the reduction of primary drives, such as hunger and thirst.
    Answer: C
    Page Ref: 269
    Skill: Conceptual
    Objective: 7.9

54) In Bowlby's theory, babies in the preattachment phase
    A) are wary of strangers.
    B) display separation anxiety when the familiar caregiver leaves.
    C) respond differently to a familiar caregiver than to a stranger.
    D) recognize their own mother's smell and voice.
    Answer: D
    Page Ref: 269
    Skill: Conceptual
    Objective: 7.9

55) According to Bowlby, during the attachment-in-the-making phase, babies
   A) understand that their caregiver will respond when signaled.
   B) respond differently to a familiar caregiver than to a stranger.
   C) protest when separated from their primary caregiver.
   D) do not mind being left with an unfamiliar caregiver.
   Answer: D
   Page Ref: 269
   Skill: Conceptual
   Objective: 7.9

56) According to Bowlby, one similarity between the preattachment and the attachment-in-the-making phase is that
   A) the main function of each stage is to attract a caregiver who will provide food.
   B) infants do not yet respond differently to a familiar caregiver than to a stranger.
   C) babies do not yet use behaviors like smiling, grasping, and gazing into the adult's eyes to help bring them into close contact with other humans.
   D) infants in either phase do not yet protest when the familiar caregiver leaves.
   Answer: D
   Page Ref: 269
   Skill: Conceptual
   Objective: 7.9

57) Nine-month-old Miguel becomes upset when his mother leaves him at child care. He is exhibiting behavior consistent with Bowlby's _____ stage of attachment.
   A) formation of a reciprocal relationship
   B) clear-cut attachment
   C) attachment-in-the-making
   D) preattachment
   Answer: B
   Page Ref: 269
   Skill: Applied
   Objective: 7.9

58) One-year-old James cries and climbs on his mother when she attempts to leave him with his babysitter. James is displaying
   A) stranger anxiety.
   B) interactional synchrony.
   C) social referencing.
   D) separation anxiety.
   Answer: D
   Page Ref: 269
   Skill: Applied
   Objective: 7.9

59) Twelve-month-old Wanda uses her mother as a secure base as she becomes overwhelmed when exploring an unfamiliar room. In Bowlby's theory of attachment, Wanda is most likely in the _____ phase.
   A) preattachment
   B) postattachment
   C) clear-cut attachment
   D) attachment-in-the-making
   Answer: C
   Page Ref: 269
   Skill: Applied
   Objective: 7.9

60) Separation anxiety declines during the _____ due to rapid growth in representation and language skills.
    A) formation of a reciprocal relationship
    B) attachment-in-the-making phase
    C) clear-cut attachment phase
    D) preattachment phase
Answer: A
Page Ref: 270
Skill: Conceptual
Objective: 7.9

61) Two-year-old Brooke knows that her mother will pick her up from childcare every day after snack and seeks her comfort whenever she is in an unfamiliar or stressful situation. These examples show that Brooke has developed
    A) effortful control.
    B) an internal working model.
    C) interactional synchrony.
    D) a categorical self.
Answer: B
Page Ref: 270
Skill: Applied
Objective: 7.9

62) The _____ is an important determinant of attachment security as measured by the Strange Situation.
    A) extent to which the child uses the parent as a secure base to explore an unfamiliar setting
    B) child's display of emotional self-regulation
    C) degree to which the child follows the parent as the parent moves from room to room
    D) child's capacity for effortful control
Answer: A
Page Ref: 270
Skill: Conceptual
Objective: 7.10

63) During the Strange Situation, a parent leaves the room in order to assess _____, and returns again to assess the infant's _____.
    A) separation anxiety; secure base
    B) secure base; reaction to the reunion
    C) separation anxiety; reaction to the reunion
    D) secure base; separation anxiety
Answer: C
Page Ref: 270
Skill: Conceptual
Objective: 7.10

64) In the Strange Situation, Aimee repeatedly makes eye contact with her mother as she actively explores the new surroundings. When her mother leaves the room, Aimee cries and is not comforted by an unfamiliar adult. However, she is comforted when her mother returns. Aimee is demonstrating characteristics of _____ attachment.
    A) avoidant
    B) secure
    C) disorganized/disoriented
    D) resistant
Answer: B
Page Ref: 270
Skill: Applied
Objective: 7.10

65) In the Strange Situation, Zachary ignores his mother and does not get upset when she leaves. When his mother returns, Zachary does not seek contact with her. Zachary is displaying characteristics of _____ attachment.
   A) avoidant
   B) secure
   C) disorganized/disoriented
   D) resistant
   Answer: A
   Page Ref: 270
   Skill: Applied
   Objective: 7.10

66) In the Strange Situation, Rabi sticks close to his mother, fails to explore, and cries uncontrollably when she leaves the room. When his mother returns, Rabi resists being picked up and cries despite his mother's efforts to comfort him. Rabi is demonstrating _____ attachment.
   A) secure
   B) resistant
   C) avoidant
   D) disorganized/disoriented
   Answer: B
   Page Ref: 270
   Skill: Applied
   Objective: 7.10

67) In the Strange Situation, when reunited with his mother, Naaman approached his mother with a flat, depressed emotion and then suddenly cried out. Naaman would be classified as having a(n) _____ attachment.
   A) avoidant
   B) secure
   C) disorganized/disoriented
   D) resistant
   Answer: C
   Page Ref: 271
   Skill: Applied
   Objective: 7.10

68) The Attachment Q-sort
   A) is a quicker and more efficient method of assessing attachment than the Strange Situation.
   B) takes place in a specially designed laboratory.
   C) is not suitable for infants and toddlers.
   D) does not differentiate between the types of insecurity.
   Answer: D
   Page Ref: 271
   Skill: Conceptual
   Objective: 7.10

69) Research on the stability of attachment indicates that
   A) insecurely attached babies more often maintain their attachment status than secure babies.
   B) infants who move from insecurity to security typically have well-adjusted mothers with positive social ties.
   C) quality of attachment is most stable for low-SES babies experiencing unfavorable family conditions.
   D) the disorganized/disoriented attachment pattern is the least stable attachment classification.
   Answer: B
   Page Ref: 272
   Skill: Conceptual
   Objective: 7.10

70) Because German parents encourage their infants to be non-clingy and independent, these children show considerably more _____ attachment than American babies do.
  A) resistant
  B) avoidant
  C) secure
  D) disorganized/disoriented

Answer: B
Page Ref: 272
Skill: Conceptual
Objective: 7.10

71) Cross-cultural research on attachment indicates that
  A) Japanese infants rarely show avoidant attachment.
  B) the most common attachment classification in all societies is the resistant pattern.
  C) American infants show higher rates of avoidant attachment compared to German infants.
  D) infants in Israeli kibbutzim usually have an avoidant attachment.

Answer: A
Page Ref: 272
Skill: Conceptual
Objective: 7.10

72) German parents encourage their infants to be
  A) expressive.
  B) vocal.
  C) nonclingy and independent.
  D) creative and exploratory.

Answer: C
Page Ref: 272
Skill: Conceptual
Objective: 7.10

73) Studies of institutionalized babies who had been given up by their mothers indicate that
  A) it is imperative that the first attachment bond develop within the first year of life.
  B) "late adoptees," placed in homes after age 4, did not display social or emotional problems.
  C) the first attachment bond can develop as late as 4 to 6 years of age.
  D) these children are likely to shy away from adult attention once adopted.

Answer: C
Page Ref: 273
Skill: Conceptual
Objective: 7.11

74) Adopted children who spent their first 8 months or more in deprived Romanian orphanages
  A) exhibited disrupted formation of neural structures involved in "reading" emotions.
  B) did not show social or emotional problems if adopted by the age of 6.
  C) displayed normal ERP brain-wave responsiveness to facial expressions of emotion.
  D) rarely developed deep ties with their adoptive parents.

Answer: A
Page Ref: 273
Skill: Conceptual
Objective: 7.11

75) Caregiving that involves prompt, consistent, and appropriate responding to infant signals is likely to promote a(n)
   A) resistant attachment.
   B) avoidant attachment.
   C) secure attachment.
   D) difficult temperament.
   Answer: C
   Page Ref: 273
   Skill: Conceptual
   Objective: 7.11

76) Mrs. Posada hears her baby, Shauna, fussing. She lifts Shauna out of her crib, talking softly to her until she calms down, then places her in an infant carrier on her chest while she finishes a few more household chores. As Mrs. Posada carries Shauna around the house, she occasionally responds to Shauna's babbles, often making eye contact and describing the things that Shauna looks at. Mrs. Posada and Shauna are engaged in
   A) attachment in the making.
   B) interactional synchrony.
   C) goodness of fit.
   D) social referencing.
   Answer: B
   Page Ref: 274
   Skill: Applied
   Objective: 7.11

77) Compared with securely attached infants, avoidant babies tend to receive
   A) well-timed and appropriate care.
   B) overstimulating and intrusive care.
   C) resentful and rejecting care.
   D) less physical contact from their caregivers.
   Answer: B
   Page Ref: 274
   Skill: Conceptual
   Objective: 7.11

78) Resistant infants tend to have mothers who
   A) match their infants' emotional states.
   B) overwhelm their infants with stimulation.
   C) engage in interactional synchrony.
   D) are unresponsive to infant signals.
   Answer: D
   Page Ref: 274
   Skill: Conceptual
   Objective: 7.11

79) _____ attachment is especially high among maltreated children.
   A) Disorganized/disoriented
   B) Secure
   C) Avoidant
   D) Resistant
   Answer: A
   Page Ref: 274
   Skill: Factual
   Objective: 7.11

80) Research on attachment suggests that
    A) avoidant attachment is especially high among maltreated infants.
    B) physical control predicts attachment security in all cultures and SES groups studied to date.
    C) persistently depressed mothers tend to promote a disorganized/disoriented attachment classification.
    D) tight but not moderate adult-infant coordination predicts attachment security.
Answer: C
Page Ref: 274
Skill: Conceptual
Objective: 7.11

81) Research on attachment reveals that
    A) preterm birth predicts insecure attachment regardless of maternal characteristics.
    B) difficult infants are more likely than others to have highly anxious mothers.
    C) children's temperaments show a very strong relationship with attachment security.
    D) siblings who differ in temperament rarely establish similar attachment patterns with their parents.
Answer: B
Page Ref: 275
Skill: Conceptual
Objective: 7.11

82) Infant characteristics do not show strong relationships with attachment security because
    A) temperament is not stable until middle to late childhood.
    B) most newborns easily form secure attachments to their primary caregivers.
    C) many infant attributes can lead to attachment security as long as the caregiver is sensitively tuned to the baby's needs.
    D) of difficulties measuring the quality of the emotional bond between parents and their infants.
Answer: C
Page Ref: 275
Skill: Conceptual
Objective: 7.11

83) Parents who exhibit objectivity and balance in discussing childhood experiences, regardless of whether they were positive or negative, tend to have infants who display a(n) _____ attachment.
    A) avoidant
    B) secure
    C) disorganized/disoriented
    D) resistant
Answer: B
Page Ref: 276
Skill: Conceptual
Objective: 7.11

84) Which of the following appears to be MOST influential in terms of whether adults become sensitive or insensitive parents?
    A) the actual history of care by the same-sex parent
    B) the actual history of care by the opposite-sex parent
    C) the actual history of care by the mother
    D) positive reconstructed memories of care rather than actual history of care
Answer: D
Page Ref: 276
Skill: Conceptual
Objective: 7.11

85) When caring for their babies, mothers devote more time to _____ and fathers devote more time to _____.
    A) playful interactions; feeding and diaper changes
    B) feeding and diaper changes; emotional closeness
    C) playful interactions; emotional closeness
    D) physical care; playful interactions
Answer: D
Page Ref: 276
Skill: Conceptual
Objective: 7.12

86) When playing with their babies, mothers more often _____, whereas fathers tend to _____.
    A) engage in conventional games; provide toys and talk to infants
    B) provide toys and talk to infants; play games like pat-a-cake and peekaboo
    C) engage in highly physical games; play conventional games
    D) provide toys and talk to infants; engage in highly physical games
Answer: D
Page Ref: 276
Skill: Conceptual
Objective: 7.12

87) Of the following, which is supported by research on fathers?
    A) In the United States, Hispanic fathers spend more time engaged with their children compared to fathers in other ethnic groups.
    B) In dual-earner families, mothers and fathers devote equal time to caregiving.
    C) In the United States, high-SES fathers devote more time to their children than low-SES fathers.
    D) Fathers in Japan spend more time engaged in child care compared to fathers in the United States.
Answer: A
Page Ref: 278
Skill: Conceptual
Objective: 7.12

88) Research on multiple attachments demonstrates that
    A) a warm marital relationship is more important for mothers than fathers in affecting their quality of parenting.
    B) when fathers are primary caregivers, they tend to lose their typical arousing play style.
    C) paternal time engaged with or accessible to children varies widely across SES and ethnic groups.
    D) mothers in dual-earner families tend to engage in more playful stimulation than stay-at-home mothers.
Answer: D
Page Ref: 278
Skill: Conceptual
Objective: 7.12

89) Of the following, which is supported by research on grandparent primary caregivers in the United States and Canada?
    A) Grandparents generally take over the role of primary caregivers when parents' troubled lives threaten children's well-being.
    B) Less than 1 percent of the child population live apart from parents and with their grandparents.
    C) Grandparents in Caucasian families are more likely to serve as children's primary caregivers than grandparents in other ethnic groups.
    D) Older children who enter grandparent care fare better than younger children who enter grandparent care.
Answer: A
Page Ref: 279
Skill: Conceptual
Objective: 7.12

90) Research on siblings indicates that by the end of the baby's first year,
    A) the security of their preschool-age brother or sister's attachment often begins to decline.
    B) preschool-age brothers or sisters rarely show affection for their younger sibling.
    C) their preschool-age brother or sister often begins to feel threatened and displaced.
    D) infants are comforted by the presence of their preschool-age sibling during short parental absences.
Answer: D
Page Ref: 280
Skill: Conceptual
Objective: 7.12

91) Between 1 and 2 years of age, coordinated interaction appears largely in the form of
    A) mutual imitation.
    B) emotional contagion.
    C) social referencing.
    D) interactional synchrony.
Answer: A
Page Ref: 280
Skill: Factual
Objective: 7.12

92) Of the following, which is supported by research on attachment and later development?
    A) Infants who display disorganized/disoriented attachment usually develop more favorably than resistant infants.
    B) Continuity of caregiving determines whether attachment security is linked to later development.
    C) Even with supportive caregiving, insecurely attached infants show few signs of developmental recovery in childhood.
    D) There is definitive evidence that secure attachment in infancy causes improved cognitive, emotional, and social competence in later years.
Answer: B
Page Ref: 282
Skill: Conceptual
Objective: 7.13

93) Research suggests that a child who is insecurely attached in infancy may fare well later on as long as
    A) the child is neglected in school but not rejected.
    B) his or her mother becomes more positive and supportive during early childhood.
    C) the family income is high enough for comfort.
    D) the child has no siblings to compete with for affection.
Answer: B
Page Ref: 282
Skill: Conceptual
Objective: 7.13

94) Newborn Safara displays a stronger sucking reflex in response to external stimulation than to self-stimulation. This finding demonstrates that Safara has the beginnings of
    A) self-awareness.
    B) effortful control.
    C) an internal working model.
    D) emotional self-regulation.
Answer: A
Page Ref: 283
Skill: Applied
Objective: 7.14

95) When shown two side-by-side video images of their kicking legs, one from their own perspective and one from an observer's perspective, 3-month-olds
    A) look longer at the observer's view.
    B) look equally long at both images.
    C) look longer at their own perspective.
    D) almost entirely ignore the observer's view.
Answer: A
Page Ref: 283
Skill: Conceptual
Objective: 7.14

96) Two-year-old Isabella has a red dot on her nose. When she looks into a mirror, she tries to rub the dot off of her nose rather than off of the mirror. This behavior indicates that she has developed
    A) effortful control.
    B) a categorical self
    C) self-recognition.
    D) empathy.
Answer: C
Page Ref: 284
Skill: Applied
Objective: 7.14

97) Two-year-old Hannah offers her brother her favorite blanket when he falls down and skins his knee. Hannah is demonstrating signs of
    A) effortful control.
    B) social referencing.
    C) empathy.
    D) emotional self-regulation.
Answer: C
Page Ref: 284
Skill: Applied
Objective: 7.14

98) Two-year-old Haakem tells his babysitter that he is a "big boy." This statement demonstrates that Haakem is beginning to develop
    A) an internal working model.
    B) self-conscious emotions.
    C) a categorical self.
    D) social referencing.
Answer: C
Page Ref: 285
Skill: Applied
Objective: 7.14

99) To behave in a self-controlled manner, children must have some ability to
    A) engage in social referencing.
    B) understand another's emotional state.
    C) display self-conscious emotions.
    D) think of themselves as autonomous beings who can direct their own actions.
Answer: D
Page Ref: 285
Skill: Conceptual
Objective: 7.14

100) Of the following, which is supported by research on the development of self-control?
   A) Children's first consciencelike verbalizations precede the development of compliance by several months.
   B) Compliance first becomes apparent during 6 to 9 months of age.
   C) Some toddlers sing or talk to themselves to keep from engaging in prohibited acts.
   D) Children who are advanced in the development of attention and language tend to lag behind their peers in delaying gratification.

Answer: C
Page Ref: 285
Skill: Conceptual
Objective: 7.14

101) Of the following, which is more likely to be found in shy, inhibited children than in highly sociable, uninhibited children?
   A) a higher heart rate from the first few weeks of life
   B) lower levels of amygdala activity in response to novel stimuli
   C) a drop in blood pressure in response to novelty
   D) lower levels of saliva concentration of cortisol

Answer: A
Page Ref: 263
Skill: Conceptual
Objective: (B&E Box) Development of Shyness and Sociability

102) Compared to sociable infants and preschoolers, shy children show
   A) greater EEG activity in the right frontal lobe.
   B) lower levels of generalized activation of the cerebral cortex.
   C) lower levels of fMRI activity in the amygdala.
   D) greater EEG activity in the left frontal lobe.

Answer: A
Page Ref: 263
Skill: Conceptual
Objective: (B&E Box) Development of Shyness and Sociability

103) Findings from the NICHD Study of Early Child Care have shown that
   A) the rate of insecurity is equal among child-care and non-child-care infants.
   B) child care in the United States and Canada is nationally regulated.
   C) child care alone does not contribute to attachment insecurity.
   D) many toddlers in full-day child care show a decrease in salivary concentrations of stress hormones.

Answer: C
Page Ref: 277
Skill: Conceptual
Objective: (SI Box) Does Child Care in Infancy Threaten Attachment Security and Later Development?

104) North American studies on infant child care show that
   A) most infants who are placed in full-time child care are insecurely attached.
   B) full-time but not part-time work during the first year is detrimental to attachment security.
   C) long hours spent in child care do not affect attachment quality.
   D) more than one child-care arrangement increases the likelihood of attachment insecurity.

Answer: D
Page Ref: 277
Skill: Conceptual
Objective: (SI Box) Does Child Care in Infancy Threaten Attachment Security and Later Development?

105) Research on child care has demonstrated that
   A) many infants and children who attend full-time child care show a mild increase in concentrations of stress hormones across the day.
   B) the rate of insecurity is equivalent among infants in child care and those who stay at home with their mothers.
   C) mother-child interaction is not affected by the quality of child care or the time spent in child care.
   D) even children in high-quality child care have higher rates of insecurity than those who are informally cared for by friends, relatives, or babysitters.
   Answer: A
   Page Ref: 277
   Skill: Conceptual
   Objective: (SI Box) Does Child Care in Infancy Threaten Attachment Security and Later Development?

106) Research in Western cultures demonstrates that
   A) mothers' affectionate involvement predicts favorable development more strongly than father's affectionate involvement.
   B) fathers who devote little time to physical caregiving place their children at risk for various emotional and behavioral difficulties.
   C) mothers' and fathers' emotional interactions with their children are not linked.
   D) fathers' warmth can protect children against a wide range of emotional and behavioral problems.
   Answer: D
   Page Ref: 279
   Skill: Conceptual
   Objective: (CI Box) The Powerful Role of Paternal Warmth in Development

107) Rescarch on the Aka of Central Africa reveals that the strong father-infant relationship is due in great part to
   A) the strong division of male and female duties in the tribe.
   B) the lack of respect for women within the tribe.
   C) the lack of respect for men within the tribe.
   D) an exceptionally cooperative and intimate marital relationship.
   Answer: D
   Page Ref: 279
   Skill: Conceptual
   Objective: (CI Box) The Powerful Role of Paternal Warmth in Development

ESSAY

108) Describe the development of children's ability to understand the emotions of others, the emergence of self-conscious emotions, and emotional self-regulation during the first 2 years.
   Answer: Within the first few months, babies match the feeling tone of the caregiver in face-to-face communications. Around 3 to 4 months, infants become sensitive to the structure and timing of face-to-face interaction. From 5 months on, infants perceive facial expressions as organized patterns. Not long after, babies engage in social referencing, in which they actively seek emotional information from caregivers in uncertain situations. By the middle of the second year, infants begin to appreciate that others' emotional reactions may differ from their own.
   Self-conscious emotions, such as guilt, shame, embarrassment, and pride, appear at the end of the second year, as the sense of self emerges. Adult instruction is also an important ingredient in the development of self-conscious emotions. Between 2 and 4 months, caregivers begin to foster the development of self-regulation by engaging in stimulating play and providing guidance in expressing socially approved emotions. By the end of the second year, growth in representation and language leads to more effective ways of regulating emotion.
   Page Ref: 256–259

109) Explain the relationship between social referencing and a secure base with respect to the emotional development of infants.

Answer: Social referencing involves relying on another person's emotional reaction to appraise an uncertain situation. A secure base involves the use of a familiar caregiver as a base from which the infant confidently explores the environment and to which the infant returns for emotional comfort. Many studies show that a caregiver's emotional expression influences how an infant will react in an unfamiliar setting (for example, meeting a stranger, playing with an unfamiliar toy). A caregiver's emotional cues may be a major reason that she is used as a secure base. In unfamiliar situations, babies show a strong desire to remain within "eyeshot" of their mother. Babies will leave an attractive set of toys to relocate within her visual field so they can retain access to her facial and vocal cues. The assumption in this situation is that the baby depends on the caregiver's cues to help assess the comfort level of his or her current situation.

Page Ref: 257

110) Is temperament a stable trait? Why or why not?

Answer: Temperamental stability from one age period to the next is generally low to moderate. Although quite a few children remain the same, a good number change when assessed again. In fact, some characteristics, such as shyness and sociability, are stable over the long-term only in children at the extremes—those who are initially very shy or very outgoing.

Temperament is least stable during infancy because early behaviors change quickly with brain development and sensitive caregiving. For example, as infants become better at regulating their attention and emotions, many who initially seemed irritable become calm and content. These inconsistencies help us understand why long-term prediction from early temperament is best achieved from the second year of life and after, when styles of responding are better established. They also reveal that biologically-based temperamental traits can be modified by experience, although children rarely change from one extreme to another.

Page Ref: 262, 264

111) Describe the three types of children identified using Thomas and Chess's model of temperament.

Answer: The easy child (40 percent of the sample) quickly establishes regular routines in infancy, is generally cheerful, and adapts easily to new experiences. The difficult child (10 percent of the sample) has irregular daily routines, is slow to accept new experiences, and tends to react negatively and intensely. The slow-to-warm-up child (15 percent of the sample) is inactive, shows mild, low-key reactions to environmental stimuli, is negative in mood, and adjusts slowly to new experiences. Thirty-five percent of the sample do not fit any of these categories, but show unique blends of temperamental characteristics.

Page Ref: 260–261

112) Describe the four phases of attachment development according to ethological theory.

Answer: According to ethological theory, the infant's relationship with the parent begins as a set of innate signals that call the adult to the baby's side. New cognitive and emotional capacities, as well as a history of warm, responsive care, support the development of a true affectionate bond. Attachment develops in four phases: The first is the preattachment phase, which lasts from birth to 6 weeks. During this phase, infants use a variety of built-in signals, such as grasping, crying, and smiling, to help bring them into close contact with other humans. The second is the attachment-in-the-making stage, which lasts from 6 weeks to 6 to 8 months. During this phase, infants start to respond differently to a familiar caregiver than to a stranger. But even though they can recognize a familiar caregiver, they do not yet protest when separated from him or her. The third stage is the phase of clear-cut attachment, which begins at 6 to 8 months and ends somewhere between 18 months and 2 years. In this phase, infants display separation anxiety and use the parent as a secure base from which to explore, indicating that a true attachment bond has formed. By the end of the second year, toddlers move into the final stage—formation of a reciprocal relationship. During this phase, rapid growth in representation and language permits toddlers to try to alter the parent's coming and going through requests and persuasion rather than following and clinging.

Page Ref: 269–270

113) Describe the Strange Situation and the four attachment patterns assessed by it.

Answer: The Strange Situation is a widely used technique for assessing the attachment security of 1- to 2-year-olds. The Strange Situation takes the baby through eight short episodes in which brief separation from and reunions with the parent occur. Observing the responses of infants to these episodes, researchers have identified a secure attachment pattern and three patterns of insecurity. Infants who use the parent as a secure base from which to explore and who actively seek contact with the parent during reunion are classified as having a secure attachment. Babies identified as having an avoidant attachment seem unresponsive to the parent when she is present, are usually not distressed when the parent leaves, react to the parent and the stranger in the same manner, and avoid or are slow to greet the parent during reunion. Infants who are resistant often fail to explore when the parent is present and display angry, resistant behavior when she returns. The disorganized/disoriented attachment pattern reflects the greatest insecurity. These babies show a variety of confused, contradictory behaviors —for example, approaching the parent with a flat, depressed gaze.

Page Ref: 270–271

114) Describe parental behaviors that are associated with each of the four attachment classifications.

Answer: Research shows that sensitive caregiving distinguishes securely from insecurely attached infants. The extent to which mothers responded promptly, consistently, and appropriately to infant signals and held their babies tenderly and carefully is moderately related to attachment security. Additional studies indicate that a special form of communication called interactional synchrony distinguishes the experiences of secure and insecure babies. This refers to a sensitively tuned "emotional dance," in which the caregiver responds to infant signals in a well-timed, appropriate fashion. Compared to securely attached infants, avoidant babies tend to receive overstimulating, intrusive care. By avoiding the mother, these infants appear to be escaping from overwhelming interaction. Resistant infants often experience inconsistent care. As a result, the baby is overly dependent, as well as angry at the mother's lack of involvement. Disorganized/disoriented attachment is especially high among maltreated infants and infants of depressed mothers.

Page Ref: 276

STUDY QUESTIONS

Erikson's Theory of Infant and Toddler Personality

Basic Trust versus Mistrust

1. How did Erikson expand upon Freud's view of development during infancy? (p. 252)

_____

_____

2. Based on Erikson's theory, summarize the psychological conflict of the first year, *basic trust versus mistrust*, and explain how it can be positively resolved. (p. 252)

Conflict: _____

_____

Resolution: _____

_____

Autonomy versus Shame and Doubt

1. In what way did Erikson expand upon Freud's view of development during toddlerhood? (p. 252)

_____

_____

2. Explain how the psychological conflict of toddlerhood, *autonomy versus shame and doubt,* is resolved favorably. (pp. 252–253)

_____

_____

Emotional Development

1. In line with the dynamic systems perspective, emotional expressions are (flexibly / rigidly) organized; they vary with the person's developing capacities, goals, and contexts. (p. 254)

2. What is the MAX system, and how does it help researchers analyze the range of infant emotions? (p. 254)

A. _____

B. _____

Development of Basic Emotions

1. Define the term *basic emotions,* and provide several examples. (p. 254)

Definition: _____

_____

Examples: _____

_____

2. True or False: Infants come into the world with the ability to express all of the basic emotions. (p. 254)

3. How does the dynamic systems perspective help us understand how basic emotions become clear and well-organized? (p. 254)

_____

_____

_____

4. Explain how caregiver communication affects an infant's emotional development. (p. 254)

_____

_____

_____

_____

5. At approximately what age do infants' emotional expressions become well-organized? (p. 254)

_____

6. What is a *social smile,* and when does it develop? (p. 255)

   A. _____

   B. _____

7. Laughter, which appears around _____ to _____ months, reflects (faster / slower) processing of information than does smiling. (p. 255)

8. How do expressions of happiness change between early infancy and the end of the first year? (p. 255)

_____

_____

9. The frequency and intensity of infants' angry reactions (increase / decrease) with age. Why does this happen? (p. 255)

_____

_____

_____

10. Describe the circumstances in which infants are likely to express sadness. (p. 255)

_____

_____

11. Fear reactions (increase / decrease) during the second half of the first year. (p. 256)

12. The most frequent expression of fear in infancy is to unfamiliar adults, a response called
_____ *anxiety.* (p. 256)

13. Cite several factors that influence infants' and toddlers' reactions to strangers. (p. 256)

_____

_____

_____

_____

14. How does a *secure base* aid infants' exploration of the environment? (p. 256)

_____

_____

_____

Understanding and Responding to the Emotions of Others

1. Early on, babies respond to others' emotions through the fairly automatic process of emotional _____, in which they match the feeling tone of the caregiver in face-to-face communication. (p. 256)

2. Define *social referencing,* and explain its role in infant development. (p. 257)

   Definition: _____

   _____

   Role: _____

   _____

   _____

3. At what age do infants understand that others' emotional reactions may differ from their own? (p. 257)

   _____

Emergence of Self-Conscious Emotions

1. What are *self-conscious emotions*? (p. 257)

   _____

   _____

2. Cite several examples of self-conscious emotions. (p. 257)

   _____

3. Besides self-awareness, what ingredient is required in order for children to experience self-conscious emotions? (p. 257)

   _____

4. True or False: The situations in which adults encourage children's expressions of self-conscious emotions vary from culture to culture. (p. 258)

Beginnings of Emotional Self-Regulation

1. Define *emotional self-regulation.* (p. 258)

_____

_____

2. Explain how caregivers contribute to children's style of emotional self-regulation. (pp. 258–259)

_____

_____

3. By the end of the second year, gains in representation and language lead to new ways of regulating emotion. Explain how this occurs. (p. 259)

_____

_____

_____

Development of Temperament

1. Define *temperament,* and provide an example of a temperamental trait. (p. 260)

    A. _____

    _____

    B. _____

2. Cite two important findings from the New York longitudinal study of temperament. (p. 260)

    A. _____

    _____

    B. _____

    _____

The Structure of Temperament

1. List and describe five of the nine dimensions of personality outlined in Thomas and Chess's model of temperament. (p. 261)

    A. _____

    _____

    B. _____

    _____

    C. _____

    _____

    D. _____

    _____

    E. _____

    _____

2.   List and describe the three types of children identified by Thomas and Chess. (p. 260)

A. _____

_____

B. _____

_____

C. _____

_____

3.   True or False: All children fit into one of the three temperament categories described above. (p. 260)

4.   Of the three styles of temperament, the _____ pattern places children at highest risk for adjustment problems. (p. 260)

5.   Cite six dimensions of temperament identified by Mary Rothbart. (p. 261)

A. _____

B. _____

C. _____

D. _____

E. _____

F. _____

6.   Define *effortful control,* and explain why it is important. (p. 261)

A. _____

_____

B. _____

_____

Measuring Temperament

1.   Discuss the advantages and disadvantages of using parent reports to assess children's temperament. (p. 262)

Advantages: _____

_____

_____

Disadvantages: _____

_____

_____

2.   Most physiological assessments of temperament have focused on _____ children, who react negatively to and withdraw from novel stimuli, and _____ children, who display positive emotion to and approach novel stimuli. (p. 262)

Biology and Environment: Development of Shyness and Sociability

1. What percentage of children identified as displaying extremes in shyness and sociability retain their temperamental style as they get older? (p. 263)

2. What area of the brain does Kagan believe contributes to individual differences in arousal? (p. 263)

3. Discuss four physiological correlates of approach–withdrawal behavior. (p. 263)

   A. _____

   B. _____

   C. _____

   D. _____

4. Heritability research indicates that genes contribute (modestly / substantially) to shyness and sociability. (p. 263)

5. Explain how child-rearing practices affect the chances that an emotionally reactive baby will become a fearful child. (p. 263)

Stability of Temperament

1. True or False: Temperamental stability from one age period to the next is generally low to moderate. (p. 262)

2. Long-term predictions about early temperament are best achieved after age _____, when styles of responding are better established. (p. 262)

3. True or False: Child rearing plays an important role in modifying biologically based temperamental traits. (p. 264)

Genetic Influences

1. Research shows that identical twins (are / are not) more similar than fraternal twins in temperament and personality. (p. 264)

2. Describe ethnic and sex differences in early temperament. (p. 264)

   Ethnic: _____

   Sex: _____

Environmental Influences

1. Explain how child rearing contributes to ethnic and sex differences in temperament. (p. 265)

2. Explain how children reared in the same family develop distinct temperamental styles. (pp. 265–266)

_____

_____

_____

3. Both identical and fraternal twins tend to become (increasingly / decreasingly) similar from one another over time. (p. 266)

Temperament and Child Rearing: The Goodness-of-Fit Model

1. Describe the *goodness-of-fit* model. (p. 266)

_____

_____

2. How does the goodness-of-fit model help to explain why children with difficult temperaments are at high risk for future adjustment problems? (p. 266)

_____

_____

_____

3. Explain how cultural values and life conditions affect the fit between parenting and child temperament. (pp. 266–267)

_____

_____

_____

Development of Attachment

1. Define *attachment.* (p. 268)

_____

_____

2. True or False: Both psychoanalytic and behaviorist theories emphasize feeding as an important context in which infants and caregivers build a close emotional bond. (p. 268)

3. How did research on rhesus monkeys challenge the idea that attachment depends on hunger satisfaction? (p. 268)

_____

_____

Bowlby's Ethological Theory

1. True or False: The *ethological theory of attachment*, which recognizes attachment as an evolved response that promotes survival, is the most widely accepted view of the infant's emotional tie to the caregiver. (p. 269)

2. Match each phase of attachment with the appropriate description. (pp. 269–270)

    _____ Attachment to the familiar caregiver is evident, and infants display separation anxiety.

    _____ Infants are not yet attached to their mother and do not mind being left with an unfamiliar adult.

    _____ Separation anxiety declines as children gain an understanding of the parent's comings and goings and can predict his/her return.

    _____ Infants start to respond differently to a familiar caregiver than to a stranger.

    1. Preattachment phase
    2. "Attachment-in-the-making" phase
    3. "Clear-cut" attachment phase
    4. Formation of a reciprocal relationship

3. What is an *internal working model,* and how does it relate to personality? (p. 270)

    A. _____

    _____

    B. _____

    _____

Measuring the Security of Attachment

1. The _____, designed by Mary Ainsworth, is the most widely used laboratory technique for measuring the quality of attachment between 1 and 2 years of age. (p. 270)

2. Provide a brief description of the *Strange Situation.* (p. 270)

    _____

    _____

    _____

    _____

3. Match each of the following attachment classifications with the appropriate description. (pp. 270–271)

    _____ Before separation, these infants seek closeness to the parent and fail to explore. When she returns, they display angry behaviors, may continue to cry after being picked up, and cannot be easily comforted.

    _____ Before separation, these infants use the parent as a base from which to explore. They are upset by the parent's absence, and they seek contact and are easily comforted when she returns.

    _____ Before separation, these infants seem unresponsive to the parent. When she leaves, they react to the stranger in much the same way as to the parent. Upon her return, they are slow to greet her.

    _____ When the parent returns, these infants show confused, contradictory behaviors, such as looking away while being held.

    1. Secure
    2. Avoidant
    3. Resistant
    4. Disorganized/ disoriented

4. The *Attachment* _____ is an alternative to the Strange Situation for measuring attachment in children between 1 and 5 years of age. Briefly describe this method. (p. 271)

_____

_____

_____

Stability of Attachment

1. Describe the link between SES and children's attachment security. (p. 272)

_____

_____

_____

2. (Securely / Insecurely) attached babies are more likely to maintain their attachment status. Cite one exception to this trend. (p. 272)

_____

Cultural Variations

1. Cite at least one example of how cultural variations in child rearing affect attachment security. (p. 272)

_____

_____

Factors That Affect Attachment Security

1. List four important influences that affect attachment security. (p. 273)

    A. _____

    B. _____

    C. _____

    D. _____

2. True or False: Adoption research shows that children can develop a first attachment bond as late as 4 to 6 years of age. (p. 273)

3. True or False: *Sensitive caregiving*—responding promptly, consistently, and appropriately to infants and holding them tenderly—is moderately related to attachment security in both biological and adoptive mother-infant pairs and in diverse cultures and SES groups. (p. 273)

4. Describe differences in caregiving experienced by securely attached and insecurely attached infants. (p. 273)

    Securely attached: _____

    _____

    _____

    Insecurely attached: _____

    _____

    _____

5. Describe *interactional synchrony*. (p. 274)

_____

_____

_____

6. True or False: Moderate adult-infant coordination is a better predictor of attachment security than "tight" coordination, in which the adult responds to most infant cues. Briefly explain your response. (p. 274)

_____

_____

7. Among maltreated infants, _____ attachment is especially high. (p. 274)

8. Explain why children's characteristics do not show strong relationships with attachment security. (p. 275)

_____

_____

_____

9. Explain how family circumstances, such as job loss, a failing marriage, or financial difficulties, affect infant attachment. (pp. 275–276)

_____

_____

_____

10. Summarize the relationship between parents' childhood experiences and the quality of attachment with their own children. Based on this information, do our early rearing experiences destine us to become sensitive or insensitive parents? Explain. (p. 276)

A. _____

_____

B. _____

_____

Social Issues: Health: Does Child Care in Infancy Threaten Attachment Security and Later Adjustment?

1. True or False: American infants placed in full-time child care before 12 months of age are more likely than home-reared infants to display insecure attachments. (p. 277)

2. Summarize three factors that influence the relationship between child care and attachment quality. (p. 277)

A. _____

_____

B. _____

_____

C. _____

_____

3. Based on findings from the NICHD Study of Early Child Care, describe factors that contribute to higher rates of attachment insecurity. (p. 277)

    A. _____

    B. _____

    C. _____

4. List three ways child-care settings can foster attachment security. (p. 277)

    A. _____

    B. _____

    C. _____

Multiple Attachments

1. Describe how mothers and fathers differ in the way they relate to and interact with babies, and discuss how these patterns are changing due to the revised work status of women. (p. 278)

    Mothers: _____

    _____

    Fathers: _____

    _____

    Work status: _____

    _____

2. Explain how fathers' involvement with babies affects family attitudes and relationships. (p. 278)

    _____

    _____

3. In which ethnic groups are grandparents most likely to assume the parenting role? Explain why. (pp. 278–279)

    _____

    _____

4. True or False: Grandparents tend to assume the parenting role under highly stressful life circumstances. Explain your answer. (pp. 278, 280)

    _____

    _____

    _____

5. When a new baby arrives, how is a preschool-age sibling likely to respond? Include both positive and negative reactions in your answer. (p. 280)

    Positive: _____

    _____

    Negative: _____

    _____

6. Discuss four ways in which mothers can promote positive relationships between infants and their preschool-age siblings. (p. 281)

    A. _____

    _____

    B. _____

    _____

    C. _____

    _____

    D. _____

    _____

Cultural Influences: The Powerful Role of Paternal Warmth in Development

1. True or False: Fathers' warmth toward their children predicts later cognitive, emotional, and social competencies as strongly as does mothers' warmth. (p. 279)

2. Describe two factors that promote paternal warmth. (p. 279)

    A. _____

    _____

    B. _____

    _____

From Attachment to Peer Sociability

1. How does culture predict the onset of peer sociability? (pp. 280–281)

    _____

    _____

    _____

2. Explain the link between attachment to a sensitive caregiver and early peer relationships. (pp. 280–281)

    _____

    _____

    _____

Attachment and Later Development

1. In a longitudinal study conducted by Sroufe and his collaborators, how did teachers rate preschoolers who were securely attached as babies? (p. 281)

    _____

    _____

2. Which attachment pattern is consistently related to fear, anxiety, anger, and aggression during the preschool and school years? (pp. 281–282)

    _____

3. Some researchers have suggested that *continuity of caregiving* determines whether attachment is linked to later development. Briefly explain this relationship. (p. 282)

_____

_____

_____

Self-Understanding

Self-Awareness

1. True or False: Over the first few months, an infant's self-awareness is limited and is expressed only in perception and action. (p. 283)

2. Provide an example illustrating how by age 2, self-recognition is well under way. (pp. 283–284)

_____

_____

3. How does sensitive caregiving promote early self-development? (p. 284)

_____

_____

_____

4. Describe two ways in which self-awareness is associated with early emotional and social development. (pp. 284–285)

A. _____

_____

B. _____

_____

Categorizing the Self

1. Describe categorizations of the self that appear in toddlerhood, and cite an example of how children use this knowledge to organize their behavior. (p. 285)

_____

_____

_____

_____

Self-Control

1. List three developmental milestones that are essential for the development of self-control. (p. 285)

A. _____

B. _____

C. _____

2. Once toddlers become capable of *compliance,* do they always obey requests and demands? Explain. (p. 285)

    _____

    _____

3. True or False: Toddlers who experience parental warmth and gentle encouragement are more likely to be cooperative and advanced in self-control. (p. 285)

4. Explain how attention and language contribute to *delay of gratification.* (p. 285)

    _____

    _____

5. List several ways adults can help toddlers develop compliance and self-control. (p. 286)

    _____

    _____

    _____

    _____

PUZZLE 7.1 TERM REVIEW

Across

5. Attachment style characterizing infants who remain close to the parent prior to separation but display angry behavior upon reunion

9. Model of attachment which states that an effective match between child-rearing practices and a child's temperament leads to favorable adjustment (3 words, hyph)

10. _____ caregiving involves prompt, consistent, and appropriate responses to infant signals

11. The _____ smile is evoked by the stimulus of the human face

12. Positive outcome of Erikson's psychological conflict of toddlerhood

14. The strong, affectionate tie that humans feel toward special people in their lives

16. Infants use the caregiver as a secure _____ from which to explore, returning for emotional support

Down

1. Negative outcome of Erikson's psychological conflict of infancy

2. Interactional _____: a sensitively-tuned emotional dance, in which the caregiver responds to infant signals in a well-timed, appropriate fashion, and both partners match emotional states

3. _____ Situation: procedure involving brief separations from and reunions with the parent that assesses the quality of the attachment bond

4. Social _____: relying on a trusted person's emotional reaction to decide how to respond in an uncertain situation

6. Attachment style characterizing infants who respond in a confused, contradictory fashion when reunited with the parent

7. The _____ theory of attachment views the infant's emotional tie to the caregiver as an evolved response that promotes survival

8. Attachment _____: method for assessing the quality of the attachment bond in which a parent sorts a set of descriptors of attachment-related behaviors on the basis of how well they describe the child

10. Attachment style characterizing infants who are distressed at parental separation and are easily comforted upon parental return

13. _____ working model: set of expectations derived from early caregiving experiences; guides all future close relationships

15. Positive outcome of Erikson's psychological conflict of toddlerhood

PUZZLE 7.2 TERM REVIEW

Across

2. Emotional self-_____: strategies for adjusting one's emotional state to a comfortable level of intensity
4. Stranger_____: an infant's expression of fear in response to unfamiliar adults
5. Stable individual differences in quality and intensity of emotional reaction, activity level, attention, and emotional self-regulation
6. A child who reacts negatively to and withdraws from novel stimuli
8. Voluntary obedience to adult request and commands
9. Temperament style characterized by inactivity; mild, low-key, reactions to environmental stimuli; negative mood; and slow adjustment to new experiences
10. _____ self: classification of the self according to prominent ways in which people differ, such as age, sex, physical characteristics, and competencies that develops between 18 and 30 months
11. Emotions involving injury or enhancement to the sense of self (2 words, hyph.)
15. Temperament style characterized by establishment of regular routines in infancy, general cheerfulness, and easy adaptation to new experiences

16. Temperament style characterized by irregular daily routines, slow acceptance of new experiences, and negative, intense reactions

Down

1. The capacity to understand another's emotional state and to feel with that person
3. Delay of _____ is the ability to wait for an appropriate time and place to engage in a tempting act
7. _____ emotions can be directly inferred from facial expressions
12. The self-regulatory dimension of temperament, called _____ control, involves voluntary suppression of a dominant, reactive response in order to plan and execute a more adaptive response
13. A child who reacts positively to and approaches novel stimuli
14. _____ anxiety: infant's distressed reaction to the departure of a familiar caregiver

CROSSWORD PUZZLE SOLUTIONS

PUZZLE 7.1

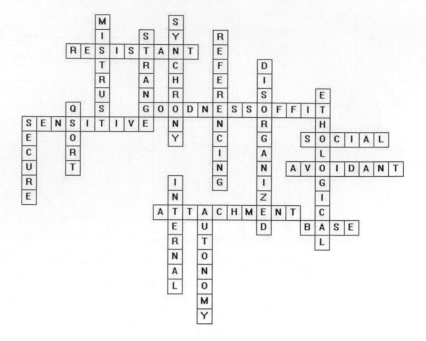

PUZZLE 7.2

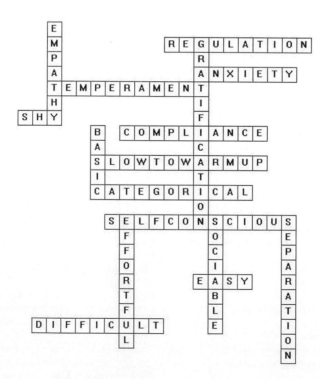

PRACTICE TEST #1

1. Expanding Freud's theory, Erikson believed that a healthy outcome during infancy depends on the (p. 252)
   a. amount of food and oral stimulation offered.
   b. frequency and severity of punishment.
   c. continual presence of the mother.
   d. quality of caregiving.

2. According to Erikson, the toddler's conflict of autonomy versus shame and doubt is resolved favorably when parents (pp. 252–253)
   a. enforce strict toilet-training rules to bring the child's impulses in line with social requirements.
   b. encourage the superego's control over the ego and id.
   c. provide young children with suitable guidance and reasonable choices.
   d. allow children to toilet train themselves.

3. According to the dynamic systems view, emotional expressions (p. 254)
   a. are flexibly organized, varying with the person's developing capacities, goals, and contexts.
   b. are determined primarily by a person's gender.
   c. directly correspond to degree of brain development.
   d. reflect a person's experiences in infancy, with little influence from later events.

4. Infants' earliest emotional life consists of (p. 254)
   a. only two emotions, anger and happiness.
   b. the struggle for oral satisfaction.
   c. attraction to pleasant stimuli and withdrawal from unpleasant stimuli.
   d. fear of unfamiliar persons and events.

5. At about 18 to 24 months, children typically begin to (p. 257)
   a. identify emotions expressed during face-to-face communication.
   b. engage in emotional self-regulation by shifting attention and self-soothing.
   c. laugh at events with subtle elements of surprise.
   d. experience self-conscious emotions of shame, embarrassment, guilt, and pride.

6. The faster processing of information that begins around 3 to 4 months of age distinguishes (p. 255)
   a. social smiling from newborn smiling.
   b. laughter from smiling.
   c. true happiness from biological satisfaction.
   d. autonomy from trust.

7. The gradual rise in infants' anger from 4 to 6 months is adaptive in that (p. 255)
   a. new motor capacities enable an angry infant to defend herself or overcome an obstacle.
   b. anger serves as a bridge between the young infant's crying and the toddler's single-word expressions of need or desire.
   c. anger occurs in a smaller range of situations as infants realize that they cannot always affect their environment.
   d. it prepares the infant for separation from the caregiver.

8. In the second half of the first year, the infant's most frequent expression of fear is to (p. 256)
   a. heights.
   b. separation from parents.
   c. unfamiliar adults.
   d. the threat of pain.

9. The rise in fear after 6 months of age serves to (p. 256)
   a. balance the infant's approach and avoidance tendencies.
   b. keep the newly mobile baby's enthusiasm for exploration in check.
   c. place necessary limits on the parent's interactions with the infant.
   d. prepare the infant to respond to discipline during toddlerhood.

10. Around the middle of the second year, toddlers begin to use social referencing to (p. 257)
    a. establish richer joint attention.
    b. block out mixed signals in vocal communication.
    c. know when to laugh at a stimulus.
    d. compare their own and others' assessments of events.

11. Self-conscious emotions generally appear in the middle of the second year because 18- to 24-month-olds (p. 257)
    a. become firmly aware of the self as a separate, unique individual.
    b. feel less stranger anxiety than before.
    c. are less motivated by basic emotions.
    d. are cognitively ready to move beyond social referencing.

12. By 4 to 6 months, infants are generally better able to control their emotions because (p. 258)
    a. they have reached a higher level of self-consciousness.
    b. their more regular sleep patterns enable them to cope more effectively with stress.
    c. they have gained in ability to shift attention and engage in self-soothing.
    d. they can crawl away from emotionally disturbing situations.

13. Studies have revealed that infant boys have a harder time than infant girls in (p. 259)
    a. responding to caregivers' lessons in socially approved expression.
    b. regulating negative emotion.
    c. developing a vocabulary for talking about feelings.
    d. understanding themselves and others as emotional beings.

14. The results of the New York Longitudinal Study showed that (p. 260)
    a. temperament may protect a child from the negative effects of a stressful home life.
    b. girls are more reactive than boys.
    c. parenting practices have little effect on children's fundamental emotional styles.
    d. temperament is influenced primarily by environmental rather than biological factors.

15. Unlike the difficult child, the slow-to-warm-up child (p. 260)
    a. is generally cheerful.
    b. has irregular daily routines.
    c. adapts more quickly to new experiences.
    d. shows mild, low-key reactions to environmental stimuli.

16. As a method of studying temperament, home or laboratory observation (p. 262)
    a. enables inhibited children to accept novel stimuli.
    b. avoids the subjectivity of parent reports.
    c. is always more accurate than parental reports.
    d. tends to calm sociable children who might "act out" in an unfamiliar setting.

17. Long-term predictions from early temperament are best made after age 3 because (p. 262)
    a. saliva concentrations of cortisol fall after age 3.
    b. older children are better able to follow caregiver directions that regulate behavior.
    c. at that point, the child's system of emotion, attention, and action is better established.
    d. older children have greater skill at effortful control.

18. Unlike North American mothers, Japanese mothers tend to believe that babies (p. 265)
    a. come into the world as independent beings who must learn to rely on parents.
    b. must be weaned away from dependence to autonomy.
    c. should be encouraged to express strong emotion.
    d. must be free to develop individualistic qualities.

19. A limitation of the psychoanalytic and behaviorist accounts of attachment is that they (p. 268)
    a. overemphasize the infant's characteristics.
    b. underestimate the importance of toilet training.
    c. underemphasize emotional bonding between children and adults who are not their parents.
    d. overemphasize the role of hunger satisfaction.

20. In response to the Strange Situation, resistant babies tend to (p. 270)
    a. use the parent as a secure base and, when the parent returns after separation, actively seek contact.
    b. be unresponsive to the parent when she is present and show no distress when she leaves.
    c. seek closeness to the parent before separation and, after the parent returns, combine clinginess with angry, resistive behavior.
    d. show confused, contradictory behaviors at reunion, such as approaching the parent with flat, depressed emotion.

21. The fact that about two-thirds of siblings establish similar attachment patterns with their parents, although the siblings often differ in temperament, suggests that (p. 275)
    a. the heritability of attachment is very high.
    b. the heritability of attachment is virtually nil.
    c. the parents established appropriate interactional synchronies with all of the siblings.
    d. the siblings probably share a few characteristics that result in similar levels of attachment security.

22. Studies have shown that paternal availability to children is (p. 278)
    a. fairly similar across SES and ethnic groups.
    b. slightly higher in Canada than in the United States.
    c. dramatically different across cultures.
    d. higher in dual-earner families.

23. Between 1 and 2 years, coordinated interaction between agemates largely takes the form of (p. 280)
    a. smiling and reaching when they see one another.
    b. mutual imitation involving jumping, chasing, or banging a toy.
    c. using words to talk about and influence a peer's behavior.
    d. playing games with rules.

24. Around age 2, children display self-recognition by (p. 284)
    a. matching facial expressions with their caregivers.
    b. looking longer at images of their own leg positions than at those of other children.
    c. empathizing with others' emotional states.
    d. pointing to themselves in photos and referring to themselves by name or with a personal pronoun.

25. A toddler's use of consciencelike verbalizations ("No, can't!") to correct herself shows that she has become capable of (p. 285)
    a. independent thinking.
    b. self-awareness.
    c. compliance.
    d. resilience.

PRACTICE TEST #2

1. According to Erikson, basic trust versus mistrust is resolved favorably by (p. 252)
   a. **a balance of care that tends toward love and sympathy.**
   b. the triumph of the ego over the id.
   c. frequent oral satisfaction.
   d. separation between child and mother.

2. In Erikson's view, adults who have difficulty establishing intimate ties or who doubt their ability to meet new challenges (p. 253)
   a. have an overdeveloped superego.
   b. had too much autonomy as children.
   c. did not toilet train early enough or with sufficiently consistent rules.
   d. **may not have fully mastered the tasks of basic trust and autonomy during infancy and toddlerhood.**

3. Basic emotions, such as happiness and surprise, are (p. 254)
   a. imprinted as the infant establishes trust.
   b. **universal in humans and other primates.**
   c. not as flexibly organized as higher emotions.
   d. the result of unrestrained biological drives.

4. At about 3 to 5 months, infants' emotions have developed to the point that they (p. 256)
   a. are attracted primarily to neutral stimuli.
   b. begin to engage in social smiling.
   c. **expect others to respond similarly to their gaze, smile, or vocalization.**
   d. become angry more often and in a wider range of situations.

5. By the end of the first month, babies start to smile (p. 255)
   a. in response to gentle touches and sounds.
   b. **at dynamic, eye-catching sights.**
   c. when they hear the mother's soft, high-pitched voice.
   d. in response to parents' complex expressions and sentences.

6. Angry reactions increase as infants grow older because they (p. 255)
   a. **want to control their own actions and the effects they produce.**
   b. get hungry more often.
   c. can perceive, but not yet interpret, caregivers' complex emotional expressions.
   d. feel increasingly frustrated by their parents' contingent control over their movements.

7. Infants most often express sadness in response to (p. 255)
   a. pain.
   b. removal of an object.
   c. hunger.
   d. **deprivation of a familiar caregiver.**

8. Of the following situations, which is the most likely to cause stranger anxiety? (p. 256)
   a. An unfamiliar adult speaks to the baby's parents in a loud voice.
   b. An unfamiliar adult sits still and stares at the baby.
   c. **An unfamiliar adult picks up the baby in a new situation.**
   d. An unfamiliar adult approaches the baby slowly.

9. Studies have revealed that a caregiver's voice is more effective in social referencing than a facial expression alone because (p. 257)
   a. **the voice conveys both emotional and verbal information.**
   b. facial expressions often confuse young children.
   c. young children's hearing is better developed than their vision.
   d. hearing the voice does not require joint attention.

10. In collectivist cultures like those of China and Japan, calling attention to personal success often evokes the self-conscious emotion of (p. 258)
    a. pride.
    b. communal satisfaction.
    c. embarrassment.
    d. envy.

11. Because young infants have only a limited capacity to regulate their emotions, they (p. 258)
    a. engage in effortful control.
    b. depend on soothing for distraction and reorientation of attention.
    c. use social referencing to calm themselves.
    d. generally cannot tolerate face-to-face play.

12. Studies have revealed that when caregivers fail to regulate stressful experiences for infants, (p. 259)
    a. the development of self-conscious emotions is delayed.
    b. infants compensate by using effortful control.
    c. infants have trouble understanding social referencing.
    d. brain structures that buffer stress may fail to develop properly.

13. Self-regulation strategies help children to modify their (p. 260)
    a. temperament.
    b. self-consciousness.
    c. reactivity.
    d. autonomy.

14. In the Thomas and Chess model of temperament, a child with high rhythmicity (p. 261)
    a. has a very regular schedule for bodily functions, such as sleep, hunger, and excretion.
    b. is extremely distractible.
    c. tends to laugh, cry, or engage in gross motor activity with great energy.
    d. requires little stimulation to evoke a strong response.

15. According to Mary Rothbart, individuals differ not just in their reactivity on each dimension of temperament, but also in their (p. 261)
    a. threshold of responsiveness to stimuli.
    b. effortful capacity to manage that reactivity.
    c. level of activity or inactivity.
    d. frequency of negative mood.

16. Jerome Kagan's research has revealed that a comparatively high heart rate and saliva concentration of cortisol are common physiological responses of (p. 263)
    a. sociable children.
    b. children with a poorly developed amygdala.
    c. children who show greater EEG activity in the left frontal lobe.
    d. shy children.

17. The role of heredity in determining temperament is (p. 265)
    a. highest during infancy, when environmental influences have not had enough time to shape temperament.
    b. virtually impossible to measure because of the complex interaction of genetic and environmental influences.
    c. higher in childhood and beyond, when temperament becomes more stable.
    d. stronger in boys than in girls.

18. In Thomas and Chess's goodness-of-fit model, an effective match between rearing conditions and child temperament is best accomplished (p. 267)
    a. early, before unfavorable temperament–environment relationships produce maladjustment.
    b. at the point when adjustment problems become evident enough for caregivers to identify them.
    c. after the child has developed pragmatic skills.
    d. at birth, when infants typically display strong temperamental traits.

19. According to John Bowlby, during the "attachment in the making" phase, (p. 269)
    a. built-in signals, such as smiling and crying, help bring newborns into close contact with other humans who comfort them.
    b. infants begin to develop a sense of trust in caregivers' responses but still do not protest when separated from them.
    c. babies display clear-cut separation anxiety.
    d. rapid growth in representation and language enables toddlers to understand and predict a caregiver's behavior.

20. Research into stability of attachment indicates that (p. 272)
    a. the attachments of low-SES babies tend to be stronger than those of middle- or high-SES babies.
    b. children often show short-term instability in attachment quality during middle childhood.
    c. stability patterns tend to be the same across cultures.
    d. secure babies are more likely than insecure babies to maintain their attachment status.

21. Recent studies suggest that sensitive caregiving is _____ related to attachment security. (p. 273)
    a. not
    b. slightly
    c. moderately
    d. highly

22. Research into the relationship between child care and attachment quality suggests that we should (p. 277)
    a. increase the availability of high-quality child care.
    b. reject the Western European model of state-funded child care.
    c. regularly monitor children's cortisol levels.
    d. encourage caregivers to foster children's independence so that they adapt more favorably to nonparental care.

23. Studies have shown that in Western cultures, paternal warmth (p. 279)
    a. is highest in middle-SES families.
    b. yields greater benefits for boys than for girls.
    c. predicts little about children's later development.
    d. protects children against a wide range of difficulties, including childhood emotional problems.

24. The sensitivity to variations in caregivers' emotional messages that comes with self-awareness sets the stage for (p. 284)
    a. self-recognition.
    b. social referencing and the emergence of self-conscious emotions.
    c. emotional resilience.
    d. complex intermodal perception that, in turn, leads to self-awareness.

25. Language enables the development of the categorical self because it (p. 285)
    a. promotes self-recognition.
    b. replaces effortful control as the main determinant of self-awareness.
    c. permits children to represent the self and others more clearly.
    d. helps children become more consciously aware of their physical distinctness from their surroundings.

POWERPOINT SLIDES

Infants, Children, and Adolescents
Laura E. Berk 6th edition

Chapter 7

Emotional and Social Development in Infancy and Toddlerhood

This multimedia product and its contents are protected under copyright law. The following are prohibited by law:
- Any public performance or display, including transmission of any image over a network;
- Preparation of any derivative work, including the extraction, in whole or in part, of any images;
- Any rental, lease, or lending of the program.

INFANTS, CHILDREN, AND ADOLESCENTS
SIXTH EDITION

LAURA E. BERK

Psychodynamic Stages

Age	Erikson's Stage
First Year	Basic Trust versus Mistrust
Second Year	Autonomy versus Shame and Doubt

Interpreting Emotions

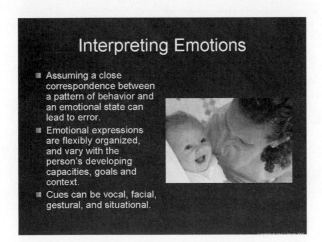

- Assuming a close correspondence between a pattern of behavior and an emotional state can lead to error.
- Emotional expressions are flexibly organized, and vary with the person's developing capacities, goals and context.
- Cues can be vocal, facial, gestural, and situational.

The MAX System

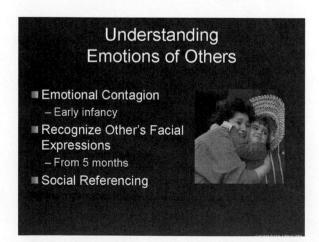

- (a) Cheeks raised and corners of the mouth pulled back and up signals happiness.
- (b) Eyebrows raised, eyes widened, and mouth opened with corners pulled straight back denotes fear.

First Appearance of Basic Emotions

Happiness	Smile—from birth
	Social smile—6 to 10 weeks
	Laugh—3 to 4 months
Anger	General distress—from birth
	Anger—4 to 6 months
Sadness	Distress to "still face"—2 to 7 mos.
Fear	First fears—6 to 12 months
	Stranger Anxiety—8 to 12 months

Understanding Emotions of Others

- Emotional Contagion
  - Early infancy
- Recognize Other's Facial Expressions
  - From 5 months
- Social Referencing

Self-Conscious Emotions

- –Shame
- –Embarrassment
- –Guilt
- –Envy
- –Pride
- Emerge middle of second year
- Need adult instruction about when to feel them

Emotional Self-Regulation

- Effortful control improves gradually, as the result of the development of the cerebral cortex and the assistance of caregivers.
- Young infants rely on caregivers to soothe them.
- Self-regulation grows over first year, with brain development.
- Caregivers contribute to child's self-regulation style.

Structure of Temperament

- **Easy – 40%**
- **Difficult – 10%**
- **Slow-to-warm-up – 15%**
- **Unclassified – 35%**

Two Models of Temperament

THOMAS AND CHESS		ROTHBART	
Dimension	**Description**	**Dimension**	**Description**
Activity level	Ratio of active periods to inactive ones	*Reactivity*	
Rhythmicity	Regularity of body functions, such as sleep, wakefulness, hunger, and excretion	Activity level	Level of gross motor activity
Distractibility	Degree to which stimulation from the environment alters behavior—for example, whether crying stops when a toy is offered	Attention span/ persistence	Duration of orienting or interest
		Fearful distress	Wariness and distress in response to intense or novel stimuli, including time to adjust to new situations
Approach/ withdrawal	Response to a new object, food, or person	Irritable distress	Extent of fussing, crying, and distress when desires are frustrated
Adaptability	Ease with which child adapts to changes in the environment, such as sleeping or eating in a new place	Positive affect	Frequency of expression of happiness and pleasure
Attention span and persistence	Amount of time devoted to an activity, such as watching a mobile or playing with a toy	*Self-regulation*	
Intensity of reaction	Energy level of response, such as laughing, crying, talking, or gross motor activity	Effortful control	Capacity to voluntarily suppress a dominant, reactive response in order to plan and execute a more adaptive response
Threshold of responsiveness	Intensity of stimulation required to evoke a response		
Quality of mood	Amount of friendly, joyful behavior as opposed to unpleasant, unfriendly behavior		

Biological Basis for Temperament

Inhibited, Shy

- React negatively, withdraw from new stimuli
- High heart rates, stress hormones & stress symptoms
- Higher right hemisphere frontal cortex activity

Uninhibited, Sociable

- React positively, approach new stimuli
- Low heart rates, stress hormones, and stress symptoms
- Higher left hemisphere frontal cortex activity

Stability of Temperament

- Temperament develops with age.
- Long-term prediction from early temperament is best achieved after age 3.
- Many factors can influence temperament, including the biological systems on which temperament is based, effortful control, and parenting experiences.

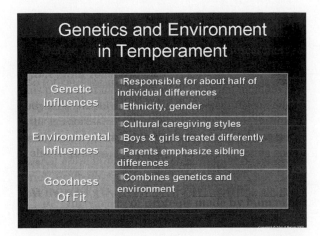

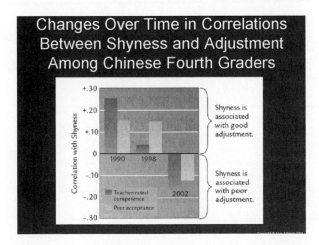

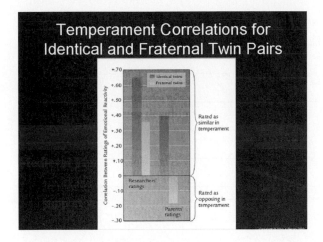

Bowlby's Ethological Theory of Attachment

1. Preattachment
2. Attachment-in-the-making
3. Clear-cut attachment
   - Separation anxiety
4. Formation of a reciprocal relationship

Measuring the Security of Attachment

- **Secure Attachment**
  - Use the parents as a secure base; actively seek contact with the parent when he or she returns.
- **Avoidant Attachment**
  - Seem unresponsive to the parent and are slow to greet the parent upon reunion.
- **Resistant Attachment**
  - Seek closeness to the parent and are distressed and angry when the parent returns.
- **Disorganized/Disoriented Attachment**
  - Pattern reflects the greatest insecurity. At reunion, these infants often show confused, contradictory behaviors.

Measuring the Security of Attachment

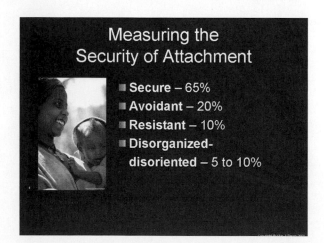

- **Secure** – 65%
- **Avoidant** – 20%
- **Resistant** – 10%
- **Disorganized-disoriented** – 5 to 10%

Episodes in the Strange Situation

EPISODE	EVENTS	ATTACHMENT BEHAVIOR OBSERVED
1	Researcher introduces parent and baby to playroom and then leaves.	
2	Parent is seated while baby plays with toys.	Parent as a secure base
3	Stranger enters, is seated, and talks to parent.	Reaction to unfamiliar adult
4	Parent leaves room. Stranger responds to baby and offers comfort if baby is upset.	Separation anxiety
5	Parent returns, greets baby, and offers comfort if necessary. Stranger leaves room.	Reaction to reunion
6	Parent leaves room.	Separation anxiety
7	Stranger enters room and offers comfort.	Ability to be soothed by stranger
8	Parent returns, greets baby, offers comfort if necessary, and tries to reinterest baby in toys.	Reaction to reunion

Note: Episode 1 lasts about 30 seconds; each of the remaining episodes lasts about 3 minutes. Separation episodes are cut short if the baby becomes very upset. Reunion episodes are extended if the baby needs more time to calm down and return to play.

The Attachment Q-Sort

- Suitable method for children between 1 and 5 years of age.
- Relies on home observations of up to 90 behaviors.
- Time-consuming method that does not differentiate between types of insecurity.

A Cross-Cultural Comparison of Infants' Reactions in the Strange Situation

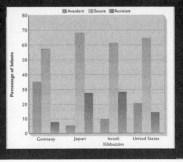

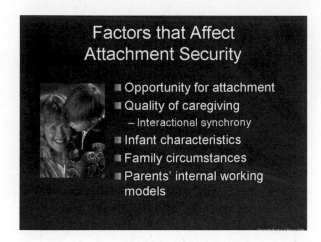

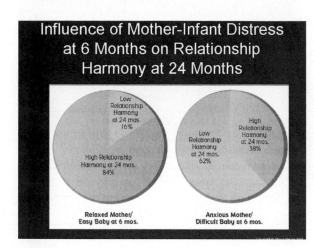

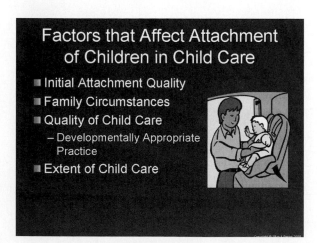

Multiple Attachments

- Fathers
- Siblings
- Grandparents
- Professional caregivers

The Powerful Role of Paternal Warmth in Development

- Fathers' sustained affectionate involvement predicted later emotional, cognitive, and social competence, as strongly, if not more strongly than a mothers' warmth.

- Some fathers express warmth through play.

Grandparent Primary Caregivers

- Over the last ten years, families in which grandparents are the children's primary caregivers have increased.
- Many are taking over during times of stress.
- Grandparent caregivers forge significant attachment relationships with their grandchildren in spite of problems.

Siblings

- 80% of North American children still grow up with at least one sibling.
- Resentment can be minimized by spending time with the older child, handling sibling misbehavior with patience, discussing the baby's wants and needs and modeling good problem solving.

Attachment and Later Development

- Secure attachment related to positive outcomes in:
  - Preschool
  - Middle childhood
- Continuity of caregiving may link infant attachment and later development.

Self-Awareness

Beginnings:

- At birth, infants have a sense of self as a distinct agent, separate from the surrounding world.
- Self-awareness is limited.

Self-Recognition:

- Sense of self as object of knowledge and evaluation.
- Aware of qualities that make self unique at 20 months.

Testing Emerging Self-Awareness

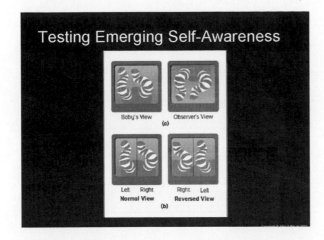

Baby's View   Observer's View
(a)

Left   Right   Right   Left
Normal View   **Reversed View**
(b)

Self-Awareness

- At the end of the first year, learn that their own goals frequently conflict with those of others.
- Empathy emerges and improves through early childhood.

Self-Control

- Effortful control
- Capable of compliance between 12 and 18 months
- Toddlers assert autonomy by sometimes not complying
- Delay of gratification shows self-control
- Warm, sensitive caregiving increases compliance

Helping Toddlers Develop Compliance and Self-Control

- Respond with sensitivity and support.
- Give advance notice of change in activities.
- Offer many prompts and reminders.
- Reinforce self-controlled behavior.
- Encourage sustained attention.
- Support language development.
- Increase rules gradually.

MEDIA DISTRIBUTION INFORMATION

Aquarius Health Care Media
18 N. Main St.
P.O. Box 1159
Sherborn, MA 01770
(888) 440-2963
www.aquariusproductions.com

Cambridge Documentary Films
P.O. Box 390385
Cambridge, MA 02139-0004
(617) 484-3993
*www.cambridgedocumentaryfilms.
org*

Cambridge Educational
Films Media Group
P.O. Box 2053
Princeton, NJ 08543-2053
(800) 257-5126
www.cambridgeeducational.com

Child Development Media
5632 Van Nuys Blvd.
Suite 286
Van Nuys, CA 91401
(800) 405-8942
www.childdevmedia.com

Concept Media
P.O. Box 19542
Irvine, CA 92623
(800) 233-7078
www.conceptmedia.com

Davidson Films.
735 Tank Farm Rd., Suite 210
San Luis Obispo, CA 93401
(888) 437-4200
www.davidsonfilms.com

Films for the Humanities &
    Sciences.
Films Media Group
P.O. Box 2053
Princeton, NJ 08543
(800) 257-5126
www.films.com

GPN Educational Media
1001 Fleet St., 9th floor
Baltimore, MD 21202
(800) 228-4630
http://shopgpn.com

Insight Media
2162 Broadway
New York, NY 10024-0621
(800) 233-9910
www.insight-media.com

Learning Seed
330 Telser Rd.
Lake Zurich, IL 60047
(800) 634-4941
www.learningseed.com

Magna Systems
330 Telser Rd.
Lake Zurich, IL 60047
(800) 203-7060
www.magnasystemsvideos.com

Meridian Education Corporation
Films Media Group
P.O. Box 2053
Princeton, NJ 08543
(800) 257-5126
www.meridianeducation.com

RMI Media Productions.
1365 N. Winchester St.
Olathe, KS 66061
(800) 745-5480
www.actmedia.org

ShopPBS
www.shoppbs.org

NOTES

NOTES

NOTES

NOTES

NOTES

NOTES

NOTES

NOTES

NOTES

NOTES

NOTES

NOTES

NOTES

NOTES

NOTES

NOTES

NOTES